SUNDERLAND
RIVER, TOWN AND PEOPLE

© Sunderland Borough Council

ISBN 0 947637 06 0

Second Edition 1990

SUNDERLAND
RIVER, TOWN AND PEOPLE

A history from the 1780s

Edited by
Geoffrey E. Milburn and Stuart T. Miller

Printed on behalf of the Borough of Sunderland by Thomas Reed Printers Limited,
with the generous support of Vaux Breweries Ltd.
1988.

Introduction

The Mayor in his kind foreword mentions the anniversary which provided the stimulus for this book. Sunderland elected its first modern borough council at the end of 1835, but its full legal right to incorporation was not established until 1837. One hundred and fifty years or so later it seems valuable to take stock of the significance of those events, in part for their own interest and importance, but more so for their indication that Sunderland had come of age as an urban self-governing community.

It is the progress and development of that community which this book seeks to trace. We begin our story some 50 years before 1837, at a period when Sunderland as a unified community did not yet exist and when the character of the area which was to become the modern borough was still as much rural and agricultural as urban and industrial. It should be pointed out that the very name Sunderland at that time referred to the riverside port and parish on the south bank of the Wear near to its mouth, while Bishopwearmouth, Monkwearmouth and other villages and hamlets were still quite separate communities. One consequence of Sunderland's growth and development was the extension of that name to the whole urban area.

From the 1780s, the book surveys the major processes of growth, and of industrial and social change, which affected the town over the following two centuries, ending virtually at the present day. The decision to confine the book to these 200 years was deliberate. Earlier histories of the town by Garbutt, Burnett, Mitchell, Corfe and others have ranged over the whole of the town's past from its most distant origins and are valuable for so doing. Our aim, however, was to put the microscope closer in order to examine in detail the town's greatest period, and to show how its present state can be better understood by a knowledge of its recent past. Yet even within this somewhat limited time-span of 200 years we cannot claim to be absolutely comprehensive and definitive. Enormous themes have had to be squeezed into single chapters and much has had, inevitably, to be left unsaid. Moreover, some important topics have been, for one reason or another, omitted from the book. These include commerce, banking, hospitals, the police and fire services, and (not least, though easily overlooked) farming. Some of these are fortunately already covered in other publications, while others await proper research. It is one of our hopes that this book will help to stimulate such research and its publication in the shape of articles, monographs and books. Much certainly remains to be explored.

Despite the limitations just mentioned, this book stands as the fullest available account of the modern history of the town. We trust it will prove to be one of interest and value to a wide range of readers. The aim of all the contributors has been to write in such a way that combines sound research with an attractive and readable style. We have tried to emphasise the human element in the town's history, both in the chapters and in the brief biographies and the appendices. And through the many illustrations, and the special 'picture insets', we have sought to bring to life much of the fascinating detail that is part and parcel of the life and tradition of the town.

A Victorian scholar once pointed out the importance of historians writing in such a way as to allow the reader to catch what he aptly called 'the sound of running history'. We hope that this has been achieved in the pages which follow and that those who read them will be stirred to a new appreciation of the history of a town which has had an important and interesting past and which will, we trust, despite contemporary problems, enjoy a prosperous and happy future.

G. E. Milburn,
S. T. Miller,
October 1988.

Acknowledgements

We are indebted to Vaux Breweries and the Sunderland Borough Council who offered most generous sponsorship towards the publication of this book. We are also grateful to our printers, Thomas Reed Printers Limited who, from the first, welcomed the subject. In these connections we must thank particularly Frank Nicholson, Tom Mills and Tony Brunton-Reed. With regard to the printing of the book we express our thanks to Cyril Scott and his colleagues at Thomas Reed, whose professional skill (and patience) we came quickly to admire, and be grateful for, during the protracted business of seeing the typescript turned into finished text.

Our thanks go also to those who have shared with us in writing the book, and who have often had to suffer the burden of revising, reducing or rewriting what they had at first written! It is sad to record that one of our contributors, John James, who had become the foremost authority on the first Wearmouth Bridge, died in January 1988.

Two of our colleagues need special acknowledgement. They are Tom Corfe who came to our editorial aid at a time of particular pressure, and Neil Sinclair who put the photographic and other resources of the Sunderland Museum at our disposal and has throughout given invaluable advice and support. Neil also provided most of the captions for the colour prints.

Our other debts must be acknowledged more summarily but not the less sincerely. We thank our typists Barbara Peebles, Pat Crossley, Ann Barrass, Patricia Osborne and Mary Milburn; the *Sunderland Echo* for a donation towards costs and for making available a number of photographic prints; Messrs Blacklock and Co, Arnott Bros, Hills Bookshop and the former Geography and History Department of Sunderland Polytechnic for help with administrative and research costs; Dr Stewart R. Craggs who prepared the index; the staffs of the Tyne and Wear and County Durham Record Offices, and of Sunderland Museum (Tyne and Wear Museums Service), Sunderland Central Library (Local Studies section), the Sunderland Polytechnic Library, and the Department of Palaeography and Diplomatic Durham University; Vera Stevens and the Council of the Sunderland Antiquarian Society; Kevin Butler for drawing some of the graphs; Billy Bell for help with photographs; Frank and Martin Preston of Hills and Co, Booksellers; Frank Manders; Ian S. Carr; the late Cyril Chester; Dr Stafford Linsley; Adrian Osler; Tim Pettigrew; Martin Routledge; Dr Helen Sinclair; Arthur Staddon.

We also acknowledge help, in the very early stages of the planning of this book, from Mrs M. E. Armstrong, editor of *An Industrial Island: A History of Scunthorpe* (1981), which book was in some respects a model for the design and layout of our own.

GEM
STM

End Papers:
Part of a plan of Sunderland and the river Wear by Stephen Dinning, 1853.

Frontispiece (opposite):
The Bede Memorial Cross, unveiled on Roker cliff tops on 11 October 1906, demonstrated renewed awareness in Sunderland during the period covered by this book of the age of Bede, the scholar-monk of St Peters Monkwearmouth and Wearside's greatest son.

FOREWORD

I am delighted to be asked to write a foreword for this new history of Sunderland from the 1780s to the present day. It has been encouraged and financially supported by Vaux Breweries, and also by the Borough of Sunderland, as a way of marking the 150th anniversary of the Act which finally recognised the town's municipal status in 1837. I would like to say how glad the Borough is to be associated in this sponsorship with Vaux, a firm of national importance which has been established in Sunderland for a century and a half. It is also very fitting that the printing has been carried out by Thomas Reed, another local firm whose history goes back even further, to 1782.

This book shows the development of Sunderland from three villages and a scattering of hamlets in the 1780s, to a major industrial town. It tells of the town's important industries such as shipbuilding, glassmaking and coal-mining, as well as describing the social, political and religious life of the community over the past two centuries. In conclusion the book makes clear the economic problems which Sunderland has faced in the 20th century, while also recognising achievements such as the establishment of Washington New Town and the introduction of new industries such as the Nissan car plant.

Sunderland: River, Town and People, should have a wide appeal to those living in the area as well as to Sunderland exiles, and be of particular value to schools and colleges. It has only been made possible by the hard work of the editors. Geoffrey Milburn and Stuart Miller, and of the other authors. I would like to thank them for this major contribution to the history of the town. Thanks are also due to Sunderland Museum and Art Gallery (Tyne and Wear Museums Service), the Borough's Department of Recreation and Libraries, Tyne and Wear Archives, the *Sunderland Echo* and all those other organisations and individuals who have provided information and illustrations.

Leslie Mann (Cllr),
Mayor.

Contents

Sunderland in the 1780s

It is unlikely that even the most doctrinaire of academic historians could resist an opportunity to be whisked back in time astride the saddle of some sort of Wellsian time machine. In fact while it is not quite possible to achieve this journey back to the Wearside of the late eighteenth century, it is nevertheless possible in imagination to amble idly through the streets and to observe inhabitants at work and play because of the existence of the unique pictorial plan drawn between 1785 and 1790 by John Rain, the parish surveyor of Bishopwearmouth. So detailed is the plan that it can be employed not only as a map but almost as one would employ a commercial directory.[1]

One has to accept the Eye Plan, eccentricities and all. The river, for instance, was straightened ruthlessly to fit the linen strip of 21 inches by 84 inches upon which it was drawn. Rain's wind blows unconcernedly in contrary directions. Churches, houses and fully-rigged ships are comfortably dwarfed by residents of Brobdignagian proportions. Nevertheless whatever its warts the opportunity to explore Bishopwearmouth and Sunderland, plan in hand and in the guise of a traveller of the day, is too good to miss.

AROUND AND ABOUT BISHOPWEARMOUTH

Entering Bishopwearmouth by the road from Chester le Street the noise of excited hounds in the large kennel in Hind Street attracts our attention. This is the property of the gentlemen members of the Bishopwearmouth Independent Hunt who indulge in the fashionable new activity of fox hunting.

Turning to the right into Green Terrace (or High Row) the first building on the corner is the Bishopwearmouth Poor House, a converted private residence which now holds up to 25 inmates. In 1788 the gentlemen of the Bishopwearmouth Vestry, concerned about the rising costs of the system of out relief, had insisted that all recipients must be badged. They ordered that:

> ... the poor have badges made for them which they are to wear at all times, and not to be paid unless they conform to this regulation.[2]

Not surprisingly, perhaps, the Poor House was in the same block as a tanyard because both premises have adverse effects on the value of property. Indeed the air is full of the stench of the human urine which is one of the tried and trusted ingredients in the repulsive broth in which animal skins are steeped in pits to remove the hair and to cure them. Between these two buildings stand the properties of the families of White, Storey and Easterby (indeed one of these still survives today in the form of the Greensleeves restaurant).

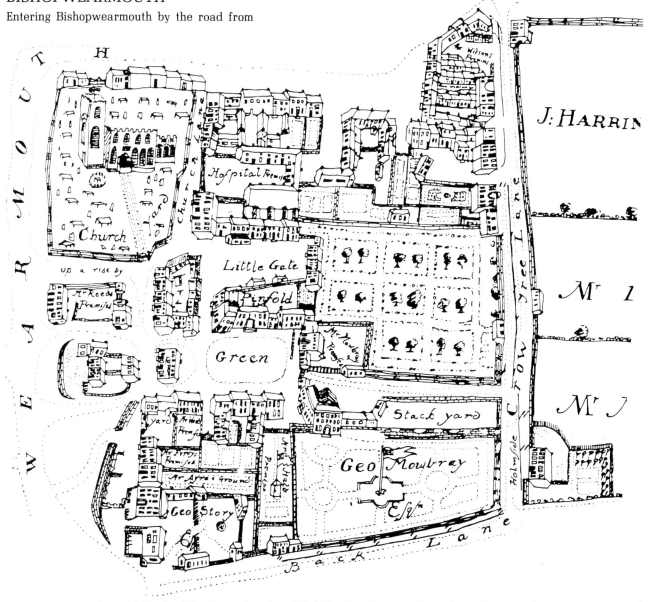

Bishopwearmouth Green and environs.

While we are in this part of the town a short circuitous tour of the Bishopwearmouth Green will be rewarding. Over the road stands a row of houses somewhat elevated above street level and fronted by a limestone wall. This block of properties is Southgate, a name reflecting the fact that this is the southern access to the parish church. Indeed the most impressive house is known as Southgate House, the residence of Mr George Storey, a very prominent member of the community.

Cutting up towards the church we encounter the Green — and a problem. The difficulty is that it is not very clear where the original heart of the village was. Perhaps the most obvious contender is the Green, surrounded by houses backing on to garths which, have become gardens or been built upon. Built around though it is, the Green is still an attractive place. Some of the properties are the modest residences of artisans, smaller tradesmen and farm workers. It still has a rural sense about it and a village 'pounder' is still responsible for rounding up stray livestock and holding it in the 'pinfold'. However there are also a number of very fine and relatively modern Georgian houses. Just to the east of the green is a block of houses owned by the coalowner Teasdale Mowbray (or rather his widow since his death in 1785) who obtained them by marriage into the Shipperdson family. The greatest of these houses is Crowtree House which stands at the south eastern corner of the Green. Moving northwards past the pinfold and through the cluster of shops and houses called Littlegate (the old namestone is still in existence at the Silksworth Hall Hotel) this small tour is completed by a visit to Bishopwearmouth Church.

The medieval church of St. Michael's dominates the village. An ancient, somewhat decrepit but still impressive structure, probably with a Saxon core, it stands at the centre of a very extensive parish. Even since the separation from it of the parish of Sunderland in 1719 this still leaves a parochial area of almost 20 square miles and a population — in 1785 — of nearly 8,000 souls. A stipend of £1,200 a year means that the rector is usually a gentleman of significant connections who can afford curates to assist him. Typical of these well-bred rectors is Henry Egerton MA, a member of the great Bridgewater clan and brother of a bishop of Durham. On his death in 1795 his successor William Paley — the eminent philosopher — would exclaim, regarding the rectory:

> Such a House! I was told at Durham it is one of the best parsonages in England; and that there are not more than three bishops that have better. There is not a shilling to be laid out upon it, and you might have rubbed it from top to bottom with a white handkerchief without soiling it.[3]

(When the rectory was demolished in the mid-19th century its fine staircase was placed in the new rectory on Gray Road — now the St. Michael's Building of the Polytechnic.)

Behind the rectory is a small garden together with outbuildings which include three stables, a cow house, a coach house and a large tithe barn to hold the farm produce received by the rector in payment of tithe. Beyond the garden is a stretch of some 30 acres reaching to the riverside, forming the Rectory park walled in by Egerton. Paley would later describe this Park thus:

> There is nearly a mile of wall planted with fruit trees, i.e. a rich field of ten acres, surrounded with

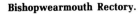

Bishopwearmouth Rectory.

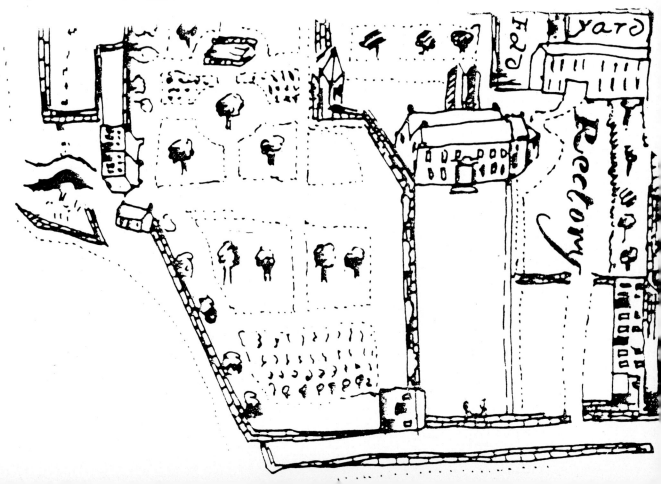

a well gravelled walk; gardens and shrubbery grounds, commanding some pretty views of the banks of the Wear, two or three hot houses and a greenhouse.[4]

On the west side of this walled retreat is the pretty dene known as the Rectors' Gill. This is the exit point of the burn which rises near Hasting Hill (and which is most visible today in Barnes Park and Burn Park). The Gill is already being nibbled away by industrial development. There is the rector's own quay, there are some workers' cottages, and the Gill is also crossed by a path and a lane which link up with the glassworks at Ayres Quay and Deptford. (The building of the Newbottle Waggonway is still some 30 years off and with it the enormous wayleave income which rectors would derive from the coal being moved down to the drops on the river bank.)

At this time the total glebe land of the rector is about 130 acres (extending — in today's terms — from the Royalty to High Barnes, and between Chester Road and Hylton Road). At the centre (near the present Kayll Road) stands the substantial Glebe Farm. Many years ago the glebe was enclosed and divided into 19 fields with hawthorn hedges. The rector's glebe is only half of the total land of the Rectory Manor which is some 240 acres in extent. The non-glebe sections are leased out to tenants and include some sections which are already being developed — as with the Sunniside district.

A short step north-west from the church takes us to the Hinds' Bridge across the burn. Its name, in fact, derives from a term used for a farm worker. However lowly the origin of its name this bridge is of considerable significance since it carries the main road to Newcastle via Ford (or South Hylton). (In 1753 an eminent local coalfitter, Mr William Maude, was drowned while attempting to ford the river there.) Near the Hinds Bridge stands a toll booth belonging to the rector of Bishopwearmouth.

Indeed this is a good point at which to stand and gaze around. Looking to the left down the lane alongside the Burn one can see a series of properties belonging to well-to-do families such as the Ayres, the Sharps and the Easterbys. Turning to look towards the west, the extensive tracts of land which can be seen belong not to the rector but to William Johnson of Silksworth, who recently inherited his brother's share of their father's estate to add to his own. Johnson's career — like that of the unlucky Maude — is as a coalfitter. The coalfitters are independent coal merchants, and in the main the wealthiest residents of Sunderland and Bishopwearmouth.[5] Some 280,000 chaldrons of coal a year are exported from Sunderland (a chaldron = 53 hundredweights) as opposed to the 400,000 from Tyneside and this trade is held together by the middlemen fitters.

Turning around and proceeding past the rectory garden we may pause again briefly at the end of Church Lane and consider our surroundings. Facing on to Church Lane itself is a block of buildings known as the Hospital House. These are almshouses built in 1727 and maintained from the proceeds of endowed lands. They were established by Jane Gibson the widow of a prominent merchant. They are meant for the reception of "twelve decayed old women who have been in better circumstances". (At a later date the Mowbray family inherited responsibility for their administration. They were rebuilt in 1863 and extensively renovated in 1983.)

Here again one is confronted with the problem of the elusive true centre of Bishopwearmouth. It is very likely that the complexity of the layout of Bishopwearmouth is due to the Normans. It was probably one of those villages wasted by the invaders during their counter-insurgency operations in the north. Then the village was laid out again along the broad street to the north of the church faced with lines of villeins' cottages. The odd twisted access points are typical defensive features of such a layout. As confirmation of this view there was the old tendency to call this area 'the Square' or 'Front Street'.

Towards Sunderland along the Sunderland Lonnin, (High Street West), the first very obvious feature is the 'blewstone' standing near the Peacock Inn. This stone represents the boundary of Bishopwearmouth village and stands at the intersection of Crow Tree Lane and the Sunderland Lonnin. The Peacock Inn — 'Mr Wilson's Premises' — is the chief inn of Bishopwearmouth. Rain does not show the stables of the Peacock which stood opposite it. Nor does he show for that matter its competitor the ancient Red Lion Inn which was founded in 1630 and stood on the west side of Crow Tree Lane. On the other hand our guide does show very clearly the high stone wall which lines the west side of Crow Tree Lane all the way to Vine Place protecting gardens and vineries. (The Peacock Inn later became — in 1831 — the Londonderry Arms. The present Londonderry is a much later building on the same site.)

ALONG SUNDERLAND LONNIN

We step out eastwards along the Lonnin, and have a splendid view of very fine gardens to the right of us which are owned by wealthy families such as the Fawcetts, Harrisons and Leightons. John Harrison is a coalfitter whose family have been for many years the agents of the Earl of Scarborough. Harrison owns that grand house ahead of us just opposite the end of Pann Lane although he normally lives at the family home in Whitburn. The Fawcetts are, of course, that very wealthy Newcastle family who own land in Boldon, Lambton, Chester le Street and Newcastle as well as Sunderland. (After the building of the Wearmouth Bridge in 1796 the 19 acres of the Fawcetts in Bishopwearmouth were to become much magnified in value as the commercial axis of the town was altered. Upon it would be built the fine terraces of John Street, Frederick Street, Foyle Street and Fawcett Street.)

On the other side of the Lonnin is the developing 'overspill' from Bishopwearmouth which is creeping eastwards towards Sunderland. Already built, upon land which had probably once belonged to Harrison, there is Hopper Lane (later Castle Street), Chapel Street (later Dunning Street), Queen Street, Factory Street (later Cumberland Street),

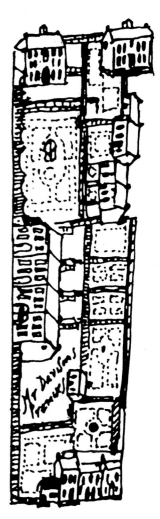

Properties between Pan Lane and Green Street.

Green Street and Pann Lane. They include the poorer houses of artisans as well as elegant Georgian terraced properties and detached houses set in their own gardens. Amongst them, at the head of Chapel Street, is Dunning House, the home of Christopher Bramwell the son of a former rector of Sunderland and the founder of a wines and spirits business on Church Street as well as part owner of a chemical works in Heworth.

On Chapel Street stands the Roman Catholic Chapel which holds up to 400 persons. To the east of it the large detached house is the meeting house of the Sunderland Baptists which was built in 1763. (The latter would be replaced in 1798 by the chapel on Sans Street. The Catholics would have to wait until 1835 for the building of their grand new church, St Mary's, to replace their old chapel.)

In the very midst of these residential properties stands a sail cloth factory. (In a few years time this factory would pass into the hands of Messrs. Mounsey and Richardson who would diversify into the production of furs and beaverskin hats.) Beyond this street and down towards the riverside there are also a number of blockyards which produce that other vital ingredient in the handling of sailing ships. (At this time, in the days before Marc Brunel, blocks were produced manually. Brunel, was to invent a mechanical device which would break the production bottleneck which so concerned the Admiralty.) Sails, blocks — the third in the trilogy is, of course, rope. However we will encounter this element elsewhere.

At the eastern end of Harrison's land stands another toll booth (where Littlewoods is today) and here we have to pay to proceed. We pass between the lands of the Fawcetts on the right and of the Lambtons on the left. The Lambtons are, of course, an ancient family of gentry whose fortunes were originally based upon salt, coal and fortunate marriage arrangements. Major General Sir John Lambton is the colonel of the 68th Regiment of Foot and MP for the City of Durham.

Attracted now by the promise of refreshment in one of the hostelries of Sunderland we pause only to admire the fine Fawcett mansion and the ornamental gardens which cover such a large part of this area. Most of them are the rather old-fashioned French-style gardens consisting of parterres of lawns, hedges and flower plots, interspersed with coloured paths formed from earths, chalk dust, coal dust and broken brick. The resultant effect is 'like a knot made of divers coloured ribbons'.

Adjacent to the Fawcett mansion is the small hamlet of Sunniside; overlooking this is the residence of the Maude family. Warren Maude, who died in 1780, left the fortune he had made from coalfitting to his son Jacob. Jacob himself is at the centre of an on-going scandal. He left the Society of Friends and married two Quaker ladies in succession — both expelled from the Society for such disregard of its conventions. A consolation for them must be the chatelaineship of the fine Maude house which, with its extensive gardens including an orchard, stands amidst lands which extends to the Back Lane (Holmeside and Borough Road of future times).

AN INDUSTRIAL PANORAMA

The western boundary of Sunderland township is another part of the Back Lane (later Sans Street). Northwards this is extended along Russell Street, named after Matthew Russell who settled in Sunderland in 1717. He was a timber merchant and shipbuilder who had prospered and bought property in Low Street. In fact at this point it might be worthwhile to pursue another digression and stroll down Russell Street into the Panns and Low Street thoroughfare, a busy hive of activity running parallel to the river. Straight ahead of us stands the Russell raffyard and the Sunderland Bank. The former is one of the very many timber yards scattered all over the town, the latter an excellent example of the country banks developing all over the country throughout the century in response to provincial needs. They tend to be established by local merchants and tradesmen dealing through a merchant in London. William Russell is a major partner in this enterprise. Such banks circulate their own paper money which is backed by bullion or Bank of England notes. They can be involved in a wide range of activities although not so typical was the payment in 1768 of £27 12s 0d to 'Russell and Co.' the proceeds of a play 'for the benefit of the Corsicans' who were then engaged in the struggle for liberation from France.

Sunniside.

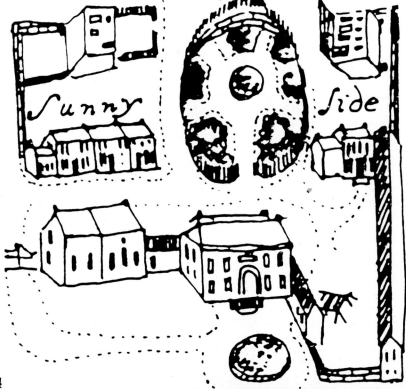

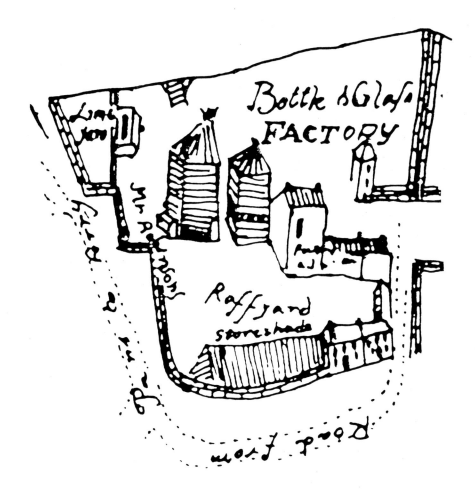

Along to the left and to the right of the junction there are many signs of industrial activity. The old salt industry has long ago disappeared leaving only place names such as 'the Panns'. Looking up river one of the most prominent features is the great glass cones. (As Dr. Dibdin, another travelling cleric, was to remark in later years Sunderland did '. . . a great shake of business in the glass way'.) Sunderland is one of the greatest glass-producing towns in the kingdom. The main bottle and glass works are concentrated in the Ayres Quay – Deptford – Panns region although glass is also produced at Southwick. (By 1818 there would be no less than 16 bottle houses producing up to 70,000 bottles a day. In that year exports from Sunderland would include 1,543 hundredweight of bottles, 1,296 hundredweight of crown glass and 463 hundredweight of flint glass.)

The local pottery industry is also a significant employer. In Low Street stands the warehouse of the Newbottle Pottery which was established in 1700 and specialises in the production of brown and white ware for local domestic use. The Garrison Pottery also opened in the early eighteenth century and is famous for its gold lustre and its lions. Then, of course, there is the North Hylton Pottery of the Maling brothers which opened in 1762 and is already renowned for its lustre and enamel ware and its frog mugs but is especially famous because of its process for printing pictures on to pottery using copper plates. (Even as the Eye Plan was drawn the industry was expanding. Scotts opened the Southwick Pottery in 1788 and John Brunton opened in the following year.)

Of course much of the produce of the potteries and glasshouses is used to hold the ales and beers which are such an important element of dietary needs. On the south side of the river is one of the many breweries — Elstob and Company. Over on the north side is the big Stafford Abbs brewery. A major site determinant is the availability of water and indeed each of these breweries has its own well. They supply the local beerhouses and inns and the weak ale used commonly as a table drink. They also supply ale and water to

the ships standing in the river and harbour. In fact even as we stand looking across the river a seaman is in a boat taking on board a barrel from the Stafford Abbs brewery.

Also on the north side of the river we can see smoke rising from the cinder kilns or coke ovens. These ovens produce an ingredient which is vital to the process of iron working because it is smokeless and does not react with hot iron so the smiths can work wrought iron without it hardening. From the middle of the century stone-built ovens have been built in the north to produce coke in commercial quantities. The coke produced on Wearside is used locally but there is also an export trade.

Just a little down river from the coke ovens is the landing of Mr Burn which is almost opposite the Pann Ferry. We can see there is a ship being built there. Burns have been building ships here and at other points on the riverside since 1691. The building of ships so close to the river can be somewhat of a problem. The River Wear Commissioners are on occasion deeply concerned by the very real danger of unfinished vessels being carried into the channel at high tide and drifting aimlessly in the midst of the busy traffic. Clearly, however, there is big money to be made in shipbuilding because how else could the Nicholson family afford the very substantial double fronted, three-storied house with pillars, steps and railings which faces their prosperous shipyard?

The only way to cross the river is to ford it further up or to cross it by ferry. At Sunderland there are two ferries — the Pann Ferry and the Sunderland Ferry. The former crosses at a point which will later be the site of the admired and controversial iron bridge. The latter would overturn one evening in 1795 and result in the deaths of 17 passengers, only a year or so before the bridge opened.

Sunderland ferry.

A PAUSE

High Street can be rejoined by retracing our steps along Russell Street or, further along, by Bodlewell Lane which takes its name from a nearby well which supplies water to many local houses and where the water costs a bodle — a half farthing — for a skeel holding two gallons. Leading off from High Street to the south is a series of streets and alleys in a fairly symmetrical pattern reflecting the old elongated burgage garths of the burgesses which had been derived from the enclosed sections of the old common fields. They back on to a lane (later to become Coronation Street and Prospect Row), and beyond lies the town moor and the open fields. By now most of the garths have been built upon and a once busy medieval borough has become a very populous modern urban community.

Along these streets and alleys are all sorts of features worth noting. However, at this point, having spent a busy morning exploring the town it might be better to roll up the plan for a while and resort to one of the inns on the main street. Much of the produce of the breweries was directed towards the many local taverns, public houses and inns. In fact there is a marked technical difference between the various types. Essentially it is a question of the

nature and combination of refreshment and accommodation provided. On the Eye Plan Rain shows plenty of each although he can do no more than show a sample of the ubiquitous alehouses and taverns. There are many public houses in Low Street alone, which serve the transient mass of sailors and keelmen. We, however, shall enter one of the better inns which cater for those with more cultivated tastes.

For instance there is the Golden Lion with its large stable yard and coach houses. It was rebuilt recently and is owned by a gentleman known as 'Willie the King' because he was once the tenant of a public house called the King George III. It is let to Thomas Jowsey a former tenant of the King's Head in High Street. Such men as Willie Irvine and Thomas Jowsey are respected members of the community. The inns are heavily involved in the network of local road communications and the innkeepers often have a share in the local turnpike trusts (cynics would say that they also have shares in highway robbery). The inns are also the main assembly rooms for local functions and gatherings. The River Wear Commissioners, for instance, always meet in the local inns and one of their favourites is the Golden Lion.

Emerging from the inn we can renew our exploration of the side streets. Playhouse Lane, which is the former Society Lane (named after the early Methodist Society which met here) contains the Theatre Royal which was established by Thomas Bates in the 1760s in a building which was once used by the Methodists and was preached in by Wesley himself. (This playhouse would later be run by Bates' own nephew James Cawdell. In the 1850s it would be replaced by another Theatre Royal on Bedford Street.)

Behind the Golden Lion, down the western side of Queen Street, stands the Phoenix Lodge which is the centre of freemasonry in Sunderland. It was built in 1784-1785 to replace the previous lodge which had been burnt down in 1783. Hence, of course, its name.

Venturing into Covent Garden we encounter one of the windmills which Rain has depicted. Usually the mills were built on high ground on the periphery of the town. In Sunderland and Bishopwearmouth, when settlement expanded, the ring of mills moved outwards. On our street guide Rain shows two types of mill. There are the lighter post mills which are suspended from a large central wooden post and are moved bodily to catch the wind. The relative lack of stability means that they have a disconcerting tendency to topple over in strong gusts of wind. Far more balanced are the heavier tower mills capped by a rotating sail mechanism.

CHAPELS AND CHURCHES

Also much in evidence in this part of the parish is the very active protestant nonconformist community. Just to the west of Russell Street stands the Quaker Meeting House with its school and burial ground. Quakers such as the Maudes, Ogdens, Mounseys, Wilsons and Richardsons are amongst the most prominent and wealthy families in the town. This house dates from the late seventeenth century, although it was rebuilt after its destruction in a riot in 1688. (In 1822 it would be replaced by a meeting house on Nile Street.) Directly to the north of it stands the Numbers Garth Methodist Chapel which was opened by John Wesley himself in 1759 during one of his 30 or so visits to the town. (In 1793 it would be replaced by another on the corner of Sans Street, the old Back Lane, and High Street.) Then to the east of Russell Street between High Street and Low Street stands the Calvinist Cornmarket Chapel which in the 1730s suffered from the secession of an element of the congregation over the issue of the introduction of hymns. In 1739 this secessionist group built their own Presbyterian chapel on Robinson's Lane east of Church Street. Further south, near the Covent Garden windmill, is another Presbyterian secessionist meeting house which was built in 1766. The present minister is Thomas Mason of Dunbar, the father of 22 children whom he must support on a stipend of £80. No wonder his wife is driven to sell tea and coffee; and he gives Hebrew classes for Jewish boys.

Wandering further along High Street towards its junction with Church Street we pass through the market area which dates back to the charter of Bishop Morton of 1634. The old market cross and stocks are just to the north of Union Lane, with the butchers' market or shambles to the east of it. Just opposite it are the shops of some of the wealthier butchers of the town with their stalls projecting. West of the cross is the bakers' market. The poultry and dairy produce markets are near Queen Street. The seed and corn market is near the Bodlewell Lane junction with High Street. A wide range of other goods — shoes, leatherware, clothing and so on — are sold on stalls along the High Street. To the east of Church Street are the vegetable stalls. It is also in this part of High Street that the town fairs have been held every May and October since 1634.

The more fashionable streets are in the district which we are now entering. Streets such as Silver Street, Vine Street and Fitters Row contain merchants, professional people, fitters, prosperous tradesmen and so on. As we walk along Church Street towards Holy Trinity Church we pass some very grand houses such as those of the Burleighs, Freemans, Maudes and Bramwells. Amongst them is the house of Bernard Ogden, the Quaker businessman with interests including a chemist shop, flour milling, copperas manufacturing and shipowning. (Nos 10 and 11 Church Street still survive, three storeys high and five bays wide.)

So on to the church. The early years of the century saw a campaign by the prosperous citizens of the growing town of Sunderland — with 6,000 inhabitants by 1719 — to establish an independent parish. By 1719 both money and parliamentary approval had become available. This church ahead of us on a corner of the Town Moor is built of brick and in the classical style.

To the north is the rectory, a substantial building. The basic stipend of the rector is only £80 — largely because there is no glebe land

attached to the living and the parochial tithes remain with the rectors of Bishopwearmouth. However other sources make his income altogether about £250. Over to the west of the churchyard stands the Assembly Garth. The building with the flag is the Assembly Room which serves as a place of assembly for the citizens, for public and recreational purposes. On the south side of the Garth are almshouses for sailors or their widows. At the north-east corner of the church yard stands the poor house of Sunderland which is considerably larger than that of Bishopwearmouth.

The building of this church has been only one episode in the erosion of the town moor, a large stretch of common pasture bounded by the river in the north, the sea in the east, Robinson's Dene in the south, and by the fields of the manor of Bishopwearmouth in the west. The rights to pasturage on this common land were recognised in Bishop Puiset's charter of c. 1180 and confirmed by Bishop Morton in 1634. By the seventeenth century it was about 80 acres in extent. It is divided by stone walls into three sections — the Great Moor, the North Moor and the Intake. The grazing rights are managed by the freemen but in fact it was the freemen who abused their power in 1715 by laying claim to the Coney Warren in the north-east corner which was growing in value as the town grew. They divided it amongst themselves and started to build the 'new town' of Sunderland upon it. In fact this was only one — albeit the main — incursion. So far throughout the century the moor has been progres-

Holy Trinity (Sunderland Parish Church).

The Old Cast Iron Bridge 1793-1796

Road traffic originally crossed the Wear by four ferries in or near Sunderland. Their inconvenience and insecurity led to demands for a bridge and in 1788 Robert Shout (1734-97), then engineer to the Port of Sunderland, proposed a large masonry arch of 170ft span. This was relatively daring and an alternative plan with two 90ft spans and a river pier 18ft wide was also mooted.

The Wear, roughly 250ft wide, was then thronged with tall masted ships and controversy arose between the land and river users as to the best form of bridge and its location. In the event Shout's design was shelved and the matter stayed unresolved until a hand was taken in the matter by Rowland Burdon (1757-1838), of Castle Eden, son of a Newcastle banker. In 1790 he and Ralph Milbanke became joint Members of Parliament for the County of Durham, one of their election promises being to improve local communications. In 1791 Burdon gathered ideas for a Sunderland bridge from various sources, ranging from reputable experts to hopeful entrepreneurs, and considered the rival merits of stone, wood and iron as construction materials.

An Act of Parliament was necessary before the bridge could be built. Burdon submitted a draft Bill to the House of Commons in March 1792 and the Act received Royal Assent in June. The Act dealt at length with tolls and ferry compensation but said little about the bridge itself, which was merely required to have a main span of at least 120ft, to provide at least 80ft vertical clearance for shipping, and be at least 26ft wide. The material was unspecified although it was tacitly assumed that masonry was intended. Unfortunately it became clear from the testimony of expert witnesses that a long-span high-level masonry bridge would cost at least £70,000 and be a risky venture. An obvious cheap alternative was timber but this was notoriously short-lived and there was a similar lack of precedents to draw upon for a span of the order of 200ft.

Burdon was at last coming to the conclusion that iron would be the best solution — it was the least tried of all, but more durable than wood, and much lighter and cheaper than stone. A famous iron arch had existed over the Severn at Coalbrookdale since 1779 but its ribs were cast in massive half-lengths which had pushed contemporary foundry practice to its limits: it was doubtful if similar principles could be applied to a span twice as long. However from October 1790 to October 1791 a much lighter

The original cast iron bridge under construction, with the centering still in place. A view from the east, by Robert Clarke.

The cast iron bridge in the mid-1850s, just before its replacement by the Stephenson version.

and simpler 100ft span iron bridge had been exhibited in London by Thomas Paine (1737-1809) who claimed that this system, patented by him in 1788, was suitable for spans up to at least 400ft. This arch had been made for him by the renowned Walker ironworks at Rotherham and, in the summer of 1791, the Walkers took a model of Paine's system to Castle Eden. In the autumn a design for a 200ft span of this type was made for Burdon.

Despite its economic attractiveness, Paine's system — which consisted of thin wrought-iron bars bent to an arch form and spaced concentrically one above another by 2ft long cast-iron tubes or blocks — was self-evidently very flimsy and it is unlikely that this proposal was given serious consideration for long. However, also in the second half of 1791, the Walkers had introduced Burdon to John Rastrick (1738-1826), a millwright from Morpeth who had devised a better system based on that of stone arches i.e. using some form of voussoir blocks made of cast iron. This concept was not original for arch systems made of iron voussoirs (although largely impracticable ones) had been exhibited and discussed throughout the previous decade in Paris. In mid-1792, faced with the fact that a long-span stone bridge was going to be prohibitively expensive and of doubtful practicality, it was decided to look more closely at the iron voussoir system. Regrettably, details of Rastrick's proposal have not survived and it is not known how far it resembled the design which was finally evolved.

In November 1792 the Bridge Committee, which had been set up in accordance with the Act's requirements, held a meeting to decide on the bridge site and the material to be used. In December, Burdon, as prime mover in the scheme, engaged a local schoolmaster, Thomas Wilson (c1750-1820), to superintend the construction of an arched bridge made of cast-iron voussoir blocks having a nominal span of 240ft, the details to be worked out in conjunction with the Walkers. During the next six months a trial rib was made and test-loaded at the Rotherham works under the auspices of the foundry foreman William Yates. Simultaneously work was started on the foundations of the bridge abutments and in September 1793 the foundation-stone ceremony was held. It was then publicly announced that the arch would be made of iron.

It took until the spring of 1795 to raise the masonry abutments to the level where the arch ribs were to be located and, during the interim, details of the centering were worked out. Because the iron ribs were very light compared with those of a stone arch, centering of

The reconstructed bridge of Robert Stephenson; with the Lambton (Newbottle) staiths and drops in the foreground. (Photograph c. 1875.)

unprecedented lightness could be used and the system chosen was a variant of one proposed earlier by John Nash (1752-1835), using two scaffolds in the river as intermediate supports. (Nash's plan however had been for a masonry arch.) This timberwork was erected in the summer of 1795 and on it the iron ribs were assembled in September. Rib assembly took only ten days but nearly a year more was required to complete the spandrels and deck. The structure was finally opened to traffic on 9th August 1796.

The bridge had six arch ribs, each consisting of 105 cast blocks about 2ft 5in. long, 5ft deep, and 4in. wide, weighing roughly 4½cwt. Longitudinally these blocks were strapped together with wrought-iron bands (three on each side — at top, middle and bottom), about 3 × 1in. Laterally the ribs were connected by cast-iron tubes 6ft long × 4in. diameter with 18in. flanges on each end. Altogether the blocks weighed about 140 tons, the wrought-iron straps and bolts 36 tons, and the cross tubes 27 tons. In addition to this the spandrel-work, decking, paving, etc., amounted to another 720 tons so that the whole superstructure totalled less than 1,000 tons. The tall masonry abutments were the most costly item in the bridge, the ironwork costing a mere £6,130. The total cost of the structure was about £28,000, although the purchase of land, ferry rights and other incidentals brought the total outlay to just over £40,000. Burdon personally contributed £30,000 of this and would have done handsomely out of the toll income, for the bridge

All tolls had been abolished by 1847 but in order to pay for the reconstruction of the bridge the Corporation re-imposed charges for all but foot passengers in 1858 and restored the unpopular foot tolls in 1875. All tolls were abolished finally ten years later.

was a great financial success, had he not become bankrupt over another scheme in 1806 and had to forfeit his shares.

There has been disagreement as to who should be awarded most of the honours for the ironwork design. Burdon patented the system in September 1795, just after the main ribs had been successfully assembled, and thus became the legal inventor although Rastrick began an inconclusive public dispute with him about authorship of the basic concept after the bridge was opened to traffic. Most modern writers accord the design honours to Wilson, who was undoubtedly the official architect/engineer, although it is probable that most of the ironwork details were due to the foundry experts at Rotherham.

The effects of unequal thermal expansion caused the arch to develop an alarming bulge on the sunniest side after a few years, many of the cross tubes falling out as a result. In 1805 a local engineer John Grimshaw (c1762-1840) installed horizontal diagonal bracing between the ribs and drew them back into line. Without his intervention it is doubtful if the bridge would have survived another decade. With his improvement the bridge survived until the 1850s when major reconstruction was undertaken by consultant engineer Robert Stephenson. A new Act was obtained in 1857 and the bridge was re-opened in March 1859. In this work the superstructure was stripped down to the arch ribs which were left in situ; tubular wrought-iron arches were then inserted between them to relieve them of load and new spandrel-work and decking raised on top. The abutments were also raised so that the new deck was almost level from end to end instead of having the inconvenient hump which was such a feature of the old bridge. In this form the arch survived until the present one was built 1927-9. To keep traffic flowing the new bridge was erected around the old one, Burdon's ribs only being finally dismantled in 1929. Incredibly, not one voussoir block appears to have been kept as a memento.

The third, and present, Wearmouth bridge.

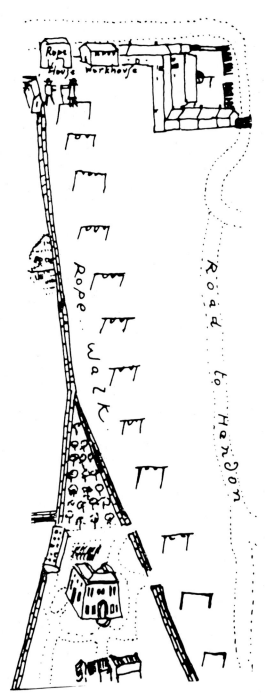

Right, A rope walk adjacent to Holy Trinity Church. Below, A coastal gun battery.

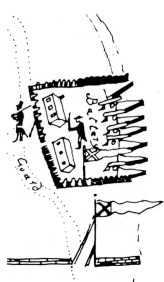

other parts of the town at least he includes these token kilns which are representative of what is one of the most important industries in Sunderland. In the production and export of lime Sunderland dominates the markets of north Yorkshire, Northumberland and Southern Scotland. Most of the output comes from the Pallion quarries of the Goodchild family, from Fulwell, Southwick, the Sheepfolds and the Town Moor. Mostly it is used in the de-acidification of agricultural land but is also important in the production of plaster and a particularly water resistant mortar.

Over towards the coast is a large pond used for watering cattle and horses. The moor acts as a vital communal centre, an assembly point for groups such as disgruntled seamen, agitating keelmen and bible-thumping religious enthusiasts. It is also available for purposes such as the drying of fishing nets and washing and as a site for village fairs and festivals. Horse racing is a regular feature; bulls, bears and badgers are bloodily baited; and fights between cockerels and bull terriers attract considerable crowds of gambling gentlemen.

Before we turn northwards and head towards the harbour, the pulsating heart of the community, there is an opportunity to call in on St. John's Church. This, the second post-reformation church in Sunderland, was completed and consecrated in 1769. It was intended to cope with the rapidly increasing population of Sunderland parish.

The chief projector and the architect of the new church was the ambitious coal exporter John Thornhill. He was a resident of Sunderland but later moved to his fine new house in Bishopwearmouth, Thornhill House. The style of the church standing before us is similar to that of Holy Trinity. (Upon Thornhill's death in 1802 St John's ceased to be a proprietary chapel and became a daughter church of Holy Trinity. In 1875 St John's became a separate parish. By then it served the most severely deprived part of the borough. The building was eventually demolished in 1972.)

Stepping out briskly towards the harbour and enjoying the scent of the sea breeze we pass, on the right, a series of formidable gun batteries which protect the town and the harbour from the depredations of French privateers and from the activities of John Paul Jones. Indeed such an impression has been made by that Scottish murderer and Yankee pirate that one of the four gun batteries is actually called after him. The guns — 24 and 32 pounders — are manned by the brave men of Sunderland's own volunteer artillery which is officered by local gentlemen. An officer and soldier are on duty as we pass.

THE HARBOUR

Now at last we have come to the harbour where so much of interest is happening. We are by no means alone because there are numerous ladies and gentlemen promenading along the quayside and observing the movement of vessels. This scene is in stark contrast to the harbour entrance of only 75 years ago. In 1717 the River Wear Commissioners were created to convert a decaying harbour and

sively reduced in size as people build houses and business premises and lay out gardens.

Walking on from Holy Trinity over the moor towards St. John's Church other aspects of Sunderland's industrial development are encountered. As well as sails and blocks the other vital ingredient in the propulsion of ships is rope. Thousands of miles of hempen rope are required every year and it is produced in rope walks throughout the seaports of the kingdom. Here on the town moor is a good example of a rope walk with its distinctive rows of skirders used to support the strands which are twisted to make rope. Normally there would be three or four strands. For shrouds for the Royal Navy a scarlet strand is included as a precaution against theft.

Beyond the rope walk can be seen lime kilns. Although Rain ignores the existence of kilns in lower river to suit the needs of the rapidly developing coal trade. The activities of the RWC are very evident in the lower harbour. The manually operated dredger is working industriously off the Watch House. It is this dredging machine which has been hired out to gentlemen like the Earl of Scarborough to dredge before their property. At the entrance to the harbour stands a new North Pier — parallelling the old South Pier which was extravagantly described in 1748 by the Swiss engineer Charles Labelye as "one of the Most Magnificent and best built in the whole world."[6] Damaged by the awful flood of 1771 the South Pier itself has also been reoriented. To the south stands the Pier House where lives the RWC resident engineer, 'over the shop' so to speak. The employees of the RWC, their horses and equipment, move and work the stone which has been supplied by the Goodchild owners of the Pallion quarries who are also prominent members of the RWC.

In various places along the river can be seen a number of vessels of various shapes and sizes. They range in size from one very large 'ship-rigged' craft down to the small brigantines and 'billy boys' with their extravagant jib booms. The bulk of the vessels though are the collier brigs, the two masted workhorses of the coastal trade, square rigged and ranging up to 300 tons.

Weaving in and out of these larger vessels are lots of small craft. Most of them are keels. Some of them are meeting the colliers to unload their return cargoes of ballast which will be dumped at sea or on designated land sites. More numerous are the flat-bottomed coal keels carrying their eight chaldrons of coal down river to rendezvous with the colliers. Some of these are propelled by means of large, red-dyed sails while in the shallower reaches they are 'puyed' along using a forked 'set'. In the early 18th century there were some 200 keels working along the Wear.

The small sturdy brigs are the main product of the growing number of shipyards. Just across the river from where we stand on Nobles Quay we can see a large yard. As we watch we can observe the sweating shipwrights wielding their saws, axes and adzes while a couple of well-girthed foremen stand and oversee their efforts. There are piles of timber lying around in the form of ribs, planking and angled knees. Materials are stored in sheds more as a protection against the pilfering which masquerades as the taking of 'lawful perquisites'. There are five vessels on the stocks here at the yard of Mr James Leithead which actually stands upon a large sandbank, created recently as a result of the building of the North Pier. At this time the output of the Wear yards is small.

RETURN JOURNEY

Weaving in and out of the ranks of spectators watching men at work on the quayside and in the harbour, and leaving behind the palls of coal dust which blacken the sails of the ships and faces of the people, we can now retrace our steps towards High Street, then back up Church Street to Holy Trinity where we can

The piers.

join the Back Lonnin which will take us back to Bishopwearmouth.

On the way, over on the left opposite the end of Walton Lane, stands a large farm house with a barn and a yard sheltered by outbuildings and in which the stock can shelter and accumulate the manure which is so important to the farmer. Nearby is a dyehouse. This is probably explained by the use of animal urine in the production of natural dyes. Actually it makes a good material for adding to the family wash and many homes will have buckets of human urine standing maturing. There are also a couple of brick grounds with solid, hand-made bricks stacked up and drying out. Just over the road is a hat factory where are produced the fashionable beaver skin hats sported by the gentlemen idling along the riverside.

Continuing along the Back Lonnin and passing along the back of the properties of Messrs. Aiskel, Walton, Trotter and General Lambton, we rejoin the Bishopwearmouth back lane and move southwards. At least as early as 1737 there was a farm here called Field House.

Continuing onwards past the grounds of General Lambton, of Messrs Coxon and Todd

A shipbuilding yard near the North Pier.

The tollgate on Durham Road.

which winds 2¼ miles through fields and farmland to the little hamlet near the Tunstall Hills. Just adjacent to it is the start of the old Ryhope Way. The two highways create between them an island of properties which will later become Albion Place. Ahead of us is the road back, via the Durham-Sunderland turnpike.

REFERENCES
1. Most of this chapter is derived from M. Clay, G. Milburn and S. Miller, *An Eye Plan of Sunderland and Bishopwearmouth 1785 — 1790 by John Rain* (Newcastle, 1984). The original of the Eye Plan is no longer available. The best copies are in the hands of the Sunderland Central Library, the Sunderland Museum and the Sunderland Antiquarian Society. Very good reproductions can be purchased from the latter at a very reasonable price.
2. H. L. Robson, "Maintenance of the Poor in Sunderland under the Parish Vestry", *Antiq. Sund.* XXIV.
3. *Sunderland Year Book* 1906 p.31.
4. *Ibid.*
5.   In 1802 the travelling cleric the Reverend Richard Warner was to describe their status thus:

> Four different bodies of people extract a profit from the Sunderland coals before they appear in a foreign market — the colliers who dig them; the proprietors of the mines who sell them to the third description of people; the fitters a sort of middlemen, who bring the article from the mines and deliver them to the fourth description of persons concerned — the merchants. The largest profit is derived to the fitters whose risque is nothing and payment prompt. They receive about a shilling a chaldron for coal sold and for the trouble of providing keels and keelmen who, however, are paid for by the shipowners; and the fortunes acquired in this place are generally by them.

Rev. R. Warner, *A Tour through the Northern Counties of England and the Borders of Scotland* (Newcastle, 1802).
6. C. Labelye, A Report relating to the Improvement of the river Wear and Port of Sunderland made after a view thereof taken in July 1748, TWAS.

to the left and of the Fawcetts to the right we now approach Crowtree Road again. We pass the end of the road to Building Hill — a name probably derived from nothing more exotic than the tendency to take good building stone from there. This is part of the estate of the Mowbrays whose house stands on the top of the hill. At the moment it is a sort of inn and spirits shop run by Messrs. Hogg and Renner whose customers are, no doubt, appropriately prepared to encounter the ghost said to haunt the wind-blown house. Over to the right now are the estates of the Maudes and Leightons. Near the junction of Crow Tree Lane and the Back Lane stands Holmside House which belongs to Samuel Maude.

In fact at this point our tour of Sunderland and Bishopwearmouth in the company of Mr Rain (by proxy) is virtually completed because we are back at the end of Green Terrace. Over to the south west is the 'Road from Tunstall'

The cartouche of Rain's Eye Plan.

Harbour and River Improvement

In 1847, following the presentation of a paper to the Institute of Civil Engineers by the Sunderland harbour engineer John Murray,[1] the eminent consultant Sir John Rennie remarked of the previous 130 years of harbour improvement at Sunderland that

> ... the entire system that had been followed was well worthy of the attention of engineers as the port was a striking example of what might be affected by adopting correct general principles and persevering in their execution ... The consideration of the whole of this question was well worthy of the attention of the younger members of the profession.

Indeed this was not entirely true. In reality the story was one of much trial and frequent error, of accident and adaptability, and of dogged persistence, only in the course of which were appropriate principles evolved.

THE EARLY YEARS OF RIVER IMPROVEMENT

At the start of the eighteenth century the basic problem of Sunderland was that the great potential of the coal trade was not matched by an adequate harbour. In fact the river was on the verge of asphyxiation by its bars and sand banks. To the Tyne coal interest the state of the port of its competitor was a joke. 'J.C.' wrote, with just an element of pleasure,

> There wants a peor ... Besides the Bar is so choaked up that there is a great want of water ... If any storm arises at sea there is no safety in offering to go into Sunderland ...[2]

An attempt to establish a river improvement commission was blocked by the Tyne coal trade in 1705-1706 but in 1717 a bill was enacted and the River Wear Commissioners were established.

The River Wear Commission (RWC) enjoyed renewable statutory powers. Its ranks were filled — until 1861 — by nomination and co-option from amongst coalowners, landowners and members of the business community of Sunderland and the Wear region. The jurisdiction of the Board extended originally as far as Durham City but in 1759 it was cut back more realistically to the Biddick ford. The main source of revenue was a bi-annual levy on coal exports from the Wear to which was added, from the early nineteenth century, a duty payable by each ship per voyage using the harbour. Within a few years, between 1725 and 1730, the RWC had completed its first major harbour work, the South Pier. This 'major piece of maritime construction', as Professor Skempton describes it,[3] was designed to shelter the harbour and direct the force of the river against the bar. However, it was in the half century, following a major report, by the eminent Swiss engineer Charles Labelye[4], that a programme of intensive improvement was undertaken by the RWC.

In the early 1750s the use of a combination of old hulks and training jetties to block the north channel and considerable "Boreing Schemes" (sic) to deepen the south channel, achieved the consolidation of the river into one channel. From at least 1749 the RWC was contracting out the dredging of the harbour. In addition it assumed the role of traffic regulator to keep the channel free from obstruction. Keel skippers and collier masters were regularly fined for depositing ballast in the river or mooring in prohibited stretches. Keels had to be regularly weighed, licensed and numbered to combat fraud. The RWC also prosecuted businessmen whose jetties and wharves were traffic hazards, irregularly sited or crumbling into the river.

The most visible activity of the RWC was its harbour works. In 1771 the great floods damaged the foundations of the South Pier. In any case it was under suspicion of being the cause of a large sand bank at the river mouth. As a result of a report by John Smeaton in 1780[5] it was largely rooted out and replaced by 1785. At the same time the then resident engineer Robert Shout also started work on a North Pier and by 1795 it was completed to a length of 700 feet. The consultant Ralph Dodd expressed himself "surprised that it was not done years ago, but better late than never".[6] Dodd also reflected the continuing suspicion that the South Pier was more productive of problems than cures and remarked that the idea of pulling it down completely was "in agitation". Indeed from then until the 1840s there was almost ceaseless work on the extension, refinement and realignment of the two piers in the same empirical manner by the harbour engineers Jonathan Pickernell (1795-1804), Matthew Shout (1804-1817), Thomas Milton (1817-1831) and John Murray (1832-1845).

It was the rather erratic Pickernell, dismissed in 1804 for misapplying the "money, wood, goods and property of the Commissioners", who was responsible for the addition of two very distinctive features to the harbour. In 1801-1802 he supervised the building of the fine octagonal lighthouse on the North Pier which became one of the symbols of the town. It was this 76 feet landmark which

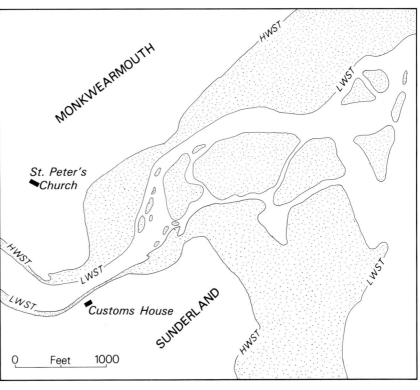

Sunderland Harbour, 1718-1719.

St. Peter's Church

Customs House

MONKWEARMOUTH

SUNDERLAND

HWST LWST

0   Feet   1000

was moved bodily along the North Pier, extended once again by John Murray, in 1841. This event, not the first or last example of Murray's originality, excited one local satirical rhymester to see Murray as the potential remover of the new workhouse and to wish

> ... they'll engage ye to shift all the bastilles (whare they part men and wife), ay, reet owre the peer ...[7]

Pickernell it was who also introduced the system of steam dredging from 1797. His steam governed dredger was the first of its kind in the world. Actually it was not very successful initially and in 1804 the old 'bag and spoon' method was restored, the steam equipment being sold off to local businessmen including Cuthbert Vaux. After these teething troubles steam dredging was reinstated in 1811.

Thomas Milton (something of a 'hi-tech' enthusiast) was the first engineer at Sunderland to make use of a diving bell to examine the foundations of the piers. A trip to London and a quick dip in one of the new gadgets made him a great advocate.

> I went down in a bell and the opinion of its usefulness which I had before entertained was the more confirmed. Small objects may be seen distinctly in it and a person may remain under water (up) to six hours at a time.[8]

According to Professor Skempton 1817 was a turning point in the development of the harbour:

> The sands and rocks on an exposed coast at the mouth of the River Wear had given way to a safe and commodious harbour with its entrance piers and lighthouse and a deep channel maintained by steam dredging. Much of course still remained to be done, but 1817 marks an important stage in the evolution of the modern harbour.[9]

In terms of the coal trade and competition with Newcastle, which is where this part of the account started, the RWC had been brilliantly successful. Over the period 1751-1790 Sunderland's export of coal rose by 63 per cent while Newcastle's rose by only 30 per cent. In the latter year 762,964 tons were exported from the Wear as opposed to 1,007,600 tons from the Tyne. The rate of growth continued to accelerate. The first three decades of the nineteenth century saw a quinquennial rate of growth of 11.36 per cent, double the average of the previous 30 years and contrasting favourably with the 8.54 per cent of Newcastle.[10] Dr. Swann sums up the previous hundred years as follows:

> The creation of a really successful harbour was in some cases the product of a century or more of progressive extension and improvement. No harbour illustrates this point better than that of Sunderland ... Only the slow process of experiment could answer the problem of how many piers were needed, how long they ought to be. Because of the limited state of civil engineering knowledge there was an element of groping in the dark.[11]

CHANGING CIRCUMSTANCES

The more mundane work of the RWC was concerned with man-made obstacles to navigation. Every user of the river and developer of the riverside was a potential cause of obstructions to navigation. Even the building of the famous bridge had, apparently, led to stones being thrown into the river. Indeed, progress was associated always with drawbacks. The steamship, for instance, was by no means an unmixed blessing. On the one hand there was a minor revolution in dredging when Milton started to use the RWC steamer *Seahorse* to tow the hoppers out to sea from 1823, with a consequent halving of the cost of removal. A fleet of tugboats also enabled a far more rapid turn around of shipping. In 1833 the ship owner Henry Tanner in evidence to a select committee of the House of Commons remarked that

> The facilities of steam vessels must increase the number of voyages; in former years a vessel would be in Sunderland harbour perhaps six weeks before she would go to sea, now she scarcely ever lies six days.[12]

On the other hand the RWC had to take steps to regulate the speed of steamships because their wakes could damage unquayed banks and cause havoc in crowded areas. Amongst other things the approach of steam vessels had to be signalled by the sounding of a bell.

From the early nineteenth century the real problem was that the economic interests of the town and of the coal trade were no longer synonymous. The economy of Sunderland was undergoing a fundamental change as it developed into an industrial town in its own right, a trend which was led and typified by the shipbuilding industry. This process served to enhance the problem of spoil and rubbish along the riverside, a greater length of quayage to be maintained, and the encroachment of local industries on the riverside and salt marsh regions. The issue was whether the river ought to be corsetted in quayed banks to strengthen its force, or whether the open salt grass regions should be

Sunderland harbour in 1819.

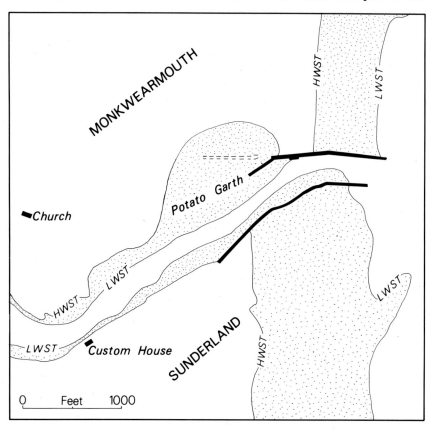

preserved to enable the accumulation of a greater volume of backwater.

The staple trade of the town was still the coal export trade. Here as well there were developments of considerable significance. In 1815 Nesham and Co. began to move coal directly by waggonway to the Rector's Gill from their Philadelphia pits. There it was loaded straight into the waiting colliers and so the use of keels was eliminated. The result was a violent riot by keelmen.[13] In 1822 the Hetton Coal Company began to move coal from Hetton Lyons to its riverside staiths along the Hetton Colliery Railway, the first line engineered by George Stephenson. A thriving coal trade had to be reconciled with riverside industrial development.

The issue came to a head between 1818 and 1824 when the RWC attempted to force the Pemberton family to reduce its encroachments on the river and especially a loading jetty built out into the channel. The Pembertons were a powerful family with extensive and diverse economic interests which included at a later date a major share in Monkwearmouth Colliery. They also exercised a solid block of votes within the RWC and could support their activities with theories about the value of quaying. In 1819 John Pemberton openly accused the RWC of being an oligarchy biased in the interests of the coal-owners. He claimed that it was attempting to

> erect the Commissioners into a junta to exclude the owners of lands from having the use of the River to prevent the River being improved for the benefit of those trading upon it and to secure the present owners of quays an extensive monopoly of the commerce of the River Wear.[14]

A long, costly and acrimonious conflict within the Board, in the courts and in parliamentary committees, eventually led to some sort of compromise involving the establishment of a legal quay line which defined the limits to encroachment on the riverside, and laid the basis for the achievement of a reasonably regular quayage.

By 1830 according to Dr. Swann "the problem had been solved" and "whereas it had

Top left, The moving of the North Pier Lighthouse in 1841. Bottom left, Sunderland harbour from the South Pier, an engraving by Thomas Allom about 1830. Below, A berthing notice of the RWC.

SUNDERLAND

Navigation Acts,

49th GEORGE III. cap. 41. and 59th GEORGE III. cap. 106

OWNERS and Masters of Ships, Pilots, and others, are hereby required to take Notice, that the Commissioners for putting the said Acts into Execution, are determined not to allow more than Nine Ships to lie, at any one time, in the Tier commonly called " The Ferry-boat Landing Tier," so that there never may be more than Two Ships on the Outside of the Mooring Chains placed there ;—Nor more than Eight Ships in the Tier commonly called " The Long Tier :"—Nor more than Four Ships in the Tier below the Long Tier and opposite the Mark Quay :—And that no Tier shall be allowed at the low part of the North Quay.

The Harbour Masters will keep a strict look-out, and all Offenders against the above Regulation will incur the Penalties imposed by the said Acts.

By Order of the Commissioners,

DAVIDSON, Clerk.

May 8th, 1822.

Sunderland, printed by Reed and Son, 189, High-Street.

once been necessary for large vessels to load coal outside the harbour the largest vessels could now come into the harbour to load".[15] Yet by 1830 the problem was changing. The extension of the Durham coalfield and the introduction of direct carriage of coal by railway were reflected in the fact that by 1830 the collieries of Hetton and Newbottle accounted for 53 per cent of the total exports through Sunderland. And railway development, as with the steamships, poses problems for the river.

The 1820s had seen the introduction by William Paterson of a system of loading Londonderry coal using chaldron tubs carried by keels and lifted by drops over the holds of colliers. Paterson also invented a floating drop which was anchored in the river and could be used in all conditions of tide — at least until it sank in 1828. Then in July 1831 Lord Londonderry started to export his coal from the new harbour at Seaham which was linked by railway to his Rainton pits. The result was that the proportion of Londonderry coal fell from 25.3 per cent of the Wear total to 10.2 per cent by 1834. In the long term though it was the development of the new harbour facilities on Teesside which represented an even greater threat. It was this development which accounts largely for the fact that in a decade of continued growth in north eastern coal exports Sunderland's share actually fell. Improved harbour facilities seemed to be the answer.

THE DOCKS QUESTION

As early as 1794 Ralph Dodd had suggested that a dock was "the greatest improvement your Harbour will admit of"[16] Then in 1828-1829 the consultant, Robert Stevenson, grandfather of the great novelist, produced two reports for the RWC in which he considered the various options, then came down in favour of a 30 acre dock on the south side of the river.[17] These reports were the background to the conflict over the site of the dock which followed.

The balance of logic lay with the south side. About 85 per cent of the coal shipped through Sunderland harbour in 1831 came from collieries on the south side of the river. The bulk of the business community resided on the south side, while Monkwearmouth was the somewhat decayed manor of the Williamson family. In addition, although the RWC was suffering from internal administrative and financial problems, and was divided over the issue, it was clear that by and large it supported the south side. On the other hand its support was not seen as being necessarily an advantage. The shipowner Solomon Chapman asked cynically in September 1831 if

> It would not be better in order to facilitate the completion of the dock without delay that its management should be placed in other hands than the Commissioners of the River Wear for if entrusted to the latter it would require half a century for the foundation of what all wished to see realised without delay . . .[18]

The project was taken up by a group of businessmen and a bill was promoted, but in April 1832 it was defeated in a committee of the House of Commons. The solicitors called it

> a prey to the selfishness of private interests, the influence of family connections and the artful machinations of professed friends but secret enemies.[19]

It may well have been, but in truth it was also a bad scheme. In the design by Francis Giles, an associate of the incomparable Brunel, the site was too exposed and required an expensive angled sea wall.[20]

In July of the same year (1832), a bill to enable the creation of a dock on the north side on the property of Sir Hedworth Williamson was also defeated. This scheme was based upon a plan produced by Brunel himself. As one of the sitting MPs for County Durham, Sir Hedworth was effective enough as a "professed friend but secret enemy" but could not carry his own legislation against concerted opposition. On the other hand he did not really need legislation because the projected site, the Potato Garth, was on land which belonged totally to the baronet and he had a strong interest in the projected Monkwearmouth and South Shields railway. A nine acre basin was excavated by the Wearmouth Dock Company in the shelter of the North Pier. In 1837 it was opened. In August 1839 following its linking to

Right, The Hetton Staiths in the 1820s, a lithograph by J. D. Harding. Below, An anonymous attack on the dock plans of Sir Hedworth Williamson (probably early 1832).

the Brandling Junction railway connecting the Wear with Gateshead and South Shields the first shipment of coal was moved. The dock was far too small for the port's needs. A bridge designed by Brunel to bring the coal from the south side was never built. Between 1838 and 1858 the coal exported through the dock never amounted to more than an average of 8.3 per cent of the total exports from Sunderland.

The RWC tried to retrieve the situation. It rejected an over ambitious compromise plan by Murray which involved a substantial compensatory cut through Monkwearmouth.[21] It did, however, take up a scheme by James Walker which would provide two docks, one on each side of the river. The interesting feature of this plan was that it involved using training groynes to accumulate a natural defence for the dock on the south side.[22] In May 1833, the RWC dropped a scaled-down version. The coalowners had too much invested in the existing systems of staiths and drops, and they opposed any increase in the river duty. The RWC for its part was uncomfortably aware of the possible illegality of using river duty to build docks.

Never a man to end a fight without a Parthian shot, Murray came up with a scheme in 1842-43 which involved placing walls and two vast 80-foot gates across the river which would be converted into a 100 acre dock.[23] Astonishingly the RWC took up the plan which Walker described politely as "ingenious".[24] By the early 1840s the RWC must have been desperate because the export of coal from Sunderland was actually falling. Walker, however, was not the only adviser to revive memories of the spectre of an ice mass crashing down the river in 1841, this time to smash and disable helpless shipping trapped by the barrier. As a result of the doubts of consultant engineers and Admiralty assessors and the opposition of the coalowners, the RWC in some embarrassment dropped yet another project.

In August 1845 Murray resigned his post. Obviously he had had a better offer from the new MP for Sunderland, none other than the "railway king" George Hudson. Hudson was looking for a parliamentary seat. Part of the price, mutually beneficial to both Hudson and the businessmen of Sunderland, was a South Dock connected to the York and Newcastle Railway and its tributary lines. As the *Times* put it

> The Railway Lord had promised great things which he will do and which he undoubtedly intends to do for his own sake as well as for Sunderland. He offers to embrace the nymph with the arms of railroads and to make the sea her tributary slave.

In 1846 Hudson's Newcastle and Darlington Junction Railway bought up the Durham and Sunderland Railway, a frequent subject of mockery, and the Wearmouth Dock Company. In 1847 the Hudson 'group' became the York, Newcastle and Berwick Railway — the basis of the North Eastern Railway formed in 1854 — and it was mainly from this that the finance came for the South Dock.

From the summer of 1846 to the summer of 1850 work pressed ahead on a scheme designed by Murray. Essentially it amounted to the creation of a 47-acre dock with a southern sea outlet into Hendon Bay and protected by a series of groynes. Over 13,000 men, 1,200 wagons and 10 steam engines were involved in the excavation of the main basin. According to the *Sunderland Herald* the opening of the main dock on the 20 June, 1850 was one of those events which marked ". . . an epoch and era in the annals of Sunderland".[25]

Between then and the end of 1856 the dock was extended to achieve a total water surface of 66 acres in a complex of facilities set in and upon land which was largely reclaimed from the sea. Over the period from 1851 to 1858 the quantity of coal exported from the Wear rose by 56 per cent. Ironically the following year the Sunderland Dock Company was taken over by the RWC. It was a victim of the incredible financial tangle arising from Hudson's breathtaking financial machinations but more immediately of the failure to reach agreement over the distribution of income from tolls and dues on coal exports and shipping.

As had so often happened before, no sooner had the RWC arrived at some sort of answer than the questions were rephrased. The old disputes about the representativeness of the RWC itself disappeared because from 1862 it

Isambard Kingdom Brunel's design for a bridge across the Wear.

Sunderland harbour entrance in the 1850s.

The start of work on the North Pier in 1883.

was an elected body (its debates were reported in the local press from the 1840s). The docks were no longer a subject of controversy. Between 1864 and 1868 the RWC added the Hendon Dock to the system. Nor was the threat to vessels entering the harbour much less. According to Admiralty returns on wrecks in 1854 there was an average of one vessel wrecked per mile of coastline of the United Kingdom but 4.5 per mile between the Tyne and the Tees and 5.5 at Sunderland. There were 38 wrecks at Sunderland in 1854. Thomas Meik the resident engineer claimed that 30 of those would have been saved with an improved harbour. Even if a ship's master reached the harbour entrance, he had the bar to cross. Records kept by the South Pier lighthouse keeper for 1854-1855 reveal that in 16 months no less than 134 ships were grounded including the unfortunate *Ellen*

which was only freed by the combined efforts of five steam tugs.[26]

What was new was the size of ships. The Wear's first iron ship was launched in 1852, and the new materials of iron and steel together with steam power led to a revolution in the scale of vessels. In 1818 the average register tonnage of vessels entering the harbour was 148 tons but by 1886 it was 342 tons.[27] Ships of far greater dimensions, and drawing far more water, were the main cause of the next wave of harbour improvements.

The dock facilities had to be adjusted very soon, Within 20 years of the completion of the system all the entrances had to be widened and the coal loading equipment had to be improved. The vaunted sea outlet of the Hudson Dock was a failure. Murray's patent sluicing system, designed to maintain a reasonable depth of water, started as it meant to continue when it led to George Hudson and the visiting party being soaked in a backwash of filthy water through the air pipes and then jammed open during one of its early displays. The result was that between 1878 and 1880 the outlet was replaced by a much more conventional and reliable lock which was also much wider than its ill-fated predecessor.

COMPLETION OF THE HARBOUR

From the 1870s an intensive dredging programme was undertaken. Murray had started to remove some of the rock outcrops from the river in the 1830s but now the dredging facilities were supplemented by a new-fangled rock breaking machine. By 1882 considerable stretches of the river and harbour still had a covering of only four feet at low water, whereas by 1914 the channel had been deepened to a minimum of eighteen feet. An 'elder statesman' of the RWC looking back to his childhood in the 1850s remarked:

When I think that 70 years ago it was no uncommon thing to 'plodge' across the river between the old piers at low water and that now on this very site there is a depth of 21 feet at low water . . . I feel that we have ample proof that the Port can be improved and developed to a yet greater degree.[28]

According to him since 1881 the astonishing total of 32 million tons of material had been removed by the dredgers *Goliath* and *Samson* and their brethren. The RWC Dredging Books do not cover the whole period but the estimate is probably reasonable and the cost of removal was down to about 3d. a ton.

Above all, the greatest objective of the RWC in this period was the building of the great protecting breakwaters on the north and south sides of the river mouth. Actually the idea of "covering piers" was an old one. During his long reign as resident engineer between 1755 and 1780 Joseph Robson had recommended that breakwaters be built on the sites which are actually occupied today by the two piers. There is some evidence that the RWC did in fact start work on the scheme. From 1849 onwards a whole series of proposals were made by Thomas Meik, David Stevenson and Sir John Coode. The main issue was whether the breakwaters should be built completely from scratch or whether one of them might be a prolonged extension of one of the old piers. All the proponents believed the breakwaters would help to reduce the scale of the bar and protect shipping. Meik remarked that

by completely breaking up the sea before it enters between the piers (it) will ensure internal tranquility: in fact vessels within them will be in an outer harbour.[29]

Following Coode's report in 1876 and some amendments by the resident engineer Henry Hay Wake in 1882,[30] work started on the Roker Pier in 1885, building initially upon the natural outcrop; further out, on a foundation of rubble and cement the great blocks — some of them up to 56 tons — were put in place by a 290 ton hydraulic crane. Along the whole length of the breakwater a subway was created to carry the cables and allow for maintenance work when weather conditions were very bad. The final blocks were put into position in 1902. The 2,800 feet long breakwater with its huge round head and quite distinctive red and white granite lighthouse containing the most powerful port light in the country was officially opened on 23 September 1903. The Earl of Durham attended the ceremony to place a polished black commemorative block on the lighthouse and to enjoy a performance by the band of the Northumberland Hussars.

It had always been intended to build a twin South Pier and in 1890 Wake laid out the options in another report.[31] On Sir John Coode's acceptance of this, with some amendments, work started in 1893. A critical point was reached in early 1902 when Wake was driven to urge that work on the two piers be expedited because the combination of the new harbour pattern and the deeper channel had the effect of turning a much greater face of water against the old piers. It was this which produced the alarming splits in the roundhead of the old north pier and caused the octagonal lighthouse to lean. Wake was instructed to remove the lighthouse. Work then proceeded on the South Pier until 1912 when it was decided not to proceed any further and to conclude it with a round-head. Coode's contribution to the two breakwaters was important but there is little doubt that they are, on the whole, as Hudson said, "Monuments to the constructive genius of Mr. Henry H. Wake".[32]

By the outbreak of the First World War the major harbourworks were completed. By then there had been substantial changes in the trade of the port. For instance the decline in the building of ships with timber was reflected in the fall from 147,900 loads of timber imported in 1874 to 77,119 loads in 1912. On the other hand the import of iron and steel and ores had risen from 26,561 tons to 132,511 tons. Some of the old trades were disappearing. Lime exports were down to 830 tons. Exports of glass and bottles were down from 14,642 tons to 3,395 tons. The staple export though was still coal. In 1904 there was a record movement of 5,117,230 tons although there had been a levelling off in the trade from the 1890s. In fact despite the problems of the national economy after 1918 the record was broken repeatedly with a peak of 5,615,847 tons exported in 1929.

The whole story of the RWC was one of incessant endeavour against great odds. Writing in 1888 the Newcastle journalist William Duncan considered that "Whether it was the River Wear which made Sunderland or Sunderland that made the River may be difficult to decide".[33] Certainly in 1922, when the breakwaters were completed, the channel was substantially deepened and coal exports were back up to over five million tons, there was every reason for the expression of pride in the work of the RWC.

Without effort nothing can be gained that is worth having, and only steady perseverance will eventually overcome apparently unsuperable difficulties.[34].

Sunderland first lifeboat the *Florence Nightingale*, 1865.

REFERENCES:

1. John Murray, "An Account of the progressive improvement of Sunderland Harbour and the River Wear, *Proc. Inst. of Civil Engineers,* 6 (1847), pp.256-277.

2. J. C., *The Complete Collier* (1708), pp.52-53.

3. A. W. Skempton, 'The Engineers of Sunderland Harbour, 1718-1817'. *Industrial Archaeology Review,* 1, 2 (Spring 1977), pp.103-125. The first Rolt Memorial Lecture originally presented at Durham University in 1975.

4. Charles Labelye, 'A Report relating to the Improvement of the River Wear and port of Sunderland made after a View thereof taken in July 1748'. It was presented to the RWC in September 1748. The papers of the River Wear Commission are held at the Tyne and Wear Record Office. They are referred to henceforth as RWC.

5. John Smeaton, 'The Report of John Smeaton, Engineer, upon Mr. Shout's Plan for Rebuilding and Extending the Old Pier of the Harbour of Sunderland', 16 January, 1780.

6. Ralph Dodd, 'Report to the Honourable Commissioner of the River Wear on the State of the River, Harbour, Piers, etc. of the Port of Sunderland', July 1794.

7. 'The Fishwife's Letter to Mr. Murray on the Removal of the North Lighthouse to the Pier End', n.d.

8. Thomas Milton, 'Report on Inspecting the Diving Bell in London', 2 June, 1824.

9. *op.cit.*

10. The coal export figures are derived from the declarations made by the representative of the coalowners and recorded in the Order Books of the RWC until 1859. Strangely they are far more difficult to come by after that date and I have used the volumes of RWC newspaper cuttings which report the statements made by the Traffic Committee of the RWC although there are gaps for 1916 and 1921-1922.

11. D. Swann, 'The Pace and Progress of Port Investment in England, 1660-1830', *Yorkshire Bulletin of Economic and Social Research,* XII, 1960.

12. Quoted by Taylor Potts in his *Sunderland: A History of the Town, Port, Trade and Commerce* (London, 1892). Potts was an employee of the RWC.

13. The best account is given by Martin Douglas, *The Life and Adventures of Martin Douglas, Sunderland Keelman* (Sunderland, 1848).

14. John Pemberton 'A letter on certain clauses proposed to be introduced into the River Wear Navigation Act by a bill this session of Parliament addressed to Richard Wharton, Esq., MP by John Pemberton, 22 February 1819'.

15. *Ibid.*

16. *Ibid.*

17. Stevenson made his first report on the 16 October 1828 and the second report on the 28 September 1829.

18. *S.H.,* 10 September 1831.

19. J. P. Kidson and J. J. Wright to the RWC, letter dated 2 April 1832.

20. Francis Giles, 'Plan for the intended Docks on the South Side of the Entrance to the Port and Haven of Sunderland', 1831.

21. John Murray, 'Report to the Committee of the Commissioners of the River Wear, etc'. 20 September 1832.

22. James Walker, 'Report to the Commissioners of the River Wear on Wet Docks at Sunderland,' 24 November 1832.

23. John Murray, 'The Engineers Report to the Commissioners of the River Wear, Port and Harbour of Sunderland on the Requirements and proposed Improvements of the Port', 2 November 1842.

24. James Walker, 'Report on the Sunderland Floating Dock', 27 April 1843.

25. *S.H.,* 21 June 1850.

26. The figures are taken from a volume of miscellaneous reports and statistics but probably came originally from the log books of the lighthouse keepers which are no longer available.

27. These figures are given by Taylor Potts (*op.cit.*) In fact register tonnage figures can be misleading because different standards were used at different times but this comparison is probably a reasonable one.

28. R. M. Hudson, 'Forty Years Reminiscences of the River Wear Commissioners', 25 January 1922.

29. Meik's report appears to be no longer available but he mentions it in his observations on Stevenson's report in April 1858. Coode's report 'Sunderland Port and Harbour Improvements', was presented to the RWC on the 18 October 1876.

30. Henry H. Wake, 'Engineer's Report upon Proposed Protecting Piers, Harbour Entrance', 13 June 1882. Wake added a lighthouse and subway to Coode's proposals. Wake (1845-1911) was born in Sunderland. He was a pupil of Meik and succeeded him as harbour engineer in 1868. He held the office until his death.

31. Henry H. Wake, 'Engineer's Report upon Proposed South Protecting Pier at Harbour Entrance', 9 December 1890.

32. *Ibid.*

33. William Duncan, *Industrial Rivers of the United Kingdom* (London, 1888).

34. R. M. Hudson, *op.cit.*

Roker Sands in 1901.

Industry to 1914

Many of the industries which became so important to Sunderland in the eighteenth and nineteenth centuries had their origins in the medieval period. Shipbuilding, coal mining, salt making and lime burning were already established and a network of trade routes developed. Iron was brought in from Spain and timber from Norway, while ships from Kings Lynn, Rochester and elsewhere along the East coast traded out of the River Wear.[1]

The development of Sunderland's industries was governed by the geology of the district and the location of the town on the River Wear and the coast. Sunderland is sited on magnesian limestone and clay, whilst easily worked coal measures are available nearby. The products of the town's industries could be taken out and raw materials brought in by sea. This was especially the case when sailing colliers returning to Sunderland needed ballast, as clay, sand, chalk and flint could be transported at virtually no cost to local industry. Ambrose Crowley, transferring his iron manufactory from the Midlands to Sunderland about 1682, wrote that from:

> anny ... places between Exon and Sunderland (which is half round England) I can have iron carry'd to my intended mill for 2s 6d a ton, but from most places for nothing beeing it savith ballis...[2]

This advantage disappeared, however, with the introduction from the 1850s of steam colliers which used water ballast. Sunderland also lost some of its geographical advantage with the development of the railway system from the 1830s onwards which removed the transport disadvantages from inland towns.

Shipbuilding, Sunderland's largest industry, is examined elsewhere in this book, although some of the manufacturing industries covered in the chapter were ancillaries to it. In addition to the manufacturing industries there also developed service industries to meet the needs of Sunderland's growing population.

For much of the nineteenth century Sunderland's major industries were in a state of continuous growth, pioneering nationally important developments in, for instance, the making of glass and paper. Several manufacturers proudly included the word 'Steam' in their titles (as in 'Steam Ropery') to signify their adoption of the latest technology. By the end of the nineteenth century, however, many of Sunderland's industries were in decline, often through the effects of continental competition, and the town's largest pottery and glassworks had both closed down.

This chapter looks first at the industrialists, then at the location of their industries in the area which by 1914 was the County Borough of Sunderland plus the neighbouring industrial villages of Southwick and North and South Hylton. It then examines individual industries, concentrating on those which have been fully researched such as pottery,[3] glassmaking,[4] and those individual firms in other fields which have been studied in detail[5] or are featured in two informative publications produced in 1898 and 1902 — *Guide to Sunderland and District* and *Sunderland Coronation Souvenir*.

THE INDUSTRIALISTS

The entrepreneurs who led the way in Sunderland's nineteenth century industrial development came from varied backgrounds. Some were landowners or land holders who often invested in more than one area of industry and commerce. Thomas Brunton (1771-1837) one of Southwick's major landowners, ran lime kilns, a shipyard, the Southwick Union Pottery and was also a coalfitter.[6] John Maling (1746-1823) was a partner in the North Hylton Pottery established in 1762 by his father William Maling and was also a partner in the Sunderland Bank of Russell, Allan and Maling (1787-1803).[7] Another landowner, Richard Pemberton of Barnes (1746-1837) was involved both in glassmaking and the development of Monkwearmouth Colliery. Other figures in the town's industrial history had humbler backgrounds. John White (1764-1833) born in Monkwearmouth, started work as a cooper but became a leading partner in the Bishopwearmouth Iron Works and the Wear Flint Glass Company, as well as a major ship owner.[8] Four of the major families in the Sunderland pottery industry — the Austins, Moores, Scotts

The river Wear, upstream of the Iron Bridge, c.1816. On the north bank (left) are lime-kilns, served by a waggonway from Fulwell Quarry, and on the south the cones of the glassworks.

and Dixons — worked in the Newbottle potteries before moving to set up their own firms in Sunderland. The Scotts not only developed Sunderland's largest pottery at Southwick (1788-1896) and established a bottle works there, but also became major landowners in the village. Peter Austin (1771-1863), who had become a partner in Moore's Pottery at Southwick, later left this to develop his shipbuilding firm, as well as becoming a partner in the firm which took over the Scott's Bottleworks. The majority of the Sunderland pottery owners were, however, skilled craftsmen who operated their businesses as relatively small family concerns.

Other entrepreneurs included John Grimshaw (c.1762-1840) ropemaker, part owner and manager of Fatfield Colliery and a man of many engineering skills; he saved Sunderland Bridge from collapse[9] and was involved in early steam locomotive developments.[10] His brother William was a grocer and the Grimshaw family became owners of several commercial and industrial concerns in the town as tea, coffee and porter dealers, candlemakers, cementmakers, silver-platers and carriage-builders.

Other industrialists had been involved in particular industries elsewhere before arriving in the town to establish or take over works. James Hartley (1811-1886), whose father had worked in glassworks in several parts of Britain and was a partner in Chance's of Smethwick, moved to the town in 1836 to establish the Wear Glassworks with his brother. Thomas Routledge (1819-1887) came to Sunderland in 1860 and developed the manufacture of paper from esparto grass at the Ford Paper Mill. Both these men had national and international reputations, but the majority of Sunderland's industrialists did not enjoy such extensive fame and were only known within the region or in the town.

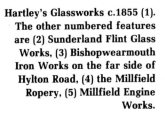

Hartley's Glassworks c.1855 (1). The other numbered features are (2) Sunderland Flint Glass Works, (3) Bishopwearmouth Iron Works on the far side of Hylton Road, (4) the Millfield Ropery, (5) Millfield Engine Works.

LOCATION OF INDUSTRY

Until the second quarter of the nineteenth century the location of industry in Sunderland was governed by the town's riverside situation, close to the sea, and four miles from the edge of the exposed part of the Durham coalfield. In the area immediately surrounding Sunderland the coal measures were covered by the Permian magnesian limestone and yellow sand which let water into the seams. It was only when more efficient deep mining and draining methods were introduced in the 1820s that coal could be taken from underneath the limestone. In the eighteenth century the coal was taken down wagonways to the tidal Wear in the Fatfield and Cox Green areas where it was loaded into keels (coal-carrying barges). The industries in Sunderland could receive the coal directly from keels, a distinct benefit when compared with many areas beyond the Wear whose coal was transferred into sea-going collier ships and then transferred again at the end of the voyage. Most of the town's products were shipped out in sea-going vessels which had often brought raw materials for industry as return ballast. Some exported goods could be packed in crates along with the coal in the holds of the colliers. The breakages from sea transport were far less than those incurred by horse transport along uneven roads. Many of the exports from the Wear went to ports on the east coast of Scotland and England, including London, and to north west Europe. The North Sea trade was of major importance to Sunderland. When Scott's Pottery was closed it was remarked:

Messrs. Scott's trade was chiefly to foreign ports and in the year 1876 they fitted out over 13 ships with the products of their manufacture, which is white and brown common earthenware. Formerly they did a thriving business with Hamburg and other German ports, now their export business is almost entirely to Denmark.[11]

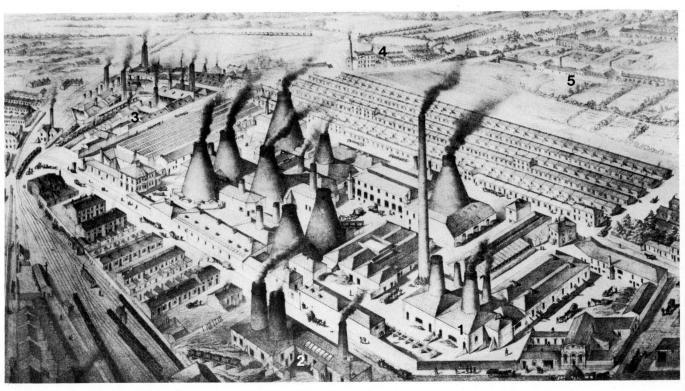

Sunderland gained many advantages as a result of its closeness to the Durham coalfield, but there were still significant costs and problems in moving coal by wagonway and keel to works in Sunderland. The village of Newbottle remained the centre of pottery making on Wearside in the eighteenth century, almost certainly because it was on the very edge of the exposed coalfield and movement of coal was easy.

A far more efficient method of transporting coal to the works in one wagon became possible once railways were built direct from the collieries to Sunderland. The Newbottle, later the Lambton, Railway was opened in 1815 and the Hetton Colliery Railway, opened from the new pit at Hetton Lyons, in 1822. The purpose of these railways was to take coal to the staiths at Sunderland for trans-shipment into the colliers, but landsale depots to supply coal to the town were opened at the same time as the lines and sidings were built into the various works. Although glass from Hartley's works was taken out in a vessel belonging to the firm, there is little doubt that the site bounded by Trimdon Street and Hylton Road was selected because it could receive coal from the adjacent Hetton and Lambton Railways.

1836 saw the commencement of public railways on Wearside with the opening of the Durham and Sunderland Railway. These railways acted as common carriers rather than being built purely to carry minerals, and accelerated the change in location of industry away from the river banks. When the Penshaw branch was opened in 1852, for instance, it ran through almost open fields until it reached Hendon, but within a few years several new works such as the Diamond Hall Bottleworks and the Millfield Engine Works were being constructed alongside the line. Sunderland's last two significant pottery works — Ball's Deptford Pottery, re-sited in 1862, and the Sunderland Pottery Company, Millfield, established in 1913, were built, not on the banks of the Wear, but adjacent to the Penshaw railway. By 1914 there were 20 industrial or commercial concerns with private sidings within a three-quarter mile radius of Millfield Station.

The change in location of industry was reflected in the attitude of R. T. Wilkinson, a Sunderland solicitor, who operated Moore's Wear Pottery at Southwick from 1861 to 1875. He provided the business with direct access to the Wear by removing substantial ballast hills which stood between the pottery and the river and by building a new quay. Yet he was also aware that the future lay with railways and was one of the industrialists who were the main promoters of the Hylton, Southwick and Monkwearmouth Railway, opened in 1876.[12]

LIME, COAL, BRICK AND CEMENT

Lime was one of the town's most important industries in the late eighteenth and early nineteenth centuries. Sunderland was one of the few ports on the north-east coast where limestone was exposed and the town became the main centre in the area for the export of lime. This was used as an agricultural fertiliser, for making building mortar and as a flux in glassmaking. Limestone had to be burned in kilns. The eighteenth century maps of Sunderland show small kilns scattered around the town, but by the beginning of the nineteenth century there were several wagonways from the quarries to kilns on the river banks. Coal could be brought easily by keels to the kilns and also lime could be loaded directly into sea-going ships.

On the south bank of the Wear the largest limestone workings were at Pallion (owned by the Goodchilds) and described by Dr. Clanny in 1815 as being "the deepest wrought of the Sunderland limestone formation, and are of great extent and value ... a steam-engine of considerable power is in constant use, to draw the lime from the quarry to the kilns."[13] The kilns appeared to be in use between the 1790s and the 1830s.

On the north bank there was a group of quarries in the Southwick, Carley Hill and Fulwell areas, all of which seem to have been linked by wagonways to kilns on the river banks in the 1790s. The most westerly quarry is shown on a map of the Grey Estate in 1746[14] as being worked by Thomas Brunton, but was disused by the 1840s. There were two quarries at Carley Hill whose wagonways ran on parallel courses to the two adjacent kilns which still survive close to the Wearmouth Colliery. The Williamsons' Fulwell Quarry served kilns adjacent to it on Newcastle Road as well as a further set of kilns on the river banks near the Iron Bridge which were reached by a wagonway running down Newcastle Road and North Bridge Street.[15]

In the 1870s the Fulwell wagonway was abandoned and a link put in to the North Eastern Railway. The Williamsons erected a kiln at the North Dock from which lime could be shipped, but ultimately concentrated lime-burning in the large kilns built in Fulwell Quarry in the 1900s, and the large complex came totally under the control of Sir Hedworth Williamson's Limeworks Ltd., who quarried it until closure in 1957.

Local limestone was often used in the side or back walls of Sunderland buildings, and in garden walls, but was generally too soft and coarse to be a satisfactory construction material. The sandstone quarries at Penshaw and Springwell supplied the material for many of the town's public buildings. There were also smaller sandstone quarries (one example being Wood House, North Hylton), all of them beyond the old Borough boundaries.

A further group of kilns visible on late eighteenth century maps of Sunderland are 'cinder kilns'. These were used for producing coke for blacksmiths and also for other trades and industries. In 1791, 844 chaldrons of cinders were shipped from the Wear.[16]

Coal was by far the most important factor in the development of the Port of Sunderland and the railway network of the area. The only pit within the boundaries of the County Borough in 1914 was Monkwearmouth, later Wearmouth, Colliery. It took nine years to sink the shaft as

Above: Scotts' Pottery mark.
Above right: Machine-throwing of bowls at the Wearside Pottery company, shortly before closure in 1957.

the coal measures were concealed by the Permian magnesian limestone and yellow sand. Monkwearmouth was the deepest mine in the world when it began shipping coal in 1835.[17] In 1900 the Wearmouth Coal Company opened Hylton Colliery which lay within the Sunderland Rural District Council's boundaries, as did Ryhope, opened in 1859, and Silksworth, one of the Marquess of Londonderry's pits, in 1873.

The clay which overlay much of the limestone in Sunderland was dug out to make bricks and tiles, and several clay pits, later filled in, are marked on the 1855 Ordnance Survey Map. Fireclay from the coal measures was a by-product of mining and was used by fire brick works, although Stourbridge clay was also used.[18] Both clay and lime were raw materials for the Sunderland cement industry. The other raw material which could be obtained at no cost to the cement makers on Wearside, was chalk from the Medway which was used as ballast by local vessels which were returning from the London area. When sailing vessels began to be replaced by water-ballasted steam colliers from the 1860s the cement manufacturers had to pay for chalk and transport.[19] The three main Sunderland firms were William Grimshaw and Sons at North Hylton, Hylton Cement Company at South Hylton, and Matteson and Chapman beside the river at Deptford and at Wellington Lane; as in the case of many of Sunderland's industries, the product went by sea to other towns on the east coast; Matteson and Chapman had, for instance, warehouses in Dundee and Broughty Ferry.[20] There was also increasing competition from the continent and the cement industry disappeared on Wearside by the end of the First World War.

POTTERY

Among the best known products of Sunderland's industries are the purple lustre jugs with a transfer of the 1796 Wear Bridge on one side and a verse on the other. Because of this, pottery making, although it was certainly an industry of importance, is sometimes given a greater significance than it merits on economic grounds. In 1851, for instance, when the pottery industry was at its height, only 395 people can be identified as being employed compared with 716 in the glass industry,[21] while in 1861 the figures were 312 and 1,105;[22] in addition to those specifically listed as being pottery or glassmakers, other classified as 'labourers' would have worked in these industries.

The Sunderland potteries did make some use of the local clay for the manufacture of their ware, but in order to match the high quality wares of Staffordshire and other pottery-making centres, they also used white clay from Devon, Cornwall and Dorset, which was mixed with ground flint; this added to the whiteness and hardness of the ware and helped to keep its shape during firing.[23] Only earthenware was made in Sunderland.

Although purple lustre is by far the best known of the products of the Sunderland potteries, it was but a small part of their output and was by no means unique to Sunderland.[24] Other types of earthenware included brown kitchenware, slipware, marbleware, yellow transfer-printed brownware, cream-coloured and yellow-glazed ware.

The Sunderland potteries were:
Bridge or 'Jericho' Pottery Company, Monkwearmouth (c.1829-1941).
Burnside's Pottery, Green Street, (1850-1858).
Deptford or Ball's Pottery (1857-1918).
High Southwick Pottery (1850-1885).
Low Ford or Dawson's Pottery, South Hylton (c.1794-1864).
North Hylton Pottery (1762-c.1850).
Sheepfolds or Rickaby's Pottery, Monkwearmouth (1840-1900).
Sheepfolds Warehouse (c.1856-1885).
Southwick or Scott's Pottery (1788-1896).
Southwick Union, later the Wear or Moore's Pottery (c.1753-1882).
St. Bede's Pottery, Monkwearmouth (1874-1885).
Sunderland or Garrison Pottery (c.1799-1865).
Sunderland Pottery Company, later the Wearside Pottery Company, Millfield (1913-1957).
For much of the nineteenth century Sunderland had a large pottery export trade to Europe. In 1819, for instance, 292,142 pieces of earthenware were exported, 145,092 of these to Holland.[25] This trade greatly declined in the last three decades of the nineteenth century because of tariff barriers. Continental countries were now exporting an increasing amount of their own pottery to Britain, taking advantage of the lack of import duties. There are several types of teapots, jugs and cups with transfers of the major buildings opened in Sunderland in 1879, the Central Station, the Wear Railway Bridge and the Library and Museum; but with one or two exceptions they are German export porcelain, and not Sunderland ware.

The most notable indication of the decline of the pottery industry was the closure in 1896 of the largest works, Scott's, only eight years after it had been entirely re-equipped. The loss of Scott's continental customers was partly due to tariff barriers, but also to the firm's own operations. Correspondence shows complaints of non-arrival of goods, breakages and delivery of 'seconds'. Scott's practice of packing common undecorated articles which carried a low import duty inside larger decorated items at the higher rate meant that importers had to pay the higher rate on both and this helped to alienate foreign customers. The latter also requested a wider range of new designs and stated that cheaper prices were being quoted by the Staffordshire potteries.[26] The Sunderland potteries had all but vanished by the end of the First World War but today their products are widely collected in Britain and abroad and are displayed in the town's museum.

GLASSMAKING

Glassmaking is one of Sunderland's oldest industries, having been established by the Sunderland Company of Glassmakers in the 1690s, but it is also one which has continued to be of importance up to the present day. Major factors in the development of glassmaking in the town were the availability nearby of coal for fuel and also of salt and later lime which were used as fluxes to lower the temperature at which raw materials would melt. Another raw material, sand from East Anglia (principally Kings Lynn), was brought in by sea transport which also took the finished goods out. Firestone (sandstone) used for lining furnaces, which had normally to be rebuilt every eight weeks, was quarried at Cox Green and Penshaw. The quarries were owned by Sunderland glass manufacturers who also supplied Lancashire glass firms.[27]

During the eighteenth century the glass industries of Wearside and Tyneside became dominant in the London market.[28] Glassmaking on Wearside continued to expand until the middle of the nineteenth century, but there was then a rapid decline leading to the closure of most of the leading firms by the early 1920s.

There were three branches of the glass industry in Sunderland — bottles, window-glass and tableware. The works known to have operated in Sunderland between 1780 and 1914 are listed in the table at the end of this chapter.

Bottles were made in Sunderland at the Ayres Quay and Bishopwearmouth Panns Bottleworks from the end of the seventeenth century. The demand for bottles increased in the nineteenth century, not only for beer, but also for mineral and aerated waters, and for the products sold in chemists' and grocers' shops. By 1833 Sunderland produced more bottles than any other area of the north east,[29] but the final Sunderland bottleworks, Ayres Quay, ceased production in 1923 in the face of competition from the more highly mechanised Yorkshire firms.

The manufacture of window glass was originally by the Crown and then the Broad methods. Crown glass was made from a blown hollow ball which was sliced open, reheated and spun out into a flat disc which was then cut into small pieces. Broad glass was made by cutting an opening in a blown glass cylinder and flattening it out into a sheet.

The older methods were superseded by cast plate glass which was flattened on iron tables with the use of heavy rollers. This system was developed by James Hartley, who had established the Wear Glassworks in 1836 and who in 1847 was granted a patent for improving its manufacture. The removal of duty on glass in 1845 benefitted Hartley, and the Wear Glassworks became of national significance. The works produced a third of all the sheet glass in England in the early 1860s.[30] Hartley's patent plate was installed in the roofs of many industrial buildings and railway stations, including those of Monkwearmouth and Paddington, London.

Hartley granted licences to produce his patent plate glass to Chance's near Birmingham, and Pilkington's in St. Helens which in the 1860s were roughly the same size as his own firm. In the following two decades, however, his competitors improved their position by better methods of production such as conversion from coal to gas-fired furnaces, while Hartley's delayed this change until 1891. James Hartley himself retired in 1869 and his son John lacked his father's abilities.[31]

The firm suffered bad industrial relations in the 1870s and 80s with several strikes. Moreover, Hartley's was facing competition not only from Chance's and Pilkington's but also from the continent, especially Belgium as import duties on glass were reduced. In 1894 when the flat glass trade was particularly depressed by strong foreign competition the Wear Works closed. Two years later the site was cleared completely and houses built there so that by the twentieth century no trace remained of what had been one of the country's most important glass factories.

In 1893 James Hartley, grandson of the founder of the Wear Glassworks went into partnership with Alfred Wood making stained glass at the Portobello Lane Works. The firm, a subsidiary of Pilkington's, operated until 1989 as the major supplier of stained glass in Britain.

The third branch of the glass industry on Wearside was tableware. Until the early nineteenth century this was produced by blowing and then decorated by cutting and engraving. Most of Wearside's products were of a cheap utilitarian nature, but there were exceptions to this, notably the engraved drinking glasses which, like much Sunderland Pottery, often showed the Wear Bridge. The finest tableware made in Sunderland was the dessert and wine service of almost 200 pieces made for the third Marquess of Londonderry in 1824 by the Wear Flint Glass Company. Made of thickly blown and deeply cut glass engraved with the Marquess's coat of arms, it cost nearly 2,000 guineas.[32] The service is now displayed in Sunderland Museum.

Pressing (using a plunger pressed into a mould) replaced blowing as the most common method of producing tableware during the 1830s. There were two notable pressed glass firms, one was Matthew Turnbull's, established in 1865, which continued to make pressed glass until 1953 when the loss of a

Codd bottle, manufactured c.1890 at the Ayre's Quay Bottle Works for Joseph Wilkinson of Sunderland and Gateshead, manufacturer of aerated water.

Sunderland's Railways

The first railways within the town of Sunderland were the wagonways which took limestone from the quarries to the kilns on the river banks. Lines from the quarries at Pallion, Southwick, Carley Hill East and West and Fulwell seem to have been built during the 1790-1800s. There were other short wagonways in the Sunderland area. One narrow gauge line took sandstone from a quarry at North Hylton to the river bank. About 1880 it was converted to standard gauge and extended to take traffic such as manure, including the contents of the town's ash-privies, up to Wood House Farm. Near the mouth of the river at the North Ferry landing a wagonway carried ballast from ships in a tunnel to the west of St. Peter's Church. It was later extended to the west of Brandling Street.

In 1815 the Nesham family replaced their wagonway from Philadelphia to the staiths at Penshaw by a new line which ran near to the mouth of the Wear. This meant that coal could be loaded directly into colliers and the use of keels avoided. This resulted in a riot on the 20th March 1815 started by a group of keelmen who saw their livelihood threatened. They set fire to the stationary engine house and damaged railway lines and a bridge. Order was only restored when cavalry were called from Newcastle. The Nesham Collieries were sold in 1822 to John Lambton (later the first Earl of Durham) who linked them to the extensive network of lines in the Penshaw area; eventually creating a system which stretched from Harraton Colliery in the north to Sherburn House Colliery in the south.

The Hetton Colliery Railway, opened from the new pit at Hetton Lyons to the staiths at Sunderland in 1822, occupies a place in railway history since it was the first complete line to be engineered by George Stephenson and used locomotives as well as stationary steam engines and self-acting inclines to move coal.

In 1836 the Durham and Sunderland Railway, promoted by several of the town's leading figures, opened to Haswell;

The Wear Railway bridge in 1984 with the 1929 road bridge behind.

it was extended to Shincliffe, outside Durham, in 1839. Unlike the earlier lines which had been built to carry minerals, the Durham and Sunderland Railway was a public railway operating as a common carrier for both passengers and freight, although coal was its most important traffic. The line terminated on the south bank of the Wear. In 1839 another public railway, the Brandling Junction Railway from Gateshead and South Shields, was opened to Monkwearmouth on the north bank. There was a short branch to the North Dock which was opened by the Wearmouth Dock Company in 1837.

In 1845 the election of George Hudson, the "Railway King", as an MP for Sunderland owed much to the benefits these railway connections might bring to the town. The Newcastle and Darlington Junction Railway, of which he was the chairman, duly purchased the Durham and Sunderland Railway, the Brandling Junction Railway and the Wearmouth Dock Company, in addition to securing the building of the South Dock. The final Sunderland railway development of the 'Hudson Era' came in 1852 after he had been removed from his railway chairmanship and details of his dubious financial dealings had emerged. This was the Penshaw branch from Hendon Junction, near the South Dock, to Penshaw, where it joined the then main line from Newcastle to Darlington south of the impressive Victoria Bridge across the Wear; Durham was reached by a branch further south from the main line. The Penshaw Branch was opened by the York, Newcastle and Berwick Railway which became part of the North Eastern Railway in 1854.

The Earl of Durham appears to have diverted some of his coal trains from the former Nesham route via Grindon to the new Penshaw branch shortly after this railway opened; they reached Lambton Staiths by a link from Millfield Station. In 1865 a new line was opened from Pallion to the Staiths and the Grindon route was abandoned.

In 1852 the Marquis of Londonderry opened the Seaham and Sunderland Railway, a public line which carried passengers and freight, as his dock at Seaham could not cope with the output of the Londonderry and South Hetton

Collieries. The Londonderry Railway remained independent until it was taken over by the North Eastern Railway in 1900. A branch with a shorter independent life was the Hylton, Southwick and Monkwearmouth Railway of 1876 promoted by the owners of the collieries, limekilns, ironworks, potteries and glassworks, along the route. This purely freight line was always worked by the North Eastern Railway and was absorbed by it in 1883.

Until 1879 the Sunderland railway system consisted of two separate networks on either side of the Wear. In that eventful year (which also saw the opening of Sunderland's tramway system and the Library and Museum building) the NER completed the Monkwearmouth Junction line linking Monkwearmouth with Ryhope Grange. The line involved a major bridge across the Wear designed by Thomas Harrison, two tunnels and a new Central Station, which replaced the former termini at Fawcett Street, Hendon and Monkwearmouth, the latter becoming a wayside passenger station. The Central Station served only passengers; the goods station at Monkwearmouth was developed as the main freight depot for the town. The opening of the Monkwearmouth Junction line meant that Sunderland was now

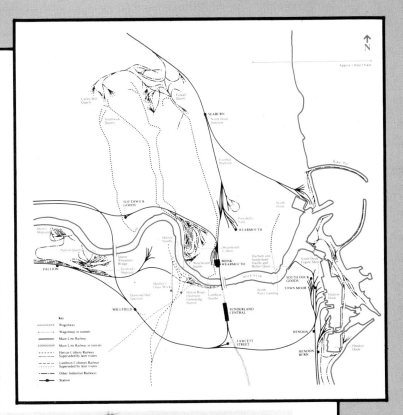

on the secondary main line served by passenger trains running from Newcastle to Leeds, Manchester and London. Their route south of Sunderland was by the Durham and Sunderland line to Haswell, but in 1905 the NER opened a new coastal route by extending the former Londonderry Railway from Seaham to Hartlepool.

Coal was the most important traffic on the railways of Wearside and it was to enable coal trains from the west of Durham to reach the South Dock without reversing that the massive Queen Alexandra bridge and its approach lines were opened in 1909. This proved to be an expensive white elephant as coal traffic, increasing when the bridge was first planned, had started to decline by the time of its opening.

In 1911 the Lambton Collieries, by now owned by Sir James Joicey, took over the Hetton Colliery Company and the two adjacent staiths on the Wear were linked by a sharply curved tunnel. The other major colliery system in Sunderland was that of the Wearmouth Coal Company with staiths close to the colliery. From 1900 the Wearmouth Coal Company ran trains from its new Hylton Colliery over the NER's Hylton, Southwick and Monkwearmouth line.

The NER became part of the London and North Eastern Railway in 1923. The new company lost some of its traffic to increasing road competition, but most of the Sunderland railway network remained intact during the London and

The Queen Alexandra bridge shortly after its opening in 1909. The railway track was carried on the top deck.

North Eastern Railways period and a new station at Seaburn was opened in 1937 to serve the town's seaside resort and new housing developments in the area. Nationalisation led to the LNER becoming part of British Railways in 1948; the collieries had been taken over by the National Coal Board a year earlier. A major contraction of the Sunderland railway network took place from the late 1950s. By 1967 only Sunderland Central and Seaburn stations retained their passenger services, albeit on an increasingly important commuter link to Newcastle, while only Monkwearmouth remained open as a general freight depot; the latter closed in 1981 leaving only private sidings for oil, scrap and shipbuilding steel. Even more significant was the decline in coal shipped from the town. Coal shipment ceased from the Lambton and Hetton staiths in 1967, and from the Wearmouth staiths in 1968, while the staiths at the South Dock which in 1983 had shipped 1,570,529 tons of coal finally closed in 1986 following the opening of new coal-handling facilities in Tyne Dock. Although coal is no longer shipped from Sunderland it remains an important railway centre for the operation of trains taking coal from Wearmouth Colliery and the South Durham collieries to Tyne Dock and electricity power stations in Yorkshire and at Blyth.

large contract with Woolworth's caused its closure.

The second major pressed glass firm was Henry Greener and Company which had its origins in the Trimdon Street Works established by Nicholas French in 1855. In 1873 the works moved to Alfred Street in Millfield. After coming close to bankruptcy the firm was taken over in 1885 by its principal creditor, James A. Jobling, a Newcastle businessman, one of the largest mineral merchants and suppliers of glassmaking chemicals in the North of England.

There was, however, a further financial crisis in 1902 after which James Jobling made his nephew, Ernest Jobling-Purser, works manager. He revitalised the production of flint glass and then in 1921 acquired the right to manufacture Pyrex heat-resistant glass in Britain and the Empire (excluding Canada) from Corning Glassworks after the American firm had been rebuffed by other British glass manufacturing firms.[33] Every item of British Pyrex domestic glassware has been made in Sunderland. The firm was renamed James A. Jobling and Company in 1921, and then Corning Limited in 1975, two years after the firm had been absorbed by the American company. The Wear Glassworks produces Pyrex today for a world market.[34]

THE CHEMICAL INDUSTRY

Salt was made locally from medieval times, or even earlier, by boiling salt water in large iron pans, and we know that the monks at Monkwearmouth leased out their salt pans in 1447.[35] In 1589 ten salt pans, said to employ 300 people, were established by Robert Bowes of Barnes in Sunderland and Edward Smith of Kings Lynn partly using coal from the new pit they sank at Offerton as well as that from other local collieries.[36] By the 1630s some 50,000 bushels of salt were being produced annually on the Wear. Sunderland's salt industry did not, however, reach the importance of that in South Shields and had disappeared by the beginning of the nineteenth century although a map of Deptford in 1801 still shows a single salt pan.

The copperas industry was one which flourished on the Wear at Cox Green, Deptford and South Hylton. The process involved extracting sulphur products by 'ripening' (in rain water) pyrites found in coal to produce ferrous sulphate or green vitriol for the making of ink and dyes, for dressing crops and for paper manufacture.

The largest copperas works were at Deptford and were founded in about 1722 by Taylor and Inman using pyrites which was then collected from Lyme in Dorset. It passed into the hands of the Biss and later the Ogden families. The latter installed pyroligneous retorts in 1826 and began the manufacture of acetate of soda and acetic acid until the works became probably the largest in the world. They closed in 1896.[37]

Other chemical works in Sunderland included the Wear Fuel Works, at the South Dock, while Prussian Blue dye was also manufactured on a small scale at Claxheugh,

and Lamp Black at North Hylton. As part of his glass-making process James Hartley manufactured alkali in the Wear Glassworks and was prosecuted for causing damage to the local market gardeners' gooseberry plants.[38] The court decided that the damage had been caused by frost, but the prosecution is a reminder of the dangerous fumes that chemical plants produced and explains why they were mainly sited in areas which had little housing nearby. The major chemical works that developed on Wearside were at Washington, some distance from the Sunderland conurbation.

TIMBER

The processing and preserving of timber was carried out by several firms in the town. Rain's Eye Plan of 1785-1790 shows several 'raff' (timber) yards beside the Wear while nineteenth century paintings and photographs of the Wear show large amounts of timber being seasoned in the river. A reminder of this today is the name 'Timber Beach' still given to the section of the river bank at Southwick where timber once was stored and seasoned. Most of the timber was imported from the Baltic and this was another industry which benefitted from Sunderland's geographical position. Wood also came from North America, India and the East Indies.

In addition to the major use of timber in shipbuilding, it was needed for coal mining, engineering, building, bridges, fences and railway sleepers. The firms were naturally situated beside the Wear, mainly in Monkwearmouth or at the South Docks and all had railway sidings for moving the finished timber out.

The two principal firms in Monkwearmouth were J. & W. Wilson and Armstrong Addison. Wilsons, established in 1851, had a small yard and timber mills to the east of the Wearmouth Bridge, with their main yard and offices, adjacent to the railway in Newcastle Road. Among their products were deck deals for shipbuilding, door and window frames and casings, mouldings and turned work for houses and furniture, and ladder and scaffolding poles.[39] Armstrong Addison was established in 1853 at Sunderland North Dock. Their main trade was in the preservation of timber by creosoting and kyanising. The firm produced railway sleepers, bridge timbers, fences and buildings for farms and, at their North Shields works, telegraph poles.[40] Sunderland's other timber firms in the 1900 included Thomas Elliot which had been established as far back as 1800, and had later moved to the South Dock where further yards such as Thompson's were also situated.

PAPER

Until the second half of the nineteenth century the raw materials used locally for papermaking were old sails, rope and cotton rags. Sunderland's first paper mill, the Wearmouth Mill, was established in Deptford by Vint, Hutton & Company about 1826, and became well known for rope brown paper. It was burnt down in 1846, but re-opened in 1848 and continued production, mainly under the control of the Hutton family, until closure in 1902.[41]

In 1838 Vint, Hutton & Company opened another paper works at Ford to produce white paper from rags. One reason for siting it here, apart from the convenience of the river access, was the existence of a spring of good clean water nearby.[42] By 1866, however, this was to prove inadequate and there were complaints in the years that followed of the large water rates that had to be paid to the Sunderland and South Shields Water Company. This reached £1,000 a year in 1889. A reservoir was completed in 1892 for water from local streams, but, it proved necessary to install a pumping station a mile south of the mill in 1898 and a second station two miles south-east in 1911.

The Ford Mill, owned from c.1839 by Fletcher, Blackwell and Faulkner was sold in 1860 to Thomas Routledge and Company. Thomas Routledge pioneered the use of esparto grass for paper making and had taken out his first patent in 1856 while working a small mill at Eynsham in Oxfordshire. In 1861 Gladstone repealed the duty on paper, so widening the market which coincided with a shortage of cotton due to the American Civil War. Making the most of this situation Routledge developed the use of esparto grass for paper-making at Ford, the first large scale use of this in the world. The mill was partially burnt down in 1887, the year of Routledge's death, but was rebuilt and continued to expand under J. P. Cornett as manager from 1883 to 1918.[43]

In 1872 Frederick Miller, manager at Ford, left to become the managing director of the new Hendon Paper Works which developed into the largest mill in the north of England. The Hendon works mainly used esparto grass, but by the late 1880s this was supplemented by wood pulp. In 1902 Hendon Mill employed 430 people, making printing and writing paper like the Ford Works. The water was drawn from a well within the works and another in Grangetown, while electricity was provided by the works own steam-powered generator.[44]

Paper making has survived for longer than several of Sunderland's other industries. The Ford Mill lasted until 1971; the Hendon Mill closed in 1980, but was re-opened a year later by Edward Thompson's to make low grade paper for their Bingo tickets.

ROPE

Rain's Eye Plan shows several examples of the traditional method of making ropes on walks. The strands were laid out along the full length of the rope walk and then twisted together. The rope walks were often hundreds of yards long and making a rope was a slow process.

There was a need to produce rope more quickly, of a more even texture and in a smaller space. This challenge was met by the firm of Webster and Grimshaw who about 1794 built the world's earliest factory for machine-made rope at Deptford. The building, recently restored, still survives. The works made use of the machinery invented by Richard Fothergill in 1793 and developed and patented by his executor, John Grimshaw, "of an entire new modern method or art of dressing hemp and making or spinning the same into ropes and cordage by the application of a machine".

There had always been a large demand in Sunderland for ropes for use on sailing ships, but the nineteenth century opened up new markets in collieries and railways. In the late 1830s a three-and-a-half mile rope without a single splice was manufactured in the town for railway haulage.[45] The vast majority of ropes were made from hemp until the 1830s when the manufacture of wire rope was developed. Webster's started producing wire ropes using a modified Grimshaw machine in 1840 and extended their business to cover collieries in the Midlands, South Wales and Scotland as well as the north east, eventually becoming one of the largest firms in the country. In 1892 they produced a steel wire rope six miles long for colliery haulage at Whitehaven; it weighed 25 tons and required 30 horses to take it to Monkwearmouth for loading on to a railway wagon.

The invention of rope machinery did not, however, mean that rope walks disappeared. Both Dawson and Usher of Hendon Road, and Craven and Speeding of Roker Avenue, had covered-in walks well into the twentieth century; Dawson and Usher's is recorded as being 450 yards in length in 1898.[46] Craven and Speeding were established in 1860 when they took over Smiths Ropery; they produced wire rope and, from 1886, 'Red Star' binder twine. Sunderland's other rope making firms included that of Glaholm and Robson, founded in 1859. They produced wire ropes which were used in lifts, mining, aerial ropeways, engineering, oil-well boring, naval and merchant ships, dredging vessels and bridges such as the Widnes Transporter Bridge.[47] David Haggie, one of the partners in Glaholm and Robsons, and a member of the family which had rope making factories on Tyneside es-

A flat rope, as used in mineshafts, being hand-stitched at Glaholm and Robson's c.1910.

tablished his own firm D. H. & G. Haggie in the former Hay's Ropery, Monkwearmouth. Haggie's, and Craven and Speeding, became founder members of British Ropes in the 1920s and Glaholm and Robson's were absorbed into the group in 1946. The last five Sunderland rope factories closed between the late 1960s and the early 1980s.

FOUNDRIES AND ENGINEERING

Much of the work of Sunderland's foundries and engineering companies was related to shipbuilding which is covered in another chapter in this book. Although iron and steel products were produced for other trades, they were of far less significance than shipbuilding, and Sunderland did not, for instance, have any major locomotive or colliery engineering firms as might have been expected in a large industrial town. Locomotives were built at the works of the three major local colliery companies but these lay outside Sunderland — the Lambton Collieries at Philadelphia, the Hetton Collieries at Hetton Lyons and the Londonderry Collieries at Seaham. Repairs to locomotives were carried out in the middle years of the nineteenth century by firms such as Close Burlinson and Co.'s Millfield Engine Works, but only on a limited scale and the town's contribution to railway engineering lay in the production of rails and track components. Sunderland's metal industries were mainly concentrated in the Deptford, Millfield, Monkwearmouth and South Hylton areas. The most important of the firms that came into existence in the first half of the 19th century was the Bishopwearmouth Iron Works of White, Sons, Panton and Kirk (later owned by Mounsey, Janson and Co.) which was situated in Hylton Road.

In the 1870s the Sunderland forges began to work in steel as well as iron. One figure involved in the changeover was the shipbuilder Thomas Oswald who owned ironworks at Pallion and also opened the Wear Rolling Mills at Castletown. Both ventures went into liquidation although the Wear Rolling Mills were reopened in 1881, lasting until 1894 when they closed for good; the site was later used for Hylton Colliery.[48] A longer-lived forge was that of T. S. Forster at Pallion established in 1880.

The range of Sunderland's metal industry at the turn of the century can be seen by looking at two of the major companies — the Sunderland Forge and Engineering Company and Samuel Tyzack and Company. The Sunderland Forge and Engineering Company was established in 1887 by ship-builder James Marr and the Thompson family. They were mainly involved with the manufacture of ship components. In the late 1890s, however, they started making electric motors and dynamos and were responsible for the electric lighting plants not only in Sunderland but also towns such as Llandudno.[49] Samuel Tyzack's Monkwearmouth Iron and Steel Works were established in 1857 and by 1902 covered almost 12 acres off Roker Avenue adjacent to the Sunderland to Newcastle railway. The iron and steel plant included Siemen's gas furnaces, puddling furnaces, and steam hammers. They produced iron and steel angles, bulbs, bars, rails, rivets, bulwark cranes and ship's ladders.[50]

The more specialised firms in the metal and engineering industries included brass foundries, the Hendon Spelter Works (which made an alloy of which zinc was the main component),[51] and Cook and Nicholson's file-works at Monkwearmouth. Established in 1864, the latter firm produced 24,000 files a month, many of which were exported. They also manufactured engineer's tools such as hammers, dies, angles and vices. The firm of Cook and Nicholson is still in business today as is the Sunderland Forge and Engineering Company. Several of the other companies survived until recent times, closing in the 1970s and '80s.

BREWING

Brewing was one of Sunderland's oldest industries. The Borough Charter of the 1180s granted to Sunderland by the Bishop of Durham established the assizes which controlled (among other things) the quality of ale brewed in the town.[52] Rain's Eye Plan shows a number of breweries in operation in the 1780s mainly in the Low Street area of Sunderland and Bishopwearmouth and on Monkwearmouth shore. There were five breweries in Low Street at the beginning of the nineteenth century. They had their own wells which according to Taylor Potts produced "soft, clear and sparkling water" without the lime which was found later in that supplied by the Sunderland and South Shields Water Company.[53] The water supply was an important point in the location of breweries. Bramwell Scurfield and Co. almost certainly chose the former Bishopwearmouth Water Works site in Westbourne Road for their new premises in 1871 because they knew they could draw their own water from the well there.

Two of the breweries shown on Rain's Eye Plan continued well into the twentieth century. One was the Sunderland Brewery in Low Street, later taken over by the Fenwick family who were already in the brewing business and operating a 'tied house' system by 1807.[54] The Fenwicks also owned a brewery in Chester-le-Street and the Bishopwearmouth Panns Glasshouse which produced bottles for their breweries.[55] The firm passed into the control of George Younger of Alloa and then Flower's Breweries before these premises closed in 1964. The other long established brewery on the river bank was that at Bonners Field, Monkwearmouth. Its ownership passed from Stafford Abbs via J. J. & W. H. Allison to James Deuchar who also supplied their Lochside Ale from their Montrose Brewery by steam coasters. The firm became part of Newcastle Breweries in 1956. The building still survives today and is used as a public house and restaurant.

By the end of the nineteenth century the largest brewing firm in Sunderland was the North-Eastern Breweries Ltd., formed in 1896 when Richard Murray, who had already taken over Bramwell Scurfield's Wear Brewery, the

Moor Street Brewery in Sunderland and the Spennymoor Brewery, merged these with his hotels into a limited company with a capital of £1,100,000. The company later purchased breweries in Stockton and Burton-on-Trent.[56]

The other major Sunderland brewery by the 1900s was Cuthbert Vaux and Sons. The Vaux family is reputed to have become involved in brewing about 1805 and to have established a brewery on their own account in Matlock Street about 1837.[57] By 1844 Cuthbert Vaux (1813-1878), founder of the firm, had purchased the brewery in Union Street,[58] but this site was required for the North Eastern Railways Central Station and in 1875 it was re-located in Castle Street/Gill Bridge Avenue. The firm has remained there ever since and has expanded to take over much of the surrounding area. The founder's grandson, also called Cuthbert Vaux, learned the brewing trade at the Ny Carlsberg and other continental breweries; on his return to Sunderland Vaux became one of the first British brewers to introduce bottled ales and stouts.[59] Although the Vaux family had brewing expertise they lacked managerial skills and to provide this Frank Nicholson, a Sunderland chartered accountant, was appointed manager and secretary in 1898; he later married one of Cuthbert Vaux's sisters, and became a director in 1914 and managing director in 1919. His business abilities saw Vaux expand and survive government restrictions during the First World War. In 1927 he arranged an amalgamation with the North East Breweries Ltd., creating the North East's second largest brewers. The firm, still managed by the Nicholson family, has continued to expand to the present day.

The manufacture of soft drinks developed from the 1840s. The best known makers were Powley & Son of Millfield established in the 1880s. The products included lemonade, 'zolkolone', champagne cider, ginger beer, unfermented fruit wines, lime juice, orange squash and cordials. In common with other aerated water manufacturers their factory was re-equipped at the end of the nineteenth century enabling the price of their products to be reduced.[60] Other firms included Ernest Lautebach which became part of the Vaux group in 1920.

INDUSTRIAL CHANGE

When Dr. Dibdin visited Sunderland in the 1830s he commented on the "increasing manufactories which vomit forth their black, broad and long extended columns of trailing smoke".[61] 90 years later there were fewer smoking chimneys and kilns on the river banks. Many of the firms on the Wear had closed and their sites had been absorbed into the expanding shipyards while others, along with almost all new industries established in Sunderland from the middle of the nineteenth century, were now situated in Millfield, Pallion and Hendon. Sunderland was still a major industrial centre at the time of the outbreak of the First World War. Some of Sunderland's industries — pottery, cement, chemicals, window and bottle glass making — had,

however, either disappeared or were on the point of extinction. There were several reasons why these industries had declined, including the loss of Sunderland's advantages as a port after the development of railways and the removal of import duties which made the home industries less able to compete against foreign imports. Other factors were the failure to re-equip with modern machinery, or the introduction of modernisation too late. Sunderland's largest pottery and glass firms, Scott's and Hartley's, both closed down within eight years of being re-equipped. Another suggested reason for industrial problems was high wage demands. It is certainly striking that a large number of the town's industries closed during the 1890s and the following years, but the full reasons for these failures have still to be established. One cause for the decline of some firms was undoubtedly the loss of the driving personality responsible for the firm's previous success. It was fortunate that in 1914 Sunderland still possessed industrialists such as Ernest Jobling-Purser and Sir Frank Nicholson who would ensure that the firms they controlled continued to develop and thrive.

REFERENCES

1. *Inventories and Account Rolls of the Benedictine Houses or Cells of Jarrow and Monkwearmouth,* Surtees Soc. xxix (for 1854).
2. Ambrose Crowley, draft letter 1684/5, Friends Library, London.
3. John C. Baker *Sunderland Pottery* (Sunderland, 1984) p. 170.
4. Catherine Ross *The Development of the Glass Industry on the Rivers Tyne and Wear, 1700-1900,* University of Newcastle Upon Tyne, Ph.D. thesis, 1982.
5. David Bean *Thomas Reed — the first 200 years* (Sunderland, 1982).
6. Corder MSS 5 p. 42. Sunderland Library.
7. John C. Baker *op. cit.,* p. 45.
8. Geoffrey E. Milburn *Piety, Profit and Paternalism* (Bunbury, 1983) p. 91.
9. J. G. James *The Cast Iron Bridge at Sunderland* (Newcastle, 1986) pp. 33-37.
10. L. G. Charlton *The First Locomotive Engineers* (Newcastle, 1974).
11. *SWE* 14 July, 1893.
12. *ST* 11 May, 1875.
13. W. R. Clanny 'An Account of the Sunderland Limestone Formation,' *Annals of Philosophy* 1815 p. 116.

Bill-head showing the Vaux Castle Street Brewery.

WORKS	DATES	FIRST OWNERS	LATER OWNERS	PRODUCTS	NOTES
Ayres Quay Bottleworks	c.1696-1880	Company of Glass Owners of Sunderland	Thomas Wilson & Co. 1756, Wilson & Russell from 1768, William Russell & Co. from 1776 proprietors of Ayres Quay from 1781, Pemberton family from c.1795, Pemberton and Featherstonehaugh 1830, William Kirk & Co. from 1849.	Bottles also Broad window glass until c.1819.	
Bishopwear-mouth Panns Glasshouse	c.1696-1883	Company of Glass Owners of Sunderland	As Ayres Quay, then Fenwick family from c.1795.	Bottles also Broad window glass c.1810-1877. Crown window glass c.1827-c.1846.	Site incorporated in Austin's shipyard.
Bishopwear-mouth Glass-house, west of bridge.	c.1765-c.1780 c.1809-c.1877	John Hopton	Hilkiah Hall Laing, Horn, Scott & Co.	Table glass Bottles and plate glass.	Demolished for railway bridge.
Ballast Hill Bottleworks	c.1800-1923		T. Bonner & Co. c.1820 (Bonner, Laing, Horn and Scott). Laing, Horn, Scott & Co. from 1821.	Bottles	Site incorporated in Laings shipyard.
Wear Flint Glassworks	c.1805-c.1844	John White	John White, Thomas Young and various partners 1816-1830. William Booth, Nicholas French and James Vint from 1830.	Cut, engraved table glass.	Sometime after 1844 enclosed in Deptford Bottleworks.
Southwick Crown Glassworks.	1805-1875		Atwoods from c.1823. Wear Crown Glass Co. (Managing Partners J. & C. Matteson from c.1869.)	Crown glass until c.1860. Blown sheet.	Site incorporated in Pickersgill's shipyard.
Deptford Bottlehouse (The Wear Glass Bottle Company)	1807-1883	Featherstone & Co.	Wear Glass Bottle Co. (Walter Featherstonehaugh managing director).	Bottles	
Wear Glass-works (1)	1836-1894	James Hartley & Co.	The Wear Glass Company from	Roller plate window glass, stained glass, tableware.	
Harrison Street Works	1853-1887	Nicholas French	J. Thomas from 1882	Table glass.	
Southwick Bottleworks	1846-c.1918	The Scott family	Alexander and Austin from 1867.	Bottles	
Trimdon Street Works	1855-1873	Nicholas French. (Sunderland Flint Glass Company)	J. Walton from c.1857 Angus and Greener from c.1869 then Henry Greener. Samuel Neville of Gateshead, 1873.	Table glass including pressed glass from 1859.	Greener moved to Alfred Street.
Diamond Hall Bottleworks	1857-1877	Snowdon and Watson	John Candlish from 1858	Bottles	
Cornhill Glassworks	1865-1953	The Turnbull family. (Southwick Flint Glass Co.)		Pressed table and utility ware.	
Hope Street/Johnson Street Works	c.1867-1900	D. Young, A. W. Phillips, C. T. Candlish	J. Ayre c.1869, T. Turnbull 1873-1900.	Table glass, later also bottles.	
Crown Road Bottleworks. (Low Southwick.)	c.1869-c.1885	H. Pool	Horn and Scott from c.1877.		
South Hylton Bottle Co.	c.1871	Cuthbert Marr		Bottles	Used furnaces of Dawson's Pottery. (Closed in 1864.)
Wear Glass-works (2) Alfred Street	From 1873	Henry Greener	James A. Jobling from 1885. Corning Ltd. from 1973.	Table glass, utility & scientific ware. Pressed glass until c.1957. Pyrex from 1921.	Greener moved from Trimdon St.
Ropery Walk Works	1877-1883	Harrison & Park		Bottles	
North East Glassworks. Pallion	1879-1899			Window glass	
Portobello Lane Works	1883-1891 From 1892	Park, Duncan & Co.	Hartley Wood (Subsidiary of Pilkington Glass Ltd. from 1982.)	Bottles Stained glass	
Monkwear-mouth Bottle Company	c.1884-1886 1893-4	James Davidson of Blyth Bottle Company	Yorkshire Bottle Company (Richard Henry).	Bottles.	

14. *A Plan of Lands Lying at Southwick in the County Palatine of Durham belonging to George Grey, Esq., by William Donkin, 1746.* Sunderland Museum TWCMS B8179.

15. Neil T. Sinclair *Railways of Sunderland* (Sunderland, 1985) p. 7.

16. Potts p. 157.

17. See p.

18. Auction Notice Fire Brick Manufactory, Ayres Quay, 9 May, 1822 Sunderland Museum TWCMS K7051.

19. A. J. Francis *The Cement Industry 1796-1814: A History*, (Newton Abbott, 1970) pp. 225-7.

20. *An Illustrated Guide to Sunderland and District* (Edinburgh 1895) p. 65.

21. 1851 Census. quoted John C. Baker *op. cit.*, p. 10.

22. 1861 Census. quoted John C. Baker *ibid.*

23. *ibid.* pp. 17-25.

24. *ibid.* p. 8-9.

25. Potts *op. cit.* p. 165.

26. J. T. Shaw *Sunderland Ware: The Potteries of Wearside* (Sunderland, 1973) p. 18.

27. Catherine Ross *op. cit.* pp. 26-27.

28. *ibid.* p. vii.

29. *ibid.* p. 258.

30. R. W. Swinburne 'The Manufacture of Glass in the Northern District', *The British Association For The Advancement of Science Proceedings Newcastle 1863.*

31. Catherine Ross *op. cit.* p. 509.

32. *Newcastle Courier* 6 November, 1834.

33. John Baker and Kate Crowe *A Collector's Guide to Jobling 1930s Decorative Glass* (Sunderland, 1985) p. 7-8.

34. John C. Baker, Stuart Evans and Cindy Shaw *Pyrex 60 Years of Design* (Sunderland, 1983) pp. 7-11.

35. *Inventories of Monkwearmouth* Surtees Soc. xxix p. 203.

36. H. L. Robson 'George Lilburne, Mayor of Sunderland' *Antiq. Sund.* xxii p. 91.

37. G. Heslop 'A Note on the Deptford Copperas Works' *Antiq. Sund.* iii p. 125.

38. Catherine Ross *op. cit.* p. 176.

39. *An Illustrated Guide, op. cit.* pp. 42-3.

40. *ibid.* pp. 39-40.

41. J. P. Cornett 'Local Paper Mills' *Antiq. Sund.* ix pp. 161-2.

42. *ibid.* p. 161.

43. C. A. Chester *History of Ford Papermill* Paper, based on the notes of Mr. W. Wilson, presented to the Sunderland Industrial Archaeology Society, 1972.

44. *Sunderland Coronation Souvenir* (Sunderland 1902) p. 108.

45. T. F. Dibdin *A Biographical Antiquarian and Picturesque Tour of Northern Counties* (London) (1838) p. 1071.

46. *An Illustrated Guide to Sunderland, op. cit.* p. 61.

47. Glaholm and Robson Photographic album (c.1910) Sunderland Museum.

48. C. E. Mountford and L. G. Charlton *Industrial Locomotives of Durham* (London, 1977) p. 147.

49. *An Illustrated Guide to Sunderland*, p. 62.

50. *ibid.* p. 61.

51. *S. T.* 30 March, 1876.

52. H. Bowling (Ed.). *Some Chapters In Sunderland's History* (Sunderland 1969) p. 23.

53. Taylor Potts *op. cit.* p. 13.

54. Corder MSS 33 p. 37.

55. Catherine Ross *op. cit.* pp. 189-190.

56. *Illustrated Guide to Sunderland*, p. 111.

57. J. M. Webb 'Vaux Breweries — 100 years at Castle Street'. *Things That Affect Us: House Magazine of Vaux Limited.* No. 19 (1975) p. 6.

58. R. Vint and Carr's *Borough of Sunderland Directory* (Sunderland, 1844) p. 15

59. *Things That Affect Us, op. cit.* p. 7.

60. *An Illustrated Guide, op. cit.* p. 77.

61. G. T. F. Dibdin *op. cit.* p. 314.

Shipbuilding 1780-1914

It is very unlikely that anyone in 1780 would have predicted that 70 years later Sunderland would be proclaimed the greatest shipbuilding port in the world. Lloyd's Register of 1776 showed ten ports with a greater aggregate tonnage than the 63 Sunderland-built vessels, which, totalling 12,222 tons, were less than one sixth of that built at Whitby. Indeed Scarborough with 26,410 tons also far exceeded Wearside. At that time on the eastern seaboard of North America a new nation was being born and the following seven years of war, ending with the birth of the United States of America, were to influence shipbuilding profoundly. Much of the British merchant fleet had been built in the American colonies. The men of Wearside seized this opportunity to advance their shipbuilding industry in the years which followed, so that the port, where shipbuilding had begun by 1346, could by the 1820s reach such a leading position.[1]

Averaging 192 tons those Sunderland ships of 1776 were larger than the average for Lloyd's Register as a whole and included two ships of 420 tons, demonstrating the port's capacity to match perhaps any port other than London for individual ship construction. During the 1780s some six shipyards were working regularly and 2,740 tons of shipping were built in 1790. Two years later Sunderland ships registered with Lloyd's reached almost 3,000 tons; however it was in the war years that the port's output was to expand massively. The local historian George Garbutt wrote in 1819 "The township of Monkwearmouth is comparatively of modern date, and owes its present consequence to the extensive shipbuilding yards which during the war were established there . . ." and 11 years later Burnett commented: "During the war orders were received from all parts of the kingdom for ships and large profits were made . . . the builders then in business generally made their fortunes."[2]

By 1804-5 the output of Sunderland (14,198 tons) was exceeded only by Newcastle upon Tyne; as a result in 1816 Surtees wrote: "In shipbuilding the Port of Sunderland stands at present the highest of any in the United Kingdom", an opinion endorsed by Garbutt three years later. The growth of trade and in particular the shipment of coal created a substantial local market for shipping. The number of ships belonging to the port more than doubled between 1752 and 1786, when the 387 registered vessels totalled 52,160 tons and by 1815 the 615 ships exceeded 90,000 tons. Such a tonnage on a 20 year replacement period would require 30 ships (4,250 tons) per year. By 1851 the port had more than 1,000

vessels (207,804 tons) so clearly the new ships required also added substantially to local shipbuilding output and many shipowners from other ports bought their vessels at Sunderland. More than 14,000 tons were built in 1814, probably the largest output of merchant vessels by any port for that year. The substantial cyclical fluctuations which characterise this industry are clearly to be seen in graph A "Total tonnage on Wear 1820-1912" and such fluctuations in addition to their disastrous effects upon shipbuilding profoundly also affected the whole town given the great local significance of the industry.[3]

THE EARLY WOOD SHIPYARDS

Timber was to remain the material for ship construction on the Wear until after 1860, (see graph B). Indeed as late as 1872 James Gardner opened a new wood building yard.

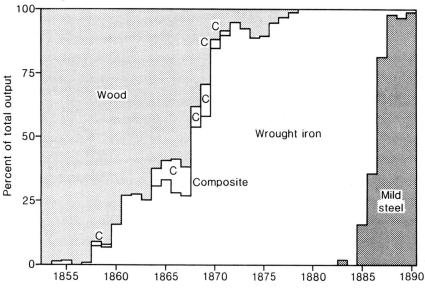

Graph B: Proportion of output on River Wear, wood/iron/steel, 1853-1890.

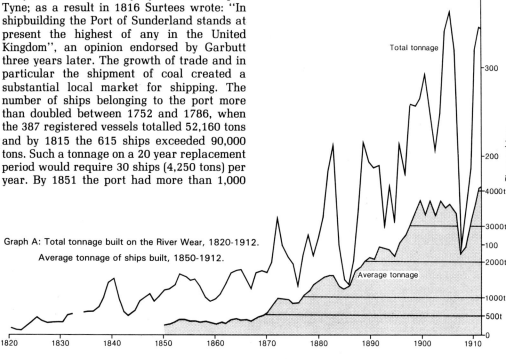

Graph A: Total tonnage built on the River Wear, 1820-1912.

Average tonnage of ships built, 1850-1912.

Many of the early shipbuilders were timber merchants, although some such as Reay and Havelock were coal fitters. Many of these yards were often built for their owners' personal use, while others would trade with the vessels until a buyer was found or else became regular shipowners, such as was the case with the Laings. By 1790 the shipwrights who built the ships were supported by 13 master craftsmen in sailmaking, five in ropemaking, ten blockmakers and three master anchor smiths; in addition blacksmiths were necessary for the iron work, which formed part of the wood vessel. A wood shipyard essentially needed some space by the river, a skilled workforce and perhaps a steaming oven, often of an elementary construction, for shaping timber. The shipwright possessed his own tools. Consequently shipyards could increase and decrease with great rapidity; probably about 25 yards were normally working during the Napoleonic wars. Twenty-four shipyards in 1804 employed 667 and as many as 60 per cent of these were apprentices (no doubt in part a consequence of the recent rapid expansion). The three largest yards each employed about 50 men, but the average yard size was 28. Fifty years later the size of yards had hardly changed, the average number employed being only 32. The average size doubled to 64 in 1861 but was still much smaller than the iron shipbuilding yards, already opening on the Wear.[4]

Many timber merchants extended credit to ambitious craftsmen shipwrights and even paid wages while ships were under construction to provide a market for their timber. Throughout the whole period of wood ship construction a large proportion were built 'on spec', that is, in advance of the ship actually having a purchaser. The leading craftsman would combine with fellow workers and build a ship. If they were successful and trade was expanding a new permanent shipyard might come into existence (e.g. Thompsons, see below) or the yard might exist for a few vessels or indeed simply for the initial single vessel. Between 1800 and 1860 very nearly 300 shipbuilders completed at least one vessel, however about one third of them did not last a single year and not more than half survived for two years.[5]

Ships were built by men "barely above the position of artisans", according to Tyneside businessman Thomas Brown in 1833, and so prices were lower than if they "had been capitalists". Nor had the situation changed by 1850 when a Sunderland shipowner stated "a great many of our Shipbuilders are Workingmen". These vigorous young shipwrights may be identified as the driving force in the expansion of the industry. Unlike many other ports in which the shipwrights were well organised in trade unions no regular union was established on Wearside until 1846. Cheap supplies of timber were important and in 1818 Tiffin introduced American elm. Low cost land may for a time have provided adequate space for spreading out the beams of timber to allow the most economical use. By such efficient use of timber there was a minimisation of waste enabling Sunderland shipwrights to build ships

at prices other ports could not match. This point was made many times by builders on both the Tyne and Mersey. As the merchant and shipowner Joshua Wilson admiringly explained in 1848:

A shipbuilder could make £100 by converting the Timber when another would make nothing because one Man could cut his timber to waste and another will fit it with much less waste ... if a Twelve Years Ship is built at Sunderland ... you will generally find a small vessel built next to it ... the refuse timber (from) the Twelve Years ship is put into the lower class vessel ... (From the Select Committee on Navigation Laws, 1848.)

In such ways for some decades the port of Sunderland established its ability to build lower class vessels at prices that other ports failed to match. This did not mean, as some have argued, that they were bad ships. They were intended to be the equivalent of the popular car rather than the Rolls Royce. All five ships launched by Robert Thompson Jnr. in 1866 were in the 14 year class and the ships built by William Pile Jnr. received acclaim by many writers on sailing ships; so of the ability to build the high quality vessels there should be no doubt.[6]

As might be expected many small wood-building yards had short lives and, as noted above, often disappeared after building a single ship. However 19 shipbuilders who first began before 1800 survived for ten years or more. Thomas Nicholson (born 1722), with a family name linked to boat building as early as 1667, worked a shipyard and graving dock at Bishopwearmouth Panns and lived in a large double fronted three-storied house almost facing the gates of the yard. By no means all of these shipbuilders had such a grand home but, almost without exception, they did live immediately adjacent to their shipyards. Nicholson was building in 1768 and his son launched ships in every year from 1789. Usually built 'on spec', the ships were often registered by Nicholson. Another character from those early years was Mr. Burn, whose yard was at Old Jackdaw Dock, Bishopwearmouth. From 1781 the yard was managed by his widow until his son took over in 1814 when the four ships built totalled nearly a thousand tons. Robert Reay in the 1770s was repairing ships and probably built a ship or two before becoming a regular builder at North Hylton in 1791. When Reay died his wife asked her shipwright brother William Potts to become yard foreman and 'partly manager' and when Potts left to open his own shipyard he recommended that Neddie Brown take his place. Brown, too, started his own yard only after many years of managing the Reay yard and shipbuilding was continuous there until 1837. From 1845 Miss Margaret Reay ran the yard and output was only sporadic until it closed in 1857. The Potts family continued to build until 1868, the end of the wood era; the first yard was just below the Ferry-boat landing. William Potts Jnr. moved the yard to Lower Hylton. After about five years Edward Potts ended the partnership with his brother and in 1803 at South Hylton started his own yard, where his foreman was William Gales. In 1812 Gales began his own shipyard and continued to build until 1841. His brother John Mowbray began in 1827. One of the two Mowbray brothers launched the highest tonnage on the River Wear in 15 of the 21 years, from 1813 to 1833. Such interactions of family and foreman were typical of the early years in shipbuilding, where, overwhelmingly, there was little social class difference between small scale shipbuilders and the craftsmen who built the ships. Eleven of these early yards lasted an average of almost 14 years, whilst three others averaged 25 years. The Laing family, who began in 1793, continued shipbuilding throughout the whole of our period.[7]

Thirteen of the shipbuilders who began in the war years 1800 to 1815 survived for ten years or more. Luke Crown began in 1807, and the Crowns were to build more or less continuously for about 70 years and a Crown yard was to emerge again in the twentieth century. One of the family's outstanding characters was 'Jacky' Crown (1840-1902), who was ever ready to join the workmen in his yard in building a vessel. Three Hall brothers began by building a single vessel of 182 tons in 1801 and although, like so many others, they failed in the depression of the 1840s (see below) the family continued building for 60 years, including such notable ships as *Daphne* 842 tons (1854) and *John Temperley* 998 tons for London in 1856. After a brief partnership with Thomas Robson in 1810 Thomas Tiffin (1766-1855) began building east of the Pottery Bank. Output was always modest and later took place at two different sites. After his retirement in 1836, his sons continued to build ships. However, the yard survived a mere two years after the death of Tiffin Snr. The only other long running yard was that of John Hutchinson commenced in 1813. However after 1840 building was sporadic and the last vessel was built in 1862; it seems likely he engaged extensively in repairs and fitting out, the more profitable side of the business.

Although Watsons were probably involved in earlier partnerships of shipwrights, the family yard began in 1817 and output was more or less continuous until the 1860s. The following are examples of the tonnage built by the Watsons:

year	1817	1818	1819	1823	1836	1838	1840	1847	1848	1855
tons	723	988	734	1315	1497	2427	2072	2102	1593	2513
ships	4	6	4	6	6	9	7	5	4	4

While it is true that the Watsons were amongst the pioneers in the construction of East Indian merchantmen, the claim to have built 317 ships seems very high but impossible to verify in the absence of yard records and also because many ships were signed over to their owner 'as builder' to avoid sequestration due to the financial difficulties of the Watsons. Thus the *Middlesex* (1,191 tons) and *Winchester* (1,157 tons) both appear in Lloyds as built by Marshall, who was in fact the shipowner. Other very large Watson vessels were: *Castle Eden* 930 tons (1842), *Kent* 815 tons (1847), *Agra* 714 tons (1851), *Anglo Saxon* 890 tons (1854), *Chapman* 750 tons (1854) and *Patricia* 1,140 tons (1859). Undoubtedly these 13 year-ships as classified by Lloyds were amongst the most superior ships built in the port. Watson like so many others failed to

launch a single ship in 1843, the central year of the depression spanning 1842-44.[8]

FLUCTUATIONS IN GROWTH

Nationally shipbuilding fell from a post-war peak of almost 90,000 tons in 1819 to just over 50,000 tons in 1822. Output also fell on the Wear. The steady upward climb from that point (see graph A above) took Sunderland's output to almost 21,000 tons in 1825 and, although shipbuilding then fell back, the average for the next five years was not far below 15,000 tons. In the early 1830s output averaged about 26,000 tons or double that of the 1820s. Eight new builders opened shipyards in 1837 and the port launched a total of 32,000 tons, an increase of 5,000 tons (i.e. 18.5 per cent). Shipbuilding increased sharply, as the graph shows, and with it the number of shipyards increasing to 76. Two hundred and fifty-one ships were built in 1841, a total of 64,446 tons. Such significant changes were bound to be reflected in a massive increase in the numbers returned as shipbuilders in the Census returns for men over 20 years. The increase for Sunderland was from 366 to 968 and the impact on young workers was even more significant as the following table shows:

Census data 1841: Shipbuilder, carpenter, wright

	20 yrs & over	under 20 yrs	youths as % of men
England	12,615	3,040	24*
Monkwearmouth	418	260	62
Sunderland	187	99	53
Bishopwearmouth	363	150	41

*22% for England without the Wear

Thus amongst working youths almost one in three in Monkwearmouth was described as 'shipwright etc' (31.8 per cent), one in six in Bishopwearmouth (16.1 per cent) and one in every eight in Sunderland (12.1 per cent) a most remarkable illustration of the importance of shipbuilding for employment and of the number of apprentices which the shipwright craftsmen were prepared to accept.[9]

Even as those census returns were being collected a crash was on hand and the fall in output was even more dramatic than the rise. Thirty-five shipbuilders went out of business in 1841 as output fell by 24,000 tons and worse was to come. Only 31 builders remained in 1843 to build the 85 ships (21,377 tons). Many of the longest lasting yards failed — Reay (started 1786), Adamson (1809), William Gale (1812), Storey (1821), Dixon (1824), Kirkbride (1824), Rowntree (1826), Gales J. M. (1827), Dobbinson (1831), Frater (1831), Ogden (1832), Mills and Sampson (1832). Trade through the port had collapsed, and duties collected almost halved between 1840 and 1842. The Wear Shipping Co.'s ships were sold by auction on 20 April 1843 when eight vessels only realised £8,605. As the local press noted there were 133 shops empty, including 13 in the High Street, and the wages of shipwrights fell from 31s 6d to 19s 6d. Such elementary statistics can in no way reflect the mass of human misery which accompanied such an extensive loss of jobs and trade by small shopkeepers and others.[10]

Once increasing output returned in 1845, with the launching of 38,260 tons, shipwrights started new yards again. William Doxford, the builder of a single ship in 1838, and three vessels in 1840, only to be bankrupt in 1841, began continuous production in 1845; at first in partnership with Crown. So began one of the Wear's most distinguished shipyards. Another was to be born in 1846 when the Thompsons, a family of shipwrights, built their first ship the *Pearl*. £200 profit was made on this 240 ton brig. Robert Thompson (Senior 1797-1860), served as foreman in many yards and his sons learned their craft by his side and within a few years this family yard would build its first A1 13 year-ship *Grahams* 668 tons. So long as construction continued in wood shipwrights came together in partnerships. During the 1850s 38 yards were started, of which only ten were able to continue for nine years, while more than half failed in under two years. The Crimean War years offered new opportunities

Robert Thompson's Shipyard at Southwick c.1850 (from a painting by Duncan McLee). Scott's Pottery is on the left.

for Sunderland shipbuilders. Production averaged almost 65,000 tons per year for the years 1853-6, but once again slump followed with the average for 1858-1860 being less than 40,000 tons. A trade unionist estimated 1,800 shipwrights and joiners were out of work in the town in 1858 and many of those in work earning only 30 pence a day and some as little as 18 pence. The price paid for ships also slumped. Sunderland followed the national pattern, which showed a fall from 323,000 tons in 1855 to 186,000 tons in 1859. Some measure of the significance of the industry for the town may be gauged from the estimated value of the shipbuilding output on the Wear for 1853, fitted ready for seagoing, as at least one million pounds. That sum amounted to about £110 per house or £15 for every person living in the town of Sunderland. Such a dependence upon shipbuilding would not have been matched anywhere else.[11]

IRON CONSTRUCTION

Long before this time, wrought iron, the new construction material for ships, had established itself firmly on other shipbuilding rivers. By 1846 20 iron vessels had been built on the Mersey, and in 1846 17 steamships (7,125 tons) were launched on the Clyde. On

the Tyne many iron vessels were already built and from Jarrow in 1852 the *John Bowes* would inaugurate the era of the steam collier. "Ere long our shipwright yards will be mere places for repairs" taunted the *Sunderland Herald* as early as September 1850. In fact no such threat lay before the wood builders for many years to come, but nevertheless what the same newspaper's words described as the greatest shipbuilding port in the world was failing to grasp the opportunities of the new material. Many factors no doubt influenced the delay but at root it was then, as now, a matter of people. Technical change results from human actions and on the Wear both the shipbuilders and their craftsmen, the shipwrights, were committed to wood. "An operative shipwright" wrote as follows in 1858:

Nothing can be equal to a good first-class wood ship, well constructed; and the safety of the nation demands that wood shipbuilding be encouraged in England ... Iron shipbuilding ... is the introduction of machinery into the art of shipbuilding, as well as an entire new class of skilled and unskilled workmen to build ships. It is unskilled labour's opportunity in shipbuilding.

Of no small importance was the fact that those young apprentices of the 1840s boom were not even 40 years of age in 1860 so that even if apprentice recruitment was stopped, there were many able-bodied craftsmen anxious to use their tools. This attachment to the wooden ship was reinforced by the timber merchants who still saw this as a major outlet for their trade and indeed there clearly was a market for wooden ships for many years beyond the mid-sixties. In the USA wood construction would continue for a very long time. Although it might be argued that iron plates would cost more at Sunderland this can hardly be a fundamental reason. The same commercial acumen that brought timber to the port at a price which enabled the Wear shipbuilders to compete successfully could also have been applied to the purchasae of iron. The attraction of repairing wooden vessels was, of course, strong, as this was always a profitable side of the shipwright's business. Wearside's 'operative shipwright' acknowledged that "iron shipbuilding (was) to a great extent displacing wood shipbuilding" and by 1861 the *Sunderland Herald* noted that "iron ships can be built at a lower price than wooden ones". Clearly under those circumstances there will be a limited period in which the wood shipbuilder can continue. It must, however, be recognised that given the size of vessel then being built there was no compelling technical reason to switch to iron. The new material added a new commercial hazard, to the cycle of boom and slump, the iron shipyards were much more capital intensive than ever the wood yard had been.[12]

Three yards on the Wear in 1861 were building in iron, those of Laing, Pile and Oswald. In only his third year T. R. Oswald was bankrupt for the first time, but for the *Herald* this was due to "the grossest of wreckless trading" and the editorial declared, that "where iron shipbuilding was undertaken by prudent capitalists conversant with details of the business it never failed ... to flourish ..." Oswald was the only one of these men to be solely building in iron and he was far more aware of the technical implications of iron construction than the *Herald's* editor. Bankruptcy was to continue to haunt Oswald but he continued to build for all his working life in Southampton and Wales after leaving the Wear in 1873. Following the tiny 77 ton *Loftus* built in 1852 by George Clark with John Barkes, Laing was to lead the wood shipbuilders in using iron: his first iron ship of 479 tons was the *Amity* in 1853. With the exception of 1858 James Laing continued to build in iron; in 1860 nine of his ten vessels built were of iron. Thereafter only three further wooden ships would be built. However the last of these was a very notable vessel, the *Parramatta* of 1,521 tons launched in 1866. The ships built at Sunderland that year averaged only 432 tons. No iron ship was as large as the *Parramatta*, indeed the average for the iron ships was 647 tons which reinforces the point made above about their being no technical reason of size for adopting iron. Also in 1866 Laing built the first of a small number of composite ships, that is vessels which have iron frames for strength but a wooden hull to enhance their sailing qualities particularly in tropical waters. Nine years later the famous *Torrens* was launched. This vessel, made famous by its one-time second mate, the author Joseph Conrad, could reach Adelaide in 64 days and was to sail for 35 years before she was broken up in 1910. Almost 60 per cent of the tonnage built by Pile in 1861 was in iron, his first year in the new material; his last wooden ship was in 1863 and from the following year he also built composite vessels. Ironically the two leading builders in 1872 Oswald (19,683 tons) and Pile (18,385 tons) would only survive another year. When Palmer of Jarrow addressed the 1863 Newcastle meeting of the British Association for the Advancement of Science the 15,608 tons of iron ships built on the Wear was less than half the output of the Tyne. The next year Doxfords began building in iron, to be followed in 1866 by Iliffe. The *SS Irishope* launched two years later was the first iron vessel built by Robert Thompson Jnr. (1819-1910), and not until 1871 did J. L. Thompsons and Short Brothers construct any iron hulls.[13]

WORKERS AND EMPLOYERS

No less a person than Sir George Hunter, builder of *Mauretania*, pointed out the hard-working characteristics of the Sunderland shipwright and his dedication to his craft, how they debated the characteristics of each ship as it stood on the slipway as well as the merits of iron ships. Many showed considerable literary talents. When finally in 1846 they formed themselves into a regular trade union they quickly established a solidarity which many would envy and their employers could rarely match. The extant rule books clearly demonstrate their desire to protect their trade and their members' jobs, including their older members, by reserving the labouring jobs for them. They firmly rejected piecework — rule 4

those who take or solicit piecework (will be) suspended during the Society's pleasure, and rule 29 members ... will not work overtime while there

are any (members) off work ... excepting at the finish of a vessel and then the ¼ day if required.

Probably very nearly a 100 per cent membership was achieved; 1,389 members in 1850 may be compared with the 1851 census return of 1,372 shipwrights over the age of 20 years. It seems more than likely that many of the small master-shipwrights retained their union membership, very wisely given the risks of business failure and their possible need to return to work as craftsmen.

Annually the Wearside men joined in great Whit Monday parades with union members from other shipwrights' associations on the Tyne. Each port usually had its own Society; nonetheless a yearly national meeting was held in different ports (they met in Sunderland in 1860 and 1874). This was a loose federation represented 24 ports in 1870. A continuous record of membership is not available and it was certainly subject to fluctuations related to the state of the trade. Numerous serious industrial stoppages inspired the Wearside employers to come together in 1853 and this was soon followed by a remarkable attempt at industrial conciliation and the stoppage of disputes through a joint board of the masters and men.[14]

At the Bridge Hotel on the evening of the 25 January 1853 the shipbuilders met "to take into consideration several regulations respecting the hours of labour, wages and other matters" and George Booth proposed: "the time has arrived, when, for the mutual benefit of shipbuilders ... and their men, a proper understanding, and a feeling of good-will should exist between them." The very next day the employers agreed to invite their work-men to nominate a representative to meet with them at the Lyceum and after various discussions the Board of Conciliation was formed. Despite a short life the Board was a bold pioneering experiment. The strong personal wish of these craftsmen to be directly involved in all trade matters was illustrated when their spokesman Gamsby told the employers they all wanted to be present at Court of Arbitration meetings. They finally elected a delegate from each of the forty-five shipyards and these delegates elected 14 representatives, nine to join the Court, with five as deputies. This Board, whose vice-chairman was William Knott, foreman black-smith with the Wear Commissioners, recognised "the principle that the interests of employer and employed are combined, and cannot be separated without disadvantage to both parties" and it was to consider "any question of dispute, either between an individual master and his men or the whole body of builders and shipwrights ... with a view to their amicable settlement". Before many months had passed it was clear that the employers did not accept this all embracing character and the Board faded away but the employers' Association, like the union, survived; though the members of the latter were more united than the former.[15]

Over the years unity was difficult to maintain amongst the master shipwrights even after the number of employers was reduced with the building of iron vessels. In the

Robert Thompson junior (1819-1910), son of the founder of the Southwick yard.

mid-1890s James Laing declared that in a boom his fellow employers might break ranks and offer higher wages to attract workers. Laing was chairman when on the 8 November 1853, the Wear Shipbuilders' Association was formed 'for mutual protection'; 45 names were recorded. The tentative character of this association in those early years is reflected in the absence of any minutes of meetings between the 6 December 1854 and 21 January 1856; some 27 builders paid £1 subscription in February 1856. They usually came together on the question of wages and so on the 14 May 1857, with Laing as chairman, they met. They held discussions with employers from North Shields, South Shields and Hartlepool. The employers' decision resulted in a strike. The action of the men and the pressures of business finally ended this effort at joint action by the employers who decided 'nem con' on the 8 January 1858 that each shipbuilder should act independently. Wages, however, were reduced towards the end of the year. The employers debated employing union or non-union men but two of their meetings had to be adjourned because too few shipbuilders were present. In May 1859 offers of work from the Naval Dockyards gave rise to demands for increased wages and in an effort to break the strike men were brought down from Scotland, and the shipbuilder Hutchinson was asked to pay off his men. A special subscription of £1 was raised for the expenses of the two men sent to Scotland to recruit strike breakers. As late as July the Association was still trying to bring the ship-repairers into line.[16]

Earlier, in May 1857, the Association set up a committee which included Laing, Spence, Pile, Alcock, Watson and Mills, to consider Lloyds rules. A year later Laing wanted the new rules modified. In 1858 they organised meetings and a petition for the repeal of the timber duties, a clear indication of the intention to continue in timber building rather than advancing iron shipbuilding. In 1864 they resolved to ask Lloyds to remove their surveyor Mumford. Again Laing was prominent, expressing his objections in 'forcible terms'. By then iron working was influencing their decisions and Oswald was playing an active role in the Association. Unless there was a dispute, or a wage reduction was wanted, Employers' Association meetings became for some years, almost just a formal annual event.[17]

The Shipwrights had three branches on the Wear in 1870 — Sunderland (779 members), Monkwearmouth (561) and Hylton (160). In the following year membership on the Wear grew by almost 100 and the Wear formed about 20 per cent of the national Federation membership. When 1,900 members were enrolled the union had reached probably its highest membership and it did not fall much below this in the 1870s. These men maintained their resistance to piecework throughout our period even though this became the norm for shipbuilding and it certainly meant their regular take-home pay was less than that of those crafts which worked in iron. Despite the formation of a national union — the Amalgamated Society of Shipwrights — the

Wear men maintained their own separate trade union until 1907. There were just over a thousand members in the early 1890s. The Hylton men were still in a desperate organisation, with about 160 members. They finally joined the Wear men in 1898 and a year later the 'Iron worker Shipwrights' (about 580 members) was also added to the Wear Society so that it had about 1,500 members when it joined the national union in the early years of the twentieth century.[18]

THE BOILERMAKERS

The craftsmen who built the iron ships were initially from the boilermaking trade and so were members of the Society of Boilermakers, which would later add 'Iron Shipbuilders' to its title. The first branch of the Boilermakers was established at Sunderland in 1856 but no membership figures are available until 1872, when the combined membership of four branches was 963. Membership of this union fluctuated rather more than that of the shipwrights because as members of a national craft union they were expected to travel in search of work; thus membership fell to 741 in 1873 but it exceeded 1,000 in 1877 and by 1906 its 11 branches included 3,832 members. In shipbuilding the boilershop craftsman's work was subdivided into platers, rivetters, etc. Each of these trades worked on piecework, normally assisted by 'helpers' and these 'non-craftsmen' would organise their own trade unions in the late 1880s after an abortive attempt in the 1870s.[19]

From the 1870s the employers had to deal with a full-time organiser from the Boilermakers' Society and its delegates ultimately won the confidence of the employers. The strong national leadership of this union with its headquarters in Newcastle strove for discipline amongst its members but also tended to act independently of the other trade unions. Robert Knight, as national secretary, no less than his Wearside delegate, was concerned with how union funds flowed away in the disputes, which haunted the shipyards, and in unemployment benefit. The following is the income and expenditure of two Wear branches in good and bad years:

Branch	1876	1878		1883	1884
No.1 income	629	967	No. 5 income		
				885	452
expenditure	1,323	834	expenditure	307	1,579
net		−694	+143	net	+578	−1,127

The strength of organisation of the Boilermakers in the shipyards was second to none amongst British trade unions; it was these men who built the iron ships and their employment could not be avoided even if shipbuilders wanted to do so. The union's leadership was embodied in men like James O'Neill, who was concerned to avoid disputes while protecting its members interests.[20]

DEPRESSION IN THE 1880s

The dominant role of iron in the 1870s resulted in larger ships. The average for 1872-9 was 1,100 tons, substantially more than double the

James O'Neill (1839-1913) a leader of the Sunderland Boilermakers' Society.

448 tons of 1862-9. The output of 134,825 tons in 1872 was almost double the best output of any year in the wood era and the annual average for 1872-8 was almost 93,000 tons, despite the very low output of 54,041 tons in 1876 which was the bottom of a very sharp decline from 1872 (as graph A shows). Output fell again in 1879, when the 60 ships launched averaged 1,457 tons which was almost the mean size of vessels built in the 1880s. At Doxford's Pallion yard they launched the 4,500 ton *Grecian*, the largest deadweight steamer afloat. The central depressed years of both decades saw the construction of smaller vessels e.g. 1875-6 average 888 tons and in 1884-5 average 1,382 tons. This characteristic fall was seen again in 1907-8 when the average size at 2,393 tons fell well below the usual size for the period. Graph A shows how the average size of ships built moved up in phases.[21]

Paralleling a national trend output swept upwards from 1879 to 108,000 tons in 1880 and this had almost doubled to 212,313 tons by 1883. In the next year, when output did not even reach 100,000 tons, disaster was about to hit the port, By 1886 output was not much above a quarter of 1883 and the total of the three years 1885-7 fell almost 10,000 tons short of that of 1883 alone. On the Wear output fell to a mere 26.7 per cent of the 1883 peak. In the rest of the country it dropped to about 42 per cent. Little wonder that the *Shipping World* commented that the trade was never before "in such a wretched state" and added; "The present suffering is among a class of highly respectable artizans, self reliant, proud workmen, who will endure long, rather than disclose their poverty and want." During 1884 the Boilermakers' Society paid out £7,700 in home donations at Sunderland. This benefit was available only for a limited period, the sum paid out being equal to the annual subscriptions of nearly 4,000 members. Some in the town were so impoverished that food was taken from pig troughs and the Medical Officer of Health reported: "Their homes are bare of furniture, their clothes are scanty, the season promises cold and fires are a luxury which they cannot afford." In April 1884 *The Shipping World* estimated "not less than 7,000 men lying idle", confirming the Boilermakers' Society report that "scarcely a quarter of our members (are) in employment. In some (yards) there are only the apprentices working." Just over a year later only on 20 of 67 berths was any work going on. The continued severity of this depression can be seen on the output graph A. It was the sequence of four years which made this a financial burden no working man could possibly have provided for. No less than four wage reductions failed to bring new orders to the shipyards. Nonetheless these years witnessed the establishment of a Conciliation Board for the shipyards and very significantly a major technical change — the introduction of the steel hull.[22]

More than 20 years of unprecedented industrial conciliation began at the Queen's Hotel on 24 June 1885 when 16 delegates representing the workmen met with Laing and five other builders. Doxford's motion to establish a Conciliation Board was seconded by one of the men and rapid progress was made. James Laing would later stress to the Royal Commission on Labour the important significance of conciliation, that is, the bringing of the parties together, and how the Wear was free of strikes for six years. Indeed the industrial relations record of Wearside shipbuilders was the envy of other centres until the National Federation of Shipbuilders ended such local arrangements. Although the Boilermakers stayed outside the new body, no doubt to emphasise their independence and prestige, they too had largely amicable arrangements with their employers. Doxford, who always played a major part in labour relations matters, declared: ". . . my personal views are strongly in favour of strong unions, both on the part of the men and the employers. I believe the stronger the unions are, the less likely there will be strikes." This was the view of many, though by no means all, north east employers. Although this Board did not eliminate stoppages it reduced them most remarkably, e.g. in the five years 1894-8 there were only seven stoppages.[23]

Even before Sunderland's shipbuilders had generally adopted iron construction a small number of steel ships had been built. It was to be the end of the 1870s before a suitable quality of Siemens-Martin open hearth steel was available to be worked under normal shipyard conditions. The extensive use of mild steel began in Scotland but even there in 1883 less than one-third of the tonnage was in the new material. On the Tyne a small amount of steel construction began in 1878. Five years later Doxford led the change at Sunderland by building four steel ships (4,877 tons in all) which was about one third of the shipyard's output. Perhaps understandably no-one followed his initiative in 1884, not even Doxford himself, and in 1885 his steel output was only one fifth of the total modest production of 6,496 tons. Eight Wear yards built in steel in 1885; for J. L. Thompson it was more than half the output. Two years later four of every five tons built was of steel and by 1888 the changeover was virtually complete. This rapid passage from iron to steel in a mere four years contrasts sharply with the prolonged period in the change-over from wood to iron (see graph B). This was in large part due to similarities in working steel compared to iron in contrast to the profound technological change from wood to metal. So short a period of transition demonstrates the skill and adaptability of the workforce and technical staff of the shipyards.[24]

The iron shipyards rang to the sound of the rivetter's hammer wielded by hand, as they would continue to do for many many decades. In 1885, however, J. L. Thompson's yard gave the lead in introducing hydraulic equipment which would eliminate hand-rivetting on parts of a ship. This equipment was invented by Ralph Hart Tweddell, a former north east apprentice who maintained close connections with the region. His type of plant had already been working for more than ten years in the French naval yards. Thompson's lead was followed by other yards and before 1889 hydraulic machines were generally used

Robert Thompson (1851-1908), son of J. L. Thompson (1827-1893) of the North Sands yard.

whenever construction permitted. Pneumatic tools would only arrive in the last years covered by this essay.[25]

The depth of the depression challenged, at least temporarily, that mainstay of the iron shipyard — piecework. John Priestman, who started his shipyard in 1882, finally decided, in the face of no orders, to build a ship on speculation by day-work payments only. Austins also abandoned piecework for a time and S. P. Austin almost passionately denounced it before his fellow north east employers at a meeting of the North East Coast Institution.[26]

Yet another very important event in these fateful years of the mid-1880s — was the formation of the North East Coast Institution of Engineering & Shipbuilding. This Institution was to be significant for the whole region, and indeed for the whole world, in terms of enhancing understanding of shipbuilding and marine engineering. Remarkably virtually none of those outstanding builders of ships had received any formal education since leaving school and, equally surprisingly, there was no Institution for the industry similar to that which existed for Scotland from the 1860s. From Wearside only J. Y. Short (in 1875) had contributed a paper to the Transactions of the Institution of Naval Architects and S. P. Austin contributed to a discussion in 1877. The story of the institution is told elsewhere (see footnote 25). Its connection with Sunderland begins in the Queens Hotel on 31 October 1884 when a meeting chaired by Robert Thompson "warmly advocated the formation" of the proposed Institution. Three of the four men from Sunderland on the provisional committee were from marine engine works. The Institution met regularly in Sunderland for some years and the second President was William Doxford, to be followed in 1892-3 by Robert Thompson. W. H. Dugdale (1859-1930) of Austins, as President in 1906-8, took the decisive step of establishing the Institutions Scholarship awards and so enabling at least some young people to receive a university education in naval architecture and marine engineering.[27] Before returning to the main chronological account the following is a brief survey of marine engineering.

MARINE ENGINEERING

Although dredging was carried out regularly by steam power on the River Wear as early as 1811 the port was very slow to adopt steampower for the propulsion of ships. That 'very curious machine' of 1811 lifting 55 tons in 35 minutes, was not moved by steam but its contribution to improving the harbour and so making the port more accessible was a factor in expanding shipbuilding. At Sunderland as elsewhere tug-boats led the way in adopting steampower to enable the sailing vessels to be hauled out to sea and, indeed, pulled into the river if the winds were in a contrary direction. In 1825 the *Wear* and *Dragon* were built and in the following year the *Neptune*.[28]

Appropriately named, the *Experiment* of 296 tons, built by T. Rowntree, was the first seagoing steam propelled ship built on the Wear. Of the 37 steam vessels registered at Sunderland in 1854 only four were seagoing vessels. No more than a tiny 1.1 per cent of the ports shipping was steam propelled compared with a national average of 7.2 per cent. Seven years later the output of the port was still only 6.5 per cent compared with national ratio of 10.5 per cent. This lack of steampowered vessels was undoubtedly related to the slower development of iron shipbuilding at the port, iron ships were overwhelmingly steampowered. While a lack of engineering capacity may be offered as an explanation this seems inadequate. In the mid-1850s 14 iron foundries were noted by Fordyce, including the Bishopwearmouth Iron Works of Mounsey, Jansen & Co. There was no shortage of engine builders nearby on the Tyne. In 1848, when George clark (1815-1883) opened his general engineering works, a foundation was laid for marine engineering on the Wear. As already noted this works built the iron *Loftus* and in 1854 constructed the first locally built marine engine for James Laing's *Alfred*.[29]

The engineering works of John Dickinson & Son began at Palmers Hill in 1852 and, with iron building in the ascendancy, in 1865 the North Eastern Marine Engineering Works was opened. When Pile entered iron shipbuilding he also decided to build his own engines and boilers. Similarly Oswald not only built marine engines for his iron ships but also made the iron for both. These companies provided a local supply of engines for Sunderland ships and, although craftsmen were recruited from Tyneside, they also created an engineering workforce of considerable skill.

There were 236 engine and machine makers over the age of 20 in Sunderland in 1861 and ten years later the census recorded a massive increase to 1,348 machine makers. Although not more than a quarter of this workforce belonged to a trade union in the spring of 1871 these Sunderland craftsmen under the leadership of Andrew Gourley, formerly of Palmers at Jarrow, fought a successful strike to win the nine-hour day for engineering workers. Between 800 and 1,000 attended the early meetings that decided on strike action.[30]

Twelve years later, in the depression of the mid-1880s, these same workers, after a strike lasting two and a half years, were defeated and almost suffered the destruction of their trade union organisation. In May 1883 the Amalgamated Society of Engineers members at Clark's Marine Engine Works struck to secure a wage increase and against the employment of a 24 year old apprentice. The union was most anxious to secure the reduction in the number of apprentices employed and so the issue was taken up by the workers throughout the town, following a mass meeting of about 1,400 men. Before long however the depression resulted in 400 union members leaving the town in search of work. The apprentices continued to work until they too briefly stopped work when men were brought in as black-legs; court action quickly sent them back to work. Despite financial assistance from all over the country the trade union's national leadership ended the strike in May 1885 but the employers stated the strike ended in December of that year.[31]

Directly this strike action threatened the four marine engineering firms formed the Wear Engine Builders' Association. By the early 1890s these firms employed some 2,500 workers. The average wage was 30 shillings (£1.50) per week and there was very little piecework, as was normal in this strongly craft based industry. The census of 1901 shows the great importance of engineering for Sunderland. The proportion of males in engineering and machine making in the town was 1,208 per 10,000 males over the age of ten years against 516 in England & Wales, i.e. 2.34 times the national average. Sunderland had the greatest concentration for shipbuilding of any town 1,642 per 10,000 compared with a national average of 71. It may be noted that for every 16 working in shipbuilding there were 12 in engineering.[32]

Doxford's added to their fame as ship-builders their considerable achievements in marine engine building. Their engine works was opened in 1878 under Robert P. Doxford (1851-1932). They began supplying the engines for their own ships and were to reach a productive capacity equal to the specialist engine builders. Indeed in 1897 Doxford's output was just above that of George Clark, amounting to 28 per cent of Wearside output. When a fire destroyed the engine works in 1901 a new and improved works was built and within three months engine building was resumed. However, the company's claim to fame rests not so much on its output capacity as on its pioneering decision to invest in a re-search programme to develop a diesel type engine work began on the project in 1906. Within three years engines were under construction and in 1912 the prototype design of the opposed-piston airless injection oil engine appeared. Before the 1914-18 war began a 450 hp single cylinder engine had been tested satisfactorily to show the potential of the new design. Doxford's were virtually alone amongst British marine engine builders in undertaking this work. The demands of war delayed work on this project and it was not until 1921 that the *Yngaren* sailed with a 3,000 hp Doxford engine. O. Keller (1877-1942) and W. H. Purdie (1888-1971) headed the research and development work on these engines.[33]

William Allan, a future M.P. for Gateshead and a pioneering industrialist, re-opened the works of Carr, Fowles & Co. as the Scotia Engine Works in 1883. While general manager at North East Marine he had written *The Shipowners' and Engineers' Guide to the Marine Engine* (1880) and he later produced a standard design of a triple expansion steam engine. The excellence of the works helped start many apprentices on the road to dis-tinguished careers. At his works and that of his friend George Short there was established the eight-hour day (48 hour week) in 1892, almost a generation before such hours were conceded by the engineering and shipbuilding industry in 1919. His 400 workmen began at 7.30 a.m. instead of 6 a.m. and finished at 5 p.m. (dinner break 12-12.45) and Saturday was a half-day. Early in the 20th century the works merged with Richardson Westgarth. This company built 25,100 hp on the Wear in 1906. The North

Eastern Marine Engine Company works was moved to Southwick in 1882 when it was substantially extended, and in 1902 the works was electrified making it one of the earliest companies to change over from direct drive by their own steam engines and boilers. On occasion this company did other engineering work as well; in 1899, for example building 6,000 hp of pumping machinery, in addition to 21,575 hp of marine engines and related boilers. In 1906 NEM built 47,054 hp on the River Wear. After that date no separate output figures are available for Sunderland but the combined figure with the Tyne for 1907 of 121,470 hp suggests that the output for that year could hardly have been less than 1906. The successor of this company, as part of the Richardson Westgarth Group, would take over Dickinsons in 1940. While Dickinson's became a limited liability company in 1895 it remained very much a company run by the family and in the boom year of 1906 delivered some 55,000 hp and also exceeded 50,000 hp in 1913. For 40 years starting in 1894 marine engines were built at Wreath Quay by MacColl & Pollock. In the early years of the 20th century this works was capable of delivering about 10,000 hp a year.[34]

Wear output of marine engines exceeded 100,000 hp for the first time in 1892 and in 1898, the year in which it was 144,000 hp, George Clark Ltd delivered 51,216 hp and was to reach 50,000 hp again in 1905 and 1906. Almost half a million horsepower (496,616 hp) was produced by the company in the years 1900-1913. During the Great War years George Clark's works built steam turbines of 34,800 shp in addition to 128,310 hp of recipro-cating steam engines, almost all triple expansion engines. Their boiler output was 168,549 hp of Scotch boilers and 20,019 hp of water-tube boilers. Dickinson's built 48 engines, a total of 112,240 hp, during hostili-ties. It also carried out repair work for torpedo boats and machining on Hotchkiss guns for the Admiralty. Building smaller engines MacColl and Pollock delivered 37 sets of engines, almost 48,000 hp. At Doxford's boilers were constructed capable of providing more than 400,000 shp for naval vessels, in addition to the engines and boilers constructed for merchant ships. Doxford's built turbines for one vessel which were of 27,000 shp and at the end of the war were building a number of other turbines. The firm carried out an historic transfer in removing the turbines from Parsons famed *Vespasian* and installing them in the *Lord Byron*. Unfortunately the war years prevented the continuance of the diesel engine research. It may here be noted that the great efforts of A. E. Doxford (1867-1937) and the North East Coast Institution of Engineers and Shipbuilders failed to convince the shipbuild-ing employers of Sunderland that they should financially support research. "After discus-sion" on 12 January 1920 the Wear Ship-builders' Association was of "the opinion . . . that a Research Association would not be of any real benefit to Shipbuilders". Thus, sadly, the lead of Doxford's was not followed but the Doxford diesel engine was to gain recognition in many parts of the world and both Keller and

Sir James Laing (1823-1901) probably taken at the time of his investiture 1897.

41

Purdie were internationally respected as experts on diesel engines.[35]

BOOM & SLUMP

More than 100 ships, with a new peak of 217,383 tons, were launched on the Wear in 1889 and although output was less in the next two years the average for the three was more than 200,000 tons and, despite the appalling fluctuations, there was remarkable growth over the years which followed. Ten years later the comparable average was 273,425 tons and in 1901 very nearly 300,000 tons were launched. During the three years 1905-7 more than a million tons (1,023,018) were built, an achievement which was repeated in 1911-13 (1,008,955 tons). In September 1906 the Wear shipyards employed 12,672 in a town with an adult male population which was 39,478 in 1911 (males over ten years numbered 54,330). Employment fell to a mere 4,068 in those same yards two years later when in 1908 a mere 92,022 tons were launched. Six months later those employed numbered 5,386. Total output for 1908-10 did not reach 420,000 tons (yearly average just under 140,000). Graph A shows the dramatic growth compared with earlier years.[36]

These economic fluctuations may be illustrated by reference to the great Deptford shipyard of Laing's who, in the 1890s, began building oil tankers, establishing a clear Wear-side lead in this new field, to be followed by passenger liners, a type of ship not usually built at Sunderland. Launching more than 40,000 tons in 1900 the yard had the highest output on the river. However not long after Sir James Laing's death a year later the company was in serious financial difficulties. Not a single ship was launched in 1909 and James Marr was invited to join the Board and help secure the company's recovery. Chairmanship of the Board and an output of almost 26,000 tons in 1912 showed his success.[37]

Doxford's in both 1905 and 1907 headed the shipbuilding output for Britain. All 86,632 tons built in 1905 were turret ships. This type of vessel was first built in 1893 and gave both a reserve of buoyancy and additional cargo capacity. In all some 178 of these ships were built. An extended shipyard with 100 ton radial crane provided Doxford's with the capacity to build vessels up to 520 feet in length. In 1906 the tonnage launched was 106,000 tons, an output exceeded by the river as a whole for the first time in 1872. Two vessels built in 1912, the *Cairnross* and her sister ship *Cairngowan*, were to make a most important comparison in marine propulsion. One was propelled by geared steam turbines, to establish the suitability of turbines for cargo vessels, and the other by a Doxford triple expansion engine. A year later the largest oil tanker to date on the Wear, the 10,150 ton *San Jeromino*, was built at Pallion. Although no other yard could match Doxford's after 1904, J. L. Thompson had been head of the river in 1898 with 40,815 tons and Thompson's were to average 46,266 tons over the years 1904-7, only then, like the industry as a whole, to collapse to a mere 10,404 tons in 1908. These

employers, managers and men, despite the buffetting of boom and slump and the initial loss of craftsmen, were to make a most valuable contribution to wartime production after August 1914.[38]

The industry, in building a million tons for 1911-13, paid an average annual wage bill of £761,162 in comparison with £671,167 for the same tonnage in 1905-7. In the depressed years the men would, of course, get much less and work would be irregular through the year. With a workforce of about 10,000 the annual average sum paid of about £70 confirms the lack of a full year's work. The official earnings survey of 1906 does not discriminate between the three rivers on the north east coast but it is safe to assume that the men of Sunderland were unlikely to be below the average of the region. The figures show the workers on the north east coast with higher earnings than the national average for all grades, earning overall £2.05 compared with £1.79 for the U.K. as a whole and £1.80 on the Clyde. The figures for individual trades was as follows:

Angle-iron smiths	Platers	Helpers	Rivet Heaters	Ship-wrights
£3.86	£4.10	£1.52	£1.20	£2.00

It is notable how much less shipwrights were paid on time-work compared with the piece-work craftsmen. The figures for north east engineering are not comparable in the same way as shipbuilding was more complicated because on the Tyne in particular many engineering workers were not engaged in marine engine construction. Nonetheless only the London area (£1.90) had earnings higher than the north east coast (£1.77) for the industry overall, but not all the individual craft grades were as well paid as elsewhere.[39]

The years of the Great War saw most remarkable levels of output, especially in view of the initial loss of many skilled men to both the army and navy. Labour controls of a kind never previously used were applied, and finally, despite the reluctance of both employers and workmen, women entered the shipyards and engineering workshops. They did not survive even a day after the men returned, despite having clearly demonstrated their abilities in doing the work, Wearside shipbuilders such as Marr were involved in national shipbuilding committees in addition to managing their individual companies.

The wartime tonnage included 87 merchant vessels as well as 32 standard design wartime merchant ships, 35 cargo steamers and 20 colliers, 14 tankers were built, 12 by Laings, and five Admiralty Oilers, and Doxford's constructed torpedo boat destroyers. At the Armistice there was a substantial tonnage in the yards under completion, e.g. at Blumers 15,625 tons and a similar amount at Short Brothers, while at J. L. Thompson it exceeded 19,000 tons.[40]

Human skill and enterprise made Sunderland a great shipbuilding port. Its greatest achievements were based upon manual dexterity and persistent hard work. Nonetheless both workers and employers regularly felt the destructive blast of cyclical depression which, in a market based economy, was the inevitable fate of a capital goods industry totally exposed to overseas competition. However their regard for shipbuilding was such that they were ever ready to come back with hope — whether in the mid-1840s or the mid-1880s or those disastrous years of the early twentieth century. Such fluctuations, and the desire to avoid loss of output by shipyard reconstruction in boom times, contributed to a neglect of sufficient capital investment to meet the challenge of newcomers to the industry in the age of steel. There was also a reluctance to acknowledge the importance of adequate technical education and systematic research in the twentieth century. None of these comments should detract from the many notable achievements, such as the pioneering efforts of the Conciliation board in an industry plagued with disputes, a vast number of notable vessels, technical achievements such as the Doxford turret ship and later the diesel engine, and the ability to quote a price for a new merchant ship, win the order, and deliver within one year. That was normal on the River Wear up to 1914!

REFERENCES:
1. Lloyd's Register (1776); See also J. A. Goldenberg, "An Analysis of Shipbuilding Sites in Lloyd's Register of 1776" *Mariner's Mirror* (1973) pp. 416-435. Goldenberg (p. 422) "Americans built one in every three British ships . . . nearly 40 per cent of the British tonnage listed was colonial built . . . English shipwrights certainly had cause to rejoice when American Independence put an end to competition from colonial builders" — W. Smith & E. Holden. A 1697 copy of a document dated 1346 states Thomas Menvill paid the bishop an annual rent of 2s to build ships at Hendon, despite some dispute around the document it is the accepted date for the start of Sunderland shipbuilding.
2. For the early period see J. F. Clarke Chap. 4 "Shipbuilding on the River Wear 1780-1870" in R. W. Sturgess edit. *The Great Age of Industry in the North East* (Durham, 1981); Corder MSS; Parl. Papers "Ships & Vessels built in Great Britain 1790-1806" (1806); Lloyds Register 1792. Garbutt p. 91. Burnett p. 141.
3. PP. 1806 *op. cit.*; Surtees Vol. (i) p. 14-16; Garbutt *op. cit.* p. 406; no. of ships registered appear in Garbutt & Burnett and papers of River Wear Commissioners; 57 of the 103 wood ships built by Thompsons were for Sunderland.
4. *S.H.* — regular reports on ships built & under construction 1851-; local directories Parliamentary papers 1805 "Ships of war . . ."; Corder MSS; Census reports for 1851 & 1861.
5. Potts p. 102 & 107; see evidence to select committee on Manufactures, Commerce & Shipping (1833); analysis of shipyards life span in Clarke (1981).

"The Turret Age" (left) and the "Sagamore" (a rare "Whaleback design) being fitted out at Doxford's Pallion yard 1893.

6. Select Committee (1833) *op. cit.* Brown Q. 8501-2; Potts *op. cit.* p. 88; Sel. Cttee on the Navigation Acts (1848) Q. 4011-3. These, no doubt, were individual shipwrights in unions before 1848 and perhaps for some years a local branch, Potts wrote of 1821-2; "A great many carpenters were . . . thrown out of employment, the want of work causing great distress . . . the carpenters union resolved to commence shipbuilding . . . give work to as many men as they could employ . . . The managers of the union yard separated from the union and each commenced on his own account . . ." p. 95-6 see Clarke (1981); evidence to Sel. Ctte (1833); S. C. (18480; Sel. Ctte. on Shipwrecks (1843); diagram from tables of class of vessels in *S.H.*; Smith & Holden *op. cit.* pp. 31-35, Corder lists a number of maritime authors, Lubbock, Fletcher and Fox-Smith all of whom cite Pile vessels, see also David R. Mac Gregor "Merchant Sail 1850-1875" (1985).

7. Details of the output of yards & notes on builders in Corder MSS, Potts pp. 87-95; Smith & Holden *op. cit.* pp. 20-30.

8. Data from Corder MSS; MacGregor *op. cit.* Lloyd's Register.

9. B. R. Mitchell *Abstract of British Historical Statistics*, (Cambridge, 1962) pp. 220-22; Census 1841.

10. Fordyce Vol. II p. 511; noted by White T. W. A. S. 730; *S.H.* 25 Jan. 1850.

11. J. L. Thompson Papers, Tyne & Wear County Archives 1045; Smith & Holden *op. cit.* pp. 72-81; *One Hundred Years of Shipbuilding* — J. L. Thompson Ltd (1946); Potts p. 116, also points to the role of Irish famine, famine migration and emigration to Australia needing ships; "Causes of Distress . . ." by an Operative Shipwright (Sunderland, 1853) p. 3 & p. 13; Mitchell *op. cit.*; p. 17, *S.H.* 6 Jan 1854.

12. Liverpool Town Council Inquiry 1850; *S.H.* Sept 1851; "Causes of Distress . . ." *op. cit.* p. 6 & 15; see Clarke "Changeover from Wood to Iron Shipbuilding" (Newcastle 1986); *S.H.* 11 Jan 1861.

13. *S.H.* 11 Jan 1861; Clarke (1981); Lloyd's certificate records owner G. Foster as builder, vessel of 77 tons was 67 ft long × 18ft and 8 ft deep. p. 285 W. Armstrong *et. al.* (eds.) *Industrial Resources of the Tyne, Wear & Tees* (1864) — data in preface on shipping owned at Sunderland (Seaham);

Sailing vessels	859	210,963 tons	£1,443,000
Merchant steamers	29	14,401 tons	£ 360,000
Tugs	59	839 tons	£ 27,000
Total	947	226,203 tons	1,830,000

compared with all Tyne ports 1,673 vessels (385,268 tons) value £2,700,000 (Newcastle 574 vessels — 118,269 tons £965,000). Tonnage for Mersey 1,406,904 for Thames 1,059,356.

14. W. Rutherford *The man who built the Mauretania*, (1934), pp. 32-33 & North East Coast Institution Vol. XXIV p. 96- (1910-11); Rules of the Wear Shipwrights' Society 1860 (rev. ed. of 1846); J. F. Clarke "Labour Relations in Engineering & Shipbuilding on the North East Coast c. 1850-1906" (M. A. Newcastle 1966); *Bulletin of the North East Group for the Study of Labour History* no. 1 & no. 7.

15. Records of the Wear Shipbuilders' Assoc. T.W.A.S. (708) see Clarke (1966); local press reports Jan. 1853-.

16. T.W.A.S. 708; Royal Commission on Labour 1892-94 Laing's evidence Q.26022-Q.26090 see Q.26082.

17. T.W.A.S. 708.

18. Membership figures from various trade union reports & notes from Angela Tucker; Annual reports on Trade Unions 1887-.

19. J. E. Mortimer *History of the Boilermakers' Society* Vol. I 1834-1906, (1973), Vol. II & earlier account D. C. Cummings *A Historical Survey of the Boilermakers & Ironshipbuilders Society* (1905).

20. Monthly & Annual reports of the Boilermakers' Society 1872-1906. Boilermakers' Society records, S. & B. Webb *The History of Trade Unions* (first edit. 1892; new edition Feb. 1920 many reprints) in 1950 impression p. 432 "Of these great Unions, that of the boilermakers . . . was incomparably the strongest, having no rival for the allegiance of its trade and including the whole body of the skilled workmen engaged in ironshipbuilding and boilermaking from one end of the United Kingdom to the other." Whatever qualification might now be made to this judgement its overall assessment is acceptable.

21. See table of output figures; Smith & Holden *op. cit.* p. 64.

22. Shipping world from March 1884 the depression is commented upon, cited Medical officer of Health in Vol. II p. 225; Boilermakers' Monthly reports.

23. T.W.A.S. 708; evidence of Laing & Doxford to Royal Comm. on Labour; R. Thompson's presidential address to North East Coast Institution Vol. IX (1892-93); Reports on Strikes & Lockouts 1887-1906.

24. J. F. Clarke & F. Storr *The Introduction of Mild Steel into the Shipbuilding & Marine Engine Industries* (Newcastle upon Tyne, 1983), for a detailed account.

25. Trans. *North East Coast Institution* Vol. II pp. 91-; Chap. 5 of J. F. Clarke *A Century of Service to Engineering & Shipbuilding* (Newcastle upon Tyne, 1984).

26. Austin in discussion on Doxford's presidential address to the North East Coast Inst. Vol. V; in T.W.A.S. 708.

27. Clarke (1984) see footnote 25; T.W.A.S. 708.

28. Fordyce *op. cit.* p. 511; Potts *op. cit.* pp. 188-89; PP Return of Steam Ships (1862).

29. Lloyd's Register 1845; Holden & Smith p. 150-58; see also footnote 13 above.

30. See Clarke "Labour in Wearside Shipbuilding c.1880-1914" in Archie Potts (ed.), *Shipbuilders and Engineers* (Newcastle upon Tyne, 1987).

31. Account of strike in Clarke (1966) and N. McCord *et. al.* *The North East Engineer's Strike of 1871* (Newcastle upon Tyne, 1971).

32. Census Reports 1861-1901; evidence of Wear Engine Builders' Assoc. to Royal Comm. on Labour (1892-94).

33. Output of marine engine output annually in *Engineering* and other trade journals; many papers on diesel engines in *Trans. of North East Coast Institution*.

34. William Allan (1837-1903) *Who's Who of British Members of Parliament* Michael Stenton & Stephen Lees (Harvester Press, 1976-1981 — 4 vols.), many obituary notices; *The Engineer* 27 Aug. 1880- an early description of NE Marine, also A. Harrison *North East Coast Institution* Vol. XXXIII pp. 161-62.

35. Output as footnote 33; *Trans. North East Coast Institution* Vol. XXXV pp. 502-3 & 516-522; T.W.A.S. 708.

36. T.W.A.S. 708; in Sept 1906 nos. in trades were as follows (incl. apprentices) 2,777 boilermakers, 723 shipwrights, 349 joiners, 451 drillers and 164 blacksmiths; Census Report 1911.

37. Smith & Holden *op. cit.* pp. 28-30; Output data.

38. Leonard Gray & John Lingwood *The Doxford Turret Ships* (World Ship Society, 1976).

39. T.W.A.S. 708; Report of an Enquiry by Board of Trade into Earnings & Hours . . ." (1906).

40. A. H. J. Cochrane "A short report . . . work . . . of North East Coast during the War" *Trans. of North East Coast Institution* Vol. XXXV pp. 479-524.

Victorian Working Life

Anyone living in the north-east of England must be aware of the hardships of work in the region's basic industries. There is abundant evidence of the conditions in coalmining in particular, but, although coal is central to the region's economy, in Sunderland it was never the most important industry in terms of numbers employed. Census returns[1] show that until 1871 seafaring was the largest employer to be overtaken by shipbuilding up to 1911, with one census excepted. It is equally important to note that throughout the nineteenth century second place was consistently taken by domestic service, which in 1881 actually became the largest single category of employment. Perhaps because the coal industry still exists, and because of the dramatic nature of the miners' work its story is one of which people are always conscious, while seafaring has diminished to the point where most people have ceased to be aware of its former importance. Shipbuilding somehow never had the dramatic appeal of coalmining, and domestic service — female, mundane, invisible — has simply been disregarded.

There is not enough space to cover every aspect of every industry. In this chapter working life will be explored by case-studies of two very different occupations in the mid-nineteenth century. Coalmining and seafaring were the subjects of numerous investigations and the reports of these Royal Commissions and Select Committees provide vivid descriptions of conditions in these major industries, including firms operating in Sunderland.

THE MINERS

In one particular Royal Commission report there is a detailed description of the life and labour of the miners at Monkwearmouth Colliery, then the deepest coalmine in the world. In 1840 the movement for factory reform had revived after years of inactivity, and the government's response to the pressure, voiced by Lord Ashley (later Shaftesbury) in the House of Commons, was to set up a Royal Commission on the employment of children in mines and unregulated industries. The Report was issued in two parts, the first on *Mines and Metal Works* in May 1842, the second on *Trades and Manufactures* almost a year later.[2]

The national impact of the publication of the Mines Report was tremendous. The unprecedented use of drawings of women and children at work underground caused a sensation and a bill by Lord Ashley passed through the Commons only a month after publication of the Report. This Mines Act forbade the employment underground of boys under 10 and all females, allowed only males over 15 to operate winding gear, prohibited the payment of wages in pubs and allowed the government to appoint inspectors to visit mines and enforce the law.

This fell far short of what the reformers wanted and even this modest Act was ineffective. A decade later the annual reports of the sole inspector appointed by the government were still showing under-age boys going down the pit. In some cases the truth about children's ages emerged only at inquests after explosions. It certainly did not come from inspection of mines, for inspector H. Seymour Tremenheere admitted in his report for 1854 that he had never been down a mine. "Everyone would be hostile to such a search", he wrote, although another Mines Act in 1850 had increased the inspectorate and enlarged its powers. Not until a new safety inspectorate was created in 1860 with new regulations was any real advance made. The same Act raised the minimum age for underground work by boys to 12 unless they could read and write and in 1872 the first restrictions were put on the hours to be worked, limiting them to ten hours per day provided the boys attended school for not less than 20 hours each fortnight.

While four named Royal Commissioners were responsible for the Report as a whole the work of investigation in the regions was done by sub-commissioners whose local reports and collections of evidence were published as appendices. Durham south of the Wear was the responsibility of Dr James Mitchell, while John Roby Leifchild reported on North Durham and Northumberland (although he descended and reported on Hetton and Eppleton collieries as well).[3]

Between them Mitchell and Leifchild covered most parts of the region and most of

---

No. 372-Richard Bell

14 in June. Driver. Gets 1s 4d a day. Gets thumped whiles when a waggon gets off the way, and it is not his fault. Sometimes they fling stones at him. The waggonway men do this. If he is long-putting the lows (candles) in the bag, the overseer whiles flogs him with a stick, as hard as he can. Makes him cry, and leaves the marks on him. Last week he did this.

Whiles he hurts him and others so as to lay him off work. Once he was hit over the head with a stick and laid off two days. The overman is Robert Robinson. Every time he gets into the pit he turns sick and dizzy; very often; twice last week, he brought up his victuals from his stomach, soon after he had eaten them. Whiles he is sore tired after work. Is very sleepy when he gets up, and is drowsy all day from the pit being so hot like. Has been lamed twice, his ancle split, and his thumb burst. Can read the bible. Writes his name. Goes to Sunday School and used to go to night-school but left off from being too sleepy.

No.373-Thirty-nine boys

The oldest is 18 in May; the youngest is 8. Six assist in putting. Eighteen drive. Five keep doors. Nine are employed in various ways and at the bank. Fifteen read an easy book. Eleven write their names. No boy goes to a night-school. Fourteen go to Sunday-schools. Fourteen have had "lames" of a more serious kind. Nearly the whole of them complain of the heat of the pit, and say that it makes them sick and bad at times.

No.380-William Hutterson

Aged 10 (apparently 8 or 9). Keeps a switch door. Has been down the pit about a year. Feels his head work often, and his belly work.

Evidence relating to Monkwearmouth Colliery from the Report on Children's Employment, 1842.

the major enterprises, not confining themselves to describing the conditions, morals and bodily health of the children as their instructions required but visiting workplaces and houses and reporting on the homes, habits and cultures of the mining and other communities.

Leifchild in particular threw himself into his task with great enthusiasm, spending weeks getting accustomed to a dialect that was incomprehensible to him on his arrival in January 1841 before trying to interview his subjects. His report is almost twice as long as its nearest rival (that for Yorkshire) and almost five times as long as Mitchell's for the neighbouring area. What is more important, he describes in detail his visit to Monkwearmouth Colliery and returns the evidence of owners, management, and adult and child workers, with perhaps the most vivid pictures coming from the evidence of the children themselves (fig 2).

Even then, the words understated the conditions. As Leifchild noted:

[the children's] vocabulary was too restricted to admit of more than common or feeble words . . . they were unable to transfuse the bitterness of their thoughts into their homely terms . . . Hence, for example, 'sore tired' would be expressive of an extreme degree of fatigue, and a boy would frequently say he had been 'hurt in the arm' when he was discovered to mean that he had fractured the limb . . ."[4]

To modern minds the very fact that "One Robert Pattison, now employed down this pit, is now six years of age, and has been down four months,"[5] is terrible enough.

The reformers' aim was to reduce the hours of work and increase the age at which it started. There were those who opposed both these aims and a fair number within the industry who supported the idea of a higher starting age without agreeing on the shorter hours. Among these was George Elliot, the viewer (manager) of Monkwearmouth Colliery, who favoured a minimum age of 12.[6] However, he was opposed to legislation to enforce such a limit, and claimed that the children's parents were even more opposed. He was "very much pressed and intreated by parents to take their children at a very early age, from five years and upwards". The owners of the colliery, Richard Pemberton and William Smith, differed slightly from their viewer, holding that ten should be the minimum age and claiming that they would not object to this being legally enforced.

WORK AND WAGES

Unanimously it was assumed, even by the reformers, that children must work. In fact they were a vital part of almost every industry. About 15 per cent of Monkwearmouth's labour force was under 13, with another 15 per cent between 13 and 18, although the proportion varied from under 30 per cent to over 40 per cent at different collieries. The youngest boys, up to the age of 12, were employed as trappers, opening and closing the doorways along the pit's underground roads. Although this was the least arduous work it was the most monotonous and solitary and at the same time the most responsible, for on the diligence of those little

boys depended the ventilation of the colliery. Their trapdoors controlled the flow of air and several major explosions in the nineteenth century were attributed to their falling asleep or other neglect.

"Driver" was the next stage up and a lad would tend the horses drawing the coal to the bottom of the shaft till about the age of 16, when he became a "putter". The putter pushed the tubs along the tramways from the coalface to the main roads or rolleyways where the driver took over. He would be assisted in the harder places by a "helper-up" and sometimes a younger boy — a "foal" — would help by pulling in front of the putter. The putter had the hardest job of all, heaving his 7cwt of tub and coal an average of around 8 miles a day, but his reward was to graduate to the rank of hewer at about the age of 20. As he approached that age he would already have been allowed to fill some tubs for himself, if he could find the time while putting for others.

With all the gradations the boys' progression was in four basic stages and paid accordingly — trappers earned about 5/- (25p) per week; drivers 7/- (35p); putters between 11/- (55p) and £1 by piece-work; and hewers from £1 to 24/- (£1.20) per week. To earn this the hewer had to fill his "score" of 21 tubs. The rates were laid down in the annual bond, the contract which legally bound the collier to his employer for a full year.[7] At Monkwearmouth in 1841 for example, the hewer was guaranteed sufficient work to allow him to earn at least £1.50 a fortnight, plus a free house (or £4 per annum in lieu) and free coals, with 3d (1p) deducted for delivery.

However, these were not the only deductions. The hewer had to provide his own pick and drilling gear and pay the blacksmith for keeping them sharp, while the putter was bound to find his own candles, grease and soams (reins for pulling the tubs). On top of this was the possibility of incurring fines for breaches of the bond. For example, the tubs were three feet long by two feet three inches wide by two feet three inches deep and the hewer was required to fill 21 of them per shift.

If the level of the coal was three and a quarter inches below the top of the tub both hewer and putter forfeited any payment for it. If when it was emptied it was found to contain two quarts of stone or splint the hewer forfeited payment and was fined 3d (1p); if three quarts, 6d (2½p); if four quarts 1/- (5p); then, of course he had to fill another tub to make up his score. If he left the pit without completing his score he was liable to another fine of 2/6 (12½p), the better part of an average day's wages.

The hewer's normal day was much shorter than that of his ancillary workers. The bond set the maximum at eight hours and in fact most hewers worked six or seven hours, although the long winding times at Monkwearmouth could mean another hour underground. In Monkwearmouth, as in most of the Durham coalfield, the pattern became one of two shifts of hewers serviced by one of transit workers. The average hours worked by transit hands did not fall from twelve to ten until 1890 and not until 1910 did eight hours (plus travelling time) become normal. To cope with the reduced hours of ancillary workers collieries adopted a system of three shifts of hewers served by two shifts of transit workers, a system which became a way of life dominated by the knocker-up and a ceaseless round of meals, baths, and bait-preparation for the women of the large mining households.

THE COMMUNITY

The miners' wives and daughters were almost as much employees of the colliery as their men and it is impossible to consider conditions at work without looking at the way of life which the pattern of work created. Long hours of hard and dangerous toil, and a year-long legal servitude to one master, who even owned the house the miner lived in, created particular types of community. On the positive side can be cited the village solidarity which was the foundation of the union, the chapel and the store. On the other hand, particularly in the period under discussion, there were the overcrowded and insanitary living conditions, over-large families, huge infant mortality and premature death rates, and a vast ignorance as the need to work overwhelmed the children's chances of education. Not just the mine but the whole village was the workplace, and its rows of houses without their own water supplies or privy facilities must be seen as part of the workplace conditions.

The resulting social character of the villages was not to the liking of Leifchild or indeed of many of the religious and medical men who gave evidence. The main incentive to shorter hours for many witnesses was the need to provide education for the moral reform of the communities, particularly those of the newer mines. "Schools where the elements of mechanics and natural philosophy are taught would not benefit the people, as workpeople, so much as schools where religious and moral instruction are imparted" said George Elliot. New collieries such as Monkwearmouth were staffed by migrants from other collieries. They were, said Leifchild, "naturally the receptacles of the refuse of the old"[8] and Monkwearmouth had a particular problem. In 1842 it was 265 fathoms (490m) deep and George Elliot claimed there was a prejudice against the depth of the pit. "Respectable families do not like to come from this circumstance," he said, and this was one reason for the prevailing immorality of the village. The other was the nearness of Sunderland. "Generally the neighbourhood of a town corrupts the colliery people. Fairs, dances, theatres, etc, seduce them. Drunkenness is prevalent here. The police prevent at present many disorders." The rector of Washington, the Rev B S Broughton, was appalled by his new parish.

> I consider the religious and moral condition of the children, more particularly of the young persons, to be at an awfully low ebb. I was not prepared to witness so much carelessness, irreligion and immorality, having before I came here lived in an agricultural district.[9]

Two points must be made about such comments. While no doubt many new pit settlements had something of the character of frontier towns, the modern reader should beware of automatically accepting those judgments on the miner's nature made by employers, clerics and a middle-class government employee. While we might share their condemnation of drunkenness we might be less hasty than those virtuous Victorians to damn the hardworking people for their pleasure in the "low amusements" of fairs, pubs and music halls.

With an 11-day fortnight, underground 4am to 5pm there could have been little opportunity for recreation other than sleep for much of the mining workforce. In terms of hours, however, there were many worse off. In other industries a 12-hour day was normal for both adults and children and in busy times it often ran on to overtime too. Across the river from Monkwearmouth Colliery, off Hylton Road, was Bishopwearmouth Iron Works, where Leifchild found children even more exploited than those in the pit.

OTHER TRADES

In 1843 Leifchild's second report appeared, on the lesser industries of the region.[10] The factories he visited were all on Tyneside, but conditions would not be very different in the potteries, plate-glass and bottle works of Wearside. Everywhere the "normal" day was of 12 hours with an hour or an hour and a half for meals, but everywhere this was a nominal time. As Leifchild noted, overtime was very frequent in the potteries:

Sinking the third shaft at Monkwearmouth Colliery in the 1870s.

. . .No.67 — aged about 10, sometimes works from six a.m. to half past eight at night, once or twice in some weeks; sometimes he comes to work at four o'clock in the morning, and stops till six at night, getting a quarter-day overtime for this. Came this morning at four o'clock. No.76 — aged 11; has been here two years taking off. Works from six to six p.m.; has a good few times worked overtime till eight at night, perhaps 30 times. Has twice come at four in the morning. A girl, aged about 12, No.87 — attends from six o'clock a.m. to eight o'clock p.m. inclusive of one hour and a half for meal times.[11]

Potteries had a particularly high proportion of child workers, many of them employed and paid by the workmen rather than the owner and the exploitation was certainly no less because of that. In the glassworks the hours varied according to the product, and depended on the techniques used. In a crown-glass factory, for example, 11 years old John Brown:

comes to work at 12 o'clock on Sunday night and finishes at 2 o'clock on the Monday afternoon then goes home. His father is a blower in these works. Then comes to work again on Tuesday night at the same time, i.e. 12 o'clock, and goes home on the Wednesday at 2 o'clock p.m. Comes again on Thursday night at 12 o'clock and goes home on Friday at 2 o'clock p.m. Comes to work again on Sunday night at 12 o'clock, and goes on as above.[12]

For this he earned 4/- (20p) per week.

In Cookson's at South Shields a 13 year old

comes at 5 o'clock in the morning and is done work at 8 o'clock at night. Has been at this work 8 months, and has always worked these hours, except on Saturdays, etc. Has sometimes worked from 5 in the morning till 9 at night; no time for meals being allowed out of that time. Gets his victuals when he can.[13]

On such a shift the young worker might blow two hundred pieces of glass. In bottle works the hours varied but usually consisted of five shifts of ten or twelve hours, the first starting at 2am on Monday morning.

Whereas the Mines Report brought immediate action from the government in the form of the Mines Act, restricting the age of labour for children, the Report on Trades & Manufactures was completely ignored. Not until a new Commission 25 years later were limitations put on the ages of children employed and the hours they were required to work.[14]

UNION GROWTH

It was, however, only for children and women that there were restrictions. One of the reasons that it took so long to get factory reform was the authorities' fear of restricting the hours of adult male labour. It was not government action which finally brought down the hours of men but the example of direct action by the engineering workers in the great strike for the nine-hour day of 1871. A four-month struggle against the employers on Tyneside made the breakthrough for many other industries to achieve the shorter working-week but the first victory was in the engineering works of Wearside, where the employers gave in to the union's demands after a month-long strike.[15]

In coalmining trade unionism was much more backward. Every attempt at combination was broken as employers held out against strikes, usually undertaken in circumstances unfavourable to the men. Almost always they were reacting to a wage cut in a period of falling coal prices, as for example, in the four-month battle of 1844, long recalled for the eviction of thousands by the owners.[16] In that terrible defeat the Northumberland miners at least got rid of the yearly bond, but it remained the basis of the Durham miners' working life. Many people blamed the fetters of the bond for their pathetic and demoralised condition after an attempt at union failed yet again in 1863. They were worse off than the miners of unionised areas and worse off too than the craftsmen of the other heavy industries in their own area. In 1865 a hewer might earn 4/- to 4/6d (20-23p) a day for eight hours work while boys were still working underground for an average of 14 hours per day.[17]

The incentive to unionise came once again from cuts of up to 33 per cent in the piece rates at Monkwearmouth Colliery in April 1869. The cuts were accepted until the men found they could not earn a living wage at the new rates, but when they went on strike in May they were prosecuted under the Master and Servant Act for breaking their contracts. At first the "Pitmen's Attorney", W P Roberts, used legal arguments in defence, then announced that the men were so opposed to the bond that they would regard it as cancelled, stay on strike, and leave their homes within nine days. A procession of 300 miners handed in their lamps and rulebooks and their example drew others, including the deputies, into the struggle.

Predictably, a single colliery could not win and, as always, the leaders were casualties. On 3rd July, however, John Richardson, victimised at Monkwearmouth, chaired a meeting of "representatives of collieries not yet united, to devise means whereby an organisation could be established throughout the county of Durham".[18] More meetings were held, leading to the inaugural meeting of the "Durham Miners' Mutual Association" on 20th November 1869. John Richardson became secretary and agent at a salary of 32/- per week and the first president was William Crake, another of the Monkwearmouth strike leaders.

The 1872 Mines Regulation Act brought the first limitation of the boys' hours to 54 four per week, their working time to fall between 6am and 8pm. Probably more important was the introduction of elected checkweighmen and payment by weight rather than measure of coal hewn, reducing the burden of fines paid by the miner. It was the union, however, which negotiated the abolition of the bond. That the employers conceded without protest perhaps indicated that the days of such contracts were over and that a fortnight's notice was more in tune with the times. However, the infant union gained the credit for ending what had come to be seen as the serfdom of yearly employment.

THE SEAMEN

While the miner might achieve equal status with other industrial workers the same could not be said of those in Sunderland's most important industry. The sailor is one of the most neglected figures in the region's history, yet for three-quarters of the nineteenth century seafaring was the largest single occupation in nearly all the large towns of the north-east. In Sunderland shipping at its peak in 1861 employed no fewer than a quarter of all the men over the age of 20.[19]

The seamen also provided the one great national union that was born in Sunderland, its founder a Sunderland sailor who set out single-handed to unite the seamen of all British ports. In 1887, at the age of 29, Joseph Havelock Wilson created the National Amalgamated Sailors' and Firemen's Union from his temperance hotel and coffee shop at 174 High Street East and was general secretary, then president, until his death 42 years later. It is a sign of the changed times that the descendant of Wilson's union, the National Union of Seamen, no longer has even a branch office in the town. A hundred years ago Sunderland was one of the major ports of the country and almost 4,000 men got their livelihood from seafaring.

Very often in writings about the town a sort of 'local patriotism' portrays the shipping industry in a romantic light — Sunderland shipyards building the finest ships in the world; honourable local owners creating sound businesses by hard work and shrewd dealings; captains unsurpassed in their knowledge of the sea, and stern but just in their dealings with their men; sailors rough and ready but second to none in their seamanship, honest service and bravery. No doubt there were some such and no doubt most of those involved in the industry were decent human beings, but there was a darker side too. When Samuel Plimsoll set out in the 1870s to expose the industry's wrongs we find a very different cast — jerry builders cobbling together ships unfit to put to sea; owners guilty of pursuing profit, unconcerned with the cost in men's lives; captains found to be incompetent through lack of skill or excess of drink; seamen described by the owners as an ignorant, disloyal, drunken rabble.[20]

Certainly the industry was different from any other. While governments were often concerned to avoid interfering in other industries, the role of the merchant marine as a naval reserve in times of war meant that the government had always been involved. For example, owners were bound to take a certain number of apprentices, a near military discipline was enforced and the press gang had the right to take any seamen for Royal Navy service. The sailor had compulsory deductions from his wages paid into a Seamen's Fund which, theoretically anyway, provided pensions in case of death or disability. (The almshouses in Trafalgar Square Sunderland were built in 1840 from the Fund to house widows and incapacitated sailors.) From the passing of the Merchant Shipping Acts of 1850 and 1854 the Board of Trade controlled a system of official employment agencies, the Mercantile Marine Offices, overseeing every part of the relations between sailors and employers. Like the miner, the sailor was bound by a legal contract — the ship's articles — and for breaking it the sailor could expect an automatic 90 days' imprisonment.

Such interest by government might lead to the assumption that the conditions of the sailor would be better than those of his land-based fellow-workers. In fact this is so far from being the case that it could be argued that the sailor was the most exploited of all working-men. He lived in the vile conditions of an overcrowded, unventilated, leaky and verminous foc'sle, his food was often old, foul and inadequate, as owners, captains and suppliers all cheated to line their pockets. He worked harder and longer than the hardest working navvy ashore for wages less than those of most common labourers, and in every port pimps, prostitutes and publicans waited to strip him of the wages he had.

In the 1860s the death rate among these young men in the prime of life was higher than that in the worst Victorian city. In 1867 the report of the Society for Improving the Condition of the Merchant Seaman showed that one

Samuel Plimsoll in 1875.

in 80 died of disease in service, one in 70 drowned and one in 20 was invalided out each year.[21] To this total of one in 12 lost to the service by accident, disease or disability must be added the large number who, each year, made their practical protest against conditions by jumping ship, often in the United States or Australia.

The report maintained that

the majority of merchant seamen who form the crews of our foreign-going ships are broken down in health soon after the early age of 35 years, and the expectation of life of seamen (... at about 20 years of age) does not extend beyond the 45th or perhaps even the 40th year.

Of course most Sunderland sailors were in the coastal and North Sea, rather than foreign-going, trade. In the 1820s about a third of Sunderland's ships and a half of the sailors were in the foreign trade but this proportion diminished as the demand for coal grew enormously in the decades after 1830. However, the substance of the complaints of the sailors in both sectors of the trade was the same. A letter from the seamen of Sunderland to the Society for Improving the Condition of Merchant Seamen set out their grievances:

They complain most bitterly of the accommodation afforded on board merchant ships to the men. There is not sufficient room for the berths, and the ventilation is always very bad, always lumbered up with ship's stores, and in most cases damp and wet from the many leaks in the upper deck.

They also complain that the Board of Trade Regulations are not properly carried out ... In many cases the water is of bad quality, improperly kept, and the quantity given out is far from sufficient. They also complain of the small quantities of anti-scorbutic stores allowed. Coffee and tea, being horribly bad, and not nearly enough. (This is most bitterly complained of.)

The bad and leaky condition of many ships, and the worn-out state of their gear, the perfect unseaworthiness of the boats, which are always lumbered up with livestock and other filth. Boats' gear are never ready or fitted, and consequently when the boats are wanted in a hurry, all is confusion."[22]

These grievances of the deep-sea sailors were echoed by a similar petition from those from Seaham, who were mainly engaged in the coastal trade. They pointed out that the conditions of the crews had worsened since the changeover from hempen to chain cables had allowed owners to move the crews' lodgings from deckhouses to wet, cramped, and unventilated fo'c's'les.

They also point out that food is probably even worse in the coastal trade since there was no Board of Trade scale for provisions, although the work in the home and coasting trade is much more laborious, more exposed to hardships from cold and bad weather, more working of tide work on passages, whether to or from the port of lading, than is ever the case in southern-going ships.[23]

It was not seamen alone who felt that conditions were deteriorating. The Society to whom those grievances were addressed had them investigated by William Burroughs, the Board of Trade's shipwright surveyor in Newcastle, and he confirmed that conditions were as bad as the men had said.[24] Many other people were also convinced that conditions were deteriorating. Mrs Janet Taylor, who had taught at a nautical academy and written books on navigation, had spent many years working among seafarers. She wrote to the Society saying that:

it is a well known fact that the seamen's berths are places where neither cargo nor animals that would take any harm by constant wetting could be stored; his food is of the scantiest and coarsest description, and he is often under the command of captains and officers who do not know their own duty, and as owners seldom see or speak to their men, they have no opportunity of reporting their grievances, and consequently there is no sympathy between them, and no anxiety on the part of the sailor to do his best to deserve future encouragements; in fact the present mode of treatment brutalises every sense, produces discontent, and a constant antagonism to superiors, unfits the men for their work, and makes them the dirty, lazy, degraded beings they are.[25]

There was no shortage of shipping employers to echo Mrs Taylor's condemnation of the sailor's character. In the nineteenth century there were enquiries, committees and commissions galore considering the state of shipping and seafaring and at all of them the owners deplored the seamen's defects. In 1836 one witness was asked, "You think the appetite for drink on the part of seamen is uncontrollable?" "Insatiable" he replied.[26] Yet hardly any of these witnesses put the blame for the seamen's faults on the vile conditions on their ships. As with the Children's Employment Commission the modern reader would do well to be wary of accepting the employers' sweeping condemnation of their labour force.

The rewards for working in such conditions varied with the state of the trade. From the 1840s to the 1860s the rate of wages fluctuated around £4 a voyage in the coal trade (of from one month to six weeks) and around £3 a month in the foreign trade. In 1860 the rate for a master in the coal trade was £9 a voyage to London. The mate and carpenter received £5, the cook £4.5.0. and four boys sums ranging from 15/- to only 3/- for the voyage.[27]

DEATH AT SEA

To this hardest of labour and worst of conditions must be added the greatest outrage of all, the enormous death rate at sea. The central figure in the campaign against the "coffinships" was Samuel Plimsoll and much of his evidence came from the north-east. From Sunderland itself he drew his example of "a shipowner who was notorious for the practice of overloading and for a reckless disregard of human life."[28] Perhaps the most vivid image of the scale of losses is seen in the Wreck Charts of 1869 (fig 4) which Samuel Plimsoll included in his book *Our Seamen: an appeal*.[29]

Plimsoll began his campaign after his election to parliament in 1868, when the total number of ships lost was rising year by year. High losses were nothing new, although in earlier periods it is more difficult to be accurate about the exact number. Forty years before, a Select Committee on the causes of shipwrecks heard that between 1827 and 1829 107 ships from Sunderland were lost, and that between 1833 and 1835 124 went down.[30] These losses were from a total of about 600 ships belonging to the port. A search of the shipping registers over a longer period shows that between 1824 and 1836 2,241 ships were registered in Sunderland and of 615 which were not sold to other ports, or whose fate is not known, 603 were lost and only 12 were broken up. (Of course a number of those sold would appear as losses in another port's register.) Of those known to have been lost five per cent were lost before they were one year old, 23 per cent were under five years old and half were under 13 years old.[31]

The east coast route to the great northern coalfield was always full of hazard. In 1667 a letter from "Sunderland-by-the-sea" to the bishop of Durham from the appropriately named John Tempest described:

a most violent storme which had a lamentable effect upon a fleet of 100 light colliers coming from the southward and being in sight of the port when the storms began. We heare of many cast away upon this coast and by the judgment of many able seamen it is doubted that at the least one-halfe of them is lost . . .[32]

By 1875 no less than 46 per cent of the 2,900

GENERAL
WRECK CHART
OF THE
BRITISH ISLES
FOR
1869

DRAWN FROM THE WRECK CHART
COMPILED & ISSUED BY THE
BOARD of TRADE

51

coastal casualties were on the east coast coal route. In the great majority of cases no life was lost but of 141 cases involving loss of life in that year, 45 were between Tyne and Thames. In any case the deaths in coastal waters were far outnumbered by those abroad, where their numbers were swelled by large ships foundering with all hands in the oceans of the world, far from shore and the possibility of rescue.

Each year the total mounted to the peak in 1881 when almost 4,000 masters and men died: 2,552 by wreck, 1,123 by otherwise drowning (being washed overboard, etc), and 273 by accident (falling from yards, etc.).[33]

The figures were put in the context of the rest of the north-east's dangerous industries by Joseph Chamberlain, President of the Board of Trade in a speech at Newcastle-upon-Tyne in 1884:

> We know that the miner's is a dangerous and perilous trade, but the loss of life has never been, even in the heaviest year, more than one in 315 of the persons employed. In the case of British shipping . . . one in 60 of those engaged in it met with a violent death in a single year.[34]

CAUSES OF WRECKS

It was the weather which accounted for much of the yearly variation in the numbers of ships and lives lost but it cannot alone explain losses on such a scale. While weather would always take its toll, critics from the 1830s to the 1880s would have agreed with the Board of Trade official who said that "well-found ships ought not to strew the ocean in every heavy gale".[35] Indeed, almost half the 20,000 coastal wrecks in the decade up to 1875 did not even have that excuse and occurred when the wind was force six or under, meaning that they went down in, at most, a strong breeze.[36]

Men, not the elements alone, were responsible. While the popular impression is that Samuel Plimsoll's campaign was solely for a "Plimsoll Line", in fact his criticism was much more wide-ranging. To overloading he added undermanning, bad storage, deck loading, bad design, defective construction and lack of repair of ships, all of which were capable of yielding profit to the owner whether or not the ship went to the bottom, as long as he could insure, and over-insure, against the huge risks that his crews had to take.[37]

Since Sunderland was the major supplier of ships to north-eastern owners the question of the quality of its production is a very pertinent and interesting one. There is perhaps a tendency in local writings to idealise the pre-1840 period when river banks were thronged with small partnerships of as few as two shipwrights and an apprentice on any little piece of shore they could find, building speculatively on credit from a timber merchant.

We may have here a picture of proud craftsmanship, but it is just as likely that it involved cheap-jack undercutting of more reputable yards. The most dramatic criticism was voiced before the Select Committee of 1835, when a witness, Henry Woodroffe, described a series of disasters involving recently built ships. When asked whether he considered Sunderland ships better or worse built than those from other ports, he replied "I conceive them the worst-built ships in the world".[38]

This might seem extreme but Woodroffe was not alone in his opinions. In the first issue of *The Northern Tribune* in 1851, an article claimed that "Until about 10 or 12 years ago . . . the character of the vessels built on the Wear was considered 'sloppy'."[39] Five years later William Fordyce wrote of the same period that "the form (of the ships) in general was exceedingly rude . . . subjecting them to the scornful designation of tubs".[40] The later critics all emphasise that after the 1840s, when most of the smaller producers were swept away, the high quality which the better yards had always produced became general.

By the time the Plimsoll campaign began, the change-over from sail to steam was speeding up. While in the long run the steamship was far safer than sail, this was not always the case in the days of transition. Sir Walter Runciman looked back on a career which took him from an apprenticeship aboard a decrepit leaking tub in 1867 to a fortune as a shipowner and the eminence of a baronetcy and his judgment on the early steamers was harsh:

> Many of the ships were faulty in design, weak in construction, with leaky boilers and defective engines which could never be relied on. Scores of wall-sided, narrow-gutted ships were built on the North-east coast, turned turtle, and took their poor sailors to the bottom with them . . . Sunderland had not a good reputation at that time, though some of its builders had produced the finest tea-clippers that had ever sailed the seas. They subsequently made amends handsomely.[41]

A shipyard in the 1830's, showing Monkwearmouth Colliery in the background.

If, as the evidence suggests, the losses from badly-built ships were confined to certain periods of time, the losses from the overloading of aged and ill-repaired ships were constant. In 1868 the Board of Trade's *Abstract of Wrecks* pointed out that about half of the 2,000 wrecks round Britain's shores were from the "unseaworthy, overloaded or ill-found vessels of the collier class". *The Life Boat* (journal of the National Lifeboat Institute) said on 1st November 1870:

> such is the notoriously ill-found and unseaworthy manner in which these vessels are sent on their voyages, that in every gale — even if it be one of a moderate character only — it becomes a certainty that numbers of them will be destroyed . . . It is overwhelming to contemplate the loss of life from these, in too many instances, avoidable wrecks.

Five years later Sir Digby Murray, the Board of Trade's Professional Officer, wrote that:

> Overloading is a disease on the East Coast; a disease too which is spreading to other localities . . . The result of the East Coast overloading is loss of steamships and human life; the vessels run very safely for a time; sometimes if they have good luck for a long time; then comes the exceptionally heavy weather which in their loaded condition they are unable to withstand and nobody comes back to tell the tale; this is what the underwriters blasphemously call 'the Act of God' .[42]

PLIMSOLL AND SUNDERLAND

Plimsoll took up the charge and repeated what he had been told by "a high authority" in Sunderland that hundreds of ships sailing from north-east ports were "utterly unfit to be trusted with human life".[43] They were in the coal trade only because they were unfit for any other. The evidence that ships sailing from north-east ports were systematically overloaded is overwhelming and the three major cases cited by Plimsoll are from the north-east. Two of them involved Sunderland and both landed Plimsoll in court on charges of criminal libel.

The first case involved the steamship *Livonia*, lost after sailing from Sunderland in November 1869 with a cargo of iron rails for the Baltic. Plimsoll claimed that such a voyage with such a cargo should never have been made at that time of year, that she was so overloaded that her main deck was actually awash, that she was so insured that there would be no loss to her owner, whom Plimsoll described as "one of the greatest sinners in the trade".[44] Neither ship nor port nor owner was actually named in *Our Seamen*, but to those connected with any of them the identities were plain, and the owner, C M Norwood, MP for Hull, took Plimsoll to court on a charge of criminal libel.

Far from providing an opportunity to expose the villain, Plimsoll found his evidence shredded and escaped being sent to prison only on the grounds that the *Livonia* was overloaded by one foot, drawing 21 feet rather than the 20 she was designed for. In court, Norwood showed that over the previous 12 years he had lost six ships but not a single life, and that the *Livonia* was the first which had foundered. He had been in Egypt when the ship was chartered and loaded and he owned not the whole ship but only 12/64ths (although he was "managing owner"), while the major share-

holder was the ship's builder, James Laing. Norwood also showed that his share was not insured and that the loss cost him £4,500. The *Livonia* had been specially built to carry heavy cargoes and when she foundered she was carrying 1,600 tons of cargo and 160 tons of coal, which was within her design capacity of 1,800 tons. In fact the cause of her loss was engine failure and the cargo breaching the hull in the consequent buffeting from the sea as she drifted.[45]

Edward Temperley Gourley in 1874.

At the same time as the Norwood case, Plimsoll was faced with a similar action by Edward Temperley Gourley, MP for Sunderland, who had also appeared anonymously in *Our Seamen* and against whom Plimsoll's accusations were even more serious. In *Our Seamen* he wrote:

> There was one ship-owner whose name was often mentioned to me in the course of the years 1869 and 1870. During my inquiries in the north and east, I heard his name wherever I went as that of a ship-owner who was notorious for the practice of overloading and for a reckless disregard of human life. I therefore made inquiry as to the ships belonging to him which had been lost, with the number of lives lost in each case, and the reply I received I will show you. It is incomplete you see; but sufficient is shown to demonstrate the necessity of Government interference.

There followed an anonymous letter:

> 20th February 1871
>
> My dear Sir,
>
> Annexed I forward a more complete list of Mr . . .'s losses, together with the number of lives sacrificed. I think I shall be able to send you a further list of sailing vessels but a melancholy list of 105 lives lost will be almost enough evidence to produce against him.
>
> I am,
> My dear Sir,
> Very truly yours, ------------[46]

The author was probably Thomas Luke, Lloyds Surveyor in Sunderland, who had given Plimsoll the information in the *Livonia* case. As in that case, the list which followed was not entirely accurate (Plimsoll's evidence seldom was) but the fact remained that Gourley had lost six steamers and 75 lives in two years. In two cases there were inquiries and in both cases blame was attached to the method or degree of loading. In three other cases no cause could be found, since those steamers simply disappeared at sea with 69 hands.[47]

Plimsoll put the blame on the managing owner, Edward Gourley, but had he checked he would have found an interesting connection between the Gourley and *Livonia* cases. The most important partner in Gourley's firm, owning more shares than Gourley in several ships, was the same man who had a half-share in the *Livonia*, James Laing, who also built many of the firm's vessels. Gourley's other partners were William Stobart, managing proprietor of Wearmouth Colliery, H T Morton, Lord Durham's agent, C M Webster, the Sunderland ropemaker, G I Wallas of Barnstaple, and C R Fenwick of London, who was also a partner in Wearmouth Colliery.[48] While it would not be likely that any of these would have much interest in the management of the concern, Laing is in a different category. He was an active shipowner, a River Wear Commissioner, a member of Lloyds Committee

Joseph Havelock Wilson at the age of 29.

and Sunderland's representative on the Chamber of Shipping, becoming its president in 1883. This organisation was set up specifically to oppose legislation that Plimsoll was proposing and if there is blame to be apportioned for overloading or unseaworthiness it would seem not unreasonable to give Laing his fair share.

Plimsoll's denunciation of Gourley did nothing to harm the MP politically for he was returned at the top of the poll in Sunderland a year later. His majority shows clearly that many working-men, including presumably some seamen,[49] had voted for him despite his refusal to support the Plimsoll programme of compulsory inspection and loadline. Indeed one of the most interesting features of Plimsoll's campaign is how little the sailors themselves were involved. One factor is, of course, that protests by the men went virtually unreported. At the height of the Gourley case, for example, the *Sunderland Times* gave column after column to the Sunderland Shipowner's Association's denunciation of Plimsoll. It gave a single paragraph to a meeting in the Golden Lion, High Street, of "captains, engineers and mariners" which condemned overloading and unseaworthiness as causing great loss of life.[50]

SEAMEN'S UNION

It was left to the coal-merchant MP, Plimsoll, to champion the sailors, with the aid of the national journalists who publicised him, the middle-class public which supported him, and the recently founded TUC, whose unions formed a fund to finance him. In this period, the seamen themselves had no national union, and the problems of organising one are clear. Certainly they had managed to combine locally for short periods, from the late eighteenth century onwards. In 1851 a great strike paralysed the coal trade of Tyne and Wear, and won better wages and modifications of the proposed disciplinary code.[51] However, the problems of organising and financing a union whose members were, as one old sailor put it, a rope of sand washed away on every tide, meant that unions had a local and transient existence.

Joseph Havelock Wilson, born in High Street, Sunderland in 1858, brought about the change.[52] By the age of 22 he had spent eight years at sea in the southern oceans and discovered trade unionism in Australia. Back home in Sunderland he joined the grandly-named North of England Sailors' and Seagoing Firemen's Association. In fact it was confined to Sunderland and was both ineffective and inefficient. Against the localism of most of the members Wilson was enthusiastic to spread the union, following the lead of the nationally-organised craftsmen he met on the newly-formed Sunderland Trades' Council.

It was with the help of a railway union member that Wilson drew up a rule book and at a meeting in his premises in High Street in August 1887 he recruited the first member into the National Amalgamated Sailors' and Firemen's Union of Gt. Britain & Ireland. At the 1888 TUC, Wilson represented 500 members but within a year 65,000 had joined. By July 1889 the union seemed secure and Wilson moved the head office from Sunderland to London.[53]

Plimsoll in the 1870s had been a hero to the young Wilson but he believed there had to be support from a union of the sailors themselves if Plimsoll was to succeed. The agitations did result in legislation in the 1870s, including, in 1875, the introduction of a load-line. However, perhaps the worth of the new laws is indicated by the fact that an amendment by C M Norwood, MP (owner of the *Livonia*) gave the duty of fixing the position of the load-line to the owner. In fact the rate of casualties, far from decreasing, soared to a peak in 1881. When the *Royal Commission on Loss of Life at Sea reported in 1887 it declared that:*

When we look at the general results of the legislation . . . upon the loss of life and property at sea in British vessels, it is most unsatisfactory to find that no sensible effect has been produced in the reduction of this loss.[54]

By the time Wilson founded the union in 1887 Plimsoll had concluded that little could be done to improve the condition of the seafarers. However, the 29-year old Sunderland man made him believe otherwise and he accepted the position of honorary President of the NASFU and rejoined the fray. It was three years later, in 1890, 20 years after Plimsoll had taken up the cause, that a new Act finally established his principle that the position of the load-line should be fixed according to rules determined by the Board of Trade.

However, it must not be forgotten that this Act, like its predecessors, made exceptions for small vessels and for those solely employed in the coastal trade. A similar rule applied in the matter of officer's certification, since under the 1850 Act a master employed solely in the coastal trade need never have passed an examination. Even where the law did not make exceptions the Board of Trade did; for example, it ordered its officers not to detain unseaworthy old coastal vessels if the crew was willing to sail in them.[55]

OWNERS AND SAILORS

Whatever the organisation, whatever the legislation, the shipowners were opposed to it. Following the load-line legislation the owners called a great meeting in London early in 1876 to denounce "fussy, meddlesome, crotchety interference" by the law. James Laing carried a resolution regretting that after so much "petting" of seamen as there had been recently, with extraordinary improvements in comfort, so many shipping casualties should be caused by their "inefficiency, intemperance and negligence."[56]

How far incompetent crews were responsible for losses is impossible to say. Certainly there are plenty of cases of masters and mates having their certificates suspended for various offences, usually involving alcohol. There was also a tendency from the 1880s for more boys and ordinary seamen (i.e. inexperienced men) to be shipped rather than apprentices and able seamen. Whereas the sailing collier fleet had once been the nursery of seamen the steamers with their shorter trips, less danger and better wages attracted the best men away from sail. As sail tried to survive the competition it produced not fully-trained sailors but "half-marrows" or "half-and-half men" on the east coast; men who were big enough and old enough to pull an oar or a rope and who could just about steer, but who could not be trusted with soundings.[57]

The old sailorly skills were not needed on the steamers, where the real requirement was for "burly lads who could steer" and "ship-navvies".[58] The seaman was becoming less of a distinctive breed, with grades from captain to engineer to deckhand and fireman, resembling more and more the structure of management, skilled and unskilled labour in manufacturing industry ashore. The impact of the changeover from sail to steam was probably greater on the north-east sailor than on others. With steam the men in the coastal trade were much more home-based, working in "weekly boats" sailing to south-east England or near-continental ports and having enough time at home to be citizens as well as seamen.

It is also true that after the initial years the steam colliers were safer vessels than the old wooden brigs, provided of course that they were soundly built, well maintained and not overloaded. The early 1880s saw many of the oldest and worst wooden vessels lost or scrapped as the Board of Trade more actively enforced the regulations on seaworthiness.

However, as the numbers of deaths from wreck declined with the number of sailing ships so the number of deaths from disease in steam ships rose. In 1895 the Medical Officer of Health for Newcastle produced a pamphlet on the hygiene of merchant ships[59] and while he maintained that many ships were still lost through overloading (and that insurance remained an incentive to risk-taking) he concentrated on loss of life deriving from the conditions of life aboard ship. Insanitary, unventilated, overcrowded accommodation in lower fo'c's'les, lack of drying facilities and bad food and worse cooking he believed were general and contributed to a death rate for sailors far above that for the equivalent population ashore. Some cases of sickness the Medical Officer had treated in the years 1892-3 were probably derived from overseas service — 208 cases of yellow fever and malaria, 351 of dysentery and diarrhoea — but the largest group of complaints were respiratory, and, as another contemporary pamphlet observed, the largest single killer disease was phthisis, or tuberculosis of the lungs, as active in sea-borne as in city slums.[60]

It is difficult to describe the life of the nineteenth century seaman without appearing to make every vessel a hulk, every owner a villain and every seaman a drunken incompetent. The scale of casualties, the number of dead, and the evidence that so much of it was avoidable distort the picture, as indeed they did for contemporaries. It remains true, however, that the bad were capable of negating the good. A handful of bad crewmen meant overwork for their shipmates and endangered the ship while a group of owners overloading and undercutting in a port pulled down the standards of those who had to compete with them.

One consequence of this was a welter of accusations and counter-accusations that produced a bitterness in industrial relations in the late nineteenth-century that was not equalled in any other industry. The militancy of Havelock Wilson's union was renowned and was matched by the ferocity of the employers' response, strike and picket being met by organised blacklegging, determined efforts to break the union and even imprisonment for Wilson himself. It was entirely appropriate that in 1887 Plimsoll became president of the union, for every struggle, whether on manning, accommodation, loading, food, or even wages, could quite literally be about life and death and hence a logical follow-on from his life-saving campaign.

It is equally appropriate that the founder of the union should be a Sunderland seaman. Havelock Wilson may serve as the type of the self-educated skilled man, proud of his craft and bitterly angry against those who exploited, often to death, his fellow seamen, and almost equally angry against the disreputable among the men. An important part of Wilson's fight was for respectability and respect for the seamen and surely the latter at least is due to the men, from dignified, bewhiskered masters to drunken, unshaven ordinary-seamen, who had the hardest job in the world. Their tough lives and too numerous deaths were the price of Sunderland's industrial eminence.

REFERENCES

1. D. J. Rowe "Occupations in Northumberland & Durham", *Northern History* Vol. VIII (1973).

2. *Children's Employment Commission: First Report, Mines and Metal Works*, PP 1842 XV and XVI; Second Report, Trades and Manufactures, PP 1843 XIV and XV.

3. PP 1842 XVI. Mitchell's report pp. 123-172, Leifchild's report pp. 523-748. Details of Monkwearmouth Colliery 659-665, Newbottle 665-6, Hetton 656-74, N. Hetton (Hazard) 674-5, S. Hetton 676-7.

4. Leifchild 1842 p. 534.

5. *Ibid.* p. 660.

6. *Ibid.* p. 660.

7. *Ibid.* p. 546-8, reprints the Monkwearmouth bond.

8. *Ibid.* p. 540. See also G. Patterson (ed) Monkwearmouth Colliery in 1851 (1978).

9. *Ibid.* p. 540.

10. PP 1843 XV pp. 251-306

11. Leifchild 1843, p. 253.

12. *Ibid.* p. 262.

13. *Ibid.* p. 267.

14. *Royal Comm. on Children's Employment* annual reports from 1863 to 1867 contain more evidence of local conditions.

15. E. Allan, J. F. Clarke, N. McCord, D. J. Rowe, *The North East Engineers' Strikes of 1871* (1971) pp. 98-104.

16. R. Fynes, *The Miners of Northumberland & Durham* (1873) (reprinted 1986) chs. IX-XXII. The other standard works on miners' unions are: J. Wilson, *A History of the Durham Miners Association 1870-1904* (1907); S. Webb, *The Story of the Durham Miners* (1921); E. Welbourne, *The Miners Unions of Northumberland & Durham* (1923); W. R. Garside, *The Durham Miners 1919-1960* (1971).

17. Wilson, p. 7.

18. Wilson, p. 11.

19. Rowe (see note 1).

20. S. Plimsoll, *Our Seamen — an Appeal* (1873, reprinted 1980). Some of the evidence for and against is in *Sel. Comm. on Causes of Shipwrecks* PP. 1836 XVII; *Royal Comm. on Unseaworthy Ships* PP. 1873 XXXVI; *Royal Comm. on Loss of Life at Sea* PP. 1884-5 XXXV and 1887 XLIII.

21. PRO. MT9/36/M5489/67 app. III, p. 94-5.

22. *Ibid.* app. IV, p. 105-6.

23. *Ibid.* p. 102.

24. *Ibid.* p. 104.

25. *Ibid.* p. 76.

26. PP. 1836 XVII, p. 592.

27. *Sel. Comm. on Merchant Shipping*, PP. 1860 XIII, p. 745. Wages from 1817-1847 are tabulated in *Sel. Comm. on Navigation Laws*, PP. 1847 X, p. 30; and from 1847-1860 in *Sel. Comm. on Merchant Shipping* 1860, XIII, p. 717.

28. Plimsoll, p. 46.

29. Plimsoll, following p. 28.

30. *Sel. Comm. on Shipwrecks*, PP. 1836 XVII, App. 8, pp. 716-7 and 745-6.

31. Sunderland Shipping Registers in Tyne & Wear Archive Department.

32. Quoted in J. Summers, *History & Antiquities of Sunderland* (1858) p. 26.

33. These numbers and those in fig. 5 are from the Board of Trade's annual *Abstract of Wrecks*, etc. There are collections in PP. 1884-5 XXXV.

34. *SDE* 17/1/84.

35. PP. 1873 XXXVI, p. 724.

36. *Abstract of Wrecks*, PP. 1875 LXX, p. 11.

37. Plimsoll, *Our Seamen*, passim.

38. PP. 1836 XVII, p. 411.

39. *Northern Tribune*, vol. 1 Jan 1855, p. 110.

40. W. Fordyce, *History of Co. Durham* Vol. II p. 509.

41. W. Runciman, *Before the Mast and After* (1926) p. 223.

42. National Maritime Museum, Parkhurst Ms. Vol. 14/1 p. 149.

43. Plimsoll, p. 62.

44. Plimsoll, pp. 48-50.

45. The legal actions involved are summarised in D. Masters, *The Plimsoll Mark* (1955) Ch. XI.

46. Plimsoll, pp. 46-48.

47. The losses were checked in Lloyds Register and Lloyds List. The inquiries are summarised in PP. 1868/9 LV, p. 86 and 91.

48. Information on owners is contained in the Shipping Registers.

49. Male householders had the right to vote from 1867, but seamen at sea at election times lost their vote.

50. *ST* 25/2/1876.

51. For early seamen's unions in the north-east see N. McCord "The Seamen's Strike of 1815" in *Ec. Hist. Review*, Apr. 1968; "Some Labour troubles of the 1790s" in *International Review of Social History* 1968 No. 3; S. Jones "Early Seamen's trade unionism 1768-1844" in *Maritime History* 1973 No. 1; S. Jones "The Tyneside Sailors' Movement 1851' in *Bull. NE Lab. Hist. Soc.*

52. For Wilson see Biographical section.

53. J. H. Wilson "*My Stormy Voyage Through Life*" (1925) p. 204.

54. PP. 1887 XLIII p. 11.

55. PRO. MT9/110/M6725.

56. *Sunderland Herald* 4/2/1876.

57. PP. 1887 XLII p. 446, evidence of John Heron (chairman Sunderland Shipowners' Association).

58. F. T. Bullen, *Men of the Merchant Service*, p. 277.

59. H. E. Armstrong, *The Hygiene of Merchant Ships* (1895).

60. *The Lancet*, 5/5/1894.

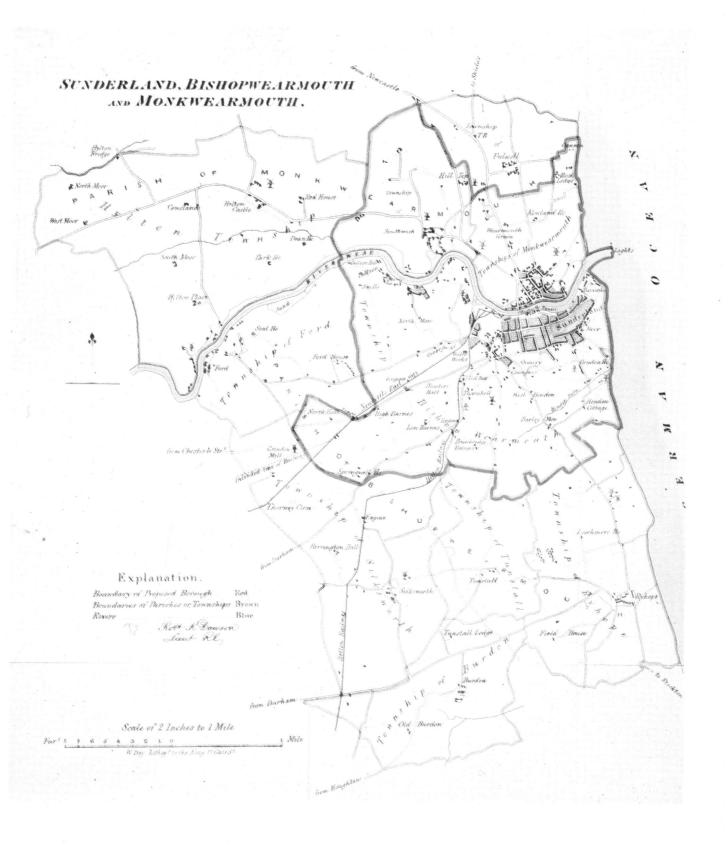

The proposed Borough boundary of Sunderland: a map prepared by R. K. Dawson, RE, of the Ordnance Survey. The original intention was to adopt the parliamentary constituency boundary of 1832, and it is this which is shown in red here. However the municipal boundary was in practice reduced (north of the river) to the two townships of Monkwearmouth and Monkwearmouth Shore, and (south of the river) to an area enclosed by a circular line with a radius one mile distant from the centre of Wearmouth Bridge. Dawson's map is incidentally very helpful in showing the topography of the area which, though still largely rural in the 1830s, was to become the town of Sunderland.

i

View of Sunderland from Building Hill, painted by John Storey in 1856. Storey has in fact adopted an imaginary aerial viewpoint above Building Hill. The hill was purchased by the Corporation in 1854 and the bottom left of the picture shows that area being laid out as the first section of Mowbray Park. The Penshaw Branch Railway and its station can be seen in the foreground, and the Grange School is in the bottom left corner. Between the old village of Bishopwearmouth (extreme left) and the Port of Sunderland are spread out the rows of terraced houses, largely built in the first half of the 19th century, which linked the two communities and formed a new town centre. The contrast between the broad streets of the new town and the narrow lanes of old Sunderland is clearly seen. Many other details can be observed, including the South and North docks, the industrial developments of Millfield and Deptford, the Monkwearmouth Colliery, and the embryonic beginnings of Roker.

John Crawford of Sunderland. This lithograph shows the sailor, popularly known as Jack Crawford. (See biographical appendix.) He was aboard *HMS Venerable*, flagship of Admiral Duncan when in October 1797 it engaged the Dutch fleet, allies of the French, at Camperdown. At the height of the battle the mast top was shot away, and to show that Duncan had not hauled down his colours, Crawford climbed the mast and nailed the Admiral's flag to it. The British won a great victory and Crawford became a national hero; this lithograph was published in the month after Camperdown. Jack Crawford was the second victim of the cholera epidemic in Sunderland in 1831. There was a revival of interest in Jack Crawford in the late 19th century when a statue in Mowbray Park, and a memorial over his grave in Sunderland Parish Church were erected.

Sunderland Museum (Tyne and Wear Museums Service).

Looking West from the Town Moor in 1960 showing (left to right) the hall of the Assembly Garth Merchant Seamen's Houses of 1727, the grave of John Dixon and Holy Trinity Parish Church and Rectory.

Photograph: James Crawley Sunderland Museum (Tyne and Wear Museums Service).

Bishopwearmouth in 1810, a watercolour copied from a painting by H. Davison. It shows the rural nature of Bishopwearmouth village and its crowded, medieval appearance. The view is looking south from Rector's Gill (the present-day Galley Gill) with Bishopwearmouth Rectory on the left. In the centre is St. Michael's Church as rebuilt 1806-1810.

Sunderland Museum (Tyne and Wear Museums Service).

J. Webster's watercolour *Roker from the South Pier* about 1888, shows the outer South Pier under construction. It was completed in 1903. On the shore are bathing huts for Sunderland's developing seaside resort. Part of Roker Terrace in the background beyond was designed about 1840 by John Dobson for the Abbs family.

Sunderland Museum (Tyne and Wear Museums Service).

The Opening of Sunderland Docks, painted by J. W. Carmichael, shows the festivities on 20th June 1850 which marked a major event in the history of Sunderland. On the left the first chaldron wagon of coal is being lowered from the staiths. George Hudson the 'Railway King', the town's MP and Chairman of the Dock Company, is shown standing above a paddle wheel at centre right. In the background is St. John's Church.

Sunderland Museum (Tyne and Wear Museums Service).

Thomas Hemy's *The River Wear from the Bridge*, 1882, shows the industry concentrated around the Wear. On the south bank is the Sunderland Glass Company's Panns Bottle Works and Austin's Wear Dock Yard. In the river beside the glassworks a paddle tug is engaged in rafting timber, probably for Wilson's Sawmills immediately opposite on the north bank. Also visible on the Monkwearmouth shore are Deuchar's Brewery, an iron works and, Dickinson's Marine Engine Works, while the Ballast Hill rises on the skyline behind.

Sunderland Museum (Tyne and Wear Museums Service).

Sunderland Bridge at Monkwearmouth, painted by James Wood in 1849 shows the view from Panns Bank with the toll gates at the south end of the Bridge. On the north bank are Monkwearmouth Station and Monkwearmouth Colliery while on the river banks are the industries of Bonners Field, the steam crane used for unloading tubs of coal from keels to colliers, and Sir Hedworth Williamson's limekilns.

Sunderland Museum (Tyne and Wear Museums Service).

Low Quay, Sunderland, 1883, painted by A. J. Moore. The section of the quay on the right of the painting had been cleared of its riverside buildings for the Durham and Sunderland Railway's staiths, which were situated there between 1836 and 1850. This area became part of the Corporation Quay in 1934. On the skyline in the centre of the painting are the Pottery Buildings financed by Edward Backhouse as a base for religious and social work among the poor and seamen. In the river are: (1) steam tug fitted out as paddle trawler, (2) brigantine dried out alongside quay on the Grid Iron, (enabling maintenance work to be carried out to hulls at low water), (3) barque-rigged vessel, (4) sloop with brig behind, (5) timber raft being poled along, (6) small steam launch, (7) paddle tug *Rescue* and (8) Wear Keel being poled.

The Wearmouth Bridges shown on Sunderland-made pottery and glass. From left to right: (1) the 1796 bridge on a jug made by the Garrison Pottery about 1815, (2) the 1859 bridge on a goblet made about 1870, (3) the 1879 railway bridge on a jug made by Ball's Pottery about the time of the Bridge's construction, and (4) the 1929 bridge on a Pyrex tumbler of 1966.

Sunderland Museum (Tyne and Wear Museums Service).

Watercolour by R. Kane of Wearmouth Colliery about 1879. One of the Colliery Company's locomotives is shunting chaldron wagons, to be taken to the adjacent staiths or handed over to the North Eastern Railway.

Beamish North of England Open Air Museum.

Herbert Simpson's watercolour *Lambton Staiths*, of 1935, shows colliers awaiting loading. Beyond on the South Bank are the Hetton Staiths, the electricity works and St. Stephen's Church, Deptford, while Wearmouth Staiths stand out from the north bank.

Sunderland Museum (Tyne and Wear Museums Service).

Watercolour showing Robert Thompson's yards about 1890 which was later reproduced as an advertisement in *England's Vast Industries*. The upper view shows the *Barnsley* at the Southwick yard where it was built in 1881. The lower view shows the Bridge Dockyard with the *Matin* built in 1873 for the Earl of Durham's (later Lambton) Collieries fleet at Aberdeen undergoing modification, and the *Lena* built by Robert Thompson's in 1881.

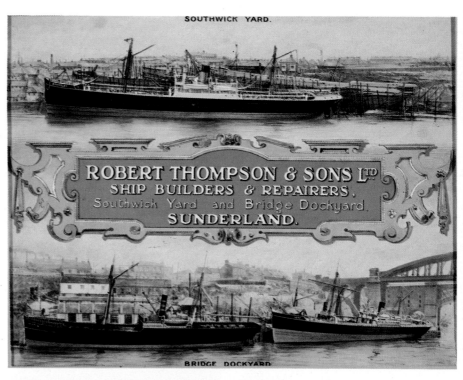

The centre two arches of the Victoria Bridge which carried the railway between Washington and Penshaw 125′ above the Wear. It was completed on Queen Victoria's Coronation Day in 1838. The engineer was T. E. Harrison. During the mid-19th century the viaduct was used by London-Newcastle main line services.

Photograph: Neil T. Sinclair.

Ralph Hedley's painting (completed in 1910) of *Hylton Ferry* showing the chain-operated ferry arriving at the North Hylton landing in driving rain. In the background is South Hylton; the white building is the original Golden Lion inn. The Ferry served the main route between Sunderland and Newcastle until the iron bridge was built in 1796. As well as the chain-operated ferry for vehicles, a rowing boat was used for passengers. The latter survived until 1957.

Sunderland Museum (Tyne and Wear Museums Service).

Growth of Sunderland

It is a commonplace of British history that, parallel with the process of industrialisation, the population of the country rose dramatically and in a sustained way. It is a further commonplace that the towns of Britain grew faster than the population of the whole nation so that the country shifted from being predominantly rural in the late eighteenth century to being predominantly urban in the late nineteenth century. The scale and rapidity of this population movement astonished the people who lived through it and has been perceived by historians as a significant framework to which the analysis of many aspects of modern history must be related. The growth of Sunderland in population terms, while having its specific features, naturally conforms to the overall picture of national population change. As a town it grew faster than the overall rate for the country, but its growth was not more striking than many other towns which were also establishing new economic bases and opportunities. This chapter will seek to outline the growth of the town in terms of the population statistics and of the spatial distribution of those people within the expanding urban fabric. In particular it will seek to relate the population pressure to the provision of housing as this was the particular facet of urban provision that was forced to respond most directly to shifts in population numbers and distribution.[1]

POPULATION

By the late eighteenth century Sunderland had already experienced considerable population growth. Hutchinson's estimate for 1781 of 20,940 souls shows an increase of 17,850 over his estimate for 1681 of 3,090.[2] Even allowing for the imprecision of these calculations it is clear that the town had grown rapidly before the period of industrialisation. The bulk of this growth had concentrated in the small parish of Sunderland itself. The contemporary accounts are clear that this population growth related directly to the increase in commercial activity on the river, especially in the coal trade.[3] The non-availability of statistics make it difficult to analyse the patterns of growth, but the creation of the separate parish of Holy Trinity in 1719 makes it clear that the area on the south side of the river mouth had become the centre of trade and of population and was to be the seat of social problems in the next century.

Through the nineteenth century the population of the town continued to grow steadily and at times sharply (see appendix 1). Although the opening of Wearmouth Bridge in 1796 gave tangible form to the increasing linkage of the three parishes and the 1835 Municipal Corporations Act formally united them there were still significant variations between the parishes in population terms. Because the Parliamentary Borough, the Municipal Borough and the Poor Law Union all had differing boundaries, population figures for the parishes remain valuable. Of course all population sequences are affected by boundary changes and Sunderland Borough boundaries were extended in 1867, 1895, 1928, 1935, 1951 and 1974. Simple comparisons

through time may therefore be misleading. Nonetheless the main patterns are clear. Within the nineteenth century Sunderland experienced roughly a six-fold increase with inter-censal rates of increase running higher than the national average until the end of the century. Equally striking is the contrast with the twentieth century in which growth rates have been generally below the national average, and showed an actual decline 1931-51. The figures confirm the general perception of Sunderland as a boom town in the Victorian period and a depressed town subsequently.[4] Within that period of growth the key decade was the 1830s which showed the highest decennial growth rate. This pattern of one decade of very high growth acting as a peak in a run of figures of sustained growth is again typical of many nineteenth century towns, though the particular decade of extreme growth differs for local reasons. However when the figures are examined at a sub-area level there are variations to be noted. Most strikingly Sunderland parish grows by only 15 per cent over the whole century, peaking in 1851, and in the 1830s it actually declines marginally. Monkwearmouth increases by eight-fold, Bishopwearmouth 16-fold, Southwick, from its very low base, by 24-fold, and the two areas to the north of the Wear have their largest inter-censal increase in the 1850s rather than the 1830s. The pattern of the eighteenth century was reversed as the town was forced to spread out into the undeveloped areas of Bishopwearmouth parish and to the north of the river.

With its very much smaller area (220 acres compared to 2,669 acres in Bishopwearmouth township) Sunderland parish was simply unable to absorb any more people. So, despite the small rate of increase, population density remained highest in Sunderland and the social problems associated with high concentrations of population continued to be more acute in the east end than elsewhere.

Given that the pattern of population growth is similar to that of other towns it is inevitable that the factors adduced to explain it are familiar from the general literature. "An obvious consequence of the industrial growth and prosperity was the speedy rise in population."[5] The repeated correlation between economic and industrial growth and population growth has been noted throughout the country. An expanding population clearly needed expanding economic opportunities to sustain it. This argument is made more precisely in Mitchell's list of 12 factors that were "the chief causes of this rapid increase in the population", though he does confuse economic factors such as the opening of collieries or the growth of shipping with political developments such as the creation of the corporation and the parliamentary constituency which more exactly follow economic and demographic change rather than causing it.[6] While accepting the logic of the economic explanations they do not go far to explain the mechanism of population growth. Robson does go further by analysing the census returns that give information about occupation. He demonstrates that in 1862 42 per cent of occupied males over 20 worked in shipping and ship-building and that if coal mining is added, then these two basic industries accounted for half of male employment. He can also show a 'marked parallelism' between two significant economic indicators (coal shipments and shipping tonnage launched) and population growth. The fastest growth in coal shipments co-incides with the highest growth in population and follows the establishment of railway links. The economic basis for the town's growth in numbers is shown.[7]

Sunderland is perceived as a magnet offering people economic opportunity and so migration into the town must have been a significant element.

Again the national pattern of a shift of population from the southern rural areas to the northern urban areas argues for some migratory patterns though researching them in detail is difficult, especially before the mid-nineteenth century. There is also an argument that the economic opportunities were more open to young active people leading to a higher than average birth rate in towns as young people established their families and so reinforced the migratory influx. Against that has to be set the acute problem of public health and high death rates in the most crowded areas that must have mitigated the rate of increase to some degree.

Two detailed population studies[8] of areas of Sunderland, both based around the 1851 census, add to our knowledge of the population patterns of the town. Patterson's study concentrates on the new, raw area around Wearmouth Colliery which was sunk between 1826 and 1834. It therefore illuminates the particular issues of the rapidly expanding new areas, though it may be more typical of a Durham pit-village than of a town. Given the sparse local population before the pit was won, and the specialist nature of the employment, the census analysis emphasises the significance of migration. Only nine per cent of the adult population came from Sunderland borough while about 80 per cent came from the counties of Durham and Northumberland. Clearly the pit owners wanted experienced workers and so men had moved from other local pits to sell their skills to the new company.[9] Patterson suggests that this typical pattern of short-wave migration is reinforced by a tendency for miners to be regularly on the move to new pits, either attracted by better conditions or moving because their poor work habits were only too apparent to their previous employers.[10] The extreme youthfulness of the population reinforces the supposition that the young and active are the most likely migrants.[11] The Monkwearmouth study gives an insight into the frontier town element of the Victorian urban experience and other areas of Sunderland would have undergone equivalent experiences at different times in the nineteenth century as their particular local phase of economic development took place.

The study by Fox of Sunderland parish centres on a different type of experience and highlights different elements in the population equation. Sunderland had experienced its growth from a small base long before the nineteenth century and by 1851 was entering a period of population stasis. Some 60 per cent of the sample analysed originated in Sunderland borough with only 15 per cent coming from Northumberland and Durham. 12 per cent were Scottish or Irish, a much larger proportion than in Monkwearmouth.[12] The migratory pattern was still the normal one of local movements, but the proportion moving in was lower than in comparable studies in other towns.[13] The lower rate of migration into the parish from the surrounding districts might have been explained by there being more poor residents employed in unskilled jobs (mobility being easier for the better-off) but Fox's occupational analysis show that 60 per cent of the residents were skilled manual workers.[14] The aspect of life in Sunderland most clearly shown is the effect of the concentration of population. The analysis of household size and the number of households per house shows that there were more than four persons per household, and 2.5 households per house. This gives occupancy levels of about 10 persons per house through the parish, with some enumeration wards producing higher figures.[15] It is this pattern of concentration that under-pins, and to a large degree explains, the evidence given in the Rawlinson Report of the dirt, disease and misery that obtained in the east end. (See Chapter 7 p. 69).[16]

By 1851 Sunderland parish had reached its lowest point in terms of quality of life and it contrasted sharply with the other parishes in terms of demographic measurement. Robson has developed this analysis further to show, by the use of indicators such as rateable value, the provision of schools, the distribution of pawnshops and the incidence of notifiable diseases, that there are clear social differentiations that can be made between different areas of Sunderland in both the 19th century and 20th centuries.[17] He has demonstrated another characteristic of Victorian towns; the tendency to spatial differentiation of social groups within the urban area. That tendency is reflected in the differing demographic patterns that are revealed by the census calculations. To fully develop this element it would be useful to have further detailed studies of more middle class areas like central Bishopwearmouth or of some of the later areas of growth like Hendon or Southwick to enable further comparisons to be made. At present these studies are not in existence.

HOUSING: MIDDLE CLASS

The most pressing problem presented to a town by a rapidly rising population is the basic one of housing the people. It may well be true that the press of population creates or exacerbates a whole range of social problems like public health, education, crime, provision for leisure and changes in moral attitudes, but housing the people is the one which is most obviously related to numbers. This element, combined with the re-defining of people's aspirations to be housed differently or better, led to both the physical growth of the town and to its particular social configurations. When the scale of the housing problem is realised, by reference to the figures of population growth, and it is appreciated that it had to be dealt with within the framework of an uncoordinated commercial building industry, then it is often striking how well Sunderland and other towns coped, despite their well known shortcomings. The key element in determining the pattern of urban housing growth was the attitude of the middle classes who had the financial power to achieve whatever housing goals they set themselves. As geographers have demonstrated it is the mobility of this group, and therefore the location of highly rated residential areas, that forms the pattern into which the working classes have to fit.[18]

In the eighteenth century prosperous members of the commercial and business classes chose to live close to their business interests. This meant that in general they lived close to the river and also close to the rest of the population. The large houses of Fitters Row, or those built in Church Street around 1720, of which only two now remain, gave them homes of space and distinction, but in areas that were also populated by the poorer class. As the town developed commercially, more men became prosperous and the move into Bishopwearmouth began with streets like Villiers Street being developed in the late eighteenth century. Again substantial terraced houses were built, but the crucial factor was proximity to High Street, which was the spine to the whole residential and business area. A few wealthy men lived at a distance in mansions set in the rural areas like Thornhill, Ford Hall or Herrington Hall, or even in large houses in extensive grounds closer to Bishopwearmouth church as can be seen on Rain's Eye Plan.[19] But most of the middle-classes did not aspire to suburban living. What changed their minds about this pattern was partly the attraction of new developments on the edge of the built-up area and partly the unattractiveness of living in the older areas as they experienced the tensions and problems of accommodating increasing numbers of people.

As Sunderland parish had relatively little land available for new housing provision any influx could only be accommodated by sub-letting the existing properties and of in-filling any space around existing houses. The sub-letting shows up in Fox's analysis of the 1851 Census. Partly this was the effect of the lodging houses, especially in Low Row, but mainly it was the division of single family homes into multiple occupancy units. If the middle classes vacated a house it could be used by several poorer families and might well generate a larger income from their aggregate rents than was payable by a single family. A combination of housing need and commercial advantage encouraged sub-letting. It also encouraged in-filling to build over gardens and back-yards to create the courts and alleys that were to be the prime exhibits of public health reformers (see Chapter 7). With the limited sanitary and drainage facilities the pressure on those who could afford it to consider alternative sites grew, and the movement of the middle classes into peripheral sites, of exclusively middle class character, accelerated throughout the nineteenth century.

The first major move away from the river and the east end was facilitated by the building of the Wear Bridge in 1796. The positioning of this bridge was to move the natural centre of the town westwards so that the High Street/Bridge Street junction was to become the focus for the town's business district. But initially it encouraged the development potential of the Fawcett Estate. From about 1820 the straight streets were planned out and building leases were sold. By 1850 a fine estate of elegant terraces had been developed as the residential centre for the prosperous businessman. Fawcett Street itself had large houses with balconies, steps up to imposing doorways and commodious accommodation: eight bedrooms, three reception rooms and two kitchens in one particular example.[20] In the parallel

Ford Hall, built 1785 and demolished in 1929 to make way for council house development on the Ford Estate.

streets which were built after Fawcett Street, rather smaller but still elegant houses were built, such as two offered for sale in Frederick Street with three bedrooms, two reception rooms, two kitchens and two attics for the servants.[21] The good proportions and the fine detailing of the houses can still be seen in John Street and Foyle Street, though the style was by this time a little old-fashioned by national standards. It was a speculative development with few if any properties being built for specific clients and it achieved its overall style through the perceived expectations of the owners and tenants who would be needed to make the venture commercially viable. To reinforce that sense of respectable superiority, churches and public facilities like the Athenaeum were included within the development, as well as some open space like the Shrubbery in Fawcett Street on which the Town Hall was ultimately built. What it did not have were retail or business premises. Nor did it have working class residents.[22]

The Fawcett Street development was barely completed when its special character was under threat, for it contained within it the forces that would change it dramatically. By removing a substantial part of the wealthiest families to a definable area retailers were encouraged to move to sites close to their potential clientele. As shops moved westwards on High Street it was inevitable that some would spill over into the Fawcett Estate at the High Street junction, and Hutchinson's Buildings of 1850 marked the first stage of that process. Over the next decades shops and offices spread southwards, with the placing of the Railway Station in Union Street in 1879 giving further impetus to the trend. When Binns' store was moved from High Street[23] to the south end of Fawcett Street, reinforcing the commercialisation begun by the opening of the Gas Office on the Holmeside corner in 1867, the predominantly residential character of the street was ended. The commercial centre of

Sunderland shifted away from roads parallel to the river on to the north/south axis. A similar, though later and less effective development, was to change Monkwearmouth by the end of the century. The process was slower in the rest of the Fawcett estate and residential use was maintained in John Street, Frederick Street and Foyle Street into the twentieth century, though progressively office use took over these streets also. This pattern of commercial infiltration had its positive causes, but it was facilitated by the fact that the middle classes were on the move again.

The cutting of Burdon Road through Bildon [Building] Hill in the late 1830s had two effects. It made Fawcett Street the main through road from the Wear Bridge to the south and so increased traffic and noise for its residents. It also gave convenient access to the Mowbray Estate lying by Ryhope Road at the top of the hill. The opening of the road made this land a prime development site in the same way as the Fawcett Estate had been a generation earlier. Here was land raised above the town, away from the pollution of the river, offering the possibility of a healthy rural situation and yet within convenient walking or carriage distance of the business centre. It was ideally situated for middle class suburban development. The cutting of the new road co-incided with the settlement after nearly 20 years of the Mowbray Estate inheritance by means of a private Act of Parliament. This finally made possible the sale and development of the estate. This Act gave the Mowbray heirs powers to approve the design of properties, to enforce binding covenants on purchasers and to forbid noxious trades. All these are characteristic of landowners intent upon middle-class development on their land.[24] Immediate attempts at development to a street plan by J. & B. Green of Newcastle failed to come to fruition,[25] but by 1850 land had been sold for others to develop at £600 per acre.[26] A. J. Moore built a mansion here for himself

Fawcett Street around 1880, showing the residential nature of the southern end. The Athenaeum (1841) can be seen on the right and in the middle distance the dome of the Subscription Library (1878) and the shrubbery where the Town Hall was later built (1886-1890).

(Bede Tower 1851) by J. & B. Green in Italianate style and some terraces for less prosperous men like Douro Terrace and St. Bede's Terrace[27]. This established West Hendon or Ashbrooke as it came to be called as the prime middle class residential area of the town. With its large mansions in extensive grounds like Ashburne House and West Hendon House that were already there, or like Nicholson House (1850), Ashbrooke Hall (1864) and Langham Tower (1889) scattered among a number of fine terraces, many of them in private gated roads like The Esplanade, The Oaks and Park Place, Ashbrooke provided a spacious, leafy environment for the socially powerful groups. The St. George's Square development, now demolished, though actually built on the Grange estate 1855-6, illustrates the quality of life nicely. Twenty-four houses grouped round a square, with gates, maintained by an annual levy, provided a private environment for a very homogenous group of professional and business families. The development was not a unified scheme, but involved six different builders, building no more than three properties at any one time. The residents' sense of social exclusivity is seen in their rules for access to the Square which was for carriages only and not for tradesmen, hawkers, dogs or children playing rough games.[28] The desirability and success of such a development explains the continued building of such schemes through the Ashbrooke area and beyond, even into this century with Holmelands Park and Beresford Park. That the middle classes came to dominate this particular area of town is not surprisng and as in Fawcett Street they provided the support facilities they wanted to make their environment complete, including a crop of fine and impressive churches — Christ Church (1864), Grange Congregational (1883), Park Road Methodist New Connexion (1887), St. John's Wesleyan (1888), St. George's Presbyterian (1890) and the Synagogue (1928). Ash-

brooke Sports Ground (1887)[29] provided for more physical recreation and the main private schools the Church High Schools for Boys and for Girls were also sited here in the 1880s.[30] Ashbrooke is Sunderland's Jesmond or North Oxford and remains a fine example of a Victorian suburb, now suitably a Conservation Area and with several individual buildings listed.

The slightly surprising element in the middle class movement within Sunderland is the apparent lack of interest in the coast line of Roker and Seaburn. Coastal sites with their sea breezes and sea views fulfilled many of the aspirations of suburban idealists and since the development of fashionable Brighton there were models to follow. Whitley Bay was to fulfil a suburban function for Newcastle. Roker was less congenial. Partly this was due to distance from the town centre and the fact that the journey lay through the working class area of Monkwearmouth; while by contrast from Ashbrooke the route was alongside Mowbray park. But it was mainly caused by difficulty of access. Roker Ravine was not yet bridged and so no coastal road existed north of the Roker Baths and Hotel which were served by Roker Baths Road. Also the sea front was a place of resort and so less exclusive. When Roker Park was laid out after the gift of land by Sir Hedworth Williamson, the corporation built a road bridge over the ravine in 1880. Williamson had made it a condition of the gift.[31] Now Williamson land running along the coast could be developed and some terraces were built from the 1880s onwards, especially close to the Park. But the area was already too identified with cottage development for it to be wholly successful and a major scheme for Seaburn in the early twentieth century came to nothing.[32] All this helps to explain why Fulwell remained a predominantly rural area for so long and only experienced any meaningful growth in its population at the turn of the century.[33] So the

A view of Bede Tower (1851) taken around 1870 from Building Hill. Christ Church was built in 1864. This view is now obscured by Park Road Methodist Church (1887).

Corporation Ferries, Trams and Buses

Sunderland Corporation operated three forms of transport — ferry boats from 1852 to 1957, electric trams from 1900 to 1954 and buses from 1929 to 1973. The oldest of these, Sunderland Ferry, had a long history before it passed into Corporation control. The crossing seems to have been in existence from the seventh century after the foundation of St. Peter's monastery at Monkwearmouth in 674. During the mediaeval period it passed into the control of the Bishop of Durham who leased out its operation. The lease was held by the Ettrick family from 1661 until 1796 when the ferry was purchased by the Commissioners of the iron bridge across the Wear. It passed to the Corporation after the 1851 Improvement Act abolished the Commissioners. In addition to the historic Sunderland Ferry there were other private ferries across the Wear. The Panns Ferry was purchased by the Commissioners, and closed when the Bridge opened, but ferries between Deptford and Southwick lasted until the Queen Alexandra Bridge opened in 1909 and that between South and North Hylton remained until 1957.

The Sunderland Ferry was operated by rowing boats until the Victorian period. A steam vessel known popularly as the "iron box" was introduced in 1843 but lasted only four years. A second steam vessel, the *Gulston*, built in 1876, proved even less successful. The third steam ferry boat, the *MAB* (short for Mayor, Alderman and Burgesses) arrived in 1877. On its demonstration trip for the councillors it zig-zagged out of control across the river and hit a Norwegian barque, much to the amusement of the crowd of onlookers on the bridge. The problem was reported solved when the steering chains were adjusted, but it was a warning of many future difficulties. The *Sunderland Echo* of the early 1880s is full of reports, editorials and letters about the *MAB*'s frequent failures. A reliable steam operation came when the *Wolston* and the *Wear* were purchased in 1884 and 1885. For these ferries floating pontoons, built at Austin's Wear Dock Yard, were provided as landing stages in 1887 and the shore approaches to the landings were also rebuilt. The ferry closed in 1957 after the demolition of houses near the riverside led to a decline in traffic. The maximum toll for the ferry remained one halfpenny (0.2p) from before the 1792 Bridge Act until its closure. Tenants of the Williamson family in Monkwearmouth were granted free passage (under an agreement of 1710) after the payment of customary tolls of five shillings (25p) for every house and two shillings (10p) for every cottage per year.

Streamlined tram 99, the "pride of the Sunderland Corporation fleet", built in 1934.

A horse tram passing Langham Tower in the 1890s.

Until the second half of the 19th century the built-up areas of Sunderland were close enough to be within easy walking distance of one another. by 1854, however, the town was expanding and a letter to the *Sunderland Echo* commended the recent introduction of horse cabs for hire in the town, and called for the establishment of an omnibus service "as the majority of businessmen live in the more airy part of the town". The need for public transport was filled by the Sunderland Tramways Company which operated horse-drawn trams. In 1879 they opened their first route, from Roker to Fawcett Street, then on to Christ Church and Gray Road and back to town via Tatham Street; a branch went to the foot of Cousin Street, serving the Docks. In 1879 local authorities were not allowed to operate tramways but could build lines for leasing to other companies as Sunderland Corporation did for additional routes from Villiers Street up Hylton Road to Peacock Street, from Fawcett Street up New Durham Road and from the Wheatsheaf to Southwick.

The tramway service began at 9.00am and charged a flat fare of two pence (0.8p), and clearly catered for the middle classes rather than working people who continued to walk to work. Working class areas such as Deptford and Monkwearmouth Shore were not served by trams.

The Tramway Company's lease of the Corporation lines was due to expire after 21 years, but in 1894 they offered to construct a new line up Chester Road if a further 21 years lease was granted. Opposition to this, led by the Labour members of the Council, resulted in the proposal failing to receive the necessary two-thirds majority on the Council in 1895. The Council eventually decided to purchase and electrify the tramways. It already had a power station in Dunning Street and a second power station was opened in 1900, the year the Corporation took over the tramways, at Hylton Road; a tram depot was added here in 1903 to supplement the Wheatsheaf depot.

In addition to electrifying the tramways the Corporation extended the New Durham Road route via Chester Road and Kayll Road to join the Hylton Road route and form the Circle service. Other extensions opened were to Villette Road, Grangetown, Fulwell and Sea Lane (Seaburn). The Docks route was re-aligned and the Gray Road lines abandoned.

At Grangetown the Corporation Tramways met those of the Sunderland District Electric Tramways Company which ran via Ryhope, Silksworth and the Herringtons to Houghton-le-Spring and to Penshaw, Fence Houses and Easington Lane. By 1905 the Corporation tram routes had reached the limits of the built up areas and there was to be no further extension until a route was opened to Barnes Park in 1925; four years later this was extended to Humbledon. By this time some undertakings were replacing their trams by buses as the Sunderland District Tramways Company did in 1925. The Corporation converted their Docks service to buses (hired for the first year from the Northern General Omnibus Company) in 1928. It seemed possible that the whole Corporation tramway system might disappear, but instead it was retained and modernised under the direction of Charles Hopkins, General Manager from 1929 to 1948. Hopkins was also responsible for the extension of the Fulwell line via Dykelands Road to Seaburn in 1937. He also introduced bus routes to areas outside the tram network, notably Ford Estate and Newcastle Road.

In the 1930s-1940s the Sunderland Tramways were notable for the construction of new trams (including eight centre entrance streamlined vehicles) and the purchase of second hand cars from systems which were closing. Unlike the horse trams the Corporation electric trams charged low fares. From 1900-1948 tram passengers could usually travel from the centre to any part of the tram system, except Humbledon, for 1d (0.4p).

A decision to replace trams by buses was taken in 1947 because of the expense of renewing track and overhead wires and the fact that new housing estates were being constructed away from the trams. There were however problems in purchasing new buses and it was agreed the Durham Road route should still be extended to Thorney Close which was reached in 1949. In 1952 it was decided to speed up the replacement and the last tram ran in October 1954. During the 1950s and 1960s further bus services

The ferry boat *Wear* in the late 1890s, with Monkwearmouth Shore in the background.

were introduced to the new housing estates on the outskirts of the town. Several of these were outside the Corporation's traditional operating territory and were operated jointly with the Northern General and Sunderland District companies.

In 1966 a start was made in replacing the largely double-deck bus fleet with one-man operated single-deck buses in which a flat fare of 4d (1.63p) using tokens, was charged. The flat fare was replaced in 1969 with a zonal system of 4d per zone. The policy of introducing single-deck buses continued, however, until the Corporation became part of the Tyneside Passenger Executive in 1973; a year later it became part of the Tyne and Wear PTE controlled by the new County Council.

Corporation trams and buses at the Gas Office corner about 1939.

middle classes took control of a bloc of land to the south of the town centre sited away from those urban elements they disliked and in an area with particular advantages. This left the working classes to look for new properties in the parts of the town the middle classes did not favour and which were not required for commercial development. The story of their movement out of the traditional centre of the town reflects different criteria and a different pattern of development.[34]

HOUSING: WORKING CLASS

Working class families had much less freedom to choose where they would live because they had to work within the constraints of a limited budget and the need to be close to their place of work. So the builders of working class houses were always working to tight costings and seeking to provide adequate dwellings with the minimum outlay on land and materials. For those who had to remain within Sunderland parish the problems of overcrowding and the progressive deterioration of the older properties were compounded by demands of industry and commerce for sites for expansion. Most strikingly this led to the erosion of the Town Moor, initially for public services such as the Church and burial ground, or the Gray Schools, but ultimately for the South Dock complex and its railway servicing. The Dock scheme even involved the demolition of some houses[35] which further exacerbated the problems.

As the shipbuilding industry, glass works and potteries, Wearmouth colliery, iron foundries and engineering works grew and spread so they created a demand for working class housing close by. While it is not possible to make watertight causal links between industrial developments and the housing of that industry's workers, it remains clear that where industry was sited, new housing followed. So as Wearmouth Colliery expanded its workforce, a knot of houses was built in streets immediately around the pit-head; as ship yards developed on Monkwearmouth Shore a band of working class houses was built running back from the river to Broad Street later called Roker Avenue; and as shipyards lined the river at Deptford, Pallion or Southwick so housing was provided for workers in those places of employment. This does not mean, generally, that employers were directly involved in this provision, but rather that the speculative builders within the town recognised that these areas would be successful developments as there would be a ready demand. The building industry expanded considerably throughout the century as shown by the directories[36] and by 1901 it was the largest employer in the town after ship-building with 4,299 men.[37] The success of these firms depended upon building houses at the right price in the right location to ensure that few were left untenanted for very long, thus avoiding cash-flow problems. The solution to the growing population of Sunderland was to provide new housing in exactly the same way that other towns were doing. What is different about Sunderland is the particular form of housing that was provided.

Most towns adopted a particular working class house type that was congenial to the tenants and within whatever local building regulations applied in the second half of the century: back-to-backs in the West Riding, tenement blocks in Glasgow, tunnel backs in the East Midlands, and Tyneside flats in the north east are well known examples. But Sunderland is virtually unique in building

One of Sunderland's earliest photographs, showing St. George's Place (later Square) soon after its construction in the mid-1850s.

single storey terraces known as Sunderland Cottages. "With the exception of some streets in Darlington and Jarrow, other urban concentrations of one-storeyed houses are unknown in England."[38] The decision to adopt a particular pattern can usually be explained by reference to keeping costs down, as with the flats or tenement styles, or with peculiarities of local land-use patterns as with back-to-backs, although they also are miserly with land. Single storey houses are not economical in land or building materials. In Leeds a plot of c.18 square yards could be the site for two houses; in Morgan Street in Southwick for example two houses occupy a site, long and narrow, of c.120 square yards. This suggests that land costs were not significant in Sunderland, possibly because of the chief rent system of land holding that is also virtually a unique Sunderland phenomenon. Single-storey houses are also expensive in materials as they require larger roof areas with extensive use of wood. Explanations linking this to the avail-ability of wood imported to the town, and the high quality of wood craftsmanship that re-sulted in the decorative detailing and the distinctive Sunderland doorcase, seem uncon-vincing as other north east ports do not exhibit similar patterns of building even though they have the same advantages.[39] A more likely influence is that of the Durham pit row which adapted traditional rural building practice for the colliery villages, many of which were sited in remote and hitherto rural areas. It remains hard to explain why Sunderland should adopt this form for urban use when other towns in the region simply do not.[40] If it is true that the earliest examples are to be found around Wearmouth Colliery and that these provided a model for later developments like that around Hartley's glass works in Millfield, then the link with the pit-row would seem to be clear.[41] But whatever the precise origin of this house-type there is no doubt that, encouraged by the building regulations, many rows were built throughout the town.

As already suggested the siting of these cottages were largely determined by the siting of industry. In Monkwearmouth Sir Hedworth Williamson was the dominant landowner, having built North Dock and railways, and he took a direct hand in development. In the 1850s he planned an estate based on Dock Street and Dame Dorothy Street for over 400 houses. The layout and the house designs, which were praised in Rawlinson's Report on Public Health, were drawn by John Dobson, but it is not clear whether Williamson then built the properties or sold plots to builders who under-took construction within the plans already drawn. Clearly it was intended to set good standards of accommodation as is evidenced by the engagement of the leading regional architect, the provision of a public bath house and the decision to build two storey houses which would give more space to the families.[42] When in the 1870s Williamson de-veloped land north of Roker Avenue he opted to have his land agent draw an estate plan and to sell plots to builders who built cottages accord-ing to the standard pattern, though in Stans-field Street for example there are several variations on the basic design.[43] The pattern in the Millfield development around the Wear Glass Works is rather different. These cottages date from the mid-1840s, but the building process was long drawn out. Within the terraces there was no uniform design with some being double-fronted, some having dormer windows and a few being of two storeys. This is typical of the piecemeal build-ing process in which small builders erected a few houses (maybe only one or two) in a build-ing season and then returned in subsequent years to add to the terrace. The seemingly uniform and monotonous terraces rarely turn out to be the work of a single developer or to be totally standard. These houses were generally occupied by single families, though that might mean sizeable numbers of people if lodgers and relatives are taken into account, which is different from the pattern in the east end. And while James Hartley was doubtless pleased to have workers' housing available near his works, only a minority of residents were in his employ and he was in no way directly involved with the processes of land development and building that took place.[44] Hartley was involved in the re-development of the area after the closure of the glass works.[45]

Another area that was extensively developed with cottages was Hendon. As the docks were extended it was natural to provide workers' housing southwards out of Sunderland parish and providing a clear boundary was maintained with the middle class development of West Hendon or Ashbrooke an acceptable balance of interest could be maintained. After 1851 Hendon had other advantages for developers especially in its outer areas. The 1851 Improvement Act, which had applied Public Health legislation to Sunderland, introduced building regulations to the town, and some builders objected to this imposition. Until the boundary extension of 1867 parts of Hendon lay outside sanitary authority jurisdiction and The Builder, comparing Sunderland mortality rates un-favourably with other towns, noted that New Hendon was unpaved and undrained and therefore rife with fever.[46] The Hendon de-velopment also illustrates the role of the Build-ing Society movement in the building process. The Middle Hendon Estate commenced in 1865 in Mainsforth Terrace was to comprise three streets of cottages to an aggregate value of £35,000 built over three years. J. C. Tone the agent argued that the cottage was the best housing for the working man because of its good ventilation. The developers were the Uni-versal Building Society who were only one of many small local societies sponsoring such de-velopments. Because of this institutional sponsorship sites were earmarked for churches and Mainsforth Terrace Primitive Methodist Chapel was opened in 1867 designed by the estate architect, John Tillman. Here was a much more co-ordinated approach to development and this particular example was to have higher standards than the regula-tions imposed by the 1867 Improvement Act.[47] It also helps to explain another striking characteristic of Sunderland's work-ing class housing: the high incidence of owner occupancy. Nineteenth century towns were dominated by private rented houses even for the middle classes and most estimates for owner-occupancy are placed at less than 20 per cent. In parts of Sunderland the rates could be much higher. Tower Street in Hendon showed 86.6 per cent owner occupiers and the neighbouring Ridley Terrace showed 50 per cent in 1870 shortly after the streets were laid out. In Millfield streets like Booth Street and Hume Street produced lower figures of 28.6 and 35.7 per cent respectively, but they were still well above national norms. Analysis of the social class of these residents shows them to be predominantly skilled artisans. If the analysis is further extended to higher social class areas like Shakespeare Street (behind the infirmary) or Argyle Square, still higher owner-occupancy rates are recorded. Although these surveys are necessarily small scale they are consistent enough to encourage the belief that Sunderland had a smaller percentage of tenants than was common in most towns.[48] This was in part the result of the high wage rates enjoyed by skilled men in the town[49] and in part the result of the multiplicity of small building societies that encouraged regular saving and which permitted repayments over long periods at low weekly sums that might hardly exceed normal rents. It is this pattern of owner occupation that maintained so many of these cottage homes right up to present times as desirable properties, so that these Victorian streets still make a valuable contribution to the town's housing stock. When transport developments made it possible for working men to live further from their workplace, the cottages simply spread. It was the tramway that allowed this. Vividly described by D. H. Lawrence as 'gondolas of the poor,' they allowed workmen to travel for a few pence a week into work and so to enjoy the advantage of housing built away from the pollution of the centre and closer to rural or seaside amenities.[50] Cottage development in Barnes or Fulwell and Seaburn followed and continued into the twentieth century.

One further element in the development of housing deserves consideration: the attempt to clear the worst slums in the east end and to re-develop with model housing. All the new development at the periphery did little to help the congested areas in Sunderland parish where people still rented cramped and overcrowded properties with poor facilities and where the toll of disease, especially amongst the young, was still disturbingly large. In parallel with the national attempt to legislate for slum clearance Sunderland used local acts to tackle the problem.[51] The original plans to demolish some 35 streets and to replan the road layout of the east end were not fulfilled,[52] but some useful work was done. A Corporation-sponsored competition for model workmen's dwellings in 1872 produced over 50 designs and two winners, Thomas Oliver and John Tillman.[53] Some were erected on the newly formed Outram, Hartley, Havelock, and Lucknow Streets by the Sunderland Dwelling Company. Although built as two storey houses they were let as flats at rents which were rather higher than the original tenants could afford.[54] The Corporation cleared a further site and laid out James Williams Street in 1872. This did clear Baines Lane and Union Lane, but as some building plots were used for a school and churches, very few houses were available to house the displaced families.[55] Those built were not cottages and tended to attract men in secure employment even though most proper-

Deptford Terrace, built around 1870. A typical Sunderland cottage row, with its end house adaptable for use as a corner shop.

ties were sub-let.[56] A similar scheme in Monkwearmouth created Roker Avenue.[57] The problem with these schemes is that while they cleared poor housing, they relied on the building industry to supply the replacements. Slum clearance and council sponsored rebuilding had to wait upon the Housing of the Working Classes Act of 1890. Sunderland used this Act to clear the notorious Hat Case where 49 houses housed some 460 persons and to provide the tenements of Harrison's Buildings on the site. Again this proved to be far less than the planned 19 areas of demolition and again the site finally provided for only about 350 tenants in the new scheme. About 100 persons were thrown back on to existing housing stock, and while rents were equivalent to those of private landlords they tended to be higher than those in the demolished buildings.[58]

Harrison's Buildings were important not so much for their contribution to housing provision but as heralds of the determined efforts made in this century by the Corporation to improve housing. The inter-war slum clearance programmes and the major council housing schemes involving both re-development like the Garths and new peripheral housing estates like Humbledon, Ford and Marley Pots were to be re-emphasised after 1945 when the authority led the country in its housing programmes and gave the town its distinctive balance of private and public housing.

The patterns of growth in Sunderland in the nineteenth century reflect those of many other towns because the same forces of economic expansion, of population growth and of pressure on housing were experienced throughout the country. Particular geographical and historical factors produced particular patterns within the town like the development along the river or the effects of the tripartite nature of the original town, but, as Robson shows, Sunderland conforms well enough to familiar models of urban growth from 1780 onwards.

And it is against the fact of this growth and the confidence that it gave to the town that Sunderland's history must be placed. On the one hand it produced the pressures and tensions that resulted in the acute social problems that were not fully tackled until the twentieth century, but it also generated the wealth that paid for the achievements of the town and for the attempts to solve problems. The change from being a boom town to being one in economic decline occurred at the turn of the nineteenth century and so the patterns of growth and development are necessarily different in the two centuries. And as perceptions of social priorities have changed so these have also influenced patterns of development as in the way in which the more slowly growing population in this century has consumed far more space for its homes and activities than the more rapid growth in numbers in the Victorian period. Yet Sunderland is distinctive especially in respect of its unique approach to working class housing via the ownership of small cottages. The few examples that are now listed buildings are aptly designated as they are tangible evidence of the processes and pressures that formed the community of Sunderland in the nineteenth century.

REFERENCES

1. For a brief discussion of national population trends see N. L. Tranter, *Population since the Industrial Revolution: the case of England and Wales* (1973). For the overall position of towns within the national growth see W. Ashworth, *Genesis of Modern British Town Planning: a study in the economic and*

Harrison's Buildings, Sunderland's first council houses, built in 1903.

social history of the 19th and 20th Centuries (1954), Chapter 1.

2. W. Hutchinson, *History and Antiquities of the County Palatine of Durham* (Newcastle, 1787), Vol. 2, pp. 525-6.

3. See Hutchinson, *op. cit.* Vol. 2, pp. 523-5 who quotes other sources.

4. See B. T. Robson, *Urban Analysis: A study of city structure with special reference to Sunderland* (Cambridge, 1971), Chapter 3 for a discussion of population that emphasises the 20th century experience.

5. Corfe, p. 93.

6. Mitchell, (reprinted 1972), p. 89.

7. B. T. Robson, *op. cit.* pp. 79-82.

8. G. Patterson (ed.), *Monkwearmouth Colliery in 1951: an analysis of the census returns* Durham University Extra Mural Department, (1977). R. C. Fox, *The Demography of Sunderland, 1851*, Occasional Paper No. 1, Dept. of Geography and History, Sunderland Polytechnic, (1980).

9. G. Patterson, *op. cit.* pp. 35-37.

10. *Ibid.* pp. 39-40.

11. *Ibid.* pp. 26-8. Almost half the population was under 15 and about half the children had been born in the town after their parents move to the colliery.

12. R. C. Fox, *op. cit.* pp. 19, 39-40.

13. e.g. W. A. Armstrong, "The Interpretation of Census Enumerators' Books for Victorian Towns", in H. J. Dyos (ed.) *Study of Urban History* (1968) pp. 67-86.

14. R. C. Fox. *op. cit.* pp. 19, 41-5.

15. *Ibid.* p. 11, 13-15, 33-34.

16. R. Rawlinson, *Report to the General Board of Health on a Preliminary Inquiry as to the Sewerage, Drainage, supply of Water and the Sanitary Condition of the Borough of Sunderland* (HMSO, 1851). Relevant extracts are quoted in R. C. Fox, *op. cit.* pp. 4-7.

17. B. T. Robson, *op. cit.*, pp. 108-120.

18. Robson, *op. cit.* discusses these issues with full references, though largely in the context of the 20th century.

19. M. Clay, G. E. Milburn and S. T. Miller, *An Eye Plan of Sunderland and Bishopwearmouth by John Rain* (1984). J. Robinson, 'Some Historic Houses in Sunderland', *Antiq. Sund.*, IV, (1903), pp. 16-22. L. P. Crangle, 'Old Houses in Sunderland', *Antiq. Sund.* xxvi, (1976), pp. 68-84.

20. Advertisement, *S.H.* July 25, 1845, p. 1.

21. Advertisement, *S.H.* April 7, 1843, p. 1.

22. T. Corfe (ed.), *Buildings of Sunderland 1814-1914* (Sunderland, 1983) p. 11. R. Hyslop, 'The Fawcett Estate', *Antiq. Sund.*, xix, 1932, pp. 29-41. For an appreciation of its architectural qualities see, N. Pevsner and E. Williamson, *Buildings of England: County Durham* (Harmondsworth, 2nd ed., 1983) pp. 456-458.

23. The precise date of this move is unclear, but it is in the mid-1880s. *S.D.E.* March 4, 1907, p. 3. D. J. Blair, *Spatial Dynamics of Commercial Activity in Central Sunderland*, Unpublished M.A. Thesis, (Durham Univ. 1977) pp. 169-173.

24. Details of this settlement are held with Deeds to Carlton House. Deed Packet 803, Borough Solicitors Dept. Civic Centre. Deeds held there can only be inspected by prior agreement. I am grateful to the Chief Administrative Officer, Sunderland Polytechnic and to the Borough Solicitor for permission to examine this and other documents.

25. *S.H.* April 9, 1841, p. 1.

26. *S.H.* Nov. 16, 1849, p. 5.

27. *S.H.* June 3, 1853, p. 5.

28. G. L. Cummings, 'Some Account of St. George's Square and the People Connected Therewith', *Antiq. Sund.*, vii, 1906. pp. 53-80.

29. E. Watts Moses, *To Ashbrooke and Beyond* (Sunderland 1963) p. 27.

30. The Boys' School had only a short life, but the Girls' School has celebrated its centenary.

31. *S.D.E.* Nov. 21, 1878, p. 3. *S.D.E.* June 23 & 24, 1880, p. 2.

32. *S.D.E.* May 23, 1901, p. 3.

33. B. T. Robson, *op. cit.*, Graph, p. 92.

34. See T. Corfe (ed.) *op. cit* p. 14 for an account of Housing the Middle Classes using some different examples.

35. N. Dennis, *People and Planning; a sociology of housing in Sunderland* (1970), pp. 147-8.

36. Pigot's Directory (1822) lists three building firms; Vint and Carr (1844) 21; Ward (1873) has 52 and Ward (1900) has 66.

37. *Report of an Enquiry by the Board of Trade into Working Class Rents, Housing, and Retail Prices and Standard Rates of Wages in the United Kingdom*, (1908), p. 448. Cited in D. H. Tasker, *Housing and Public Health in Victorian Sunderland c. 1840-1905*, unpublished B.A. Dissertation, (Hull, Univ., 1986), p. 24.

38. S. Muthesius, *The English Terraced House* (1982) p. 104. This is the most authoritative source on housing styles.

39. T. Corfe (ed.) *op. cit.* p. 13.

40. S. Muthesius, *op. cit.*, pp. 102-106.

41. See T. Corfe (ed.), *op. cit.*, p. 13; D. H. Tasker, *op.cit.* pp. 18-20; H. G. Bowling (ed.) *Some Chapters in the History of Sunderland* (privately printed, n.d.) pp. 104-5.

42. Fordyce, ii, p. 480.

43. See P. Emmerson, *The Williamson Family of Whitburn; some aspects of its history*, Unpublished B.A. dissertation (C.N.A.A. Sunderland Polytechnic, 1986) pp. 49-53.

44. D. H. Tasker, *op. cit.* pp. 20-24.

45. *S.D.E.*, June 2, 1896, p. 3.

46. *Builder* 19, Feb. 2, 1861, p. 81; April 20, 1861, p. 274.

47. *S.H.*, April 7, 1865, p. 8.

48. E. A. Longstaffe, *New Housing in Sunderland, c. 1860-1870*, unpublished B.A. dissertation (C.N.A.A. Sunderland Polytechnic, 1982).

49. E. H. Hunt, *Regional Wage Variations in Britain 1850-1914*, (Oxford, 1972).

50. The first routes to Roker, Christ Church, Tatham Street and Docks all opened in 1879 with a flat fare of 2d. See S. A. Staddon, *The Tramways of Sunderland*, (Huddersfield, 1964).

51. *Sunderland Improvement Act, 1867*.

52. See the plan showing *Proposed New Streets for Commercial and Sanitary Purposes* drawn by G. A. Middlemiss in 1866. Copy in Sunderland Museum Collection, TWCMS B10359.

53. *Building News* 22, Feb. 16, 1872, p. 132.

54. D. H. Tasker, *op. cit.* p. 50.

55. T. Corfe (ed.) *op.cit.* p. 8.

56. Census Enumerator's Book, 1881 Census.

57. D. H. Tasker, *op. cit.* p. 51.

58. See. G. Patterson 'Harrison's Buildings — Sunderland's first council housing', *Sunderland's History*, 3 1985, p. 5-34.

Prosperity and Poverty

Nineteenth-century visitors to Sunderland tended to remark on two complementary aspects. On the one hand you had a busy, prosperous, fast-growing town, teaming with industrious and well-paid workers who were noted for their enterprise and proud of their skills and strength; industrial and technological progress was everywhere spectacularly evident. On the darker side, though, there was filth and overcrowding that made some areas notoriously unhealthy. Henry Irving's description in a letter written shortly after his debut at the Lyceum in 1856 summed up pithily: "A very large ship-building, coaly town".[1] A. B. Granville, like many other visitors, hastened first to wonder at the Wear Bridge "the stupendous structure — one of those projections which show the power of man so strikingly".[2] But then he regretted that he had necessarily to pass through "a long and dirty street, the prolongation or tail of High-Street, inhabited by the lowest class of people, principally mechanics and sailors, and from which branch off, to the right and to the left, many very narrow passages or alleys . . . all presenting, at the time of my visit, the very sink of gloom and filth — an apt nest or rendezvous for typhus and cholera".[3] William Chambers, visiting in 1849 to preside at a soirée of the Lit. and Phil., where he was pleased to be "brought into contact with many intelligent minds" in a town "growing up to be one of the greatest seaports on the east coast",[4] regretted that he found also "accounts of mis-spent means — intemperance, and the evils that follow in its train were much too prevalent".[5] Even immigrant Scotch glassmakers, he was distressed to find, were too fond of drinking; and almost everyone spent their high earnings on liquor. Murray's

Handbook for Travellers of 1864 was uncompromising: "The whole town is black and gloomy in the extreme, and the atmosphere is so filled with smoke that blue sky is seldom seen, especially in the lower part of the town, which consists for the most part of a maze of small dingy houses crowded together, intersected by lanes rather than streets; dirt is the distinctive feature; earth, air and water are alike black and filthy".[6] But Murray, too, was impressed by the booming port and the "famous Cast Iron Bridge over the Wear, consisting of one stupendous arch . . . spanning the black gulf crowded with coal staiths and collier vessels . . ."

There was no doubt about the prosperity. Sunderland in Victorian times was generally accepted as the fourth port in the kingdom and "the most extensive shipbuilding port in the world",[7] while its working people were often admired for their industry, intelligence, enterprise and good looks. That there was a sharply contrasting darker side was a matter of concern to visitors, to the national press and public, and to government itself. Sunderland's unhealthier areas were a prime target for the numerous official enquiries into public health and related matters that kept conscientious administrators and legislators so busy in the 1840s. Lurid descriptions of conditions in the east end frequently found their way into state papers and into the newspapers.

Edwin Chadwick's great *Report on the Sanitary Condition of the Labouring Population* of 1842 spelled out with fearful clarity the links between hygiene and health, becoming the bible of Victorian sanitary crusaders. But the relationship between urban filth and disease had been forcefully brought to public attention in the cholera outbreak of a decade

A cartoon of 1831 satirises the Sunderland authorities for the continuation of road traffic during the first cholera epidemic while the port was quarantined.

earlier. In October 1831 the long-expected Asiatic Cholera had at last reached Britain, and it struck first at the port of Sunderland. An apprehensive press and public sought scapegoats. One was speedily found in the obtuse and selfish conduct of Sunderland's local authorities, doctors and business community; another in the appalling conditions revealed in its hard-hit port area.

It was not that the town was unprepared for the emergency. During the previous summer the magistrates had, anticipating government instructions, set up a local Board of Health, with advice from the town's medical men. Their subsequent mistakes were understandable but deplorable. They failed to identify the first cases as anything other than normal autumnal ill-health. They yielded to local opinion which feared that the government's panic measures would cripple Sunderland's trade. The town's leading figures united to belittle the cholera alarm, and made rash statements that became the subject of much hostile comment.[8].

The behaviour of Sunderlanders brought widespread ridicule. "More suitable to the barbarism of the interior of Africa than to a town in a civilised country",[9] Charles Greville thought the conduct of Sunderland people. The "human misery" of the crowded east end caused equal and more lasting concern. Most of the 534 cases of cholera occurred in the parish of Sunderland, and 156 of the town's 202 deaths.[10] One in 109 of the east end population died, compared with one in 706 in the more spacious and salubrious Bishopwearmouth. The lesson was patent for those concerned over public health.

Dr William Clanny 1777-1850, an Ulsterman who became one of Sunderland's leading doctors, played an important role in the fight against cholera, and invented a variety of miners' safety lamps.

THE CROWDED EAST END

Sunderland parish, carved out of Bishopwearmouth in 1719, was confined to 120 acres, of which 20 made up the dwindling Town Moor. The rest of the parish was completely built up. On either side of High Street narrow entries led to dark alleys between built-up burgess strips, or to airless courts. The parish faced northward, on slopes dropping to the river, so that many houses were constantly dark and the lower parts in particular suffered from recurrent drainage problems. Large houses left over from more spacious days were now subdivided into tenements. By 1851 there was an average of two-and-a-half families (or between 10 and 11 people) to each house of the parish;[11] and of these fewer than seven per cent could boast their own privies. The area, as a seaport, was dense with pubs, clustering along the High Street, and down to the riverside. Eden had reported 187 ale-houses as long ago as 1797;[12] in 1850 their number was variously estimated at from 150 to 250.[13] Common lodging-houses were another hazard, where "crime, vice and human misery"[14] flourished; they were frequented by "vagrants, thieves, tramps and beggars".[15] Pig-keeping added its stench and filth, and there were 19 slaughterhouses.[16] Investigators recorded in righteous horror the profitable middens and stinking pools that added a distinctive flavour to east end life. Nearly 19,000 people lived in this packed parish, one to every 38 square yards according to the calculation that Mordey and Brown submitted to Rawlinson's enquiry, whereas folk in Bishopwearmouth could spread themselves over 260 square yards.[17]

The influx of industrial labour was the principal factor causing this overcrowding, for prosperous industries were attracting those displaced from less fortunate parts of the country. In 1846-50 conditions in the east end reached their worst as labourers working on the new dock flooded in. In those years of the Great Famine, there was naturally an Irish invasion. 5.7 per cent of the town's population in the 1851 census were Irish-born, and most lived in squalid conditions in the east end streets. Hat Case, a notorious close near the dock, which had warranted a particularly lurid description in the 1845 report, was, by 1851, crowded with Irish immigrants. One in three of the families in its tenements was of Irish origin, most of the men working as labourers or excavators.[18] North of the river more Irish settled in John Street, Monkwearmouth, in similarly overcrowded conditions. Many found employment linked to the expanding Wearmouth Colliery; but they were not accommodated in the relatively spacious pit village built by its proprietors.[19]

Even as population reached a peak of density in Sunderland parish, more spacious working-class housing was being built on the fringes of the town, at Monkwearmouth, Deptford, Pallion, Hendon and Southwick. Here, better-paid skilled workers, native and immigrant, tended to live close to their jobs. Often these, too, were incomers. In Southwick (administratively distinct from Sunderland but closely reflecting its pattern of development) young craftsmen in a demanding but well-paid occupation sought employment in the bottle-works. Eight new houses added to Victoria Street about 1850 were speedily occupied by 25 glassworkers and their families; only three were Sunderland born, while the rest, apart from two Scots and an Irishman, had moved in from South Shields or elsewhere on Tyneside.[20]

GAS AND WATER

It was conditions in the east end that demanded intervention. Faced with wide-spread public concern over the many graphic reports, Sunderland's leaders were driven to action. The division of authority in the town after 1836 may have contributed to the slowness of progress. None of the bodies claiming to exercise local authority, Improvement Commissioners, parish vestries, and elected Borough Council, saw itself as responsible for dealing with this kind of problem. The first years of the Council were in any case spent in defending its right to exist and levy rates. But from 1844 rivalry between the different local bodies helped in speeding improvement. In the changed climate that followed Chadwick's *Report* and, more locally, the publication of Dr. Reid's damning comments in the *Second Report on the State of Large Towns* of 1845, Council and Commissioners each sought to blame the town's disgrace on the other's shortcomings and irresponsibility, and each determined to outshine its rival in ostentatious activity.

The 'Health of Towns' faction was active in Sunderland from 1844. Its leaders were the public-spirited doctors William Mordey and Robert Brown. Their enthusiasm also carried them into the Borough Council, so that Council soon became identified with the demand for public health reform. It found backing from a new generation of activists who included the Quakers Joshua and Caleb Wilson and the Chartist bookseller James Williams. In opposition stood the Ratepayers' Protection Association (dubbed by its enemies the 'filth of towns' faction), apprehensive of what might follow from any growth of the Council's powers and its financial requirements. The RPA naturally looked for support from the Improvement Commissioners, resentful rivals of the Corporation. A number of prominent citizens who had once spearheaded the radical campaign to secure Sunderland's borough status had by now drifted into sympathy with the Corporation's opponents. They included Richard Spoor, who had presided over the birth of the Borough, J. P. Kidson, who, as the first town clerk, had led the campaign for statutory and legal recognition, and David Jonassohn, who had been unable, as a Jew, to take the Council seat to which he was elected. A major factor in this transfer of loyalty was the Commissioners' link with the gas-light and water services of the town; enterprising and public-spirited businessmen should obviously seek to share in ventures that showed every prospect of future expansion. Thus, when the Council launched its attack on the

inadequacies of the Commission-sponsored companies as contributing towards the town's unhealthy reputation, there was an element of resentment over their opponents' control of a valuable source of patronage and profit.

An obvious target for reformers, and the focus of sharp dispute, was the Bishopwear-mouth Water Company, set up by the Commissioners in 1824. Though several times reorganised since, it still included a number of Commissioners on its Board of Directors. The Council was anxious to emphasise the dangers of collusion between Commissioners responsible for cleansing the streets and Commissioners acting as directors of the Water Company. Further, the water supplied by the Company's two steam pumping engines in Fountain Street was deemed wholly inadequate for a growing town, and unjustifiably expensive.[21]

Late in 1844 Mordey launched the attack on the Water Company, and the Corporation set about seeking parliamentary backing for a new company. Simultaneously an attack was mounted on the Commissioners' other enterprise, the Gas Company they had set up in 1823, and again parliamentary support was needed. Here, there was less obvious reason for the 'Health of Towns' movement to complain; but much was made of the inadequacy of the street lighting, and tales were told of the ill-lighted privies by the river where, it was said, four men had drowned early one morning through missing their way in the dark.[22] A. J. Moore, chairman of the Watch Committee, opened the assault on the Gas Company, and the latter only confirmed suspicions when it promptly found it possible

Spring Garden Lane in Sunderland's east end, a photograph taken in the early twentieth century.

Cholera in Sunderland

The first outbreak of cholera in the British Isles was in Sunderland in the winter of 1831. The national epidemic which led on from this and the impact the new killer had on public opinion contributed much to the eventual winning of public health legislation and attempts to contain the problems associated with over rapid urban growth.

With an aggregate population of some 40,000, rising rapidly, appalling living conditions in the riverside parish of Sunderland particularly, and considerable trade links with the Baltic where cholera had blazed since June 1831, the town was, in retrospect, a likely candidate for the first outbreak. It is probable that the first victim was a river pilot called Robert Henry but it was the 12 year old Isabella Hazard who died on the 17th October, the famous "blue girl", who displayed the classic and unmistakeable symptoms of the disease in its extreme form. It was the death of the 60-year old keelman William Sproat on the 26th October which led the local Board of Health on the 1st November to inform the government of the presence of the "continental cholera". The upshot of this was the declaration of a fifteen day quarantine on the harbour.

So far the lead had been taken by the only two medical men in the town with any degree of independence and sufficient experience and knowledge. James Kell the garrison doctor had dreamt this nightmare once before — on the island of Mauritius when he had been garrison doctor. William Reid Clanny, on the other hand, made up for a lack of specific experience with a wealth of theoretical knowledge. The chief physician at the Infirmary, he already possessed developed views as to the causes of cholera believing that it was due to atmospheric disturbances producing a gaseous miasma and the resultant "hyper-anthraxis".

The problem was that cholera was no longer an academic medical problem. The local business community and the coal trade especially felt themselves threatened by the quarantine. Since there was no inland quarantine anyway the government action seemed inconsistent. Apart from

The 12-year old Isabella Hazard, the famous "blue girl". This sketch was originally published in the *Lancet*.

anything else the new disease in its milder forms could be compared to other zymotic diseases. It was very debateable whether this was really the dreaded "Asiatic Cholera" or just commonplace old "English Cholera" born from the stench of backyard filth. If it was this latter there was no point in quarantine which would probably just lead to more unemployment and poverty.

This explains the discovery revealed to all on the 10th November by the Sunderland Select Vestry that ". . . the Town of Sunderland is now in a more healthy state than has been usual in the Autumnal Season . . .!" so that the pernicious quarantine operated enthusiastically by a young naval officer was a waste of time. The next day local businessmen at a meeting in the Exchange Building attacked the letter of the 1st November as a "most wicked and malicious falsehood" and they insisted that transmission of such ill informed communications without consultation with the leading members of the community must cease.

Easily pulled into line by the representatives of that class which paid their fees the doctors met on the 11th November and recanted. Of course this put Clanny into a very difficult position. He was accused of duplicity although not in fact involved in the vote of the doctors and very concerned that the prevailing view should not obstruct proper remedial action. His own theories as to the cause of cholera also meant that he could see little value in the quarantine. The result was that on the 12th November he was able to draw the leading physicians and surgeons to agree to a compromise declaration that the disease was present but had not been "imported", that it was caused by environmental and dietary factors and that anything retarding the trade of the town would only make matters worse.

The disease raged on throughout November and December. A total of 418 cases were diagnosed and there were 215 deaths. Special ground was set aside in an extension of Bishopwearmouth's burial ground on Hind Street near the Infirmary for the burial of the victims. The magistrates took steps to regulate the communications between Sunderland and the surrounding towns and, with a somewhat exaggerated view of medical capacities, to encourage patients to allow themselves to be removed to

Cholera Morbus!

NOTICE.

REPORT OF THE VISITORS the Townships of Bishop-Wearmouth and Panns.

ÆSCULAPI.. Sunderland SELECT VESTRY.

CAUTION FROM THE SUNDERLAND Board of Health.

hospital for treatment. By January however the disease had been loosed into South Shields, Newcastle and Gateshead. Interestingly the barracks, although in the midst of the stricken area, suffered no victims at all. Dr. Kell attributed this to the closure of the gates from the 1st November and the implementation of a firm quarantine.

The effect of the affair was that Sunderland appeared in a very bad light. The *London Medical Gazette* remarked:

> The good people of Sunderland appear in no very favourable light, it seems very clear that the public safety is in their estimation a very secondary object when brought into competition with the sale of coals.

In fact given all of the circumstances of the time the local reaction is less worthy of the opprobrium which the event attracted and when set against the panic responses to novel diseases in this century it is almost understandable.

Sunderland's Infirmary, built by private subscription in 1822. Dr Clanny worked here. It was replaced by the new infirmary on New Durham Road in 1867. Photo dated c. 1870s, at which time the old infirmary housed a Primitive Methodist Theological Institution. It was later used as a PM chapel and a Roman Catholic School, and is now leased by Sunderland Polytechnic. The building as it stands today is different in a good many details from this photograph.

to reduce charges from 10s.0d. to 6s.8d. per thousand cubic feet, and from £10 to £5 per street pillar lamp. Moore maintained that these charges were still excessive, and moreover that the quality of the gas was poor, a charge flatly denied by the Company. The Corporation proceeded to set up its own Gas Company, which purchased the works of the small Monkwearmouth Subscription Gas Company.

There followed a war of words in the Council and its committees, in the local press, and by poster and pamphlet. Kidson, Jonassohn, Charles Taylor (Clerk to the Bishopwearmouth Commissioners) and 'Royal' Coates (the Gas Company's secretary and manager) were singled out as targets for criticism and ridicule; respected people like Spoor and Clanny, equally opposed to the Council's moves, were let off more lightly. A local versifier, William Chapel ('Peter Flint')

made his contributions in pamphlet form: *Gasocracy: A Tale of Smoke* in 1845 was followed by *Waterocracy: a Tale of Fire* in the following year. Both humour and verse were somewhat laboured; *Gasocracy* showed Company directors panicking over the effect of Corporation competition on the price of gas; *Waterocracy* had Jonassohn complaining, in execrable mockery of a German-Jewish accent, of reforming doctors who

Vant de fountains for to play
An vash mine tirt an filth avay;
Him ruin de ould cumpanee
An make de shares cum down, ye see.

The Commissioners and the old companies were doubtless equally rude about their opponents, but they were less well supported in print. However they sought to appeal to ratepayer opinion through public meetings and rally support against Council pretensions. As the Herald, firmly on the side of 'reform', loftily remarked, their meetings were attended by many with no real financial stake in the

controversy, by "the labouring classes ... blacksmiths and shoemakers ... men not at all interested in the welfare of Sunderland".[23] The 'shopocracy' had no doubts as to where its interest lay.

By 1846 there was a sympathetic Liberal government which accepted the Corporation's gas and water bills, despite opposition in committee from Taylor and J. J. Wright for the Commissioners. The new companies were naturally closely linked with the Council. Four councillors (Wright, Muschamp, Hills, and Richardson) appeared on both boards (of 11 and 12 members respectively), while Moore chaired the Gas Company and Andrew White the new Water Company.

While the Corporation-backed Water Company was able to take over the assets and equipment of the former Bishopwearmouth Water Company, the Gas Company faced a stiffer fight, and there was no amalgamation until 1854. The Commissioners naturally rejected the new Company's tenders for public lighting and refused it permission to lay pipes in the streets or to use existing mains for its gas. This brought to a head the long-standing rivalry of the two main claimants to exercise local authority. The Corporation's response was to apply for an Act to enhance its own powers, and the Commissioners promptly retaliated by doing precisely the same. Each side argued that the general problems of poverty and squalor, as well as the specific issue of street lighting, could only be handled by a strong authority enjoying public confidence. The Council claimed popular support, the Commissioners that of responsible property owners. The one sought to reassure potential ratepayers of its moderation, the other claimed to represent respectable folk who feared punitive rate demands.

1851 AND AFTER

The inspectors, or "Surveying Officers" (Rawlinson and Hosking) who duly investigated the rival claims in January 1847 agreed that the only way to deal with Sunderland's many problems — the filthy and ill-lit streets, the stinking drains, untidy ashpits and middensteads, the generally inadequate local services — was to set up a single local authority. "The streets of a town", they concluded, "cannot be maintained ... in a proper condition when there are other bodies, in the various capacities of Commissioners of Highways, Commissioners of Sewers, Gas Companies and Water Companies ... who may and must be at liberty, when it is required, to break up pavements and open the streets. If all such matters were placed under the same executive authorship, things which might be necessary to be done to any of the works might be done at the same time, in the same place, and not at the same time in several places".[24] Perhaps they were being unduly optimistic.

The inspectors opted for the Corporation. Before anything was done Robert Rawlinson arrived as emissary of the Board of Health. His enquiry was necessary both because the Health of Towns party was clamouring for it, and because Sunderland's death rate was substantially above the 23 per 1,000 set up by government as the acceptable limit. Rawlinson's own report,[25] taken in conjunction with the earlier one, formed the basis for the 1851 Borough of Sunderland Act (14 & 15 Vic. cap lxvii), which brought all strands of local government into the hands of the Corporation and greatly extended its powers.

The 1851 Act was followed by the first official moves to improve the quality of life for Sunderland's less affluent residents, though it needed a further act of 1867 before the Council was empowered to demolish slum property and start on a more spacious rebuilding of the streets and houses in the east end. One urgent requirement was to build an adequate network of sewers and drains. The inspectors of 1847 had pointed out that "Sunderland was wholly unsewered", in the sense that it had no

in Hendon Road in April 1851, designed by Thomas Oliver with 12 warm and cold baths, four shower baths, two vapour baths, and a spacious wash-house and drying-room. Before the end of the year more than 15,000 people had used the baths.[28] Crozier designed a similar but rather smaller set of baths for Monkwearmouth, opened in February 1854. Further baths were proposed for the former workhouse site at the end of High Street West in 1856, and before these were completed it was agreed to include a swimming bath; they were opened in March 1859.[29]

The Public Health Report also brought Sunderland its first public park. Already close-packed and airless, the town was in process of swallowing such stretches of open country as remained around it, notably the Hendon Valley Gardens, known romantically as the Valleys of Love. By the 1850s streets and housing were extending over this area. The open ground

The corporation water works on Humbledon Hill. c.1855.

"subterranean conduits for the removal . . . of such fluids and matters soluble in water as are, or soon become, offensive to sight and sound". As for such scattered drains as did exist, "in dry weather they stink", remarked the inspectors.[26] It was not until 1855 that the Council really got down to the problem. In October of that year the Corporation Engineer, William Crozier, came up with a comprehensive scheme for 55½ miles of drains, drawing together all existing systems and providing new culverts and tunnels in various dimensions; the cost was estimated at £83,802. After some debate his plans were adopted, and the new system was built over the next six years.[27] As the town continued to expand, further expenditure was frequently needed — another £25,000 was proposed in 1878; but the sewerage installed after 1855, coupled with the much improved water supply, gave the town the system it needed.

Another step was taken in the provision of baths and wash-houses. The first was opened

around Building Hill was also under some threat, and the Mowbray estate (with Hill House itself) seemed about to be carved up. Burdon Road had been cut through the hill in 1836-40 to provide direct access from the Ryhope Road to Fawcett Street and the Wear Bridge. The northern end of Building Hill was acquired by George Hudson's railway companies in the 1840s as a site for the Penshaw line, linking with the new south dock. The Hill's limestone had long been available to townspeople as of right; it served as their principal building material, though its coarse texture made it useless for more elegant buildings.

From 1844 the Corporation had been half-heartedly negotiating to purchase what was left from the Mowbrays. The existence of common quarry rights was one factor delaying completion of the deal, and only the Report and the 1851 Act revived the proposal. In 1852 the Corporation agreed on purchase of the Mowbray land for £2,000 (to which government contributed £750), and the deal was concluded by 1854. The quarry floor was elegantly landscaped, planted with trees and criss-crossed by winding gravel paths. Edward Backhouse came forward with a grandiose plan to build a 'crystal palace' in the new park, with winter gardens, school of design, museum, concert hall, meeting room, bazaar and exhibition. It was to cost £7,000, and although much of this was speedily subscribed, the scheme fell through. Without this addition, Mowbray Park was opened to the public amid great rejoicing in 1857. Nine years later the ground to the north, up to Borough Road, was purchased from the North-East Railway and linked to the original park by an iron bridge over the railway cutting. In this extension the Corporation proposed to build itself a Town Hall, but the scheme ran into legal difficulties and the Council settled instead for the Museum and Art Gallery, opened in 1879. Mowbray Park became a popular and respected town centre playground, adorned with statues commemorating local worthies.

THE POOR

Just as these developments were making conditions pleasanter and healthier for town dwellers, the work of those responsible for the town's poor reached its own culmination: in 1855 the Board of Guardians opened the new Union Workhouse in Hylton Road, The

Guardians had come into existence in the same year as the Borough Corporation (under the Poor Law Amendment Act of 1834), and they had inherited a complex situation.

For two centuries each parish had cared for those who, through age, illness or misfortune were unable to fend for themselves. Almshouses sustained by local charity supplemented their efforts. In general, Sunderland's workforce was employed in fairly lucrative occupations: a coal-heaver, at the end of the 18th century, could earn £30 to £50 a year, according to Sir Francis Eden,[30] a sailor from £40 to £100. For those who were past employment, there was support from the rates; in Eden's time (1797) for 279 families; 176 others, mostly old women and prostitutes but including 36 children, were housed in the workhouse. Built on the Town Moor in 1740, Sunderland workhouse was "in a very good situation. Each apartment has four or five beds with wooden bottoms, and are filled with chaff. Each bed has two blankets, one sheet and rug".[31] Bishopwearmouth's workhouse, built at the west end of High Street in 1827, though much newer when the new Board of Guardians took it over, was nevertheless found to be damp, crowded, ill-furnished and lacking in adequate provision for, among others, the feeble-minded.

But apart from the usual poor supported from the parish rates, Sunderland had a special problem. It was burdened with many discharged and exhausted seamen, and with roughly three times as many widows or orphans of lost and dead seamen. By the middle of the nineteenth century relief had to be provided for an average of 800 widows, 800 orphans and other children, and 300 worn out, disabled or temporarily unemployed seamen.[32] Many were supported by the Muster Roll Charity, whereby since the reign of George II seamen (or, in Sunderland, their employers) had contributed 6d. a month from their pay to assist their less fortunate fellows; [33] and this provided for almshouses at the

The old Sunderland workhouse of 1740 (left), and the Donnison Charity School on Church Walk, in the east end.

Assembly Garth, supplemented from 1840 by further accommodation in the Trafalgar Square Almshouses, built in the garden of the old workhouse. In Bishopwearmouth, the Maritime Institution near Crowtree Lane catered for the widows and unmarried daughters of master mariners. These provisions proved inadequate as the numbers of Sunderland seamen (and consequently those of widows and orphans left by a notoriously hazardous occupation) grew rapidly. In 1791 an Act (31 Geo III) set up commissioners to levy payments from all ships registered in and trading from the port of Sunderland, at ½d. per ton burthen per voyage, or 2d. per ton annually. Another measure in the following year provided similarly for the support of the Wear skippers and keelmen, levying ½d. per chaldron on their coals and proposing a hospital such as the Tyne keelmen already had.

The new boards of guardians elected all over the country after 1834 were widely regarded at the time with suspicion and resentment. The Act itself had resulted from a noisy propaganda campaign, and those carrying out its provisions faced a similar campaign. But in the North generally the new guardians and their workhouses were accepted as an improvement on previous confusion and inefficiency. In Sunderland, as elsewhere, most of those newly elected had served in a similar capacity under the old parish councils; while existing poor law officials were given posts under the new Board. Most guardians, too, were already borough councillors, and the mayor, Andrew White, also became chairman of the Board. There was in fact no noticeable change of personnel or policy,[34] and the speed with which the new men were elected argues, P. A. Wood suggests, a considerable degree of preliminary agreement.

The new Board of Guardians in due course set about providing more adequate workhouse accommodation for the poor of the eleven parishes now linked in the Sunderland union. They sought a site just out of the town, on Hylton Road, and in 1855 opened their new building. It was designed by J. E. Oates of York, on similar lines to the other 'bastilles' rising all over the country, with accommodation for some 500 inmates in separate men's and women's wards; there was room for up to 33 able-bodied, 225 aged and infirm, four married couples, 119 children, 45 idiots, 30 lying-in, 70 sick and infectious and 12 vagrants.[35]

The new workhouse was under some pressure, particularly because of the influx of Irish and Scots then at its peak, which caused the guardians much concern. In 1853 they appointed a Removal Officer, who was able to get rid of some 80 persons a year by returning them to their homelands. By 1857 there was already a scandal over dirty and verminous conditions in the new workhouse, for the Guardians remained highly vulnerable to public concern over their activities.

Through the later decades of the century, the workhouse buildings between Hylton and Chester Roads were continually added to, as hospital and educational provision became more elaborate. By the mid-twentieth century (when it had become the General Hospital) the original buildings of 1855 were completely swamped amid later accretions; and in 1971 they were demolished to make way for the massive central block of the District General Hospital.

Periodically, harsh weather or trade depression added to the problems of poverty, and on such occasions mayor and corporation

The 'Trafalgar Square' almshouses on Church Walk (1840), for aged Sunderland seamen, and their wives and widows.

joined with public-spirited nobility, gentry and townsfolk to organise the relief of distress. Soup kitchens provided some help in times of distress from the winter of 1875; in December, 1878, when a sharp decline struck commerce and shipbuilding and unemployment soared, an emergency committee soon set up soup kitchens again, which provided bread and soup for 1,700 people south of the river and 700 in Monkwearmouth; in addition, 'cocoa rooms' ladled out hot drinks and bread for hungry children, while coal, groceries, and 560 pairs of children's clogs were distributed to the needy.[36]

WORSENING CONDITIONS

Efforts to relieve poverty made no difference to the atrociously crowded conditions of the east end. The local press, and such outspoken citizens as alderman James Williams, from time to time reminded Sunderland of its problems; but it took another outbreak of cholera, on top of endemic typhus and smallpox, to produce action. The cholera returned briefly in 1866, and brought the setting up of a joint committee by the Guardians and the Corporation, which received a forceful report from their medical officer reiterating the well-known problems: "the lanes of the infected district are too closely built to permit human health . . . faults of construction . . . appalling nuisances . . . to

grapple with the evil . . . sweep away entirely the two blocks of lanes west and east of Church Street . . . and rebuild on ordinary sanitary principles model dwellings for the poor. I do not doubt that such a scheme would repay both capital and interest in thirty years".[37] Somewhat hurt by Dr. Evans' assertion that such steps were of more importance than the new extension park on which they were spending so much money and effort, the joint committee and the Council devised schemes for purchase, demolition and road-building to open up the east end.

So came about the Sunderland Extension and Improvement Act of 1867, which authorised the building of new streets, giving powers of compulsory purchase to "erect improved Dwelling Houses for Mechanics, Labourers and other Persons of the Working and Poorer classes . . . with proper Conveniences", to rent or sell. The streets and buildings authorised were to set very different standards from the lanes they replaced: streets were to be 30 feet (for single-storey houses) or 35 feet wide, rooms to be nine or ten feet high. Though the far-reaching demolition and rebuilding envisaged in some plans did not take place, and no fine new avenue thrust its way into the slums, one street did emerge, the modestly pleasant James Williams Street. Much of one side was occupied by houses very suitable for prosperous and respectable artisans. Further slum demolition and street widening took place north of the river, where the Irish-occupied John Street was replaced by a new wide road linking Broad Street (the sometime Monkwearmouth village green) with North Bridge Street at the Wheatsheaf.

By this time, in fact, many artisans tended to move outwards, to the new estates appearing

James Williams Street, laid out in the early 1870s as part of a proposed east end improvement scheme and named after the notable Sunderland reformer. The chapel (1878) was built for the members of one of the Christian Lay Churches (Independent Methodists) who seceded from the Primitive Methodists in 1877.

on the town's outskirts. On either side of Chester Road, north of Roker Avenue, and east of the railway between Hendon and Grangetown, there appeared rectilinear grids of streets, all laid out around 1880. These were lined with the typical Sunderland cottages, the usual local housing type for skilled workmen and lower middle classes of the town.

The rebuilding of 1868-73 that produced Roker Avenue and James Williams Street did not, of course, solve the problem of the east end slums. It initiated a cyclical pattern of building, deterioration, scandal and concern, followed by fresh rebuilding that continued over thirty-year periods into the latter half of the twentieth century. In 1891 the Council began the protracted process of clearing away such notorious slums as the Hat Case to provide new flats for the poor — "Sunderland's first Council housing".[38] But before the scheme was really off the ground two fresh reports drew attention once more to the problems of the east end slums. These resulted from the concern of the Rev. T. Nicholson, vicar of St. John's parish, and of Bishop Westcott who, in 1892, had spoken out at St. John's annual parish tea on the pitiably overcrowded homes of the parish.[39] The vicar and his colleagues duly produced a report covering both the architectural problems of his church and the social shortcomings of the parish, appealing for funds to help deal with them. At the same time a commission (made up of equal numbers of clergy and laymen) was set up by the ruridecanal conference to produce a wide-ranging report on the east end as a whole.[40] They produced some appalling statistics and observations. The east end death rate was 30.3 per thousand compared with 21.2 in the rest of the borough. Worse was an infant mortality rate of 239.2 compared with 168.3 elsewhere, and 150 in the large towns of England generally.[41] Both reports were outspoken about the depressing surroundings of the slums, blaming them for the moral short-comings of parishioners. Homes had degenerated into tenements, houses were built back to back, yards were so covered in buildings "as seriously to interfere with the ventilation and lighting of the dreary dwellings, and to make the provision of needful sanitary conveniences a practical impossibility".[42] A block of five houses in Maling's Rigg had 20 families of 83 people living in 24 rooms; another of ten had 166 in 62 rooms. Squalid common lodging houses persisted; in 1894 more than half of the 843 cases sent to the workhouse hospital were tramps. There were still 144 public houses in the area, and boys and girls drank copiously long before they reached adulthood. Gambling was rife; 90 per cent of the impoverished residents could still afford to bet on horses, and even children risked their pennies; calculating the odds, the commissioners thought, might be good for their mathematics if for nothing else. A large number of pawn-shops and 51 brothels added to local colour. Petty crime flourished; one person in 22 was convicted for some offence in 1894, the vast majority for drunkenness but 37 for assaults

on the police. In general, the East End Commissioners concluded, the condition of the people was worse than it had been a quarter of a century earlier; and they were particularly concerned about the children: generous and obedient, perhaps, but led by home influences into lying, foul language, brawling, thriftlessness, idleness, drink, dirt and untidiness.

Poverty and squalor, depravity and ignorance, did not necessarily mean that the east end was an unhappy place. On the contrary, outsiders and residents alike felt that its inhabitants for the most part enjoyed life; there was a strong sense of communal loyalty and good neighbourliness; they worked and played hard, and looked to the future with cheerful optimism. But there were already disquieting hints that the industrial growth that had borne Sunderland along so buoyantly for a century and more was at last coming to an end. Some of the town's old-established industries were already in decline. By 1907, when a sharp slump hit trade and shipyards, even those employed in the town's major industries faced an uncertain future. The twentieth century virtually eliminated the grinding poverty so familiar in Victorian Sunderland; but it also destroyed the steady growth in prosperity that was the town's other characteristic feature.

REFERENCES:
1. L. Irving, Henry Irving (1951) p.79.
2. A. B. Granville, The Spas of England and Principal Sea-Bathing Places (1841) p.266.
3. Ibid., p.268.
4. Chambers' Edinburgh Journal, 30 March, 1850, p.193.
5. Ibid., p.196.
6. John Murray, Handbook for Travellers in Durham and Northumberland (1864) p.124.
7. R. Rawlinson Report to the General Board of Health on . . . the Sanitary Condition of the Borough of Sunderland (1851) p.22.

8. W. R. Clanny, *Hyperanthraxis, or the Cholera in Sunderland* (1832); J. B. Kell, *On the Appearance of Cholera at Sunderland in 1831* (1834); T. W. Ede, 'Cholera in Sunderland in 1831', in *Bulletin 13, DCLHS* (1970) pp.22-41. A Heesom 'This Unpleasant Affair ... Lord Londonderry and Cholera in Sunderland 1831-32' in *Bulletin 30, DCLHS* (1983).

9. Quoted in N. Longmate, *King Cholera* (1966).

10. Rawlinson, *op.cit.*, p.18.

11. R. C. Fox, *The Demography of Sunderland 1851*, (1980).

12. Sir F. M. Eden, *The State of the Poor* (1797) p.185.

13. Fox *op.cit.*, p.6.

14. Fordyce, II p.527.

15. Rawlinson *op.cit.* p.84.

16. *Ibid.*, p.82.

17. *Ibid.*, pp.34-35.

18. Census Enumerators' Returns, 1851.

19. G. Patterson, *Monkwearmouth Colliery in 1851* (1977).

20. Census Enumerators' Returns, 1851.

21. G. Bennett Gibbs 'The Early History of Sunderland's Water Supplies' in *Antiq. Sund.*, XII (1911).

22. Rawlinson *op.cit.*, p.46.

23. *SH*, 10 Jan., 1845.

24. *Report . . . of the Surveying Officers appointed under the Sunderland Improvement Acts* (J. J. Rawlinson and W. Hosking) (1847) p.xx

25. Rawlinson *op.cit.*

26. *Report . . . op.cit.*, p.xii.

27. Fordyce II, p.420; *SH*, 5 October, 1855.

28. Fordyce, II p.479; *S. Herald*, 28 March, 25 April, 1851.

29. *SH*, 15 Feb, 1856, 15 Jan, 1858, 7 May, 1858, March 1859.

30. Sir F. M. Eden, *op.cit.*, pp.185-187.

31. *Ibid.*

32. B. Morton 'The History of the Assembly Garth and Trafalgar Square Merchant Seamen's Homes' in *Ant. Sund.* VI (1905, reprinted separately 1951) p.8.

33. *op. cit.* p.5.

34. P. A. Wood *The Activities of the Sunderland Poor Law Union 1834-1930*, Newcastle M. Litt. Thesis (1975). See also P. A. Wood, 'Finance and the Urban Poor Law: Sunderland Union 1836-1914' in M. E. Rose (ed) *The Poor and the City: the English Poor Law in its urban context* (1985).

35. *Ibid.*

36. *SH*, 21 Dec. 1878.

37. *SH*, 28 Sept, 1866.

38. G. Patterson 'Harrison's Buildings — Sunderland's first council housing' in *Sunderland's History*, 3 (1985) pp.4-33.

39. *The East End of Sunderland. St. John's Parish: its work and its limitations* (1896) p.9.

40. *Report of the East End Commission of the Rural Deanery of Wearmouth* (1896)

41. *Ibid.*, pp.6-7.

42. *The East End . . . op.cit.;*, p.11.

Local Government 1810-1851

When the setting up of a municipal corporation for Sunderland was proposed in 1835, a local newspaper, the liberal *Sunderland Herald*, threw its influence behind the cause, and, in a leader, claimed that "Sunderland is, and has long been, an overgrown family without a head to direct and govern it".[1] The family referred to was the group of five separate townships which had become known, collectively, as Sunderland. The township of Sunderland, which gave its name to the whole, was a mere 120 acres on the south bank of the Wear, bounded on the east by the sea, on the west by Russell Street and Sans Street and on the south by Coronation Street. Bishopwearmouth Panns, even smaller (6 acres), also lay on the river bank. The much larger Bishopwearmouth was centred on the built-up area around St. Michael's church and included Pallion on the west, reached the Grindon Mill at its southwest point and contained Barnes, Bainbridge Holme and the Hendon Burn within its southern boundary. On the north side of the river lay the built-up township of Monkwearmouth Shore and the more rural Monkwearmouth. Southwick, included in the Parliamentary Borough of Sunderland by the 1832 Reform Act was not to join the municipal 'family' until 1928.

The family had grown in two senses. The population of the area included in the municipal borough more than doubled from 24,500 to 51,500 between 1801 and 1841, and in the next ten years was to increase by a further 12,500. The built-up area had grown too, so that by 1835 Sunderland and Bishopwearmouth, which not long before had been "two distinct towns separated by a considerable distance",[2] formed one town. This growth, and the immense problems which came with it, had seen the family outgrow the myriad organs of local government which had accumulated over the years.

The townships were sub-divisions of the ancient parishes of Bishopwearmouth and Monkwearmouth. The ratepayers of these parishes would periodically elect vestries, committees of respectable inhabitants, who would attend to the affairs of the church and also, until the mid-1830s, exercise administrative functions such as the appointment of overseers of the poor, constables and scavengers.

In 1719 an Act of Parliament removed the township of Sunderland from Bishopwearmouth and made it a parish in its own right; it was said to contain six thousand souls, and upwards. The Act directed that the inhabitants contributing to parish funds "shall chuse 24 substantial and creditable inhabitants"[3], with freehold property of £10 annual value, to be vestry-men for the parish for periods of three years. The vestry was to impose a rate on the parishioners in order to provide for the upkeep of the church, pay the rector a stipend of £80, the parish clerk a salary of £10, and the scavenger "a competent sum yearly". Churchwardens, overseers of the poor and other parish officers were to be appointed. The minute books of Sunderland parish vestry show that the fire engines were under their control and that later they appointed inspectors of butcher's meat and fish, and of weights and measures. They also appointed constables of the watch, church constables and constables to examine lodging houses. By 1837 Sunderland parish had 26 constables and Bishopwearmouth 19, but in the following year, when the borough police force had been formed, each parish appointed only eight constables.

The Poor Relief Act of 1819, also known as the Select Vestries Act, was adopted in Sunderland in that same year. A 'select vestry' was established consisting of 12 respectable householders chosen out of the 24 and charged with managing the concerns of the poor. Later the select vestry was increased to 20 members, appointed annually by public meeting. It continued in existence until 1836 in which year the administration of poor relief for the whole of the parishes of Sunderland, Bishopwearmouth (except Burdon township) and Monkwearmouth was placed under the control of the Board of Guardians for the Sunderland Poor Law Union.

The townships, as well as the parishes,

Seats for parochial officers in a special pew at the west end of Sunderland parish church.

appointed officers. Monkwearmouth township's minutes record the appointment of overseers of the poor, constables and surveyors of highways "at a meeting of the ratepayers . . . in vestry assembled". The overseers of the poor were, according to one authority, "the principal executive servants of the vestry"[4] and had a number of functions including the preparation of rating valuation lists, the registration of electors, the making of jury lists and the responsibility for summoning certain vestry meetings.

Until the appointment of borough magistrates under the provisions of the Municipal Corporations Act of 1835, county magistrates dispensed justice at the Sunderland Petty Sessions. The county rate paid by Sunderland ratepayers (almost £700 for the five townships for 1833) helped maintain the county gaol and its inmates. The county was put to no expense in maintaining bridges and their approach roads in Sunderland, as the Wearmouth Bridge was, until 1851, the responsibility of the Bridge Commissioners. Until the establishment of the borough fund under the 1835 Municipal Corporations Act, fines for summary convictions were paid to the county treasurer. It was reported that only in the cases of Sunderland and Durham petty sessions did the fines actually paid over to the county agree with the amounts due to be paid. The county authorities complained that the overseers of the poor (who were responsible for paying over the fines) were "a numerous and fluctuating body . . . nearly out of the reach of wholesome supervision".[5] It was suspected that in some cases the fines had been diverted to local funds for poor relief.

IMPROVEMENT COMMISSIONERS

The inadequacy of the traditional organs of local government in dealing with the problems arising from increasing population led to the passing, from the later eighteenth century, of hundreds of local acts of parliament establishing bodies of improvement commissioners. Two such acts were passed (not without local opposition) in 1810, one for Sunderland Parish and the other for the townships of Bishopwearmouth and Bishopwearmouth Panns. These acts were obtained on the initiative of local people and provided in the case of Bishopwearmouth for lighting, watching and cleansing and paving of footpaths; in Sunderland for paving, lighting, watching and cleansing, the building of a town hall or market house, and the establishment of a watch on the River Wear. The powers of the Sunderland commissioners were increased by an amending act in 1826.

The idea of bodies of private citizens, unelected and self-perpetuating, being responsible for duties undertaken today by local councils and paid officials, may seem strange. In the early nineteenth century however, "local government" (the phrase itself was new then) was perceived as being to do with keeping the King's Peace rather than with public health and sanitation. The idea that a municipal council should concern itself with the provision of a system of sewerage and drainage was novel. The job could perfectly well be carried out by public spirited private citizens — improvement commissioners. There is an interesting parallel with the debate taking place today as to which services are appropriate to be provided by the public and private sectors.

Each of the acts referred to above named more than 100 commissioners to put its provisions into effect. Commissioners who had died were from time to time replaced by the nominees of those remaining. Only a fraction of the total number were active. In Bishopwearmouth no more than about 20 and often only eight commissioners attended meetings in the 1840s when important developments were projected.

The Sunderland Act of 1826 permitted the levying of a rate of 2/6d (12½p) in the pound to pay for its purposes, while the act for Bishopwearmouth allowed only one shilling (5p) in the pound. An alleged defect in the drafting of the latter act meant that owners of property in some parts of the township were able to avoid paying the rate at all, while others, where street lighting was provided, paid only sixpence (2½p) in the pound. The commissioners claimed to have no jurisdiction in the streets omitted from the act and in the new streets formed after the act was passed, although this view was disputed by William Snowball, the town clerk appointed in 1848.

The commissioners ceased to appoint watchmen when the borough police force was established in 1837. These watchmen had a poor reputation as law enforcers. The mayor, Richard Spoor, spoke contemptuously of them in 1838, describing how, when a disturbance had broken out during the county election, only two watchmen could be found who were not drunk.[6] These two were later to become inspectors in the borough police.

Both the Bishopwearmouth and Sunderland Commissioners were strongly criticised for the inadequacy of the lighting they provided in their respective townships. The borough police

BISHOPWEARMOUTH
SELECT VESTRY.

A

Meeting

Of the Inhabitants of the Township of Bishopwearmouth, who pay Poor Rates, will be held at the Vestry Room,

On Thursday next, the 15th instant,

AT TEN O'CLOCK IN THE FORENOON,

for the Purpose of appointing a Select Vestry for the ensuing Year, for the Management of the Poor ; and when a Statement of the Accounts of the late Overseers will be laid before the Meeting.

JOSEPH TREWICK,

Clerk to the Vestry.

9th of April, 1824.

complained of it and the government surveying officers of 1847 said "it was most disgracefully neglected".[7] At that time oil lamps were still used in parts of Sunderland parish. The police complained that "they do not give a particle of light"[8] while the surveying officers described them as "begrimed with soot and almost as filthy as the streets themselves".[9] Not all the Bishopwearmouth streets were lighted and such lamps as there were were not lit throughout the hours of darkness. There were insufficient lamp-lighters and it took more than an hour to light the lamps. The surveying officers J. J. Rawlinson and William Hosking, appointed in 1847 to report on the proposed new Improvement Act, condemned the 'niggardliness' of the lighting after sunset and the early extinction of the lights.[10]

The Sunderland Commissioners had built a market in 1830 which by 1847 had vacant stalls, suffered from a falling-off in rents, and was said by its users to be too small and so inconveniently laid out that it had been necessary to employ a man to prevent quarrels and fighting.[11] The construction of the market had cost £11,000 and had saddled the Commissioners with a huge debt which by 1849 had not been reduced. The rents received from the market covered the interest on the debt with a surplus of £200 a year if no account was taken of the cost of maintaining the fabric of the market.

The Commissioners complained that they did not have sufficient income to carry out their functions. They had nonetheless expended substantial amounts from their funds in unsuccessfully opposing legislation intended to improve gas and water supplies in the town, and Rawlinson and Hosking concluded that they had generally failed to exercise their responsibilities properly.[12] No Improvement Act existed for the townships of Monkwearmouth and Monkwearmouth Shore, but the ratepayers had chosen in 1833 to adopt the General Lighting Act passed in that year and lighting inspectors were appointed in each township.

The shape of local administration in Sunderland was changed in 1835 by the passing of two measures, the Municipal Corporations Act and the Highways Act.

THE BOROUGH REBORN
1835-1837

It was through the passing of the Municipal Corporations Act that Sunderland, almost by accident, became a borough. Two earlier attempts to incorporate the town had been made long before. The Port of Wearmouth (Sunderland as it was to become) had been raised to borough status by a late twelfth century charter of Hugh du Puiset, Bishop of Durham. In course of time this ancient borough decayed, but in 1634 Bishop Morton granted a new charter under which a mayor, alderman and common councilmen were appointed for the Borough of Sunderland. This attempt was shorter-lived than that of Bishop Puiset. After only a few years, perhaps because of the disruption caused by the Civil War, no new

mayor, aldermen or councillors were elected and the charter fell into disuse.

Throughout these attempts to establish an early corporation there survived in Sunderland, right up to the nineteenth century a body of men calling themselves "the freemen and stallingers of the Borough of Sunderland". They were sometimes described as an ancient corporation and claimed their foundation to have been centuries earlier, beyond the memory of man. They did not pretend to have any authority over the inhabitants of the borough, or claim any rights of local government. Their principal claim (often disputed by Sunderland people) was to property rights over the Town Moor.

Because of the existence of the charters and the ancient Corporation, the Municipal Corporations Commissioners visited Sunderland late in 1833. Since they could find nothing in the way of a municipal corporation their report was brief. They concluded that the incorporation of the Borough was obscure and questionable and that "the members of the Corporation (if it had one) do not exercise any jurisdiction or municipal authority".[13] However by the time the commissioners came to collate their reports on the different boroughs and had drafted a covering report for presentation to the Home Secretary, they had decided to include Sunderland in the list of corporations "possessing or exercising Municipal functions".[14]

When the Municipal Corporations Bill was in committee, David Barclay, one of the Members of Parliament for Sunderland discovered (as he afterwards stated) that Sunderland was named in a schedule as a borough to which the bill was to apply. Upon enquiring of the Attorney General as to whether it would be obligatory for the inhabitants of Sunderland to elect a mayor and councillors, Barclay was advised that this was the case. Not knowing the wishes of his constituents on this matter, he gave notice of his intention to move an additional clause to the bill which would have

NOTICE
Is hereby given,

THAT A PUBLIC

MEETING

Of the Parishioners paying Scot and Lot

WILL BE HELD IN THE

VESTRY-ROOM,

This Evening, at Six o'clock,

On very particular Business, relative to the late Overseers' Accounts, when it is requested that as many as have opportunity will attend.

Sunderland, Monday, Jan. 5th, 1824.

Printed by T. Hodge, 37, High Street, Sunderland.

Dr Gerald Wellesley, 1770-1848, brother of the Duke of Wellington, rector of Bishopwearmouth 1827-1848, and figurehead of the party opposed to the incorporation of Sunderland.

made its provisions non-obligatory for boroughs in a similar position to Sunderland. Still hearing nothing from his constituents and facing government displeasure at his proposed clause, Barclay let it drop.[15] The Municipal Corporations Act, naming Sunderland in its schedules, received the Royal Assent in September 1835.

The pro-liberal *Sunderland Herald* edited by Thomas Marwood junior was in favour of a municipal corporation being established in the town, and letters and editorials appeared in its columns pointing out the advantages of incorporation. A public meeting in support was held at the Exchange on 16 December 1835, chaired by Andrew White. A meeting was called to take place the next day by the opponents of the scheme, led by the Rev. G. V. Wellesley, rector of Bishopwearmouth. This too was held at the Exchange, but it was packed with the supporters of the municipal party so that Andrew White and not Wellesley was chosen to chair the meeting and resolutions were passed in favour of setting up a corporation.

Support for and opposition to the establishment of the corporation did not correspond with political party allegiances. Andrew White who led the municipal campaign and became mayor was a Whig and he was supported by Thomas Reed Junior, a Tory, who, as an alderman, was to be one of the most assiduous attenders of the new council and chairman of the important watch and finance committees. J. J. Wright, a prominent Tory party activist, opposed the campaign because he feared that a town council would lead to party political strife, and that it would be a cause of heavy expense. It is worth recalling at this point that owners of property in Sunderland at that time were already paying separate church and county rates, as well as rates for the maintenance of the poor, for the upkeep of the highways and, in some cases, for paving and lighting. The more substantial property owners were laying out large sums of money in rates, which, in some instances, under a system of

plural voting, gave them as many as six votes and corresponding influence. The Municipal Corporations Act gave only one vote to male ratepayers of three years standing, thus reducing the influence of the large ratepayers.

Supporters of incorporation argued that money could be saved because, if certain conditions were met, the borough would be exempt from the county rate. They hoped for better paving, lighting and street cleaning, an efficient police force and a degree of control over the appointment of magistrates to serve in the borough, complaining of "the capricious decisions" of some of the "eccentric and incompetent" county magistrates.[16] A town council was seen as a single effective voice for all classes and interests in the town, while the tradesmen hoped that a court for the recovery of small debts could be established under the provisions of the Municipal Corporations Act.

A practical difficulty arose concerning the election of a town council. There was no mayor to act as presiding officer as required by the Municipal Corporations Act. The opinion of the Attorney General was sought and he advised that Bernard Ogden, the senior freeman of the corporation of freemen and stallingers should officiate, or if he refused, the most senior freeman willing to act should do so. Bernard Ogden, an elderly man, did refuse, as did the next three freemen in order of seniority. The fifth freeman, Richard Spoor, a Tory, agreed to preside and the first election took place on 26 December 1835. Six councillors were elected for each of the seven wards of the borough: Monkwearmouth, West, Bishopwearmouth, Bridge, Sunderland, East and St. Michael's. Among those elected were Andrew White and his brother Richard, Dr. Clanny, Richard Spoor, freeman of the ancient borough, Thomas Reed junior, printer and Thomas Marwood junior, editor of the *Sunderland Herald*.

The new council met at the Arcade on 31 December, appointed the borough's first town clerk, J. P. Kidson, a lawyer, and elected two aldermen for each ward. They met again on New Year's Day 1836 and unanimously elected Andrew White mayor of the borough. At their third meeting on 6 January it was decided that the mayor and aldermen would each lend ten pounds and the councillors five pounds until rates could be collected. On 9 January 1836 another election took place to fill the vacancies caused by the aldermanic appointments.

Even in those early days it was clear that the opponents of the council were not going to accept its authority. Proceedings were begun in the Court of King's Bench, the case being founded upon the weakness earlier referred to, that there had been no mayor to act as presiding officer and also on the fact that there had been no town clerk to compile and distribute the electoral roll. (These latter tasks had been performed by George Stephenson, the solicitor to the corporation of freemen and stallingers.)

The opposition's case was so strong that it was decided that further legislation was required to legitimise Sunderland's corporation. This was brought into parliament early in 1836, but because the clauses relating to the standing of the presiding officer were in the

Andrew White thanks his electors. He received 132 votes from the 261 registered electors in Bishopwearmouth ward. He was also elected for West Ward but opted to represent Bishopwearmouth.

TO THE

Burgesses

OF

Bishopwearmouth Ward.

GENTLEMEN,

Having been elected, by your almost unanimous Suffrages, one of the Councillors of this Ward, I have to return you my most unfeigned Thanks, assuring you it is my Determination to use every means in my Power, to promote the Prosperity, of not only this Ward (in which I reside), but also the general Welfare of the Borough.

I am, Gentlemen,

Your very faithful Servant,

Andrew White.

Frederick Lodge, Dec. 29, 1835.

same bill as other controversial clauses relating to administration of charitable funds under the control of municipal councils, the bill did not pass in 1836. The necessary legislation was not enacted until after the death of William IV, receiving the Royal Assent from Queen Victoria on 17 July 1837.

THE BOROUGH'S EARLY YEARS

After prescribing the method of election of councils, authorising a borough rate and establishing a borough fund, the Act was almost exclusively concerned with the management of the borough police force and the administration of justice in the locality. Even the powers of street lighting were to facilitate the watching of the town rather than for the convenience of the public. The commissioners of local improvement acts were permitted by the Municipal Corporations Act to hand over their functions to the council, but were not required to and in Sunderland repeatedly refused to do so. Even these minimal powers could not be exercised in Sunderland until the Municipal Corporations Act was amended in July 1837.

The Council and its committees thereupon promptly set to work drafting byelaws and making plans for the establishment of a police force. William Brown, a senior police inspector from London, was appointed superintendent of the borough force at a salary of £120 a year. The report of the watch committee chaired by Alderman Thomas Reed was adopted. This recommended that the force should consist of two inspectors (to be paid 26 shillings [£1.30] per week), nine sergeants (£1.00 per week) and 41 constables (17 shillings [85p] per week). The entire cost of paying, equipping, clothing (allowing one great coat in two years) and accommodating the police force for the first year was estimated at £3,399 8s. 0d. To meet this, with the town clerk's salary of £200 and sundry other expenses, the Council ordered a rate of 10d (4p) in the pound. This followed hard upon a rate of 1/4d (6½p) in the pound

ordered by the Council to pay all the expenses incurred since 1835, amounting to £3,164. Of this approximately £2,500 had been spent in defending the Council against legal action. The Council's opponents applied again to the Court of Queen's Bench which ordered the £2,500 to be struck out of the Corporation's accounts. The Council ignored the Queen's Bench order and the opposition chose not to press their case any further.

The Corporation also had problems over the municipal boundary which was provisionally fixed by the Municipal Corporations Act to coincide with the parliamentary constituency boundary and included the whole of the townships of Southwick and Bishopwearmouth, as well as Sunderland parish. This meant that the owners of a considerable tract of agricultural land would have been liable to pay the borough rate. In the eyes of some Council members there was nothing wrong with this since the value of the land just beyond the built up area was enhanced by its proximity to the town, which provided a market for the farm produce. Furthermore the farmers had the use of the facilities of the town when they came to sell their produce. Nevertheless some of the landowners were induced to drop their opposition to the incorporation of the borough when the boundary on the south side of the River Wear was fixed along a radius of one mile from the centre of the Wearmouth Bridge (approximately as far as the Hendon Burn which runs through Backhouse Park). On the north side of the river, only the townships of Monkwearmouth and Monkwearmouth Shore were within the revised boundary. This boundary was temporarily determined by an act of parliament passed in August 1836.[17]

Late in 1837 a bill was brought into parliament which would have extended the boundaries of several municipal boroughs, including Sunderland. The bill was lost in the Commons on its second reading in March 1838. William Ettrick in a letter to his son Anthony a few days later must have expressed the feeling of many local landowners: "the villainous Bill is kick'd out — Huzza!".[18]

Andrew White 1792-1856, Sunderland's first mayor 1836-1837. (From the painting by William Bewick.)

The Exchange on High Street (built 1812-14), was used as the meeting place of the borough council for several years from 1836. (A late nineteenth century photograph, when the Exchange had become the home of the Seamen's Mission.)

Printing: Thomas Reed

Alderman Thomas Reed, VD, DL, JP in 1890.

There have been many printers in Sunderland, ranging from one man printing and bookselling businesses of the late eighteenth and early nineteenth centuries, through firms such as Vint and Carr, which also published newspapers, to Edward Thompson Ltd, the world's largest producers of bingo tickets in the 1980's. The firm of Thomas Reed stands out among the town's printing businesses because it has been run by one family from the earliest days of trade in the town, to the present day and has developed a world-wide reputation for its nautical publications.

Thomas Reed (1760-1840) was an apprentice of Roland Wetherald, Sunderland's first printer in 1762, before setting up his own business in High Street East in 1782. Sermons, schoolbooks, handbills and posters were the main output of the firm in its early years. The appearance of the *Steamship and Young Mariners Guide* in the 1830's marked the beginning of the firm's maritime business. This developed in 1834 with the first accurate *Tide Tables* for Sunderland and in 1850 Reed's became the first firm in the world to publish text books for the Board of Trade mariners' examinations. By the First World War, Reed's were producing many maritime technical publications, ranging from guides to electrical lighting in steamships and drawings of turbine engines, to stoker's guides to the firing and care of steam boilers.

Reed's Nautical Almanac, the Home Trade Merchant Navy and yachtsman's "Bible" first appeared in 1931, and was issued to all small craft for use on the 'D' day Normandy landings, and has become the largest publication of its' kind in the world.

Today the firm is best known for the *Almanac*, but this is only one of the many activities, which in addition to the maritime books, include magazines, decorative packaging and the organisation of international business conferences. Among Reed's books are two notable histories of Sunderland industries — *Where Ships are born* (1946), and the revised and extended *Sunderland Pottery* (1984).

The Works and offices were originally in High Street East. In 1879 they were moved to High Street West, and later they extended back into Nile Street with later additional new factories at Hendon, opened in 1961 and 1986.

TO THE

Rev. R. Gray, A.M.

Rector of Sunderland.

WE, the undersigned, request you will call a PUBLIC MEETING of the Inhabitants of Sunderland, paying Scot and Lot, at the Vestry-Room, on the 14th inst. to take into consideration the present state of the Poor of this Parish.

CALEB WILSON,
GEORGE BINNS,
S. WATSON,
THOS. REED,
JOHN WILSON,
RALPH DAUSON,
B. BRAY,
CLEMENT GOWLAND,
JOHN CAMERON.

Dec. 10th, 1831.

In compliance with the above Requisition, this is to give Notice, that a PUBLIC MEETING of the Inhabitants of the Parish of Sunderland, will be holden in the VESTRY of SUNDERLAND CHURCH, on WEDNESDAY next, the 14th inst. at 12 o'Clock at Noon.

Dec. 10th, 1831.

ROBERT GRAY,

RECTOR.

SUNDERLAND: PRINTED BY REED & SON.

NOTICE.

THE COMMISSIONERS under Sunderland Paving and Lighting Act, do hereby give Notice, that if any Person or Persons shall permit or suffer any

BULL DOG,

OR

Mastiff Dog,

to go at large *unmuzzled*, in the Streets, Lanes, Alleys, Public Ways, or Passages of the Parish of Sunderland, every such Person will be proceeded against, in manner directed by the said Act.

By Order of the Commissioners,

GEORGE WOOD,

Clerk.

Sunderland, November 22nd, 1822.

Sunderland; printed by Reed and Son, 183, High-Street

Sunderland

SELECT

VESTRY.

THE Select Vestry for the Parish of Sunderland, assembled at a Meeting this Evening, deem it a duty they owe to the Public, in the present excited state of Public Feeling, to declare that in their opinion, founded upon the Reports of the Forty-eight Gentlemen who have twice visited every house in this Parish, within the last three days, that the Town of Sunderland is now in a more healthy state than has been usual in the Autumnal Season; and that the information which appears to have been given to His Majesty's Most Honourable Privy Council, that the Indian Cholera exists in this Town, is not justified by the general Health of the Inhabitants.

ROBERT DIXON,

CHAIRMAN.

Sunderland, November 10th, 1831.

Sunderland; printed by Reed and Son, 183, High Street.

EMIGRATION

TO

CALIFORNIA.

THE FINE A 1. COPPERED BARQUE

JOHN HUTCHINSON

550 TONS BURTHEN,

John Hutchinson, Commander,

Will sail from Hartlepool direct for the Port of Panama, in the Pacific, in about Ten Days. There is direct communication between Panama and California.

This Vessel has excellent accommodation for Cabin and Steerage Passengers.

For Particulars apply to the Owner, MR. RALPH HUTCHINSON, at the Three Cranes' Wharf, Monkwearmouth; or to MESSRS. LUMSDON & BYERS, Brokers, Sunderland.

Sunderland, 17th February, 1849.

SUNDERLAND: PRINTED BY THOMAS REED & CO.

Borough of Sunderland.

The Watch Committee hereby give Notice that Mr. BROWN, the Superintendent of Police, will be ready to receive applications from such Persons as may be desirous of serving as

POLICE
Constables

For this Borough, on Wednesday next, the 18th instant, at the Station House, in Villiers Street.

No Person will be employed who is above 35 Years of Age, or under 5 feet 9 inches in height, and preference will be given to unmarried Men.

Certificates as to Character will be required, and the Parties must apply personally.

By Order,

KIDSON, Town-Clerk.

Oct. 12, 1837.

An advertisement regarding the appointment of Sunderland's first policemen, October 1837.

Police Station (left), Police Court and Mayor's Parlour/Municipal offices, in 1876. The Police Court was built by the corporation 1843-4 and was used for council meetings from then until the Town Hall was built on Fawcett Street in 1890. The buildings to the right and left of the Police Court were converted houses. These premises stood on West Wear Street, at the northern end of East Cross Street (off High Street).

The boundary of the borough was not to be extended until 1867, the first of a series of expansions, but the legitimacy of the Corporation was established beyond serious challenge by the Act of 1837. From its limited beginnings as little more than a police authority, the Council gained greater powers in the borough of Sunderland Act of 1851 and since then the responsibilities of the Council, like the boundary have steadily grown.

Robert Rawlinson, the government inspector who visited Sunderland in 1849 to enquire into the state of public health in the borough reported that "the Town Council have assumed all the powers with which the Municipal Corporations Act invests them".[19] The main responsibility, and that which consumed the bulk of the rate income, was of course the police establishment which was overseen by the watch committee. There was no municipal town hall with Council chamber and offices; a building in West Wear Street had been purchased and fitted out to serve as a police court and the Council met there. Offices had also been provided and equipped for the police. In 1846 one of the first municipal museums in the country was established in the

Athenaeum, on the produce of a special rate for the purpose of a halfpenny in the pound. The first investment in the area of public health was not made until 1850 when land was acquired in Hendon Road for the public baths and wash-houses which were opened in the following year.

Apart from these concerns the Council busied itself by petitioning parliament and debating motions on a variety of matters — income tax, 'papal aggression', repeal of the window tax, the postal services — and did what it could to spoil the chances of rival ports which threatened the trade of Sunderland.

The speed at which the Council could progress was hampered not only by the limits set by legislation and the intransigence of the Sunderland Improvement Commissioners but also by the economic recession of the early 1840s which limited the amount of rate the council felt able to impose. In the years 1842-43 and 1843-44, three half-yearly rates of £1,000 and one of £1,100 were set, compared with the average of £1,600 per half-year in the following six years. The shortage of money forced the Council to cut the size of the police force as well as reducing their pay for a time.

HIGHWAYS ACT

The Highways Act of 1835 repealed much old legislation and empowered parishes and townships of more than 5,000 population to set up boards to supervise the repair of the highways. Bishopwearmouth township quickly took advantage of this Act. In 1836 a meeting of ratepayers under the chairmanship of the rector, the Honourable and Reverend G. V. Wellesley, resolved immediately to form such a board and elected 20 members to serve on it. A committee of five board members attended to the day-to-day running of things until a full-time salaried assistant surveyor, William Buck, was appointed in October of the same year. Buck served until 1840 when he was replaced by John Cox, who served for nearly 12 years.

Sunderland township had no highways board, the streets being under the jurisdiction of the Improvement Commissioners. Monkwearmouth Shore did not form a Highway Board until 1848, while Monkwearmouth township did not have a large enough population to

justify one. Rather than appoint a salaried "person of skill and experience"[20] this township chose to elect unpaid surveyors each year. The Bishopwearmouth Highways Board did set about repairing its highways and surfacing its roads with a certain amount of energy as the orders recorded in the minute books for hundreds of tons of stones testify. Under arrangements with the Poor Law guardians, the board had their stones broken by the inmates of the Poor House. Nevertheless there were always complaints about the state of the streets. Both Bishopwearmouth and Monkwearmouth Shore Highways Boards were constantly remonstrating with the gas and water companies about the damage caused to the streets by their excavations and botched repairs. The highways boards cleared the streets of snow in winter and watered their macadamized surfaces in summer. They authorised the making of street crossings and paid for their sweeping. They bought up property for demolition so that streets could be widened and did what they could to protect rights of way. More than once the Bishopwearmouth Highways Board had to act on complaints that James Laing's "new ship now building projects over the cart road 24 feet"[21] and an ancient right of way across Building Hill was threatened by the cutting of Burdon Road by the Bridge Commissioners. In 1844 the Board took steps to reopen an alleged right of way across the Thornhill Estate, from the lodge in Tunstall Lane to Broadmeadows in Durham Lane. The ensuing litigation cost the Highways Board over £900 in trial costs. Its annual income at this time was only in the region of £1,100.

An adjunct to the maintenance of the highways was cleansing, which the Bishopwearmouth Board undertook in association with the Improvement Commissioners. The scavenger with whom they contracted was required to "lead away all manures, dirt, rubbish and filth of every description".[22] This too was a source of constant complaint never satisfactorily resolved. The Board tried different arrangements, contracting with different scavengers, organising the township into divisions, and even deciding to manage the operation themselves. It was done neither thoroughly nor promptly. Besides receiving complaints about this, and about the men employed by the scavenger begging in Tatham Street, the Board was always frustrated in its efforts to find a suitable dump for the filth. The problem must have been aggravated when the Sunderland Commissioners gave notice in 1840 that they would no longer allow the manure collected in Bishopwearmouth to be deposited in the midden on the Town Moor. Richard Chilton leased the 'depot for manure' in Littlegate in November 1839 "provided he undertake to keep the same clean", but three months later he was ordered to quit possession of it.

Highways boards were responsible for the prevention and removal of nuisances and annoyances and in doing so the Bishopwearmouth board encountered a great variety of challenges. Dr. Cowan, proprietor of the Grange School, complained to them in September 1838 about the danger from flying rock caused by blasting on Building Hill. At the time work was going on cutting the new Burdon Road through the hill. Complaints about danger from blasting persisted until 1846. Other public safety hazards included the railway crossings in Hylton Lane. In 1838 the clerk to the Highways Board was instructed to suggest to the agents of Lord Durham and the Hetton Coal Company that the waggons crossing the road should slacken their speed. The danger continued until the coal companies were prevailed upon to erect crossing gates. Even as late as September 1845 the collieries were urged as to "the necessity of immediately putting up the gates".

Although the Highways Board had no power to levy a rate for making common sewers it did from time to time give financial assistance to private individuals who were making their own drains "in order that the public may not be inconvenienced". It also reopened after 20 years, a well in Tunstall Road, and provided it with a pump and water trough. An intractable nuisance was the state of the Bishopwearmouth Burn near Hinds Bridge. Privies emptying into it turned it into an open sewer. A decision in 1845 to have the privies removed was evidently ineffective as a decision was taken in 1849 to culvert the 'insufferable nuisance'. No sooner had the board paid for the work than a middenstead and privies were built on the culvert by a Mr. John Ewan who insolently refused to quit when ordered.

THE BOROUGH OF SUNDERLAND ACT 1851

Many other bodies were involved in local government: the River Wear Commissioners, the Commissioners of the River Wear Watch Act of 1846, the Bridge Commissioners, the trustees of the various turnpike roads that ran into the town and the Board of Guardians which (in addition to its Poor Law duties) had, from 1848, responsibility for the removal of nuisances. These illustrate the chaotic state of local government and the resulting impotence of authorities to deal with major problems.

Committees were unsure of their powers. In 1840 the Bishopwearmouth Highways Board and Improvement Commissioners jointly sought counsel's opinion as to which of them should appoint the scavenger. On other occasions authorities denied that they were responsible. In 1849 the Monkwearmouth Shore Highways Board pleaded with the Bridge Commissioners and the Newcastle turnpike road trustees to repair a road at the north end of the bridge at their joint expense until a dispute between them as to which was liable for the repair could be settled. The road had become so deep in mud that a cart-horse which had fallen nearly suffocated before it could be extricated from the traces.

Some of the bodies had unpaid and unwilling officers to serve them. Their attitude was no doubt exemplified by John Ewart, Surveyor of Highways for Monkwearmouth Township, who in 1847 told the surveying officers Rawlinson and Hosking:
> you will find me a very inadequate witness, because I come quite unprepared to answer any

William Snowball (1807-1883) a Sunderland-born lawyer, Town Clerk from 1848. Important for his work in helping to secure the Borough of Sunderland Act 1851 and the Town Improvement Act 1867.

questions likely to be put to me; more particularly as the surveyor of Monkwearmouth Shore receives no pay for what he does, and therefore, we do not take so much interest in these matters.[23]

Even among the paid officials there was a lack of professionalism. The evidence given before the surveying officers showed that some of the town's surveyors had only hearsay knowledge of the drainage of their townships. They only knew the dimensions and construction of the drains where they had recently been excavated and exposed to view. Detailed records appeared not to have been available.

The responsibilities of one body in a particular sphere were not complemented by those of another body. Although the Bishopwearmouth Water Company would lay on a supply of water to a house for a nominal charge of five shillings, this was of no use to households which had no drainage and no authority to turn to to supply it.

The surveying officers of 1847, J. J. Rawlinson and William Hosking, favoured a single executive authority in Sunderland and in 1851, Robert Rawlinson, the inspector of the General Board of Health, unhesitatingly recommended that "one local board" with "a superior and efficient staff may be employed with much greater advantage and far more economy than by having divided and conflicting boards".[24] Rawlinson intended that the new authority should cover the whole of the Sunderland parliamentary borough.

The 1851 Borough of Sunderland Act vested the powers of the Bridge and Improvement Commissioners, and the highways boards, in the Corporation, but did not extend the boundary of the municipal borough. This act provided a head for the 'overgrown family' and the basis of a local government which could begin to tackle the manifold problems of a populous industrial town.

REFERENCES

1. *S.H.,* 21 November 1835.
2. *Reports from Commissioners, Municipal Corporation Boundaries (England and Wales). Report on the proposed municipal boundary and division into wards of the borough of Sunderland (1836).*
3. *An Act for Making the Town and Township of Sunderland a Distinct Parish from The Parish of Bishopwearmouth, in the County of Durham,* 1719 (5 George I).
4. W. E. Tate, *The Parish Chest, A Study of the Records of Parochial Administration in England* (C.U.P. 1979) p. 30.
5. General Account of the Treasurer of the County of Durham for the Year 1833, p. 32.
6. *S.B.,* 24 October 1838.
7. *Report of the Commissioners of H. M. Woods and Forests, etc., enclosing the report of the Surveying Officers: Sunderland Markets, Bridge, Ferries, etc., Sunderland Improvements, Markets and Bridge* (1847) (hereafter referred to as *1847 Report*) p. xiv.
8. *Sunderland Markets, Bridge, Ferries, etc., Sunderland Improvement, Markets and Bridge. Minutes of Evidence,* (hereafter referred to as *1847 Evidence*) question 2151.
9. *1847 Report* p. xiv.
10. *1847 Report* p. xiv.
11. *1847 Evidence,* question 522 (evidence of William Drysdale, surveyor to Sunderland Improvement Commissioners).
12. *1847 Report* p. xix.
13. *Report of Royal Commission on Municipal Corporations* 1835, xxv, p. 1734.
14. *Ibid.,* xxiii, p. 5.
15. *S.H.,* 19 December, 1835.
16. *Ibid.*
17. *An act to make temporary provision for the boundaries of certain boroughs* (6 & 7 William IV cap. 103).
18. Letter in T.W.A.S., ref. 839/332.
19. *Report to the General Board of Health on a Preliminary Enquiry as to the Sewerage, Drainage, Supply of Water and the Sanitary Condition of the Borough of Sunderland* (1851) (hereafter referred to as *1851 Report*) p. 84.
20. *General Highways Act,* 1835 (5 & 6 William IV cap. 50), clause 9.
21. Bishopwearmouth Highway Board minute for 29 October 1849. A similar complaint was minuted for 3 August 1846.
22. *ibid.,* 25 January 1837.
23. *1847 Evidence,* question 920.
24. *1851 Report,* p. 85.

Parliamentary Politics 1830 to the 1860s

Sunderland had no representation of its own in Parliament before 1832. Since County Durham's enfranchisement in 1675, Sunderland freeholders had played their part in electing its two MPs; no less than 424 had voted in 1790 out of a county total of 3,407. Sunderland, increasingly populous and prosperous, stood firmly for a reform that would give it members of its own.

Sunderland was not the first north-eastern borough to demand MPs of its own in the Reform crisis of the early 1830s; that honour went to South Shields. But by February of 1831 Sunderland, too, was demanding representation. A meeting in the Assembly Rooms on the 8th February attended by the leading reformers of the town petitioned Parliament in favour of Reform. The meeting was consciously moderate, insisting that the details of Reform should be left to the House of Commons themselves, trusting that they would produce such a reform "as may secure the country from having, on the one hand, its general interests sacrificed to those of a few, or from becoming, on the other, the prey of anarchy and confusion".[1] The petition was forwarded for presentation to Lord William Powlett, one of the MPs for the County, but Powlett, when presenting it on 2nd March 1831, while welcoming the additional members which the Government's plan proposed for the County of Durham, objected that it would mean substantial disfranchisement elsewhere. Sir Matthew White Ridley, MP for Newcastle supported Sunderland's petition, and rebuked Powlett, echoing the sentiments of the Sunderland meeting, and expressing the hope that "the reformers would not, by any dissensions on the minor details of the bill, allow ministers to be defeated on the great and essential measure of Reform".[2] A second meeting was held in Sunderland within a month; on 11th March speakers like Drs Clanny and Brown, Joseph John Wright, Ogden Brown, and George Pemberton were unanimous in favour of the Government's proposals. As Taylor Potts put it,

> during the agitations and struggles that preceded the passing of the Reform Bill, the inhabitants of the borough seem to have laid aside, for the time being, all their trifling differences, and acted together.[3]

This unanimity was made easier because, from the first, Sunderland was proposed to be included in schedule C of the new Reform Bill, the list of new boroughs that were to have two MPs each; it was thus set in a short list alongside such great industrial towns as Manchester, Birmingham, or Leeds. Thus though the agitation and excitement of the Reform crisis affected the town, the citizens were able to pull together to ensure its enfranchisement. Open meetings were held on the Town Moor, and indoor meetings in the Assembly Rooms in Church Street. The press at such meetings was sometimes so great that the audience spilled out on to the steps, and on one occasion spectators climbing for a better view brought down a stone coping and themselves with it. Taylor Potts, a witness, said that the crowds were so great that he could only see "the heads and faces of the

surging mass".[4]

While Sunderland was still represented by the county members of Parliament, all the town's solicitors pledged themselves to work for the return of reforming MPs, and condemned the "pernicious influence of the boroughmongers".[5] At the general election caused by the defeat of the government's first Reform Bill a large and influential committee of 35 prominent Sunderland citizens was formed to secure the return of the Reformers William Russell and Sir Hedworth Williamson for the county, and William Chaytor for nearby Durham City, and all three candidates sought to appeal to the electors of Sunderland. Russell was praised at a public meeting in Sunderland for being prepared to forego his own borough influence in the south of England "in behalf of a salutary and efficient reform", while Sir Hedworth Williamson, though most closely connected with Sunderland, told the town's freeholders that he thought the unanimity of support in his favour was

> owing to no personal merit of my own, but to the great cause in which we are all engaged, and which, in conjunction with the other freeholders of the county, you are determined to carry to a successful conclusion.[6]

Chaytor, for his part, was a regular visitor to the borough, had spoken at the first reform meeting in the town on 8th February 1831, and had previously been guest of honour at the Bridge Inn, Bishopwearmouth — the Liberal headquarters of the town — where he had denounced the man who was now his fellow liberal candidate, William Russell, for not being radical enough![7]

Not surprisingly, perhaps, Tory candidates fared less well in unrepresented Sunderland. Sir Roger Greisley, Lord Londonderry's nominee for Durham City, was driven out of the town when he attempted to canvass the Durham freemen who lived there. The three reformers, with the help of their Sunderland supporters, were duly elected, and the new county members returned to Miss Jowsey's at the Bridge Inn to hold a victory dinner.

The boundary commissioners appointed to draw up the new parliamentary constituency

The Bridge Hotel (or Inn) on the corner of High Street and Sunderland Street was the headquarters of the Liberal interest in Sunderland in the age of reform.

of Sunderland agreed on its importance and confidently predicted continued expansion for the newly enfranchised town. They initially contemplated drawing the boundary for the parliamentary borough around the whole of the three parishes of Sunderland, Bishopwearmouth and Monkwearmouth, but this would extend the boundary five miles into the already small county of Durham, and they eventually restricted their recommendation to the parish of Sunderland, together with the townships of Bishopwearmouth, Bishopwearmouth Panns, Monkwearmouth, Monkwearmouth Shore, and Southwick. The vote was to be given in new boroughs to the occupants of houses valued at £10 *per annum*, and the commissioners recorded 1,968 qualifying houses within their more restricted area, the majority being in Bishopwearmouth (1,298) and Sunderland (864). The fact that the inclusion of Hylton, Fulwell, Ford, Ryhope, Tunstall, Burdon and Silksworth would only have added another 170 qualifying houses altogether was another reason for the commissioners choosing the smaller borough. Even on the restricted area proposed by the commissioners, however, Sunderland had three-and-a-half times as many qualifying houses as Gateshead, three times as many as South Shields (each of which were to have one MP), and nearly four times as many as Durham City which was to retain its two members.[8]

The Reform Bill, with its provision for the new parliamentary borough of Sunderland to send two representatives to Westminster, finally became law in 1832, and was cause for great rejoicing in the town. Monday 27 August was proclaimed "a day of general joy in Sunderland;" the Reform Committee requested all shops to be closed at noon, and the members of the Reformers' Political Union were to assemble with their colleagues from Newcastle for a great dinner in celebration.[9] When Sunderland at last came to elect its own MPs later that year, the returning officer, Addison Fenwick, doubtless reflected the feelings of the townspeople when he congratulated them from the hustings: "You have been placed in a situation of political importance, which, from the extent of your trade, wealth, and population, you are justly entitled to."[10]

Yet as Taylor Potts noted, no sooner had the royal assent been given to the Reform Bill, than the leaders of the reforming agitation in the town,

> who had been acting together to secure the passing of the bill and the enfranchisement of the borough, separated into parties, each one striving to secure the return of representatives according to their own peculiar political bias.[11]

The *Durham Chronicle*, commenting on the political prospects in Sunderland, believed that, as a consequence of their opposition to parliamentary reform, "the fate of the Tories is sealed for ever",[12] but they calculated without two factors. The first was a national one, which Sunderland was to share with other newly-enfranchised towns like Manchester; in unenfranchised towns the inhabitants were united in their desire to secure representation, but once that had been achieved, differences of opinion, submerged for the duration of the reform struggle, reappeared on the surface, and tended to express themselves in party political terms. The second factor was, however, peculiar to Sunderland, and had to some extent been anticipated during the reform struggle itself; this was fear of the political domination of the newly-enfranchised town by one or other of the local magnates. And this fear was itself compounded by the major preoccupation of Sunderland's new electorate, the construction of new docks for the town, and the stand taken upon that issue by rival local grandees.

ARISTOCRATIC INFLUENCE

Even while the Reform Bill was going through parliament, Lord Durham (formerly John George Lambton, until 1828 MP for the county, and thus Sunderland's representative), son-in-law of the Prime Minister Lord Grey, and Lord Privy Seal in his cabinet, had been accused of gerrymandering the new representation, which he had been instrumental in formulating, for his own political purposes. Lord Londonderry, Lord Durham's county neighbour and, until the reform crisis, political and business colleague and rival, told the House of Lords that it was self-evident that, under the proposed scheme, Lord Durham would have "great influence in the return of the members" for Sunderland, Gateshead, and South Shields. Lord Durham had hotly denied it.

"I solemnly disclaim any wish or intention to procure for myself any personal advantage or influence whatsoever," he claimed; "I should be ashamed of myself if I had entertained any such desire." Besides, he insisted, even if he had wished to do so, "the attempt would have been futile, for the constituency to be created is so numerous, intelligent and independent, as to be above all influence, either of mine or of any other person."[13] Yet according to the *Durham Advertiser* the lie was given to Lord Durham's protestations by the first parliamentary election for Sunderland, held in December, 1832. Among the candidates who presented themselves was Captain George Barrington, yet another son-in-law of Lord

Penshaw Monument was erected on a prominent site to the west of Sunderland in 1844 as a memorial to the first Earl of Durham, John George Lambton, (1792-1840).

Grey. Barrington said: "he hoped not to see the influence of any of his noble and illustrious relatives exerted in his favour," because "he wished to stand or fall by his own merits," but it was clear that he was Lord Durham's nominee. It was also clear from the first that he was an unsuitable candidate. As Hedworth Lambton told his brother, Lord Durham, "three or four of your warmest admirers told me how disappointed they were to find Barrington, a man of such little talent and political information."[14] Worse was to follow. It became clear during the election contest that Barrington was unwell; he failed to canvass, or make speeches to his supporters, or to be chaired after he had won, blaming on each occasion his "indisposition". Much of the one speech he did make to the electors on nomination day was taken up with apologies for his ill-health. After the election it became clear that he was seriously mentally ill, and was unable to take his seat in the House of Commons. As an unkind handbill put it, Barrington "had not half an inch of sound mind to spare", and subsequently another handbill protested to the electors of Sunderland that

it is known to every person in this borough, and throughout the neighbourhood, that at the time Captain Barrington was elected one of your representatives, he was suffering from mental affliction, and this fact was kept from your knowledge.[15]

As Barrington was Lord Durham's nominee, such ill luck (or, perhaps, deception) was bound to reflect on his patron. Hedworth Lambton warned his brother that he must in future ensure "whenever you send down a candidate either now or hereafter, to be *very*, *very careful* to send one who is *most highly eligible* in every respect", and was sure that Lord Durham's "staunch supporters", many of whom were "very susceptible chaps", would desert him if they thought "you meant anything like positive dictation, or even that you sent any one down at any time who was not in every way *most eligible*".[16] For all his warning, however, Hedworth Lambton himself compounded the problem by writing to Sunderland to announce that, during Barrington's illness, Edward Ellice, MP for Coventry, and yet another of Lord Grey's sons-in-law, was going to undertake Barrington's constituency business. Naturally there was indignation in Sunderland; why should their interests be transferred among the members of the Grey family, or entrusted to a distant MP with no connection with the town? The Lambtons were accused of double dealing, of engaging in "nomination and borough-mongering" which they professed to denounce, and for "lordly domination". Rumours of a secret meeting of the Lambton agents at Miss Jowsey's Bridge Inn to plot what to do if and when Barrington was forced to resign leaked out, and the cry that Lord Durham was seeking to undermine the independence of the borough became a powerful weapon in the hands of the opposition.[17]

Yet the opposition to Lord Durham was handicapped by similar charges. Lord Londonderry's accusation that Lord Durham was seeking to manipulate the Reform Bill for his own political advantage could be — and was — thrown back at him. His particular complaint that those who lived more than seven miles from the borough for which they voted were to be disfranchised was (rightly) seen not as a complaint about the new reformed system, but a personal *cri-de-coeur* that his Seaham Harbour employees would no longer be eligible to vote for Durham City, while the very creation of that harbour — dismissed by one Sunderland voter as his Lordship's "duckpond" — made him all the more anxious to maintain a precarious footing in Sunderland politics. The Tory candidate at Sunderland's first election, Alderman William Thompson, was simply dismissed by many as the Londonderry nominee.

The third powerful local magnate was Sir Hedworth Williamson, with his estates in Monkwearmouth. Though politically a Liberal like Lord Durham (as opposed to Lord Londonderry's Toryism), Williamson had an uneasy relationship with the Sunderland electors. *The Times* estimated in 1841 that Williamson could "command between 200 and 300 votes" as a result of his property in the borough, but this did him little good when Lord Durham's newspaper, the *Durham Chronicle*, condemned him in 1832 for pushing the candidature of his brother-in-law, David Barclay; the electors of Sunderland, the *Chronicle* insisted, should resist such dictation by "the Whitburn clique".[18] Though in 1832 Lord Durham and Sir Hedworth Williamson had been rivals, each promoting their own nominee before the Sunderland voters, after the Barrington fiasco, Lord Durham found himself forced to compromise with Williamson. As his brother warned him, if he put up his own man against Williamson's candidate, Barclay, at the by-election in 1833, brought on by the final recognition that Barrington was unfit to be an MP, not only was the man Lord Londonderry backed, Thompson, bound to be elected, but Lord Durham would "materially injure" his

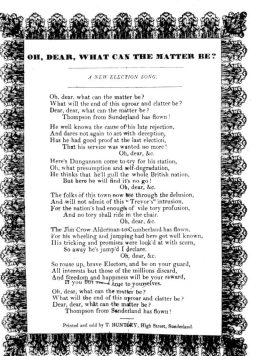

A handbill of 1841 referring to William Thompson's resignation as MP for Sunderland.

own interests in the borough. It would be better, counselled Lambton, to support Barclay who was after all a Liberal, in the by-election, and bring his own man forward on a subsequent occasion with his interest uninjured.[19]

Magnate politics thus played a significant part in the newly enfranchised borough of Sunderland. In spite of his denials that he sought to influence the electorate, Lord Durham supported Barrington in 1832, and only the disaster of his initial choice forced his later compromise support of Barclay. The Lambton influence was put behind Andrew White in 1837, and after Lord Durham's death his influence, personified by his agent, Henry Morton, was used to support the successful candidature of Lord Grey's eldest son, Viscount Howick, in 1841. Lord Londonderry supported Thompson in 1832, and subsequently until he resigned in 1841; and later was to be found among the backers of George Hudson from 1845 onwards, while Williamson supported Barclay until the latter went bankrupt, when he took over the seat himself.

THE DOCKS ISSUE

Such aristocratic manoeuvring was complicated by another local peculiarity of Sunderland, the building of the town's new docks, which became a significant — perhaps the most important — political issue in the borough.[20] Sir Hedworth Williamson wanted the docks on his own property in Monkwearmouth on the north side of the river Wear, and thus opposed schemes for the intrinsically more viable south docks. As the *Durham Chronicle* said in disgust, it would not have been surprised if such a scheme had emanated from Lord Londonderry "or any man who has fattened upon the innumerable abuses to which the people of this country have, under the curse of Tory domination, been exposed," but it was shocked that a Liberal, like Williamson, should support a plan that put his own self-interest before the true concerns of the people of Sunderland.[21] Londonderry had initially opposed the south docks proposal, in an attempt to protect his investment in his embryonic harbour at Seaham, but subsequently, recognising the potential political damage such opposition would do to his influence in Sunderland, became a firm supporter and condemned the north docks scheme, or even any proposal to advance both plans simultaneously. Like Lord Londonderry,

Lord Durham's main coal interests were to the south of the Wear, so he, too, became a supporter of the south docks. Battle lines were thus drawn not only on the issue of personal allegiance, but on the question of the location of the docks.

Thus in 1833 a handbill, calling on the electors to support Thompson, "the advocate for the south docks," dismissed David Barclay as "the nominee of the Lambtons, the adopted of Sir Hedworth Williamson," who, it was said, had cost the people of Sunderland thousands of pounds by frustrating the bill they had promoted to commission docks on the south bank, and merely wanted to return Barclay "to promote his own end". Barclay, while dismissing the charge that he was any man's nominee as a "gross fabrication" of "Tory malevolence" was nevertheless forced to compromise on the docks issue. He conceded that the scheme for south docks seemed to be "approved of, and desired by a large majority of the inhabitants of the borough", and therefore agreed to support the idea, but added that it north docks were built, too, he should "hail the event".[22]

Williamson eventually went ahead by himself and built his north docks, though at enormous personal cost. The original estimate of £30,000 soon became £120,000, and Williamson was forced to resign his seat as MP for the county because of his financial difficulties in 1837. Heavily mortgaged, forced to manage without a carriage, Williamson's career in politics was reduced to a local one, as mayor of Sunderland, and though his brother-in-law Barclay sat from 1835 till 1837, and again from 1841 to 1847 (when he went bankrupt), and though Williamson was a vigorous partisan on behalf of Viscount Howick in 1841, his popularity declined almost as fast as his financial resources. His election as MP for Sunderland after his brother-in-law's failure in 1847 was a last effort to retain his political power in the town, and owed not a little to the fact that the docks crisis was, at last, on its way to solution.

The saviour of the town, as far as docks were concerned, was George Hudson.[23] The south docks, initially blocked by Williamson and Londonderry, had been unable to obtain financial backing, especially when Williamson went ahead with his docks on the Monkwearmouth shore. The scheme was kept alive, but Williamson's financial difficulties were not an incentive to investors in rival docks. In spite of the construction of the Sunderland and Durham Railway, which was designed to attract more coal to the port, the coal trade was in decline, and the railway, too, was in financial difficulties, and unable to pay a dividend. Those Sunderland businessmen who had invested in the scheme found the value of their £50 shares had fallen, by 1845, to a mere £24. At this low point for the economic life of the town, the Sunderland Tories persuaded George Hudson to become their candidate, on the elevation of Viscount Howick to the House of Lords.

The Sunderland Tories favoured businessman candidates, especially those whose commercial interests fitted in with those of the

Sir Hedworth Williamson (1779-1861), landlord of Monkwearmouth, said to command two to three hundred votes in Sunderland. MP for the town 1847-1852. (Portrait 1831.)

A handbill denouncing Sir Hedworth Williamson for his support of the North Dock scheme (1830s).

NO WILLIAMSON!

No Enemy of Sunderland!
No PARLIAMENTARY Jobber!

Freeholders!
Reject Williamson, that Traitor
TO HIS SUNDERLAND CONSTITUENTS, WHO WOULD ENRICH
HIMSELF AT THE EXPENCE & RUIN OF SUNDERLAND.

SUNDERLAND
Expects every Man to do his DUTY.

(SUMMERS & SON, PRINTERS, SUNDERLAND.)

borough. Indeed, such views were not confined to the Tories; the Whig *Sunderland Herald* described the ideal candidate for Sunderland as a man with intimate local knowledge, business aptitude, and devotion to the interests of the town.[24] Until the 1860s, though, it was the Tories of the town who managed most effectively to find candidates who fulfilled the formula. Their choice in 1832, who had gone on to win the by-election in 1833, and to remain the town's MP until his resignation to stand for the more prestigious county seat of Westmorland in 1841, had been William Thompson. As well as being an alderman of London, Thompson was chairman of Lloyd's, a director of the Bank of England, and a railway director. He stood, initially, as the friend to the shipowners, and it was in that light that he was elected. "You received your elective franchise chiefly on account of your trading and shipping interests," a handbill on Thompson's behalf reminded the Sunderland electors in 1833, and should therefore support a man "intimately conversant with commercial and shipping subjects".[25]

When Thompson resigned, Sunderland's Tories once more looked to a shipping man. Besides being a merchant and banker in London, Matthias Wolverley Attwood was chairman of the Steam Navigation Company, and as he told the electors, "we want to place the interests of shipping in the hands of men who know what shipping is". The crudity of Attwood's approach[26] perhaps alienated many of the traditional Tory shipowners, but in Hudson, four years later, they found an ideal candidate. "The industrial, commercial, and shipping interests of the place are those by which we subsist," an elector reminded his colleagues, and pointed to Hudson's commercial record as the guarantee of the town's future prosperity.

At the time of his election for Sunderland, Hudson was at the height of his success, the "Railway King" for whom no speculation could, apparently, go wrong. Even his opponents in Sunderland conceded that he was a "formidable" candidate. As Richard Cobden, campaigning on Peronnet Thompson's behalf for the Anti-Corn-Law League put it,

> He would go into every constituency with an *intangible* bribe for every class — the capitalists would hope for premiums — the smaller fry would look for situations for their sons in the vast railway undertakings over which he rules absolutely, and the rope, iron, coal and timber merchants will all bid for his patronage.[29]

And Cobden's predictions were fulfilled. Once it was known that Hudson had agreed to contest Sunderland, shares in the Sunderland and Durham Railway rose three pounds in two days. Such stock-market expectations were fulfilled when Hudson duly triumphed, and bought out the shareholders at £31.50 for a £50 share, well above their market price. Moreover, in one of those deals which were later to annihilate his reputation, Hudson unilaterally decreed that the Newcastle and Darlington Railway should put up £75,000 towards the construction of the longed-for South Docks in Sunderland. The shareholders, who were later bitter in their complaints,

allegedly laughed when Hudson told them "I hope you won't think me guilty of a *job* in this matter."[28] As Cobden had prophesied, it was not simply the prospect of instant wealth for investors that enhanced Hudson's reputation in Sunderland. As his agent, the Tory solicitor J. J. Wright, told a banquet in Hudson's honour after his election victory in 1845, not only had Hudson's enterprise "benefitted the rich," but it had also

> disseminated advantages through every class of society in this great commercial community. He has provided engagements for the artisan, employment for the labourer, trade for the shopkeeper, a market for the manufacturer, channels for industry, and oceans for business, unequalled in the history of this empire.

Not surprisingly, such a eulogy was greeted with "great applause", but Hudson himself, on the same occasion, added a vision of even greater prospects. Thanks to the improvements which his business acumen could provide for

A handbill advocating the cause of William Thompson, 1833.

ELECTORS

OF

Sunderland!

VOTE FOR

THOMPSON

THE FRIEND OF THE

Shipping & Commercial Interests

The Constitutional Advocate for Civil & Religious Liberty,

THE

Enemy of the Corn Bill,

The determined Opposer of the Impressment of SAILORS,

A FRIEND TO THE FINAL ABOLITION OF SLAVERY,

And the unflinching Advocate of

Economy and Retrenchment,

In the Expenditure of every

DEPARTMENT of the STATE !!!

Thompson for ever!!!

HUDSON

FOR EVER.

Sunderland, there was no limit to the horizons of Sunderland's future. "I do not see why merchandise from Petersburgh and China should not come to Sunderland," he told his audience, "provided you give facilities for its entrance. Gentlemen," he concluded,

> there is something in imagination; I do not say that imagination ought to govern us, but, once we have formed our judgement, let imagination have a little play; let us imagine we are going to make Sunderland and Newcastle the Liverpool and Manchester of the world.[29]

The electors had been urged to vote Tory, as they had done for Thompson, to "promote the prosperity of your town and port"; even more emphatically than with Thompson, the electorate followed what they saw as their natural self-interest, inspired by the spectacular future that Hudson held out for them.

GEORGE HUDSON'S CHANGING FORTUNES

By 1847, rumours of the instability of Hudson's financial enterprises were beginning to surface. The Whig Sunderland Herald tried to belittle Hudson's pretensions. In contrast to their favourite, David Barclay, the representation of Sunderland was to Hudson "only one other in the train of occupations which this mighty engine carries in its tail, and by no means the most important truck either". It was

absurd, they claimed, for the electors to "suppose in him any disposition to support the interests of Sunderland at the expense of his own". Moreover the Herald pointed out that in the long term Hudson's railway interests were positively hostile to the best interests of Sunderland; if Hudson succeeded in his project of linking up all the East coast lines to London, what would become of the coasting trade? The Herald was not Luddite, in that it was prepared to acknowledge that in the long run railways were bound to replace the more irregular and hazardous coasting trade, but, they said, "surely it does not belong to Sunderland to accelerate the process" by returning Hudson. "It may be awful audacity," said the Herald, "it may be sacrilege, it may be madness", to suggest that the electors reject the saviour of the docks project, but they, at least, were willing to contemplate it.[30]

The electors were not. The Radical candidate, Wilkinson, boldly called for the abolition of the Navigation Laws, claiming this would be "a great gain to the nation at large, and the shipowners, shipwrights and seamen of Sunderland in particular". David Barclay, who in principle favoured free trade, was enough of a Sunderland man to insist that the Navigation Laws were an exception to the general rule, and that they must be maintained for the protection of shipping. Hudson, who was anyway an opponent of free trade, simply dismissed the notion of an end to the Navigation Laws as "disastrous". Such attitudes doubtless had their effect on the result of the election, but Hudson's triumph at the head of the poll owed as much, according to the Sunderland Herald, to the fact that he was "money personified", adding that "this makes him more formidable than would the eloquence of a Canning, the foresight of a Burke, and the sagacity of a Peel, all united."[31]

In the course of the next few years, however, Hudson's financial reputation collapsed, and his misdealings were revealed to the world. Francis Meaburn, the Secretary to the Stockton and Darlington Railway, who at the time of Hudson's first election for Sunderland in 1845 had described him as "the most wonderful man who has appeared and astonished the railway world", was by 1849 complaining that "it is impossible to defend his conduct".[32] By 1850 rumours were strong that Hudson would be forced to resign his parliamentary seat.

Lord Londonderry was one of those who, at the height of Hudson's powers, had patronised and profited from him; now he began to suggest that an alternative Tory candidate, in the person of his own son, Lord Adolphus Vane, should be put up for Sunderland in Hudson's place, and Wright had to assure Londonderry (as a friend of both men) that his revised views of Hudson's worth were mistaken: "Your Lordship never was further wrong than in the opinion you entertain of Mr. Hudson."[33] Hudson not only did not resign, but at the next general election in 1852 was once more returned at the top of the poll.

Whatever Hudson's difficulties with his Eastern Counties or York, Newcastle and Berwick shareholders, he remained a hero in Sunderland. In 1850, two years after he had

OFF THE RAIL.

. Mr. Hudson, M.P. for Sunderland, who was commonly called the Railway King, came badly to grief at this time.

laid the foundation of the South Dock, and a year after his financial bubble had burst elsewhere, Hudson triumphantly opened the dock with great pageantry. 50,000 spectators assembled, cannon were fired, and a water procession with bands and banners hailed what was seen as Hudson's personal triumph. J. J. Wright, as well as eulogising the personal "extraordinary talents, indomitable energies, wonderful character, and mighty achievements" of Hudson, recalled his theme of 1845 when he claimed that Hudson had "diffused a profuse expenditure of money in this district, and throughout the North of England, furnishing employment to the trading and labouring classes," which, he suggested, had kept Sunderland prosperous while the rest of Europe had been plunged into revolution in 1848![34] When the general election came two years later, Hudson rubbed the point in:

> I trust that my efforts to promote the shipping and commercial interests . . . of your enterprising and advancing port . . . have been such as to ensure me a continuance of that entire confidence, invariable kindness, and triumphant support, I have hitherto received at your hands,

he told the electors.[35]

They were. Even the Radical *Sunderland News* was forced to confess "Mr. Hudson's election, it is well known on all hands, is safe".[36] Though he was hissed when he mounted the platform on nomination day, a crowd of navvies from "his" docks surrounded Hudson's portion of the hustings, and cheered him vociferously, especially when Christopher Bramwell, echoing Wright, emphasised that Hudson had proved himself not only "a friend to the town, but more than that he had proved himself a friend to the lower classes, a friend to the working man."[37] Hudson himself was suitably grateful to the Sunderland electorate for his victory in 1852; as he told the electors, "You have supported me in many trials; you have comforted me when almost every comfort seemed to have forsaken me. When all had forsaken me, Sunderland has remained firm to me. My right hand shall forget her cunning," he concluded, in a revealing comment, "before I forget the favours I have received at your hands".[38]

After the election, though, his personal affairs deteriorated still further. A series of chancery judgements against him in 1853 forced him to mortgage his country properties; a high court judgement against him in 1854 forced him to vacate his London house. In desperation, he sought to recoup his fortunes by railway undertakings in Spain, but no sooner had he arrived there than he was struck down by illness, from which he took more than a year to recover. It was assumed in Sunderland that a man who chose to pursue his business interests abroad, rather than attend at his place in the House of Commons, would not seek re-election.

When, therefore, a sudden general election took place in 1857, and Hudson, from Paris, issued an address soliciting re-election in Sunderland, there was considerable surprise. "Wonders will never cease!" exclaimed the *Herald*; "Our truant representative desires re-election!" He had been out of the country for two years; he had failed to represent the interests of Sunderland, for which above all he had been elected; he had, said the *Herald*, reduced the representation of Sunderland to "a delusion and a sham." Yet here he was, once more appealing for their votes. Gratitude, proclaimed the *Herald*, had its limits:

> So long as he continued to attend to his duties in Parliament, the country could partially understand how it was that Sunderland remained true to him; but when the constituency is left for nearly two years with only a single representative, when his vote has been lost on questions vitally affecting the interests of that port . . . the nation at large would unfailingly denounce his re-election as a political crime, and a glaring abdication of one of the highest duties of British citizenship.[39]

Hudson threw himself on the mercy of the electors. He acknowledged his failure to attend Parliament, but claimed that illness (rather than the demands of his creditors) was to blame; he was now, he said "a wiser and better man". His speech to his supporters, following his hasty return from Paris, was greeted with "loud and protracted applause". He was, he protested, an "honest man", who had done nothing to forfeit the confidence of the electors. Should that confidence be renewed, he would, he promised, serve them in a "more efficient and better manner" than in the last two years. His chief appeal remained, though, to the electors' gratitude for his "very humble but not inefficient" efforts to provide the town with docks. Moreover, he held out the prospect of more to come, by adopting the project to build a harbour of refuge at Hendon as his own, and claiming that "the day is not far distant when I may again be further able to assist in extending the commercial enterprise of your port".[40] Once more the appeal worked. Though he was defeated by Henry Fenwick, Hudson managed comfortably to hold off the challenge of the third candidate Ralph Walters.

In 1859 the Sunderland Liberals at last produced a match for Hudson. In spite of his promise, Hudson had once more been erratic in his attendance in Parliament. Once more, too, he was forced to rely on a personal appeal for support. "I appeal to you," he told the electors, "in recollection of the invariable kindness shown me under circumstances of great difficulty." But now he had little to offer. The South Docks, whose provision had ensured such lasting loyalty from the electorate, proved

The opening of Sunderland's South Dock, 1850, from the painting by Mark Thompson.

Sir William Chaytor (1777-1847), known popularly as 'Tatie Willie'. His idiosyncracies were caricatured by Thackeray in *Vanity Fair*. MP for Sunderland 1832-35. (Portrait 1837.)

less successful than anticipated; the company's dividend declined until just before the election, to the disgust of the shareholders, it had been unable to pay a dividend at all.[41] Rival docks had been opened at Hartlepool and Middlesbrough, and a new dock was under construction at Jarrow. The great coal magnates like the Londonderrys had been reluctant to ship their coals through the docks, and J. J. Wright, so long Hudson's greatest ally in the town, faced bankruptcy.

It was at first thought that in the general election there would be no opposition to the return of Fenwick and Hudson, but the Liberals then brought forward a second candidate in the person of William Schaw Lindsay. Like Hudson, Lindsay was a rags-to-riches figure; he had risen from orphan cabin-boy to become a wealthy shipowner, and while MP for Tynemouth in the preceding Parliament had been popularly seen as the voice of the shipping interest in Parliament. Both he and his fellow Liberal candidate Fenwick were members of a Royal Commission on shipping then sitting, and both were able to hold out prospects that they would be able therefore to relieve the shipping industry from its present distressed condition. All Hudson could offer, in contrast, was memories of past glories:

> I have spent my time, money, and labour for the working classes; I have given employment when labour was not abundant, and when no other man could have done it. There are thousands on whom I have conferred happiness and prosperity, and if I have not made a large fortune for myself, I do not regret it. When I look to the noble works which have been executed by my intelligence and industry, if I have not made my fortune, I have erected a large number of monuments to my name in this district which will never be blotted out.[42]

It was not enough, and Hudson finished a humiliating bottom of the poll. His appeal to past successes and benefits was insufficiently attractive when compared with the prospects that Fenwick and Lindsay held out for future gains.

It was clear from Hudson's career that what the Sunderland electors valued was an MP who would be useful to the town, and from

1859 onwards both sides in Sunderland's politics sought to provide this. The Tories seemed to have re-established their position of the Hudson years when, in 1865, they ran James Hartley. The Whig *Sunderland Herald* had admitted in 1857 that "a more suitable representative than Mr. Hartley could not be found, "combining as he did local knowledge, patronage of employment, and large scale business contacts in the country and abroad.[43] The Liberals responded in kind, with a fellow-Alderman of Hartley's, and like him a Wear Commissioner, the bottle manufacturer and shipbuilder James Candlish, who, though defeated by Hartley in 1865, won a by-election in 1866, to secure to Sunderland for the first time since its enfranchisement wholly local representation.

ELECTIONS

Henry Morton, Lord Durham's agent, had a cynical view of what Sunderland wanted from its MP. "I am much mistaken," he told Lord Durham, "if any Sunderland man will sacrifice one shilling on the score of political feeling."[44] Indeed, elections were seen in Sunderland (as elsewhere) as occasions for making money, as candidates resorted to either direct or indirect bribery. The Tory Attwood, in 1841, was accused of both direct bribery and of offering £125 to the Chartists to field a candidate and split his opponent's vote. The Whigs in the same election spent large sums on treating; Lord Howick was eventually presented with bills for nearly £5,000, mainly for refreshments. The Radicals, less generous threatened in 1845 to withdraw custom from those who had failed to support them.[45]

There were legitimate expenses to be met by candidates as well, the cost for example of erecting wooden hustings some 16 or 18 feet high on the north side of High Street, with 20 constables to guard them overnight.[46] It was costly, also, to ensure that supporters were on the electoral register, and as many opponents as possible struck off. There were lawyers' fees to be met, and agents were essential for canvassing voters. J. J. Wright described his experience of 1837:

> It is certainly awful work — I have been upon my feet since last Monday morning applying to any electors no less than 12 or 13 times, and with the lower class of electors it is desperate as they can only be seen at night after their work, which keeps one constantly moving in the crowded lanes and alleys until 10 and 11 o'clock at night.[47]

Wright was accused of threatening to raise the rent of an elector if he failed to vote Tory, a charge which he denounced as 'an atrocious calumny'.[48] Canvassing could be exciting, and sometimes led to exuberant rivalry.

In 1832 burning tar-barrels were rolled through the streets and fireworks were thrown.[49] 'Judas' Wright was hissed by 'a hired rabble from Monkwearmouth Shore," and rival factions exchanged stones.[50] In 1841 a near riot occurred when a disaffected publican discharged a blunderbuss loaded with paper pellets at Lord Howick who had to be rescued from an irate mob by the constabulary.[51]

Yet it would be wrong to give an impression

Candidates exhorting their friends to support them at the nomination (1832).

BOROUGH OF
Sunderland
ELECTION.

Sir William Chaytor, Bart.

Respectfully requests the favour of the attendance of his Friends, at his Committee Room, on Monday Morning next, at Ten o'clock precisely, and from thence to accompany him to the place of Nomination.

Committee Room, 8th Dec. 1832.

T. Hodge, Printer, 37, High Street, Sunderland.

of Sunderland elections as a combination of riot, mayhem, bribery and intimidation, culminating simply in the return of that individual who would do most to line the pockets of the voters. Such elements were present, but like the attempted aristocratic domination of the town's electorate in the 1830s, they were part of the contemporary election scene in British politics. The electorate took their politics seriously, and it was partly because of this that Sunderland's politics assumed the character that it did.

THE RADICAL ELEMENT

Those who like their politics simple would have preferred to see Sunderland's electors simply in terms of pro- and anti-Reform; hence their shock at what they regarded as the betrayal of the erstwhile Reformer "Judas" Wright, and the virulence with which they continued to attack him. The Sunderland press in the later 1830s represented this simple dichotomy of view, and indeed, if the borough's politics had not been clouded by the docks issue, this might have been a tenable position. The *Sunderland Herald*, founded in 1831, at the height of the Reform struggle, saw itself as the champion of liberal views within the borough, dismissing the Tories of Sunderland as "an unintelligent set", "men of grovelling and sordid views", incapable of independent judgement. In 1838 the *Herald's* simple anti-Toryism was challenged by the equally virulent *Sunderland Beacon* which took a strong pro-Tory stand, dismissing the editor of the *Herald* as an "ignorant, impudent, and low-bred fellow" and the Whig MP Andrew White, whose cause the *Herald* upheld, as "wandering, weak, and garrulous".[52]

While local politicians might have been happy to see the struggle in terms of black and white, and the partisan press hurling abuse at the rival camps, there was a third force in Sunderland politics. Its appearance had been signalled even before the borough was enfranchised. At Sunderland's first meeting in favour of the Reform of Parliament, in February 1831, George Pemberton had alarmed the meeting by proposing that they should support vote by ballot, then regarded as an extreme radical position. Only with difficulty had other reformers present, like Bernard Ogden, Drs Clanny and Brown, and J. J. Wright, induced Pemberton to withdraw his resolution, so as to preserve unanimity amongst Sunderland's Reformers.[53] But this tactical withdrawal did not mean that Radicalism in Sunderland disappeared, and indeed in the late 1830s it was to reappear in violent form.

By the terms of the Reform Act some 2,500 of Sunderland's inhabitants were entitled to vote, but this was out of a population of around 43,000; naturally many were disappointed and frustrated. By the late 1830s such disaffected people, having abandoned the hope that a reformed House of Commons would be sympathetic to their cause came together in the Chartist movement. By June, 1838, Sunderland had held a meeting to endorse the Charter, with its call for a dramatic extension of the suffrage, the secret ballot, and so on, and the following year the Sunderland Charter Association was formed.[54] Some of the language of the Sunderland Chartists was violent; Robert Knox claimed that "the majority has a right to use any means that will gain its rights. If fighting in the field with the pike or musket will get those rights, the people have the right to use the pike and the musket," while Sunderland's Chartist leaders, the booksellers James Williams and George Binns, warned the middle classes that if they did not at once concede the necessity of further reform, "vengeance swift and terrible will then overtake you . . . your warehouses, your homes will be given to the flames, and one black ruin overwhelm England!"[55] Binns and Williams were subsequently arrested, and given six months in Durham gaol for sedition.

At the general election of 1841 George Binns, whose imprisonment had made him a martyr to the cause, and who had been feted throughout Tyneside and Wearside on his release, was nominated as a candidate. The middle-class electorate dismissed the Chartists as "beggars and blackguards of every degree", "thieves, pickpockets, and cheats" whose only recourse was violence.[56] But this was a caricature. It was probably true, as the *Times* claimed in 1841, that the Chartists could be, to all intents and purposes, equated with the non-electors,[57] but aside from the fact that Williams lived on to become a respected Alderman the Chartists were significant for the strain of radicalism they represented in the borough. Binns doubtless recognised his true voting strength when having won the show of hands in 1841 (when, of course, the non-electors could make their presence — and sentiments — felt) he declined to go to the poll. Within three months there was a by-election, and Binns, though not on this occasion standing, took the opportunity of nominating the prominent Radical, Thomas Peronnet Thompson, claiming that only such men as Thompson would provide those necessary "measures of reform commensurate with the wants and demands of the country."[58]

Sunderland
ELECTION.

Mr Ald. Thompson

Respectfully solicits the honour of the attendance of his Friends, at the Assembly Room, on Monday Morning next, at Ten o'clock precisely, being the place appointed for the Nomination of the Candidates.

Committee Room, 8th Dec. 1832.

T. MOORE, PRINTER, 37, HIGH STREET, SUNDERLAND.

Thompson declined, but agreed to stand at the next election.

It was in the course of this speech that Binns revealed that the Tories of Sunderland had attempted to induce the Chartists to put up a candidate, in order to split the Liberal vote. Most attention at the time was concentrated on the fact that the Tories had offered £125 towards the cost, but as significant is the fact that there was a possibility of securing such a split. Binns, Williams, and their colleagues wanted a thorough-going Radical candidate; Sir Hedworth Williamson, on the other hand, was on record as saying that "it was only so long as the electors of Sunderland supported such men as Lord Howick ... that he would retain his influence in the Reform cause."[59] This division in the ranks of the Reformers of Sunderland was to be a persistent feature of subsequent elections.

In 1845 Lord Howick succeeded his father as Earl Grey, and, at the subsequent by-election, Thompson fulfilled his pledge to stand. Thompson was a well-known Radical, an out-and-out reformer, and an early advocate of free trade. His extremism was alarming to many. The *Manchester Guardian* labelled him a "Chartist of the wildest school", while the *Tyne Mercury* reported that others had labelled him a "socialist" or an "infidel".[60] Such radicalism was anathema to those whom Thompson dismissed as "the pretended Reformers" of Sunderland, but who saw themselves as moderate Whigs in the tradition of Lord Grey and as those who had enfranchised the borough in 1832. Faced with the prospect of such a candidate as Thompson, they looked for a more moderate alternative, and found him in the person of John Bagshaw, a moderate Whig, an East India merchant with experience of shipping, who shared an interest in railways with his potential rival, George Hudson.[61] But if the Whigs were fearful of Thompson's extremism, the Radicals were resentful of this attempt to split the Liberal vote; it was, as one of Thompson's supporters wrote, "a downright insult to the more extreme men of Sunderland that the Whigs should attempt to get hold of both of the seats". The sitting member, David Barclay, was, he pointed out

> a fine Whig, and represents that part of the constituency. It is not right that they should oppose or thwart Colonel Thompson — as he may fairly be taken to represent the other section of the constituency which has a perfect right to one seat both from numbers and influence.[62]

With two Liberals in the field, compromise was essential. George Wilson, the Chairman of the Anti-Corn-Law League (who sent their leading speakers to support Colonel Thompson, to the disgust of the locals, who resented such outside interference) put it thus: "If you both go to the poll, the Tory of course wins easily." To simply drive Bagshaw away would not do, for to secure Thompson's victory, the Radicals needed the cordial cooperation of the Sunderland Whigs. "Depend upon it he has no chance unless the Bagshaw party assist," wrote Wilson. "There is only one way of doing the thing," Wilson told his fellow Leaguer, Richard Cobden, "and that is by a joint canvass or ballot, and the weakest to give way".[63] The irascible Colonel Thompson however indignantly rejected such a notion, which, as John Bright, remarked, "put him in the wrong with almost everybody." Bright was particularly upset as he believed such a primary run-off would have resulted in Thompson's favour, but "his obstinacy has endangered his election." But for that obstinacy, which he felt was "beyond all belief", Bright felt some compromise could have been reached with the local Whigs, who were "almost to a man" free traders, and though alarmed by Thompson's extremism on the franchise, not, on the whole, "a bad set ...; to have got up a quarrel with them is very annoying".[64]

Bagshaw did withdraw before the election, but as Wilson had foretold, this forced withdrawal did not heal the breach. Most crucially, Henry Morton, the Whig agent, was reluctant to aid Thompson. Though the local press was wrong when it asserted that Morton was working for the Tories, there were others among the leading Sunderland Whigs who were prepared to do so, rather than support the Radical Thompson. Walker Featherstonehaugh, who had been chairman of Lord Howick's election committee in 1841, was reported as saying that Sunderland electors should assert their independence of the Anti-Corn-Law League, and support Hudson as the man who would do most for the borough, and George Wilson, gloomily admitted that such was Whig discontent that, "from what I hear some of them say, they will vote for Hudson."[65]

The result of the 1845 by-election showed that of those who had supported the Whig Viscount Howick in the 1841 by-election, 12 per cent now supported the Tory Hudson, while a further 16 per cent abstained. The abstentions are perhaps most significant, for Howick himself had attracted considerable numbers of erstwhile Tory votes in 1841. The greatest swing against Thompson was in Sir Hedworth

In the absence of secret voting hourly reports on the state of the poll were placarded round the streets of Sunderland. An example from 1841.

OFFICIAL STATE OF THE POLL.

One o'Clock.

HOWICK - - - - - 621

ATTWOOD- - - - - 394

Reformers, Relax Not! Sweep In the Stragglers!

Poster, probably produced during the 1866 election showing (second left with cigar) James Hartley, the Conservative MP from 1865-8, and (far right) probably George Hudson, Hartley's only predecessor as a Tory MP. The setting is Fawcett Street Station with Mowbray Park in the background.

The banner of William Digby Seymour (July 1852) 'presented by the ladies of Sunderland', is a surviving reminder of early election marches and parades. (A similar banner of 1837 presented to Andrew White also survives.)

Williamson's bailiwick of Monkwearmouth. But the result also showed that, in a straight fight between a Radical and a Tory, 44 per cent of Sunderland's electorate were prepared to cast a Radical vote — a higher figure than could be found in contemporary Gateshead or Newcastle.[66] If the result showed that some Whigs preferred a Tory to a Radical, it also demonstrated the underlying strength of Sunderland Radicalism as a force to be reckoned with for the future.

After the election the Sunderland Tories were jubilant. "The contest and victory were expressly a Conservative contest and victory," proclaimed Joseph Wright. The Tory *Durham Advertiser* also claimed that the result showed that "the Liberals had no chance of a majority"; Thompson was defeated "because the Liberals happen to be in a large minority among the electors". Such analyses were false, however; the result showed simply that Sunderland Liberalism was disunited, and that a candidate with the strong market power of a Hudson would attract floating or luke-warm voters. Though the *Advertiser's* boast about the strength of Sunderland Toryism was a vain one, it was more accurate when it spoke of the disarray among "the 'Liberal' politicians — the Whigs — if there be any of that genus left — the Radicals, the Chartists, the Leaguers, the Socialists . . . Such a medley of Liberalism was styled the union of Reformers!"[67]

The electoral history of Sunderland in subsequent years confirmed the pattern established in 1845. At the next general election, the Radicals challenged the sitting members Barclay and Hudson with another Corn-Law-Leaguer, William Arthur Wilkinson, but the result, as the *Sunderland Herald* recorded, demonstrated a "political paradox — at once showing the overpowering strength of the Liberal party, and its self-constituted weakness." The Liberals, claimed the *Herald*, had 2,093 votes; but while 1,560 of these had gone to the two Liberals — the Whig Barclay and the Radical Wilkinson, — 533 had gone to the Tory, Hudson.

> The number of Liberal voters is such that, being united, would operate beneficially to the Reform party, and enable them to carry into Parliament men thoroughly suited to express their views. The want of that unity constituted their lack of power in the present instance. The fears of one party laid them willingly open to the advances of the Tories, and they chose the coalition rather than the more patriotic endeavour to return two Liberal members, which they could have done.[68]

Worse was to come, for when Barclay resigned the subsequent by-election was a straight fight between Liberal and Radical. Sir Hedworth Williamson replaced his brother-in-law, but only by defeating Wilkinson, once again. Whig and Radical were now firmly opposed to each other in Sunderland.

The degree of bitterness engendered was apparent in the general election of 1852. The *Sunderland Times* threw its weight behind William Digby Seymour, denouncing the Whig candidate, Henry Fenwick, and those who supported him as "the whiggling toadies dangling about at the heels of the sensitive and gentlemanly whiggling candidate for the honour of degrading Sunderland by getting it to send him to Parliament". Fenwick's only claim on the electors, they said, was that he was the friend, "if he be not the nominee", of Sir Hedworth Williamson. His pretensions to Liberalism were false; having opposed Wilkinson in 1847, he now (in order to gain support) claimed to be his political heir, but was in reality allied with Hudson. "The mass of the free and thinking electors," said the *Times*, would vote for Seymour, and "convince the imperious and haughty local Whigs that they cannot, whether of their own free will, or in submission to dictation, longer trample down the independent and uncorrupted electors of Sunderland".[69] The Whig press was no less backward in its attacks on Seymour and the Radicals. Seymour was a convert to Radicalism, and was, moreover, the son-in-law of Hudson's agent, J. J. Wright. The *Sunderland Herald* insisted that the "clique" who supported him did so only on the hope of "some little picking or other some day" from the fruits of the Hudsonian table. If an honest Liberal — "not an Orangeman of bygone days — not a Tory of yesterday, and a mock-Reformer of today — but a straightforward and trusty man" were to stand, said the *Durham Chronicle*, then Hudson might be beaten; the Liberals would not win with Seymour, who was "nothing but a Tory-Chartist", whose "wires are worked" by his father-in-law.[70] In the event Seymour won, but the *Times* was premature when it said that "the haughty Whig dictators have been humbled by the Liberal electors of Sunderland".[71] The result really showed how deep was the division in Sunderland Liberalism. Only 103 voters cast both their votes for the Liberals, while over 600 gave one of their two votes to the Tory, Hudson. Rather than vote for another Liberal, 322 Radicals cast only one vote (for Seymour) while 249 Whigs equally gave a "plumper" for Fenwick.

When the Tories and their allies were safe (as in the by-election of 1855, following Seymour's appointment as Recorder of Newcastle) then the relative position of Radicalism was exposed. In another bitter contest, Fenwick reversed his defeat at the general election of 1852. Expecting Hudson to retire, the *Sunderland Herald* looked forward to the general election in 1857 as a favourable opportunity "for re-uniting the shattered ranks of the Liberals of Sunderland." If old feuds could be forgotten, and the recent differences of 1855 "decently buried (as well they may!)", then Sunderland could once more elect two Liberals. Richard Hoare, a banker and merchant, had contemplated standing in the Liberal interest when it was felt that Hudson would withdraw; but with Hudson's announcement, the Radicals brought forward Ralph Walters, and Hoare abandoned his candidacy; "as the Liberal party is already so divided," he told the electors, "I feel my remaining as a candidate would be injurious to the cause." With Fenwick, the Whig and Walters, the Radical, still in the field, and Hudson having announced his candidacy, the *Herald* gloomily declared that "the dream of union in the ranks of the Liberals is over," and then proceeded to denounce the local Radicals, showing the hollowness of its call for buried hatchets. The opposition to Fenwick was, it claimed, the work of "men who have all along shown themselves averse to any arrangement which did not sufficiently flatter their self-importance, or which tended to restrain their ambition within its proper limits." Though the straight Radical vote rose to 524, much larger numbers than in 1852 divided their votes between the Whig and the Tory, and, to the *Herald's* relief, Fenwick came top of the poll.[72]

The chief beneficiary of these divisions within Sunderland Liberalism was, of course, George Hudson. And from the first, Hudson had attempted to attract cross-party, or non-party support. At the banquet to celebrate his victory over Colonel Thompson in 1845, Hudson urged his largely Tory audience to "cultivate good feelings towards those who are politically opposed to us, and prevent political feeling from interfering with our endeavours to promote the local advantage of the town". If his vision of transforming the port of Sunderland into the commercial hub of the world was to be realised, "we must not suffer political feeling to interfere, we must not allow politics to intermix with the management of these affairs".[73]

In 1857, facing criticism for his absenteeism, he told his supporters:

> As to supporting any particular government, I beg to assure you that if you return me I shall be quite free in that respect . . . If you elect me I shall go to Parliament upon entirely independent grounds

a sentiment that was greeted with great applause by his audience.[74] In 1859 Hudson made a rare (and as it turned out, rash) excursion into party politics, when he denounced Lord John Russell and the Liberals for what he described as their factional opposition to Lord Derby's Tory Government. By 1859, though, the Hudson bubble — even in Sunderland — was burst, yet even then the *Herald* conceded that, in "other circumstances than the present," he might have "reckoned on a very large measure of support from men of all shades of politics."[75]

The "other circumstances" to which the *Herald* alluded were not simply that Hudson had exhausted Sunderland's fund of gratitude for its docks, but that there was at last an issue before the electors which could divide them on simple two-party lines. Fenwick and Lindsay not only represented the shipping interests of the future, but also both were pledged (in marked opposition to Hudson) to Lord John Russell's new Reform proposals. "For years past", said the *Sunderland Herald*,

> it has been a common remark that if the Liberal electors of this town could only arrive at a common understanding, they would, beyond all question, secure the return of a couple of representatives after their own hearts. Never until now has that much desired unity of purpose been realised.

When Hudson was finally defeated, the *Herald* claimed that the result "unmistakably demonstrated" that for the last 14 years he, "as an avowed Conservative, had been allowed to sit in Parliament as the representative of a constituency in which the Liberal party predominated to a very considerable extent." It was clear, admitted the *Herald*, that

Hudson had owed his return to Whig support, "a support which could not have been given because of his political views, but simply out of regard to the great service which he rendered the town." They briefly skated over the "unhappy divisions among the Liberals" which had reinforced the attractions of Hudson as a candidate to many of the Whigs.[76]

The wheel was almost come full circle; that unity which had characterised Sunderland politics on the eve of the first Reform bill, was beginning to re-emerge in anticipation of a second. But Reform was not, as many in Sunderland expected, enacted in 1859, and two more bitter contests were to take place before the Radicals of Sunderland emerged triumphant.

In 1832, under the restricted franchise conferred by the first Reform Act, Sunderland had been given its MPs, but they were elected by a very small section of the population of the town. That electorate had been subjected not merely to the normal pressures inherent in early nineteenth century electioneering — of bribery, of aristocratic pressure, of the lure of a free drink — but also severe pressure on their pockets, in the form of self-interest in the town's docks, in employment prospects for the shipping of the town, in the lure of easy dividends. The town had grown fast, and with it the electorate had grown. From 1,378 registered electors at the time of the first election, there were 1,973 in 1852, and 2,905 in 1860.[77] Moreover, the percentage of the working class within that electorate was growing; by the eve of the second Reform Act, over 17 per cent of Sunderland's 3,468 voters were officially recorded as being working class.[78] The radicalisation of Sunderland's politics, so long delayed, and frustrated by the conservatism of the Whigs, and the manipulations of Hudson, came at last with the passage of further Reform in 1867, and the massive increase in Sunderland's electorate in 1867 to some 11,000.

REFERENCES

1. *Durham Advertiser*, 11 Feb. 1831, *Durham Chronicle*, 12 Feb. 1831.

2. *Hansard's Parliamentary Debates*, 3rd series, ii, 1155 (2 March 1831).

3. T. Potts, *Sunderland; A History of the Town, Port, Trade and Commerce* (Sunderland 1892) pp. 309-10.

4. *Ibid.*, p.309.

5. *Durham Chronicle*, 30 April 1831.

6. *Durham Chronicle*, 7 May 1831.

7. *Durham Chronicle*, 9 Oct. 1830, *Durham Advertiser*, 11 Feb. 1831.

8. *Reports from Commissioners on Proposed Divisions of Counties and Boundaries of Boroughs. Parliamentary Papers*, 1831-32 (141), xxxviii, pp.171-2. *Parliamentary Representation: Abstract of the Population, Assessed Taxes, &c., of the Boroughs contained in the Boundary Report . . .*, pp.1831-32 (232), xxxvi, p.322.

9. Raine MSS, VII, 48.

10. *Durham Advertiser*, 14 Dec. 1832.

11. Potts, *op. cit.*, p.309.

12. *Durham Chronicle*, 8 June 1832.

13. *Hansard*, xii, 363, 1378-9 (13 April, 23 May 1832).

14. Hedworth Lambton to Lord Durham, 1 Jan. 1833. Lambton MSS. I am grateful to Lord Durham for permission to see his family papers, and to Miss H. Borron for allowing me access to them.

15. Raine MSS, VII, 3, 1. Taylor Potts, *op. cit.*, p.314 n., says Barrington was driven mad by the excitement of the contest; he was however, clearly already ill.

16. Hedworth Lambton to Lord Durham, 1 Jan. 1833, Lambton MSS.

17. Raine MSS, VII, 1.

18. *The Times*, 17 Sept. 1841. *Durham Chronicle*, 22 June 1832.

19. Hedworth Lambton to Lord Durham, 1 Jan. 1833. Lambton MSS.

20. For the following paragraph, *cf.* T. J. Nossiter, 'Dock Politics and Unholy Alliances, 1832-1852,' H. Bowling (ed.) *Some Chapters in the History of Sunderland* (Sunderland 1970) pp.78-88.

21. *Durham Chronicle*, 23 March 1832.

22. Raine MSS, VII, 4, 12.

23. For the following paragraph, see N. McCord and P. A. Wood, 'The Sunderland Election of 1845,' *Durham University Journal* new ser., xxi (1955-56), pp.11-21.

24. *SH*, 6 March 1857.

25. Raine MSS, VII, 9.

26. A. J. Heesom, 'The Sunderland By-Election, 1841,' *Northern History*, ix (1974), pp.62-78.

27. L. G. Johnson, *General T. Peronnet Thompson, 1783-1869* (London 1957) p.253.

28. R. S. Lambert, *The Railway King: A Study of George Hudson and the Business Morals of his Time* (London 1934) p.158.

29. *SH*, 24 Oct. 1845.

30. *SH*, 18, 26 June 1847.

31. *Ibid.*

32. *The Larchfield Diary: Extracts from the Diary of the Late Mr. Mewburn, First Railway Solicitor* (London and Darlington 1876) pp.68-9, 99.

33. Robert Anderson to Londonderry, 28 May 1851; Londonderry MSS (Durham County Record Office), D/Lo/C 158 (143). *Cf.* Lord Castlereagh to Londonderry, 11 Feb. 1847: "I have nothing in common with your old friend Hudson. I always wondered how he could ever have got to Wynyard, or how you could have been so civil to him." *Ibid.*, D/Lo/C 104 (79). J. J. Wright to Londonderry, 25 July 1848. *Ibid.*, D/Lo/C 489 (9).

34. Lambert, *Railway King*, p.281.

35. *Durham Advertiser*, 4 June 1852.

36. *Sunderland News*, 3 July 1852.

37. *SH* 9 July 1852.

38. Lambert, *Railway King*, pp.284-5.

39. *SH* 13 March 1857.

40. *Ibid.* 13, 20 March 1857.

41. Lambert, *Railway King*, pp.292-3.

42. *Ibid.*, p.294.

43. *SH*, 6 March 1857.

44. Morton to Lord Durham, 15 Jan. 1837; Lambton MSS, T. Fordyce, *Local Records, IV, 1867-1875* (Newcastle, 1876), p. 85.

45. John Bright to Richard Cobden, 29 July 1845. Bright MSS. (British Library) Add. MSS, 43383, f.154-6. *Durham Advertiser*, 29 Aug. 1845.

46. Return of Official Expenses, 1832, *PP*, 1833 (189), xxvii, pp.223-4. Potts, *Sunderland*, p.311. H. L. Robson, 'Extracts from the Churchwardens' Accounts, Sunderland Parish', *Antiq. Sund.*, xxv (1970-73), p.59.

47. Wright to Londonderry, 17 June 1838, 23 July 1837; Londonderry MSS, D.Lo/C 489 (4, 1).

48. *Durham Advertiser*, 14 July 1837.

49. Potts, *Sunderland*, pp.316-17.

50. Hedworth Williamson to Lord Durham, 26 Dec. 1832. Lambton MSS.

51. Heesom '1841 By-Election', pp.76-7.

52. P. Storey, 'Sunderland Newspapers, 1831-1873,' *Antiq. Sund.*, xxvii (1977-79), p.104. *S.H.*, 8 July 1837.

53. *Durham Chronicle*, 12 Feb. 1831.

54. For Sunderland Chartism, see K. Wilson, ' "Whole Hogs" and "Sucking Pigs"; Chartism and the Complete Suffrage Union in Sunderland', M. Calcott and R. Challinor (eds.) *Working Class Politics in North-East England* (Newcastle 1983) and works therein cited.

55. W. H. Maehl, 'Chartist Disturbances in Northeastern England, 1839', *International Review of Social History*, viii (1963), pp.394-6. D. Thompson (ed.) *The Early Chartists* (London 1971) p. 133.

56. Handbill, 'Hurrah for the Chartists!', Sunderland, June 1841 (British Library).

57. *The Times*, 16 Sept, 1841.

58. Handbill, 'Binns' Speech at the Nomination', Grey MSS, Subject Files (Parliamentary Elections — Local).

59. *Ibid.*, Heesom, 'Sunderland By-Election', pp.70-71, 75.

60. Johnson, *Thompson*, pp.256-7.

61. As a fellow director of the Eastern Counties Railway, he was implicated in Hudson's fall in 1849, and defended Hudson in Parliament.

62. McCord and Wood, '1845 Election', p.14.

63. Wilson to Cobden, 24 July 1845. *Ibid.*, p.15.

64. Bright to Cobden, 28 July 1845; Bright MSS, Add. MSS, 43383, f.153-4.

65. McCord and Wood, '1845 Election', p.16.

66. T. J. Nossiter, 'Elections and Political Behaviour in County Durham and Newcastle, 1832-74,' (unpublished D.Phil. thesis, University of Oxford, 1968), p.379. For Howick's vote in 1841, see Heesom, '1841 By-Election', pp.75-6.

67. Wright's speech, 21 Oct. 1845; *Sunderland Herald*, 24 Oct. 1845; *Durham Advertiser*, 29 Aug. 1845.

68. *SH*, 6 Aug. 1847.

69. *ST*, 3, 10 July 1852.

70. *SH*, 2 July 1852. *Durham Chronicle*, 2 April 1852.

71. *ST*, 10 July 1852.

72. *SH*, 6, 20 March, 3 April 1852.

73. *Ibid.*, 24 Oct. 1845.

74. *SH*, 20 March 1857.

75. *Ibid.*, 22, 29 April 1859.

76. *Ibid.*, 29 April, 6 May 1859.

77. Returns of Electors, *PP* 1852 (8), xliii, p.318; *PP* 1860 (130), 1v, pp.65-6.

78. Return of Working Class Electors, *PP* 1866 (170), 1vii, pp.48-50. By 1868 there were over 4,000 trade unionists in Sunderland; R. Harrison, *Before the Socialists* (London, 1965), p.160.

Plan of Borough of Sunderland prepared by R. S. Rounthwaite, the Borough Surveyor, to accompany the Sunderland Corporation Bill of 1899. The area in red shows new housing built since 1878.

Sunderland Museum (Tyne and Wear Museums Service).

Tommy Sanderson, Town Crier, painted by Gillis Brown in 1884. In the background are the Donnison School for poor girls, and Holy Trinity Parish Church. Tommy Sanderson, born 1808, was a well-known character-poet, inventor, musician, umbrella-mender and last town-crier of Sunderland. An eccentric, he lived in 'Metal Hall', an iron hut on wheels on the site of the present Museum. Evicted by the Council he left Sunderland, but returned eventually to become Bellman and Town Crier until his death in 1892.

Sunderland Museum (Tyne and Wear Museums Service).

Phoenix Hall, Queen Street, designed by John Bonner in 1785. This is the oldest purpose-built Freemason's building in England, still used for its original purpose. The interior is thought to be a replica of the previous Lodge Hall in Vine Street, which was severely damaged by fire in 1783. In the late 18th and early 19th centuries many prominent Sunderland residents belonged to the Phoenix Lodge.

Sunderland Museum (Tyne and Wear Museums Service).

An advertisement from the cover of the *Sunderland Year Book* for 1911, showing Jopling and Tuer's Department store in High Street East. The firm, established lower down the High Street as a drapers shop in 1804, moved westwards to the 'Beehive' building about 1878, and was one of the last major businesses in the East End. The westward move continued. In 1921 Jopling's moved to High Street West and, after these premises were destroyed by fire in 1954, built their present store in John Street.

Sunderland Museum (Tyne and Wear Museums Service).

Gillis Brown's 1884 painting of the *Salvation Army* in Numbers Garth, a small square of houses which lay between High Street West and the river. This was one of the poorer parts of the town, where the Salvation Army held their meetings. The painting shows members of the Army selling the *War Cry*, the Army's newspaper.

Sunderland Museum (Tyne and Wear Museums Service).

Mackie's Corner. **A night scene of the corner of High Street West and Bridge Street painted by Daniel Whitley Marshall in 1884. The Corner was part of Hutchinson's Buildings (architect, G. A. Middlemiss) completed in 1850. Partly rebuilt after being damaged in the Havelock House Fire of 1898, it still dominates the view towards the north end of Fawcett Street. Beyond is the National Provincial Bank (architect, John Gibson, 1876).** *Sunderland Museum (Tyne and Wear Museums Service).*

The Elephant Tea House (architect, Frank Caws, 1877) at the corner of Fawcett Street and High Street West, one of several commercial buildings designed by Frank Caws which made extensive use of terracotta. Built for William Grimshaw, one of Sunderland's best-known tea and coffee merchants and grocers, it featured pagodas and elephants with tea-chests on their backs. This photograph shows the building, now the Royal Bank of Scotland, soon after being restored in 1983. *Sunderland Museum (Tyne and Wear Museums Service).*

1988 view of the central section of the west side of Fawcett Street, which has developed as the town's major financial centre. The two nearest bank buildings were built for North Eastern banks which later were absorbed by national groups — Lambton's (architect, C. R. Gribble, 1981), now Lloyd's, and Wood's (architect, Austin Johnson and Hicks, 1870), now Barclay's. Beyond was the Subscription Library, and the headquarters of the Sunderland Workingmens' Building Society. The National Westminster Bank has replaced the former, while the Building Society, now part of the North of England Building Society, has its headquarters in the 1979 block on the former Town Hall site.

Photo: I. S. Carr.

This tinted postcard of 1900 shows the south end of Fawcett Street dominated by the Town Hall. The section of Binns Draper's shop beyond the near sign was the firm's first Fawcett Street premises. Established in the 1800s, Binns moved here from High Street West in 1884. By the 1900s they had taken over adjacent shops and in the following 70 years they expanded to occupy much of both sides of Fawcett Street between Borough Road and Athenaeum Street. Binns, Sunderland's largest department store, established branches in other parts of the North East and Scotland, and in 1953 became part of the House of Fraser group.

Sunderland Museum (Tyne and Wear Museums Service).

Looking over the newly completed Market Square in 1970 to the Town Hall, then about to be demolished. The area in the immediate foreground was covered over in 1988 as part of the 'Bridges' shopping development.

Photo: by James Crawley, Sunderland Museum, (Tyne and Wear Museums Service).

The exterior and council chamber of Sunderland Civic Centre (Sir Basil Spence, Bonnington and Partners), opened in the former West Park in 1970. It replaced the much-loved Town Hall, demolished in 1971 and several other buildings which had housed the town's various local government departments.

Borough of Sunderland.

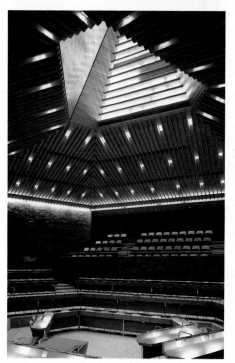

The Infirmary in New Durham Road in the 1900s. It had moved from the 1823 building in Chester Road in 1867. The original central building was designed by Joseph Potts, and several extensions designed by John Eltringham were added between 1882 and 1911. Nursing staff were provided between 1873 and 1888 by the Tottenham Sisters, a Protestant version of the Roman Catholic Sisters of Mercy. The Infirmary was granted the title 'Royal' by King George V in 1911.

Sunderland Museum (Tyne and Wear Museums Service).

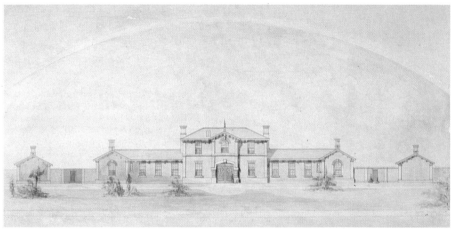

Design by the York architect John Oates for the first buildings of the Sunderland Union Workhouse, opened in 1855 to replace the separate parish workhouses of Sunderland, Bishopwearmouth and Monkwearmouth. Many later buildings were added on the site between Chester Road and Hylton Road and the Workhouse had its own hospital, schools, farm and mortuary. Some of these remain as part of the General Hospital, although the 1855 building was demolished for the new central hospital block opened in 1978.

Sunderland Museum (Tyne and Wear Museums Service).

The *Winter Gardens* painted by Daniel Whitley Marshall in 1895. The large heated glass conservatory attached to the Mowbray Park side of the Library and Museum building contained tropical plants, birds and fish. It was demolished after bomb damage in 1941.

Sunderland Museum (Tyne and Wear Museums Service).

The Briery, built for Hiram Craven, the ropemaker, in 1869. This was one of several large houses for industrialists in the Ashbrooke area in the second half of the 19th century. It is now part of St. Aidan's School.

Sunderland Museum (Tyne and Wear Museums Service).

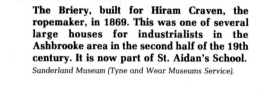

A variety of later 19th century housing styles from the Ashbrooke area. They are (in ascending grandeur) Ashmore Street, The Grove (taken from St. John's church tower) and The Elms East.

Photos: Geoffrey Milburn.

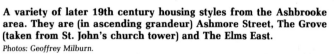

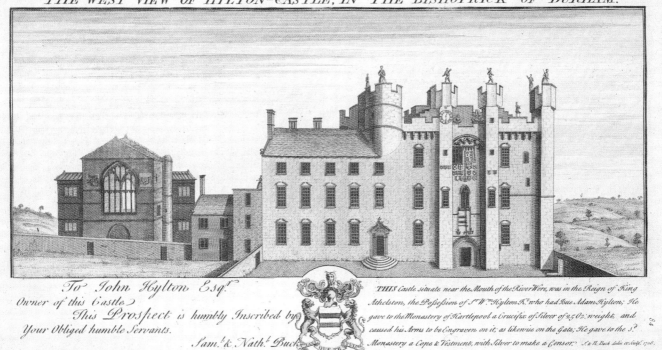

To John Hylton Esqr
Owner of this Castle
This Prospect is humbly Inscribed by
Your Obliged humble Servants.
Saml & Nathl Buck

THIS Castle situate near the Mouth of the River Were, was in the Reign of King Athelston, the Possession of Sr Wm Hylton K.^t who had Bue Adam Hylton; He gave to the Monastery of Hartlepool a Crucifix of Silver of 25 Oz: weight; and caused his Arms to be Engraven on it; as likewise on the Gate; He gave to the S.^d Monastery a Cope & Vestment, with Silver to make a Censor.

Hylton Castle shown in S. and N. Bucks' engraving of 1728. The Castle was built about 1400 by the Hylton family, owners of estates at Hylton, Usworth, Follingsby and elsewhere until the mid-18th century. The north wing shown here had been added in the 1700's, and a similar wing on the south was added in the 1730's; both were demolished in 1869. In the 19th century the castle was used as a residence and as a school. St. Catherine's chapel on the left was the private chapel of the Hylton family; its structure as shown by Buck dated mainly from the 15th and 16th centuries. Now surrounded by 1950's housing, the castle is an English Heritage property open to the public. *Sunderland Museum (Tyne and Wear Museums Service).*

Fulwell Mill in 1987. The windmill is the last survivor of many which existed in, and around Sunderland. It was built about 1821 for grinding corn, and went on later to produce animal feed until 1949. Latterly the power was provided by a gas engine instead of sails; these were removed, but were replaced by Sunderland Corporation in 1955. A second restoration by the Tyne and Wear Industrial Monuments' Trust took place in the 1980s.

Sunderland Museum (Tyne and Wear Museums Service).

This view of the interior of Ryhope pumping station shows the two beam engines built by R & W Hawthorn in 1868 for drawing water from below the limestone. They are still steamed occasionally by the Ryhope Engine's Trust. Ryhope was one of several pumping stations designed by Thomas Hawksley for the Sunderland and South Shields Water Company.

Photo: Ryhope Engines Trust.

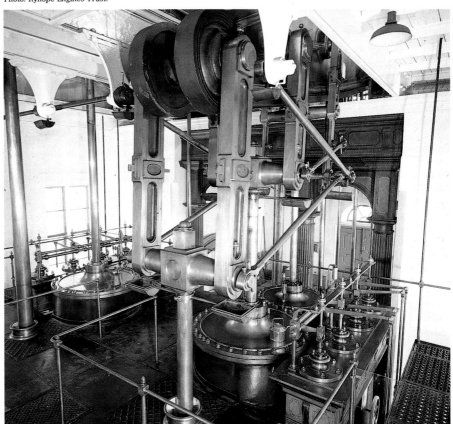

Watercolour of Tunstall Hills painted in 1866 by Edward Backhouse, a member of the Sunderland branch of the Quaker banking family. (See biographical appendix.) He was a philanthropist, natural historian and antiquarian as well as a talented amateur artist. The building in the foreground is Tunstall Hills Farm. Tunstall Hills' twin summits ('Grassy' and 'Rocky') which dominate Sunderland's southern skyline were formerly known as the 'Maiden Paps'. Sailors used them as a landmark when coming into the Port of Sunderland, and they have long been a popular place of recreation for local residents.

Sunderland Museum (Tyne and Wear Museums Service).

The aerial view of the Docks in 1985 shows the small North Dock of 1837 on the far side of the Wear, the Hudson Dock of 1850 and the Hendon Dock of 1868. The outer piers (above), and the former sea entrance to the Docks, extend well out into the North Sea. By 1985 only two coal shipment points remained in use and these also closed in 1986. Much of the industry that would have appeared in a similar view 20 years earlier had disappeared by 1985, leaving only oil and chemical depots and ship-repairing at the Wear Dockyard.

Photo: Air Fotos.

Hetton-le-Hole Primitive Methodist Chapel (Architect, Martin Greener, 1858), a good example of a traditional Methodist preaching house with a broad rostrum pulpit, large choir and enormous gallery. The Miners' Lodge banners are reminders of the strong links that existed between Methodism and pit workers in many villages in the 19th and early 20th centuries, not least at Hetton. There are extensive ancillary premises below the chapel. The stained glass windows are modern features.

Photo: Michael le Roy.

Religion and Society 1780-1914

PART I

> 'Come let's away to Tunstall Hill!
> In 20 minutes we'll be there,
> And on the top we'll take our fill
> Of the pure bracing country air!'

So begins a poem written a hundred years or so ago by William Brockie. Despite the encroachment of modern housing developments the Tunstall Hills (a limestone ridge on the southern side of Sunderland) still provide a precious oasis for exercise and refreshment. They also form one of the best vantage points in the locality, affording splendid long-distance views to all points of the compass. At shorter range can be seen most of the area which constituted the borough of Sunderland up to 1974, the very area with which this book is concerned. From here one can see the town in perspective, and consider its position, its shape, its topography, in a way not possible at a lower level. Moreover to those prepared to bring to their aid some map-work, a pair of binoculars, a willingness to delve in a few books, and a sense of historical awareness, the top of Tunstall Hills is in fact a splendid spot to think not only about Sunderland as it is but as it used to be, about its growth and development, and about the social character of the town as it has evolved over the centuries.

Let us illustrate this by reference to the aspect of that past which is the subject of this chapter, the religious life of the community of Sunderland.[1]

PARISHES OLD AND NEW

To begin with, the whole area spread out below us, stretching southwards from the river Wear to Ryhope, Tunstall and Silksworth, and westwards from the coast towards (but not quite reaching) Penshaw Monument, constituted the ancient parish of Bishopwearmouth, with its boundaries laid out in early medieval times. The parish church of St. Michael, standing near what is today the urban centre of Sunderland, but once at the heart of what remained a farming village up to the end of the eighteenth century, is visible as we look to the north. Though much rebuilt in the opening decade of the nineteenth century and again in the 1930s it yet retains the character (and indeed some of the original features) of its medieval origins, and stands proudly as the ancient mother church of the vast parochial area over which its rectors presided, and from which they drew the handsome stipend attached to the living.[2] St. Michael's roots were in a medieval, rural society, but the old church saw that society utterly transformed by industrial and urban growth, slowly at first in the seventeenth and eighteenth centuries, and then with gathering and inexorable speed in the nineteenth.

We are reminded of a similar process of change north of the river as we look beyond the valley of the Wear to the parish of Monkwearmouth. St. Peter's (the other ancient church of the town, which was extensively restored and rebuilt in the 1870s) is out of sight from Tunstall Hills but its ancient parish boundaries can be broadly discerned, stretching westwards from the sea to North Hylton (whose medieval castle is visible) and bordering the parish of Whitburn to the north.[3]

St. Peter's origins link us of course with the age of the first conversion of the English to Christianity, so that here, as at St. Michael's, we are forcibly reminded of the long tradition of Christian work and witness on Wearside, at first in the name of the medieval Catholic Church, and then from the sixteenth century in the name of the protestant Church of England. We are also reminded, however, of how these churches, which had been built to serve relatively static and stable societies, were to be caught up in all the social traumas resulting from the industrial revolution.

Even with enlargements and improvements these two ancient churches were quickly shown to be ludicrously small as industry developed and as the population of their parishes grew. The need for daughter churches and for the subdivision of the old parishes into a number of smaller ones was an increasingly urgent priority if the Church of England was to attempt to preserve (with any vestige of reality) its claim to be the Church of the people, ministering effectively to their needs and retaining their loyalty. A beginning had been made in 1719 when the eastern end of the town became the newly independent parish of Sunderland; its fine Georgian church is visible from the Hills though from certain positions concealed by the tower blocks of the east end.[4]

After the formation of Sunderland parish the Church of England proved slow to respond further to the challenges of the age, partly due to inertia and lack of vision, partly to the legal and financial problems involved in building new churches, founding new parishes and endowing the stipends of extra clergy. There were at last some significant developments in the second quarter of the nineteenth century when several new churches were built to serve the most rapidly growing parts of the old parishes. One of these, Holy Trinity, Southwick (1842) can be seen from Tunstall Hills, standing now in a relatively open situation but in the nineteenth century serving a busy industrial area with a burgeoning community of artisans and labourers and their families.

South of the river the rectors of Bishopwearmouth were, by the mid-nineteenth century, showing themselves increasingly willing to sacrifice some of the wealth of their living to promote church extension, but such were the legal complexities that it took the Bishopwearmouth Rectory Act of 1867 finally to crack the nut.[5] The outcome of the Act was that the rectors of St. Michael's were to receive a reduced (but still handsome) stipend, while the extra income of the living was to be administered by the Ecclesiastical Commissioners to support existing daughter churches, and to build new ones. Two direct products of this Act are visible from Tunstall Hills — St. Matthew's, Silksworth (1872) and St. Mark's, Millfield (1872), both built to serve new parishes that were largely if not predominantly working class in character. St. Luke's, Pallion (1874) was another. St. Paul's, Ryhope (1870), clearly seen to the south, was also, in part, a product of these developments;

Canon William Cockin, rector of Bishopwearmouth 1864-1883, during whose incumbency the Bishopwearmouth Rectory Act was passed (1867).

a smaller, simpler daughter chapel of Bishopwearmouth had existed here since 1827 and still stands (though now in secular use) with its small graveyard adjoining.[6]

ANGLICAN LANDMARKS

Other churches visible from our vantage point illustrate further the energy and initiative revealed by the Church of England in the later Victorian and Edwardian decades. St. Ignatius (1889) was a gift to the town by Bishop Lightfoot as an act of thanksgiving for the first seven years of his episcopate.[7] The bishop took a close interest in the design and layout of the church, and its first vicar, Edgar Boddington, had been a member of the Auckland Brotherhood, one of a considerable number of young Oxbridge graduates who trained for the Church's ministry under Lightfoot's own direction at Auckland Palace.

Obviously a new breed of bishop, dedicated and energetic, was at the head of the diocese of Durham by this period. In fact Lightfoot's predecessor, Charles Baring, had, in less than 20 years (1861-1879) built 120 new churches in the diocese, restored another 130, and founded 82 new parishes. Under such dynamic leadership the Church of England was certainly making vast efforts, even if belatedly, to offer its ministrations to rapidly expanding industrial and urban areas.

St. Ignatius was built specifically to serve one of the most populous areas in the entire diocese — the rapidly growing suburb of Hendon. Hendon itself was predominantly working class in social character but it is interesting to note that St. Ignatius was placed not in the heart of Hendon but on its western boundary (Suffolk Street), on the borderland between two zones, one (to the east) working class and the other (to the west) lower-middle and middle class. It is interesting to note how many other churches, both Anglican and nonconformist, were built along this particular social 'border', on or very near the line of Tatham Street and Suffolk Street: St. Paul's and St. Barnabas of the Church of England; Tatham Street and Mainsforth Terrace, both Primitive Methodists; Herrington Street Wesleyan; Lindsay Road Baptist and the Bethesda Free Chapel. (Only Bethesda is still in use for worship and of the others only Lindsay Road Baptist and Tatham Street Primitive Methodist still stand, the former clearly visible from Tunstall Hills.) Instances of other churches similarly situated might be quoted from other quarters of the town. It was in such places that the most lively, flourishing and energetic religious life was to be found in the nineteenth and early twentieth centuries. These places of worship had congregations which are hard to categorise in terms of social class. Their congregations were made up neither of the very poor nor of the very rich, but of respectable folk drawn from a broad social band between those two extremes. These 'classless' congregations reflected the openness and egalitarianism of Sunderland society at that time — a society in which there might be no great distinction between a shipbuilder and the craftsmen who worked for him

or in which even working men might be owner-occupiers of their houses. Of course there were distinctly middle class churches, Christchurch for instance, built in 1864 to serve the tree-lined suburb of Ashbrooke, or at Roker, where Sir John Priestman and his family built St. Andrew's in memory of old Mrs. Priestman in 1907. Both are visible from Tunstall Hills. Inevitably these churches drew members away from other older and more centrally situated churches which suffered financially in consequence.

Two other suburban churches which were built in the Edwardian period to serve the expanding suburbs within the ancient parish area of Bishopwearmouth can be seen from Tunstall Hills: the redbrick St. Aidan's, Grangetown and the massive stone-built St. Gabriel's on Chester Road. These, like St. Ignatius, were neither distinctively working class nor middle class but were placed where they might minister to either or both groups. The great bulk of St. Gabriel's dwarfs the church hall behind it but it was this hall (and an iron church or 'tin tabernacle' which preceded it) which served the embryo congregation, built up by two active young curates, before the parish was fully founded and the main church erected.[8] This reveals the Anglican practice by that time of gathering together a congregation before commencing the erection of a new parish church, a healthier and more sensible policy than that pursued earlier in the nineteenth century of building a church and then looking for a congregation to fill it.

One other Anglican Church, this time north of the river, demands our attention. This is St. Columba's in Southwick (1889) whose massive red-brick nave with semi-circular (apsidal) chancel make it easily identifiable from Tunstall Hills.[9] The unusual basilican style of this building, contrasting markedly with St. Ignatius, by the same architect, may have been suggested by the first incumbent, William Bird Hornby, who was appointed when the parish was formed five years before the church was built. What St. Columba's definitely does owe to Hornby is the introduction of high-church (or Anglo-Catholic) practices which survive there to the present day. These were not entirely novel in Sunderland, moderate high-churchmanship having been established at St. Mark's Millfield from its opening in 1872. But at St. Columba's it was all done with greater conviction and greater boldness. Sung mass, confession, the daily celebration of the eucharist, the use of the term 'Father', the introduction as soon as practicable of incense, and the employment of Sisters of an Anglican religious order to serve the parish, all showed that the Catholic revival in its fulness had entered into the spectrum of Anglican church life on Wearside. The shock was considerable, though perhaps moderated by the relative lateness of St. Columba's, much of the rancour nursed by evangelicals against ritualism having been drawn out some 16 years earlier over the St. Mark's case.[10] St. Columba's also benefitted from the high standards of pastoral care shown by its clergy and sisters. The church was in fact a good example of what was becoming a feature of Anglican life by the later nineteenth century — the introduction of Anglo-Catholicism into certain working class parishes, where the colour, incense, vestments, candles, pictures, processions and ritual, along with the overall sense of worship as celebration, formed a dramatic contrast with the drabness of the neighbourhood in which such churches were set. At the other end of the spectrum of churchmanship, and in a different style, the Salvation Army offered a similar antidote to drabness.

Two of Sunderland's great mid-nineteenth century cemeteries can be discerned from Tunstall Hills — Bishopwearmouth (on Chester Road) and Sunderland (on Ryhope Road). Along with Mere Knolls cemetery north of the river, these were opened in the later 1850s in response to public concern over the threats to health and decency caused by overcrowded burials in the ancient churchyards, and the practice of laying some of the dead to rest in family vaults beneath the floor of the very churches themselves, particularly at St. Michael's. The restricted size of the churchyard at the latter had led earlier in the nineteenth century to the consecration of extra burial plots on Hind Street, where the enclosure walls used to be seen, and in the Rector's Gill, where some of the memorial stones still survive. But these were only temporary expedients, and the provision of the great municipal cemeteries could not long be delayed. One regrettable consequence of this necessary development has been the removal of all but a handful of grave stones from the old churchyards of Bishopwearmouth, Monkwearmouth and Sunderland, thus causing the loss of an interesting source of social history and of many moving and evocative memorials.

Public cemeteries may not inspire the kind of poetic thoughts found in Gray's famous elegy but the thoughtful and sympathetic browser can learn much in them all the same. One immediate and obvious feature of the cemeteries is their division into Anglican and non-Anglican burial areas, and the provision of separate cemetery chapels, whose upper parts can be seen above the trees which surround them. We are here forcibly reminded of the great historical divide in English religious life, between the established Church of England on the one hand, and the non-conformists, Catholic and protestant on the other.

STRONGHOLDS OF NONCONFORMITY

From the Tunstall Hills it is possible to pick out a number of nonconformist buildings of various denominations, though those which are visible are by that very fact the grander and more prominent examples built in the later nineteenth and earlier twentieth centuries when nonconformity was enjoying unprecedented freedom, confidence and prosperity. The chapels of an earlier period were more restrained in style and size, and kept a lower profile. The most obvious chapels (some so grand with towers and spires that it has become customary to call them churches) are the Ashbrooke quartet of West Park and St.

George's, both belonging to the United Reformed Church, and Park Road and St. John's, both Methodist. These descriptions conceal a greater diversity of denominational origin than is apparent today. West Park, for instance, was formerly 'The Grange', a Congregational church, built in 1883 for a congregation which had previously worshipped at the Ebenezer chapel on Fawcett Street (built 1851-2), and before that at the Bethel Chapel on Villiers Street (1817) from where the congregation traced its origins to a secession from the old Presbyterian meeting house on Robinson's Lane (1739) in the east end of Sunderland.[11] The transition during one and a half centuries from a plain unadorned meeting house in a back lane of the old town to a Gothic mini-cathedral on the edge of middle-class Ashbrooke suburbia is an epitome of the progress of nonconformity in those years. Whether it was appropriate for non-conformists (or some of them) to make this transition from simplicity to splendour is a matter of debate; it certainly was hotly debated at the time. But it was a natural and almost inevitable consequence of the steady increase of prosperity and of social and cultural opportunities enjoyed by the more respectable nonconformists in the nineteenth century. Non-conformity was (and is) a 'voluntary' religious system, in that the chapels and ministers were paid for by the members; and if those members wanted to worship in dignified style in pleasant surroundings, and were willing to pay the price, they got what they wanted. By the later nineteenth century some of these members were becoming rich and were moving out to live in the pleasant suburbs. They were convinced that if these suburbs were not to be dominated by the resurgent Church of England, represented for instance by Christ Church, it was necessary to provide equally grand churches for the nonconformist middle class.

A similar story lies behind the other nonconformist churches in the Ashbrooke area. St.

Sir John Priestman (1855-1941), who paid for the building of St Andrew's, Roker (1907), and the rebuilding of St Michael's Bishopwearmouth (mid-1930s).

St Ignatius (1889), the gift of Bishop Lightfoot to Sunderland.

St John's Wesleyan Methodist Church 1888, designed by Robert Curwen on Anglican lines.

chapel built on the corner of Chester Road and Sorley Street in 1896, and now a community centre. The last is an example of the New Connexion strategically placing a chapel to minister to an area with a lot of working class housing, no doubt in an attempt to offset the middle-class bias of its Park Road Church. The other two were grander buildings aimed at middle class folk as well as the working class. Both replaced earlier buildings. Burn Park church was originally called Thornhill, and belonged to the United Methodist Free Churches who opened it in 1903 to replace their earlier Brougham Street chapel of 1841. Ewesley Road Wesleyan church was the result of an extension from the Fawcett Street Wesleyan chapel. A new chapel was first built at Burn Park (more or less opposite the site of the U.M.F.C. Thornhill church) in 1885, but within a relatively short time it was decided that a larger church, farther out of town, was needed to serve the areas of new housing development along the Hylton and Chester Roads. A small temporary school-mission was built on Kayll Road (now the Church of the Nazarene) and replaced by the large red-brick and stone building on Ewesley Road, completed in 1904.[15] The Burn Park chapel was sold and now houses the Elim Congregation.

Had we been standing on Tunstall Hills 15 years or so ago yet another large Methodist chapel would have been visible in the Chester Road area. This was the Cleveland Road Primitive Methodist chapel (1901), a grand replacement for the old infirmary premises at the very bottom of Chester Road, which the Primitives had used first as a college in which to train their ministers, and then as a chapel. Yet one more building in the Chester Road area should be mentioned here, the Sorley Street chapel, whose short spire, standing among row upon row of terraced bungalows, can be discerned just beyond the Mount Tabor chapel. Sorley Street (now St. Bede's U.R.C.) was a Congregational chapel whose members originated in a secession from the United Methodist Free Churches chapel on Franklin Street. It united in 1981 with the congregation from St. Peter's Presbyterian chapel on St. Mark's Road which originated in 1884 as a daughter of the Trinity Presbyterian Church on Toward Road. Such was the complexity and variety of nonconformist chapel life in just one area of Sunderland!

A nonconformist church across the river which, because of its elegant spire, is easily visible from Tunstall Hills is the church on North Bridge Street now used by the Assemblies of God but built in 1891 for a Presbyterian congregation. In this case the building of a grand Gothic church did not result in a change of site; the earlier and plainer building of 1827 had stood in exactly the same place. Also to be seen in Monkwearmouth, though modest in size compared to the North Bridge Street Church, is Roker Methodist Church (1905), representing a relatively late thrust into prosperous suburbia by the Wesleyans from their ancient base in Whitburn Street, Monkwearmouth, where the chapel was founded in Wesley's time (1761).

Two Roman Catholic buildings are visible

George's was by origin a Presbyterian church, built in 1890 to replace an elegant but much simpler chapel on Villiers Street (1825) which in turn replaced the meeting house on Robinson's Lane from which the Bethel congregation also sprang.[12] Park Road church was built in 1887 by the Methodist New Connexion, one of the half dozen varieties of Methodists then active in Sunderland. It replaced their previous chapel on Zion Street near to the heart of old Sunderland.[13] And St. John's (1888) was the result of a scheme to replace the large, venerable, but financially hard-pressed Wesleyan Methodist Sans Street chapel (built in 1793, two years after Wesley died) by a splendid new church in an area where the richest Wesleyans were then living.[14] The proposal was hotly contested, and the upshot was that two of the leading supporters of the new church, John Wallace Taylor and Charles Lilburn, undertook, largely at their own expense, to maintain the old Sans Street chapel until its financial problems were resolved. Sans Street lived on a good many years after that until its closure in 1963, but as a 'Mission' chapel, in other words a centre of Christian religious and social work in the poorest part of the town, largely maintained and financed by Methodists living in more attractive areas. Most denominations had their down-town missions by the later nineteenth century, usually in the very areas where their strongest support had originally been based, but which had been seriously affected by social changes and the physical deterioration of the environment.

To the west of Bishopwearmouth three other Methodist churches are visible — Burn Park and Ewesley Road which are still active, and the former 'Mount-Tabor' New Connexion from Tunstall Hills. The church of St. Leonard, Silksworth (1873) was the gift of Mrs. Beckwith of Silksworth House, with the aim of providing a church for the Catholic workers (mainly Irish) who were being drawn to this part of Sunderland as a result of the opening of the Silksworth Colliery a few years before. And towards the west of Sunderland, at High Barnes, stands the prominent block of buildings (opened in 1902) where the Little Sisters of the Poor, who first came to Sunderland in 1882, pursue their caring work on behalf of the elderly and disabled. Two very typical aspects of Roman Catholic Church life — parochial ministry among the working class, and the devoted service of a religious order — are here very nicely illustrated, and remind us of the remarkable flowering of this particular Church in nineteenth-century Sunderland. This flowering is best illustrated by St. Mary's church on Bridge Street, the mother church of Catholicism on Wearside. Deep in the heart of the town, it is out of sight from where we stand, but we shall return to it.[16]

THE JEWS IN SUNDERLAND

The Jewish Synagogue on Ryhope Road, though much nearer to Tunstall Hills than St. Mary's, is also lost to view, virtually obscured by the trees on the slopes of Backhouse Park. Nearby however can be seen the upper parts of the tall terraced houses on the Cedars in one of which (until early in 1988) was based the local Yeshiva, or Talmudical College, a reminder of a lively Jewish presence on Wearside.[17]

There is something very appropriate in the name of the first recorded Sunderland Jew — Abraham Samuel. It would be hard to think of a more typical name. Abraham, a silversmith and jeweller, who died in Sunderland in 1794, was one of those Jews who during the eighteenth century were crossing the North Sea from their homes in Holland and Germany to settle in English coastal towns where their mercantile and linguistic skills found ready employ. A small Jewish community gathered in Sunderland as a result of this process. In 1781 they converted part of an old house on Vine Street, once the property of the Lilburne family, into a simple place of worship, and soon afterwards opened a private Jewish cemetery on the Ballast Hills, Ayres Quay, near the end of what was to become Crescent Row. More migrants swelled the community in the early nineteenth century, but as they were from eastern Europe (especially Poland), they did not at first mix easily with the more established, prosperous and westernised Jews. It seems that the latter left the Vine Street synagogue in the hands of the Polish Jews, and settled in 1829 into a new place of worship on High Street, converted from a house next to the home of their Rabbi, Jacob Joseph. Jacob and his nephew David ministered to the older Jewish community of Sunderland, or 'Israelites' as they were apparently known, from 1790 to 1861.

This latter date was significant since in that year the foundation stone of a new synagogue, to cater for all the Jews of the town, and where "the service of the Most High might be conducted in perpetuity and in a more decorous manner", was laid by Asher Moses Lotinga, president of the town's Hebrew congregation, on Moor Street in the east end. The following year the Chief Rabbi himself came north to consecrate the building which was to serve as a synagogue until 1928 when it was replaced by the splendid new building on Ryhope Road. Any hopes of permanent unity within the Jewish community of Sunderland, which the Moor Street synagogue had been intended to embody, were not yet however to be fulfilled. The major reason was another influx of migrants, this time of Lithuanian Jews, mainly from the Krottingen district, who had sought refuge from oppression by crossing the border into neighbouring East Prussia only to find themselves driven from there also. Very many refugees were involved, and they sought new homes in various western countries; a substantial number came to Sunderland. The first of them arrived in the town in 1859, a few others followed, and in due course the families and relatives of the first pioneers also made their way to Wearside. The main wave of immigration took place in the 1870s, and soon the newcomers outnumbered the older Dutch and German Jews in the town. Rabbi Salis Daiches, who was not himself of this particular Jewish tradition, admitted that the newcomers brought much vitality and that without them the local congregation might have dwindled seriously.

The Lithuanian Jews introduced a distinctly new element. They were closely bound together by language, culture and family connections; they shared the common bond of folk who had suffered for their faith; they were poor compared with the settled and relatively prosperous older community; above all they preserved a high degree of traditional and orthodox piety, and found it difficult to live in

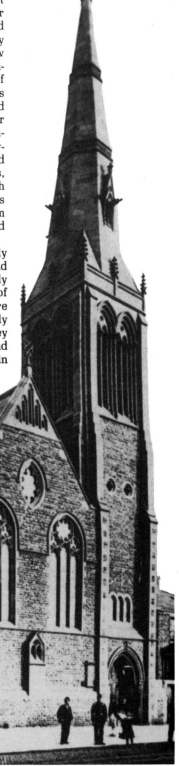

The "New Scotch Church" on North Bridge Street 1892 designed by W. L. Newcombe. (Formerly Presbyterian, now Assemblies of God.)

Rabbi Jacob Joseph (1769-1861), a leader of the Sunderland Jewish community for many years.

harmony with the Moor Street congregation. By 1891 they had seceded from Moor Street and a new Chevra (or religious union) was formed, later to become a Beth Hamedrash (house of study) with its home in a new synagogue consecrated in 1899, on Villiers Street South. (This building closed in 1938 and its congregation moved to Mowbray Road.)

In the early years of the twentieth century the congregation was served by a distinguished Lithuanian scholar Rabbi Hurwitz who had a great influence in the town and helped to found the Yeshiva. This had a short life but was re-founded in 1946, moving to the Cedars in 1950. The Moor Street synagogue also had first rate ministers in the persons of Rabbi Samuel Daiches (1905-8) and his brother Salis who succeeded him (1908-18). Under these men a closer understanding was effected between the two Sunderland congregations, and the prestige of the Jewish community in general was enhanced.

The place of the Jews in the town (even those who had arrived last, with few worldly possessions) was much strengthened by their increasingly successful commercial activities. When the Jubilee of the Moor Street Synagogue was celebrated in 1911, the crowded congregation contained leading representatives of various Christian denominations in the town — Sir Theodore Doxford (Anglican), E. H. Brown, the mayor (Primitive Methodist), T. W. Backhouse (Quaker), Alderman William Bruce (Wesleyan), and G. W. Bain (Presbyterian). By the same date a variety of Jewish cultural and welfare institutions were active in Sunderland — the Hebrew Board of Guardians, the Hebrew Ladies Benevolent Society, the Jewish Social and Literary Club, and the splendidly named Mount Pisgah Beacon of the Ancient Order of Maccabeans!

MORMONISM AND TOLERATION

Finally, as we look north from Tunstall Hills there stands immediately below us the most obvious and most modern of all the religious buildings visible from this vantage point, the Church of Jesus Christ of Latter Day Saints (1963), known more familiarly as the Mormons. In a bold architectural style with American overtones (as befits a building belonging to a Church whose origins are in the United States), built on a spacious site, and housing a valuable genealogical research unit much appreciated by non-Mormons, the Mormon church today is a respectable and accepted feature in Sunderland's religious life. How surprising then to find that some elderly folk in the town still recall passionate public demonstrations against the Mormon community in the early years of this century.

At the time of these happenings the Mormons had been in Sunderland for some 70 years.[18] The first member was recruited here in 1841 and the first formal organisation of a church occurred in 1843. For many years after that the numbers were relatively few and worshipped in hired halls and rooms — the Lyceum, the Athenaeum, the Phoenix Masonic Lodge, the Park Hall and so on. Some were persuaded to emigrate to the great Mormon settlement at Salt Lake City, Utah, where they encountered the practice of polygamy, not formally renounced until 1890. As well as offending Christian convictions in this respect, the Mormon scriptures were seen as challenging the supreme authority of the bible, so that animosity against the Mormons in a town with strong evangelical instincts is easily understood. What is perhaps surprising is to find an outburst of this feeling as late as 1912. The heart of the problem seems to have been a wave of rumours alleging the recruitment of young women to be sent to Utah to enter into marriage there. Concern was expressed both in weighty pronouncements by Christian leaders, and by popular anger which brought crowds to the Mormon chapel, a featureless brick building, still standing on Tunstall Road, to make their protests. Obviously the Mormons, or at least the dark suspicions which gathered round them, touched local sensibilities in a particularly acute way. Wearsiders had learned over 200 years and more to accept Quakers, Methodists, Roman Catholics (and their nuns), Jews, and the Salvation Army, all of whom had at first roused some degree of public feeling; but here was a challenge not only to their beliefs but to their daughters, or so it seemed. Not until their suspicions were dispelled, and the Mormons had renounced any lingering taint of polygamy, could the Mormon Church be regarded with the toleration it desired and which Sunderland was generally prepared to accord (mingled no doubt with a good deal of indifference) to all expressions of religious enthusiasm.

PART II:

Our imaginary stance on top of the Tunstall Hills has provided a vantage point not only to view a good number of the town's existing churches and chapels but also to consider something of the history which lies behind them. But it cannot show us all, and it is high time to come down off the hills and to consider in rather more straightforward fashion the influences that shaped the religious character of the community of Sunderland, throughout the period from the eighteenth century to the early twentieth.

ANGLICANS UNDER PRESSURE

In 1780 the three parish churches of St. Peter's, St. Michael and Holy Trinity, with St. John's, were the grandest, most imposing and most obviously venerable of the town's ecclesiastical buildings, and represented the status and social influence of the established Anglican Church. The Church had deep roots in Wearside society and, apart from public worship, it impinged on the lives of the people in many ways, through local government (rudimentary though it was), poor law administration, and education. Most people were baptised, married and buried by the parish clergy, and many were called upon to pay tithes and church rates, as a statutory duty, in support of the Church.

How popular was the Church of England? It certainly had its loyal and committed supporters, who came regularly to worship at the parish churches and believed strongly in the fundamental claim of the Church to be the true and lawful religion of the English people. Yet Sunderland was not a town in which Anglican loyalties were dominant. There were all kinds of reasons why this was so, among which may be mentioned the huge parochial areas of Bishopwearmouth and Monkwearmouth which made both pastoral oversight and church attendance difficult; the somewhat decrepit state of St. Peter's and St. Michael's by the later eighteenth century; the practice of pew ownership at all the Anglican churches which reserved most seats to folk of some substance and left the rest to fend for themselves; and the formal and somewhat dry worship which prevailed in Anglicanism at that time. What is said here refers primarily to the two ancient churches. In the east end of the town things were different. Here there were two relatively modern and spacious churches (Holy Trinity and St. John's), clean, light and attractive, and built largely as a result of local civic pride and local subscriptions to serve the busy mercantile community gathered round the far end of High Street. Moreover, Sunderland parish was compact and coherent in its geographical and social character. For all these reasons the Anglican churches could be seen as obviously central to its community life. Under earnest and evangelical rectors like John Hampson and Robert Gray (see biographical appendix) the religious impact of Anglicanism in Sunderland parish was obviously considerable, though never, one must stress, universal in its appeal.

The greatest problems faced by the Church of England were undoubtedly to be found in Bishopwearmouth parish. The paradox is that the rectoral living here was one of the wealthiest in the land, and the rectors themselves were usually distinguished by their family and ecclesiastical connections like Egerton (1776-1795) and Wellesley (1827-1848), and sometimes by their ability like Paley (1795-1805) and Dr Gray (1805-1827).[19] Yet with all this wealth and splendour the Church in Bishopwearmouth had to suffer the humiliation of representing a minority interest. Perhaps the heart of the problem was, in fact, the wealth itself, which stamped the rectors as belonging to the landed gentry and detached them from a community which was increasingly commercial in its interests and activities. As population grew and Bishopwearmouth parish became ever more affected by industrial and urban development, the anomalous position of the Church was more and more apparent. A further twist in the paradox was that the rectors' income rose astronomically as a result of industrialisation, in particular through the way-leave charges for coal carried on the waggonways that ran across the glebe land to the riverside staiths. To unsympathetic eyes the rectors could easily seem to be comfortable profiteers, receiving much for doing litttle, an anachronistic irrelevance obstructing progress.

The whole matter indeed reached crisis proportions by the early nineteenth century. Not only was the restoration and enlargement of St. Michael's an urgent necessity but new churches were needed to serve the increasingly populous parts of the parish, some of them distant from St. Michael's itself. For all this money was needed. The rectors had the money. Were they prepared to spend it, or would it have to be prised out of them? For 50 years longer the resolution of these urgent questions was left to the voluntary decision of the rectors themselves. To their credit they began if not in all cases actually to promote church extension, at least to indicate their willingness not to impede it. In the first decade of the nineteenth century St. Michael's church (under Dr. Gray) was extensively restored and the nave completely rebuilt and enlarged, becoming (with its north and south galleries) an enormous preaching room in accordance with the prevailing Georgian taste for auditory church interiors. (It retained this character until the major rebuilding, financed by Sir John Priestman, in the early 1930s.) St. Peter's at Monkwearmouth had been laid out in similar Georgian fashion a decade before, but with east, north and west galleries and a three-decker pulpit on the south wall.

The more urgent need was for the building of daughter chapels, and gradually these appeared, at first mainly serving the outposts of the parish: South Hylton 1817, Ryhope 1827, Deptford 1841, and Silksworth a school chapel, 1852). St. Thomas' on John Street (1829) had a different catchment area, the attractive middle class 'new town' then being created west of Villiers Street. In 1852 St. Paul's was opened at the northern end of what was soon to become the suburb of Hendon. Between 1844 and 1854 independent parishes were created for all these daughters of Bishopwearmouth except Silksworth (1868), and stipends were endowed for their clergy, though modest ones compared with the income of the rectors of St. Michael's. By the 1860s well-to-do Anglican families were leaving the town centre for the suburbs, and the Church built yet another daughter of St. Michael, Christ Church, to cater for the middle class folk of the Ashbrooke area.

Seven churches, three of them small, in nearly 50 years is not exactly a building boom, and compared with the population explosion in the Bishopwearmouth parochial area in those years the Church's response was patently inadequate to maintain an effective Anglican presence. During those years the Church of England lost the battle for religious leadership in Bishopwearmouth parish, and particularly in the central area around Fawcett Street which had become the new heart of Sunderland. When the Religious Census was held in 1851 it showed that in this central zone the Church was well and truly swamped by nonconformity.[20] It is a strange irony that the church at the same time was also losing out in its traditional area of strength in old Sunderland, owing to the serious decline in social conditions there and the westward migration of the more respectable families. In Monkwearmouth the Anglican response in the first half of the nineteenth century was to build two churches in crowded and largely working class areas, Holy Trinity Southwick and All

Sunderland Parish Church

In 1719 the residents of the fast-growing port of Sunderland, numbering (so they claimed) upwards of six thousand souls, petitioned for a parish of their own, separate from the large and unwieldly parish of Bishop-wearmouth. St. Michael's Church, an uphill mile away and always full, could no longer meet the needs of the distinctive river-mouth community.

The Act granting their request recorded that Sunderland's inhabitants had already "at their very great expence, and by the voluntary contributions of several neighbouring gentlemen, and by money collected by a Brief, erected and built a beautiful Church and a Vestry-room, within, or adjoining to the same, and a dwelling House for a Minister".

Holy Trinity, consecrated on 5th September 1719, still stands in the east end of today's town, epitomising the moment when the rising port hived off, a confident infant leaving a staid parent. The new church was packed each Sunday by the prosperous, hard-working merchants and seamen of a community that had for a century been growing in wealth and importance.

Daniel Newcombe, the rector appointed in 1719, was credited with having designed the church himself; but it seems likely that William Etty of York, clerk of works to Sir John Vanbrugh at Seaton Delaval and Castle Howard, was mainly responsible. Their building certainly echoes Vanbrugh and Hawksmoor, though perhaps it is a rather shabby, provincial echo. It is built of small, dark hand-made bricks, with sandstone dressings; and early settlement of the tower has given a somewhat insecure look to the west front. But inside all is light and spacious.

Holy Trinity is a church of its time, with emphasis on the sermon and the congregation rather than on ritual and its celebrants. It had originally no chancel, and Newcombe added the present near-circular apse at his own expense in 1735. The chancel arch, with Corinthian pilasters, broken pediment and cherubic heads, is the most vividly baroque part of the church. The tall Corinthian pillars lining the nave and the seven pairs of round-headed clear-glass windows emphasise the post-Renaissance character of the building, just as the serried ranks of pews underline its post-Reformation purpose. Once, the pews faced an imposing three-decker pulpit, while there were galleries on each side as well as the remaining western gallery.

Holy Trinity represented the establishment Church of England at a time when it was under challenge from both

An interior view looking east, showing how the church has looked in recent years. Note the ornate plasterwork round the chancel arch.

nonconformity and Roman Catholicism. Hence the fine array of coats-of-arms adorning the gallery: the royal arms of George I of Hanover are flanked by those of Lord Crewe, the Bishop of Durham and the Bishop of London, who actually consecrated the church.

One feature of Holy Trinity is the prominence given to its function as a centre of local government. Sunderland residents wanted administrative autonomy as well as their own place of worship; hence the stress laid by the Act on their vestry-room. It was here that the 24 Gentlemen, annually elected by parishioners gathered in the church, met to run the parish's civil affairs, under chairmanship of the rector. They sat around the oak table that still survives, and they kept the minutes and records preserved now in Durham Record Office and once stored in the parish chest under the gallery stair. They appointed local officials to collect the rates, keep law and order, care for the poor, and cleanse the streets; and in 1724 properly labelled pews were built under the gallery for those officials: churchwardens, constables and overseers — though none was provided for the scavenger.

Robert Gray, rector from 1819 to 1838, was perhaps the last holder of that post to play a prominent part in town matters. His fine statue stands in the disused central porch, complete with a lengthy inscription recording his many virtues. The once crowded churchyard is now empty of most of its memorials, and of the public buildings that once clustered around — Assembly Hall, workhouse, rectory — only the little Donnison School and the Trafalgar Square almshouses are left from the great days. The church stands in splendid isolation, the most interesting and attractive building remaining in a part of Sunderland that no longer flourishes as it once did.

The decline of the east end, and the breakdown of the community life which once flourished there, began in the later nineteenth century, and was completed by slum clearance in the twentieth. Inevitably, church life was also affected. St. John's church, built as a daughter chapel of Holy Trinity in 1769, was closed in 1970 and suffered demolition soon after. Grievous as the loss of a fine Georgian church was in architectural terms, its demolition also symbolised the virtual end of two and-a-half centuries of fruitful involvement by the Church of England in east end life. Holy Trinity of course continued to minister to the

Exterior view from the south east showing the circular chancel added in 1735.

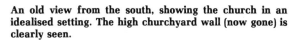

An old view from the south, showing the church in an idealised setting. The high churchyard wall (now gone) is clearly seen.

The arms of Nathaniel Crewe, bishop of Durham 1674-1721, on the western gallery. Above is the Revd James Thompson, at that time (1972) curate in the United Benefice of St. Ignatius and Holy Trinity.

neighbourhood, but now no longer as a parish church in its own right, being served by the clergy of St. Ignatius, with which church it was linked as a united benefice. Sadly, the congregation continued to dwindle.

By 1988, with its structure in urgent need of costly repairs, the closure of Holy Trinity had become inevitable. The final services were held on 26 June 1988 and a few days later the care of the church was handed over to the Redundant Churches Fund. This ensured the survival and maintenance of the property, but Holy Trinity had now ceased to be a place of regular worship or a base for Christian ministry and mission in the east end. However Church leaders believed that the sacrifice of the venerable building, which had become a financial millstone round the neck of the congregation, would make possible more flexible approaches to evangelism in the community, hopefully on an ecumenical basis, with worship being held initially in the old Donnison School and the modern school of St. John and St. Patrick.

From the point of view of conservation and social history the assured survival of Holy Trinity under the wing of the Redundant Churches Fund is very heartening. It stands as a splendid evidence of Sunderland's historic past, and has much to tell those who are prepared to study it with care and imagination. The church continues to be accessible to visitors.

The narthex of Holy Trinity, containing the attractive font. Michael Whitehead and the churchwardens (Messrs Prince and Reay) superintend the old Easter Monday ceremony of Dame Dorothy's Dole. (Photograph c. 1970.)

Revd. Robert Gray (1787-1838), rector of Sunderland from 1819.

Saints Monkwearmouth, both fine buildings of their type, and with spacious vicarages, but representing once again a response which was too little and too late to meet the challenges and opportunities created by the great age of industrial development.[21]

The Church's difficulty was in part due to a desire to provide (where possible) churches that were large and expensive to build, with handsome vicarages, and adequate endowments. All this cost much money. And whenever a new parish was carved out of an old one it meant some inevitable loss to the mother parish and complicated legal procedures to transfer some of the endowments and income to its daughters. The complexities of Bishopwearmouth finances were so great and the money involved so considerable that (as we have seen above) an Act of Parliament was finally necessary to divert part of the rector's enormous income towards church extension. It was after this happened (in 1867) that a new approach to church building and parish extension was possible, and by then a new spirit was already re-activating the Church of England, from the episcopate downwards. The Church of England revival came late to Sunderland, but it did come and the achievements of the Church in the later nineteenth and earlier twentieth centuries were considerable.

Yet Anglicans in Sunderland remained outnumbered by the overall strength of nonconformity, at least when measured by the number of churches and chapels, and the attendance at them, and we turn therefore to consider Sunderland's non-Anglican denominations and sects.

FAITH AND FREE CHOICE

The roots of Sunderland's nonconformity go deep. Roman Catholicism though illegal and persecuted had retained the loyalty of some local families after the Reformation; Presbyterianism was fostered by Scots arriving on Wearside from the early seventeenth century onwards; dissenting sects like the Baptists, Independents and Quakers were introduced and took root in the town during the upheavals of the Civil War and the Cromwellian period, when Sunderland stood with the Parliamentary side; and all of those groups survived the difficult years following the Restoration in 1660. They blossomed more freely after the Toleration Act of 1689, and as public attitudes on matters of religion became more liberal in the eighteenth century.

Sunderland, like many sea ports, was relatively open and free in its social and religious attitudes; its sea-borne trade, both English and continental, familiarised its citizens with the wider world and a wide range of beliefs and attitudes. The town also attracted an increasing number of immigrants, many of whom brought their own faiths and practices with them. The Scots and other groups from different parts of the British Isles all helped to add new shades to the town's religious spectrum or add strength to those already there. The majority of incomers came from the rural parts of north eastern England and

included, for instance, Presbyterians from Northumberland, Quakers from the dales (Methodists too, when that movement became established in the region in the second half of the eighteenth century), and Catholics deserting the declining rural estates of recusant gentry to seek better prospects in the busy industrial and commercial life of Wearside. In the nineteenth century of course the Irish were to swell Catholic numbers beyond all previous imagining. A more exotic immigrant group were the Jews, who began to settle in the port from the middle years of the eighteenth century.

At first the number of nonconformists in Sunderland was not great, but their significance should not be measured simply by statistics but rather by the fact that here were serious, committed, and courageous groups of believers who had deliberately opted out of the state-sponsored Church in order to be true to their own faith, and were prepared to accept the social disadvantages which this entailed. These folk, usually the families of mariners, artisans, traders and pioneer entrepreneurs, were prepared to stand on their own feet in religion as their menfolk did in their daily occupations. Not surprisingly they lived and worked at first mainly in Sunderland (the east end) and Monkwearmouth, and it was in these two communities that the early nonconformist chapels and meeting houses were to be found. Usually they were converted out of older dwelling houses, as with the Catholics and Jews; or purpose-built in simple vernacular styles with limestone walls and pantile roofs, like the Quaker meeting house on High Street, the Calvinistic Corn market chapel on Half-Moon Lane and the Presbyterian chapels on Robinson's Lane, Spring Garden Lane and Maling's Rigg. Some of them emphasised their separateness by providing their own burial grounds, the Quakers for instance on High Street, and the Jews in Ayres Quay. Several other nonconformist congregations were to follow this practice in due course.

Despite their stubborn independence in matters of religion these earlier dissenters were not in general eager to proselytise, but minded their own business and kept low profiles. (Despite this both the Quaker and the Catholic places of worship were extensively damaged by mob violence in 1688 and 1746 respectively.) Moreover their worship was usually plain and even dour, and, in the case of the Quakers, conducted with a complete absence of ritual, ceremony and music, in favour of a solemn and silent waiting upon the Spirit.

METHODISM

The advent of Methodism brought an entirely new element into Wearside's religious life, and it takes a real act of historical imagination to appreciate the novelty of this movement which was to transform the character and numerical strength of nonconformity in Sunderland, as it did in the nation as a whole, despite the fact that its principal founders had never intended that it should be nonconformist at all![22] Charles Wesley and his brother John preached in Sunderland High Street for the first time on separate visits in 1743, as part of their national mission whose north eastern base in Newcastle was established the year before. Of the two, John Wesley was to exert the profounder influence on Sunderland, not only through his repeated visits up to 1790 and the force of his character, but also through the unique religious system which he devised. As Church of England parsons, the Wesleys urged those who joined the Methodists to maintain loyalty also to their parish churches. This might be possible where the parish clergy were in sympathy with the evangelical work of Methodism (as at St. Peter's Monkwearmouth) but could obviously cause difficulties elsewhere, as at St. Michael's for instance. After Wesley's death in 1791 the Wesleyan Methodists of Sunderland, as elsewhere, were to abandon any attempts to maintain formal links with the Church, though some retained for it a love and respect of a kind untypical of nonconformity as a whole.

In other ways too Methodism contrasted strangely with the older dissenting groups — in the warmth and fervour of its worship and hymn-singing, its dramatic emphasis on conversion, its use of an army of lay preachers (some of them full-time 'travelling preachers', most of them part-time 'local preachers'), its deployment in many other ways of lay talents both male and female, and its unique circuit and connexional organisation.

Methodism won an immediate and growing response on Wearside and in the mining villages round about. Its first efforts were directed mainly towards manual workers and their families, and many of these found in it much that was appealing, not only for its religious message but for the warmth of its fellowship, and the social and educational advantages which it was able to transmit. But Methodism also won an increasing number of members from the upper-working and middle

Interior of St Michael's Bishopwearmouth as it was before the 1930s restoration.

classes, who found its general ethos and style of life particularly congenial, and approved of its puritanical emphasis. Those who became committed to Methodism were presumably dissatisfied (at least in part) with the Church of England and dissent, or else they had been converted from religious indifference or from atheism itself. It is an intriguing question why many ordinary working folk who were often divorced in any real sense from church life, responded to Methodist preaching and threw in their lot with the movement. All kinds of factors were no doubt at work, among which it is worth stressing that to those in dangerous occupations (mining and sea-faring being the most obvious local examples), or to people fearful about the uncertainty of life in a growing industrial town with many health hazards, Methodism was not afraid to speak about ultimate questions and to offer positive assurances about the reality of a life beyond this present one. In the early period of industrialisation when life was hard for many people, and when community facilities were scarce, the chapels also brought fellowship, music, an opportunity to serve in some capacity, and the chance of gaining a basic

The 'Georgian' interior of St Peter's as it was between the 1790s and the 1870s. (Looking West).

education. Methodism was a principal provider of Sunday Schools in the Sunderland area from the mid-1780s onwards, under the leadership of men like Michael Longridge (1757-1815) a prosperous Wesleyan mercer who devoted much of his time, energy and money to enhancing educational opportunities in the town.[23]

All this was happening as Sunderland was being transformed by socio-economic development, and the two processes, social and religious, interacted with each other. The years from about 1780 to 1850 were remarkable for the way in which the social context of Sunderland seemed to be particularly congenial for the flowering of Methodism. It grew apace, and built more and more chapels, while also dividing into a number of groups all regarding themselves as Methodist but differing significantly in organisation and ethos. Thus there emerged the Methodist New Connexion, the Primitive Methodists, the Wesleyan Methodist Association, and the Wesley Reformers, the latter two combining in 1855 (1857 nationally) to form the United Methodist Free Churches. Each of these divisions, along with the original Wesleyans, built its own chapels, employed its own ministers and lay preachers, and developed its own circuit organisation. With all this energy, growth and diversity it is not surprising that, overall, Methodism had become the dominant religious force in the town by the middle of the nineteenth century. This is borne out by the findings of the Census of Worship, which attempted to assess the numbers attending churches and chapels on Sunday 30th March 1851. The Census showed that, of all the worshippers in Sunderland on that day, 40 per cent sat in Methodist chapels, compared with about 25 per cent in Anglican churches and 28 per cent in the meeting houses of the various dissenting congregations.

It was not Methodism alone which had enjoyed an extraordinary period of growth in Sunderland during the first half of the nineteenth century. To a different degree but in the same manner the other nonconformist groups had also flourished as a result of the same mixture of circumstances which helped the Methodists. Moreover the evangelical revival,

as well as producing Methodism, had reinvigorated some of these older dissenting sects, making them more conscious of the call to evangelise, and leading to the foundation of new congregations. The Baptists and the Congregationalists were particularly affected in this way, but even the Quakers in Sunderland became almost Methodistical in their concern to reach out and make converts.

Tension might arise within a congregation between the more aggressively evangelical members and those with more staid and quiet attitudes. But these tensions often resulted in yet more growth when the disaffected part of a congregation went off to found a new cause. It was a process of this kind which created the Bethel Congregational chapel on Villiers Street in 1817 after a secession from the Robinson's Lane Presbyterian meeting house. But this is only one instance out of many. The Church of England itself experienced such a secession when several hundred Anglicans followed Arthur Augustus Rees, a young Welsh curate of Sunderland parish, into nonconformity after he fell foul of his rector and his bishop on issues of doctrine and style of ministry. Rees built the Bethesda Free Chapel on Tatham Street 1844-5 and added a colourful element to the town's dissenting religious life through his ministry there over the next 40 years.[24]

TOWN CENTRE CHAPELS

Bethesda is one of the few survivors of the many nonconformist chapels built in Sunderland during the period of great growth from the late eighteenth century to the middle of the nineteenth. To get some visual impression of the number and distribution of these buildings we can look at one of the fine mid-nineteenth century town plans, such as that made by Captain Dinning in 1853, and then endeavour to comprehend the immense variety of worship and congregational life of the chapels and churches shown, and the impact of all this activity on the communities of largely new terraced streets in which the buildings were set. This is not an easy exercise but it is a rewarding one, because it opens up for us an aspect of Sunderland's social history which the changes of time and circumstance have in many ways obliterated.

We might imagine a walk through the town as it was in the mid-1850s, and consider the places of worship along our route. Fawcett Street at its southern end makes a good starting place. Just off to the west in Waterloo Place stands the newly built Jireh Chapel (1855) replacing the Old Cornmarket Chapel as the home of an independent Calvinistic congregation;[25] nearby in Brougham Street the Wesleyan Association congregation (shortly to be merged with the Wesleyan Reformers who had for some time met in the Athenaeum on Fawcett Street) worships in its two-storeyed 'Tabernacle' (1841), the chapel upstairs, the Sunday School below[26]; on the corner of St. Thomas' Street and Fawcett Street is the grand new Ebenezer Congregational chapel (1851-2), designed, in part, by its versatile and thrusting young minister Robert Whitaker McAll, who was shortly to leave the town and

The Quaker meeting house, High Street, 1688, rebuilt 1718. (Replaced 1822 by the Nile Street meeting house).

in due course to launch a protestant mission to the working men of France;[27] looking along St. Thomas' Street we see the Anglican church (1829) after which it was named, an important daughter of St. Michael's Bishopwearmouth and a bastion of Anglicanism in an area dominated by nonconformity; a little further north, on the west side of Fawcett Street, stands the gothic-fronted Wesleyan Methodist Chapel (1836) built to serve the more bourgeois Wesleyan families of Sunderland who felt confident enough to challenge the ruling of their Connexion by installing an organ when such instruments were still discouraged; then on to Bridge Street, dominated by St. Mary's Roman Catholic Church (1835), the product of the energy, faith and money-raising abilities of Canon Philip Kearney who helped the Catholics of Sunderland in the years after Emancipation to emerge from the shadows into the fulness of civic life; behind St. Mary's, between Pann Lane and Green Street, the Sisters of Mercy who were invited from Cork by Kearney in 1843 have their convent, their garden and their schools;[28] and on the opposite side of Bridge Street from St. Mary's stands the neat Unitarian chapel opened in 1831 by the famous Newcastle minister, William Turner, to house a congregation of thoughtful and questioning believers who found the doctrine of the Trinity too hard to accept.[29]

Nor do we have to walk far to find yet more varieties of Christian work and witness in the heart of the town. If we walk again to the southern end of Fawcett Street and along Borough Road we soon see, along Tatham Street, the Bethesda Free Chapel (1844-5); we then pass on the corner of Nile Street the large red-brick meeting house of the Society of Friends, or Quakers, (1822) where gather for worship some of the industrial and commercial élite of the town, including the eminent Backhouse family;[30] we next look along the length of Villiers Street which contains among its elegant terraced houses two equally elegant Georgian chapels belonging to the Church of Scotland Presbyterians (1825)[31] and the Congregationalists (1817); further on, in the area of Hedworth Terrace and South Durham Street, we come upon John Halcro's independent 'Bethany' chapel (1849), another 'Tabernacle' of the Wesleyan Association (1836), and the 'Smyrna' chapel (1832) of a Presbyterian secession;[32] we turn north towards Coronation Street, and not far off to our right is the Zion Methodist New Connexion chapel (rebuilt in 1846); and then, heading west again along Coronation Street towards the town centre we pass the end of Flag Lane in which stands one of the most famous chapels of north eastern Primitive Methodism (1824), its position in a narrow working class alley illustrating both the relative poverty of the Primitives and their commitment to evangelism among the poor;[33] in Spring Garden Lane we note the former Presbyterian secessionist meeting house of 1766 which has since 1844 been adopted as an Anglican mission chapel of the parish of Sunderland, a small and belated measure taken by the established Church to enlarge its accommoda-

tion for worship in the crowded east end; on the left of Coronation Street stands the Union Chapel (1822) belonging to the United Presbyterians; and finally we pass the southern end of Sans Street which contains half way along its length a neat Particular (Calvinistic) Baptist chapel (1798) where both John Candlish and E. T. Gourley have worshipped,[34] and at its northern end the large and handsome Wesleyan Methodist Chapel (1793), still the centre of Wesleyanism in the Sunderland area despite the building of the Fawcett Street chapel and the decline of the environment in which the older chapel stands.[35]

THE SOCIAL IMPACT

It is something of a shock to realise that of all these buildings only two (St. Mary's and Bethesda) are still in use for worship today; two others (Sans Street Baptist and Villiers Street Presbyterian) still stand but are in secular use. All the others have been demolished. While it is true that some of the congregations moved on to other buildings later in the nineteenth century, it remains a fact that an entire world of organised religious life within the heart of the town has virtually disappeared. Moreover our walk has taken us round only a fraction of the total community of Sunderland, and would have to be repeated in Monkwearmouth, Southwick, the Hyltons, Deptford, Ayres Quay, Millfield, and the east end for a full appreciation of the total presence and character of organised religion on Wearside.

Everywhere there were churches and

Dec 7 SUNDERLAND. 1867.

JOHN BROADBENT'S Engagements on Sunday First:—at 10, Theatre Royal, Bedford Street, a LOVE-FEAST will be held, at which Converted Drunkards, Blasphemers, Infidels, Pugilists, Sabbath-Breakers, and Criminals will declare what God has done for their Souls. Psalm 66, verse 16. At 2, Theatre Royal, Subject—"Mercy and Grace." At 6, Fawcett Street Chapel. Subject—"The Devil, who he is, what he does, and what he aims at."

N.B.—Those who do not attend any Place of Worship are invited to come; the poor and ill-clad, and unemployed are most welcome to come in such clothes as they ha

A revivalist Wesleyan minister endeavours to convert the working classes in mid-Victorian Sunderland.

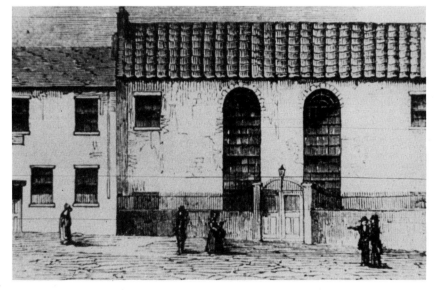

Presbyterian meeting house, Spring Garden Lane, 1766. Acquired by the C. of E. in 1844 as a daughter chapel of Holy Trinity.

chapels, some grand, some humble, representing a kaleidoscopic range of religious tastes and persuasions. And compared with church attendance today the congregations could be enormous. We have the evidence of the 1851 Census of Worship to help us here, and also of another census privately organised by John Candlish 10 years later. The total numbers of worshippers attending all services at a few selected churches and chapels on the two Sundays concerned (30 March 1851 and 21 April 1861) make interesting reading:

	1851	1861
Sunderland Parish Church	2168	1178
St. John's Chapel (C of E)	1996	389
St. Michael, Bishopwearmouth	1849	1576
St. Peter's, Monkwearmouth	1310	557
St. Mary's R.C.	?950	3170
Sans Street Wesleyan	1205	1168
Fawcett Street Wesleyan	798	1165
Flag Lane Primitive Methodist	1830	1013
Ebenezer, Congregationalist	932	1028
Villiers Street Presbyterian	871	878
Bethesda Free Chapel	1680	1028
Dock Street (United Methodist Free Churches)		
	—	974
Union Chapel, Presbyterian	1050	717
Sans Street, Baptist	351	558

The discrepancies between the 1851 and 1861 figures raise interesting questions. Perhaps there had been some 'pew-packing' in 1851 as Candlish suspected, and which his unannounced count ten years later was meant to avoid. But the figures do seem to indicate a rapid decline in church attendance in the east end of the town where social conditions were rapidly becoming inimical to organised religion. The obvious increases were due in large part to Irish immigration (St. Mary's) or to the recovery of the Wesleyans from a shattering secession which had badly affected their 1851 showing (see the Fawcett Street figures for instance).[36]

Nevertheless the broad fact is that organised religion, measured by the numbers of places of worship and those attending them, was remarkably strong in mid-nineteenth century Sunderland. The 1851 census figures indicate that something like one third of the town's population attended at least one service at Church or Chapel on the day the count was made, a percentage which may in fact be the high water mark for religious activity on Wearside. A comparable figure today would certainly be much lower, certainly below one tenth, and possibly even one twentieth of the population. We see here a fundamental fact about the Victorian age, its religiosity. Nor was it by worship alone that the churches and chapels made their presence felt and exerted an influence on people's lives. We have to imagine a multitude of other agencies by which Christian values and teachings (fragmented through the prism of church disunity into a many-coloured spectrum) were transmitted — Sunday Schools, Day Schools, books and tracts, lectures, Bible classes, charitable organisations, the discipline of serving in an official capacity in church or chapel, and the pervasive code of evangelical morality.

Canon Philip Kearney, Priest of St Mary's Roman Catholic Church, Sunderland, and a pioneer of the Catholic revival on Wearside from 1829 to 1856.

Without discounting the sincerity of faith of many church-goers at that time, it remains a fact that religion was in large part strong because it served useful social purposes. To incomers to the town, chapel life in particular provided contacts, friendship and a sense of community; to the aspiring artisan evangelical religion offered both an incentive towards self-improvement and some of the means to achieve it; to the business man, the puritan code which included an emphasis on hard work, frugality and self discipline was one which, he believed, had done him good, and would do his workers and the poor of the town good as well — he usually did his best to persuade them to accept it![37] Moreover, the rival allegiances of 'Church' and 'Chapel' were closely related to the social and political divisions and rivalries within the town. The nonconformists in general were motivated by reforming and radical ideals, and many of their leaders became active in civic life and in parliamentary politics, on the Whig and Liberal side. In the propagation and defence of their convictions, religion and politics mingled together as is seen clearly in the case of the activists who worshipped at the United Methodist Chapel on Dock Street, Monkwearmouth (see chapter 11). In different ways Churchmen and Roman Catholics saw the defence of their own beliefs as part of their socio-political stance. Whether it was good for religion and secular affairs to be so bound up together is open to question, but it helped to give allegiance to 'Church' or 'Chapel' a relevance and a force not possible in the same sense today.

LATER VICTORIAN AND EDWARDIAN RELIGION

The most obvious surviving evidences of Sunderland's religious life in the later nineteenth and early twentieth centuries are those impressive church and chapel buildings with which this chapter began. Outwardly, therefore, the image is of prosperity and growth. But the reality is more complex, reflecting the increasing complexity of the social character of the town itself.

It is not surprising, in a community with a dominant and prosperous middle class and with many well-paid, serious and respectable artisans, that nonconformity itself should become increasingly respectable. This trend affected all the established denominations, even the Primitive Methodists, who as early as the 1850s were deeply concerned to keep pace with the improved educational and social opportunities of their members. Local laymen such as J. Gordon Black, and talented ministers such as Colin Campbell McKechnie (a Scot, needless to say), did much to advance the education of Primitive Methodist preachers by launching a high-powered journal (*The Christian Ambassador*) in the early 1850s, and by reopening the old infirmary on Chester Road in 1868 as a theological institution for the training of P.M. ministers.[38] The building of the large and expensive chapel on Tatham Street in 1875, and the replacing in 1881 of the modest chapel on Williamson Terrace, Monkwearmouth, by an ambitious double-decker chapel (with Sunday School on the upper floor) are simply two further examples of how the Primitive Methodists were responding to changing circumstances and new opportunities.

Yet there was always an undertow of doubt about such developments. Among all the nonconformists there were some who looked back with nostalgia to the former days, and longed for a return of puritan simplicity or evangelical enthusiasm, or both. Once again the Primitive Methodists illustrate these tensions most clearly, because in 1877 they suffered an actual secession from their chapels in Sunderland and the surrounding mining villages of several hundred members who left to establish the Christian Lay Churches. Significantly the secessionists employed no paid or professional ministers, and erected modest chapels in working class districts, the first to be built being that opened in 1878 on James Williams Street, in the east end of the town. After some years the Lay Churches adopted the name they bear today, the Independent Methodists.[39]

The Lay Church secession was a clear protest by those who thought that Primitive Methodism had lost its way and was deserting the work which had been its raison d'être, evangelism among the poorer working class, and was becoming too respectable and polite. Similar concerns, though on a broader canvas, led to the origins of the Salvation Army, since William Booth (General Booth as he came to be known) had been a Methodist minister in the New Connexion. The Army was not born in Sunderland but it arrived here early in 1878, and soon established a strong foothold in the town. Despite horrified protests against its tactics by lovers of propriety, it won converts among the roughest classes for whom most other denominations had little appeal. By 1884 four Corps had been established, one of them (number two) housed in the great Barracks on Roker Avenue. The Lambton Street Citadel (still standing though in secular use) was built to house number one Corps in 1891.[40]

It would be quite wrong to conclude that the major denominations were blind to the need to minister to the poorer section of the community. For the Roman Catholics it was indeed part of this very section, the Irish migrants, who constituted their greatest challenge and their greatest opportunity. The problem was to raise the money to pay priests and build new chapels where they were most needed. By launching missions and using temporary or dual-purpose premises for some years, new churches were established: St. Patrick's in the east end in 1861, St. Benet's Monkwearmouth c.1861 with a handsome new church built in 1889, St. Joseph's Millfield 1872-3, rebuilt in 1907, St. Leonard's Silksworth 1873, and Our Blessed Lady Immaculate, Washington, 1878. St. Hilda's Southwick (1909) and St. Patrick's Ryhope (1915) were also the culmination of several years of mission work. Two new orders were introduced into the town to supplement the work of the Sisters of Mercy — the Little Sisters of the Poor who arrived in 1882 and the

Redemptorist Fathers, who adopted St. Benet's in 1900.

In ministering to the poor the Catholics were in a special category since large numbers of the Irish poor were, at least nominally, already members of their Church. The other denominations had no such claim on the allegiance of the masses, who it was obvious were more and more deserting organised religion, if they had ever had much meaningful connection with it. The problem had various aspects. Among the destitute, welfare work was the more compelling need, and Sunderland had many charitable agencies, usually founded through Christian initiatives and staffed by Christian folk. A major example is that which was launched by Edward Backhouse, the Quaker philanthropist, in the Pottery Buildings in the east end in 1868. A different challenge was to convince working class men, disillusioned by organised religion, that Christianity could mean something to them in a positive and practical way. Two interesting ventures towards this end were the opening in 1906 of the Thompson Memorial Hall, Monkwearmouth, by T. R. Blumer, a United Methodist shipbuilder, to serve as a chapel and working men's institute, and the launching of the Brotherhood Movement in Sunderland by William Walker, a Wesleyan Methodist businessman.[41] Both these ventures were inspired by an intensely pious evangelicalism. A broader and more relaxed approach to working men was envisaged by George Garcia, the able young minister of the Royalty Congregational Church, but he died in 1904, and never saw his visions fully implemented.[42]

It is one sign of the revival of the Church of England in Sunderland by the later nineteenth century that just as the nonconformists were abandoning their older chapels in the declining areas of the town the Church was eager to snap them up as bases for a determined effort to re-assert its influence among the working classes. This happened with the Spring Garden Lane meeting house; later examples included the acquisition by the Church of Primitive Methodist chapels on Hopper Street and Flag Lane, the Baptist chapel on Sans Street and the Presbyterian chapel on Hamilton Street Monk-

Revd. John Petty (1807-1868) a pioneer Primitive Methodist who worked in Sunderland in the early 1830s.

Ebenezer Congregationalist chapel, Fawcett Street, 1851, designed in part by its minister, R. W. McAll.

wearmouth, which was actually consecrated in 1880 as the church of the new parish of St. Cuthbert.

Other evidence confirms the newly-discovered vision and zeal which the Church of England increasingly brought to its work in the later Victorian and Edwardian years. In part it was a response to the nonconformist challenge, revealed by the 1851 and 1861 counts of attendance at worship. But there were powerful currents flowing in the Church, some stemming from evangelical sources, others from the High Church Oxford Movement or from Christian Socialism, all of which helped to impart new enthusiasm and vigour. The leadership of the bishops was important in all this. Charles Baring (bishop from 1861 to 1879) was a positive dynamo of evangelical energy. Joseph Barber Lightfoot (1879-1889) and Brooke Foss Westcott (1890-1901) brought deep scholarship, zeal, and a more broadly tolerant spirit to their work. But all of them, and Handley Moule (1901-1920), another evangelical, helped not only to promote a vigorous campaign of church building but to stir up a deep sense of purpose and conviction about the Church's mission to society.[43] Sunderland, by far the largest urban community in the diocese of Durham after the creation of the separate diocese of Newcastle in 1882, was of the greatest strategic importance in this mission, and merited a high place in the list of diocesan priorities with regard to money and manpower.

Some of the fruits of all this, especially regarding new churches and new parishes, have already been indicated in the earlier parts of this chapter. By 1914 some 30 parishes were serving the vast area which had been only two, Bishopwearmouth and Monkwearmouth. Moreover there was within all these new parishes a style of ministry and of parish organisation quite different from that prevailing up to the middle of the nineteenth century. This sprang in part from an awareness that the Church could no longer assume a privileged role but had to justify its existence in competition with nonconformity. But the Church also realised that it might adopt some of the practices which had proved so valuable to the nonconformists themselves, by allowing lay men and women an active share in parochial administration and ministry, making the teaching of Scripture more central, stressing the commitment implicit in Church membership, promoting the social side of Church life, and recruiting new members by evangelical efforts. Twice in the closing decades of the nineteenth century, in 1874 and 1890, the Church of England organised missions to the community of Sunderland. These were ambitious undertakings with teams of visiting missioners working alongside the parish clergy. But it was the changing patterns of work within the parishes themselves which, though less obvious, were of deeper significance. By the closing years of the nineteenth century the majority of parishes in Sunderland had a Parochial Church Council; parochial institutes and clubs were common; bible classes, usually led by lay people, were a regular feature; the use of laymen as preachers and evangelists, and of lay women as parish workers, was widely practised; and in many other ways the talents and energies of Church members were employed in a style of ministry in which clergy and laity worked closely together.[44] The Church of England had discovered some of the prerequisites necessary to its becoming a popular institution in an urban and industrial society. The style of churchmanship employed in its work varied widely by the later nineteenth century, with some Sunderland parishes being Anglo-Catholic, some Evangelical, and others somewhere in between these two. However, despite obvious outward differences, these distinctions should not be pressed too hard. The various streams of Anglican life and thought were by this time flowing together and intermingling in interesting and often surprising ways. What was in any case far more important than styles of churchmanship was the endeavour to regenerate parish life and make institutional religion more effective and powerful. A highly interesting example of this on the Evangelical wing of the Church was the adoption by Alexander Boddy, vicar of All Saints, Monkwearmouth, of Pentecostalist doctrines and methods, and the introduction of these into his parochial work in 1907.[45]

EPILOGUE

With the renewal of the Church of England, the prosperity and confidence of the Free Churches, the growing solidity of Roman Catholicism, and the lively work of more recent movements such as the Salvation Army and the Lay Churches, religious life in Sunderland by the eve of the First World War was patently vigorous and well organised. The quality of church and chapel buildings, of ministerial training, of worship, of congregational life and social awareness was in many respects an improvement on what had prevailed before. Moreover there was a growing realisation of the need for increased cooperation and united effort between the various denominations, perhaps evinced most clearly at that time by the nonconformists with the formation of the Sunderland Free Church Federal Council in 1902,[46] and by a union of three of the strands of Methodism in 1907. (Full Methodist Union had to wait until 1932).

Yet it is ironic that qualitative improvement was accompanied by quantitative decline. As the population grew so the percentage of that population which was actively associated with organised religion declined. In this respect Sunderland was no different from many other urban communities, in which the prevailing social, cultural and mental climate made the claims of Christianity apparently less relevant and less appealing, no matter how hard the various denominations tried. We have no Religious Census to measure the strength of religion in the town in the Edwardian period but it seems likely that perhaps something like one sixth of the population was attending church or chapel then, compared with about one third in 1851. This relative decline was to

**Rt. Revd. Charles Baring,
Bishop of Durham 1861-1879.**

continue during the twentieth century, and one consequence of it has been the loss not only of many church and chapel buildings as physical reminders of the rich story of religious faith and work in Sunderland, but also the erosion of the insight, knowledge and sympathy necessary to appreciate that story. Through historical delving and imagination we can begin to discern something of its scope and interest, and understand afresh the role played by the churches and chapels in the period of the town's greatest period of social and industrial expansion.

REFERENCES

1. In addition to the references below, information on Sunderland's churches and chapels can be found in chapters in Garbutt and Burnett; in the Sunderland sections of the county histories by Surtees and Fordyce; in the introductions to the Sunderland entries in the larger nineteenth century directories published by Kelly and Whellan; in T. H. Corfe and G. E. Milburn *Buildings and Beliefs* (1984); in G. E. Milburn *Religion in Sunderland in the mid-nineteenth century*, Sunderland Polytechnic, Department of Geography and History Occasional Paper No. 3, 1983; in various articles printed in the volumes of *Antiquities of Sunderland*, and in certain of the biographies in Brockie's *Sunderland Notables* (1894). Old maps and plans of the town are invaluable for locating and identifying churches and chapels. A very considerable body of original source materials survives in church and chapel archives, held either in the churches themselves or at the Tyne and Wear and County Durham Record offices.

2. On St. Michael's see T. J. McKitterick *Bishopwearmouth Church* (1923), D. Goldie *The Story of a Mother Church* (1964), and B. Myers *The Rectors of the Ancient Parish Church of Bishopwearmouth* (1982).

3. On St. Peter's see R. H. Lowe *Monkwearmouth Church in the 19th Century* Wearmouth Historical Pamphlet No. 6, n.d.

4. On Holy Trinity see Richard Hutchins, *Sunderland Parish Church: A Short History* (1982).

5. The Bishopwearmouth Rectory Act received the Royal Assent 31 May 1867. The text (a copy of which is in Sunderland Central Library, Local History Section) sets out the background to the Act, and its provisions, in detail.

6. On St. Luke's parish see C. H. G. Hopkins *Pallion 1874-1954: Church and People in a Shipyard Parish*. Mr. Brian Myers has written a typescript history of St. Mark's, which I am grateful to have been able to consult. On St. Paul's see David Goodfellow *How the Gospel came to Ryhope*, a brief pamphlet of 1977, and James Duncan *Knight of Ryhope: the man and his ministry* n.d. (c. 1934), about Percival Young Knight who became vicar of St. Paul's in 1902.

7. M. Richardson *The Church of St. Ignatius the Martyr, Sunderland, 1889-1949*, (1949). See also G. R. Eden and F. C. Macdonald *Lightfoot of Durham*, (1932), chap. ix. There is a short but interesting section on Edgar Boddington in Duncan *Knight of Ryhope*; pp. 40-43. On a later vicar of St. Ignatius see *A North Country Preacher: Sermons by the late Revd. F. L. Cope M.A. Hon. Canon of Durham*, 1911 (with a memoir of Cope by H. E. Savage).

8. C. H. Walker *A History of St. Gabriel's Church, Bishopwearmouth* (1938).

9. F. H. *An account of the Parish of St. Columba, Southwick 1885-1935*, (1935).

10. Henry Ritson *The 'Ritual' of St. Mark's* (1873). Some of the press correspondence relating to the St. Mark's controversy was published by Ritson in a pamphlet entitled *Diamond Cuts Diamond or The 'Detective in Plain Clothes' outwitted* (1872).

11. W. J. L. P. *The Courts of the Lord: Grange Congregational Church, Sunderland*, (1951).

12. R. Hyslop *Two Hundred Years 1739 to 1939: St. George's Presbyterian Church Sunderland*, 1939. F. H. Hawkins *History of the Presbytery of Durham* n.d. (1975); and J. T. Middlemiss and Robert Hyslop *A Short History of Presbyterianism in Sunderland* (1897).

The Lambton Street Citadel of The Salvation Army, opened 1891.

13. On Park Road Church see the jubilee and centenary booklets published in 1937 and 1987.

14. On St. John's Methodist Church see the seventieth anniversary booklet of 1958, and the centenary book, *St. John's Ashbrooke*, ed. G. E. Milburn (1988). On Sans Street Chapel see the historical souvenir published in 1937 written by F. F. Bretherton.

15. B. Cowie and E. W. Dykes *The Church on the Move: Ewesley Road Methodist Church 1904-1979*, (1979). On the former Thornhill Methodist church (now called Burn Park) see Ernest H. Sinclair *Fifty Years On: A Short History of Thornhill Methodist Church 1903-1953*, (1953).

16. On Catholicism in Sunderland see Leo Crangle, *The Roman Catholic Community in Sunderland from the Sixteenth century* (1969); St. Mary's Church 150th anniversary booklet of 1985; and D. Milburn (ed.). *Parish Histories from the Northern Catholic Calendar* (1986), pp. 55-62.

17. On the Jews in Sunderland see Arnold Levy *History of the Sunderland Jewish Community* (1956); Lewis Olsover *The Jewish Communities of North East England 1755-1980*, (1980), esp. pages 264-293; and Rabbi Salis Daiches 'An Historical Sketch of the Jewish Congregation in Sunderland', *Antiq. Sund.* xvi 75-87.

18. I am grateful to Mrs A. Power of South Shields for details regarding the history of Mormonism in Sunderland.

19. See biographical appendix for Gray. Egerton was a member of the aristocratic Bridgewater family and a brother of a Bishop of Durham. Wellesley was the brother of the Duke of Wellington. An interesting account of Paley can be found in G. W. Meadley *Memoirs of William Paley* (Sunderland 1809).

20. G. E. Milburn *Religion in Sunderland in the mid-nineteenth century*, a study based on the Religious Census 1851, and John Candlish's Census 1861.

21. On All Saints Monkwearmouth see Norman Joyce's centenary booklet, 1949, and Peter Lavin *Alexander Boddy*, (1986). Boddy was vicar of All Saints 1886-1927.

22. On early Methodism in Sunderland see G. E. Milburn *The Travelling Preacher* (1987), chapter seven, and F. F. Bretherton's articles on John Wesley's visits to Sunderland and Monkwearmouth in *Antiq. Sund.* xx and xxi.

23. See biographical appendix on Longridge. The minutes of the Sunderland and Bishopwearmouth Sunday Schools (founded by Longridge) covering the years 1802-1853 are in the Tyne and Wear Archives. See also G. E. Milburn 'Wesleyanism in Sunderland in the early nineteenth century', *Antiq. Sund.* xxvi and xxvii.

24. On Rees and Bethesda see his entry in the biographical appendix.

25. On the Cornmarket chapel see *Antiq. Sund.* v. pp. 50-69.

26. There is much information on the Wesleyan Methodist Association and the Brougham Street Tabernacle in G. E. Milburn *The Diary of John Young* (Surtees Society, cxcv, 1983).

27. On McAll see his entry in the biographical appendix.

28. On St. Mary's see the references in note 16 above. On the Sisters of Mercy in Sunderland there is very interesting material in *Leaves from the Annals of the Sisters of Mercy* by a Member of the Order, (New York, 1883) vol. ii, chapter xli. I am grateful to the Sunderland Convent of Mercy for access to this volume.

29. R. W. Davidson *The Origins and History of the Unitarian Free Church of Sunderland 1830-1930* (Sunderland, 1930).

30. See biographical appendix on the Backhouses. There is an interesting collection of Sunderland Quaker records in the Tyne and Wear Archives.

31. See note 12 above.

32. On John Halcro see Brockie pp. 293-298. On the South Durham Street Tabernacle see *The Diary of John Young*, note 26 above.

33. On Primitive Methodism in Sunderland see W. M. Patterson *Northern Primitive Methodism* (1909) chapter 16, and the *Primitive Methodist Magazine* (1886) pp. 19-23 and 85-87. On the later history of the Flag Lane chapel see G. E. Milburn 'Tensions in Primitive Methodism in the 1870s', *Proceedings of the Wesley Historical Society*, vol. xl, parts 4 and 5, Feb. and June 1976. See also reference 39 below.

34. For the Sans Street Baptist chapel a major source is a manuscript volume begun in 1757 entitled *A Book of Records and Particular Transactions of and belonging to the Baptised Church of Jesus Christ assembling in Sunderland, Durham*. It contains records to 1861. I am indebted to Mr Donald Elsdon for access to this volume. See also the Lindsay Road Baptist Church Jubilee Souvenir, 1927 — this church was the successor of the Sans Street chapel.

35. On Sans Street Wesleyan Chapel, see notes 14 and 23 above.

36. See note 20. On the difficulties faced by the churches in the east end of Sunderland there is graphic evidence (for the 1890s) in Thomas Nicholson *et al, The East end of Sunderland: St. John's Parish, its work and limitations* (1896).

37. On some of the Methodist businessmen of Sunderland see *The Diary of John Young*, and G. E. Milburn *Piety, Profit and Paternalism* (1983).

38. G. E. Milburn *A School for the Prophets*, (1982).

39. G. E. Milburn *The Christian Lay Churches* (1977), and the references given there.

40. I am grateful to have been able to read Isobel Horsburgh's account of the Salvation Army in Sunderland (written as a research project for the Wearside Church History Group).

41. On T. R. Blumer and William Walker see G. E. Milburn *Piety, Profit and Paternalism* (1983) pp. 27 and 46, and references there given.

42. J. G. Henderson *George Henry Russell Garcia: Memoir, Sermons and Addresses* (1904).

43. A useful introductory account of the bishops of Durham in this period can be found in Chapter 33 of Sir Timothy Eden's *Durham*, vol. ii, (1952). See also G. R. Eden and F. C. Macdonald *Lightfoot of Durham* (1932); A. Westcott *Life and Letters of Brooke Foss Westcott* 2 vols. (1903). *The Durham Diocesan Calendar* (annual volumes) provides much information on Victorian developments. See also H. E. Savage *A Review of the Church's Progress in the Diocese of Durham in the Nineteenth century*, a paper read at the Church Congress held in Newcastle 1900, and later printed.

44. Based mainly on episcopal visitation returns for 1896, held on microfilm at the Department of Palaeography and Diplomatic, University of Durham.

45. See note 21 for a reference to Peter Lavin's study of Boddy.

46. F. H. Hawkins *A History of the Sunderland District Free Church Federal Council* (1985).

Additions

A fuller account of the subject of this chapter can be found in G. E. Milburn *Church and Chapel in Sunderland 1780-1914*, Sunderland Polytechnic, 1988.

On the rebuilding of St. Michael's, Bishopwearmouth, especially in the 1930s, see Peter Nicol 'Bishopwearmouth Church 1790-1981' in *Bulletin of the Durham County Local History Society*, 40, May 1988, pp. 4-42.

Personalities and Power 1860s-1914

Sunderland's political history in the second half of the century may be seen through the careers of some of the town's leading political figures. Men like James Williams, John Candlish, Samuel Storey and Thomas Summerbell all played leading roles in the struggle for political power within the town at a time when only one important elected body, the Board of Guardians, escaped the political battles fought on the hustings, in the Council chamber and in the local press.[1]

JAMES WILLIAMS

Williams played a central role on Sunderland's political stage from the time he and George Binns emerged as the joint leaders of the Chartist movement in Sunderland in the late 1830s.[2] In the early 1840s, however, Williams began to move away from Chartism and towards the idea of working-class co-operation with the middle-class to secure both repeal of the Corn Laws and the extension of the franchise. In November 1847 he was elected as a councillor for Bridge Ward, beginning a career on the Council which lasted with one brief interruption until his death on 1 November 1868. His election to the Council came at a time when sanitary reform was about to become a major issue and for the remainder of his life he was a prominent and increasingly influential supporter of this cause. In 1858 he wrote to Joseph Cowen of Newcastle, regarding plans for agitation on behalf of Parliamentary reform, that

> My public speaking days are I think nearly done — Municipal affairs, sanitary reforms, temperance and . . . the business management of . . . the *Sunderland Times*, occupy all my time . . .
>
> I am not conscious of any abatement of interest in the advancement of the people, but a conviction . . . that political reformers generally attached too much importance to the value of political change has grown stronger upon me every year and made me more and more devoted to what are usually called moral and social reforms.[3]

Williams worked to secure the passage of the 1851 Sunderland Borough Act under which the Council took on responsibility for paving, lighting, drainage and building regulations, and embarked on other ventures for the public welfare. These included the opening of public baths and wash-houses in Hendon Road (1851) and in Monkwearmouth (1853), the establishment of the free library in (1858), the widening of the Wearmouth Bridge (1858-62) and the acquisition of land for both the Mowbray Park (1857) and the Extension Park (1866). Williams worked closely with the Council's other leading sanitary reformer, Dr William Mordey, in support of these measures. Mordey died in 1863 and Williams, now an alderman and Chairman of the Council's Sanitary Committee, led the campaign to secure more powers for the Council by means of another local act, the 1867 Sunderland Extension and Improvement Act. Williams made the need for action painfully clear during the Parliamentary Committee stage of this Bill when he stated that the ordinary death-rate in Sunderland Parish (the most densely populated and poorest area) was seven deaths per 1,000 inhabitants higher than elsewhere in the borough and that it was between ten and 12 per 1,000 higher when an epidemic occurred; fever and cholera the previous year had increased it to 33 deaths per 1,000 compared to 23 elsewhere in the town.[4]

The 1867 Act gave the Corporation increased powers in such matters as building and street regulations; authorised the Council to borrow money to pay for the compulsory purchase and demolition of specified blocks of slum housing within the next ten years; extended the borough boundaries to take in Hendon, Pallion and more of Monkwearmouth, but not Southwick; and enlarged the Council by creating two new wards, Hendon and Pallion.[5] Sadly, Williams' death the following year deprived his supporters of his able and respected leadership and almost certainly increased the difficulties faced by the Council in implementing what was an ambitious programme of slum clearance. James Williams' efforts in this behalf were however to be commemorated when a new street in the east end, built in the early 1870s to replace several of the infamous narrow lanes, was named after him.

Another interesting aspect of Williams' work was newspaper ownership. Sunderland had had newspapers of its own since 1831 and, as was normal in towns where more than one paper was published, they were usually strongly partisan in their political views. In a number of instances indeed they owed their existence to the political party or faction whose views they advocated. Thus Sunderland's first paper, the neutral *Gazette*, was quickly ousted by the Liberal *Sunderland Herald*, which was challenged in the later 1830s by the Tory *Sunderland Beacon*, started in 1838 with the financial backing of Lord Londonderry and his friends.[6] The *Beacon's* successors, the *Northern Times* and the *Sunderland Times*, continued to advocate Tory views, mildly for much of the 1840s, more vehemently after a change of proprietorship in 1851.

In 1851 a Radical paper, the *Sunderland News*, was started by John Candlish. This

The *Sunderland Times* office, corner of High Street West and William Street, c.1865, during James Williams' proprietorship.

John Candlish (1816-1874), glass manufacturer (Londonderry Bottle works, Seaham Harbour), Liberal MP. 1866-1874.

James Hartley (1811-1886), glass manufacturer (Wear Glass works), Conservative MP 1865-1868.

achieved a reasonable circulation — indicating the existence of a Radical readership in the town — but failed to build up a satisfactory advertisement base, and was discontinued in 1855. In the 1857 election the Radical candidate, Ralph Walters, was bitterly attacked by the Tory *Sunderland Times* and the Whig *Sunderland Herald*. A few months later, however, in November 1857, James Williams was able to buy the *Times* for £1,000. Produced from the secure base of Williams' printing business the *Times* was converted from a negligible Tory paper in deep financial trouble into a highly effective Radical organ.

CANDLISH AND THE 1860s ELECTIONS

Williams' acquisition of the *Sunderland Times* enhanced his political importance and had repercussions in the mid-1860s when the Radicals were divided over who was to stand as the second Liberal candidate with Fenwick in the 1865 election, William Schaw Lindsay, MP since 1859, or John Candlish.[7] Since his election in 1859, with the backing of a united Liberal party, Lindsay had lost support among the Radicals by his conduct in Parliament and because of his support of the South in the American Civil War. Candlish, on the Council since 1848, mayor in 1858 and 1861, an alderman from 1862, Guardian, River Wear Commissioner, magistrate, as well as a large employer, had started from nothing — as did so many of Sunderland's leading men. He was not universally popular. Some considered him over-ambitious. Roman Catholics in particular disliked him for his attitude to their religion, especially over the religious upbringing of Catholic children in the Workhouse during his chairmanship of the Board of Guardians.[8] A four-cornered fight in 1865 between two Radicals (Lindsay and Candlish), a Whig (Fenwick) and a Conservative (James Hartley) was prevented when Lindsay retired shortly before the election because of ill-health. Fenwick was returned with a large majority and Candlish was narrowly beaten into third place by Hartley.[9]

The choice of Hartley as the Conservative candidate was a good one. Proprietor of the important Wear Glass Works, an alderman since 1853, three times mayor, borough and county magistrate, Guardian, River Wear Commissioner and a director of the North Eastern Railway Co. since 1856, he followed the same pattern as his two predecessors as Tory MPs, Ald. Thompson and George Hudson, playing down his Toryism (he was often described as a Liberal-Conservative) and stressing his concern for local business interests.

Apart from Hartley's strengths as a candidate, two major factors contributed to Candlish's defeat: firstly, the damage done by the alienation of Lindsay's friends from Candlish, particularly the influential trio Edward Capper Robson, Joshua Wilson and James Williams, together with Williams' *Sunderland Times*;[10] and secondly, Fenwick's policy of theoretical neutrality, which secured him a large number of split votes with both Candlish and Hartley, but infuriated Candlish's supporters.

A few months later Fenwick accepted office as a Civil Lord of the Admiralty and had to stand for re-election. The Radicals were quick to seize their opportunity for revenge. A Requisition was got up asking Candlish to stand against Fenwick. This was presented to Candlish on 26 January 1866 at a crowded meeting of his supporters by Samuel Storey, joint secretary of the recently formed Monkwearmouth Advanced Liberal Association. Candlish allowed himself to be persuaded to stand and after a fierce month-long campaign was elected, gaining 1,430 votes against Fenwick's 1,296.

Candlish's victory in what was basically a Whig v Radical fight demonstrated the growing strength of Radicalism among Sunderland's electorate which was confirmed in the 1868 general election. By then the 1867 Parliamentary Reform Act had increased the number of Sunderland's registered electors from 3,468 to 11,364, which posed enormous problems for party organisation in two areas; registration work — elections could be won or lost on the state of the register and it was vital for a party to ensure that as many as possible of its supporters included; and electioneering — personal contact between candidates and most electors was simply no longer possible and mass meetings of electors increasingly supplemented personal canvassing. To meet the need for some form of permanent, representative party organisation to deal with these problems the Monkwearmouth and Sunderland Advanced Liberal Associations, formed after the 1865 election, were replaced by the Sunderland Liberal Political Union, a more broadly based body which, however, included the most active Radicals among its members and office bearers.

The 1868 election in Sunderland is most notable for deciding the power struggle within the Liberal party in favour of the Radicals. In the unusually long run-up to this election it was assumed that Hartley and Candlish would stand for re-election but the big question for the Liberals was who their second candidate should be. Two contenders emerged: Thomas Charles Thompson, barrister and landowner, who received Whig and some Radical, support; and Edward Temperley Gourley, shipbroker, shipowner and the then Mayor of Sunderland. The Liberal Political Union organised a trial ballot but Thompson's committee withdrew from the arrangements at the last moment and only one third of the 11,000 forms issued to electors were returned — 3,271 in favour of Gourley, 419 for Thompson — and both went on to stand in the election.[11] Hartley withdrew soon after active canvassing began in late September because of ill health and reluctance to enter on a long and expensive contest. The campaign, fought by three Liberals of very similar views, concentrated on local issues, with arguments and recriminations over the trial ballot providing much ammunition for Gourley's and Thompson's supporters. The result of the poll was Candlish 6,203, Gourley 4,886, Thompson 3,580, figures which proved beyond doubt the strength of the

Radicals as opposed to the Whigs in a straight Liberal contest after the 1867 extension of the franchise. One of Thompson's friends sardonically commented that the electors

preferred Mr Gourley because he managed to lose six steamships during the election, and Mr Thompson had none to lose; besides not being a Dissenter, and not being in favour either of the Permissive Bill or general intemperance, he lost both publicans and teetotallers.[12]

Gourley's oranisation had also been better than Thompson's on polling day. He employed more workers and spent more on printing and advertising. Candlish stayed genuinely neutral and drew support from all sides.[13]

This Radical success was achieved despite the opposition of the Sunderland press. In January 1865, the *Times* and the *Herald* had been joined by a third paper, the *Sunderland Penny Weekly News*, started by Richard Ruddock for Joseph Cowen, proprietor of the *Newcastle Chronicle*, and thus of staunchly Radical parentage. The *News* provided some press support for Candlish but was still in its infancy when he most needed it in the 1865 election and was discontinued in March 1868, leaving the Radicals yet again without their own paper, both the *Times* and the *Herald* having become increasingly moderate in tone. In the 1868 election the Radicals had to look to two papers published outside Sunderland, the *Newcastle Chronicle* and the *Shields Gazette*, for support, but a new generation of Advanced Liberals was about to take the stage. Their need for press support was to lead at last to the successful establishment of a Radical paper: the *Echo*. Much of the credit for that outcome belongs to Samuel Storey.

SAMUEL STOREY

Samuel Storey's father and grandfather had been tenant farmers in Whitburn and then in Monkwearmouth before Samuel's father moved to Sherburn, near Durham, where Samuel was born in 1841. His father died when he was two and Samuel was brought up in Newcastle. After teaching for several years he moved to Monkwearmouth late in 1864 to embark on what proved to be a highly successful business career. At the same time he had also resolved to try and follow Joseph Mazzini's teaching, laid down in *The Duties of Man*, that

it was the duty of every citizen of means and with the capacity to serve the public; . . . to do so . . . without any reward except the sense of good work accomplished and of duty done.

This high ideal Storey thought had been carried out by another man under whose influence he had come as a young man, Joseph Cowen.[14]

Fired by such idealism Storey came to Sunderland to make his way in both business and politics. Politically, he came to the fore in getting up the Requisition which persuaded Candlish to oppose Fenwick in the 1866 by-election. During this campaign he seems already to have shown the ability as a popular and effective speaker which was to serve him well throughout his long career. The following year he campaigned vigorously for increased representation for Monkwearmouth on the Town Council when the 1867 Sunderland Extension and Improvement Bill was before Parliament, and he and two other ratepayers went to London to put their case before the Parliamentary Committee considering the Bill. In the 1867 annual council elections he and another member of that deputation, Robert Swan, stood in Monkwearmouth Ward but were defeated only to be elected the following year.[15] Both were active members of the United Methodist Free Church on Dock Street, Monkwearmouth.

Swan's and Storey's election to the Council marks the revival of active politics there. The Radicals, encouraged by success in parliamentary contests, began to put up more candidates for the Council, ignoring their opponents' jibes that as 'small ratepayers' they were not suited to have control of council expenditure since they would not be the men who had to pay. Few in number, these new councillors acted as a ginger group. Storey in particular lost no time in acting as the proverbial new broom once he had been elected to the Council. He was a member of the Sanitary Committee (renamed the Health Committee in 1871) and of the Improvement Committee and it was largely due to his efforts on the latter that action was taken to implement the improvement clauses of the 1867 Act in Monkwearmouth as well as south of the river in Sunderland parish. The overall results of these improvement clauses were limited and disappointing in terms of both money and effort. Some areas were opened up and some of the worst fever dens cleared away but many areas were not tackled, and, while the total estimated sum was spent, less than half the planned clearances had been carried out by the time the ten years allowed for the scheme expired.[16] One major problem faced by the Council was the lack of a simple system for the compulsory purchase of insanitary property until the 1890 Housing of the Working Classes Act. In Sunderland parish the committee had to pay high prices for some essential properties but in Monkwearmouth

Cartoon of the 1868 election showing the Liberal candidates (Candlish and Gourley) balanced on the shoulders of Samuel Storey, co-founder and manager of the Atlas Building Society.

The Hustings erected outside the Exchange for Nomination Day in the 1866 Election.

Storey and the other two councillors responsible for negotiations there were dealing with smaller areas and made only conditional agreements to buy houses until they had reached agreements for all the property in a particular block and so could not be blackmailed by a single owner into paying an exorbitant price for his property.

Storey's abilities soon made him the recognised organiser and leader of the Radical group in the Council. He, Swan and Robert Preston (elected in 1865) were gradually joined by other new councillors like S. S. Robson and John Cameron, elected for Sunderland Ward in by-elections in January 1870 and November 1873 respectively.[17] The growing influence of this radical group was helped by the establishment of the Sunderland and North Durham Liberal Club, based in the Athenaeum in Fawcett Street and officially opened by Sir Hedworth Williamson in January 1874, and by the founding of the Echo, first published on 22 December 1873. The Liberal Club provided a meeting place for Liberals of all shades of political opinion while the Echo proved to be not only Sunderland's first successful daily evening paper but also a valuable political weapon for the radicals — putting their side of any political question in editorials, supporting their candidates in elections, reporting Liberal meetings at length and generally criticising their opponents.

THE ECHO AND THE POST

Fifty years later Samuel Storey recounted how the Echo came to be founded. The Sunderland Herald and Sunderland Times were, he wrote,

> well conducted and well edited . . . but were inadequate to supply the desires of a large population for more up-to-date news.

The Shields Gazette, a Liberal paper, sent some 3,000 copies of its afternoon edition to Sunderland, but it

> did not contain much Sunderland news, and its leaders from time to time were very inimical to the new Party of Constitutional Progressives which had risen in the town . . . and which was also busy in returning younger and more progressive councillors to replace the steady-going old gentlemen whose jog-trot ways in local government did not conform to the need of the new times.[18]

Tired of this situation, Storey and six partners resolved to start a paper of their own to supply local as well as general news and, in the words of the Echo's opening editorial, to 'advocate progress with moderation'. Of the seven founders, only Richard Ruddock knew anything about newspaper management and the prospects of success soon seemed very remote. Gourley, Palmer and Ruddock withdrew from the enterprise rather than invest more capital but Storey took on their shares, the money was raised and the Echo began to make headway. It was as well, however, that the proprietors' principal aim was political influence rather than profit: a period of intense competition was about to begin in the Sunderland press and it was to be several more years before they began to see a return on their investment. In July 1876, not only was the Echo first printed on a new press in its new offices in Bridge Street, its home for the next century, but the Sunderland Times was converted from bi-weekly to daily publication and the Tories started a paper of their own, the Sunderland Daily Post.

Squeezed between the Radical Echo, the weekly Whig Herald and the Tory Post, the Sunderland Times failed to survive. It was sold to the Echo in 1878. The Post suffered the same difficult early years that the Echo had had to face and in 1879 seemed likely to die. However, taken over by new proprietors, principally John Wright Wayman, building society manager and councillor for Hendon Ward since its creation in 1867, the Post survived and for the next quarter of a century it and the Echo provided Sunderland with rival, and often bitterly hostile, views of both local and national questions of the day.

THE RADICALS AND THE COUNCIL

While these developments were taking place, the Radicals were gaining ground elsewhere. More Advanced Liberals were elected to the Council and in 1875 they unsuccessfully

Founders of the *Sunderland Echo*, Edward Backhouse (1808-1879), Quaker banker, E. T. Gourley (1826-1902) shipbroker and MP, Charles Mark Palmer (1822-1907) shipbuilder and MP for North Durham/Jarrow from 1874, Richard Ruddock (1837-1908) reporter and editor (from 1878) of the *Newcastle Chronicle*, Thomas Glaholm (1834-1888), rope maker, Thomas Scott Turnbull (1825-1880), draper, and Samuel Storey (1841-1925), principal proprietor of the *Echo* and other newspapers, MP 1881-95 and 1910.

THOMAS GLAHOLM.

EDWARD BACKHOUSE.

T. S. TURNBULL.

SAMUEL STOREY.

RICHARD RUDDOCK.

The seven original PROPRIETORS OF THE ECHO. 1873.

SIR E. T. GOURLEY.

SIR C. M. PALMER.

nominated their own candidate, S. S. Robson, as Mayor. The following year, knowing that they intended to nominate Robson again, the Tories put up a strong candidate, Francis Ritson, who defeated him when he stood for re-election to the Council in the annual elections on 1 November. Deprived of Robson as a candidate the Radicals instead nominated Samuel Storey, who was elected Mayor unopposed. A contemporary pamphleteer commented that with frantic energy the Tories had sought to

> thrust Storey into political nothingness, and in the very elation of apparent victory, they discovered to their disgust and amazement that they had thrust him into the (Mayor's) chair.[19]

Storey's election as Mayor emphasised the substantial changes taking place in the composition of the town council during the 1870s. After the November 1874 elections there were 31 Liberal and 17 Tory councillors while the Aldermen were equally divided, eight and eight. Between November 1874 and November 1877 five Tory councillors were replaced by three new ones while four Liberal councillors were elected Aldermen and ten left the Council. The new Liberal Councillors who filled these vacancies were nearly all 'Storeyites' — men who were already friends of Storey or whom he backed and on whose support he could generally rely.

Several of these, like Storey and Swan were members of the Dock Street Chapel, and many Tory attacks on the Radicals at this time refer to either the Liberal Club clique or the Dock Street Chapel clique as trying to run the town.[20] By October 1878 the council was formed of three major groups: Storey's party numbering 28, Simey's party of 19 Tories, and 17 independents of all political shades.[21] The following year the Tory position within the Council was further weakened by the loss of two of their most able councillors: Ralph Simey, who retired, and C. H. Reed, who was defeated. Increasing Radical strength in the Council enabled them to use their power in much the same way as they had earlier objected to the Whigs and Tories doing: no Tory was elected to fill an aldermanic vacancy between George Barnes in August 1874 and John Nicholson in 1883, and the mayoralty was held by Storey or his friends from 1876 until 1882, when John Wright Wayman was allowed to fulfil his long-cherished ambition of becoming Mayor.

SUNDERLAND SCHOOL BOARD

Two months after Storey's election as Mayor had visibly demonstrated Liberal control of the Council, the Unsectarians won control of Sunderland School Board which had been set up under the 1870 Education Act.[22] Religion provided the main factor in School Board politics, opinion being divided between those in favour of expanding the existing system of voluntary schools and those preferring a system of secular or non-sectarian education. In the main, the denominations with most schools — the Church of England, the Roman Catholics and (initially) the Wesleyans — favoured the former while the smaller nonconformist denominations with few, if any, schools of their own preferred a system of secular

education. Other political issues, for example the drink question and the disestablishment of the Church of England, meant the equation of the denominationalists with the Tories (the 'Beer and Bible Party') and of the nonconformists (except the Wesleyans) with the Liberals.

The first Sunderland school board election, held in January 1871, was notable for Church unity and nonconformist divisions. The cumulative voting system meant each ratepayer had as many votes as there were places to be filled (13 in 1871, increased to 15 from 1877) and could give all of them to one candidate or divide them among as many candidates as he or she wished. On the nonconformist side four denominations were said to be strong enough to return their own candidate but if they worked together they could return six candidates.[23] However, they failed to agree among themselves on their candidates and the two strongest denominations, the Primitive Methodists and the Presbyterians, insisted on nominating their own candidates, who were both elected with large majorities. The Church party, on the other hand, agreed on a team of seven candidates and organized their supporters so that their voting strength was equally divided among the seven, all of whom were elected. The remaining places were filled by Canon John Bamber (RC), Robert Cameron (Baptist) and one of the two Wesleyan candidates, making up a Board with ten members in favour of denominational and three for unsectarian education. The editor of the *Sunderland Times* summed up the position when he commented that the Church party had subscribed liberally, organised effectively, worked vigorously and won, while the nonconformists, split among themselves, neglected to raise funds, made no joint canvass of the town, trusted for success to the well-known high character of their nominees, frittered away their strength on election day, and lost.[24] The Liberal Political Union tried to give an effective

The Dock Street Chapel (United Methodist Free Churches). Monkwearmouth, built 1867.

lead to the Unsectarians in this election but nonconformist jealousies and divisions proved too strong for it.

Three years later when the next election was due to be held the Unsectarians were robbed of possible victory by a last minute compromise. The campaign was marked by considerably better nonconformist organisation with the establishment of a Central Committee made up of representatives from each ward and from religious and other interested bodies. Six Liberal or 'Non-sectarian' candidates were chosen, including a working-man representative, William Whittle, a dyer. The idea of putting up a lady candidate was discussed but abandoned because of the difficulty of finding one willing to stand. Last minute negotiations, however, resulted in a Board of eight Denominational and five Nonsectarian members being elected unopposed. The Church party was happy but there was considerable dissatisfaction among the Liberals.[25]

Before the next election was held Liberal party organisation had been improved. In the summer of 1876 the Liberal Political Union was replaced by a Sunderland Liberal Association, based on the model used with conspicuous success by the Birmingham Liberal party. Ward committees were set up in each municipal ward and in Southwick and annual meetings were to be held to elect these committees, together with representatives on the Association's Executive Committee and the General Council of Four Hundred, a number which was later increased to keep pace with the rise in the number of electors. Parliamentary candidates were to be chosen by a public meeting of Liberal electors summoned by the General Council and ward committees were to be able to choose candidates for municipal elections if they wished.

Speaking at the ward meetings held to establish the new body, Samuel Storey and F. M. Bowey argued that such an Association would encourage all Liberals to take an interest in political matters, that Liberals would be ready to unite and work together in any emergency that arose, and that candidates would be chosen publicly and not by a clique.

One of the first tests faced by the new Association was the third School Board election held in January 1877. By then most Wesleyans had joined their nonconformist brethren on the Unsectarian side, opposing an alliance of the Church (i.e. the Church of England) party and the Roman Catholics, who, the nonconformists alleged, would both have liked to have supported their own voluntary schools at the expense of the Board's, and also, in the case of the Church party, to have had their own brand of religion taught in the Board schools.

Unlike 1874 there seems to have been little desire to avoid a contest. The Unsectarians were well organised, united and determined to secure the majority of which they had been robbed by disunity in 1871 and compromise in 1874; the Church party would not concede this without a fight. The poll on 8 January 1877 more than justified the Unsectarians. The strength of the Catholic vote, aided by his personal standing, returned Canon Bamber at the head of the poll with a large majority. The next eight elected members were all Unsectarians except for James Hartley, the retiring chairman of the old Board, who came fifth; the shipbuilder S. P. Austin followed, ahead of the eighth successful Unsectarian candidate, and the Board was completed by four more members of the Church party. One Church candidate, W. Scott Moncrieff, only recently arrived in Sunderland as Vicar of Christ Church, was defeated. Both 'teams' were well organised, with their supporters following careful instructions on how to split their votes to ensure that all members of the team were elected.[26]

The *Echo* celebrated the Unsectarian victory with an editorial headed 'Union is Strength', and attributed much of the credit for the result to the work of the Liberal Four Hundred which had brought together representatives of the nonconformist churches and the recognised social, political and trade organisations to choose candidates as well as holding meetings all over the town. The *Post* on the other hand attributed the result not only to improved nonconformist organisation and better relations between the various denominations but also to the Church party having allowed their organisation to lapse.[27] Certainly organisation was important, but the Church was numerically weaker than dissent in Sunderland and without the divisions and jealousies which had wrecked hopes of nonconformist co-operation in 1871 had little chance of success, especially after the loss of Wesleyan support. The Church candidates were men of wealth, influence and position but Liberal party organisation was now powerful enough to ensure the selection of a strong and representative team, co-operation between the various churches and the even distribution of votes.

Subsequent elections confirmed the Unsectarian majority on the Board. The Church party fought a strong campaign in 1880

An election cartoon of 1874 commenting on the alliance between the publicans and the established church, against the Liberal, dissenting and temperance interest.

"Whoso rewardeth evil for good, evil shall not depart from his house"
Proverbs XVII. 13r.

"PULLING TOGETHER!"

DEDICATED TO THE "BEER & BIBLE" PARTY

alleging mismanagement, extravagance and neglect of religious instruction in the board schools. The result was still the return of eight Unsectarians (seven of them in the top ten places), six Church candidates and one Roman Catholic.[28] Even with a good election cry, such as Bible teaching the Church party could not defeat a united Unsectarian party and the work of the Board subsequently proceeded quietly and steadily, causing little, if any, dissension. There was no contest in 1883 or 1886, while in 1889 and 1892 the Unsectarians retained their majority with little difficulty in elections notable more for apathy than excitement. The only noteworthy changes in the Board occurred in 1892 when not only were two Catholics elected for the first time, but also the first, and only, woman member, Mrs Hancock, wife of the Vicar of the Venerable Bede, Monkwearmouth.[29]

PARLIAMENTARY ELECTIONS 1874-81

As well as gaining ground in the Council and School Board, the Radicals also retained control of Sunderland's parliamentary representation during the 1870s. The 1874 election confirmed the change which had taken place within Sunderland's Liberal party in the previous decade. Candlish was ill and could not stand for re-election so the Liberals urgently needed a second candidate. Robert Cameron, Samuel Storey and Joseph Cowen, MP, persuaded Sir Henry M. Havelock to contest his father's native town.[30] Havelock came to Sunderland and spoke at two Liberal meetings before he and Gourley were formally adopted as candidates. Hartley declined to stand again so the Tories selected Laurence R. Baily of Liverpool as their candidate. Baily was closely acquainted with commercial and shipping matters but had no local connections and the result was a decisive Liberal victory — Gourley 6,172, Havelock 5,920, Baily 3,871 - with very few Liberal plumpers or cross-party splits.

This election is thus noteworthy not only because it was the Radical leaders who found the second candidate, who was then adopted by a mass meeting of Liberals, with none of the internal disagreements which had marked 1868 (there was little time for these — news of the dissolution reached Sunderland on 24 January and the poll was held on 3 February), but also because Havelock was supported by the entire party on polling day despite

dissension over events in the neighbouring county division of North Durham. There Radical pressure forced Sir Hedworth Williamson, the retiring Liberal member, to withdraw as candidate when it was rumoured that he had tried to reach an agreement with the Tories by which he and the retiring Tory member, George Elliott, would be returned unopposed. Williamson, unwilling to fight an expensive contested election, retired on 29 January leaving Charles Mark Palmer and Isaac Lowthian Bell to defeat Elliot and the second Tory candidate, Richard L. Pemberton, and so complete the return of the 'Durham Thirteen': 13 Liberal MPs for the County's 13 seats.[31].

The next election was held in 1880. For a time it seemed that Gourley and Havelock, who somewhat confusingly became Havelock-Allan just as the campaign started, might be returned unopposed for Sunderland. However, Col. John Joicey's adoption to fight North Durham with Palmer for the Liberals against Elliot encouraged the Tories to contest the borough and Edward Brooke, a Middlesex chemical dye manufacturer and merchant, agreed to stand. Storey, acting as Returning Officer, decided that the poll should be held on 31 March, the first possible day. This both further handicapped the Tories, already at a disadvantage fighting with a newly adopted candidate who was a stranger to the town, and freed the borough Liberals to work in North Durham where the poll was not held for another week.

The only real problem facing the borough Liberals was Havelock-Allan's relations with the Irish over Home Rule for Ireland. A deputation of Home Rulers had interviewed Havelock on this question during the 1874 election, but there was disagreement about what was actually said at this interview and Havelock voted against various Home Rule resolutions during the 1874-80 Parliament, while the Irish claimed he had agreed to vote for Home Rule. The incident embittered Havelock's relations with the Irish in Sunderland, who formed a substantial group of voters, estimated at five to six hundred strong by Robert Cameron in 1874, and probably at least twice that by 1880.[32] In 1880 the Irish ultimately agreed to support Gourley and Havelock-Allan on national grounds but the poll suggests that some Home Rulers may have split Gourley/Brooke or plumped for Gourley. The result was Gourley 7,639, Havelock-Allan 6,995, Brooke 4,262, and a week later the Liberals were equally triumphant in the county.[33]

The 1880 election highlighted two problems facing Sunderland's Tories. Firstly there was the lack of a broad-based political organisation able to fight at short notice. A Conservative Association had been in existence for some time but it was a much less public organisation than its Liberal counterpart; several attempts at ward organisation along similar lines to that of the Liberal Association were made in the late 1870s but they met with little success until a few months after the 1880 general election when such an association was at last established. Secondly, the Tories lacked strong leadership. James Hartley's active days were

Mrs Mary S. Hancock, wife of the vicar of the Venerable Bede, Monkwearmouth and the only lady member of the School Board (1892-1903). She became a member later of Sunderland Council's Education Committee.

John S. G. Pemberton (1860-1940), Conservative candidate 1892, MP 1900-1906.

The Victoria Hall Disaster

The death of some 183 children on the 16 June 1883 in the Victoria Hall at Sunderland is comparable only to the more recent Aberfan tragedy. The scene of the disaster, involving children mostly between seven and eleven years of age, was the great gothic Victoria Hall which had been erected at a time when huge structures like the Crystal Palace and the Albert Hall were popular. It was not built as a theatre but a hall hired out for public meetings and entertainments by the 'Victoria Hall and Temperance Institute Ltd'. It was opened in 1872 having cost £10,000 to build, and stood, a very distinctive building, on Toward Road facing Mowbray Park.

The most publicised event at the Hall in the summer of 1883 was a visit by the travelling entertainer, Alexander Fay, whose tickets were distributed widely amongst local children promising a very attractive show and offering the inducement of small presents. The offer of free toys and baubles, together with the high spirits of the weekend holiday, led to the attendance of about 2,000 excited children on the fateful Saturday. Of these 1,100 were in the gallery. There were very few adults present amongst the crowd of youngsters.

As the show drew towards its conclusion many children began to flood from the gallery to claim their share of the largesse. Streaming noisily down the winding staircase they were confronted by a door which had been partly bolted and would only open inwards. It is likely that this trap had been laid quite unwittingly by an assistant of Fay called Hesseltine who was seeking to regulate the alarming flow of children to the stage.

In fact the children were soon reduced to a struggling heap, magnified as more and more of their fellows under pressure from behind fell to join the sprawling crush, layer upon layer. The *Sunderland Weekly Echo and Times* of 22 June described the scene graphically:

Children were tumbled head over heels, one on top of the other. Shrieks and screams vibrated through the stair-

case. More pressed down from above inconsiderate of what might happen from this thoughtlessness. Accordingly the children at the bottom of the stairs got packed, as it were, in a well. The heap of writhing and rolling humanity became higher and higher until it rose above the heads of those who were first jammed in the doorway and became a mass of struggling and dying children over six feet in height.

A caretaker and a few others soon on the scene managed to pull through the gap a few of the children who were still breathing:

Alfie Dixon . . . one of the rescued, states that the feeling which came over him was like going to sleep and someone got hold of him and pulled him out. His little brother Charley said "Don't let go of my hand as someone is standing upon my face". He was drawn out however and the little brother was subsequently found dead.

Survivors were whisked away by cabmen to the new Royal Infirmary on Durham Road. The blackened and broken bodies of the dead were laid out in the dress circle and in appalling scenes of anguish the frantic parents were allowed in to identify their children. One father pointed his way down the lines saying "That's one . . . That's another . . . My God! All my family gone!". Some families lost all of their children. A Mr. Hughes lost only one son, but he had already lost the other two in an accident on the Hetton Waggonway as a result of which his wife had killed herself. The whole 30 children of one Sunday School class were annihilated. In one awful case of mistaken identity a man took back to his wife the body of their little boy only to discover that it was their neighbour's son and that their own had died of his injuries in the Infirmary. There were a few amazing escapes such as that of little Georgina Coe who escaped because she was crippled and used her crutches like pit props to prevent the pressure crushing her.

Donations of money and condolences in all forms flooded into the town. Amongst other things the money was used to

The Victoria Hall as it was in 1883, showing also the memorial to the disaster in Mowbray Park. The statue which stood there, can now be seen in Bishopwearmouth cemetery, without the original canopy.

Victoria Hall after its extension. The Central Library and Museum and the Town Hall also stand out in this rather panoramic view across Mowbray Park. It is very clear from this photograph where the Hall actually stood, at the junction of Toward Road and Laura Street.

pay for the statue of a grieving mother with a dead child on her lap. Originally this stood in Mowbray Park but was moved later to Bishopwearmouth Cemetery. The Queen sent a telegram from Balmoral, and expressed concern especially about a few cases of injured survivors of whom she required that she be kept informed. The quaint Scots poet William McGonagall added to the flood of verses his own "The Sunderland Calamity":

I hope the Lord will comfort their parents by night and by day,
For He gives us life and He takes it away,
Therefore I hope their parents will put their trust in Him,
Because to weep for the dead it is a sin,
Her Majesty's grief for the bereaved parents has been profound,
And I'm glad to see that she has sent them £50,
And I hope from all parts of the world will flow relief,
To aid and comfort the bereaved parents in their grief.

In fact the most lasting memorial of the affair, if its least conspicuous, was the passing of legislation to provide for adequate exits at all places of public entertainment and that such exits should always open outwards.

The Hall itself survived of course. For another 58 years it glowered over the park as a dark monument of a great Victorian tragedy. It remained open but became very delapidated. In 1903 it was bought by the Corporation which spent £30,000 on modernisation and reopened it in 1906. In 1941 it was destroyed by a German parachute mine.

The stage as seen from the gallery.

The frantic scene outside the hall during the disaster, according to the artists of the *Illustrated London News.*

Edward Capper Robson (1812-1893), miller, first president, Sunderland Liberal Association, 1876-1885.

Robert Vint (1807-1890), senior partner (1841-1867) in Vint and Carr, Proprietors of the *Sunderland Herald* 1841-1881. Chairman Sunderland S. Shields Water Co. 1863-1889. Father of alderman W. F. Vint.

over, although he remained the acknowledged head of local Conservatism until his death in 1886, and there was no one of real standing to take his place. Ralph Simey, a solicitor and a leading member of the Town Council during the 1870s, was appointed Clerk of the Peace for County Durham early in 1880 and thereafter concentrated on his legal career; C. H. Reed, an iron manufacturer, virtually disappeared from the political scene after he left the Council in 1879; Francis Ritson (shipbroker), his brother Henry Ritson (solicitor) and John Wright Wayman (building society manager) were all locally prominent Tories but they lacked the social standing and influence which Hartley possessed as a wealthy industrialist.

A more serious challenge to Radical supremacy was posed in 1881 when changes in army regulations forced Havelock-Allan to choose between taking up an active military appointment before July or remaining in Parliament and being placed on the Retired List. He chose the former course, but not before he had done his best to ensure that his successor was not the Radical leader, Samuel Storey. Storey had been one of those who persuaded Havelock to come to Sunderland in 1874 but by the late 1870s Havelock was suspicious of his motives and thoroughly distrusted him. It is not clear what first caused this — possibly criticism of Havelock's views by the *Echo*, which Havelock took personally,[34] or the Irish issue, or simply that Havelock thought Storey was casting ambitious eyes at his seat. Robert Cameron, on friendly terms with both men, tried to reassure Havelock, writing to him in 1879:

I am far more afraid of the unhappy feeling between Mr Storey and yourself than of any mischief Parnell can do (over Havelock and Home Rule). Believe me when I say you may, and it is at present the wisest thing to do, to consult him and trust him. I am certain there is no ground for distrust. The idea of a seat in Sunderland while Mr Gourley and yourself are in possession or candidates he does not entertain — all rumours to the contrary I know are groundless.[35]

Lack of trust probably led to lack of consultation and so to further misunderstandings, especially as Storey's position in the local Liberal party organisation should have necessitated close co-operation between him and both local members. Havelock was not the easiest of men to get along with anyway and, apart from Cameron, his Sunderland friends seem to have been moderate Liberals, especially James Laing and E. C. Robson, neither of whom were friendly with Storey. In these circumstances it is not surprisng that in March 1881 Laing, Robson and Havelock-Allan tried to ensure that whoever might replace Havelock-Allan it should not be Storey.

Here the issue of Liberal policy on Ireland came to their aid. In recent years Liberal and Tory Governments had generally followed alternating policies of Tory Coercion and Liberal Reform to deal with Irish unrest. Following the formation of a Liberal government after the 1880 general election the activities of the Land League in Ireland led to the introduction of a Liberal Coercion bill early in 1881. Storey spoke out against this policy,

arguing strongly that reform of the land laws should come first and that a just settlement would make coercion unnecessary. He was supported by Robert Cameron but by few other prominent local Liberals.

The unpopularity of his views gave Robson and Laing reason to hope that if they could find a suitable moderate Liberal candidate they would be able to exclude Storey from the succession to Havelock-Allan's seat, especially when he played into their hands by going abroad. They were thwarted, however, when both Sir Hedworth Williamson and James Laing himself refused to stand and it quickly became clear once the vacancy was announced that Storey was regarded as the strongest possible candidate despite his stand on Irish coercion. A mass meeting of Liberals approved his candidature shortly after his hasty return to Sunderland, the Tories failed to find anyone to oppose him, and he was elected unopposed.[36] The danger of a Liberal party split on the Irish issue had been a very real one but, faced with a common enemy, the Tories, the Whig and Radical wings of the Liberal party joined forces behind the latter's candidate. Gone were the days when the Whigs would have joined forces with the Tories against the Radicals.

This by-election had repercussions for the Sunderland press. In April 1880 the Whig *Herald* had belatedly gone over to daily publication. It needed to bid positively for the centre of the Sunderland market if it was not to be squeezed out of existence by its two extreme rivals, the *Echo* and the *Post*, as the *Sunderland Times* already had been. Letters from H. A. Cave, one of the *Herald*'s proprietors, to Havelock-Allan in 1880-81 suggest that Sir Henry was supplying the *Herald* with London political news and gossip and that early in 1881 Cave was hoping that he and his political friends in Sunderland — specifically James Laing — might be persuaded to put the paper on a firmer financial footing.[37] In return the *Herald* would be able to provide improved press support for their moderate wing of the Liberal party to counter the Radical *Echo*, which was, of course, supporting Storey in his opposition to the Liberal government's Irish policy. Havelock-Allan's resignation and Storey's election as MP probably ended Cave's hopes of financial support. In August 1881 the *Herald* was sold to the *Post* and the papers were merged as the *Sunderland Herald and Daily Post*.

IRELAND AND THE 1885-86 ELECTIONS

After his election to Parliament in 1881 Storey continued to oppose the government's Irish policy and his stand divided Liberal opinion in Sunderland, with E. C. Robson, President of the Sunderland Liberal Association until his resignation in October 1885, leading the opposition to his views. Despite this Storey and Gourley were both approved as Liberal candidates for the 1885 general election, while the Tories ultimately persuaded the shipbuilder, S. P. Austin, to stand. Austin was the strongest candidate they had had since Hartley's retirement in 1868 and they worked hard to capture the moderate Liberal vote for him rather than Storey.

Irish politics again intervened when Parnell's famous Manifesto was issued on 21 November, only three days before the poll was held in Sunderland, ordering Irish voters in Britain to vote against the Liberal candidates in their constituencies. Four exceptions were named, including Storey, because of their opposition to Coercion. At the same time the Catholic clergy were urging their flocks to vote Conservative because of fears that a Liberal government would introduce free education in the board schools, thereby undermining the position of Catholic schools.[38] Storey issued an urgent appeal to the Irish electors to vote for himself and Gourley, not Austin. Gourley, he declared, had voted and spoken against Coercion in Parliament and, if they voted for himself and Austin, they would be voting "for the man who led the town against Coercion, and for a Tory who supported and applauded Coercion"; he had "lost many friends" by standing up for them and he would be defeated, not Gourley, if only one Liberal was elected.

In fact the result was Storey 8,295, Gourley 7,759, Austin 6,703. The detailed analysis of the poll and contemporary comments suggest that the Irish vote, now some 1,400 strong, was split: the *Echo* thought Austin received about 1,000 Irish votes, half as plumpers, half as splits with Storey, who also received about 100 Irish plumpers, while some 300 voted Storey/Gourley.[39] The increase in the Conservative vote since 1880 can thus be partly attributed to the Irish and partly to Austin's personal standing. In addition, Austin had bid for the temperance vote and, because of the trade depression, may have received votes in support of 'fair trade' proposals, including a tax on imported manufactured goods.

Nationwide the election left the 86 Irish Nationalist members holding the balance of power. Gladstone took office early in 1886 and, converted to the idea of Home Rule for Ireland, brought in a Home Rule bill. It split the Liberal party into Home Rulers following Gladstone and Liberal Unionists following Lord Hartington and Joseph Chamberlain in opposition to Home Rule. The bill was defeated, Gladstone dissolved Parliament and appealed to the country. The election held in July 1886 resulted in a resounding Conservative and Liberal Unionist majority over the Gladstonian Liberals and Irish Nationalists and ushered in six years of Tory rule. In Sunderland Storey and Gourley were re-adopted as the Liberal candidates and were opposed by William Stobart, managing proprietor of Wearmouth Colliery, standing as a Liberal Unionist and receiving Tory support. The result of the poll was Storey 6,970, Gourley 6,839, Stobart 6,027, with the Irish vote going solidly to the two Liberal candidates.[40]

THE COUNCIL IN THE 1880s

Locally the Liberals retained control of the town council in a period which saw the build-ing of the Library and Museum on the north end of the park in the late-1870s, the Town Hall in Fawcett Street, eventually opened in 1890 after many delays and lengthy debates about alternative sites, and the Infectious Diseases Hospital in Hylton Road, also opened in 1890. In the early 1880s it became clear that a new local Act was needed. Three years of intensive discussion both inside and outside the Council resulted in the 1885 Borough of Sunderland Act, which gave the corporation increased powers over house-building, sanitary and health matters and power to fund the borough debt, but proposals to extend the borough boundaries and re-arrange the wards were dropped.

The Radicals' supremacy in the Council was gradually undermined during the 1880s, partly by internal divisions, including the Home Rule split, and partly by over-confidence. Storey's election to Parliament in 1881 and his expanding business interests outside the town also deprived his followers of his day-to-day leadership and organisational ability which had contributed much to Radical successes during the 1870s and to which they had become accustomed.

In the early 1880s the growth of a group of 'independent' Liberal councillors was encouraged by the Tory party and its organ, the *Post*. The cries of 'independence', i.e. independence from the Liberal caucus as led by Storey, and of 'No politics in the Council', summarise Tory policy at this time. This group of independent Liberals was responsible for J. W. Wayman's election as Mayor in 1882 and his re-election in 1883, despite Storey's opposition on both occasions. In 1882 the Council was made up of 44 Liberals including nine aldermen, and 20 Conservatives including seven aldermen. In the 1882 mayoral election 16 Tories and 15 Liberals actually voted for Wayman — a majority of the 60 members present — while the main Radical group, including Storey, abstained. This group of 15 Liberals was large enough to hold the balance of power between the straight Tory and Radical sections in the Council. It was made up of 'independents', moderates, future Unionists and discontented Liberals, as well as a few genuinely independent-minded men, who on this occasion may have felt that their party could afford to be generous as Wayman personally was generally popular.

In the mid-1880s a number of municipal contests took place apparently between rival Liberal candidates. Closer examination of these shows that they were cases where a Radical, or a Liberal, approved by the ward's Liberal Association, was being opposed by a moderate Liberal with Tory support. The old policy of Tory success by means of Liberal disunity had been resurrected in a slightly different guise. By supporting 'independent' Liberals the Tories were able to whittle away at the Radical majority in the Council more effectively than they could by putting up a Tory candidate against whom the Liberals would probably successfully unite. Improved results by this means brought greater confidence, and in the late 1880s more and better Tory candidates appeared and were elected. One

Robert Cameron (1825-1913), headmaster, chairman of Sunderland School Board (1877-1885), Liberal MP Houghton-le-Spring from 1895.

problem for the Tories in the early 1880s had been the reluctance of eligible candidates, who might have received Liberal as well as Tory support, to stand for the Council and the drink interest in particular had become over-represented.[41] The Home Rule split in 1886 was followed by the election of several able Liberal Unionist councillors and, as the split on Ireland clearly became a permanent one, co-operation between Liberal Unionists and Tories increased at municipal as well as parliamentary level, with Storey and his party as the enemy at both levels. By 1892 the *Post* was able to claim that the Independent and Unionist parties had gained 14 seats from the Liberal clique since 1885-86.[42] Three years later the first contest for the mayoralty since 1875 took place when the Liberals nominated Ald. William Burns and the Unionists W. F. Vint. Burns was elected, with 31 votes to Vint's 29, a victory which emphasised the importance for the Liberals of their majority on the Aldermanic bench.[43]

The Radicals were slow to respond to this challenge, possibly because Storey's absences at Westminster and abroad for reasons of health during successive winters in the late 1880s deprived them of the strong leadership needed even before his resignation from the Council in November 1890. At the same time both the Liberal Club and the Liberal Association were badly affected by the Home Rule split, ceasing to provide the stalwart support for the Liberal cause which they had done since their foundation. Liberal Unionists were gradually purged from the Association and more slowly from the Club but not before their presence had caused substantial political damage.[44]

By the time of the 1892 general election co-operation between Tories and Liberal Unionists had reached the point where it was possible for their respective candidates to run jointly. The Unionists adopted the Hon. F. W. Lambton, brother of the Earl of Durham, as their candidate and the Tories selected J. S. G. Pemberton; but the Liberal candidates, Storey and Gourley, were re-elected with comfortable majorities.[45]

One change in the Sunderland press also helped Storey's opponents at this time. J. W. Wayman's sudden death in August 1886 led to the sale of the *Post* early in 1887 to George Howitt, editor and manager of the *Echo*. Howitt bought the *Post* without telling Storey of his intentions. Their relationship had been strained for some time and Howitt disagreed with Storey's position on the Irish question.[46] Howitt improved the *Post* and a more balanced coverage of political events was given in the news columns but editorially the paper was Unionist on Ireland and opposed to Storey and his friends on all fronts. Howitt was able to use his close knowledge of Storey and the Liberal party to good effect in constant jibing, making the *Post* a more effective counter to the *Echo* than it had been, while the combination of Liberal Unionists and Tories widened its potential readership. The embittered personal relationship between Howitt and Storey led to Storey suing Howitt for libel in the early 1890s and contributed to Storey, not Gourley, losing

his seat in the Tory landslide in the 1895 general election.

SUMMERBELL, LABOUR AND THE COUNCIL

Radical decline was influenced not only by the split on Ireland but also by another national factor, the growth of a movement for independent Labour representation as opposed to working-class representation within the established political parties. The Council had for a good many years included a number of men, often first generation inhabitants of Sunderland, who had started with little or nothing and had worked their way up to a position of at least comparative affluence before standing for the Council. However, an Act passed in 1880 removed the property or rating qualifications required for town councillors and made it possible for working men to stand for election, the first being Thomas Smith, a glass mould maker, who stood as Liberal candidate for the Council in 1881 and was elected for West Ward the following year, remaining on the Council until he resigned in April 1886 in order to become poor rate collector for Ryhope. It was several years before another working man stood for the Council and by then the idea of independent Labour candidates was being promoted by a hard core of activists who believed the working-classes needed their own representatives if their class interests were to be advanced. Three local organisations played key roles in this development: Sunderland Trades Council, under the guidance of its long-serving Secretary (1888-1906) Thomas Summerbell, a printer, and the Sunderland branches of the Labour Electoral Association (formed in the autumn of 1889) and of the Independent Labour Party (formed in February 1892).[47]

In November 1889 three independent Labour candidates ran for the Council, of whom two were Trades Council officials who polled respectably against strong retiring councillors. Two years later the first Labour councillor was elected to represent East Ward. This was Henry Friend, Secretary of the North of England Sailors' and Firemen's Association, and Chairman of Sunderland Trades Council, 1890-93. Late in November 1892 Friend was joined on the Council by Thomas Summerbell and Philip Pratt, a checkweighman at Wearmouth Colliery, who were elected for Hendon and Bridge Wards respectively in by-elections caused by aldermanic elections. Both men received Liberal support in straight fights against Tory opponents.

As well as being Secretary of the Trades Council Summerbell was also an active member of the Independent Labour Party (ILP), as were at least three other early Labour councillors, David Bell, a watchmaker, who represented Monkwearmouth 1893-1911, R. D. Craig, a tailor, who represented Bridge Ward from June 1894 until he retired at the November 1897 elections, and his successor in Bridge Ward, George New, who represented the ward until he was elected an alderman in 1917. Craig and New were also prominent members of the Trades Council and this

Thomas Summerbell (1861-1910), printer, Sunderland's first Labour MP 1906-1910.

overlap in membership between the Trades Council and the ILP may well have helped Sunderland to avoid the friction experienced in some other towns where the various local Labour organisations competed with each other rather than working together.[48]

In the years up to 1914 Labour gained some Council seats but also lost others as their opponents fought back. Pallion Ward provided mixed fortunes for more than one Labour candidate. Ralph Baxter, a shipyard joiner, won it for Labour in August 1902, lost it in 1907, won in 1910 and lost again in 1926, after which he represented Bridge Ward from 1930 until his election as an alderman in May 1932. Andrew Hutton, another joiner, also represented Pallion, 1902-8, being defeated by the Tory candidate Frank Nicholson (James Williams' grandson) who was general manager of C. Vaux & Sons. The North Side maintained its long radical tradition by electing a number of Labour councillors including Robert J. Wilson who represented Colliery Ward (the old North side area of Bridge Ward) from 1907 until his election as MP for Jarrow in 1922. In other areas Labour fared badly; by the outbreak of World War I there was still only a handful of Labour councillors and it was not until 1935 that they became the majority party on the Council.

Despite their small numbers the early Labour members did have some effect on Council policy. In particular Summerbell argued for the municipalisation of the tramways system and, as vice-chairman and (from 1902) chairman of the Corporation's Tramways Committee, played an important role in its takeover and subsequent expansion.

THE SCHOOL BOARD'S LAST YEARS

The new demands for independent Labour representation in the 1890s had repercussions in both School Board and Parliamentary elections as well as in municipal contests. In January 1895 the Denominationalists briefly regained control of the School Board. The defeat of the Unsectarians was mainly due to the divisive effect of two Labour candidates (Harry Barnes, a Socialist selected by Sunderland ILP, and George New, backed by Sunderland Trades Council) standing in addition to the two working-men representatives included in the Unsectarian Eight (Robert Hindmarch and Philip Coley). Barnes and New were selected as candidates when the Unsectarians failed to choose a working man representative in place of James Chambers, a member of the Board since 1877, who had recently resigned. The Unsectarians belatedly added Philip Coley, chairman of the Co-operative Society, to their team but too late to heal the divisions created by their initial blunder. In a very low poll (41.8 per cent) in which many working-men did not vote because of the weather, all four working-men were defeated, resulting in a Board with six Church, three Roman Catholic and six Unsectarian members.

The Unsectarians regained control at the next election in November 1897, held early to avoid electioneering over Christmas, when two of the three Catholic candidates and Thomas Summerbell, the sole Labour candidate, who had refused to canvass, were narrowly defeated.[49] In the last election in 1900 no working-man or Labour candidate stood and the Catholics reverted, successfully, to running two candidates, winning their second seat at the expense of the Church party.[50] Three years later the School Board's duties passed to Sunderland Town Council under the 1902 Education Act.

LIBERAL DEFEAT: THE 1895 ELECTION

The Unsectarians' defeat in the 1895 School board election was followed by a greater disaster for the Liberals when Samuel Storey lost his seat in the July 1895 general election. The Tory candidate responsible for ending the Liberals' monopoly of the town's parliamentary representation after 27 years was the shipbuilder William Theodore Doxford. Doxford headed the poll while Storey was narrowly pushed into third place by Gourley, the result being Doxford 9,833, Gourley 8,232, Storey 8,185. This result was in line with the national trend, which resulted in a massive Conservative majority, but it was a startling outcome locally. The seeds of defeat lay in the Liberal split over Home Rule which meant that the Liberal Unionists supported Doxford, not Storey and Gourley. But while this accounts in part for the improved performance of Unionist candidates in both parliamentary and local elections after 1886, it does not account for Gourley's defeat of Storey, who had headed the poll in the last three elections. To explain this we must look at personal and purely local issues, particularly the smear campaign against Storey by Howitt and the *Post* during the election.

During the short campaign Howitt and the *Post* took every opportunity to attack Storey's record, especially as an employer. Old issues were unearthed and recirculated, despite denials and explanations. One of the most damaging was the question of low wages paid by the Monkwearmouth iron manufacturing firm of Tyzack & Co. Ltd, of which Storey had become a shareholder and chairman on the company's formaton in December 1889. A wage reduction was made in 1893 by the managing director, William Thackray, jun., and Storey found himself in a minority when he tried to get wage rates increased the following year.[51] Two leading members of the Sunderland ILP, William Key and David Bell, later testified that Key told Howitt between the dissolution and the election in 1895 that Key had seen correspondence between Storey and Thackray and that he and Bell were satisfied that Storey's hands were clean in the matter. Howitt, however, merely remarked that they did not know Storey as well as he did, continued to print the allegations in the *Post* and later denied remembering any such conversation with Key.[52] Other allegations against Storey related to a wages dispute at the *Echo* in its infancy 20 years earlier, and to the purchase of foreign newsprint for his papers, which Storey denied, claiming that

William Theodore Doxford (1861-1916), Shipbuilder, Conservative MP 1895-1906, Knighted 1900.

over 90 per cent of the paper bought since 1887 was of English or Irish manufacture. Despite this, the allegations were repeated in a leaflet headed 'Election Facts and Fictions', based on an article in the *Post* on 10 July, which was circulated with Doxford's polling card on the eve of the election.

Besides the damage done by these attacks on Storey, two other factors have to be taken into account: Liberal organisation, and education. Liberal party workers seem to have been slow to get to work in this election, probably partly due to over-confidence,[53] while the education issue meant that Catholic Irish electors were faced with a choice between voting Liberal because of Home Rule for Ireland or Unionist in the hope that a Conservative government would give financial help to the denominational schools, with their priests urging the latter course on them. It is not clear how many votes this issue gained for Doxford, but both Storey and Gourley believed it contributed to the result.[54]

After the election Storey petitioned against Doxford's return under the new Corrupt and Illegal Practices Act, which had made it illegal to "make or publish any false statement or fact in relation to the personal character or conduct" of a candidate for the purpose of affecting his return. The petition was heard at the end of January 1896. It concentrated on the circular sent out with Doxford's polling cards and the allegations made in it. The outcome of the hearing cleared Storey's character, and cleared Doxford of all personal responsibility for the circular, but it did not affect the election result as the judges held that the statements complained of did not come within the scope of the Act.[55] Storey, hurt by the allegations and by the number of electors apparently prepared to believe them, largely withdrew from active involvement in Sunderland's political life in the next few years, turning instead to Durham County Council, of which he was a member from 1892 to 1913, and where he continued his long-standing interest in both sanitary improvement and education.

Storey's defeat in 1895 marked the end of Radical control of Sunderland's parliamentary representation. He declined to stand for Sunderland at the next election, held in October 1900 during the Boer War, when the Conservative government reaped the reward of going to the polls at a time when victory seemed imminent and the Liberal opposition was divided over the war. The Sunderland Liberal Association began seeking a candidate to run with Gourley early in 1899 and it was hoped that John Candlish's nephew, Joseph John Candlish, would agree to stand. However, Gourley waited until the dissolution of Parliament had been announced and then declined to stand again in a contested election on the grounds of ill-health. It is likely that he had been hoping for an uncontested return with Doxford but any possibility of this was removed when J. S. G. Pemberton came out in July 1900 as a Unionist candidate running independently of the Conservative Association. Candlish declined to stand except with Gourley, and the Liberal Association was left with the election imminent and no candidate at

all as it refused to adopt Gourley as sole candidate. Instead it resolved to fight the election in conjunction with the prospective Labour candidate, Alex Wilkie, General Secretary of the Associated Shipwrights Society, who had agreed to stand provided there were not two Liberals in the field. Rapid negotiations enabled the Liberal Association both to endorse Wilkie's candidature on 24 September and to adopt a candidate of its own, George B. Hunter, partner in the Wallsend shipbuilding firm, Swan & Hunter, and a native of Sunderland.[56] Liberal and Labour co-operation was relatively easy at this time because the recently-established national Labour Representation Committee (LRC), which was to be re-named the Labour Party six years later, had not yet agreed on a policy of strict independence for the candidates it endorsed. The LRC's members ranged from extreme Socialists in favour of a completely independent Labour party, to moderate Trades Unionists who saw the Labour party as a pressure group which would continue to co-operate with the Liberals in the interests of Labour. Wilkie was easily acceptable to Sunderland Liberals as he appeared to belong to the Lib-Lab tradition represented by such respected figures as the Northumberland and Durham miners' MPs, Thomas Burt, William Crawford and John Wilson.

Faced with a Liberal and a Labour candidate the Tories, having failed to persuade Pemberton to retire, joined forces behind both Unionist candidates, fearing that any split in their ranks would lose them both seats. The remainder of the campaign passed comparatively peacefully and the result was a narrow victory for the Tories — Doxford 9,617, Pemberton 9,566, Hunter 9,270, Wilkie 8,842. If Gourley had been prepared to fight with Candlish it is unlikely that a Labour candidate would have stood and the result might well have been the return of the old members, or even of both Liberals.

Less than two years later Gourley died at the age of 73. His lifelong connection with shipping had made him a highly suitable representative for his native town. He had never figured prominently in parliamentary life except as a persistent asker of questions in the House, but he had been a good constituency MP, earning the knighthood which he received in the 1895 Dissolution Honours by hard work and loyalty to his party. Only the manner of his retirement in 1900 was a matter for regret.

Wilkie's performance in the 1900 election encouraged Sunderland Trades Council and the other local Labour organisations and they began early to prepare for the next election. A number of possible candidates were considered but Thomas Summerbell emerged as favourite. The only local candidate, and well-known and respected both as Secretary of the Trades Council and town councillor, he was formally adopted in April 1903.[57]

TARIFF REFORM

By the time the next election was held, in January 1906, a major new political issue had come to the fore, Tariff Reform. Britain had

Alexander Wilkie (1850-1928), first General Secretary of the Associated Shipwrights Society 1882-1928. Labour candidate Sunderland 1900, MP Dundee 1906-1922.

been firmly committed to a policy of Free Trade since the repeal of the Corn Laws in 1846. But now competition for markets for manufactured goods, agricultural depression and the movement for imperial preference (a protective tariff against imported goods with preferential treatment for Britain's colonies) led by the Colonial Secretary, Joseph Chamberlain, culminated in 1903 in proposals for fiscal reform. These proposals divided the Unionists while allowing the Liberal party, split over the Boer War, to reunite in defence of Free Trade. Not all Liberals agreed, however, and one of these exceptions was Samuel Storey. Early in 1904 he failed to persuade Sunderland's Liberals that there should at least be an inquiry into the issue. The Liberal Association resolved to seek a Free Trade and Home Rule candidate and soon afterwards selected Professor James Stuart.[58] It also left itself free to endorse Thomas Summerbell's candidature, the Liberal and Labour candidates having worked harmoniously together in 1900 and there being no reason why this should not happen again. This decision was in accord with the private electoral pact reached in September 1903 by Herbert Gladstone, Liberal Chief Whip, and Ramsay MacDonald, Secretary of the LRC, which placed Sunderland among those constituencies where a Labour candidate would not be opposed by a Liberal; but it is not clear whether Sunderland Liberal Association was acting independently or being guided by Liberal headquarters in London at this time. In the event the LRC adopted a policy of complete independence for candidates it endorsed which made close liaison impossible in the 1906 election. Stuart favoured a 'progressive' alliance with the LRC, unlike most other North East Liberal candidates, who regarded Labour's place as being within the Liberal party. Summerbell, however, was a Socialist and a staunch advocate of an independent Labour party; he recommended Stuart as the most suitable second choice for his supporters but otherwise largely ignored him.[59]

Tariff reform versus Free Trade provided a major element in both the 1906 and January 1910 elections in Sunderland and in 1906 it meant that the two Unionist candidates ran independently of each other. David H. Haggie, the official Unionist candidate, was a Tariff Reformer in favour of protection while J. S. G. Pemberton stood as a Unionist Free Trader. Labour fought the campaign on the premise that tariff reform would increase the cost of living so that the working-classes would suffer while landlords and manufacturers gained from higher prices. The Tariff Reformers reversed this argument, claiming that a measure of protection would lead to prosperity with higher wages and more jobs so that the working classes could afford to pay the higher prices. The Liberal and Labour candidates were not only in agreement on the fiscal issue but also on most of the other important questions in this election, attacking the government's record and arguing the need to reform Trade Union law in the light of recent legal decisions.

Sunderland joined the national Liberal land-slide and returned Stuart and Summerbell with huge majorities over Haggie and Pemberton in a poll which included an unusually high number of plumpers for all four candidates, especially Haggie, the only Protectionist (2,450) and a very solid Liberal-Labour split vote (11,323). There was also a substantial Unionist vote unaffected by the fiscal issue (4,936), while Pemberton received a number of presumably Free Trade votes split with either the Liberal (810) or the Labour (974) candidate.

Six months later the *Post* was discontinued. A few months before his death in October 1902 Howitt had sold his majority interest in the paper to J. S. G. Pemberton,[60] who as Unionist MP for Sunderland from 1900 had good reason to want the *Post* to survive as a Unionist paper. However, Unionist divisions over Tariff Reform, together with the differences between Pemberton and elements in the local Tory party which had led to him coming out independently in 1900, meant that when he lost his seat in 1906 he presumably decided that there was no longer any point in keeping the *Post* going.

In the next election, held in January 1910, Tariff Reform again provided the main theme in the Sunderland campaign. Summerbell and Stuart stood for re-election, and were opposed by James Knott, a shipowner, and by Samuel Storey, standing as an Independent Tariff Reformer. Storey had been adopted as candidate by the Sunderland branch of the Northern

Caricature of Samuel Storey with proposed coat of arms incorporating references to his roles as newspaper owner and tariff reformer.

Tariff Reform Federation in July 1909 and his and Knott's joint candidature was announced in mid-December. Free Traders had by now been largely purged from the Unionist ranks but close liaison between the two Tariff Reform candidates was no doubt made easier by the fact that they had been working closely together in the Northern Tariff Reform Federation since its foundation in January 1905. Storey's election address made his position clear: he argued that Tariff Reform would make agriculture prosperous and able to absorb workers who would then be able to buy manufactured goods. Flourishing manufactures would in turn mean an enlarged home market for a prosperous agriculture. He saw the budget, whose rejection by the House of Lords had led to the dissolution, as based on socialistic principles and, opposing these, wanted to deal with unemployment and its consequent miseries by Tariff Reform.[61]

The two year slump in shipbuilding which began late in 1907 meant that Sunderland was all too recently familiar with depression. Unemployment and distress and the month-long campaign resulted in the return of the two Tariff Reform candidates: Storey 12,334, Knott 12,270; Stuart 11,529, Summerbell 11,058. This result, it was widely felt, was due to Storey and his eloquence.[62]

Sadly, only a few weeks later, Thomas Summerbell was taken ill at a town council meeting and died soon afterwards at the early age of 48. Overwork and the strain of the election had taken their toll and Sunderland's Labour party was deprived of its leader at an important stage in its history. Six years later, and equally suddenly, they were to lose the services of another leading member of their local party when Thomas Dale, who had been Summerbell's election agent, was one of the victims of a Zeppelin attack on the town.[63]

The 1910 Parliament was a short one. The next election was held in December 1910 and was fought on the questions of curtailing the House of Lords' powers, and Home Rule for Ireland. Storey and Knott both retired on grounds of health and the January result was reversed. Joseph Chamberlain had written to Storey in November hoping that he would not retire as "No one but yourself, I believe can carry Sunderland".[64] His fears were justified.

Frank Goldstone was in the field as the prospective Labour candidate from July, after W. Walker had been withdrawn when the LRC Executive Committee decided that he would be better suited to a constituency "in which there is not such a strong Nationalist vote" — a comment confirming that the Irish vote was still a major factor in Sunderland politics.[65] The other candidates were not adopted until November. The Liberal candidate, Hamar Greenwood, formerly MP for York, was supplied by Liberal headquarters in London. He campaigned vigorously on the constitutional question of the House of Lords, a stand in sympathy with the radical traditions of Sunderland so long nurtured by Storey. The Unionists also had their candidates, William Joynson-Hicks and Samuel Samuel, supplied from London.

The result was a comfortable win for the Liberal and Labour candidates: Greenwood 11,997, Goldstone 11,291, Joynson-Hicks 10,300, Samuel 10,132. Greenwood was to hold Sunderland until he was defeated in the 1922 general election, but in 1918, with only three candidates in the field and no Liberal-Labour electoral pact, Goldstone was decisively defeated by the Conservative shipowner Ralph M. Hudson. Hudson retired in 1922 and the elections held in the 1920s saw a series of three cornered fights for control of Sunderland's parliamentary representation, with the new Conservative champions, Walter Raine and Luke Thompson, encouraged by Storey[66] and supported by the *Echo*, holding off both Liberal and Labour challengers until 1929. The fight for independent Labour representation still had a long way to go at all levels when war broke out in 1914.

REFERENCES

1. This chapter (an expanded version of which is to be published as occasional publication No. 5 of the History Section, Sunderland Polytechnic) is largely based on the writer's M. Litt. thesis, 'Samuel Storey of Sunderland (1841-1925): his life and career as a local politician and newspaper proprietor up to 1895', Edinburgh University, 1978. The principal original sources of material are Sunderland's newspapers to be found in Sunderland Public Library and the British Library's Newspaper Library at Colindale, London. On the Board of Guardians, see P. A. Wood, 'The Activities of the Sunderland Poor Law Union, 1845-1930', M. Litt. thesis, Newcastle University, 1975.

2. See entries for Binns and Williams by the present writer in J. O. Baylen & N. J. Gossman, eds., *Biographical Dictionary of Modern British Radicals, vol. 2, 1830-1870*, pp. 61-64 & 544-548.

3. J. Williams to J. Cowen, jun., 22 Aug. 1858, Cowen Papers, C156, TWAS.

4. *SH* 12 April 1867.

5. Hendon and Pallion each had three councillors and one alderman whereas the seven existing wards had six councillors and two aldermen; in 1898 the borough was divided into 16 wards with three councillors and one alderman apiece.

6. *SDE* 3 Jan. 1888, *SH* 4 Oct. 1839.

7. On the 1865-66 elections see T. J. Nossiter, 'Elections and Political behaviour in County Durham and Newcastle, 1832-74', D. Phil. thesis, Oxford University, 1967, pp. 392-399, and Storey, thesis, pp. 87-97.

8. Candlish, a Baptist, regarded Roman Catholicism as a political force, as well as a religious one, and consistently excluded it from his general view of religious liberty and equality. Many Sunderland Catholics were poor Irish who had migrated to Sunderland during and since the 1840s and the Workhouse was an important element in their lives. The Catholic vote was put at 70 strong in *SWN* 16 June 1865.

9. *SH* 14 July 1865: Fenwick, 1,826, Hartley 1,335, Candlish 1,305; Fenwick received 823 votes split with Hartley, 914 split with Candlish.

10. *E. C. Robson* (1813-93) miller, first President, Sunderland Liberal Association, 1876-85; *Joshua Wilson* (1806-77) grocer, alderman; both men were Quakers and leading members of the Sunderland Anti-Corn Law Association in the 1840s; *SDE* 10 May 1893, 3 Sept. 1877, *The Alderman* 29 July 1876, 8 Sept. 1877.

11. *ST* 18 Aug. 1868; on the trial ballot see H. J. Hanham, *Elections and Party Mangement*, pp. 97-99; on this election generally see Nossiter, thesis, pp. 399-404 and Storey, thesis, pp. 105-119.

12. *The Durham Thirteen*: T. C. Thompson.

13. The declared result was Candlish 6,237, Gourley, 4,901, Thompson, 3,596, later analysed as: Plumpers — Candlish 148, Gourley 614, Thompson 931; Splits — Candlish/Gourley 3,844, Candlish/Thompson 2,221, Gourley/Thompson 428.

14. *SDE* 8 Oct. 1921, speech by Storey when receiving the honorary freedom of Sunderland.

15. Swan was elected at a by-election in Feb. 1869, Storey at the annual elections on 1 Nov., when he was unopposed. *Robert Swan* (1822-97), builder, temperance worker, trustee of Dock Street Free Methodist Chapel: *The Alderman* 7 Oct. 1876, *SDE* 23 April 1897.

16. *SDE* 28 Oct., 7 Nov. 1878, Improvement Committee's final report.

17. *Robert Preston* (1829-1914), slater, councillor, 1865-78, alderman, 1878-92, Mayor, 1884-85. *Samuel Sinclair Robson* (1824-98) rope manufacturer and iron-founder in partnership with his brother-in-law, Thomas Glaholm, Mayor 1878. *John* (1830-1901) and *Robert* (1825-1913) *Cameron*, born Perthshire, sons of a Baptist minister, came to Sunderland as teachers, served on the Board of Guardians and Town Council; John became Registrar of Births and Deaths for Bishopwearmouth North in 1887; Robert, M.P., Houghton-le-Spring, 1895-death.

18. *SDE* 22 Dec. 1923.

19. G[eorge] H[erring], 'Samuelus Storius (surnamed 'Gracchus'), the Plebian who became Consul of Rome. A hitherto unpublished fragment of Roman history . . .', in Sunderland Public Library, *Local Pamphlets*, vol. 8.

20. Members of Dock Street Chapel serving as councillors at this time were Swan (Monkwearmouth, Feb. 1869-1883), Storey (Monkwearmouth, 1869-77), Robert Shadforth (Bridge Ward, 1875-91) and Thomas J. Rickaby (Monkwearmouth, 1876-92), who all became aldermen, and William Harty (Bridge, 1875-78). Dock Street's high political profile was maintained; *SDP* 22 Feb. 1892 complained one-eighth of the Council belonged to Dock Street Chapel.

21. *SH* 18 Oct. 1878.

22. Sunderland School Board covered the area of the municipal borough only; school boards were set up voluntarily in Southwick and Ford, compulsorily in Fulwell and Hylton, between 1874 and 1876; *Parl. Papers* 1883 (205) LIII.

23. *ST* 27 Dec. 1870, speech by Storey at meeting of the Liberal Political Union and Nonconformist representatives.

24. *ST* 17 Jan. 1871.

25. *ST* 2 Jan. 1874; three Wesleyans and a Quaker non-sectarian candidate withdrew, the latter at the last minute and despite objections by Storey, chairman of the Liberal election committee.

26. *SDE* 29 Dec. 1876, 9 & 15 Jan. 1877.

27. *SDE* & *SDP* 10 Jan. 1877.

28. *SDE* 8 & 12 Jan. 1880.

29. *SDE* 23, 28 Dec. 1882, 2 Jan. 1883, 30 Dec. 1885, 5-10 Jan. 1889, 11 Jan. 1892.

30. *Havelock-Allan Papers*, N. Yorks. County Record Office, 1874 Sunderland Election Diary including R. Cameron to Havelock, 20 Jan. 1874, ZDG(H)III/7.

31. Nossiter, thesis, pp. 495-6; V. A. Williamson, *Williamson Family Memorials*, II, pp. 79-80; *SDE* 21 Feb. 1974, p. 17, the 1874 Sunderland and N. Durham elections.

32. Cameron to Havelock, 20 Jan. 1874, *Havelock-Allan Papers*, ZDG(H)III/7; *SDP* 3 May 1882 put the Irish vote at 1,300. Estimates of the Irish vote vary as they can be for Irish-born voters or they can include the growing number of voters born in England but of Irish descent and whose voting behaviour was governed by Irish considerations.

33. *Havelock-Allan Papers*, Scrapbook and Diary, 1880 election, ZDG(H)III/10; Havelock-Allan attributed the increased Tory vote since 1874 to the Irish splitting Gourley/Brooke rather than Gourley/Havelock-Allan, but the Tories had made a strong effort to get splits with Gourley. The full result, with the 1874 figures in brackets, was: registered electors 15,021 (14,008); Plumpers — Gourley 146 (162), Havelock-Allan 42 (109), Brooke 3,596 (Baily 3,472); Splits — Gourley/Havelock-Allan 6,890 (5,711), Gourley/Brooke 603 (Gourley-Baily 299), Havelock-Allan/Brooke 63 (Havelock-Allan/Baily 100); Totals — Gourley 7,639 (6,172), Havelock-Allan 6,995 (6,520), Brooke 4,262 (Baily 3,871).

34. *Havelock-Allan Papers* ZDG(H)III/10, Havelock to Storey, 18 Jan. 1879, and Storey to Havelock, 1 Feb. 1879, re *SDE* report of speech by Havelock on Afghanistan; Havelock, an imperialist, and Storey, a 'Little Englander', can have had little in common on such foreign policy issues.

35. *Havelock-Allan Papers* ZDG(H)III/10, Cameron to Havelock, 17 Jan. 1879.

36. *SDE* & *SDP* 1-11 April 1881, reports of meetings, etc.; *Havelock-Allan Papers* ZDG(H)III/10, Scrapbook, 1881, letters and telegrams to and from Havelock-Allan; Storey, thesis, pp. 382-392.

37. *Havelock-Allan Papers*, Cave to Havelock-Allan, 16 April 1880, 28 Feb. & 4 March 1881, in 1880-81 Scrapbook.

38. C. H. D. Howard, 'The Parnell Manifesto of 21 Nov. 1885 and the Schools Question', *English Historical Review* LXII (1947), pp. 42-51.

39. *SDE* 30 Nov. 1885, Local Notes by Asmodeus.

40. The detailed figures for the 1885 (and 1886) elections, fought on the same register with 17,978 registered electors, were: Plumpers — Storey 177 (238), Gourley 166 (75), Austin 5,732 (Stobart 5,575); Splits — Storey/Gourley 7,370 (6,522), Storey/Austin 748 (Storey/Stobart 210), Gourley/Austin 223 (Gourley/Stobart 242); Totals — Storey 8,295 (6,970), Gourley 7,759 (6,839), Austin 6,703 (Stobart 6,027).

41. Thomas Burlinson's election in August 1886 meant seven out of 18 Tory members of the Council were connected with the drink trade; *SDE* 24 Aug. 1886.

42. *SDP* 19 Sept. 1892.

43. *SDP* 21 Oct., 11 Nov. 1895; the *Post* divided the Council at this date into 29 Unionists, 29 Liberals and 6 Labour representatives, of whom 15 Liberals and 1 Tory were Aldermen. In the mayoral election 1 Labour councillor was absent, 1 abstained, 1 voted for Vint and 3 for Burns.

44. *SDE* 11 Nov. 1895, Local Notes by Asmodeus; c. 150 out of 400 members of the Liberal Club were said to be Liberal Unionists in 1889, *SDE* 25 Nov. 1889.

45. The full result was: Storey 9,711 (67 plumpers), Gourley 9,554 (44), Lambton 8,394 (174), Pemberton 8,002 (34); Splits — Storey/Gourley 9,324, Pemberton/Lambton 7,841, Storey/Lambton 241, Gourley/Lambton 138, Storey/Pemberton 79, Gourley/Pemberton 48.

46. Howitt to Thomas Graham, 20 Sept. 1885, Carnegie-Storey Newspaper Syndicate Papers at Wolverhampton *Express & Star*, quoted in Storey, thesis, p. 401; *SDP* 27 & 31 Jan. 1896, Sunderland election petition hearing.

47. B. Charlton, 'The Origins and the History of Sunderland and District Trades Council (1874-1906)', Ruskin College Oxford, Labour Diploma thesis 1985; *SDE* 2 Oct. 1889, 3 Feb. 1892.

48. On the early history of the Labour party in N.E. England see A. W. Purdue, 'Parliamentary Elections in N.E. England, 1900-1906: the advent of Labour', M. Litt. thesis, Newcastle University, 1974.

49. *SDE* 13, 15, 29, Nov. 1897; only 400 votes separated the last elected candidate from the candidate at the bottom of the poll.

50. *SDE* 10, 15, 29 Nov. 1900; Summerbell declined to stand and the Unsectarians promised to support the Labour choice in the event of a vacancy — a promise kept when the Trades Council's nominee, Hugh Lynas, was elected to the Board following the death of William Branfoot, an Unsectarian, in Nov. 1902; Sunderland Trades Council *Annual Report, 1902-3*.

51. The company was formed to take over the old established (1857) business of Samuel Tyzack & Co., Wm. Thackray, jun., was re-appointed managing director, a post he had held since 1865, and Storey was appointed chairman of the new company; Thackray held just over one-third of the 6,000 issued £10 shares, Storey only 200. *SDE* 18 April 1887, 22 March 1888, 2 Dec. 1889, 28 Jan. 1896; Companies Registration Office file, Co. No. 30337; Tyzack Letter Book, TWAS.

52. *SDE* & *SDP* 27-29, 31 Jan. 1896, Sunderland election petition hearing; David Bell was Labour councillor for Monkwearmouth Ward where Tyzack's works were located.

53. Appeals for more canvassers were made in *SDE* 2, 4, 6 & 11 July, and ward meetings were held soon after the election to revitalise Liberal organisation at ward level.

54. *SDE* 22 July, 2 Aug. 1895, and c.p. 17 & 19 July; the full result was: Doxford, 9,833 (9,393 plumpers), Gourley 8,232 (67), Storey 8,185 (110); Splits — Gourley/Storey 7,900, Doxford/Gourley 265, Doxford/Storey 175. The small number of cross-party splits means that, unlike 1885, the Irish either plumped for the Tory candidate or voted Liberal.

55. *SDE* 2 & 4 Sept. 1895, 23 & 27 Jan. 1896; Doxford was helped by doubt as to the interpretation to be placed on some of the statements in the election leaflet.

56. *SDE* 19-27 Sept. 1900. Alex Wilkie (1850-1928), first General Secretary (1882-1928) of the Assoc. Shipwrights Soc., a national union, based in New-castle from 1888; MP, Dundee, 1906-22; Bellamy & Saville, *Dictionary of Labour Biography*, III, pp.206-8, D. Dougan, *The Shipwrights*, esp. pp. 21-22 & 224-5.

57. Wilkie was Summerbell's most serious rival and the Shipwrights Society was upset by local preference for Summerbell after Wilkie's efforts in the 1900 election. *SDE* 24 Jan., 25 Feb., 17 & 23 April 1903; Sunderland Trades Council *Annual Report 1902-3*; Harvester Press microfilm of British Labour Party Archives: LRC records 1900-1906, 6/192, 6/394-8, 7/395-9, 8/346-8, 9/412, letters to Ramsay MacDonald re-Sunderland.

58. *SDE* 28 Jan., 8 & 22 March 1904. James Stuart (1843-1913), first Professor of Mechanism & Applied Mechanics, Cambridge University, 1875-89; Liberal MP Hackney and then Hoxton, 1884-1900; *Who Was Who*; *Sunderland Year Book*, 1907 & 1910.

59. Purdue, thesis, pp. 186, 200.

60. Sunderland Post Co., PRO file BT31 3931/24887.

61. *SDE* 22 Dec. 1909.

62. Comments on the result are quoted in *SDE* 19 Jan. 1910.

63. *SDE* 3, 5 April 1916 (death), 29 Sept., 1 Oct. 1917 (memorial).

64. J. Chamberlain to Storey, 23 Nov. 1910, *Storey Papers, Settrington*.

65. Harvester Press microfilm, British Labour Party Archives, Labour Party National Executive Com. Minutes, 21 April & 30 June 1910.

66. Storey to Raine, 1 Oct. 1922, *Storey Papers, Settrington*.

Education and learning 1780-1914

Sunderland's educational history has been similar to that of many other large industrial communities, though certain distinctions may be noted. For instance Sunderland had no ancient endowed grammar school. Moreover, no Victorian philanthropist founded a college of higher education here, as was the case in towns such as Nottingham. Manchester, Sheffield and Newcastle, or (nearer to Sunderland) South Shields, where Dr. Thomas Winterbottom founded the Marine and Technical College in 1862. Sunderland's benefactor in this respect was Sir John Priestman but his contributions were made after the Technical College had been established. On the other hand Sunderland had a private secondary school (the Grange) which for at least two decades had a national reputation, and the town also was the home of an interesting and significant educational venture (now largely forgotten) when in 1868 the first ever specialist theological college to train men for the Primitive Methodist ministry was established in the former infirmary on Chester Road.

Until 1870 there was no state system of education in England. In 1833 there began a system of government grants to promote schools, the money however was not spent directly by the state on its own schools but was channelled into the work of the two great educational societies, the National, and the British and Foreign. These had been founded in the early nineteenth century to encourage the provision of Church of England and interdenominational schools respectively. In due course other church bodies such as the Wesleyans and the Roman Catholics were able to receive similar grants. Those grants (which involved state inspection) were made in response to local initiative and expenditure. Quite distinct from these schools, and not grant-aided by the state, were the 'private venture' schools. Sunderland in common with other towns had both varieties. Before looking at local examples of these however, we ought to consider the role of charity and philanthropy in providing some of Sunderland's first recorded schools.

CHARITY SCHOOLS

The eighteenth century was the age of the English 'Charity School'; small local establishments endowed by bequests from generous benefactors, usually in association with a church or chapel, and often built in their shadow.[1] Within four years of each other, in 1764 and 1768 respectively, Elizabeth Donnison (an Anglican) and Edward Walton (a Quaker) each made provision in their wills for Charity schools in Sunderland.[2] The Donnison School, established under Church auspices in Sunderland parish, offered free education for 36 poor girls between the ages of seven and 16. They were taught religious knowledge, reading, writing, arithmetic, spinning, sewing and knitting, and were provided with clothing and shoes. In 1827 Mrs Elizabeth Woodcock built a house for the mistress in Church Walk and a former schoolroom adjoining was taken over by the Charity. Both buildings still survive though are not used

for educational purposes. Under Walton's Charity a small number of Quaker children, or those with some disadvantage or infirmity, were given free schooling, first in a separate building but later by being sent to the larger British and Foreign School.

Mrs Woodcock, whose charitable record in Sunderland is notable, was also one of the principal benefactors in promoting a large parochial school for boys and girls in Sunderland parish.[3] A parish school for boys had in fact been started in 1808 in a building adjoining the workhouse; a girls' section was added in 1816, in which year the school became associated with the British and Foreign Society, implying that its religious education should be non-sectarian in character. When Robert Gray succeeded John Hampson as rector of Sunderland in 1819 he quickly showed his desire for a change, both in the siting of the school and in its religious character which he wanted to be avowedly Anglican.[4] A subscription fund was opened, and a redundant Wesleyan chapel on Vine Street was purchased in 1822 as the school's new home. Mrs Woodcock endowed it with a bequest of £1,000, and added further donations for specific projects, so that the school shared some features of the older Charity schools, while also being affiliated to the Church of England National Society. An infants school was added in 1835, situated close to St. John's chapel. Gray himself regarded the care of the schools as one of his first priorities, and poured much of his own money into them, to the extent of something like £200 per annum.[5] A financial crisis arose therefore on Gray's early death in 1838, but this was partially averted by the Gray memorial fund, some of which was used to further endow the school which was henceforth named after the deceased rector. The children attending the school paid one penny a week. As was the custom at that time the school consisted of two large rooms, that on the ground floor housing the boys, and that above the girls. The inspector's report of 1853 makes interesting reading:

> The returns of the Gray School for the past year show in a striking manner the fluctuations of a school which has to contend with a disorganised population. With an average attendance of 392 (218 boys, 174 girls), there have been 450 fresh admissions during the year. Whenever I have visited this institution at least one half of the children, both on account of age and attainments, would have been more profitably employed in an infant school.[6]

The Gray School was able to benefit financially from the Act which in 1853 founded the Sunderland Orphan Asylum, by offering schooling to 42 boys from the Asylum.[7] Money was also made available from the Asylum fund (created by the sacrifice of the rights of the Freemen and Stallingers with regard to the Town Moor) for the rebuilding of the Gray School in 1857. The Asylum or Orphanage itself was built in 1862 on the edge of the Town Moor, and still serves the east end of the town as a community centre. For many years it was the home of young boys who were the orphans of seafaring men, and who usually in turn made sea-faring their profession.

Another enormous bequest of around £160,000 was made in 1884 by George Hudson (not to be confused with the 'Railway King') to assist and educate orphan children of the town, 20 of whom were to be the sons of pilots or sailors. The children were to live at home and attend their local schools, while being supported by the Hudson Charity, which generally had around 300 children on its books at any one time. (See biographical appendix on Hudson.)

Individual philanthropy therefore played a not insignificant role in the fostering of elementary education in Sunderland, but its scope was inevitably limited.

CHURCH DAY SCHOOLS

Churchmen of all persuasions became committed to the provision of schools for working class children around the beginning of the nineteenth century. There was a mixture of motives at work, including a strong desire, especially by evangelicals, to see the hearts and minds of the young brought under the influence of Christian morality, discipline and habits of obedience, especially at a time when the French and Industrial revolutions seemed to be challenging the stability of English society.

John Hampson put the point very forcefully with regard to the children of Sunderland as early as 1788 in a sermon in St. John's Chapel of which he was then the curate:

> In travelling in most parts of the three kingdoms and much of America [he had been a Wesleyan travelling preacher] never have I beheld children so rude and uncultivated. Their behaviour in the streets, their fierce and brutal quarrels, the oaths and curses they lisp before they are well able to articulate, and the manner in which they spend the Sabbath, call loudly for a reformation; and in the brutal and savage ferociousness of many of the men in the lower class you may discover the dreadful consequence of a vicious or neglected education.[8]

Hampson was in fact commending the provision of Sunday Schools in this sermon, but his point was equally applicable to day schooling. There is no doubt that such sentiments fired the enthusiasm of promoters of church schools in that period. Their disciplinary instincts were often tempered in practice by humane and philanthropic feelings, but the expressions of churchmen on education often had a reactionary sound even when well meant. Dr Robert Gray (the rector of Bishopwearmouth) urged the creation of a national system of education since not only would it expand the minds of the poor, but they "would be more content and productive if they understood the natural laws creating their laborious station".[9] His nephew (also Robert Gray, rector of Sunderland) sought to allay the anxieties of the upper class about popular education by assuring them that there would be nothing in the new schools "to excite vain or aspiring ideas, nothing to generate amongst the lower orders a spirit of insubordination".[10] Such expressions are very typical of the early years of the nineteenth century. But we need to remember not only the words but the deeds of these men, who worked hard to provide

Revd. John Hampson (1760-1819) rector of Sunderland from 1795.

St John's Church of England School, built 1884.

schools for the poor where there were none before.

The humble beginnings of the church day school system in Sunderland were partly in the charity schools already described, but more particularly in the parochial schools of the early years of the nineteenth century.[11] That in Sunderland parish has been outlined above. In Bishopwearmouth and Monkwearmouth schools were launched in 1808 and 1809 respectively, the latter (Lady Williamson's school) being for pauper girls; a boys school for Monkwearmouth was added, built by subscription in 1812.[12] In that same year the school in Bishopwearmouth was provided with a new two-storey building on Low Row, where something like 500 boys and girls were educated. It applied for union with the National Society in 1819. The pride of the parishioners in their new school ought surely to have been tempered by the fact that an extension to the church burial ground lay just to the rear of it, with some burial vaults literally under the floor of the school itself. Oddly enough when the new Rectory Park School was built in 1854 it also was adjacent to the cemetery in the Rector's Gill. Despite that, the new building was vastly superior to the old, with provision for over 1,000 boys and girls, and for 300 infants in an adjoining building (1866). Education had progressed a great deal in the first 50 years of the century, and the Rectory Park Schools went on to play an important role in Sunderland's school system for over a century.[13]

As the old parishes of Sunderland were subdivided to provide more churches so new church schools were opened. The dates are those of the opening of schools and of their enlargement or rebuilding:

Ryhope 1810, 1836. (The old church was used from 1870.)
Deptford 1829, 1842, 1863.
S. Hylton 1836.
Low Southwick 1837, 1846.
N. Hylton 1850.
Silksworth 1851 (a School — Chapel).
Hendon (St. Paul's) 1856.
Bishopwearmouth (St. Peter's) 1869.
Pallion 1870 (services also held here until St. Luke's built 1874).
Sunderland (St. John's) 1884.
Southwick (St. Columba's) 1893, 1901, 1903.

To these have to be added the schools already mentioned above.[14]

In some cases local landowners or industrialists provided the sites for these buildings and helped with the costs. In Ayres Quay a Church of England school was actually built by Laings, the shipbuilders (1861). In that same year a school was built to serve the Wearmouth Colliery area, partly financed by contributions from the miners' educational fund, the site being donated by the Durham Dean and Chapter. (The building still stands at the bottom of Southwick Road, though is in commercial use.) These schools offered very basic facilities. Thus the Hendon (St. Paul's) school, which catered for nearly 400 pupils of both sexes, had only two large rooms of 77 feet by 19 feet, and two smaller classrooms of 20 feet by 14½ feet.

It was state aid (in response to local initiatives) which made possible the great flowering of Church elementary schools in the nineteenth century. For example the state grant towards the Rectory Park School, which cost over £2,000, was £777, compared with £135 from the National Society; and in the east end the rebuilding of the Gray Schools in the mid-1850s cost £3,292, of which £1,150 was granted by the state, with only £50 from the National Society.[15] The rest of the costs had of course to be made good from local sources.

NON-ANGLICAN SCHOOLS

The non-Anglican religious groups in Sunderland despite being numerically stronger than the Church in terms of worshippers, provided fewer day schools. This was partly due to the superior wealth of the Church of England and to the organised campaign to put a Church school in as many parishes as possible. But it was also due to a readiness of many parents, including some nonconformists, to accept Church schools for their children. Nevertheless a very significant contribution was made by non-Anglican day schools. The British and Foreign Society itself was represented by only one school, dependent largely upon the initiative of the Quakers. After a number of years in sites on Garden Street and Nicholson Street (or Coxon's Fields as it was sometimes called) it found its permanent home from 1856 on the corner of Norfolk Street and Borough Road, adjacent to the Nile Street meeting house of the Quakers. (The building still stands.) As late as 1910 old boys recalled marching from Coxon's Fields to the new school, led by their remarkable headmaster, the Scot, Robert Cameron.[16] Under him the British School acquired a highly deserved reputation; old photographs of the boys exude an air of disciplined respectability, and explain why, when the school was at Coxon's Fields, the pupils were popularly known as 'Coxon's dollies', so smart was their appearance. On the whole they were the children of the better-off artisans of the town, and many went on to professional careers and to municipal service. The Presbyterian schools of Sunderland likewise were of a somewhat superior kind, catering for the children of the upper working and lower middle class. The Villiers Street school, opened in 1849 next to the handsome St. George's chapel, soon acquired the title of 'Academy', and offered a classical and commercial education for some 300 boys and girls which was considerably more advanced than could be had in the normal public elementary school.

It was the Wesleyan Methodists and the Roman Catholics who provided the majority of school places in the non-Anglican sector. For a good many years the Wesleyans had been happy to see the Church of England take the lead in day-school education; indeed, leading Wesleyans of the town such as John White, John White junior, Andrew White, William Kirk and Stephen Watson were on the management committee of the Bishopwearmouth parochial school when it applied for union with the National Society in 1819.[17] However the development of the high church Oxford Movement disillusioned many Wesleyans and drove

them in the 1840s to the conclusion that they should accept state aid and launch their own building campaign to provide schools over which they had control and which could be 'nurseries' for the nurturing of Christians on the Methodist pattern. The Wesleyans devised an ambitious definition of education: "What we search for" they said "is an education which may begin in the infants school, and end in heaven . . . to fill the world with saints and heaven with glorified spirits"![18] With that grand hope they began their campaign. By 1873 they had built over 900 schools, 52 in the north-east, including five in Sunderland — Whitburn Street (Monkwearmouth), Trimdon Street, King Street, Nicholson Street and Robinson Street. The other Methodists in the town had a handful of schools — such as the Primitive Methodists on Mainsforth Terrace and the United Methodist Free Churches on Brougham Street. Generally the Methodist schools tended to cater for the children of their

own chapel members, and while not being exclusive they set higher standards (and charged higher fees) than most other day schools.

Like the Wesleyans the Roman Catholics had a strong impulse to provide schools for the children of their own members, though their schools were never exclusively Catholic.[19] Soon after St. Mary's Church was built in 1835 a school was opened on its north side in Pann Lane, replacing an earlier school near the former chapel on Dunning Street. The parish priest Philip Kearney wanted the staff to include members of religious orders and he was able to persuade teachers first from the order of Christian Brothers and then the Presentation Order to serve the boys school. Their stay however was brief. Kearney was more fortunate with the nuns, members of the Order of Mercy, who came to Sunderland in 1843 and established a permanent base in the town. One of their first duties was teaching, which they practised in the Pann Lane girls school and later, after the Brothers had left, the boys school also, alongside lay teachers.

From 1847 (like the Wesleyans) the Roman Catholics accepted state aid for educational

Above: Robert Cameron (1825-1913) and boys of the British School.

purposes. Channelled through the Catholic Poor School Committee it was mainly applied towards the augmentation of the salaries of teachers who reached approved standards. Grants were also received for pupil teachers. State aid involved state inspection; St. Mary's School received glowing reports from the first, thanks largely to the influence of the Sisters of Mercy. "Such schools deserve to be ranked amongst the most valuable institutions which a nation possesses" wrote the inspector in 1849. A separate infants school was soon provided and also a school for older girls, housed first in the Convent itself and then in a special school building in the Convent garden. Known at first as St. Bede's it took the name of St. Anthony's in 1902. (The transfer of this school to buildings on Tunstall Road and Thornhill Terrace took place in the 1920s and 1930s.)

Other Catholic schools had been developing meanwhile — St. Patrick's c.1860 (the school was actually held in the church for a decade or so before transferring to Coronation Street), St. Benet's from about the same time, St. Joseph's (a school-chapel at first) from 1872, and St. Hilda's 1903 (the school housed a chapel for mass before the church was built in 1909). The Sisters of Mercy taught in some of these schools also. The Pann Lane schools moved in 1902 to the building which had been a former infirmary and Methodist college on Chester Road, where they were housed for over 70 years.

To this survey of church and chapel schools should be added also a handful of 'industrial' schools where poor and undisciplined children were given instruction in useful skills and crafts; the Ragged School which opened in 1849 on Silver Street in the east end; and the undenominational school opened by the Baptist John Candlish at the bottom of Waterworks Road.[20] The list is far from complete.

The relative strength of the various church day schools in Sunderland by 1870 was as follows[21]:

Church of England/ National Society	15 schools	6046 pupils
R.C. (not counting St. Bede's which was private)	4 schools	1515 pupils
Wesleyan	5 schools	1656 pupils
British Society	1 school	815 pupils
Other	2 schools	564 pupils

The Grange School, opened in 1830.

PRIVATE SCHOOLS

Education was a 'free market' in the nineteenth century. The churches seized their opportunity by launching a wide range of schools which were in the main 'public' (in the sense that they were supported by subscriptions and grants, and open to all who could afford the fees, a penny to six pence or so each week), and elementary, meaning that the education offered in them (with some important exceptions as we have seen) was of a basic kind, not usually pursued far beyond the age of 11 or 12. But church schools could not cope with all children, and many 'private venture' schools sprang up to fill the gap. Not supported by public grants or subscriptions, but dependent upon fees, these schools varied enormously in size, quality and prestige, ranging from humble 'dame schools' to well organised and highly regarded establishments.

Parson and White's directory (1827) lists 42 'academies' in Sunderland that fall within this category. They are classified in the directory as follows: Gentlemen's boarding schools (offering a classical education) 2; ladies' boarding schools 5; gentlemen's day schools 2; ladies' day schools 1; classical day schools 1; day schools 26; dancing schools 1; music schools 2; plus one French academy, and one drawing school.[22] One of the day schools listed is against the name of Josiah Cormack, Sans Street, Bishopwearmouth. Cormack (a Scot, born in Wick, who married an American wife) was an ardent Baptist of strong evangelical convictions, serving the Particular Baptist chapel on Sans Street as a non-stipendiary minister while having a paid occupation as a teacher. John Young, one of his pupils, said that Cormack was "familiar with Hebrew, Greek, Latin and a little French" and that "the critical study of the scriptures" was one of his passions. Moreover it is clear from the way John Young writes about him that Cormack had inspired his pupil not only with a love of learning but with respect and affection.[23]

Another Scot, James Cowan, was in 1827 the master of a school on Green Street, where he taught the children of well to do Quakers and others.[24]. The quality of the teaching attracted a growing number of pupils (including a good many from north of the border) and in 1830 Cowan transferred the school to a large house called the Grange, which stood on what we know today as the West Park near to the Civic Centre; its extensive twelve-acre grounds stretched towards Toward Road on the east and to where Christ Church now is on the south. Cowan ruled at the Grange from 1830 until his retirement (in prosperity) in 1846, during which time the school became one of the most highly regarded boarding schools for boys in the north of England and southern Scotland. A lot of prosperous middle class families of Sunderland sent their sons as day scholars. (Girls incidentally had been taught at Green Street, but were not brought to the new school.) The published account of the school by C. S. Collingwood, rector of Southwick, who was an old boy, reveals a well-conducted establishment, with firm but fair discipline, good teaching, sensible rules, and a well-rounded curriculum.[25] What perhaps best gives a clue to the atmosphere of the Grange under Cowan is the sense of fun in the verses found in the old magazines, as in this pupil's poem on an autumn outing to Castle Eden dene which begins:

"Before the trip began
The doctor, with much fun,
Cried 'Mr Wilson, may I beg you,
    to take the leading, Oh!
Mr Archer! Mr Wear!
Mr Flint! bring up the rear,
While the pony takes me
    down to Castle Eden, Oh!' "[26]

Some 600 boys were educated at the Grange under Dr. Cowan,

that distinguished teacher and trainer of youth ... to whom so many men who afterwards rose to a high station in public life and in various walks of literature owed the first impulse given to their talents and genius.[27]

After Cowan's retirement the school continued for some time, but never with the same distinction or popularity.

Another good quality boarding/day school in Sunderland in the early Victorian period was that directed by Dr. John Wood, a Scots clergyman. It had several homes including Hendon Lodge, the chapel of Hylton Castle, and Broad Street, Roker. Joseph Swan, inventor of the incandescent electric lamp, was perhaps its most eminent pupil.[28]

To this brief survey ought to be added church private schools. One, St. Bede's (later St. Anthony's) R.C. school, has already been mentioned. A Church of England high school for boys had a brief life in Bede Tower in the later nineteenth and early twentieth centuries. An equivalent school for girls, founded in 1884, is of course still very much in existence.[29] It is rather surprising that no moves had been made to found a Church of England girls high school in Sunderland before this date, but it was the arrival in 1883 of Archdeacon Robert Long, the new rector of Bishopwearmouth, which provided the necessary impulse. Under his energetic initiative public meetings were held, a committee appointed, money raised, and a school with 16 pupils opened in a house on Park Terrace on 29 April 1884, under the auspices of the Church Schools Company. Within less than three years the school was transferred to its new purpose-built premises on Mowbray Road, a choir of boys from Bede Tower high school providing the music at the opening ceremony on 23 February 1887. The fees for day girls were between three and five guineas a term. The school struggled in its early years but under the fourth head, Edith Ironside (1905-1938), there was a turning of the tide. In her first decade she trebled the number of pupils to about 180, and helped to put the school on a reasonable financial footing.

THE BOARD SCHOOLS

An educational census made under government auspices in March 1851 produced some interesting figures for Sunderland. Out of a total of over 15,000 children aged between five and 15, living in the area of the three old parishes, less than one half attended school on the day the census was held. The precise figure was 7,343 (3,925 boys and 3,418 girls), with names on the school registers totalling 8,516.[30] Education was of course not yet compulsory nor was it to be so for another 30 years. But there was increasing concern both locally and nationally that large numbers of the nation's children were growing up with little formal schooling, though some were receiving some kind of education, through the Sunday Schools of the town.[31] Sunderland had a particularly good record in this respect, having launched Sunday Schools under Wesleyan initiatives as early as 1786. By 1851 the 62 Sunday Schools (of all denominations) had 7,409 children on their registers, with well over 5,000 attending. Yet even allowing for the fact that those attending were taught reading and writing as well as biblical knowledge, Sunday Schools could never hope to offset the lack of a proper system of day schooling.

William Webb, rector of Sunderland 1838-48, diagnosed the situation in his parish thus:

The reason why the children of the parish of Sunderland are so ignorant arises, I think, from the following causes. In the first place our schools are inadequate to the number. Secondly they can at a very early age obtain employment; and thirdly their parents are ignorant and consequently do not appreciate the advantages of education.[32]

A double programme was needed — to provide more schools, and to persuade or enable more children to attend them. Who was to provide the schools? The census revealed that there were in the town only 24 'public' schools (that is voluntary schools provided by the churches and chapels, with help from the educational Societies and the State) and that they were attended by 3,360 children, compared with 120 private schools attended by 3,983.[33]

Some of the private schools were of very high quality indeed, some were less good, but most were well outside the reach of poor children. Any moves towards a national system of education seemed therefore to lie with the churches, backed by increased state aid. But there were some very real problems. The churches found their efforts continually swamped by population growth; the poorer children in any case were slipping through their net; and the churches' efforts were beset by acute denominational rivalry. Some dissenters, in Sunderland as elsewhere, began therefore to call for a national system of compulsory, non-sectarian elementary education, financed and organised by the state, and outside church control altogether.[34]

The answer of the government, Forster's Act of 1870, was a typically English compromise. The voluntary schools were to continue with increased state aid; but where they obviously could not cope with the demand, extra schools were to be provided by locally elected School Boards and financed out of fees (until abolished), government grants and a local education rate. Thus began the era of the Board Schools, which was to last some 30 years.[35] Sunderland elected its first Board on 13 January 1871 and it included men such as Canon William Cockin, rector of Bishop-wearmouth, James Hartley the glass maker, James Laing the ship builder, (all Church of England men), Revd. Dr. William Antliff, principal of the Primitive Methodist Theological Institute, Robert Cameron the Baptist head of the Quaker (British) boys school, and Thomas Coke Squance a well known Wesleyan accountant.[36] There was some rivalry on the Board between the Church and Non-Sectarian parties, with the latter having a majority throughout most of the Sunderland Board's existence.[37] However it does not appear that Board elections generally excited much feeling or denominational rivalry; indeed one local Congregational minister (Revd. G. H. R. Garcia) was to bemoan the apathy of the public in this respect.[38] Yet this may have been a blessing. It allowed the Board to concentrate on its true role which was to 'fill the gaps' in Sunderland's elementary school system.

Sunderland's first Board School, James Williams Street, 1874.

The task facing the Board was daunting.[39] Local surveys showed that in 1870 the deficiency in Sunderland's school provision totalled 7,000 places and this figure was to grow dramatically when elementary education became compulsory and free in 1880 and 1891 respectively.[40]

The Sunderland Board began by taking over the control of several existing schools, mainly those under nonconformist ownership. Its first purpose-built school was on James Williams Street, an area of urban re-development in the east end of the town. This school was built in 1874, cost £9,000, and had accommodation for 1,000 pupils. Standing until quite recently, this long, low building with its prominent bell tower (a feature of Board Schools) had the air of a school which fitted naturally into its communal environment. The carving of 'Boys', 'Girls', and 'Infants' over the various entrances was an indication of the internal organisation of these schools, and a reminder also of late Victorian

attitudes with regard to teachers' salaries and the relative value of men and women — the head of the boys school received a basic £130 a year (plus various additions for pupil teachers and so on) while the headmistresses of the girls and infants schools received basic salaries of £80. Assistant masters' and mistresses' salaries ranged between £60 and £120 according to qualifications, experience and sex. Pupil teachers began at £15 (male) and £10 (female).[41]

The James Williams Street school was followed by 17 others, including Diamond Hall (1878, £13,700, 1,200 pupils), Stansfield Street (1883, £9,200, 1,350 pupils), and Valley Road (1885, £16,000, 1,700 pupils). By 1903 when the Board was wound up it handed over to the new Local Education Authority 18 large schools with 21,242 scholars on their registers. Some of these buildings still stand as monuments to Victorian education. All were erected in working class areas of the town, and were surrounded by rows of brick terraces where the artisans, sailors, and labourers of the town lived. Parts of the town such as Fulwell, Southwick and North and South Hylton, which were not yet included within the borough, elected their own Boards, and schools were erected under their initiatives at Fulwell (1877, to accommodate 350 pupils), South Hylton (1887, 500 pupils), High Southwick (1877/1894, 1,600 pupils), and Castletown (1882, 650 pupils).

One of Sunderland's Board Schools was a venture into secondary education.[42] This was the 'higher-grade' school opened in 1890 on the West Park (near to the site of Dr. Cowan's Grange School) for 380 boys and 340 girls, who were housed on the ground and upper floors respectively. The school was open to those children who had passed Standard III in the elementary schools, with a fee of 1/- a week, though there was a limited number of free places almost from the start. There was the usual curriculum with additional maths and Latin for the boys and French and German for the girls. Science was soon added. The school honoured the town's most famous scholar by adopting the name 'Bede' in 1898, becoming the Bede Collegiate School in 1905. (It was to move to its splendid new site on Durham Road in 1929.)

The launching by many other School Boards of higher-grade schools like Bede precipitated a crisis, since it was argued that under the terms of Forster's Act Board Schools should be limited to elementary education. This issue became caught up in pressures for Board Schools to be placed under the new county and county borough councils, a move which was effected by Balfour's Education Act of 1902. The Act was widely resented by the better School Boards such as Sunderland, who could take just pride in their record. They also argued that the local councils could not take the strong and close interest in education which the Boards had done since their members had many other concerns apart from schools.

The Act came into force on 30 June 1903, and in the *Sunderland Echo* the following day there appeared a black-framed obituary notice under the bald heading 'Executed':

What added to the resentment against Balfour's Act in towns like Sunderland was that under its terms aid from the rates was to be given for the first time to church schools. Many nonconformists saw this as a compulsory local subsidy to Church of England and Catholic schools, whose religious teachings were abhorrent to them.

Nonconformist opposition to the 1902 Act was cogently but moderately expressed by the Revd. G. H. R. Garcia, Congregationalist minister of the Royalty Church, in a speech to the Board on 6 May 1902.[43] He believed that the government, in granting voluntary schools rate aid, was bestowing favours upon the Anglican Church in particular, with an inevitable aggravation of 'sectarian animosities', 'denominational jealousies' and 'theological rancour'. Garcia was grieved that the Act should threaten a revival of suspicion and bitterness between the churches.

Garcia died tragically young in 1904. Others however had by then taken up the campaign against the Act, forming a Citizens' League in February 1903 to unify their protests. Some called for passive resistance by the withholding of rates. But, despite strong language and crowded meetings, there was minimal support in Sunderland for passive resistance, no more than 13 local folk refusing to pay a portion of their rates between 1903 and 1906.[44] The truth was that in Sunderland, with its large number of Board Schools now transferred to the local education authority the threat of Anglican domination of education was non-existent. Nevertheless one permanent product of the controversy was the Sunderland Free Church Federal Council, formed in 1902 to unify nonconformist activity in the town and give Free Church folk a coordinated voice on matters of social and political concern.[45]

The Education Committee of Sunderland Borough Council held its first meeting on 14 July 1903. With its co-opted members, in addition to aldermen and councillors, it was several times larger than the old School Board. There was a certain amount of continuity between the two bodies, in the persons of R. A. Bartram, T. W. Backhouse, Peter Wood, and Mrs Mary Hancock, at that time the only woman to have served on a public educational body in the town.[46] Wood and Bartram had each served as Chairmen of the Board. Another link between the two bodies was in the person of Thomas Wood Bryers who had been head of the Monkwearmouth Colliery school 1861-1879, Inspector under the School Board, 1879-1881, and Clerk and Accountant to the Board, 1881-1902. He became Secretary to the Committee on its inception.[47] On his retirement in 1910 he recalled how, in 1879, the Board had had in its employ 16 head teachers and 28 assistant teachers (only six of them certificated), whereas in 1910 the LEA employed 92 heads and 532 assistants, 300 of them with teacher's certificates.

The scope of the LEA was much broader than that of the Board. By 1910 it was responsible for the Technical College (opened in 1901); the Day Training College (1908); the Bede Collegiate School, which now had become in effect the town's grammar school; and 19 local authority elementary schools. There also were in the borough by that date seven Church of England elementary schools, the Donnison Charity School, six Roman Catholic Schools including St. Anthony's High School, the High School for Girls (C of E) on Mowbray Road, one surviving Wesleyan School, two industrial schools and a girls Reformatory.[48]

To round off this survey it is necessary to mention schools which by 1914 were available for children living in those parts of the town not then included in the borough of Sunderland. At Southwick there were two Council elementary schools (the Central built in 1909 and the former High Southwick Board School) as well as St. Columba's C of E Schools begun in 1893, and St. Hilda's RC Schools of 1904/1906. The Board Schools at Castletown, Fulwell and South Hylton continued under the direction of their respective Councils. At Ryhope it appears that the Colliery schools (with an infant extension) had come under Council control, while a large new block of Council schools had been built in 1909 for older boys and girls, juniors and infants, accommodating nearly 1,400 pupils altogether. The Church of England school was also active in the village. Silksworth Village also had its small Church of England school; it was enlarged in 1896 to accommodate 96 pupils. The bigger schools in Silksworth were of course a consequence of the opening of the colliery — the Londonderry National School of 1874 (with accommodation for 850 pupils) and St. Leonard's RC school (accommodation, 240) given to the village by Lady Beckwith of Silksworth House. An all-age Council School was built in 1908.

ADULT EDUCATION

The pattern of adult education in nineteenth century Sunderland is surprisingly complex. All kinds of agencies were at work, with different motives and interests. The nonconformist denominations encouraged the education of their lay members since they held extensive responsibilities within the life and work of their chapels, particularly as Sunday School teachers and lay preachers. James Everett (a flax-dresser) began preaching in the Sunderland Wesleyan circuit in 1806 and, we are told, spent long hours in study each day as opportunity allowed, reading books on 'science, philosophy, biography, biblical criticism and exposition, theology and sermons', and even 'giving some attention to Greek and Hebrew'.[49] The reading list which can be compiled from the diary of another Sunderland lay preacher, John Young, shows a remarkable range and depth for a busy chemist in the early 1840s, covering heavy tomes on theology, biblical studies, history, war studies, literature, grammar, science and fiction, together with the leading contempo-

Revd. G. H. R. Garcia (1869-1904).

147

rary reviews.[50] These may be two outstanding examples but the impulse towards self-improvement under the challenge of preaching or the general stimulus of church and chapel life was shared by many other young men and women of the town. It is worth pointing out here the provision by churches of libraries. Indeed probably the first public library in Sunderland was that in an upstairs room at the west end of Sunderland parish church. The Sunderland Wesleyan Methodists and Quakers both promoted libraries for their members in the early years of the nineteenth century.[51] And most Sunday Schools of that age had libraries, often containing surprisingly serious and advanced reading matter.

In the mid-nineteenth century and later, chapels and churches became aware of the need to provide discussion groups, lectures, mutual improvement societies, debates, guilds, and so forth, especially among the young. The leadership of a cultured and lively minister was always a stimulus, as in the ministry of Robert Whitaker McAll at the Bethel Congregational chapel on Villiers Street, and later at Ebenezer, Fawcett Street. The members of his Young Men's Class had to prepare papers and even deliver public lectures as part of the obligation of membership.[52] The best of the town's ministers and lay leaders were very conscious of the need to promote an interest in education among the workers. An interesting example was a series of public lectures delivered in the Lyceum on Lambton Street in the winter of 1853-1854 by a group of nonconformist ministers of Sunderland and addressed to working men. The lectures were earnest, lengthy and solid, yet the audience on some occasions reached at least 2,000 people. McAll's was perhaps the most interesting — it was entitled 'Chaos or Cosmos: The Great Artificer, or God in Nature'.[53]

By the end of the century pretty well all churches, Anglican and nonconformist, had their institutes, providing not only lecture halls and reading rooms but a games room, a gymnasium, and even a billiards room, with penny concerts on Saturday nights. The Villiers Street institute was particularly popular. George Garcia used this institute as a base from which he could open up links with working men, inviting them in for "free and easy discussion of social and religious problems" in which, "over a pipe, the men opened out on the question as to why men held aloof from the churches". This was in the winter of 1901-2.[54]

It was out of similar concerns that the Young Men's Christian Association was established in Sunderland towards the end of 1871, on the initiative of a group of local laymen. The secretary of the first committee was the Congregationalist architect, Frank Caws, a pillar of the Association in its early years.[55] Part of a house on Borough Road was hired, and meetings began. It was all very earnest at first, and the young men were urged towards a strongly evangelical commitment. From 1876 the YMCA while retaining its strong Christian basis, launched itself into a gradually extending programme of educational and social activities, proving an asset to the town.

William Brockie (1811-1890), author, editor, and one of the promoters of Sunderland's public library.

Premises on Foyle Street replaced those on Borough Road, but in 1878 the Association was able to purchase a permanent home on the corner of John Street and Borough Road, Edward Backhouse proving a munificent benefactor towards this end. This grand suite of premises, in a prominent and central position, was enlarged and extended twice in less than 20 years, so popular and active had the YMCA become.[56]

More secular educational activities included the libraries the first being the Subscription Library launched in 1795, with the backing of some of the leading citizens of the town.[57] The later development of the town's libraries, obviously central to the theme of education, is not enlarged on here since one of the picture insets in this book is devoted to that topic. Suffice it to say that, beginning with relatively modest voluntary initiatives in the later eighteenth and early nineteenth centuries, Sunderland had by the eve of the first World War a central public library with 32,000 volumes, and three branch libraries each holding some 7,500. The branch libraries built 1908-9 on Villette Road, Kayll Road and Church Street North, Monkwearmouth, were donated to the town by Andrew Carnegie. The Subscription Library was still in existence by this date and it too had a very considerable stock of over 20,000 books.

Though William Brockie lamented "Sunderland is not a very literary town and there are only a few book buyers in it,"[58] there was nevertheless in the town a minority of eager and serious readers. This is evident for instance in Brockie's own accounts of George Wilson Meadley, Sir Cuthbert Sharp, Dr. F. H. Johnson, Reginald Orton, John Ferguson, Dr. Joseph Brown, Robert Renney, John Halcro, James Everett, Robert Robson, J. G. Grant and Thomas Dixon, to which list many names could be added of individuals who do not find a place in Brockie's book. Most of these men were middle class, had strong literary tastes and often possessed large private libraries. They were the type of Sunderland residents who helped to launch the Literary and Philosophical Society in 1834, the Natural History and Antiquarian Society 1836, the Polytechnic Society 1838, the Athenaeum in 1841, the Sunderland Students Association in 1886, and the Antiquarian Society in 1899. Three of Brockie's 'Notables' listed above were, however, not middle class — the shipwright poet John Ferguson, the cork cutter Thomas Dixon and the flax-dresser James Everett. Though remarkable examples of their type, they serve to remind us of the many artisans in Sunderland who sought to further their own education and culture in adult life. Let us hear one of that number, a shipwright:

> It is an erroneous idea that the working class generally have no desire for education. I have never met with a man yet but what had a desire to know more than he really did know. Give working men the means of self-culture and they will educate themselves. The obstacles you want removing are excessive labour, irregularity in the supply of labour, and the remuneration for labour so that men can afford time for self-culture.[59]

He added that what the working class really needed was "working class literature, working class journals and newspapers''. This was perhaps too much to hope for. The tendency rather was for well-meaning but paternalistic middle class folk to offer the workers the kind of 'improving' education which they thought was good for them, and to attempt to persuade them to aspire to a middle-class cultural outlook.

The Sunderland Mechanics' Institute, which was inaugurated in 1825, is an illustration of this trend. Its aims were to:

educate the illiterate, to direct the studious, and to afford everything necessary to the intelligent and ingenious, and to assist every mind aspiring to knowledge.[60]

The Institute struggled for some years in rooms on Sunderland Street, Sans Street and Bridge Street, moved to the Athenaeum for a few years in 1845, then found a home in the newly built Lyceum on Lambton Street in the early 1850s, though still with indifferent support. By this date the young Thomas Dixon was its secretary, and was struggling to make the Institute more effective, and to raise the cultural aspirations of his working class contemporaries. Dixon deserves to be remembered in Sunderland and it is good to have two portraits and a bust of him in the town's Museum and Art Gallery, an honour which obviously marks him out as somewhat unusual among working men.[61] He was in fact a self-employed craftsman, and in time employed a few others in his cork-cutting business on Sunderland Street, but he certainly earned his living by the skill of his own hands.

Dixon shared the urge of many artisans to better themselves not only materially, but culturally. In his case however he pursued this desire to remarkable lengths, and in the process forged links with an amazingly wide circle of friends and correspondents. These included in particular the artist William Bell Scott (then working in Newcastle), William Rossetti (brother of Dante Gabriel and Christina), and John Ruskin, the art critic and social prophet. It was his desire to see an art school launched in Sunderland which emboldened him to contact Bell Scott in the early 1850s, and the friendship which developed between the two (if somewhat patronising from Bell Scott's side) was real and lasting. He soon developed a passion for corresponding with the leading literary and cultural figures of mid-Victorian England, partly to discuss intellectual, artistic and social problems, and partly to invite them to donate copies of their books to the library of the newly formed Sunderland Industrial Equitable Society (the local Cooperative Society) of which he was the zealous librarian. One connection made through this correspondence was with John Ruskin, who soon came to see Dixon as a model working class man, and exploited the contact between them to address to Dixon a series of letters on social and political issues in the early part of 1867, when excitement over the second Parliamentary Reform Bill was intense. Dixon made thoughtful replies, and had Ruskin's letters published in several newspapers. Subsequently Ruskin published his side of the correspondence (with extracts from Dixon's letters as an appendix)

in a book entitled *Time and Tide by Weare and Tyne: 25 letters to a Working Man of Sunderland on the Laws of Work*, one of those pocket-sized works which poured from Ruskin's pen and which were read avidly by his admirers, many of them working class men.

There is something rather poignant about Thomas Dixon, not only in his early death at 49 but in his passionate if somewhat naive desire to soak himself in culture, and to build a bridge between working men and the literati of his day. Yet he was a seminal influence in important developments in higher education in the town, through the Mechanics' Institute, the School of Design (1857), the Cooperative Library which he helped to launch (and which by 1902 had over 11,000 volumes), his active campaigning for a public library and his eagerness to encourage other working men to seek self-improvement and find outlets for their talents as he had done.

Other opportunities for adult education in Sunderland were much stimulated by grants from the Science and Art Department of the Board of Trade (founded in 1853) to help educational ventures promoted by local voluntary initiative. A School of Navigation appeared in 1855 (in Lodge Terrace, Hendon), a School of Science and Art in Monkwearmouth in 1861, and another in Bishopwearmouth in 1869. This last had several homes, finally coming to rest in the top floor of the new Town Hall in 1891, being known by then as the Central School of Science and Art. It was in origin a private institution under a managing committee of local businessmen and benefactors, but in 1894 it began to receive substantial funding from the borough council, through its Technical Education Committee, and in 1902 became fully a local authority institution.

By the 1870s there were something like 22 other centres offering evening classes in a variety of subjects, and in receipt of Science and Art grants. Robert Cameron, was one of the leading pioneers in this movement:

Long before the days of University Extension Lectures Mr Cameron was doing the very work in his own town and district. He is indeed one of the pioneers of the Higher Education of the people. He organised science and literary classes; and to

The new YMCA building opened in Borough Road by Bishop Westcott, 19 October, 1896.

The Central Library and Museum

The Central Library and Museum in Borough Road is one of Sunderland's best known buildings. When opened in 1879 this was possibly the most important project completed by the Corporation during its first half century and showed the high priority given to library and museum provision.

Private libraries and a museum existed in Sunderland before the Corporation could operate these services. In Sunderland the most significant institution was the Subscription Library founded in 1795. The fee of 2 guineas a year (£2.10) limited the membership of the Library to the relatively well-off.

It was almost certainly the Subscription Library building which housed the collections of the Sunderland Museum founded in 1810 and financed by subscribers. The most notable of these was Dr Clanny; a fossil fish he found in Pallion Quarry in 1815 and presented to this museum is still on display in the Borough Road building today. By 1819 the number of subscribers had fallen to five, and two years later the Museum was presented to the Subscription Library.

The collection appears to have moved later to the Literary and Philosophical Society rooms in Villiers Street and the responsibility for them was eventually taken over by the Sunderland Natural History and Antiquarian Society formed in 1836. The Villiers Street premises were replaced by the new Athenaeum building in Fawcett Street opened in 1840. The Museum there seems to have been opened to the public in 1843. In may 1846 the Museum was transferred to Sunderland Corporation which was one of the first two local authorities to implement the 1845 Museums Act which allowed town councils to finance museums from the rates. Colchester Corporation also decided to establish a public collection the same month as Sunderland but as the museum in Colchester was not open to the public until 1860 Sunderland has a good claim to be the oldest provincial local authority museum in the country.

The Public Libraries Act of 1850 allowed the establishment of rate-supported libraries, but Sunderland was slower to adopt this than the Museums Act. It was not until 1858 that the Public or Free Library, also housed in the Athenaeum, was opened. The nucleus of the stock was provided by the donation of the Mechanics' Institute

The Library in 1901 before open access to the shelves had been introduced and borrowers had to consult the indicator board on the right to see which books were available.

The natural history gallery in the late 1950s. Apart from the addition of new exhibits, this gallery had changed little since the Museum was opened in 1879.

Library (founded 1825). The books were initially for reference only; lending was introduced in 1866, but books had to be requested at the counter as there was no public access to the shelves.

The Subscription Library still continued to flourish for many years. A move was made later in 1878 to a new building in Fawcett Street with a glass-domed lecture hall (now the National Westminster Bank) where it remained until closure in 1938. Only a handful of its books subsequently found their way to the Public Library.

By the 1870s larger space was needed in the rooms in the Athenaeum and the Corporation decided to build a new Library and Museum in Mowbray Park. At first it was also envisaged that a Town Hall would be included as part of the scheme, but this had to be dropped. The competition for the new buildings was won by the local architects J. and T. Tillman. The foundation stone was laid in the presence of General Grant, the ex-President of the USA in 1877 and the Library and Museum was opened on 6th November 1879.

On the ground floor of the building were the Library and a museum gallery (mainly natural history) while on the first floor was a small room which became the antiquities gallery and a large room which was initially intended to be a school of art and science, but was opened as an art gallery in 1881. Although other services were free, a charge was made for admission to the art and antiquities galleries. Visitors to these areas also had to leave their walking sticks and umbrellas with an attendant for which further fees were levied. At the back of the Museum and Library building was the Winter Garden, a large conservatory with tropical plants. By 1896 the Library and Museum building was already too small and a plan was prepared by the Borough Surveyor for a new Museum to the east of the existing building, but nothing came of this proposal.

In 1904 Charlton Deas, a forceful and dominating personality, was appointed Librarian and in 1906 the Museum, which had previously been administered separately, was placed under his control. Among the changes he introduced to the Museum in 1906 were the abolition of charges for the antiquities and art galleries and the introduction of a programme of temporary exhibitions. Library developments in the 1900s included the opening of three branch libraries funded by the Scottish-American philanthropist Andrew Carnegie. Hendon (opened in 1908) was the first "open access" library in the North East where readers were able to browse along the shelves. The Central Library followed suit in 1911.

For 30 years there was little further expansion in the service in spite of increased public usage. A branch library was opened at Southwick in 1931 as agreed when the area was incorporated into the Borough. No finance was, however, forthcoming for an extension scheme for the Central Library designed by C. A. Clayton Greene in 1934. The Winter Garden at the rear of the Library/Museum was severely damaged by a parachute mine in 1941 and had to be demolished. The site was eventually used for the long-hoped-for extension to the Central Library and Museum which was started in 1960 and was opened by the Queen Mother in 1964. This allowed adequate space for the first time for facilities such as the reference library and the display of Sunderland pottery.

Provision of three new branch libraries to serve the town's growing housing estates began with the conversion in 1955 of the former home at Grindon of H. S. Short, the shipbuilder. A museum, later redisplayed with Edwardian rooms and shop interiors, was provided on the first floor. A further museum at Monkwearmouth Station was opened by the Duke of Edinburgh in 1973. The exterior and the ticket office of the station were restored and the remainder of the building was used as museum of land transport.

The Library and Museum services were separated in 1974. The Libraries, amalgamated with the Recreation department from 1984, remained with the Borough. Nine libraries formerly in County Durham were added to the

The Central Library and Museum building at the time of its opening in 1879.

service in 1967 and 1974 and a major new library, Washington New Town, was opened in 1976. The Museums passed to the County Council; since the abolition of the latter in 1986 the Tyne and Wear Museums Service has been run by a joint committee of district councils with some funding from central government. The Museums too gained a building in Washington with the transfer of the "F" Pit Museum from Washington Development Corporation.

The centre of libraries and museum provision in Sunderland still remains, however, the Central building in Borough Road. The increasingly overcrowded building has undergone more internal adaptations for new services provided during the 1970s and 80s.

The 1964 Central Library extension from Mowbray Park.

popularise science lectured on different aspects of Astronomy and Geology; and to acquaint the masses with the literature of the nation he introduced the writings of Wordsworth, Carlyle, Burns and Emerson to the public notice.[62]

By 1889 the various Science and Art classes in the town had almost 1,000 students, just over two thirds of them pursuing scientific subjects and the other third art. By 1897 the total number of evening students was 1,430. The emphasis in almost all the courses was essentially practical, relating both science and art to the industrial and educational life of the community. Nevertheless the work at the Central School was also helping to promote skills in fine art, and to foster artistic tastes among Wearsiders.

The borough council was slow in launching a college which would help to unify and develop this educational activity, and give to it an academic depth and professionalism. However by the 1890s the mood was changing.[63] The Government gave encouragement towards the founding of municipal technical colleges by the Technical Instruction Act (1889) and the Local Taxation (Customs and Excise) Act of 1890. By the latter act certain sums arising from customs and excise duties were allocated annually to local authorities, either to relieve rates or to subsidise technical education. In Sunderland there was lively debate as to the use of the grants (popularly known as 'Whisky Money'!). That those in favour of higher education won the day, was largely owing to Dr. Gordon Bell, a Scottish surgeon and a town councillor. He and others, including a solicitor, W. Mills Roche, persuaded the Corporation to make grants from 'Whisky Money' to finance the School of Art from 1894, and at the same time they began to promote a campaign for the building of a local Technical College. A special committee to consider the plan was set up with Mills Roche as chairman and Bell as vice-chairman.

THE COLLEGES

There had been an earlier college in Sunderland, the Theological Institute founded in the old infirmary in 1868 to train Primitive Methodist ministers, which it did for some 15 years.[64] Despite its interest the Methodist

college was a short-lived venture and, though rooted in local initiatives, was not fully local in character or administration. The Technical College, opened in 1901, was a very different institution. The Council approved such a college in 1894, and in 1896 a site was purchased on Green Terrace, partly occupied by Southgate House which had for some years been used as a small private school.[65]

Benchara Branford, first principal of the new Technical College on a salary of £500[66] had four lecturers (each at £200 p.a.) in charge of the four departments of Chemistry, Mechanical and Civil Engineering, Physics and Electrical Engineering, and Commerce and Languages, with part-time lecturers in other subjects including, navigation, naval architecture, Latin and even farriery, and a group of demonstrators and laboratory assistants. It was expected that some 200 students would enrol at the college's opening, but in the event 671 did so, all but 30 as part-timers. The college was understaffed and pressed for space from its very origins.

A very interesting development occurred in 1903 (apparently the brainchild of Dr. Gordon Bell in coordination with local industrialists) when the Technical College introduced 'Sandwich Courses' whereby local engineering apprentices would spend six months in full time attendance at the college, and six months in their places of employment over a period of three or four years. The time at college was to count as part of their apprenticeship, and most students were to be paid during that time. By 1908 25 local firms were participating. It is claimed that the Sunderland college was the first to introduce such a scheme.

Principal Branford's view of education was liberal and comprehensive. At his speech at the college's opening he stressed his ideal of a liberal education for artisans. Coupled with this aim went a wider vision of the college promoting a broad range of courses and coordinating higher education throughout the town.[67] Branford seems to have hoped to become in effect the director of Sunderland's higher education, and head of a university college. It was not to be and Branford resigned in 1905. But the college's reputation grew and it won excellent reports from the inspectors.

Those other institutions which Branford had hoped might become part of a unified higher education system all remained independent of the Technical College. The Central School of Art, despite its cramped quarters in the Town Hall, was consolidating its reputation as a fine regional college. Various plans to find new premises were constantly thwarted until finally, 'Ashburn', the former Backhouse home on Ryhope Road, was acquired and opened by Dr. Bell's widow on 6 June 1936, as a College of Arts and Crafts.

Meanwhile teacher training had also developed independently, both in the pupil-teacher training centre attached to the Bede Collegiate School, and in the Day Training College which opened in 1908 in Westfield House, directly opposite the Technical College. The first principal of the Day Training College was George Readdie, former head of the Commerce and Languages in the Technical

The Athenaeum, Fawcett Street, opened 1841.

College. His move led to the virtual abandonment of commercial and humanities courses by the Tech., and was therefore a further nail in the coffin of Branford's larger hopes for that institution.

The Teacher Training College had a stout advocate in Dr. Gordon Bell, and it needed such an influential ally, being threatened on one side by an angry local ratepayers' association who complained it was an unnecessary and expensive luxury, and on the other by the Board of Education who complained incessantly about the inadequacy of the premises, occasionally threatening closure. There was a distinct possibility of closure in 1914 but the war postponed any decision. When war began there were 32 men and 39 women students, on a two year course. During the war, no men were enrolled, but a new mixed intake was admitted in 1919. A move to Langham Tower on Ryhope Road took place in 1922, and it was then decided to use the College only for women students.

By the First World War a pattern of higher education had been established in Sunderland in which the three local authority colleges pursued their separate existences. This continued for another half century, until in 1969 the Polytechnic was formed from a union of the former Art and Technical Colleges, to be followed a few years later by amalgamation of the College of Education with the Polytechnic. By the mid-1970s therefore the vision held by the first principal of the Technical College as to how that institution might develop had found at least a partial realisation under his successor Dr. Maurice Hutton, the Polytechnic's first rector.

REFERENCES

1. M. G. Jones, *The English Charity School Movement* (1964).
2. Fordyce, ii, 452-3.
3. *ibid., 452-3.*
4. When curate at Bishopwearmouth Robert Gray preached a powerful sermon advocating a national system of Church of England schools. See note 10.
5. *A Memorial Sketch of the late Revd. Robert Gray* (Sunderland, 1838) p. 14.
6. Fordyce, ii, 455.
7. *ibid.*, 454. *Endowed Charities (County Durham and County Boroughs of Gateshead and Sunderland)* 1904, ii, 454-462.
8. John Hampson, *A Sermon delivered on the establishment of Sunday Schools in Sunderland, 7 Sept. 1788*, Sunderland 1788. See *Antiq. Sund.*, xxvii, p. 14.
9. Peter Bull, *The Development of Church of England and National Schools in Sunderland, 1800-1870*, B.A. (Combined Arts) dissertation, Sunderland Polytechnic, 1985, p. 4.
10. Robert Gray, *National Education: A sermon . . . in aid of a subscription school* (Sunderland 1816) p. 10.
11. Peter Bull, *op. cit.*, F. Watson, *An Inquiry into the place of the Voluntary School in the education system with special reference to the primary schools of Sunderland and district*, M. Ed. thesis, Durham, 1955.
12. An interesting printed document in Sunderland Public Library details the establishment of the Monkwearmouth Subscription School on 1 Jan. 1812, and the regulations adopted on 7 Jan. 1812.
13. *Centenary booklet 1854-1954 of the Bishopwearmouth C. of E. School, Rectory Park, Sunderland* (Sunderland, 1954).

14. The difficulties faced by St. John's school as the east end declined are graphically described in two printed reports of 1896: *The Report of the East End Commission* (Rural Deanery of Wearmouth) and *St. John's Parish: its work and its limitations* (both published in Sunderland).
15. Peter Bull, *op. cit.*, appendix B.
16. On Cameron see biographical appendix. The Quaker Boys' School minutes are in the DCRO reference SF/SU 32.
17. Peter Bull, *op. cit.*, p. 39 and appendix.
18. T. Greener, 'Methodist Primary Education', part (i), *Wesley Historical Society (North East) Bulletin*, 36, Aug. 1981, p. 17. See also the series of articles on this theme in Bulletins 36-38.
19. Keith Rudd, *The Growth of Roman Catholicism and Roman Catholic Education in Sunderland*, B.A. (Combined Arts) dissertation, Sunderland Polytechnic, 1985. Also *St. Mary's Jubilee, 1835-1985*, the 150th anniversary booklet of St. Mary's R.C. Church, Sunderland, 1985.
20. Brockie, p. 326.
21. Watson's, pp. 62-3, drawn from School Board minutes.
22. W. Parson and W. White, *History, Directory and Gazeteer of Durham and Northumberland*, vol. i, 1827, p. 354.
23. G. E. Milburn (ed.) *The Diary of John Young* (Surtees Society, cxcv, 1983) p. 109.
24. On Tom Taylor, Brockie, pp. 396-405. Also on J. W. Fletcher, another of Cowan's pupils, pp. 422-427.
25. C. S. Collingwood, *Dr. Cowan and the Grange School, Sunderland with recollections of its scholars* (London and Sunderland, 1897). See also *Antiq. Sund.*, vii, p. 53 ff. The fees at the Grange ranged from 40 to 60 guineas a year at the school's opening, with washing and library charges extra (contemporary handbill).
26. Collingwood, *op. cit.*, p. 30.
27. Brockie, p. 422.
28. T. Corfe, *Swan in Sunderland* (1979). *Antiq. Sund.*, vii, p. 27n.
29. Helen G. Bowling, *The First Eighty Years: A History of Sunderland Church High School, 1884-1964* (Sunderland, 1965). Audrey B. Sayers, *Sunderland Church High School for Girls: A Centenary History*, (Sunderland, 1984).
30. Fordyce, ii, 463.
31. Fordyce, ii, 466. See also 'Wesleyanism in Sunderland', pt. 2, in *Antiq. Sund.*, xxvii, pp. 13-18 (and the references there quoted) by G. E. Milburn. On Michael Longridge see the biographical appendix.
32. Fordyce, ii, 464.
33. *ibid.*, p. 463.
34. Patricia J. Storey, *Samuel Storey of Sunderland, 1841-1925*, M. Litt. thesis, University of Edinburgh,

Thomas Dixon (1831-1880), cork cutter and man of culture. (From the bust in Sunderland Museum by Sir J. E. Boehm, RA)

Southgate House, Green Terrace, in 1886. Used for some years as a private school, the house was demolished to make way for the building of the Technical College opened in 1901.

1978, pp. 130-148. See also Miss Storey's chapter in this volume.

35. *Sunderland Year Book*, 1904, pp. 27-37. C. J. Turner, *The Development of Elementary Education in Sunderland, 1870-1902*, M. Ed. thesis, Durham University, 1984.

36. The Board first met at the Police Buildings, East Cross Street, but soon leased 57 Fawcett Street as their offices.

37. Storey, *op. cit.*, and the same author's chapter in this volume.

38. *Sunderland Year Book*, 1904, pp. 35-37. Andrea Milburn, *Sunderland and the Balfour Act, 1902-1906*, B.A. dissertation, Huddersfield Polytechnic, 1985, p. 19.

39. The Board's 'catchment area' was equivalent to the borough.

40. Fees in the Board Schools were 2d. a week for infants, and 4d. and 6d. respectively for the older girls and boys. The Board could remit fees for poorer children before elementary education became free in 1891.

41. Turner, *op. cit.*, p. 286.

42. W. Ellis, *The Development of Secondary Education in Sunderland, 1945-1970*, M.Ed. thesis, Newcastle University, 1973, Chapter 2.

43. Andrea Milburn, *op. cit.*, p. 17.

44. *ibid.*, p. 29.

45. F. H. Hawkins, *A History of the Sunderland and District Free Church Federal Council*, n.d. (1985-6).

46. *Sunderland Year Book*, 1906, p. 75. Mrs. Hancock was the wife of Dr. J. H. Hancock, vicar of the church of the Venerable Bede, Monkwearmouth.

47. *Sunderland Year Book*, 1913, p. 106.

48. *Kelly's Directory*, 1910, pp. 438-440.

49. Brockie, p. 304.

50. *The Diary of John Young*, p. xxviii, and *passim*. (See note 23 above).

51. The Catalogue of the Quaker library, published in 1824, survives; the Sunderland Antiquarian Society possess Bernard Ogden's copy. Michael Longridge initiated the Wesleyan library, see Fordyce ii, 462, and Garbutt, pp. 325-6; also the biographical appendix on Longridge.

52. *In Memoriam Robert Whitaker McAll* (anon.), 1898, pp. 8-9.

53. M. Baxter and R. W. McAll (editors), *Ten Lectures addressed to the Working Classes delivered in the Lyceum, Sunderland, by Dissenting Ministers* (Sunderland, 1854).

54. J. G. Henderson, *George Henry Russell Garcia: Memoir, Sermons and Addresses* (London, 1904) p. 168.

55. On Caws, see *Sunderland Year Book*, 1906, p. 130, and the chapter in this book on architecture.

56. C. Thompson, 'The Early Days of the Sunderland Y.M.C.A.', *Flashes*, vol. ii, 1894-1895 — a series of monthly articles in the Sunderland Y.M.C.A. journal.

57. Garbutt, pp. 317-324. J. J. Kitts 'The Sunderland Subscription Library,' *Antiq. Sund.*, ix, pp. 1-48.

58. Brockie, p. 427.

59. Anon. *A Defence of Trade Unions in general and the Sunderland Shipwrights' Society in particular*, quoted in Dorothy Faughey, *Leisure in the Nineteenth Century especially with regard to Sunderland*, an undergraduate thesis, Sunderland Polytechnic, 1974, p. 16.

60. *ibid.*, p. 18.

61. G. E. Milburn, 'Thomas Dixon of Sunderland,' in *Sunderland's History*, vol. 2 (being vol. xxix of *Antiq. Sund.*) 1984, pp. 5-45, with an extensive list of sources on Dixon.

62. J. G. Bowran, 'An interview with Mr. Robert Cameron,' *Primitive Methodist Magazine*, 1897, pp. 510-514.

63. W. G. Hall, *The Provision of Technical Education in Sunderland prior to 1908*, Durham M.Ed. thesis, 1964, and J. Makkison, *The Development of Higher and Further Education in Sunderland since 1908*, Durham M.Ed. thesis, 1969, particularly useful since it appears that some of the materials on which they were based no longer exist. On the technical college, see also short accounts in the *Sunderland Year Book*, 1902, pp. 63-65 (and 67), and 1912, pp. 33-37.

64. G. E. Milburn, *A School for the Prophets: The origins of ministerial education in the Primitive Methodist Church* (Sunderland, 1981).

65. The original technical college is that part of the present Polytechnic known as the Galen Building. Its cost was £28,000, for the site, construction and equipment, of which £18,000 came from the accumulated subsidy under the 1890 (Whisky Money) Act.

66. Benchara Branford, M.A. (Edin.) was formerly a lecturer in Mathematics at the Yorkshire College (soon to become the University of Leeds).

67. On Branford's speech see W. G. Hall, *op. cit.*, pp. 145-6; Branford's wider aims for the college were set out in the first prospectus, Hall, pp. 141-2.

The Technical College in its setting (upper right). On the left, the old infirmary of 1822, used as a Primitive Methodist Theological college 1868-1883, and subsequently as a chapel, a Roman Catholic School, and as the Polytechnic's History Section.

Buildings and Architects 1780-1914

The history of architecture is usually written in terms of the development of styles and movements, or through the consideration of individual architects who played a significant role in that stylistic development. A few towns of great architectural importance like London, Bath or Manchester have been analysed, but it is unusual to consider the architectural history of an ordinary provincial town of mainly nineteenth century creation which has apparently no claim to significance or importance. Yet the architectural development of Sunderland, while it largely conforms to the national pattern of debate about styles and fashions in building, and so illuminates that pattern, does exhibit some local curiosities and achievements that are worthy of record and analysis. This chapter is an attempt to present Sunderland's architectural history in the context of the national background and also as a factor in determining the environment in which the community of Sunderland lived and worked and fulfilled itself.

Up to the end of the eighteenth century Sunderland lacked a centre and had few buildings of architectural distinction. On the outskirts of the town were a few old farmhouses and some more recent residences for gentlemen, like Thornhill or Ford Hall, now largely demolished. In the centre were two medieval churches, both in some disrepair, and a few town houses of some size for prosperous business families largely built in the Georgian domestic style that is so familiar in many other towns. The designers of these houses are unknown as the practice was for builders and craftsmen to provide their own design drawings for their clients and then to erect and decorate houses for them, working within a familiar tradition of construction. The publication of pattern books allowed fashion to be followed. No doubt Sunderland followed this system of design and construction using its local building firms for housing and other routine buildings. More significant public buildings required a rather grander sense of design and more sophisticated designers. Apart from the very few famous architects of eighteenth century England whose training in drawing and design can be traced and whose buildings are very familiar — men like Vanbrugh, Hawksmoor or Adam — it appears that buildings were designed by building craftsmen who also undertook larger responsibilities for planning and supervising constructions, or by gentlemen amateurs who took an interest in architectural matters. The emergence of these two groups is explained by the increasing interest in the classical orders of architecture which demanded a break with the traditions of English vernacular design and by the need for a clear appreciation of the overall plan of the building before work could start on its construction.[1] The eighteenth century churches of Sunderland illustrate these two alternative architectural approaches.

Holy Trinity Church, opened in 1719, was more than the first post-reformation Church in the town. It was a symbol of the growing significance of Sunderland as opposed to Bishopwearmouth, a token in bricks and mortar of the town's loyalty to the Hanoverian monarchy and the first major building in the new style of architecture. The most probable architect was William Etty of York, a carpenter-cum-designer with substantial credentials.[2] The rector and his wealthy supporters sought an experienced man from outside the town to provide them with a church that because of its style, its brick construction and its simple design as an auditory church marked it out as being quite different from the two existing churches of the town.[3] The second church was St. John, Prospect Row, which was opened in 1769 and demolished in the early 1970s. The designer here was John Thornhill who was also the most enthusiastic financial supporter of the venture and initial patron of the living.[4] Architecturally St. John's took its style from Holy Trinity, using brick and classical ideas to provide another auditory chapel, but Thornhill was a wealthy landowner and businessman whose architectural interest was purely amateur. He may also have designed Thornhill House late 1760s, now demolished.[5] So in the two prestige buildings of the eighteenth century the two main sources of architectural advice are tapped. A third building conceived in that eighteenth century tradition was the Exchange Building opened in 1814 to act as a commercial centre and a newsroom. This "chaste, elegant structure" is again classical, but this time built of stone. The architect was John Stokoe of Newcastle,[6] a builder's son who had designed the Moot Hall in Newcastle. As he was not the contractor for the Exchange Building it is possible he was trying to establish himself purely as an architect.

The nineteenth century saw major changes in the practice of architecture largely because of the new demand for buildings and because of the variety of architectural convictions and styles. All towns, like Sunderland, were faced with the problems of rapid physical expansion. Much of this was directly concerned with housing the growing population[7] and had little impact on the profession of architecture. But there was also a demand for industrial and commercial buildings, public buildings, for new churches and chapels and for buildings representing quite new requirements such as railway stations, office blocks, washhouses and, later in the period, working men's clubs and cinemas. Here was the opportunity for growth in the building trades and the numbers of builders in Sunderland increased accordingly.[8] There was also opportunity for designers to break their links with the building trade and to emerge as fully professional figures concerned wholly with matters of aesthetics and the supervision of building work. Nationally this was expressed most forcibly in the establishment of the Institute of British Architects in 1834 which gained royal status in 1837. The long-term work of the RIBA in defining the role and remuneration of the architect, encouraging and then defining appropriate methods of training, and laying down codes of professional conduct ultimately culminated in the Architects' Registration Act of 1938.[9] Locally there was a similar development. Local architects responded to the same opportunities and offered their versions of the fashionable architectural styles, while clients also had the option of calling in prestigious figures from London to create buildings that would express their importance both personally and corporately.

THE FIRST SUNDERLAND ARCHITECTS

It is difficult to establish precisely who was Sunderland's first architect as the boundary line between builder and architect was at that time indistinct. When John Dobson started practice in Newcastle c.1811 he claimed to be the only architect in Northumberland, as Ignatius Bonomi was the only one in Co. Durham.[10] Dobson was excluding builder-architects like John Stokoe and thinking solely of designing architects who had received some appropriate training. In Sunderland the emergence of such a designer was to be longer delayed. Thomas Wilson, whose main work was the supervision of the construction in cast iron of Sunderland Bridge for Rowland Burdon in 1796, was called an architect and he did put a new roof on Holy Trinity Church in 1803, but his role as a designer is open to doubt and his

other significant work was mainly as a bridge engineer.[11] The first man to appear in a local directory[12] with the appellation 'architect' was James Hogg (1785-1838). While he did design two important buildings in Villiers Street, Bethel Congregational Chapel of 1819[13] now demolished and the splendidly austere Greek style facade of St. George's Presbyterian chapel of 1825,[14] he was also a builder, auctioneer and surveyor. His father had been an auctioneer and joiner and Hogg appears to be a good example of a trained craftsman emerging as a designer.[15] Other early figures follow a similar pattern. Thomas Pratt (1794-1878) was predominantly a builder who became a successful and wealthy man through large contracts like Penshaw Monument and much house building, but who began to style himself 'architect' in the 1840s and whose son William D. Pratt (1821-1890) continued the tradition. Very few buildings can be attributed to either of the Pratts as designers and most of them are insignificant.[16] William Drysdale (1793-?) was a builder who acted as surveyor to the Sunderland Improvement Commissioners and designed Trafalgar Square Almshouses of 1840[17]; and the more obscure Dowell

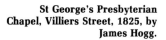

St George's Presbyterian Chapel, Villiers Street, 1825, by James Hogg.

brothers, Bartholomew and Richard (1762-1843), may have designed the Fawcett Street housing development as well as being involved with the building.[18] Similar career patterns can be discovered for John Hartforth (1799-c.1836) whose design for the Customs House of 1837 was highly praised,[19] and for Joseph Potts (1799-1885) who established a long-lived architectural practice in the town, but who always regarded himself primarily as a building craftsman.[20]

The most significant of these emergent architects in the town was Thomas Moore (1796-1865). Son of a blacksmith, he appeared in directories first as a joiner, then builder and surveyor and in 1844 as architect and surveyor. In his later career he practised solely as an architect, training his sons in the profession, being the only Sunderland founder member of the Northern Architectural Association in 1855 and acting as surveyor to Wearmouth Bridge. He was described as " 'the father of his profession' in Sunderland, and indeed, we believe in the North of England"[21] which is clearly an exaggeration given the development of architectural practice in Newcastle, but which reflects the importance of his work in Sunderland. His Monkwearmouth Railway Station of 1848 remains not only as a fine addition to the townscape but one of the most significant of early railway stations. For many years attributed to John Dobson, its splendour is a result of George Hudson's exhibitionism and it shows Moore's ingenuity as he adapted the classical orders to the entirely nineteenth century demands of the steam railway. With the neighbouring Royal Hotel and Savings Bank of the 1850s, both demolished in the mid-1970s, Moore offered the possibility of a classical redevelopment of Sunderland to match that of Newcastle. This was never achieved except in a piece-meal way and Moore accepted a variety of commissions for different buildings. Chapels for the Unitarians in Bridge Street (1830) and the Primitive Methodists in Williamson Terrace (1840), theatres like the Lyceum (1856), shops in Sunniside of c.1850 and houses like Low Barnes and Ashbrooke House (later Corby Hall) of 1864 all show him working in classically derived styles and all have been destroyed. However, an architect working in the middle years of the century also had, in response to popular taste, to design in Gothic styles and Moore produced St. Andrew Deptford (1840-41), the Register Buildings, High Street (c.1850) and Bishopwearmouth Cemetery and Mortuary Chapels (1856). These designs are less convincing than his classical work. The significance of Moore is not that he was the first architect in the town, but that he was the first to show that a man could be successful solely by the exercise of his professional skills. Without any evidence of formal training of the sort enjoyed by Dobson or Bonomi he emerged as a fully professional architect whose practice continued till the death of his son Thomas Angelo Moore (1840-1891) and who established the fact that Sunderland could support such a practice with a sufficiency of commissions.[22]

DEBATE ABOUT STYLES

Thomas Moore's ability to design in more than one style illustrates the central pre-occupation of architecture in Victorian England: the problem of determining what was the proper style for the new industrial age. A variety of forces like the emergent training opportunities for architects which had a strong historical cast, the growing distaste for some of the effects of social and economic change, and the expression of religious and philosophical ideas in aesthetic terms, tended to make architects look to past ages for inspiration. The primary models were the classical world, with its balance and symmetry and rules for the choice of order and the relationship between the parts of a building; and the medieval world with its pointed arches, romantic detail and individual craftsmanship, made manifest in the churches of pre-Reformation England. The moral issue of classical paganism versus medieval Christianity added fervour to the practical and aesthetic aspects of the debate. In an architecture based on revivals the architect had to become increasingly aware of the originals and more correct in his use of their motifs. Yet he also had to respond to demands for buildings that no previous age had needed to design, while new materials like iron and new techniques of machine-produced details in stone or brick or terracotta gave new opportunities for an architecture that was truly contemporary.[23]

This national debate is reflected in Sunderland. The early nineteenth century tradition was firmly based on classical designs. The houses in John Street and other streets on the Fawcett Estate dating from 1820 to 1850 conform to notions of contemporary taste although they continued later than might be expected. Nonconformist chapels like those of James Hogg and Sans Street Wesleyan Chapel of 1793[24] together with later ones like Ebenezer Chapel, Fawcett Street of 1852 by Thomas Oliver and Revd. R. W. McAll[25] took classical models as did public buildings like Bonomi's Infirmary of 1823[26] or the Athenaeum, Fawcett Street of 1841 by William Billinton of Wakefield.[27] For some types of building the classical styles remained fashionable throughout the century. Commercial buildings especially banks attempted to look like Renaissance palazzi as with the National Provincial Bank Building of 1876 by John Gibson.[28] In the North East this pattern of building was re-inforced by the success of Newcastle's extensive redevelopment by Richard Grainger in which architects like Dobson, Thomas Oliver, John and Benjamin Green and John Wardle exhibited a range of sophisticated re-workings of the basic design elements to produce one of the most effective nineteenth century town centres in the country.[29] Sunderland made various attempts to emulate this achievement, as with Hutchinson's Buildings of 1851 by G.A. Middlemiss[30] or the Woods' Bank development in Fawcett Street by Austin, Johnson and Hicks begun in 1875, but not carried to completion.[31] Designs based upon classical tradition continued throughout the century especially in housing, where Italianate terraces provided middle-class accommodation throughout the century; and in Edwardian times the revival of more baroque forms gave classicism a new vigour as in John Hall's River Wear Commissioners' Offices[32] and the Water Company Offices by W. and T.R. Milburn,[33] both in John Street and both opened in 1907.

GOTHIC REVIVAL IN SUNDERLAND

However it was the Gothic Revival that became the most significant architectural style of Victorian England and Sunderland's architects came to be proficient in its use and adaptation. The first medievally based buildings in the town were designed by outsiders: St. Thomas' Church of 1829 designed by a member of the prolific and important Wyatt dynasty, P.W. Wyatt, who was working for Lord Londonderry at Wynyard,[34] and the Roman Catholic Church of St. Mary opened in 1835 to designs by Ignatius Bonomi of Durham[35] architect of several Catholic churches in the region. But perhaps the building that indicated that Gothic was truly to be revived in Sunderland was Fawcett Street Wesleyan Chapel of 1836

Fawcett Street Wesleyan Chapel, 1836, by Joseph Potts.

designed by Joseph Potts.[36] That a Methodist society should instruct a local builder/architect to design their chapel in Gothic shows how far Gothic ideas had permeated. Of course Potts showed little understanding of medieval building forms and simply applied Gothic details to the facade of a plain rectangle in which preachers could be heard, but then Wyatt and Bonomi had achieved little more with their designs. As research progressed architectural design became more accurate, and long debates ensued about the particular medieval styles that were most desirable. So later churches became progressively more convincing. St. Andrew, Deptford and Holy Trinity, Southwick,[37] although more than facades, still tended to apply Gothic detail to a simple rectangular church rather in the manner of the Commissioners Churches of the early nineteenth century. But by the 1860s architects like James Murray of Coventry were designing much more convincing churches like Christ Church,[38] and at the end of the century the prolific Charles Hodgson Fowler of Durham could turn his scholarship in medieval architecture to a variety of designs from the basically correct such as St. Ignatius, Hendon, to the cheaper, but effective, as at South Hylton or to the much freer brick design of St. Aidan, Grangetown. Fowler, a highly professional architect who was trained by Scott (the most famous and successful of Victorian Gothic architects), based his entire career on church building almost wholly within the Gothic idiom,[39] but most local architects had to offer Gothic as one element in a more mixed architectural practice. Indeed in building churches the Anglicans preferred to go to regionally based figures like J.P. Pritchett of Darlington,[40] John Henry of Durham[41] or W.S. Hicks of Newcastle[42] rather than to Sunderland firms. Only Joseph Potts at St. Mark, Millfield[43] and G.A. Middlemiss at St. Peter, Cumberland Street[44] were able to essay High Victorian Gothic efforts and perhaps the most striking of the local architects' Anglican churches is St. Gabriel by C.A. Clayton Greene[45] which was designed right at the end of the Gothic tradition and which shows the influence of other architectural ideas of the early twentieth century. In addition to new churches there was a passion for restoring old ones; St. Peter, Monkwearmouth had a virtually new church added to its Saxon tower by R.J. Johnson, and as late as 1935 St. Michael, Bishopwearmouth was completely recast in a final flowering of Gothic Revival architecture by W.D. Caröe.[46]

The most striking evidence of how far Gothic styles influenced nineteenth century architecture lay in the way in which a style seen predominantly as ecclesiastical spread beyond that particular sphere. Nonconformists found it gave their chapels the right tone and many major public buildings looked to the pointed arch, the carved capital and the irregular outline of Gothic to give a strongly national character to their designs. Adaptation was widespread. Gothic could survive construction in modern materials, especially brick and tile, despite the medieval precedent of stone, in a way which classical designs could not. It could

St Thomas, 1829, C. of E., by P. W. Wyatt.

also be adapted to secular use in town halls, schools and museums or even to such un-medieval buildings as railway stations, office blocks and water works. Sunderland architects produced a series of designs of varying quality that reflected the debate in architecture that they could follow so conveniently in periodicals like *The Builder*, published since 1842. Each of the major non-conformist denominations produced a substantial Gothic styled church. The finest was St. John's Wesleyan Church, Ashbrooke, designed as a major scheme in 1888 by Robert Curwen of London. With its attached hall, classrooms, caretaker's house and the manse that was not built, it was the most expensive nineteenth century church in the town. Although it looks thoroughly Anglican, the ancillary buildings tie it firmly into the Methodist tradition and make it one of the finest examples of its type in Methodism.[47] Scarcely less impressive are Grange Congregational Church by J.P. Pritchett(1883) with its wonderful sweep of classrooms in a semi-circle around the apsidal end of the church[48] or St. George's Presbyterian designed by John Bennie Wilson of Glasgow in 1890 with its striking tower incorporating elongated arches and its use of red sandstone. The Presbyterians even demolished a Dobson church in North Bridge Street to replace it with a Gothic design by W.L. Newcombe in 1892.[49] These grand examples were supported by a mass of small chapels, some very humble, that took just the simplest Gothic detail like the pitch of the roof or a couple of lancets in the facade to indicate their religious purpose. Most local architects designed some of these buildings, though John Eltringham and John Tillman dominated the scene in terms of number, if not quality. Secular buildings in Gothic style are less prominent in the town, especially as many have been demolished. The leading architect

here was G.G. Hoskins of Darlington who was a pupil of Waterhouse, the Manchester-based architect famous for Manchester Town Hall and the Natural History Museum, Kensington. Hoskins made his reputation with a design for Middlesbrough Town Hall which was strongly influenced by his master's design for Manchester and which was awarded first premium by Waterhouse himself.[50] He worked extensively for the Backhouse family and designed their bank in High Street[51] and the Victoria Hall which the Backhouses supported financially.[52] His only surviving

St John's Wesleyan Church, 1888, by Robert Curwen.

building is the Gas Company Offices, now part of Binns Store, which shows the influence of Ruskin in the use of Venetian models.[53] The Railway Station of 1879 by William Bell, architect to the Northern Railway Company, was also Gothic with a clock-tower to High Street almost to defy Moore's classical design in Monkwearmouth.[54] The adaptation of Gothic to shops and offices was much more eclectic; the leading figure was Frank Caws[55] who worked in the late years of the century when other influences were also important. Most of this work is demolished or radically altered. Only in housing did Sunderland resist the influence of Gothic. Apart from Nicholson House, Mowbray Road (1850) by J. & B. Green of Newcastle[56] there are few houses which do not continue classical ideas in an Italianate form until later in the century. Architects like G.A. Middlemiss[57] and Martin Greener,[58] and doubtless many others, devoted much of their time to variations of the terrace style of housing for all classes of house including the "Sunderland Cottage" which is the highly idiosyncratic local house type for the working classes.[59]

By the last decades of the nineteenth century the rigid division between Classical and Gothic had lost much of its force, If architecture was to be based upon the revival of historical styles then a whole range of alternatives could be considered. The European variants on Gothic were pursued by some, though not noticeably in Sunderland, and non-Gothic church forms were tried like the Byzantine basilican style, of which St. Columba, Southwick (1890), by C. Hodgson Fowler is a striking example with its stark brick forms externally and its quite un-English interior space. Whether it is wholly appropriate to a north country industrial suburb is a matter of taste.[60] Similarly European traditions from the Renaissance and Baroque periods proved of interest to architects, especially for commercial buildings. Edwardian baroque has already been noted, but the most striking local example of this continental influence is Sunderland Museum and Art Gallery opened in 1879. J. & T. Tillman's design is like a French chateau with its pilastered facade and the dome and turrets on the roof and seems to have been chosen to give a sense of grandeur to an important public building, though some have found the design rather overblown and pretentious.[61] There was also interest in English architecture of other than medieval date. The vernacular styles that had continued despite changes in fashion, such as the so called 'jacobethan' motifs, and the 'Queen Anne' style encouraged by Norman Shaw, had their impact nationally and faint traces can be picked up in Sunderland's buildings. Langham Tower, 1890 (on Ryhope Road), by William Milburn is an exuberant attempt to use a bewildering variety of detail to create a romantic gentleman's house which owes a lot to Norman Shaw's Cragside[62] while C.A. Clayton Greene followed the important Manchester architect Edgar Wood in his design for Hammerton Hall, Gray Road, in 1911.[63] Art Nouveau, and Arts and Crafts decorative details, can be seen applied to a few buildings, but generally these amount to little more than a few flourishes derived from contemporary architectural journals. While it is true that a good deal of building done between 1900 and 1914 today looks dated and 'of its period', it has to be admitted that our concern for, and appreciation of, Edwardian architecture is still waiting to be fully awakened.[64]

MORE LOCAL ARCHITECTS

Most towns generated enough work to sustain some firms of architects in the nineteenth century, but many remained within the orbit of regional centres in which the best known local architects were based. Sunderland firms had to compete with at least three such centres. While it is generally true that few architects from London or the south built in Sunderland, regionally based practices certainly made significant contributions. Most importantly Newcastle provided the north east's 'big guns', led by John Dobson. The longstanding misattribution of Monkwearmouth Station to Dobson is proof of the dominance he has exerted over the minds of architectural historians. Inevitably he was commissioned to build in Sunderland, notably by Sir Hedworth Williamson on his estates in Monkwearmouth[65] and to provide churches for Presbyterians[66] and Anglicans.[67] More unusually he also designed the first large warehouse on the Docks.[68] None of his Sunderland work does much to enhance his well-established reputation.[69] The successors to Dobson's practice, Austin and Johnson, especially in the person of R.J. Johnson,[70] gained at least thirteen commissions including schools,[71] churches[72] and most importantly the redevelopment of part of Fawcett Street for Woods' Bank. The bank (now Barclays), the Subscription Library (now National Westminster Bank), and offices now used by an estate agent give an indication of the massive classical block that was intended to fill the whole site from St. Thomas Street to Athenaeum Street.[73] W.S. Hicks, who began with Austin and Johnson, emerged as a significant church architect in the North East and designed St. Hilda, Westbourne Road, with its outside pulpit, but which proved too close to St. Michael, Bishopwearmouth, to establish a viable independent parish, and which was demolished c.1970.[74] Many other Newcastle architects contributed occasional buildings in the town, often in their specialist areas, like Dunn, Hansom and Dunn who designed St. Benet (R.C.) in Monkwearmouth[75] and B.F. Simpson who designed the Dun Cow Hotel in High Street West.[76] When centres like Darlington, the base for J.P. Pritchett and G.G. Hoskins,[77] and Durham, which attracted church architects like John Henry, Charles Hodgson Fowler, G.L. Jackson[78] and T.C. Ebdy[79], are taken into account, it is clear that local men faced fierce competition for commissions. It is also largely the case that Sunderland firms won only a small number of clients outside the town.

The first architect in Sunderland known to have had a formal training was Thomas Oliver. He had been trained in Newcastle by his father, also Thomas Oliver, whose office was involved in Grainger's re-development of Newcastle centre. Thomas jr. practised in Sunderland only briefly from c.1849 to 1857 when he took over the Newcastle office on the death of his father. In that brief period his work included classical public buildings, though the bulk of it was housing for middle class clients. The quality of his work is best seen in the Londonderry Institute, Seaham. His main contribution to the town was Hendon Baths and Washhouses built for the Corporation. The research, and the three designs he prepared, left him out-of-pocket on the commission, but the final building was very successful and profitable. It became the model for later baths in the town and Oliver designed several more throughout the country. But the bulk of his work was in the Newcastle practice of Oliver and Leeson, a large and powerful firm of regional importance.[80]

In the middle years of the century many local architects were still with out formal training. George Andrew Middlemiss (1815-1887) began as a workman in a building firm, but by 1844 is described as an architect. Hutchinson's buildings of 1850 brought him to prominence through his design of a classical facade for an important corner. Despite its shortcomings the building was much admired[81] and Middlemiss gained other important commissions in the High Street area like the Theatre Royal (1855) and commercial developments. But he always remained a builder at heart. He developed large housing estates at Hendon and Southwick for artisans as well as providing designs for middle-class terraces on the Mowbray estate. He ran brick works at Cornhill and Villette Road and maintained an auctioneer's business. As a result he became wealthy, a town councillor, church warden of St. Peter, Bishopwearmouth, which he had designed in 1870; he died in the spacious splendour of Ashbrooke Tower, which he also designed.[82] He won first premium for James Williams Street Board School and then planned the next four schools which brought accusations of jobbery through his council connections. For a part-time architect the practice was impressive, though the individual buildings are usually quite routine.

In competition with Middlemiss was Joseph Potts (1799-1885) who always described himself as a mason despite his design work.[83] Potts' practice appears to have had little housing work, but equally little work of real prestige. The Infirmary in Durham Road of 1867 was the most important commission and by that time Joseph Potts jr. (1836-1914) was in effective charge of the firm. He regarded himself purely as an architect though how he was trained is not clear. Again much of the work of the practice is undistinguished and much of it is in the Gothic style. Basically, the Potts worked to small budgets so that a church like St. Mark, Millfield (1872), though successful in its interior design, hardly compares with the more expensive Christ Church, and the many non-conformist chapels they designed are at best homely. However, the practice was busy (they brought Frank Caws to Sunderland as a manager) and long-lived, not finally closing until after World War II.[84]

The first local firm to be headed by a formally qualified architect was that of J. & T. Tillman. John Tillman (1835-1899) was F.R.I.B.A. and his younger brother, Thomas (1852-1892) was A.R.I.B.A. John established the practice about 1860 and while many other firms were successful in the town the Tillmans had a particularly significant role in the latter half of the century. Their major commission was the Museum and Library (1879), but the bulk of their work lay in chapels for Methodists and other denominations. Most have now been demolished, but some like Hood Street United Methodist Free Church (1867) are very effective, simple chapels that fit into their setting. Others, like Tatham Street Primitive Methodist Chapel (1875), seem somewhat pretentious and overblown in their decorative fancies. Undoubtedly the Tillmans also designed many housing layouts, especially of artisan cottages, for both speculative builders and Land Societies. Evidence of their more professional approach can be found in the notes they sent to periodicals like *The Builder*, *Building News* or *British Architect* giving details of new commissions and of estimates received and accepted. Few Sunderland architects bothered to do this. Also they played an important role in the training of architects. By the 1860s articled clerkships had become the main way of entering the profession. The Tillmans trained both the Milburn brothers and John Hall, who all went on to be awarded the qualification of F.R.I.B.A. and to have significant local practices. The Tillman practice ended with the retirement of John Tillman about 1894.[85]

One of the difficulties in researching local architects is that much of their work was routine and so did not attract public notice. House building, surveying work and alterations are only traceable through the mass of plans in Sanitary Committee records in the Tyne and Wear Archives. Public attention focussed on important buildings like churches and central re-developments and so the newspaper records give a biased picture of the work of a practice. With regard to prestigious

Monkwearmouth Railway Station, 1848, by Thomas Moore.

jobs the local firms found themselves in competition with outsiders, and sometimes were excluded even from competing. Banks liked to use the same architect for their branches throughout the country, so National Provincial had John Gibson design their solid and distinguished classical building in High Street[86] and the Yorkshire Bank (now Midland) used W.H. Brierley of York in 1905.[87] The North Eastern Railway found it worthwhile to maintain an architects department and so William Bell designed Sunderland's new station in 1879.[88] To some extent this trend was balanced by a tendency for locally-based companies to use local architectural firms as for example the number of Co-operative Society shops designed by W. & T.R. Milburn. And local architects certainly expected the local council to look favourably on local talent when planning new buildings as they were increasingly doing.

ARCHITECTURAL COMPETITIONS

The emergence of councils and other public bodies as the providers of buildings led to great problems as to the proper way of selecting architects to fulfil commissions. As expenders of public money they had to be seen to be getting good value for that money and to be free of favouritism. For contractors the accepted mechanism was to invite tenders. For designs they favoured architectural competitions. In theory these gave the client a range of alternative designs from which to choose and they gave the architect an equal chance, under strict rules of anonymity, to win the commission on merit. In practice they were fraught with difficulties and the pages of the professional journals are full of complaints about competitions in general and accounts of the unfairness of particular ones.[89] Several competitions were held in Sunderland. The

most important, and least well managed, was that for the Town Hall, which is more fully described elsewhere (see picture inset). More difficulties arose with the School Board Competition for James Williams Street School. Professional architects were outraged that G.A. Middlemiss, whom they described disparagingly as an auctioneer, won the competition over fully trained practitioners with experience of school design. When Middlemiss was engaged to build the next four Board Schools without further competition they could see no explanation other than personal connections. This was especially so because there was no qualified assessor to advise the Board members on their decision. It was assumed that such Boards were easily swayed by pretty perspective drawings and unrealistic costings. In fact Middlemiss produced a perfectly workable design for a very inconvenient site and actually developed a unique ventilation system for the classrooms.[90] Local architects were more unhappy about the way in which outside architects tended to take important commissions. Competitions were a way for young architects to get work and therefore become known. Indeed some established firms refused to compete, claiming that much design work would be done with no guarantee of payment. So the Orphanage Buildings competition was won by Childs and Lucas in 1858. As they were based in London Thomas Moore effectively took control of the erection of the building.[91] Harrison's Buildings, the first council housing in the town, were put to competition and the unknown London partnership of Perry and Angell won the dubious advantage of enduring protracted disputes with the Council before the buildings were opened in 1904.[92] Some competitions went more smoothly like that for Sunderland Lunatic Asylum won in 1892 by G.T. Hine who

Sunderland Railway Station, 1879, by William Bell.

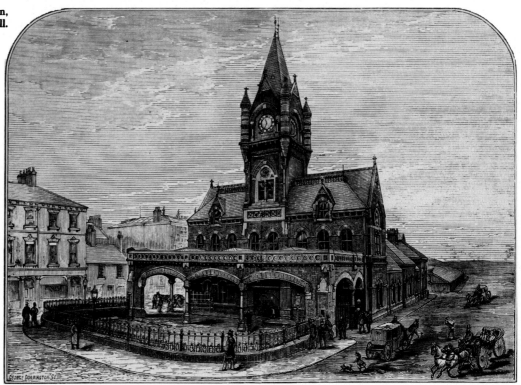

was the leading national specialist in this particular field.[93] Indeed local architects could be successful as when Joseph Shields won the premium for the new Infirmary at the Workhouse for the Board of Guardians in 1893. In the event he died before building commenced and the Milburns became responsible for the building that was opened in 1902.[94] The significance of these competitions was partly that they made architectural decisions issues of public concern and debate, since exhibitions were often held of short-listed designs, and partly that architects who normally would have had no contact with the town were able to contribute to the pattern of building within it. Except where entry was limited to local architects, they were generally not well regarded by local firms who had few opportunities to design and build on a grand scale and who resented losing some of those opportunities. Few of the chosen designs were by architects of significance, and few of the buildings were better than might have been achieved by direct commission.

FRANK CAWS AND THE MILBURNS

Two Sunderland-based firms of architects active in the last years of the nineteenth century deserve more than passing mention. They represent the two polarities of the profession: the eccentric individual, and the highly professional team with a large and significant practice. The eccentric was Frank Caws (1846-1905) who was the town's own local "rogue architect".[95] Born in the Isle of Wight and trained there, he came to Sunderland via Wolverhampton and Darlington (where he worked for the North Eastern Railway) as manager for Joseph Potts and Son in 1867. He began his own practice in 1870[96] and after his death his son continued in partnership with William Steel. He was more than an architect — "artist, scientist, poet, guide, philosopher and friend".[97] At his death his work with the Y.M.C.A., the Waifs' Rescue Agency, and with several churches was much better known than his buildings. Yet he was an idiosyncratic designer with strong preferences in terms of style and building materials. His surviving buildings are few but striking. The Elephant Tea Rooms of 1873-7 in Fawcett Street represent his powerful style precisely. Basically Gothic, with a flamboyant use of polychrome effects in brick, terracotta and faience, it has Eastern details like the Elephant gargoyles and the pagoda-like projections in the roof line to reflect its function as a tea room. Caws called it "Hindoo Gothic" which is as eclectic as is possible to be.[98] Amazingly a drawing exists in his sketch book of a Bazaar in similar style running down Fawcett Street to St. Thomas Street with a central Eastern-style dome to crown the whole bulding. If built it would have given Sunderland the most extraordinary main street in the country. Only slightly less striking are two linked buildings in bright red terracotta, also in Fawcett Street from about 1890. Again they stand out from the rest of the

street by their whole-hearted commitment to a mass of decoration in a loud colour scheme.[99] Much of Caws' output was shops in the town centre which have subsequently been replaced,[100] but he also designed the Y.M.C.A. Building in Borough Road in 1884,[101] as well as houses and schools, and what must have been a bizarre little chapel in Ballast Hills in the Norman style with a doorway decorated with elaborate zigzag design.[102] As an engineer Caws proposed a bridge at Southwick long before it was achieved,[103] designed construction sheds for Swan Hunters on the Tyne[104] and a pier at Sea View on the Isle of Wight, using the suspension principle.[105] Probably a little of Frank Caws goes a long way, but his buildings gave a zest to Sunderland's architecture that few of his contemporaries could match. Indeed Corder in his *Family Pedigrees* records the baleful judgement; "Caws and effect".[106]

A very different firm of architects, but one which was also significant was that of W. and T.R. Milburn. William Milburn (1858-1935) and his brother Thomas Ridley Milburn (1862-1943) formed their joint partnership in 1897 after both had practised independently for a time. Born into a local seafaring family they were trained by J. & T. Tillman, and Thomas had a period with Liverpool Corporation while William practised in Sunderland. Each became F.R.I.B.A. and two of William's sons, William and Stanley Wayman, came into the practice which still continues in the town though without family involvement. The firm came to dominate the architectural scene in the years before 1914 with a long list of commissions both substantial and routine. Among their more significant work is the exuberant Langham Tower already mentioned[107] and a group of public buildings: Police Courts and Police Station,[108] the Fire Station[109] and the Sunderland and South Shields Water Company Offices[110] which were all opened in the same year 1907. They show a confident handling of styles derived from the classical model though with more baroque detail as was favoured by the Edwardians. The Children's Hospital[111] of 1912 may reflect the special interest in hospital design of William jr. who had just joined the firm. Subsequently the Milburns were involved with several important hospital designs. Thornhill United Methodist Free Church of 1902 is surprisingly their only major church and it shows the last phases of the Gothic revival.[112] All these designs are competent if not very exciting, and when combined with a mass of work in estate design, shops, schools and cinemas they show how the firm led the profession. In 1907 the Sunderland Empire built to their design was opened.[113] They had acted as supervising architects on the Empire, South Shields, which had been designed by Frank Matcham who was the outstanding theatre architect of the period.[114] The incorporation of the Sunderland Theatre into the Moss Empires chain gave the Milburns an opportunity to build theatres throughout the country. These included buildings at Southampton, Cardiff, Birmingham and the Dominion Theatre in

Sunderland Town Hall

Compared with many towns Sunderland was very late in providing itself with a town hall to house its councillors and officials with dignity. Council meetings had been held since 1835 in the Exchange Building, which had been built by the rival Improvement Commissioners, and the East Cross Street magistrates court, which fell far short of the imposing facilities that other councils enjoyed. By 1870 the pressure to remedy this situation was increasing and for about 20 years the matter was debated and actions were taken in a way that did little to enhance the reputation of the Corporation or the town. In terms of public debate and dissatisfaction, only the decision to demolish the Town Hall in 1971 matched the decision to build it.

The first definite proposal to have been traced came from the architect Joseph Potts in 1868. He suggested developing the Fawcett Street site back to Union Street (the Railway Station was not yet built), for the erection of a council chamber, administrative offices, concert hall, library, museum and police courts. This centralised facility would have been paid for by renting out accommodation to the Post Office, the Inland Revenue and to 11 shops. The cost was estimated at £45,000. The Corporation declined to pursue the idea, largely because of the Victoria Hall scheme that was being undertaken privately and which would have overlapped some of the facilities. An imaginative opportunity was lost and the Corporation was to embark on a decade of travail in order to achieve less for greater cost to the ratepayers.

In 1873 the Council decided to hold an architectural competition for a Town Hall to cost no more than £20,000. Such a competition was the fashionable way to resolve the problems of public commissions, but competitions require an effective judge to decide the winners and a clear brief to competitors to avoid disputes over the rules. No assessor was appointed and the brief offered a choice of two sites at the north end of Mowbray Park. From this lack of forethought came the difficulties. Thirty designs were submitted, few from established designers, and they were exhibited in April 1874. Two sets of premiums were awarded, with the L-shaped site winner being John Johnstone of Newcastle and the Oblong site winner, Edward Godwin of London. Not only did the Corporation have two winners, but neither of them was the design they liked best.

Their favoured design was by Frank Caws who had just started practice in Sunderland. He submitted three designs for the two sites and his Gothic design for the L-shaped site was considered the best. However, objections that designs which would exceed £20,000 must be disqualified led to Caws being unplaced. He complained bitterly that he was only technically in error as the extra £2,000 in his estimate was for furnishings. He rightly pointed out that as a young architect trying to make his way in his profession a competition victory would have established his career. In the event the loss he suffered was less severe than he feared. Alderman Reed felt that building in Mowbray Park was infringing the rights of citizens who had been guaranteed access to their park in perpetuity. His legal proceedings halted progress with the scheme and a second competition in 1875 was abandoned in the middle of the designing period. The final judgment on appeal was that Mowbray Park was dedicated to public use, and as a result a town hall would infringe the trust, but a library, museum or art gallery freely open to the public would not. The Corporation had held a competition for a site it could not use and subsequently built the Museum upon it. A decision in 1877 to commission G. G. Hoskins, who designed the Victoria Hall, to design a town hall came to nothing as did Frank Caws' modification of his original design to be sited opposite the Museum where the YMCA and later Binns Store were to stand.

After several years of effort no progress had been made and the project fell into abeyance for a time. Further discussions about a suitable site continued with the two shrubberies in Sunniside and Fawcett Street being the front

Frank Caws' entry in 1874, in the Classical-Renaissance style. Intended for the Mowbray Park site (where the Library, Museum and Art Gallery were built in 1879). Caws' design combined town hall, museum and library.

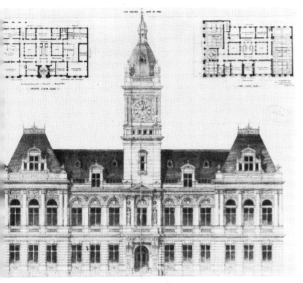

Binyon's drawings, from the *Builder*, show the Italian Renaissance design which won the competition. The Town Hall, built to this design, was opened in 1890.

The main staircase of the Town Hall.

runners; it was not until 1883 that the decision in favour of Fawcett Street allowed that site to be acquired. With the building of the railway station in 1879 the site was now smaller and less suitable than when Joseph Potts suggested it in 1868. A new competition was announced in 1886 with a cost limit of £27,000. The Corporation's own report suggested £55,000 was a more realistic figure. No assessor was at first appointed, leading to complaints from architects in their professional journals. Waterhouse, famous for Manchester Town Hall, was then appointed assessor at a fee of 100 gns, roundly condemned as a waste of money by some councillors. Waterhouse awarded the prize to Brightwen Binyon of Ipswich (who was a regular and normally unsuccessful entrant in competitions) because he felt that the plan met the rules of the competition and was of "unusual merit". The Corporation wisely accepted this judgment and offered the contract to Binyon. Building work could now commence and the new town hall was opened with much ceremony on November 6th 1890.

At that time the building was described as a credit to the town though there was disagreement as to its style. Some called it Henri Quatre with Mansard roofs, others saw it as Italian Renaissance. Its non-Gothic character was determined by Woods' Bank who sold the land and demanded a building to fit in with their own classically designed bank on St. Thomas Street corner. It placed the council chamber away from Fawcett Street and close to the noise of the station, but that was a problem which faced all the designs. The main contract was let to Allisons for £25,270 and, with the architect's fees, the building can be said to have come within the £27,000 limit. However with the cost of land, furnishings, decorations and services the total bill was almost £50,000. This figure was cheap compared with many other schemes, but still seen as needless extravagance by many.

To round off the story briefly, the town hall was found to be inadequate for its function almost at once and a competition for its extension was won in 1904 by Wills and Anderson with a scheme merely to reproduce the existing facade northwards along Fawcett Street. It was never built. The building survived only 80 years, with an increasing number of departments being housed elsewhere in the town before a new civic centre was to replace the town hall proposed on a site that had been suggested in the 1870s, and rejected because it would damage park land amenities. Suddenly the old building became an important Victorian design and a much prized part of the townscape. Alternative uses were proposed and rejected and the building was demolished to give way initially to a return to the open space that had existed in the 19th century. The process of achieving the town hall had been poorly managed and the process of demolishing it caused similar criticism. As the most public of all buildings in Sunderland it was bound to be surrounded by controversy.

London.[115] This work together with the hospitals and the commission to be supervising architects to the North East Coast Exhibition in 1929[116] gave this Sunderland firm a national standing and reputation which also led to both Milburns being elected to the R.I.B.A. Council after World War II. Specialists in theatre architecture do not rate their work highly, arguing that they had "no feel whatsoever for the theatre" and seeing the Sunderland Empire as more satisfactory from without than from within.[117] Nonetheless the Milburns were the only local firm to gain a significant practice outside the town in which they were known.[118]

ST ANDREW'S ROKER

The buildings of Sunderland were largely designed by the architects of Sunderland or of the surrounding region. On only one occasion did an architect of the first rank come to the town to design a building of substance. Edward Schroeder Prior (1852-1932) was one of the leading figures of the Arts and Crafts Movement in architecture and design. His influence through his writings and teaching was substantial, but his architectural output was small. St. Andrew, Roker, completed in 1907 is his finest church and possibly his masterpiece. Commissioned by Sir John Priestman and intended to serve the rapidly growing area being developed along the coast, the church gave Prior the opportunity to carry out his ideas with little control from his client. The great nave space, with the arches springing from low down, and the aisles reduced to narrow walkways, met Priestman's major requirement that everyone must be able to see the altar clearly and provides the most memorable architectural effect. In every respect the church is a model of the Arts and Crafts movement — it was built of local stone using traditional craftsmanship, roofed with stone slates, by a team of craftsmen under the control of an associate architect, Randall Wells, with authority to adapt the design in detail. Within the church the furnishings were provided by the leading figures of the day; tapestry by Burne-Jones, lectern and altar furnishings by Ernest Gimson, the font by Randall Wells, stained glass by Henry Payne, and roof painting by Macdonald Gill. These furnishings combine to off-set the plain simplicity of the building. And yet modern techniques were also employed in the use of reinforced concrete in the structural members, and the complicated heating system. St. Andrew, Roker is exceptional in any context. In Sunderland, tucked away in a quiet suburb, it is the finest building in the town standing equal in significance with the Saxon tower at St. Peter, Monkwearmouth.[119]

CONCLUSION

Sunderland is typical of many towns which experienced rapid growth in the nineteenth century in that it has a legacy of Victorian buildings largely designed by men whose names are now largely unknown and whose reputation barely extended outside their own locality. Much of their work was routine and severely constricted by limited budgets; some of it was frankly poor. Yet it formed the townscape in which the community lived, and with the passage of time familiarity led it to be viewed favourably by the townspeople. In that routine, and sometimes drab, townscape some buildings of real merit and genuine interest were put up and, even though they may now be assailed by changes in the environment against which they are seen, they represent important links with the taste and aspirations of Victorian Sunderland. They should be better known and better appreciated, If the general context of the town's architectural development is more fully understood the more important buildings will be more cherished. The award of listed building status and the designation of conservation areas have done much to protect this heritage, but its best protection is the informed interest of the people who live and work within its ambit.

REFERENCES

1. For a full account of the emergence of the architect in the pre-industrial period see F. Jenkins, *Architect and Patron* (Oxford, 1961) and B. Kaye, *The Development of the Architectural Profession in Britain* (1960). These two volumes continue the story into the present century and provide a useful background to this chapter.

2. R. Hutchins, *Sunderland Parish Church, A Short History* (Sunderland, 1982) p.6. This attribution is not fully accepted and Etty's contribution may only have been as a craftsman carpenter. Etty did design Holy Trinity, Leeds (1722-27) and worked for Vanbrugh on Castle Howard and at Seaton Delaval from c.1719. See D. Lindstrum, *West Yorkshire Architects and Architecture*, (1978), pp.26-7 and H. Colvin, *Biographical Dictionary of British Architects, 1600-1840*, (1978) p.301.

3. Although Holy Trinity is an important example of an early Georgian church it has experienced several alterations since 1719. Apse added 1735, interior and roof re-modelled 1803 by Thomas Wilson, new galleries added 1842, and a restoration in 1887 by C. Hodgson Fowler that re-ordered the east end. See N. Pevsner & E. Williamson, *The Buildings of England; Co. Durham* (Harmondsworth, 2nd ed., 1983) p.450; S.H., Sept. 9 1842, p.3; SDE, Oct. 31 1887, p.3.

4. Fordyce ii, p.427. This attribution is in doubt and may only mean that Thornhill paid for designs to be made.

5. Corder M.S.S., vol 29.

6. Fordyce, *op.cit.*, p.474.

7. See Chapter 6 above.

8. Directories give the following numbers of builders: Pigot, 1822-3, Pigot, 1834-15, Ward, 1857-54, Ward, 1900-66.

9. See Note 1 above.

10. Obituary, John Dobson, *Building News* 12, January 13, 1865, p.25.

11. W.C. Mitchell, *History of St. John's Lodge No. 80 Sunderland 1761-1906* (Sunderland, 1906) p.85. J.G. James, 'Thomas Wilson's Cast-Iron Bridges, 1800-1810'. *Trans. Newcomen Society*, 50 (1978-79) pp.55-72.

12. *Parson & White's Directory*, 1827, p.357.

13. Garbutt, pp.255-6.

14. J. Black, *Presbyterianism in Sunderland and the North* (1876) p.10.

15. Corder M.S.S., Vol. 6, pp.423-4.

16. Information from Census 1841 and 1851, and Obituaries, *SDE*, Sept. 27 1878, p.3 and Dec. 24 1890, p.3.

17. *Northern Times*, April 10, 1840, p.1.

18. R. Hyslop, 'The Fawcett Estate', *Antiq. Sund.* xix, p.38 Corder M.S.S., Vol. 4, p.343-45.

19. *SH*, Nov. 25 1837, p.3.

20. Census, 1881. Obituary, *SDE*, Mar. 24 1885, p.4.

21. Obituary, T. Moore, *ST*, August 28, 1869.

22. See *SE*, Dec. 27 1972, p.2. Obituary, T.A. Moore, *Builder* 61, Nov. 28 1891. p.408.

23. For a fuller account of the national debate see R. Dixon and S. Muthesius, *Victorian Architecture* (1978): R. Furneaux Jordan, *Victorian Architecture* (Harmondsworth, 1966).

24. G.E. Milburn, 'Wesleyanism in Sunderland in the later 18th and the early 19th Centuries', *Antiq. Sund.* xxvi, pp.95-6. Possibly by Bartholomew Dowell.

25. Fordyce, *op.cit.*, ii. pp.447-8.

26. W. Robinson, *The Story of the Royal Infirmary, Sunderland* (Sunderland, 1934) pp.46-7.

27. H.M. Colvin, *op.cit.*, p.112

28. Pevsner & Williamson, *op.cit.*, p.456.

29. See L. Wilkes & G. Dodds, *Tyneside Classical*, (1964); [A. Greg], *The Tyneside Classical Tradition*, (Newcastle, 1980).

30. *SH*, Jan. 25 1850, p.5.

31. *ST*, Dec. 17 1875, p.8.

32. *Builder* 98, June 18 1910. p.696 & plate.

33. *SDE*, Aug. 8 1905, p.4.

34. Fordyce, *op.cit.*, ii, p.322. For a fuller account of

Wyatt and his family see J.M. Robinson, *The Wyatts: An Architectural Dynasty* (Oxford 1979). St. Thomas was demolished after bomb damage.

35. *St. Mary's Jubilee, 1835-1985* (Sunderland 1985).

36. *SH*, Aug. 13, 1836, p.3. See also T. Corfe (ed), *Buildings of Sunderland 1814-1914* (Sunderland, 1983) p.24.

37. By George L. Jackson of Durham, 1843. Pevsner & Williamson, *op.cit.*, p.470.

38. H.G. Bowling, *A Century at Christ Church* (Sunderland, 1964).

39. St. Ignatius, 1889. Pevsner & Williamson, *op.cit.*, p.464. St. Mary, South Hylton, 1880 *Goodhart-Rendel Index*, R.I.B.A. Library, St. Aidan, Grangetown, 1911 *SDE*, Sept. 28, 1911. Obituary *Builder* 99, Dec. 24, 1910 pp.794-5.

40. St. Luke, Pallion, 1874. *Kelly's Directory* (1894) p.359. Ven. Bede, Monkwearmouth, 1870 *ST*, Aug. 6, 1870, p.8. Obituary, *Builder*, 101, Sept. 29, 1911, p.375.

41. St. Matthew, Silksworth, 1871. *ST*, Sept. 3, 1870, p.8. Obituary, *Durham Directory* (1894) pp.67-8.

42. St. Hilda, Westbourne Road, 1893 *Kelly's Directory* [1906] p.431. Obituary, *R.I.B.A. Journal*, 10 Dec. 1902, pp.141-3.

43. *SH*, Mar 17, 1871. *ST*, Ap. 30, 1872. H. Ritson, *The 'Ritual' of St. Mark's* (Sunderland, 1873).

44. *ST*, Feb. 21, 1871, p.8 & Nov. 29, 1872, p.8. Obituary, *SDE*, Dec. 20, 1887, p.3

45. *Building News*, 98, June 10, 1910, pp.794-5. *SDE*. July 6, 1910, p.3 and May 22, 1912, p.5.

46. R.H. Lowe, *Monkwearmouth Church in the 19th Century*, Wearmouth Historical Pamphlet 6, (n.d.). *SE*, May 3, 1935, p.2.

47. *SDE*, Feb. 22, 1887, p.3. G.E. Milburn (ed.) *St. John's, Ashbrooke 1888-1988* (Sunderland 1988). Robert Curwen A.R.I.B.A. is an architect about whom little is known. His major work was the Leys School, Cambridge, also for the Wesleyans.

48. *SDE*, April 20, 1881 & Jan. 26, 1883, p.3.

49. *SDE*, Feb. 6, 1889, p.3. J.B. Wilson A.R.I.B.A. is a little known figure who seemed to concentrate on church designs in Scotland. Crescent Presbyterian Church, Belfast 1887 is a design similar to St. George. See C.E.B. Brett, *Buildings of Belfast 1700-1914* (1967) p.43. *SDE*, April 22, 1892, p.3.

50. *Monthly Chronicle of North Country Lore and Legend* 3, March 1889, pp.110-112.

51. *Kelly's Directory*, 1894, p.361.

52. *Kelly's Directory*, 1894, p.361.

53. *Building News*, 15, Sept. 18, 1868, p.643.

54. *SDE*, April 8, 1878, p.3. N.T. Sinclair *Railways of Sunderland* (Tyne and Wear County Council Museums, 1985) pp.49-51. The engineer for the station was T.E. Harrison for whom see Obituary, *SDE*, Mar 20, 1888, p.3. & Mar. 21, 1888, p.2.

55. See below.

56. Now Carlton House, *Newcastle Weekly News*, Jan. 1, 1887.

57. See above, note 44.

58. Although several of Greener's buildings can be identified he remains a hidden figure about whom more research is needed. *Buildings of Sunderland*, p.15.

59. *Buildings of Sunderland*, pp.12-13. S. Muthesius, *English Terraced House* (New Haven & London, 1982) passim.

60. *SDE*, June 16, 1888, p.4. *Parish of St. Columba 1885-1935* (Sunderland, 1935) pp.4-8. *Buildings and Beliefs*, pp.15-16.

61. *Sunderland Library & Museum Centenary 1879-1979* (Sunderland, 1979). Pevsner & Williamson, *op.cit.*, p.453.

62. T. Corfe, *Langham Tower* (Sunderland Polytechnic Information Officer's Dept., n.d.).

63. Pevsner & Williamson, *op.cit.*, p.461n.

64. A general account of the period is A, Service, *Edwardian Architecture* (London, 1977).

65. Fordyce, ii, p.422, *SH*, Ap. 10, 1840, p.1 and June 18, 1841, p.3.

66. 'Scotch Church', N. Bridge Street, 1827. Demolished c.1890. J. Middlemiss & R. Hyslop, *Short History of Presbyterianism in Sunderland* (Sunderland, 1897) p.46.

67. All Saints, Monkwearmouth, 1849. Fordyce ii, p.443. St. Paul, Hendon, 1852. Demolished c.1960. *SH*, Nov. 19, 1852, p.7.

68. Dated 1856. *SH*, June 20, 1856, p.4.

69. There is an extensive range of references to Dobson's work in L. Wilkes, John Dobson, *Architect and Landscape Gardener* (Newcastle, 1980); A. Greg & T. Faulkener, *John Dobson* (Newcastle, 1987).

70. Thomas Austin died young (1822-1867) leaving Johnson (1832-1892) in charge of the practice. Johnson was considered the best architect in Newcastle by his contemporaries. For Austin see Biographical File in R.I.B.A. Library, London; *Archaeologia Aeliana* 3rd ser. Vol. 10, 1913, p.239-40. For Johnson see Obituary, *Building News*, 62, Ap. 22, 1892, p.584.

71. Gray Schools, Sunderland, 1856-7. Demolished. *SH*, Nov. 21, 1856, p.1. Monkwearmouth Colliery Schools, 1861. *Building News* 7, Sep. 20, 1861, p.771.

72. St. Barnabas, Hendon, 1866-8. Demolished. *SH*, Aug. 10, 1866, p.5. St. Stephen, Ayres Quay, 1868-69. Demolished. *Goodhart-Rendel Index*, R.I.B.A. Library. Restoration and effective rebuilding of St. Peter, Monkwearmouth, 1867-68. *SH*, Dec. 13, 1867, p.7. R. Lowe, *op.cit.*

73. *Planned in 1875 the buildings took five years to erect.* ST, Dec. 17, 1875, p.8; *SDE*, Feb. 15, 1876, p.2; Mar. 3, 1876, p.2; July 15, 1879, p.3.

74. See above, Note 42.

75. Dated 1888. *SDE*, July 28, 1888, p.4. For details of the practice see S. Welsh, *Biographical Notes, Dunn, Hanson & Dunn*, (1974). Typescript in R.I.B.A. Library.

76. Dated 1901. Pevsner & Williamson, *op.cit.*, p.459. See L. Gettings, 'Benjamin Simpson, F.R.I.B.A.', *Northern Architect*, Nos. 12 & 13. April & June 1977.

77. See above.

78. See above.

79. T.C. Ebdy practised briefly in Sunderland, but was more based in Durham during a brief career. *Biographical File*, R.I.B.A. Library. He designed St. Paul, Ryhope, 1870. *Builder* 28, Aug. 20, 1870, p.673.

80. R.D. Giddings, *Thomas Oliver (1791-1857)* unpublished B. Arch. Thesis, Newcastle Univ., (1981). Catalogue to the Victorian in Edwardian Architects exhibition, Laing Art Gallery, Newcastle, (1981), p.11. On Hendon Bathhouse see Letter to *S.H.* Nov. 12, 1852, p.8. Oliver's Newcastle firm also built in Sunderland, especially schools.

81. *SH*, Jan. 25, 1850, p.5.

82. Obituary, *SDE*, Dec. 20, 1887, p.3.

83. See Census 1881.

84. Obituaries, *SDE*, March 24, 1885, p.4; May 13, 1914, p.7.

85. There are no substantial sources about the Tillmans except the record of their buildings and references in other architects' obituaries. The family grave is in Sunderland Cemetery, Ryhope Road, Ward 13.

86. *SDE*, Feb. 2, 1878.

87. *SDE*, June 2, 1902, p.5; May 10, 1905. p.3.

88. *British Architect*, 1, Jan. 9, 1874, pp30 & 32. *SDE*, April 8, 1878, p.3.

89. For the debate about architectural competitions and details of many in Sunderland see R.H. Harper, *Victorian Architectural Competitions: an index to British and Irish competitions in 'The Builder' 1843-1900* (1983).

90. *Building News*, May 9, 1873, pp.525-6; *ST*, Jan. 9, 1874, p.6; *Building News*, 32, Mar. 23, 1877, p.306.

91. *SH*, Aug. 20, 1858, p.5 and Dec. 14, 1860, p.7.

92. G. Patterson, 'Harrison's Buildings — Sunderland's first Council Housing', *Sunderland's History*, 3, 1985, pp.5-33. The architects are given inaccurately as Berry and Angell.

93. *Builder*, 62, Feb. 20, 1892, p.143 and Mar. 5, 1892, p.183.

94. *Building News*, 65, Dec. 8, 1893, p.773. *SDE*, Nov. 27, 1901, p.3 and Sep. 16, 1902, p.3.

95. For an explanation of this term see H.S. Goodhart-Rendel, "Rogue Architects of the Victorian Era", *R.I.B.A. Journal*, 56, April 1949, pp.251-259.

96. *ST*, April 19, 1870, p.1.

97. Rev. Luther W. Caws, *The Unveiled Glory or Sidelights on the Higher Evolution* (1912). Dedication to his brother.

98. The architect for the excellent restoration of this building for William & Glyn's Bank has written a brief account of that process in *Yorkshire Architect*, 78, May/June 1981, pp.17-18. ST July 10, 1874, p.8

99. *SDE*, Sept 24, 1890, p.2.

100. Blacketts, High Street (1880), *SDE*, Dec. 3, 1880, p.3. Cobden Exchange, High Street (1885), *SDE*, July 15, 1885, p.3. Pearman & Corder, Union Street (1880), *SDE*, Aug. 18, 1880. pp.2-3.

101. *SDE*, March 24, 1884, p.3.

102. *SDE*, Oct. 18, 1881. p.4 and May 3, 1882, p.3.

103. *SDE*, Feb. 6, 1879, p.2.

104. Obituary, *SDE*, April 10, 1905, p.3.

105. A. Serle, *Seaview Pier — The Case History*, (Newport, I.O.W., n.d.). pp.8-10. Reference kindly supplied by J. O'Donnell of the Isle of Wight, County Record Office.

106. This section is mainly based on obituaries and other materials collected with Frank Caws' sketchbook now in the possession of his granddaughter. Copies of this material are in Sunderland Museum. Corder M.S.S., Vol. 8, p.163.

107. See above.

108. *SYB*, 1913, p.70. Designed in conjunction with Wills and Anderson of London.

109. *SYB*, 1908, p.112.

110. *SDE*, Aug. 8, 1905, p.4.

111. W.C. Mitchell, *History of Sunderland* (1919; reprinted 1972) p.179.

112. *SYB*, 1903, p.109.

113. *Builder*, 94, June 13, 1908.

114. *Builder*, 76, Feb. 18, 1899. Reference in G. Spain & N. Dromgoole, "Theatre Architects in the British Isles", *Architectural History*, 13, 1970, pp.77-89.

115. *Curtains* (1982) p.214. Catalogue and supporting book to exhibition on theatre architecture by various authors.

116. G. Baglee, *The North East Coast Exhibition*, *Newcastle-upon-Tyne* (Newcastle, 1979).

117. *Curtains, loc.cit.*

118. This section is largely based on obituaries. William Milburn: *R.I.B.A. Journal*, 42, April 27, 1935, p.738. *Builder*, 148, April 5, 1935, p.628. *S.E.*, March 20, 1935, p.3. T.R. Milburn: *R.I.B.A. Journal*, 51, Dec. 1943, p.42. *SE*, Nov. 6, 1943, p.4.

119. The literature on St. Andrew, Roker is extensive. See C. Grillet, 'Edward Prior', in A. Service (ed.), *Edwardian Architecture and its Origins* (1975); D. Hawkes, "St. Andrew's, Roker" in D. Cruickshank, *Timeless Architecture*, (1985); A. Walker, "Sunderland: Historic Building: The Church of St. Andrew", *Northern Architect*, N.S. 17, 1979, pp.19-24.

Between the Wars

The period between the wars is fixed in the minds of most people as 'The Depression', a time of unemployment and poverty that meant ruin for thousands of families. Of course, any account of those two decades must have at its centre the economic decline of the 1920s and the awful collapse of the town's staple industry in the 1930s. Typical reminiscences by people who lived through the period tell a dismal tale of hardship and deprivation. "Unemployment was all you could expect . . ."; ". . . there were no benefits as we know today . . ."; "In the 30s everybody was unemployed . . ."; "Most working-class children went to school and played in their bare feet".[1]

Of course none of these statements is literally true and the image of absolute misery is certainly a false one. There *was* massive unemployment, but the fact is that for all but a short time during the period the majority of people were in work, and that for many of them the 1930s were years of relative prosperity.

In a parliamentary debate in 1938 Lady Astor spoke of a tour of the distressed areas, and said the government had made an astounding difference in four years. "Four years ago Sunderland was the most derelict and depressing spot she had ever seen in her life, but now she would not have known it was the same place."[2] This of course is a politician making a party point, but it was true that Sunderland's situation had changed. Sunderland in the 1920s was not the same as in the years of slump from 1930-35, and the years to 1939 were different again.

Between the wars Sunderland grew and altered, beginning a pattern of change that was not fully worked out until after the second world war. The expansion of the boundaries in 1928 to bring in Southwick, Fulwell, and other areas was one aspect of this, but the building within the boundaries is of greater significance. The development of private and council housing began the transformation of living conditions, accompanied by equally important changes in health, recreation, employment, transport, shopping and many other aspects of life.

RECESSION AND COLLAPSE

The greatest change was in the heart of the town, as the decline, then collapse, of shipbuilding marked a permanent change in the industrial structure. Earlier chapters have shown how Sunderland grew as a port, and as a centre of wooden, then, iron and steel shipbuilding. At the end of the First World War engineering and the building and repairing of ships employed around a third of the adult male population[3] and the collapse of so dominant an industry was a disaster for the town.

Cycles of depression and boom and serious unemployment were always features of the economy of Sunderland, and indeed of the whole north east.[4]

The war, of course, meant maximum production with employment on the Wear for over 17,000 men. Immediately after the end of hostilities the need to replace lost shipping and the high level of world trade kept up the demand. 67 ships of a third of a million tons were built in 16 Wear shipyards in 1920. Indeed, in 1918 a new yard, the EGIS (Ellerman, Gray, Inchcape & Strick), was opened, employing 1,000 men at Pallion.[5]

The boom, however, was brief. British goods, and the British ships which had carried them were both in declining demand, and the great over-capacity in shipbuilding created during the war made its collapse especially dramatic. On the Wear, output dropped from the 67 ships of 1920 to only 16 in 1923, then in 1926 a mere eight ships were launched from five yards. Osborne Graham's at S. Hylton had shut down in 1925; then the Sunderland Shipbuilding Company and John Blumer's closed for ever. Eight yards launched no ships at all in 1926 and unemployment in Sunderland topped 19,000.

By the standards of the period the years 1927-29 must be regarded as relatively prosperous, and in 1929 58 ships of quarter of a million tons were launched. This was still only three-quarters of the total for 1913, and very few people believed that British yards could regain their former eminence in competition with rivals in Europe, Japan, and particularly the USA, which had, during the war, become the leading builder.

The Wear might have survived by retaining a diminished share of a growing market, but this hope was dashed as the world economy collapsed into the worst depression in history in 1929. The total number of ships built on the Wear in the five years to 1935 would have been the output of only six months in a decent year before 1914.

It was not only on the Wear that there was huge over-capacity. In 1930 the shipbuilding industry created the National Shipbuilders Security Limited to buy up and close redundant yards. Its most famous purchase was of Palmer's at Jarrow, but in Sunderland four yards disappeared under this scheme: Osborne Graham's, Robert Thompson's, Swan Hunter's and Gray's. Priestman's, although not bought by NSS, closed in 1933 and did not re-open until halfway through the Second World War. By 1939 only eight of the 16 yards of 1918 were still open.

In the 1930s the marine engineering industry suffered along with shipbuilding, although only MacColl and Pollock of Wreath Quay closed (in 1935). The response of other firms to the depression was amalgamation and between 1938 and 1940 George Clark's, NE Marine Engineering, the Scotia Engine Works and John Dickinson of Palmer's Hill were merged with Richardson Westgarth.

The most important of all the engineering firms, William Doxford's, became part of a combine with yards on the Clyde and at Belfast. It was bought by the Northumberland Shipbuilding Company, a subsidiary of the London finance group Sterline, which was involved in a spectacular collapse in 1924. Doxford's closed in September of that year and did not re-open until 1927. However, amalgamation and rationalisation could do very little to counter the effect of world-wide depression. Doxford's completed the outfitting of eight vessels in 1930, two in 1931, none at all in 1932 and only two more in the next four years.[6]

The substantial rise in shipping output in 1937 was largely due to the introduction of the British Shipping (Assistance) Act of 1935. This provided government loans at a low rate of interest for shipping firms provided they scrapped two tons of shipping for every ton which they built. Wearside benefitted more than most centres from this, since it was exclusively concerned with merchant shipping. Of the 50 ships built under the scheme 24 were constructed on the river. However, as the amount of tonnage available to be scrapped declined the underlying problems re-asserted themselves.

By the end of 1938 the shipbuilding industry was again in deep trouble. The carry-over from the scrap-and-build schemes meant that the tonnage launched in 1938 was the highest since the collapse of 1930 (35 ships, 168,898 tons) but at a launch in December Major R. N. Thompson pointed out that four of the Wear yards were without work and four of them were 'on starvation level'.

> If, he continued, shipowners cannot earn enough money to pay for the replacement of ships and if, as I contend, the wages of the workmen should not be reduced, then the problem has passed out of the hands of the shipbuilder, and has become a national problem in which the assistance of the State is immediately required.[7]

Three months later the government finally accepted the industry's arguments about subsidised competition and introduced its own subsidies for merchant shipping and a £10 million loan scheme to encourage owners to build new ships in British yards. The results, with 40 orders within three weeks of the announcement[8] and the return of thousands of men to work, made their own condemnation of the government's policy throughout the worst years of the depression of refusing to create employment by spending money.

UNEMPLOYMENT

The world economic collapse after 1929 hit all of Britain, but its most devastating effects were on the areas most reliant on the staple industries of the Victorian economy. New industries, freed from the coalfields by the development of electrical power, went to the midlands and the south. Wearside could well claim to be the hardest-hit area in the country, with 11.794 shipbuilders idle, and only 2,375 at work, an unemployment rate of 74.9 per cent.[9] By 1934 the industry had practically come to a standstill.

The census of 1931 allows a more detailed analysis than the usual bald figures of numbers unemployed issued by the Ministry of Labour. The population was classified by sex, industry, employment, and (an innovation) by unemployment.

While the overall level was appallingly high, it is clear that the core of the problem was in shipbuilding and marine engineering. Total male unemployment stood at 36.6 per cent, but without shipbuilding and the metal trades it fell to 20.7 per cent. They provided one third of the town's male employment, but about two-thirds of the unemployment, and a large amount of the unemployment in the service sectors, especially the retail trade, was the result of the lack of purchasing power among those unemployed in the town's staple industries.

The destruction of the town's economic base meant disaster for many of Sunderland's citizens but it is difficult to be accurate about the total number of unemployed in the town. Almost every published figure understates the problem, particularly after 1931 when the government ceased to count many people who were judged to have little chance of ever finding employment again. As always, women were most seriously undercounted; most were not entitled to benefit and anyway had little hope of finding a job, so they did not bother to register and did not appear in the statistics.

However, the course of the depression, although not its full extent, can be seen in the figures for registered unemployment published in the *Ministry of Labour Gazette*. The record numbers of almost 19,000 at the worst point of the 1920s (in 1926) gave way to the relatively moderate levels of 1927-30, so that in February 1930 there were 11,339 registered at the town's three labour exchanges at Sunderland, Pallion and Southwick. In October there were 18,960; by May 1931 24,163; by November 1931 24,965; by May 1932 27,322. Nationally the peak of unemployment was reached in January 1933, with 2.9 million, or 22 per cent of the population registered. Sunderland peaked over a year later, with officially 29,071, in reality over half the working population, unemployed. By 1935 national unemployment had dropped by a third, Sunderland's by less than a quarter, and even that slow recovery ground to a halt in 1937. At the outbreak of war a quarter of Sunderland's workers were still unemployed.

Observers from outside the region had no illusions about the possibility of a quick return to a high level of employment in the north east's basic industries. The Special Areas Commissioner's suggestion that the only hope for Sunderland was the introduction of a car factory must have been more of a wish than a hope, since the north east got only 900 out of

Public Assistance Committee Office, Church Street (a former eighteenth century merchant's house).

83,250 new factory jobs in 1932/3. The region was unattractive to potential employers, he said, with a reputation for high rates, difficult trade unions, socialist local government, an atmosphere of decline and a remoteness from markets.[10] By 1939 the only new industries in Sunderland were in four small factories on the new Pallion estate.

MIGRATION

In a series of articles on the problems of County Durham a *Times* special correspondent saw little hope of improvement by bringing in new industry and stressed the need for migration.[11] That a large-scale migration did take place is shown by changes in population, for although the birth rate was always greater than the death rate the population of Sunderland fell from 185,903 in 1931 to 182,400 in 1938, a decrease of 1.9 per cent. (The population of Newcastle rose by 1.9 per cent in the same period, while England's rose by 3.7 per cent.) Yet for many the major opportunities for migration had passed by the time the depression hit bottom. There was a substantial movement in the late 1920s but as the crisis affected the whole country migration practically ceased in 1930 and emigration ended as the receiving countries were themselves hit by unemployment. By 1934 the outlook was so bad that the *Times* correspondent could say that

> far the most promising opportunity at the present time of gradually reducing the surplus population of Durham is by enabling and encouraging girls to go away into service.

Official and private agencies found jobs for over 7,000 Durham girls in the south of England, almost all in domestic service.

However, many quickly returned home. As one observer noted, "the homing instinct still remains with them very strong, as many mistresses engaging Durham maids have no doubt discovered".[12] Much of the scornful comment on such girls betrays a complete lack of understanding of how a young north-eastern girl must have felt hundreds of miles from family or friends in the alien atmosphere of the houses of the rich in the nation's capital.

If travelling south to go into service was a frightening experience, how much more so must emigration have been? There were many schemes to train young people for life abroad — as always, the girls for service, the boys and men mainly for work on the land. However, in 1929 the *Echo* reported that the response to a Boy Scouts' emigration scheme had been practically nil:

> South country ladies are visiting the various centres of the county where unemployment is most pronounced and they are disappointed at the attitude of the young people and their parents.[13]

While the motives of the sponsors of such schemes were no doubt humanitarian and worthy, they showed a lack of understanding of the feelings of parents who were being asked to see their children as problems to be exported. There was nothing 'unaccountable' about the lack of success of the schemes. Family ties were not completely destroyed by depression.

THE DOLE

Yet the depression was a catastrophe that brought deep suffering to many thousands, blighting hopes and wrecking lives. The most obvious effects were those of living in grinding poverty, but the deprivation was also of prospects — of apprenticeships missed, of scholarships lost because of lack of money, or (particularly in the case of girls) of family rejection of education in favour of the few shillings earnings the girl's employment meant. What long term unemployment meant in terms of mental strain, embitterment and destruction of personality and relationships cannot be measured.

To those who lived through it, the system of unemployment relief seemed to have been designed to torment and humiliate the recipients.

The popular memory is of the Means Test, and the favourite images that survive are those of being told to sell the sideboard before qualifying for benefit, of parish boots with holes punched in the ankles to prevent their being pawned, and of daughters having to support parents with their meagre earnings. Almost equally popular is the memory of evading the authorities; of young people with fictitious addresses to avoid having their incomes taken into account when their fathers' relief was assessed, of passing possessions to neighbours via the back door while the 'Means Test Man' was at the front, and of little schemes to earn a few unofficial shillings.

The means of support available to the unemployed varied over the period. In 1920 unemployment insurance was extended to cover virtually all workers earning under £5 per week, except civil servants, agricultural workers and domestic servants. The intention was to cover people against short-term unemployment, for up to six months, but in November 1921 allowances for dependants were introduced, which meant that a payment intended to provide short-term relief became an amount on which a family was assumed to be able to subsist while unemployment lasted.

In 1931 the National Government's economy measures included a ten per cent cut in unemployment benefit and the imposition of a means test for those who had received the 26 weeks unemployment benefit to which their contributions entitled them. From being claimants as of right, they became applicants to be considered. The payments were made from central government funds, but the examination was made by the local Public Assistance Committee, the successors to the pre-1930 Poor Law Guardians — 'the parish'.

The bitterness brought about by the introduction of the means test was not simply because it meant investigation into personal circumstances. It was hated because of manner in which it was carried out, the motives behind it, and for its associations with forced labour, humiliation and the workhouse. The 1931 cut, combined with the PAC's stringent means test meant, for example, that the payment to a man and wife with two children under 16 fell from 30/- (£1.50) to 27/3d (£1.36). If, however, a child under 20 was working, everything earned over 12/6 a week for a son, and 10/9 a week for a daughter, was deducted from the father's dole. Although the ten per cent cut was restored in 1932 the family means test remained.

Those receiving these extended benefits, if the PAC allowed them, at least got the same rate as those on unemployment benefit. Those who had been in uninsured occupations, or had been self-employed, had to seek relief from the Poor Law Guardians. They went 'on the parish', where the payments came out of the local rates. The means test had always operated here and the amounts paid could be 5/- (25p) less per family than unemployment benefit, and before 1932 part of the relief might come in the form of vouchers exchangeable only for certain goods at specified shops.

The rates paid, the methods used and the allowances made by the PAC were all highly contentious political issues. In Silksworth during the 1926 miners' strike there was much argument over the parish relief given to miners' families by Guardians who were themselves striking miners.[14] When the Sunderland Guardians became the PAC in 1929, the Labour members kept up a running battle to raise the allowances and the rates paid to the unemployed, but were regularly defeated by the Moderate majority.[15] ('Moderate' was the label used by conservative and liberal anti-socialists in local elections.) The only concessions came not from the Moderates but from government. Worried about disincentives to seeking work, it instructed that the first 10/- (50p) of the earnings of members of a family should be disregarded, as well as the amount of benefit they would have received, when assessing the head of household's benefit.[16]

In November 1934 the Labour Party for the first time achieved a majority on the PAC and the change in attitude was immediate. While the registered and formerly insured unemployed were taken over by a new government-financed body, the Unemployed Assistance Board, the Labour PAC set about raising the payments to those 'on the parish'.

Some idea of the issues and attitudes of the time can be found in the response of the PAC's deposed Moderate chairman, Alderman George Lawson. At the AGM of the Sunderland Property Owners' Association (President, Sir Walter Raine, the town's Conservative MP) Ald. Lawson made a speech which brought the headline 'Socialist Orgy of Extravagance'[17]. He denounced the raising of the rate for a couple from 20/- (£1.00) to 26/- (£1.30) and other increases to widows and pensioners, and the automatic granting of the maximum so that many, he claimed, were getting more than they could have earned by working. "And," he asked, "how is this extra relief spent? I know of scores of cases where it simply goes for the hire purchase of gramophones, wireless sets and the like."

Before the election he had pointed out that the cost of relief was already £3,900 per week, and that the Labour proposals would raise it by nearly 40 per cent. To prevent such inducements to the electorate, he supported a resolution that people in receipt of poor relief should be deprived of their local government vote, as had been the case before 1918. With such Victorian views prevailing in the group which governed the borough for almost the whole period, it is hardly surprising that one legacy from the depression was the bitterness of those forced to seek the cold charity of 'the parish'.

CONSUMER SPENDING

Paradoxically, this period of the greatest collapse of the economy is at the same time the period when the age of mass consumption really begins. As the old staple industries declined so the new consumer industries grew; as employment in shipbuilding languished, that in retail trade expanded. It was the expanding sales of furnishings for the new houses, the carpets, curtains and wallpapers, which provided what little new employment arrived in the town. In 1932 2/- (10p) per week would buy a new washing machine with attached wringer

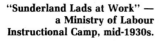

"Sunderland Lads at Work" — a Ministry of Labour Instructional Camp, mid-1930s.

(handpowered) and no new modern house would be complete without a radio, from £5, or 2/6 (12½p) weekly.[18] For those really getting on in the world the new house would also have a garage. Between the wars the national birthrate fell steadily, and in Sunderland it dropped from 30.7 per thousand in 1929 to only 13.7 in 1939. For some, poverty was the stimulus to birth control, but there was a section of the population which was choosing (in the phrase of the time) to have a baby Austin rather than another baby. In 1934 a Morris 8 cost £118 from Turvey's, while Binns Motor Stores in Holmeside had an Austin 7 for just £100. With tax at £6 a year and 45 miles to the gallon the number of cars on the town's streets rose steadily.

Spending on 'luxuries', however, was not confined to those who could aim as high as a motor car. The real revolution was in the manufacture and retailing of cheap luxury goods to a mass market. It was the age of Woolworth's, with everything for 3d and 6d, of Boots the Chemist, of the Fifty Shillings Tailor, of chain stores which spread throughout the country. It was the age, too, of the department store although here the local element remained strong, with Binns, Joplings, Blacketts, and others. Chain and department stores were increasingly outlets for branded goods, factory-packaged and nationally advertised. New goods (gramophone records, custard powder, cosmetics) and new materials (cellophane, bakelite, rayon or 'artificial silk') bought from new retail outlets, showed that not everyone was ruined by the depression.

Such developments meant a major change in the employment pattern. In 1923 shipbuilding and marine engineering were by far the largest employers, with almost a third of the insured population. By 1937 they had only a sixth, and there were actually more people in the distributive trades than in shipbuilding.[19]

The figures demonstrate again how much Sunderland's depression was centred on shipbuilding. In west Durham the position in mining was desperate, but employment in the deep mines near the coast increased, and Sunderland's other old industry, the shipping of coal, was not too badly hit either. Although it could not counterbalance the job losses in shipbuilding, the large growth in the service sector cannot be ignored.

The major reductions were in male trades, while many of the new jobs were for females, all too often only part-time and poorly paid. Yet with all the qualifications the newer industries are indicators of a relative prosperity for at least some of the citizens of Sunderland.

Of course a major contributor to the rise in spending on consumer products and luxuries was the steady fall in the cost of living. The price inflation of the war years continued until 1920, when the working-class cost-of-living index[20] reached its peak then started a steep decline. It rose again from 1933, but in August 1939 the cost of living stood some 35 per cent below the 1920 average, with prices of food, clothing and fuel all well down. The only elements in the cost of living which rose were rent and rates.

Of course, following the wartime boom, wage rates and earnings had fallen too, but they never fell as far as prices, and indeed slowly rose again over the period. The result was that the average wage earner had a rise in real wages (the amount the money would buy) of around 18 per cent. By comparison with the years before and just after the First World War, for those in employment the 1930s could be described as years of improvement.

LEISURE AND PLEASURE

One of the main recipients of the rising real incomes was the entertainment industry. New forms of entertainment grew up and older forms prospered, in spite of the problem of the local economy.

Between the wars the cinema came of age. The first regular moving pictures had been shown in 1901 in the Victoria Hall and there were over 20 picture houses in existence by 1915.[21] Some of these closed within a few years, but were more than compensated for by new openings and by the greatly improved quality. Following the Havelock's installation of sound in 1929 most others were equipped with the new machinery within two years, and between 1932 and 1937 five new cinemas opened, including the Regal and the Ritz, huge picture palaces which between them could transport over 4,000 Sunderland citizens

Left: A Morris 8 for £118 in 1934.

Below: Street advertising off Chester Road in the 1930s.

173

Sport

Since the end of the nineteenth century much of Sunderland's sporting activity has been centred on two sports grounds, with Roker Park becoming nationally known as the home of Sunderland Association Football Club, while Ashbrooke has developed as the centre for amateur sport, notably cricket, rugby, athletics, tennis, bowls, hockey and squash.

The records of sport in Sunderland go back to the eighteenth century, when cock-fighting took place at locations such as the Fighting Cock Inn in Monkwearmouth, bull-baiting at Bishopwearmouth Green, and horse-racing on the Town Moor. Sunderland Races were revived at Tunstall Hope in the 1830s and, after a further break, near Southwick in the 1850s. Between 1898 and 1906 National Hunt meetings took place on Colonel Vaux's land at Grindon.

Rowing and, to a lesser extent, "pedestrianism" (athletics) gained a wide appeal in the 1850s and 60s; rowing was a feature of the Wear Regatta held betwen 1834 and 1914. In the 1870s cycle racing emerged as a popular sport. Cycling had many attractions for leisure as well as racing, and numerous clubs sprang up. The first locally was the Sunderland Cycling Club, established in 1877. Many others followed, and by 1900 there were 40 or 50 clubs in the area.

Cycle racing was the first major spectator sport for the working classes. In the 1890s this was overtaken by football which soon became the town's most popular spectator sport. The workers' weekend half-holiday had developed from the 1870s, and the new railway network made nationwide competition an exciting possibility.

The Football Association came into existence in 1863 and its rules soon spread. In 1879 James Allan and colleagues founded the Sunderland and District Teachers' Association Football Club which two years later became Sunderland AFC and in 1883 a founder member of the Durham Football Association. In 1890 Sunderland joined the Football League, then consisting of 12 clubs, and formed two years earlier. The team, by now professional and backed by industrialists such as the shipowner Robert Thompson, won the Championship four times between 1892 and 1902. It was during this period in 1898 that Sunderland established their ground at Roker Park.

In 1913 Sunderland again became First Division champions, and just failed to achieve the League and Cup double, being beaten by Aston Villa in the FA Cup final. The Club's third period of success came in 1936 when they won their sixth First Division championship and the following

Sunderland AFC's "Team of all the Talents" in 1894. Standing on the far left is Tom Watson, Secretary and Manager from 1889 to 1896. The player with the cap is John Doig an outstanding goalkeeper. In the three seasons after his signing in 1890 the Club only lost one match at home.

Aerial view of Roker Park football ground in 1930. The top stand was erected in 1929, and the bottom (the clock stand) in 1936; both were designed by Archibald Leitch.

year they gained their first FA Cup triumph, beating Preston 3-1.

The Club's fortunes have been more mixed in the years since the Second World War. In 1958 Sunderland was relegated to the Second Division and although promoted in 1964 was subsequently relegated again in 1970. There was a second Cup triumph in 1973. Promotion and relegation followed again in 1976 and 1977 and 1980 and 1986. In 1987 the Club was relegated for the first time to the Third Division, but a year later returned to the Second. Although Sunderland's attendance began to decline after the peak years of 1949-50, when 1,004,483 spectators paid for admission to the games at Roker Park, support for the Club remained strong.

Ashbrooke Sports Ground was acquired in 1887 by the Sunderland Cricket and Rugby Club, newly formed from two previously separate organisations in order to develop the ground. Sunderland Cricket Club originated in 1850 from a union of Bishopwearmouth Cricket Club and Hendon Terrace Cricket Club. The Club had several grounds, including one at Holmeside from 1861-1876, where it developed links with the Rugby Football Club (formed 1873) which led to the amalgamation of 1887.

At Ashbrooke it was always intended that other sports besides cricket and rugby should be played. These included "gymnastic and athletic exercise, lawn tennis and quoits, the physical training and development of the human frame . . ." Bowls, hockey and, in 1960, squash were added to this list.

The various sports sections at Ashbrooke gained some notable successes, as did individual members. Between 1903 and 1912, Sunderland won the Durham Senior League Cricket Championship seven times. Ashbrooke members who won national fame included tennis player Helen Aitchison who was Wimbledon Ladies Double Champion in 1909 and an Olympic Silver Medalist.

The ground was the venue for various sporting championships as well as playing host to international touring teams. Between 1887 and 1962, for instance, nearly every touring side of importance visited Ashbrooke to play cricket against a Durham County side. England rugby union trials were also held there, as were three hockey internationals. The

The Sunderland and Durham County Open Lawn Tennis Championship at Ashbrooke (1929) showing Helen Aitchison, a club member, who won the title five years in succession. In the background is the Diamond Jubilee Pavilion opened in 1899.

Sunderland and Durham County Lawn Tennis Championships were events which attracted national attention. The annual Sunderland police sports which included leading athletes and cyclists drew crowds of over 10,000.

Ashbrooke's role as a major provider for amateur sport has become less important since the local authority developed sports centres from the 1970s. As far back as 1859 the Corporation included swimming or "plunge" baths among the other facilities which had been provided, mainly for public hygiene reasons, at the High Street Public Baths. The pool was rebuilt in 1890 to cater particularly for swimming clubs and schools; it was later described as "the finest bath for swimming in the North". The Corporation opened Swimming Baths in Newcastle Road in 1936 and also provided various playing fields. The major municipal contribution to sporting facilities came with the opening of Crowtree Leisure Centre in 1977. This was one of the country's largest indoor sports and recreation centres and included a leisure pool, ice-rink, indoor bowling green and squash courts. Other indoor sports centres were provided at Hetton, Houghton and at Washington, while the Silksworth Sports and Recreation area developed from 1981 on a former colliery site, included a dry ski-slope, athletics track and a large indoor tennis centre.

The North Eastern Cyclists Meet, photographed outside the Winter Gardens, Sunderland Museum, Easter 1881. The North Eastern Cyclists Meet was an annual gathering of clubs which began in 1878 and lasted till the late 1940s. Twenty-five clubs and 216 cyclists were represented at this early meet.

nightly to a more exotic and luxurious world. The Regal's prices, from 2/- (10p) down to 7d (3p) in the front stalls, were beyond the means of the unemployed, although a contemporary survey found that in Glasgow and Liverpool more than half the unemployed went to the cinema twice a week. The 2d or 3d seats at the Cora at Monkwearmouth were more likely places to find the unemployed, as were the Gaiety in High Street and the Victory in Borough Road which offered grocery prizes for talent nights as well as low admission prices.

The great growth of the cinema was at the expense of the theatre. The Avenue, the Palace, the Royal, and the King's had all gone over to films by 1913, and while a cine-variety policy survived for some time, the cinema part was clearly predominant. Even the Empire went over to films in 1931 before reverting to its variety role in 1933.

The cinema appealed right across the classes, although there was a large amount of physical segregation of audiences by price and location of the cinemas. Football had the same broad appeal although the segregation was by sex. A great majority of the male population of the town could identify with the team and the period between the wars saw Sunderland AFC reach a peak of popularity and success.[22]

Roker Park's main stand was built in 1929, and the Clock Stand was rebuilt in 1936.[23] Until then the theoretical capacity of the ground had been 60,000, but in fact this had been far exceeded in the record attendance of 75,118 in a cup tie against Derby County in March 1933. The very largest attendances were all in cup ties, but derby matches in the league came close, with 58,519 against Newcastle United in 1929 and 59,586 against Middlesborough in 1935.

This last attendance was in the first of the three seasons of the club's greatest success of modern times. In 1934/35 they were runners up, then in the following year won the championship by eight points. In 1936/37 came the greatest triumph of all when Sunderland beat Preston 3-1 at Wembley to win the FA cup for the first time. The heroes of the fans were the Sunderland-born players who scored two of the goals — Bobby Gurney and team captain Raich Carter, who in the previous season's league triumph had scored 31 goals each.

Yet the rewards for those who played in what has often been called the working man's game were hardly large. First team stars could expect a maximum wage of £8 per week in the season with an annual £1 per point bonus and a reduction to £6 per week in the summer. In the reserves or in the lower divisions the wages were close to the £3 or so of the working men who supported the team, with contract conditions more akin to serfdom than to modern employment. For all that, to become a professional footballer remained a dream of escape for many a working class lad.[24]

As crowds rose, the successful football club was in a very prosperous condition. There is, however, a familiar ring to the reports of boardroom quarrels in the season after the Cup triumph, as Sunderland slid towards the relegation zone.

The town's rugby and cricket club was far from prosperous. The Ashbrooke Club's new stand of 1923 was built with timber given by members, and when the roof was added in 1926 the cost of £256 was raised by subscription.[25] By 1935 the membership was below 900, and there was such a shortage of players that the rugby fixtures could not be completed. This was despite the fact that the game itself was in a reasonably flourishing condition, with 6,000 spectators attending the County Durham Diamond Jubilee game in 1936.

Indeed, the gates for these amateur games were quite remarkable, and paralleled in the Durham Senior Cricket League, with, for example, 4,000 turning up in 1921 for a game versus Whitburn. Perhaps the play was brighter then. In a 1926 match, again against Whitburn, 522 runs were scored in only five hours' play.

Cruder excitement was available in the boxing arenas. At the Olympia (on the Regal site), at the Royal between its theatre and cinema lives, and at other smaller venues, champions like Jack Casey made their names, and semi-professionals had their brains scrambled for shillings. The amateur sport flourished too, often associated with muscular Christianity and character building, as for example at St. Mary's or Matlock Street churches and Lambton Street Club.

If numbers at religious worship were declining, the social function that church-based activities performed remained important. Broadly, women's and youth organisations thrived, while the men's participation declined. In 1938 Samuel Storey attended the 40th anniversary of the Men's Bible Class at Thompson Memorial Hall in Monkwearmouth. Although the 200 present was a formidable total by today's standards, it compared with a previous membership of 1,400 and average attendances of 700 in the past.[26]

One flourishing branch of church activity was amateur dramatics, as it was in many other organisations, and the Echo had a regular page of reviews. In December 1938 for example, the public was invited to productions by St John's Methodist Players, Hetton Downs Methodist Church, Sunderland Tramway Players, Sunderland High School Old Girls and the Royalty Players, as well as by the premier amateurs, Sunderland Drama Club, which used the Victoria hall and charged 2/6 (13p) admission to its productions.[27]

Pub and club retained their power over the working class male, in spite of the efforts of the temperance movement, itself an alternative life and leisure style for many in the town.[28] The hole-in-the-wall pubs of the older parts of the town were one of the centres of what was (after drinking) the main male leisure interest — gambling. A Church of England report on the East End in 1896 described gambling as universal, even among children,[29] and little had changed since then. Bookies operated from the back yards of cottages, with their agents in pubs, billiard halls, shipyards and factories. The periodic fines were regarded simply as minor overhead costs of a thriving business.

'Buying a bit of hope' for pennies pulled the punters in, and a prize like the £40 promised by the big pitch and toss school at Trow Rocks in

South Shields was a powerful lure, although, as always, the real winners were the bookies from Shields and Sunderland who operated there.[30] The women's equivalent was altogether more modest. Those playing bingo in the organiser's house, with a deduction of 1d in the shilling for heat and light, could not have envisaged the growth of their pastime into the huge business of half a century later.

The most ambitious leisure plan of the period came to nothing. In 1938 a Tyneside syndicate produced a plan for a quarter-million pound 'Sportsdrome' in Silksworth Lane (just outside the borough). There was to be a speedway stadium, dog track, baseball park and an ice rink that could convert to swimming pool or spectator space for boxing.[31] Although it was never built, the Sportsdrome is further evidence that the poverty of very high unemployment was mirrored by the growing prosperity of the majority who were employed.

Of course, not everyone approved. The leisure habits of the young in particular always find critics among their elders. If the young still sought each other's company by parading up and down Crowtree Road on Sundays, as they had for generations (the Chief Constable's report in 1917 had deplored their raucous behaviour), the new trysting places were the dance halls. The Regal and the Ritz had their counterparts in ballrooms like the Rink, which took its name from the roller-skating arena which occupied the site before. Some saw decadence in the swing music that turned young people 'witless and cabbage like' as they emerged from their stuffy halls 'numbed by dancing and sensual crooning'.[32] Most, however, saw the smart dress and glitter ball as signs of better times and a more pleasurable way of life than earlier generations of Sunderland's people had enjoyed.

PUBLIC HEALTH

Of course, the standard of living must be measured by more than the consumption of goods and services. The state of public health is at least as important a guide, and here again there are marked contrasts by place and social class within the town. The effects of economic depression on public health have always been controversial. The marked differences in birth rates, death rates, infant mortality rates, etc, between north and south usually find governments denying and critics asserting that the figures are directly related to the level of unemployment.

In the period between the wars the controversy was focussed on a letter to the *Times*[33] by Dr G. F. Walker, who lived in Grange Crescent, Sunderland. He claimed that for all the efforts of local authorities and voluntary activity 'there had been a substantial and progressive deterioration in public health', and the government's response was to set up a Ministry of Health Enquiry whose Report was published in April 1935.[34]

The official answer was that Dr Walker was wrong. The investigators spent 17 days in the area, then took Dr Walker's six points and refuted them one by one. Not only was health not worsening with depression, the statistics for the previous decade showed a steady improvement. The general death rate was down, infant mortality was down, deaths from bronchitis, pneumonia and TB were down. Malnutrition was declining and affected a tiny part of the population, while rickets, the disease so closely associated with poverty, was rapidly becoming a rarity.

Only four days before the publication of the Enquiry Report the annual report of the School Medical Officer reinforced the impression of improvement.[35] In 1924 the proportion of children requiring treatment on entering school was 53 per cent and in 1934 it was 16 per cent. The report also confirmed that rickets was becoming a rarity. In 1928 there were 81 cases; in 1934 only 11 cases, out of a school population of 33,000.

The report also announced that a third full-time dentist had been appointed which meant one for each of the three areas of the borough. Yet that item helps put the level of achievement in perspective, since by the Board of Education's recommended level of staffing there should have been twice as many. Such omissions have to be borne in mind as the official accounts of success and improvement are produced. The reality is that at almost any time in the past century it would be possible to show that things were getting better for most people, while at the same time being much worse than they ought to have been for many others.

Of the general tendency to improved health over the period there can be no doubt. Between 1920 and 1939 the birth rate fell from 35 per thousand to 19, the death rate from 16 per thousand to 14. The end is clearly better than the beginning, but this does not mean that the investigators' dismissal of Dr Walker's allegations should be uncritically accepted.

Commenting on the responses to their questionnaire the investigators said "Most of our informants have indicated that any concern they feel is primarily as regards the women. If sacrifice is called for she will usually consider children and husband before herself", they believed, and so "it is in the woman that one would expect any stress of circumstance first to be manifest". Yet when considering the rise in maternal mortality they simply noted for County Durham and Sunderland "a slight rise in each instance".

The investigators ignored the possibility that the 'slight rise' might actually be a trend. The world depression which started in 1929 only began to have serious effects on the level of employment in Sunderland in 1930. The impact of this on such guides to health as maternal mortality rates would come a year later, then continue to be felt while the depression lasted. If, then, the two five-year periods 1926-30 and 1931-35 are considered, very different conclusions might be drawn. Average maternal mortality 1926-30 was 4.01 per thousand births, and from 1931-35 was 5.22, a rise of 30 per cent. Infant mortality in the first period was 93.8 per thousand and in the second 91.4, a fall of only 2.6 per cent which means that for the worst-off sectors there must have been a worsening of their conditions.[36] Equally significantly, the still-birth rate rose from 36.6

BLACK'S · REGAL · THEATRE

The Regal (now Odeon), Holmeside, from the opening souvenir brochure.

to 39.8 per thousand. It seems at least to be arguable that the wives, infants and unborn children of the unemployed were the depression's real victims.

HOUSING

The 1931 census showed Sunderland to be the most overcrowded county borough in England and Wales. Overcrowding meant two or more persons per room, and by that definition one in five of the families of Sunderland was overcrowded. Its only rivals were other north east towns (Hebburn and Jarrow were even worse than Sunderland) with London's crowded east end some way behind. This meant that 53,079 persons, or 30 per cent of Sunderland's population, were living in overcrowded conditions. A major reason was tenemented housing "... There are on average 1.45 families per dwelling and ... only 50 per cent of the families are in undivided occupation of a separate dwelling".[37]

Although Sunderland had for much of the nineteenth century been in the same position, the publicity in the 1930s contributed (along with government legislation) to making the corporation do something. Legislation in the 1920s had subsidised council and private housebuilding, and although grants were cut, new legislation compelled action after 1930. A slum clearance plan to build 3,500 houses in five years from 1933 was begun but was overtaken by the Housing Act of 1935. Its intention was to make overcrowding illegal, and required local authorities to complete a detailed survey by 1st April 1935. Although the corporation had built 1,002 houses and private enterprise 1,719 between 1931 and 1935, the medical officer of health had to report that 8,650 families, one in five of all the families in the town, were still overcrowded.

One surprising fact emerged from the survey. By 1936 there were in the borough 3,913 families living in corporation houses, and no less than one in five of them was overcrowded. This might not be too surprising in the case of East Ward, with council flats such as Harrison's Buildings built before the first world war, but that over a quarter of 734 recently built houses in Southwick should fail the test is more remarkable.

However, it is doubtful whether those who moved into a council house from a room in a tenement off High Street would have felt overcrowded no matter what official definitions told them, since overcrowding was only one aspect of the problem of bad housing. The overcrowding was most likely to be in rooms in houses which were damp, bug-infested and falling apart, either tenemented former dwellings of well-to-do owners in the oldest parts of the town, or jerry-built products of the nineteenth century boom years.

It might be thought that rehousing people from the slums was an unmitigated good, and there is no doubt that great benefits resulted from removal, but caution is required in assessing the results. The Medical Officer of Health surveyed 445 families removed by 1936 to Ford Estate, Marley Potts, Grangetown, Carley Hill and High Southwick, all of them 'greenfield' sites.[38] Travel expenses, hire purchase for furnishings and the increased cost of heating and lighting larger houses were heavy burdens.

The vast majority — 91 per cent — of the tenants were satisfied with the change, but the price was real. A quarter of the families had under 3/- (15p) per head per week to spend on food, and reported that they did not have enough to eat. Among other costs, 60 per cent of those surveyed remarked on the higher price of food in the new neighbourhood. "Missed the ½d and 1d shops", said one.

The rent itself was a substantial increase. The average rent in their previous slum accommodation had been 5/6¾d (28p) while the new rents averaged 9/2½d (48p). The average space was doubled, but each amenity increased the necessity for expenditure. The average income of the families was £2 3s 4d (£2.17) and it is obvious that the cost increases pressed hard upon those below the average.

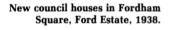

New council houses in Fordham Square, Ford Estate, 1938.

Three quarters of the families rehoused were living on unemployment relief and the survey emphasised again the difference between the way of life of the employed and those without a job. While hundreds struggled along with under 3/- (15p) per head for food, one family had the astonishing sum of 27/1d (£1.36) for each of its five members.

Of course, no such monitoring went on in the thousands of private houses built in the same period. Some notion of the price of property and the cost of buying can be gained from advertisements. In 1938, £395 would have bought a house in Fox Cover Lane, Middle Herrington, £420 one off Sea Road.[39] Alongside the house advertisements were those of building societies. At an interest rate of five per cent, "2/8d (14p) per week repays £100 mortgage". A ten per cent deposit and around 10/- (50p) per week would have bought the houses advertised above, and while the cash deposit was beyond the means of the council tenant, the weekly repayment was little more than the average council house rent. Indeed, buying seems an even better option when compared with the rents for better quality rented accommodation: "well-adapted six roomed house close Roker park 24/- (£1.20) clear; Elmwood Street three rooms, all conveniences, 15/- (75p) per week". The other side of the life is seen in advertisements for one room in Ayres Quay, 5/3d (26p) per week; and two attic rooms in Liddle Terrace, Monkwearmouth, 4/- (20p) per week.

That there were plenty of people in the town with regular employment and sufficient income to satisfy the building societies' need for security is testified to by the large numbers of houses built for private sale in the period. On Durham Road, Queen Alexandra Road, in Seaburn and Fulwell, the pre-war semi-detached and detached houses and bungalows are still there to show that for some the 1930s were years not of deprivation but of improvement.

In Britain as a whole housing completions in 1936 reached the then record level of 370,000, a figure not surpassed till the 1960s, and which compares with the 200,000 of 1980.[40] This in itself was a major contribution to the lessening of unemployment, as was the supply of the household goods and services required by the new occupants. When the housing programme was stopped by the outbreak of war, Sunderland council had built nearly 5,000 dwellings, the Special Housing Association over 2,000 (including the garths on the site of the slums) and private builders as many again. They changed the size and shape of the town, and the contrast between their semi-detached style and the nineteenth century terraced rows is sharp.

MUNICIPAL SERVICES

The great improvements in electrical and motor-vehicle technology did almost as much to transform town life.

For those within its area the Sunderland Corporation Electricity Undertaking could supply any type of equipment for sale or for hire. An electric iron came with the supply to new consumers, and cookers, boilers, water-heaters, kettles etc, could be hired for a small extra sum, or bought on hire purchase. The Sunderland Gas Company was no less eager to sell its fuel and in the mid-1920s its head office and showroom at the corner of Fawcett Street and Borough Road was renovated.[41] Although the town's street lighting was changed over from gas to electricity in the 1920s, many houses were lit by gas until after the second world war.

In 1927 the Corporation Electric Tramways Department could boast a five minute service on most of its routes[42] Private buses, and from 1928, corporation buses served the newer areas, but the re-equipped tram service continued to carry the bulk of the passengers in the crowded central area throughout the 1930s. On trams or buses passengers could travel an average of $1\frac{1}{2}$ miles for 1d, and before 9am a 2d return ticket could be bought which covered any distance and could include one change of vehicle. For those in surrounding areas the motor bus brought about a 'revolution in transport'[43] as the Northern General Co used its "speedy motor saloons fitted with pneumatic tyres" to bring people into the borough.

The combination of the older forms of transport — horse-drawn carts and electric trams — with the new buses and private cars resulted in accidents and serious congestion at various parts of the town. In 1929 the first traffic lights were introduced at Mackie's corner and at the junction of Waterloo Terrace and Holmeside.[44] That year 18 people were killed on the roads, and this rose to 24 in 1939, with 581 seriously injured.

Another aspect of the impact of the motor car can be seen in the six-fold increase in motoring offences over the two decades. The increasing amount of police time this occupied is partially balanced by the equally dramatic fall in some other offences. Arrests for common assault for example fell by 77 per cent, and this may be related to the remarkable drop in arrests for drunkenness. There was a long-term decline from the huge and brutal drunkenness that was such a prominent part of urban life in the nineteenth century, which was well under way by the first world war. There were 1,634 drunkenness offences in Sunderland in 1906, and only 739 in 1913. In 1920 there were 276 pubs or beerhouses in the town (one for every 700 citizens) and 115 off-licences, but by 1939 this had fallen by 18 per cent, and the number of arrests for drunkenness fell from 530 to only 195. For one section of the population shortage of money may have been a reason for falling consumption, and the decline of seafaring may also have been partly responsible. A third factor was certainly the measures taken during the first world war, enforcing afternoon and earlier evening closing, and reducing the strength of beer and spirits.

The figures for arrests for assault tell us only a small portion of the truth about violence. Arrests depend on police being informed, being available, and being willing to arrest. We have no way of measuring the degree of domestic violence, especially against women, where police were (and are) reluctant or legally unable to interfere. Oral evidence suggests that much violence was not only not prosecuted, but that police preferred to turn a blind eye. This included weekend pub-door brawling, but also more serious events. Patrick McLaughlin describes a running battle through the streets around the Johnson Street area, ended by a woman knocking one protagonist unconscious with a flat-iron. There was no sign of the police although the fracas lasted at least two hours and was followed through the streets by most of the neighbourhood.[45]

The number of prosecutions for indictable offences was 271 in 1920-22, and 382 in 1936-38; the corresponding figures for less serious offences were 1,776 and 1,884. The figures are for prosecutions only, They do not indicate the number of offences for which no arrest was made, and we cannot know how many crimes went unreported. With all the qualifications, however, it would seem to be true the period was one of relatively low criminal activity.

The total number of offences was very small, as was the police force which dealt with them. In 1923 a police box system came into use, partly under pressure to cut costs and partly because of the inadequacy of the old station house system. The estimated saving was over £15,000, about 25 per cent of the cost of the police force, some of whom were made redundant.

The total establishment in 1939 was 219, only five more than in 1920, with 180 constables for a population of over 180,000. So carefully was spending controlled that it was later said that Sunderland recruits could be recognised by their ill-fitting or second-hand uniforms.[46]

The corporation was more willing to spend where its outlay was supplemented by government assistance. Construction of the ring road went on almost throughout the period, but a high proportion of the expenditure was concentrated in the later years. From 1934 the Commissioner for Special Areas subsidised around £½m expenditure on sewage schemes, the construction of the sea wall and promenade at Seaburn, the building of the incinerator, and closet conversions in Ryhope and Tunstall.[47] The major expenditure was, however, on hospitals. The Royal Infirmary (which remained private until after the second world war), the General Hospital (taken over from the Poor Law authorities in 1929), Cherry

Knowle and the Infectious Diseases Hospital (Havelock) all had major additions built to accommodate new equipment, staff and patients. Grindon Hall was acquired as a sanatorium, and two new hospitals, the Eye Infirmary in Queen Alexandra Road and the Monkwearmouth Hospital, were built to replace old inadequate buildings. The Commissioner's subsidies even extended to the provision of 550 allotments and 6,000 unemployed people took advantage of free provision of materials and loan of brushes to redecorate their houses.[48]

The major educational building of the period was of the new Bede Collegiate Schools in Durham Road in 1929. Selection was by examination at the age of 11, when some 1,000 pupils were allowed to proceed to fee-paying secondary education. There were free and subsidised places, with a means test to determine the amount contributed by the local authority towards the cost, although at the same examination 160 boys and 160 girls were selected for the Central secondary schools which charged no fee. A third selective route was to the Junior Technical School (in the former St George's Chapel in Villiers Street) but for the remaining 95 per cent of the town's 32,000 pupils the elementary school was the whole of their education, ending at the age of 14.

Many of the teachers for these schools trained at the Teacher Training College for women at Langham Tower. In 1933 the College of Art, too, moved to Ryhope Road into the Backhouse Park building, and the status of Sunderland Technical College was raised by its taking students to external degrees in engineering, science and pharmacy.[49]

POLITICS

Perhaps alongside the false impression that 'everybody' was unemployed goes the idea that Sunderland was politically Labour territory. In fact through all the political realignments taking place nationally, and most noticeably in the peak period of unemployment, Sunderland was completely dominated by Conservatism. In eight parliamentary contests between the wars, the Labour Party won only once, and not until November 1935 did it secure a majority on the Council, only to lose it again three years later.

The electoral system changed substantially

Private housing, Durham Road and Thornholme Road.

between the wars. Before the First World War only about 60 per cent of men had had the vote, and no women. From 1918 all men over twentyone and most women over thirty were eligible and from 1928 all women over twentyone could vote. Fears or hopes that the new electorate would rally to the re-organised Labour Party were equally confounded. Sunderland was a two-member constituency, and in the 1918 election returned its sitting member, Sir Hamar Greenwood, as a Coalition Liberal, allied with the local Conservative ship-owner, R. M. Hudson.[50] The three-cornered contests in the general elections of 1922, 1923 and 1924 put local Conservative businessmen Walter Raine and Luke Thompson (the former knighted in 1927, the latter in 1934) at the top of the poll, ending a Liberal supremacy which had begun in the middle of the nineteenth century. The divided Liberal party shrank, then disappeared in 1931, when its voters went over en masse to the Conservatives.

The Labour party had succeeded early in Sunderland, returning Thomas Summerbell in 1906 and 1910 and Frank Goldstone in the second election in 1910, both in alliance with the Liberals against the Conservatives. As a separate party in the period between the wars Labour found life much more difficult. Chronically short of money, riven by internal disputes, with constant problems in finding good candidates willing to fight such an un-promising seat, only in 1929 did its imported representatives defeat the strong local businessmen Conservatives. Dr Marian Phillips, the party's national Women's Officer, and Alf Smith, an official of the Municipal & General Workers' Union, won this first election fought under universal adult suffrage, which raised the electorate from 78,361 to 101,875.

Smith died in 1931 and in March Luke Thompson won the seat back for the Conserva-tives. In the general election in November he was joined by Samuel Storey, the proprietor of the *Echo*, crushing the Labour Party with an almost 2 to 1 majority in the aftermath of the Labour government's collapse. In 1935 Thompson resigned and Storey was joined by Stephen Furness, the barrister son of the MP for Hartlepool, who stood as a National Liberal in alliance with the Conservative.

The Labour Party once again imported candidates. Leah Manning was the left-wing general secretary of the National Union of Teachers, while George Catlin (father of Shirley Williams of the SDP) was Professor of Political Science at London University. The Liberals did not stand and although their candidate of 1931, Dr Betty Morgan, urged Liberals to vote Labour the voting figures make it clear that they ignored her advice.

More radical politicians fared even worse. Lights, bunting, street parties and patriotic fervour marked the celebration of King George's Jubilee in 1935, and the local communist who tried to hold a street corner meeting in the east end found himself marched out of the area, unwillingly draped in a Union Jack, his *Daily Workers* shredded.[51]

Yet it was in the same month as defeat in the general election that Labour won control of the council with Tom Summerbell, son of the town's first Labour MP, as mayor. The party won only one extra seat which gave them a majority of councillors, and the ability to replace the Moderate aldermen with their own nominees. That Labour could win locally while Conservatives held the parliamentary seats was at least in part due to the greater size of the parliamentary constituency and its inclu-sion of suburban areas and more middle class voters.

The result was an administration more willing to spend money to try to diminish the fearsome unemployment rate and to mitigate its effects (as with the PAC described above). The Labour Party's hold was always tenuous, and property owners' complaints about spend-ing were given voice in the council chamber and space in the *Echo*. When Labour lost a single seat and thus control of the council in 1938 the *Echo* rejoiced that power was now "in the hands of businessmen who have pledged themselves to the utmost economy". It pro-fessed to believe that the Moderate mix of Conservative and Liberal businessmen was somehow non-political, while Labour stood for 'political domination'.[52]

The constant cry of 'economy' was one reason why the pace of change and improvement in Sunderland was so slow. Even when more enlightened Conservatives saw that spending was actually justified as invest-ment or job creating or socially improving, vic-tory often went to the immoderate econo-misers. In 1931 Councillor E. Embleton told the Rent and Ratepayers' Association of the successful fight he had led against the 'faddists' who wanted to introduce nursery schools. Lady Astor opened Sunderland's first nursery school three years later, and although she returned in 1938 to open an extension, the grant from the local authority was only a small part of the school's income. Similarly, Alderman Swan in 1931 fought a rearguard action against the scheme to develop Roker and Seaburn on the grounds that Sunderland was a town of industry, not of pleasure.

In such matters the council had to be pushed hard by individuals and adverse publicity, as, for example, when a League of Nations report on international comparisons of infant mortality[53] put the borough among the worst cases. The reluctance to act and spend was perhaps less when the investment was obviously industrial, as with the new deep water quay. The scheme originated in 1927 and was formally opened in 1934. While a warm approval might be appropriate to the creation of modern facilities on the site of two centuries' decay, the *Echo*'s headline — 'Era of Prosperity' — was perhaps overstating the potential.[54]

Yet although the pace of change was slower than it could have been, and the scale of change was less than it might have been, Sunderland was a substantially altered town by 1939. Physically it had grown, and the map shows a ring of new developments surrounding the town of 1918. However, the severity of Sunderland's problems can be seen in the fact that in June 1939 there were 12,052 unemployed in receipt of poor relief, a rate of

Prospects of property ownership for those in work.

661 per 10,000.[55] In a league table of 47 large towns in England & Wales this rate put Sunderland at the bottom, 15 per cent worse than the town above it, and over six times as bad as the towns at the top of the league. For many people the 1930s were years of steady improvement, but to the long term unemployed they brought little but suffering and waste of human lives.

REFERENCES

1. For reminiscent accounts see *Living between the Wars*, a series of oral history interviews by Durham University Adult Education Department (1984 to 1987), and *Them were the Days*, Community Arts Project, Sunderland (1985). All such accounts must, however, be treated with caution.

2. *SE* 29th November 1938.

3. D. Rowe 'Occupations in Northumberland & Durham', *Northern History*, Vol. VIII (1973).

4. D. Dougan *History of North Eastern Shipbuilding* (1968) p. 221-2. See also N. McCord *The North East — the region's development* (1974) for an overall view.

5. W. Smith & E. Holden, *Where Ships are Born* (2nd ed. 1953) covers the whole history of shipbuilding on the Wear, although in an uncritical fashion. The following material is based on their figures.

6. Doxford outfitting records, Sunderland Antiquarian Society Collection.

7. *SE* 8th Dec. 1938.

8. Smith & Holden, p. 123.

9. 1931 Census Report, Table C, p. 340. The census district includes areas outside the Borough, so figures are not comparable with later figures produced by Labour Exchanges.

10. Special Areas Commissioners Report PP 1933/4 XIII p. 379.

11. *Places without a future* by a Special Correspondent, reprinted from *The Times* as a pamphlet 1934. The special correspondent was W. R. Barrington-Ward, Editor of *The Times* 1941-48.

12. *The Times* 24th March 1934. There are many accounts of life in service in the literature of reminiscence quoted above.

13. *SE* 26th February 1929.

14. *SE* 2nd and 5th October 1926.

15. PAC Minutes 28th October, 4th December 1931, 3rd February 1932, and many other occasions.

16. PAC Minutes 14th January 1932.

17. *SE* 3rd May 1935.

18. Any issue of the *Echo* will provide similar examples.

19. Figures from evidence to the Barlow Commission, tabulated in M. P. Fogarty, *Prospects of the Industrial Areas* (1945) p. 177.

20. The Index was actually called this, because of its heavy weighting towards the basic necessities of life — food, clothing, fuel and shelter — on which almost the whole of working-class income was spent.

21. A. Anderson, *The Dream Palaces of Sunderland* (1983) is full of details.

22. For detailed histories of Sunderland AFC see A. Appleton, *Centenary History* (1979) and W. Simmons & R. Graham, *History of Sunderland AFC* (1987).

23. S. Inglis *The Football Grounds of England & Wales* (1983). The architect was Archibald Leitch, whose XXX steel balcony trademark could be seen at many grounds, eg Ibrox Park, Glasgow, and Goodison Park, Liverpool.

24. For example see J. Seed, *The Jimmy Seed Story* (1957).

25. E. W. Moses, *To Ashbrooke & Beyond* (Sunderland, n.d.) p. 36.

26. *SE* 2nd December 1938.

27. P. D. Lathan, *50 Years On — Sunderland Drama Club 1925-75* (1975). The Club owned its own little theatre in Tavistock Place, which was destroyed along with the Victoria Hall in an air raid in 1941.

28. There is a summary history of the Temperance Movement in Sunderland in 'Sunderland Case that went to Lords' *SE* 23rd December 1935.

29. Wearmouth Rural Deanery *Report on the East End* 1896.

30. N. Gray (ed.) *The Worst of Times* (1985) p. 133.

31. *SE* 16th December 1938.

32. *SE* 25th November 1935.

33. *The Times* 11th December 1934.

34. 'Effects of existing economic circumstances on health in Sunderland' PP 1934/5 IX 627-678. The full text of Dr Walker's letter and practically the whole report are in the *Echo* 30th April 1935. There is also lengthy discussion in J. Hadfield *Health in the Industrial North East 1919-1939* (1977).

35. *SE* 26th April 1935.

36. Figures are from Sunderland Medical Officer of Health's annual reports.

37. Quoted in MoH report 1934 p. 129. The MoH reports are sources of information below unless otherwise stated.

38. MoH report 1936.

39. These examples and those following are all from the *Echo* 10th October 1934 but every issue of the *Echo* carried similar advertisements.

40. B. R. Mitchell & P. Deane, *British Historical Statistics* (1962) p. 239.

41. *Sunderland Corporation Handbook of Services* 1939.

42. See S. A. Staddon *Tramways of Sunderland* (1964).

43. *Corporation Handbook* 1939.

44. Chief Constable's annual reports are the source of the figures that follow.

45. P. McLoughlin, *Johnson Street Bullies* (1980).

46. J. Conlin, *History of Sunderland Police* (1969) p. 87.

47. Annual reports of Special Areas Commissioner.

48. Special Areas Commissioner's report, 1938, p. 287.

49. *Sunderland Yearbook* 1933.

50. Full details of all elections are in W. W. Craig, *British Election Results 1900-79*. The later results are analysed in M. Callcott *Parliamentary Elections in County Durham* (unpublished M. Litt Thesis, Newcastle University, 1975).

51. *SE* 6th May 1935.

52. *SE* 2nd November 1938.

53. *SE* 5th May 1929.

54. *SE* 10th October 1934.

55. *Ministry of Labour Gazette* July 1939. Figures for major towns were published monthly from 1930.

The Home Front 1939-1945

The Second World War was a total war. Britain's armed forces were only the steel tip of a huge national effort which tested the economic and social structure of the country as never before. The population was mobilised to a greater extent than in any other participatory nation, including the Soviet Union. Demands for a more collectivist and egalitarian society were felt keenly in a conflict in which "the nation's rulers, whether they liked it or not, depended upon the willing co-operation of the ruled".[1] The people of Sunderland shared fully in this national challenge. As a major producer of merchant marine the town was bombed. Yet the yards that were a target for the German airforce had been idle through much of the thirties; ironically it took a war to bring work back to Wearside. The underprivileged of the community, the long-term unemployed, unskilled manual workers, and women, suddenly found that a government, which had thrown them to the whims of market forces, now acknowledged their importance. New opportunities opened up as they were deployed into the services or industry. Indeed the pace of life for most people quickened. In retrospect those involved realised that they lived through a special experience, leaving them with both fond and poignant memories. The incentive to pull together to get the job done was a powerful influence. Many Sunderland people recall a heightened sense of community, common purpose and excitement. They responded with hard work and bravery, but also a good deal of grumbling, cynicism, humour and the desire to keep life as normal as possible.

The German bombing campaign put the people of Sunderland in the front line. The town suffered 42 air raids which resulted in casualties and/or damage, the first on 27 June 1940, the last on 24 May 1943. These attacks never reached the intensity of a blitz, but Sunderland was, nevertheless, the most heavily bombed English town north of Hull.[2] A compact overcrowded target, the borough took considerable punishment from larger raids.

Local authorities were instructed to plan for civil defence in 1935. In line with accepted military thinking Sunderland prepared for devastating aerial attacks. With hind-sight a great deal of time was spent preparing for appalling events which never occurred. The Corporation made ready to deal with 4,000 dead. Earth burial was held to offer the necessary flexibility and rapidity which war time demanded. The town's four cemeteries were each to allocate one acre for 1,000 burials. Several schools were to act as emergency mortuaries. Valley Road was earmarked for South District and Hudson Road for East District. It was estimated that 12 vehicles (covered cars of low loading type) would be needed to move bodies.[3]

Many casualties were expected from gas attacks. A 1937 scheme called for Gas Detection Officers "recruited as far as possible from Analytic Chemists, Colliery Officials and Chemistry Masters of Schools".[4] Some capital outlay was needed. A Cleansing and Decontamination Station at Railway Row Depot cost £1,566.[5] The Munich crisis provoked by Hitler's designs on Czechoslovakia, saw Sunderland's population in a dress rehearsal for war. On Saturday, 24 September 1938, 22 Fitting Centres, mainly schools, were opened to hand out and train the public in the use of respirators. Between 10 a.m. and 7 p.m. they dealt with some 50,000 people.[6] No masks were available for babies, an alarming aspect for parents, which had not been fully rectified by September 1939. Ford Parish Council expressed concern and reported that mothers at the Child Welfare Centre has been "given a formula for soaking a cloth which would be beneficial".[7]

In the months following Munich Sir John Anderson was put in charge of Air Raid Precautions (ARP) nationally. With clearer government guidance and a great deal more finance local ARP schemes took firmer shape. Nevertheless it was still difficult to prepare for the unknown, and early planning was characterised by a 'make do and mend' approach. It was not until early 1939 that an ARP structure with permanent staff was arrived at. Council Officials doubled up as key figures. The town clerk, Mr. G. S. McIntire, was controller; the medical officer of health's

ARP (Air Raid Precaution) trenches on a cleared slum site in Monkwearmouth, October 1938. Roker Avenue is on the left and St. Benet's RC Church in the background.

department was in charge of Casualty Services; the borough engineer's department ran Rescue and Demolition; the chief constable's department took charge of Air Raid Wardens, the Auxiliary Fire Service and the Warning System. ARP headquarters was set up at Thornholme,[8] a large house on Tunstall Road. This became the centre of an intricate communications network to receive reports and respond to incidents.

Staff set about their work with dedicated enthusiasm. The borough engineer, T. E. Lewis, believed "There is no doubt that Sunderland must be considered particularly vulnerable in time of war".[9] In response to the danger he proposed a remarkable system of underground car parks. These were to be filled with earth on the outbreak of hostilities to give protection to concrete air raid shelters built beneath them. The shelters were to be linked together by an extensive tunnel system several miles long, a minimum of 30ft underground and with access points every $\frac{1}{4}$ mile. This enormous construction programme would have protected almost 50,000 people. The cost of £500,000 proved prohibitive. The town was to rely on trench shelters, basement accommodation and steel shelters supplied to householders. All of these, according to Lewis, were inadequate for much of the population. Had Sunderland ever faced a raid of Coventry intensity he would have been right.

Tempered by practicalities, and relieved by the absence of Armageddon, ARP services responded to the realistic needs they had to deal with. Reporting on casualty services, the medical officer of health commented, from "early beginnings the schemes have been reorganised to such an extent that services now bear little resemblance to their former selves".[10] Older men who were physically unfit had been replaced by those opting to do their national service in a civil defence unit. Adequate equipment, uniforms, vehicles and training had filtered through. Sunderland ran a Rescue School for County Durham. By the end of 1940 casualty personnel stood at 1,339, a mixture of paid staff and volunteers, "ample to deal with the number of casualties which have occurred".[11]

Public response to war time dangers was mixed. During the summer of 1939 many took active preparations, others adopted a more casual approach. Stocks of heavy curtain material were sold out as householders made ready for the 'black-out'. Churches were fuller than usual, and on 28 August a prayer was offered in St. Michael's, Bishopwearmouth, for Adolf Hitler that "he might be rightly led in the exercise of the great powers placed in his hands". Over 7,000 householders were issued with free Anderson Shelters, but by late August 2,000 had failed to erect them. Slackness among ARP volunteers was criticised. Several forgot to notify changes of address, leaving squads shorthanded. In the rescue and demolition squad alone there were seven letters out of 30 returned, marked 'gone away'.[12]

AIR RAIDS

Within minutes of Chamberlain's speech announcing the declaration of war, the air-raid warning sounded. The *Echo* remonstrated with the incredulous attitude of many citizens. Failing to take cover, they came out of their houses and talked in groups. Police attempts to emphasise the seriousness of the situation did not always succeed "... 'We'll take cover as soon as the pubs open', was the reply of a number of men to one officer".[13] Later, familiarity with raids encouraged the same kind of relaxed approach. In May 1943 the Mayor felt it necessary to issue a warning to '"raid rubbernecks" who risk serious injury by leaving shelter to "watch the fun"'.[14] The number of false alarms also affected people's attitudes. The sirens sounded 247 times between 1939-45, over 200 without immediate danger. A crisp response could not be expected on every occasion and from the point of view of morale life had to be allowed to go on as normally as possible. It became customary for cinemas and theatres to open their exits during warnings to allow members of the audience to leave; but the shows continued, usually to almost full houses.

The adaptability of the population belied Sunderland's grim war record for a provincial English town. 267 civilians were killed and over 1,000 injured whilst ARP personnel suffered disproportionately high casualties, 28 being killed on duty.[15] During the intensive blitz period of 1940-41 the town escaped relatively lightly. Perhaps this encouraged a sense of security which was to be rudely shattered in May 1943.

The raids on Sunday 16 and Monday 24 May 1943 involved no more than 25 aircraft on each occasion. Using moonlight and flares they were able to concentrate their bombing pattern, the same technique that British planes were attempting over German cities. Sunderland was hit by parachute mines, high explosive bombs, fireports and hundreds of incendiaries. Many industrial premises suffered, including T. W. Greenwell's ship repairers at South

Morrison steel shelters, made from bolt-together kits and supplied for domestic use, saved some lives in the blitz including (in this case) those of six people on Seaforth Road, 14 March 1943.

Dock, British Ropes at Monkwearmouth, Laing's shipyard at Deptford and Austin's Wear Dockyard. Thompson's took the most serious punishment. On the 16th there was a direct hit on the office block at the North Sands Yard. The following week two parachute mines exploded at Manor Quay, damaging several sheds and sinking a new liberty ship, the *Denewood*, at her moorings. However, damage to industry was remarkably light and production only marginally affected. The town took the brunt.

Dawn after both raids revealed great distress and disruption. Scenes of carnage and acts of bravery were commonplace. 153 people were killed, more than half the total wartime figure. The mortality rate was high, 27 per cent of all casualties.[16] Sunderland's civil defence services were fully extended and help was requested from other authorities and the military. Surprisingly the records dealing with the actions of ordinary people are thin. Few ARP incident reports have survived, whilst the *Echo* was subject to censorship and often deliberately vague. Oral accounts are an invaluable supplement.

On 16 May Maisie and Ted Wilkinson knew the raid was going to be heavy when the glare of German flares lit up the interior of their shelter at 1, East Grange, Monkwearmouth. Eight months pregnant, Maisie sat with a cushion pulled firmly to her stomach. Ted, walking on crutches from an injury sustained in the Home Guard, insisted on standing up by the blast wall to see what was going on overhead. An explosion nearby blew him over, breaking his leg, the force of the blast filling Maisie's hair with soil. Help came quickly when two wardens moved the Wilkinsons to the cellars of the Grange Hotel. It was at that point that they realised they were one of the luckiest families in Sunderland; a parachute mine had dropped only yards from their shelter, but had not exploded. Others were not so fortunate. At Waterloo Place a 1,000 kg and a 250 kg bomb exploded within yards of one another. Fifteen people died. John Feeney, an air raid warden, was outside his home, number 4, when the bombs fell. He was found on the edge of a crater pinned by a joist. His two children, Mary and John, aged 12 and 10, were both killed when the house was demolished by the blast, and his wife Veronica was seriously injured. First Aid posts struggled with the stream of injured. By 4 p.m. the floor of the waiting room at Monkwearmouth Hospital had been cleared of seating. Lines of blanket-wrapped casualties lay awaiting the attention of doctors too pressed to change their blood-soaked gowns. Problems were made worse by the urgent need to evacuate patients because of nearby unexploded bombs.

At about 3.10 on the 24 May Dr. Ethel Browell staggered, bruised and shocked, from the shelter behind her home at 75 Alexandra Road. The house next door had taken a direct hit from a high explosive bomb which left a crater 30ft across. With the raid still in progress she began to attend the stricken Thompson family in number 71. Thomas and Hannah Thompson were both Fire Guards and died, standing by to go on duty. The worst incident of the war, caused by a single explosion, occurred at the communal shelter at Lodge Terrace, Hendon. The brick and concrete building took a direct hit from a 250 kg bomb. It was ripped open and though a handful of occupants were able to crawl out through a hole in the wall 40 people were trapped. The first rescue party on the scene were local firewatchers

who knew their wives and kiddies were trapped so they needed no urging on. Working by the light of a fire nearby they lifted and heaved on the blocks of stone with their bare hands.[17]

Twelve people were killed and ten badly injured.

In the aftermath of the May raids Wearsiders faced a host of difficulties. The mopping-up operation was if anything, more of a test of the efficiency of the ARP and local authority services. The urgent needs of thousands had to be attended to. 1,298 homeless were found billeting accommodation following the events of 16 May. A large number

Fulwell railway crossing after being hit by a parachute mine on 16 May 1943. There was widespread damage and two serious injuries but no-one was killed.

Picking through the wreckage of one's bombed home was a heart-breaking task.

seriously damaged and a staggering 17,200 needed extended repairs. Main services and public transport were severely disrupted. With the risk of disease sewerage and water supplies were given high priority. Usually repairs could be effected within a day but at times the damage was too great. On 16 May the main Low Street outfall sewer was shattered and raw sewage discharged into the river Wear. On 25 May the water supply to Hendon was cut and could not be restored until bomb craters were filled. Water carts were sent into the district.

A quick and humane response from those in authority was important in maintaining the spirit of the individual or family. General morale is harder to judge but northern regional headquarters at Eskdale Terrace, Newcastle, reported no sign "of any serious moral effect upon the general public".[18] Censorship and propaganda were carefully balanced. Headlines in the *Echo* for 16 and 25 May respectively read 'OUR NON STOP AIR WAR' and 'HEAVIEST RAID ON GERMANY'. News of the Sunderland raids appeared on page 4, referring anonymously to 'A North East Coast Town'. Relatives of casualties were interviewed and named, but locations were not given. Attempts to deny any information of value to German intelligence were more successful in irritating local people. Readers became accustomed to piecing the news together. Following a heavy air raid the previous day, the *Echo* for 15 March, 1943 contained two apparently unrelated items in separate articles.

> Among the people still missing . . . is the Vicar of a church. He was firewatching and was probably near to the church entrance or conversing with firewatchers at a block of offices across the street when both church and offices were wrecked.

> Vicar of St. Thomas' Church, Sunderland, for the past four years, Rev. James Fraser Leyland Orton, died suddenly last night.

were evacuated temporarily from their homes whilst unexploded bombs were dealt with. On the 25 May, 13 rest centres were opened immediately after the raid, and 3,500 homeless accommodated. 12 emergency feeding centres provided meals for 3,791 people. Administrative centres handled one of the most important public needs, giving advice about what to do next. Representatives from departments such as the Assistance Board, Billeting Office, Military Assistance Office, and the Food Office, answered urgent questions about accommodation as well as about destroyed possessions and ration cards, gave advice on financial aid, and assisted in contacting relatives in the services. 14,000 enquiries resulted from the two raids.

Rescue and demolition work continued for days. It was an onerous task as the borough engineer indicated in his report on the site at St. George's Square (behind Grange Crescent):

> During the period 24 to 28 May portions of bodies were found . . . On the 29 and 30 May, 11 badly mutilated bodies were recovered.

Housing had suffered badly. 534 houses had been or required to be demolished. 2,000 were

Reporters themselves often faced an unsympathetic attitude from the authorities. Enquiries to ARP control centres were not encouraged. Regional headquarters commented: "The press has on occasions been a nuisance", and indicated that reporters should be kept as far as possible from rescue sites.[19]

Two hard raids within ten days left Sunderland tense and scarred. Preparations were put in hand for further attacks but the town's 'active service' was over. The German air force was losing its capacity to direct attacks by plane on the British mainland. London was the priority for the flying bomb attacks of 1944, a horror the northern conurbations were spared. The Ministry of Home Security sent Wing Commander Hodsoll to review Wearside's recovery in early June 1943. His comments are a fitting tribute:

> It is quite obvious to me that not only did your civil defence services work extremely well, but that all other sides of the organisation, which are perhaps the most complicated, were functioning with remarkable smoothness.[20]

EVACUATION

The prospect of saturation bombing had led to one of the most pathetic and alarming events

St. George's Square, one of Sunderland's most prestigious private streets, was destroyed by bombing on 24 May 1943.

of September 1939, the evacuation scheme for the country's mothers and children. Cheering newsreels portrayed smiling, well-organised parties boarding trains to leave the major cities for a great rural adventure. They contrasted sharply with the sorrows and fears of parents. Nationally one and a half million people were evacuated by the state whilst a further two million made private arrangements. This was the largest exodus from the conurbations, but not the last. Two further, though smaller, waves of English evacuees followed, escaping the blitz of 1940 and the flying bomb attacks of 1944. This mass movement of peoples of all classes was felt by many contemporaries to carry a social message which would be difficult to forget. Britain's two nations, rich and poor, urban and rural, were thrown together. Accounts of the reactions of slum children to their wealthier billets are almost apocryphal.[21] Marwick broadly supports this view, citing evacuation as an outstanding example of how war tested and exposed existing social institutions.[22] However, the importance of evacuation can be exaggerated. The scheme was entirely voluntary and the majority of those eligible stayed at home.

Despite being one of the most densely populated industrial areas in the country Sunderland was designated a neutral zone. By July 1939 heated lobbying led the Minister of Health to agree to change the status of the crowded central areas to a Class C zone. The grave international situation led the government to implement evacuation on 31 August 1939 as a 'precautionary measure'. On 1 September children from Newcastle and Gateshead, Class A zones, began to disperse. Sunderland's Education Authority could only advise parents to prepare, "pending arrangements being put into force".[23] An appeal for residents in the suburbs to accept children from the town centre, in the interim, met with a poor response.

With the go-ahead given on 7 September plans were put into effect for a two-day evacuation. On Sunday 10 September children were to leave, followed on 11 September by mothers and under fives, cripples able to walk, and expectant mothers. Millfield, Pallion and Monkwearmouth stations were used to transport 7,910 children and 1,785 adults from the other 'Priority Class'. Despite administrative smoothness the operation was very far from a success. Less than a third of the town's children in danger zones moved to the safety of the countryside.

In the weeks immediately prior to the outbreak of hostilities parents had to decide whether they wished their children to leave. Warnings were dire. The scheme was portrayed as being "as much and as necessary a defence measure in these days as the provision of a strong air force and efficient anti-aircraft guns".[24] In the frightening period of late August 1939 there was an upsurge of registrations, reaching 16,000 by early September. The poor final result shocked the authorities and led to the widespread condemnation of indifferent parents.

The unpopularity of evacuation arose from several causes. The commonest was the desire of families to stay together in time of danger. The idea of parting with the children was simply too upsetting. One evacuee remembers:

> It must have been a dreadful experience for my parents. My mother wasn't given to weeping . . . She told me years after that she absolutely cried until she was past herself.[25]

Many parents could not face such a sad experience, let alone handing over the care of their children to strangers. The absence of air raids gave a welcome sense of security and perhaps affected many last minute changes of mind. With regard to mothers leaving, financial considerations may have weighed heavily in a town still struggling with unemployment. In a letter to the Echo 'W.S.' believed many mothers had not left because:

> Most of their husbands are still on benefit or U.A.B., and they have considered how men are going to pay rent and clubs out of the men's 17s (85p) income.[26]

The cost of kitting out evacuees was beyond the income of some families and the government released funds in November through the Unemployment Assistance Board and public assistance officers. This move belatedly recognised:

> That essential garments for children who are living in the country are different from those used in the towns. Many children have long distances to walk to school and they need strong shoes, Wellington boots and macintoshes.[27]

It was not acknowledged that the poverty of city children, so openly on view during evacuation, had raised an outcry which necessitated some response. The rumour that parents would be asked to pay the cost of billeting their children gained currency in early September. Perhaps this accounted for some of the withdrawals. Certainly the government was short-sighted when it announced on 4 October that assessments would be made from the end of the month.[28] The move damaged the credibility of the scheme and added to the substantial numbers returning home.

Sunderland evacuees were distributed across much of Durham and the North Riding of Yorkshire. Although press reports painted a

Firemen extinguish the last of the blaze which destroyed the premises of Messrs. Binns Ltd, on Fawcett Street, after an aerial attack on 10 April 1941. After having been under the control of the Sunderland Police, local firemen became part of the National Fire Service during the war. An independent Fire Brigade was established after the war had ended.

The First World War

Within a chapter devoted to life in Sunderland during the Second World War it is of interest to look back, if only briefly, to the First, and to consider the impact which that earlier great conflict had upon the town in the years 1914 to 1918.

News of the outbreak of war reached Sunderland soon after midnight on the 5 August and was announced to a noisily patriotic crowd assembled outside the *Echo* offices. The town was to contribute a substantial proportion of its manpower to the direct war effort over the next four years. One of the units raised, was the 7th (Sunderland) Territorial Battalion of the Durham Light Infantry. They embarked for France in April 1915 as part of the Northumbrian Territorial Division which fought at the infamous Ypres Salient.

The town's most striking contribution to the war effort was in ship building. Most of the 360 ships built on the Wear during the war were merchant ships, totalling some 900,000 tons. On 15 June 1917 the Wear's efforts were recognised officially when King George V and Queen Mary visited Doxford's shipyard and toured the overworked shipbuilding and engineering complexes on both sides of the river. A number of destroyers were also built at Sunderland.

The townspeople experienced war at first hand. As early as December 1914 Scarborough, Whitby and Hartlepool had been subjected to a bombardment from sea. Sunderland's worst experience was on Saturday 1 April 1916 when Zeppelin No. LII dropped 14 high explosive bombs and seven incendiaries. The resultant casualties were 22 dead and over 100 injured. Initially the town's air defences were minimal but in 1916 anti-aircraft guns were sited in various areas. Hopefully the Chief Constable advised the populace:

Indications that enemy aircaft are in the vicinity are as follows: First, the cutting off of the electrical supply. Second, the noise caused by the explosion of bombs.

One of the outstanding features of the war was the extent to which women were drawn into occupations usually reserved for men. By 1918, for instance, 90 per cent of munitions workers were female. This trend was even more marked in public services such as tramways. In Sunderland the first ten female conductors were employed in June 1915 and soon all of the conductors were women. Here can be seen Sally A. Holmes of the Sunderland Corporation Tramways who was, in fact, injured in the air raid of 1916. Women were also employed in very heavy work such as chipping and painting, and even cleaning and scaling boilers.

The tram conductress, Sally A. Holmes, who was injured in the Zeppelin air raid on 1 April 1916.

Mrs L. Burnop, a VAD nurse at Ashburne during its use as a military hospital in the First World War.

A typical recruiting poster.

THINK!

ARE YOU CONTENT FOR HIM TO FIGHT FOR YOU?

WON'T YOU DO YOUR BIT?

WE SHALL WIN BUT YOU MUST HELP

JOIN TO-DAY

King George V and Queen Mary visit J. L. Thompson's shipyard in June 1917.

The Torpedo Boat Destroyer HMS *Opal*, with three of her sister ships nearing completion at William Doxford's yard in December 1915.

A notable feature of wartime life was the number of public appeals, usually for recruits in the earlier stages, but increasingly for money to support the war effort. There were Tank weeks, Cruiser weeks, Feed The Guns weeks and (more prosaic) War Loan, War Savings and Victory Loan weeks.

Daily life was most affected by government regulations. Amongst the more obtrusive interventions were daylight-saving regulations, curtailment of licensing hours and conscription for military service and work. Food rationing was a surprisingly late addition. Sunderland's Food Economy Campaign began in 1916 with lectures in cinemas, theatres and music halls, and exhortative public meetings in work places. Shortages and queues became commonlace and the national introduction of rationing in 1918 was actually welcomed.

Medical services were overwhelmed by the casualties, and various big houses had to be taken over and staffed by a corp of professional staff supplemented by Voluntary Aid Detachments. Sunderland had five such hospitals — Hammerton House in Gray Road, Ashburne House in Back-house Park, Jeffrey Hall in Monkwearmouth and others on Kayll Road and the Royalty. In 1917 the War Hospital of 500 beds was opened in Chester Road. When Ashburne closed in 1919 a total of 1,493 wounded men had been treated there.

Some 18,000 Sunderland men joined the armed forces, about ten per cent of the population. Probably about a third of them were killed or wounded.

A War Memorial was erected in Mowbray Park in 1922, based upon the plans of Mr Ray the head of the art school. The theme of an angelic Winged Victory is an uncommon one as far as British war memorials are concerned.

The wounded soldiers victory procession in July 1919.

determinedly cheerful picture the reality was mixed. At best evacuees had their horizons widened and were treated with great kindness. The *Echo* reported on 19 September:

> Among the happiest of the Wearside children are 18 who are living in Middleton Hall, the home of Mr. W. Prince-Smith, member of a well known Yorkshire family. Thirteen year old Ian Forbister of Collingwood Terrace, Southwick, proudly showed me over the huge mansion which has hundreds of acres of parklands adjoining. 'We have two helpers, three servants and a cook to look after us.'

Country life could be invigorating with an abundance of fresh food, clean air and exercise. A new environment to explore, with proximity to wild and domestic animals, and work on farms or small holdings, was exciting. The medical officer of health regretted the return of large numbers of children to Sunderland:

> Although the primary reason for evacuation was the dispersal ... from the danger zones, those remaining in the reception areas are likely to benefit in health.[29]

Unfortunately not everyone was able to look back on a pleasant experience. The influx of city children was viewed by some in the country as little better than an invasion, and their resentment focussed on the evacuees thrust upon them. There were bitter complaints at the inadequacy of the billeting allowance.[30] Some Sunderland parents sent additional money but this added to the dissatisfaction of those attempting to feed children on the basic amount. Between November 1939 and the end of January 1940, 120 Bede boys in the Northallerton area had had to be rebilleted. Some householders simply refused to accept evacuees and by February the urban council and police were considering prosecutions. Sunderland children, reluctantly taken in, could suffer. Catherine, aged 9, from Redby School stayed with a labourer and his wife:

> a hard woman ... I never heard one affectionate word either to her own daughters or the evacuees ... Back at school the Headmaster, Mr. Benson, was angry with mum for bringing me home but she said I could be bombed to death in Sunderland or starved to death in the country...[31]

Sunderland Education Authority attempted to take a firm line to preserve the evacuation scheme. The director of education, Mr. Thompson, and members of the Education Committee, set a strong moral tone in the local press, emphasising the contentment of children in their new surroundings and appealing to "the mothers of Sunderland to refrain from bringing their bairns home".[32] The Christmas festivities provided an opportunity to persuade the community to support evacuation with collections of funds and gifts and Santa Claus excursions to the reception areas. The town's élite institutions, the Bede School and the Junior Technical Schools, were moved as complete units. It was stressed that this would enable secondary education to continue in the country, a strong pressure on examination-conscious parents. Of 583 pupils on roll at Bede Boys School in early September 486 were evacuated. By Christmas only 54 had returned. With 74 per cent of the school's population in Northallerton the Education

Ready to go! An evacuee awaits the long journey to his new home.

Authority insisted that the boys were receiving an adequate amount of training to enable them to take School Certificate at the normal time. At first recalcitrant parents were sharply dealt with. In October 1939 Robert S—. from Bede Boys was suspended for making a trip home from Northallerton without the headmaster's permission. A full apology was demanded from Robert's father before he was allowed to resume his education. However a grass roots dissatisfaction amongst parents continued to grow.[33]

Sunderland schools had stayed closed since evacuation had been announced, although over 20,000 children of school age remained in the town. By October 1939 parents were angrily demanding a resumption of lessons. Mr. Thompson was "almost inundated with letters — many of them abusive".[34] Whilst the LEA insisted that parents were largely to blame for not availing themselves of the evacuation scheme, the core of the problem lay with the perceptions of central government. The Board of Education refused to allow the opening of schools in danger areas of the town, still fearful of heavy raids. The LEA was only slowly able to open buildings in the neutral areas, beginning with Havelock School on 6 November.

To limit criticism a number of temporary and makeshift measures, largely relying on the enthusiasm of teaching staff, were put into effect. Informal lessons using private houses, and a wonderful assortment of temporary accommodation, brought almost 10,000 children back to schooling on 16 October.[35] An emphasis was placed on fieldwork with trips to museums, parks and the coast. In January several schools opened, including Barnes Boys, "on a half time voluntary basis ... 252 boys presented themselves for duty".[36] Full time education for most pupils did not resume until the summer of 1940.

By June 1941, 2,546 children remained in the reception areas. This was despite a third evacuation on 7 and 8 July 1940 which moved a further 1,761 to the North Riding of Yorkshire. As a way of saving lives evacuation proved to be a complicated irrelevance. For those involved it was an unforgettable experience, fixed sharply in young minds as a notable period of their lives. The scheme's main effect was however the worry and disruption caused to the majority of families who stayed together in Wearside.

HOUSING

Many evacuees returned to sub-standard housing. The report of the Registrar General following the 1931 census cited Sunderland as the most overcrowded borough in England and Wales. The pressures of an economy geared to the war effort compounded the problem. At the beginning of 1939 the corporation planned to continue its vigorous housing initiatives of the inter-war period. 1933-38 had been record years in Sunderland with 1,455 occupied houses being demolished and 3,849 families rehoused. A further five year slum clearance programme involving 1,918 houses and 5,000 families was planned. The war brought an abrupt halt. The Housing (Emergency Powers) Act 1939 deferred slum clearance

> in view of the possible destruction of housing accommodation by attack from hostile aircraft . . . Sunderland was considered to be . . . 'in the happy position of having the majority of work on existing schemes completed.[37]

In terms of the potential loss of life in later air raids the town was indeed fortunate. Large parts of the densely populated east end and central areas had been cleared including Monkwearmouth, Monkwearmouth shore and the area around the old infirmary on Chester Road. Those rehoused on the outskirts of the borough were rarely endangered by bombing.

Council and private house building was also stopped. The prestige council estate of 1,062 houses at Plains Farm was almost finished. The Borough Engineer reported the houses, roads and sewers complete, the flagging 80 per cent so, but the site in need of cleaning up. Perhaps its untidy condition influenced some of the problems the estate was to develop. In 1943 a letter to the *Echo* commented:

> The tram shelter is a wreck; the telephone kiosk is unusable; the road signs smashed; trees stripped of their bark and branches broken; gardens and allotments rifled, fences torn down; windows broken by stone throwing and general pandemonium.[38]

Work on other estates was less advanced. At Springwell Farm the sewers had been laid but no houses started. No work had begun on the High Southwick or North Hylton sites.

The inability to complete pre-war schemes meant that Sunderland began the war with a housing shortage, compelling many families to endure a further five years in overcrowded, insanitary dwellings. The inactivity of the 'phoney war' period encouraged the council to press for limited slum clearance and building. In common with much of County Durham there was "need of especial urgency for dealing with unfit housing".[39] Throughout the war however the national shortage of materials and labour meant that new civilian homes were a low priority. In January 1943 the town's predicament was shown when, "in view of the shortage of working class houses in Sunderland"[40] the Ministry of Health was prepared to permit the completion of 76 private houses, provided they were in an advanced state of construction and the amount of controlled material needed was not extensive. The desperate lack of accommodation led to inflated purchase prices. Building societies attempted to control this by advancing mortgages based on 'fair value' rather than 'current value', but at best they could only slow the trend.[41]

If building could not take place, planning could. Early in 1942 the Housing sub-committee was set terms of reference, "to give full and detailed consideration to the question of post-war housing construction".[42] By 1945 the problem was acute. Sunderland was faced with an estimated shortfall of almost 13,000 homes. The Medical Officer of Health argued that rehousing "should and will take priority over any other post war scheme".[43]

Bomb damage and billeting increased the pressure on available accommodation during the war years. The demolition or repair of damaged properties became a major task. In the first place a house was made structurally fit, wind- and water-tight, and sanitary. Thereafter more substantial repairs could be carried out if the building could be refurbished at reasonable expense. Typically a light air raid on 30 September 1941 led to the council repairing 66 houses and demolishing 14. An unlucky owner could face repeated repairs. Number 74 Stratford Avenue, Hendon is an example of the moderate damage that occurred to so much of Sunderland's housing stock. In February 1941 the property was damaged by an explosive incendiary. Repairs to the roof, ceilings and window cost £25, including 42 hours skilled labouring time by a bricklayer, joiner and painter at 2s 4d an hour. Bomb blast and the effects of anti-aircraft fire during the raids of May 1943 again damaged ceilings. These further repairs cost £33. Between 1939-45 1,030 houses were demolished, 2,700 seriously damaged, and 30,000 slightly damaged. This amounted to 90 per cent of the borough's housing being affected to some degree. Coping with the demands created was labour intensive. It was estimated in August 1943 that 140 skilled and 270 unskilled men could be redeployed for war production work if no further serious air raids occurred.

WARTIME REGULATIONS

As well as a shortage of accommodation the war brought a host of restrictive laws and a stream of propaganda, to organise and persuade the participants in a 'People's War'. The introduction of peacetime conscription in June 1939 was only a foretaste of future regulations. The Emergency Powers Act gave the government absolute control of the freedom and property of the individual without recourse to Parliament. Citizens were registered and rationed, their labour was mobilised and directed. The media exhorted them to do their patriotic duty, whilst avoiding careless talk and waste. For seven years Britain took on many of the characteristics of a totalitarian state.

Men of the Sunderland Home Guard resist a mock invasion — South Durham Street, 1942.

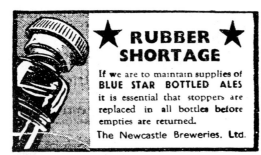
Security was comprehensive. Sunderland
police undertook surveillance of organisations
of a hostile, subversive or doubtful character.
A formidable list of investigations resulted
including reports on aliens, naturalised
Germans and Italians, Japanese sailors,
political and racial minorities such as the
British Union of Fascists and the Irish,
refugees including Poles and Czechs, pacifists,
suspected acts of sabotage and enemy agents.
The Communist Party of Great Britain took the
lion's share of attention. With 20,000 members
nationally, the CPGB was viewed by the
authorities as a tool of the Third International.
Generally little action was taken but local communists working for Rediffusion in Sunderland
in 1940 were dismissed. The communists represented themselves as the only party carrying out systematic opposition to the government and achieved some sympathy. A particularly successful campaign drew attention to
inadequate Air Raid Precautions, and a petition organised in Gateshead received 3,000
signatures. Party activists in Sunderland were
less successful. A hall was booked for a
meeting of the Wearside Apprentices Movement in July 1941, but no one attended. With
the entry of Russia into the war, the CPGB
raised the call for a second front at the earliest
opportunity. Increased interest in the Soviet
Union as an ally led to a lively local debate.

Food rationing epitomised the war time
discipline imposed on consumers. The system
was introduced on Monday 8 January 1940,
with the bacon ration at 4 ounces, sugar at 12
ounces and butter at 4 ounces per week. As the
war continued more commodities were controlled and allowances tightened, but there
were several ways of supplementing the basic
diet. Works canteens supplied additional
meals, with those catering for heavy manual
workers permitted generous supplies of meat,
cheese, butter and sugar. 'British Restau-
rants', looked after the general public providing self-service meals at about a shilling (five
pence). The corporation planned to provide six
centres in Sunderland during 1941, accommodating a minimum of 794 people at an estimated cost of £9,177. The first, at South
Durham Street Unemployed Social Centre, was
opened on 10 October 1941 by the Mayor. The
government's programme for national self-suf-
ficiency in food production emphasised tending
gardens and allotments as a patriotic duty. In
May 1940 Sunderland Council tenants who refused to cultivate their gardens were
threatened with eviction. Two months later
local restrictions on the keeping of poultry,
pigs and rabbits were lifted. The DIG FOR
VICTORY campaign ran throughout the war.
In March 1943 a major exhibition was held at
the New Rink. The Secretary of the National
Allotments Society stoutly told the audience
"The battle of the brussel, the broccoli, the
cabbage and the cauliflower is as important as
any that has been fought".[44] An accompany-
ing poster competition for Wearside schools
produced an apposite winning slogan: 'Mind
your Peas and Avoid the Queues'. A flourishing
blackmarket provided an alternative source of
supplies. Every shop had its 'special
customers', usually peacetime regulars whose

loyalty was rewarded. Shopkeepers found themselves with an enviable bargaining power. Jean R., an assistant at Moore's Store on Chester Road, recalls the manageress securing first refusal on the purchase of a cottage with a liberal supply of ham shanks and bacon bones. Those denied favourable treatment could be incensed by long, fruitless queues. A letter to the *Echo* on 9 March 1943 complained about a local fishmonger:

> Practically every morning I look in his shop and see parcels of every type of fish . . . under the counter . . . I am always given the same answer, "It's only for old customers, no orders are taken or wanted!".

Wartime regulations were viewed from two standpoints. They might be necessary measures for the defence of the country, but also uncomfortable, irritating and avoidable. Dabbling on the black market was so common that it was hardly viewed by the public as a real crime, more a practical response to difficulties. Mrs. T. for instance paid well above shop prices for material for a dress and 'a set of pink undies' supplied by a workmate with no questions asked. Her wedding dress was made from parachute silk brought back from Africa by her prospective brother-in-law. The cloth was superb but it took three weeks to unpick the stitching.

As never before, having useful contacts was important. In a fully mobilised population it could make the difference between having a son called up to the services or deployed into a 'safe' job in industry; between having a daughter taken on locally or directed to the Midlands. Local magistrates were conscious of setting a strong moral lead and wartime sentences often reflected the determination to deter others. Mrs. Hordahl of Queens Parade, Seaburn, banked up her fire before going out. By night-fall a respectable blaze flickered through the windows of a room that had not been blacked out. She was fined £3, the presiding J.P. admonishing her, "It was a very foolish thing to leave a fire burning all day. Apart from the blackout the offence was a shocking waste of fuel". Leonard Salter, a local businessman, had been allocated a petrol ration for commercial travelling. His trip to the Empress Hotel for a lunchtime drink cost him a 40/- fine for using petrol for a purpose other than that for which it was issued. Looting was regarded as particularly heinous and more persistent than the authorities cared to admit. At one level it involved local people picking up wood or scrap metal from bomb sites, on other occasions it was the distressing theft of personal possessions from wrecked homes. Mrs. S. was a child in 1940 when the family home in Suffolk Street was hit by a crashing German bomber. Her mother's treasured wedding gifts were kept in a cupboard on the stairs, but the structure of the house was so weakened that her brother was not allowed to collect them. When a demolition squad cleared the ruins the presents were gone. ARP personnel were in a trusted position and their behaviour was to be beyond reproach. William Hay and John Overton were members of a squad cleaning up after the heavy raid of 14 March 1943. They were brought to court for picking up cigarettes worth 6/- (30p) from the wreckage of a bombed confectionery shop. The magistrates felt that with such conduct "no person will be safe in their own houses after a raid" and sent them to jail for six months.[45] Later the same month the *Echo* condemned rumours of widespread looting.

MORALS

As the war progressed, the thrills and dangers of the period eroded traditional moral restraints. A generation of young people left their home backgrounds whilst many women found themselves financially independent for the first time. Sexual licence and criminality were perceived as evidence of falling standards. Nostalgia focussed on the interwar years as a time of struggle against the grim conditions which had bound the community together. The war economy brought wealth, mobility and the disruption of familiar patterns.

The rise in illegitimacy caused great concern nationally. The rate of births among married women actually fell, while the number of illegitimate births per thousand single or widowed women nearly tripled by 1945. Those women unlucky enough to become pregnant

COME ON! —FANTASTIC PRICES AND IT DOESN'T HELP THE WAR A BIT!

LUXURY STORES

BEWARE THE SQUANDER BUG!

He's EVERYWHERE—in the streets, shops and market places, trying to get you to buy things you don't need. He's on the side of the Nazis, devouring good money that ought to be fighting for Britain. Turn your back on the little brute! See that your money does a war job! Join a Savings Group and buy one or more Savings Certificates every week!

Savings Certificates cost 15/- and £1, and can be bought by instalments with 6d., 2/6 and 5/- Savings Stamps through your Savings Group or Centre or any Post Office or Trustee Savings Bank. Buy now!

ISSUED BY THE NATIONAL SAVINGS COMMITTEE

faced widespread censure but attitudes were changing. Of the 109 notified illegitimate children in Sunderland in 1944, 76 mothers kept their babies with help from grandparents or because they were able to take them to work. Social Services were moving away from a poor law mentality towards an understanding of wartime pressures. In 1943 the town's moral welfare officer emphasised the difference between the present conflict and the last. Unmarried mothers were younger and there was a far greater disintegration of family life with many girls having to leave home. This was particularly true of Sunderland, where factories and war work had not been started to the same extent as in other towns. The increase in casual sexual contacts led to the rapid spread of venereal disease. Faced with what amounted to an epidemic the government launched a blunt advertising campaign in the press, 'Ten plain facts about V.D.'. Defence Regulation 33B enforced compulsory treatment for those named by two others as a source of contact. On Wearside a pre-war decline in the incidence of V.D. turned into a 30 per cent increase by 1944.

Unease over shifts in morality was reflected in a growing concern over crime. The number of indictable offences in England and Wales had risen from just over 300,000 in 1939 to 478,000 in 1945. The local pattern was less alarming with 723 indictable offences in 1939 and 828 in 1945. This was a modest increase of 14.7 per cent compared with over 50 per cent nationally. The blackout was blamed for providing a perfect cover for petty theft and vandalism. In 1943 several Sunderland women's groups including the National Union of Women Teachers and the Thornhill Townswomen's Guild wrote to the Chief Constable requesting a curfew for children. He politely refused, pointed out that his statistics showed a reduction of mischief in the early evenings during the war and suggested that "interfering with the liberty of the subject was not conducive to good citizenship".[46] Petrol rationing led to markedly safer streets with most private cars stored for the duration. Road accidents fell from 561 with 25 deaths in 1939 to 296 with 19 deaths in 1944.

ENTERTAINMENT

Exaggerated fears of enemy bombing raids led the government to close places of public entertainment on the outbreak of war. The shutting of Roker Park seemed almost welcome to 'Argus' in the *Echo* of 4 September 1939:

> At such a time it seems highly improper to go into much detail of Sunderland's game at Arsenal Stadium, for criticism is merely destructive if not based as a guide to the future ... For the time being at least Manager Billy Murray has been relieved of his worries.

Official attitudes quickly changed and most sports arenas, theatres, cinemas and dance halls were reopened by the end of September 1939. It was recognised that entertainment was vital for morale. At times of heightened national tension such as Dunkirk or the blitz of 1940 people flocked to enjoy themselves as never before. More usually there was the dull routine of long working hours, overtime, reduced holidays and endless blacked out winter nights to face. Companionship and fun were an essential escape.

Dancing became a wartime craze, though some dance halls tried to preserve a calmer atmosphere with notices proclaiming, 'no jitterbugging'. The Rink and Black's Regal offered cheap weekend dancing whilst the Seaburn Hotel catered for more sophisticated tastes, presenting nationally famous bands such as 'Harry Gold and his Pieces of Eight'. Chain dances like the 'Lambeth Walk' and 'Hokey Cokey' gave dance halls a party atmosphere. This was useful when couples were only too likely to be separated and courtship rituals had to be kept as short as possible.

A night out at the pictures almost inevitably began with queuing. A two-hour wait was not unusual, whilst the queue was an accepted feature of British wartime life which at best became a cheerful social occasion. National cinema audience figures boomed, trebling through the blitz to over thirty million weekly attendances. In Sunderland 18 premises were granted Cinematographic Licences in 1940. These included the Villiers Electric Theatre

Ten plain facts about

and the Cora Picture Palace. Three were destroyed in raids, the tiny Victory in April 1941, and the King's Theatre and the Bromarsh in May 1943. Each cinema had its own special features, the organist at the Ritz always played 'Goodnight Sweetheart' as the last tune for an emptying house. Most films of the period were propaganda, of varying degrees of subtlety. Robert Donat in 'The Young Mr. Pitt', or (Churchill's favourite) Laurence Olivier as Nelson in 'Lady Hamilton', looked to glorious episodes in the past for inspiration. 'Gone with the Wind', with its epic portrayal of a nation at war, drove Goebbels, the Nazi Minister of Propaganda, wild with envy. It played to packed houses at the Ritz in 1942. Escapist musicals and comedies proved the most popular with audiences, but they too served the cause. Military backdrops with thin plots were in vogue. 'Rookies', starring Abbot and Costello, was one of the last films shown at the King's.

The theatre in Sunderland shared in the boom in audience ratings. There were new and revived musicals, radio shows on tour, plays, ballet, orchestral and vocal performances by well known stars. The propriety of acts was tightly supervised by the Chief Constable. A striptease routine by Phyllis Dixey and the 'Eve takes a Bow Company' was considered particularly objectionable. Sunday performances had to be of a 'refined nature'. However detailed reports by police sergeants studiously watching shows at the Empire, the Regal and the King's, on Sunday 14 January 1940, illustrate that music hall was alive and well. At the Empire the patter of Yorkshire comedian Jack Lane came thick and fast.

This blackout is getting me down. I got lost the other night when I was out for a walk. I met a policeman and asked for Roker Avenue, he replied, "Man I don't know, I'm a Shields policeman! . . ." One of my married pals goes out with single girls; he met one the other night called Maggie Wood — and Maggie would![48]

In the best show business tradition the air raid of March 14 1943 failed to stop the production of 'Damaged Goods' at the Empire. Members of the touring company were injured but the play went on the following night with a full supporting cast to perform before bumper houses.

As a result of the blackout and travelling difficulties, entertainment at home with family and friends became important. Listening to the wireless was a social activity, with 'ITMA', 'Much Binding in the Marsh' and 'Variety Band Box' being particular favourites. Sewing could be done in company and provide a useful supplement to the clothes ration. The demand for reading material soared. Sunderland libraries saw a steady increase in the total issue of books, from 849,004 in 1939-40 to 1,083,374 in 1941-42. To cut unnecessary journeys the government encouraged councils to organise 'Holidays at Home'. The programme in Sunderland for 1942 included Sunday Evening Services on the Winter Garden Terrace in Mowbray Park, a Children's Fun Fair at Backhouse Park on August Bank Holiday Monday and a 'Cavalcade of Sunderland' in Barnes Park.

INDUSTRY

An economy geared for war meant full employment and gave most people the surplus income to enjoy their leisure. By August 1943 there were only 429 unemployed men in Sunderland, but the figure was deceptive.[48] Little had been accomplished in using wartime investment to rebuild the town's economy. A report of the Northern Regional Board of the Ministry of Production noted that 3,000 men and 3,500 women had been transferred to other industrial areas. It was further noted that, apart from shipbuilding:

No attempt had been made . . . to provide additional employment in the town . . . Much better use could be made of the labour by providing work near their homes . . . Action on these lines would be in accordance with the policy of bringing the work as far as possible to the workers . . . but (there has not been) any appreciable effect in Sunderland.[49]

By the end of the war the situation had not improved. Referring to a lone example of government investment, the town clerk observed "there are practically no new factory buildings".[50]

Wearside's economy and contribution to the war effort continued to rest overwhelmingly on shipbuilding. From September 1939 to the end of 1944, 249 ships were completed, 1,534,980 gross tons. This was equivalent to 27 per cent of the total output of merchant shipping from all British shipyards. A summary of the number of industrial firms employing 20 or more people in the Sunderland Labour Exchange area reveals the dominance of the yards. On 24 May 1943, 148 firms employed

32,151 people. Of these, 17 firms in shipbuilding, ship repairs and marine engineering and repairs had 15,022 employees. In other industries, such as wire and hemp-rope manufacturing, four firms employing 1,584, were substantially reliant on orders from the yards. With national survival at stake, government concern concentrated on the capacity of the Wear to build ships quickly. Investment in shipbuilding was substantial but a major restructuring of the industry was not undertaken. Any improvements had to be pushed through without interrupting vessel construction. In June 1942 the Admiralty offered contributions of 50 per cent of the cost of extending the use of electric welding provided "that there will be no decrease in production while any works or training of labour involved is being carried out".[51] This principle precluded large scale modernisation.

Management and unions approached wartime changes cautiously. The Wear was an intimate river with a family firm tradition. It was hoped that most issues could be sorted out in-house. The Labour Supply Committee, a tight unit, with three members of the Wear Shipbuilders Association and three union representatives met regularly. It achieved notable successes. There were no major strikes, whilst stoppages were generally short-lived and confined to individual yards. Independent moves by workers were firmly resisted. In March 1942 W. L. Barker, district secretary of the Confederation of Shipbuilding and Engineering Unions, expressed concern over the unofficial shop stewards movement. To stifle any rebel organisation he agreed with management that "no meetings could be held, notices posted, or collections made in any shipyard except by special permission".[52] The impact of wild cat strikes such as those on the Clyde in 1941 or the Tyne in 1944 barely caused ripples in Sunderland. Working customs and attitudes cumulatively had a much greater effect.

The prospect of women workers was not welcome. In early management discussions memories turned to 'Unfortunate experiences' in the last war when the result had been to "positively retard production rather than to help it".[53] The threat of a labour shortage opened employers' minds: thereafter opposition came from the unions. In spite of a national agreement a host of local objections were raised. There were still men unemployed; some ex-shipyard workers could be redeployed from non-essential industries; the Wear was making more efficient use of its male labour through transfers from yard to yard. Nationally female labour made little headway in shipbuilding and repairing; it constituted only two per cent of the workforce by October 1942. In Sunderland this figure was 1.3 per cent. Those women who were accepted were largely confined to less skilled work. Typically the National Society of Painters insisted they should only be allowed to do the undercoating in accommodation areas.

The reopening of the derelict site at Southwick formerly occupied by Swan, Hunter and Wigham Richardson was one of the apparent achievements of wartime adaptability. Thompson's took responsibility for the venture and work began on refitting the site in July 1942.

Prefabrication was used to a greater extent than in other yards and the first ship, *Empire Trail*, was launched just over a year later. However, far from being a crisp response to the need to increase production the scheme was devised as a cover to meet a coming threat to the Wear's labour supply. In May 1942 R. C. Thompson had been summoned to a meeting with Sir James Lithgow, Controller of Merchant Shipping. In effect the Sunderland firms were told to snap out of their parochialism. Nationally there was going to be an increase in the numbers employed on

King George VI and Queen Elizabeth visit J. L. Thompson's shipyard on 14 March 1943. There are some women workers in the crowd greeting them.

merchant and naval shipbuilding, but whilst other rivers were requesting additional manpower "the Wear had practically no demands at all".[54] Unless this was corrected quickly then skilled men would be transferred from Sunderland. Lithgow suggested that reopening one of the disued yards would result in

> placing an immediate and considerable demand for labour with the Ministry of Labour in which case it would be less likely that any of the existing establishments on the river would be interfered with.[55]

The WSA seized on this idea with alacrity. The Shipbuilding Corporation Yard was an answer to a number of other nagging difficulties. Every firm had troublesome workers who could be redeployed to the new yard. Moreover a higher proportion of women might be employed, again deflecting government criticism of the Wear's quotas. The remaining men on the dole, whose case the unions used to limit dilution, could also be absorbed. The Corporation Yard was to prove a temporary expedient, largely manned by unskilled and semi-skilled workers. It was closed down in 1947.

PEACE RETURNS

The formal announcement of VE day came late on Tuesday, 8 May 1945. The Mayor, Councillor John Young, proclaimed the official declaration of Germany's surrender from the town hall steps. The police band provided a fanfare of trumpets, while the biggest crowd since Sunderland won the cup in 1937, an estimated 10,000, packed the central block of Fawcett Street. Celebrations were heartfelt, and as extravagant as rationing permitted. The town was strewn with flags and buntings. Two adjoining houses in Coronation Street captured the mood of jubilation, their walls were

> covered with flags of the Empire, portraits of the King and Queen, Churchill, Montgomery and a banner containing the words "God Bless Our King".[56]

Perhaps most symbolic and most welcome of all was the ending of the blackout. Yet elements of disillusion set in quickly. A BBC broadcast on 18 May paid tribute to shipbuilding on the Clyde and Tyne but failed to mention the Wear. Would Sunderland again become the forgotten town it had appeared to be in the 1930s?

The slump had provoked sharp criticisms of national social policy, but the common struggle of the war years gave a huge impetus to reformers. The determination to build a more just society was exemplified by the Beveridge Report. Published on 1 December 1943 it became a best seller and the centre of an intense debate on reconstruction. An editorial in the *Echo* of 3 April 1943 followed Churchill's lead to attack "the present vogue for forgetting about the war and concentrating upon conditions that will follow". Nevertheless expectations emerged that were to bring a labour government to power in the election of July 1945. Stevenson refers to "the triumph of Mr. High Mind",[57] a view that an interventionist capitalist government could initiate the social amelioration which the British people had shown they deserved. A consensus that no government could again strengthen the pound

with mass unemployment held sway for the next 30 years. Sunderland took benefit from the full order books of the 1940s and the promise of positive discrimination for the depressed regions.

REFERENCES
1. Calder, Angus, *The Peoples War* (Jonathan Cape 1969) p. 17.
2. This follows Tom Harrison's definition, "a blitz is one where over one hundred German piloted bombers were involved at one conurbation on one night". *Living through the Blitz* (Collins 1967) p. 15.
3. TWAS 170/20, Sunderland County Borough Council Wartime Files *Civilian Deaths due to War Operations — Old Scheme.*
4. TWAS SDB/AA/1/40 Minutes of Sunderland C.B.C. (signed), 9 March 1938.
5. Thankfully never used in anger, Sunderland's Gas Cleansing Centres had their finest hours in response to the 'itch'. Personnel were repeatedly called upon to treat outbreak of scabies. Hot showers, towels and sulpher ointment were provided for sufferers, many of whom were children.
6. Carrying bulky gas masks was inconvenient. During the early years of the war public anxiety at the news could be judged by the numbers encumbering themselves with respirators.
7. TWAS T12/462 *Minutes of Ford Parish Council* 14 September, 1939.
8. Previously the home of Samuel Peter Austin, the shipbuilder, on the north side of Thornhill Park.
9. TWAS SDB/AA/1/40 *Minutes of Sunderland C.B.C.* (signed), 8 March 1939.
10. County Borough of Sunderland. *Annual Report of the Medical Officer of Health* (1940).
11. *Ibid.*
12. *SDE*, 25 August 1939.
13. *Ibid.*, 4 September 1939.
14. *Ibid.*, 15 March 1943.
15. No official historical record of Sunderland's casualties has ever been completed. In 1947 figures supplied by the Town Clerk to the Imperial War Graves Commission were as follows:
Casualties (Members of Civil Defence)
  Killed by enemy action — On Duty 28
  Killed by enemy action — Off Duty 1
Casualties (Civilian)
  Killed by enemy action — 267
  Seriously injured — 362
  Slightly injured — 639
In May 1967 the Civil Defence Officer gave slightly contradictory figures:
  Killed — 273
  Seriously injured — 389
  Slightly injured — 639
No separate figures were given for Civil Defence personnel.

16.	Killed	Seriously injured	Slightly injured
May 16	70	73	125
May 24	83	109	113

17. *SDE*, 24 May 1943.
18. TWAS 209/113 *Reports on Air Raids*, 1940-68.
19. *Ibid.*
20. TWAS T170/19 *Awards for Gallantry August 1940 — July 1953.*
21. On 20 September the *SDE* reported a typical vignette:

> One little girl on having a bath remarked "It's the first time I have been washed all over but it's nice". Two little girls were billeted with a very respectable family. On the fourth day the eldest girl approached her hostess with a puzzled look "Doesn't your old man ever take you to the pub for a drink?"

22. Marwick Arthur, *Britain in the Century of Total War* (Bodley Head 1968) p. 266.

23. *SDE*, 2 September 1939.
24. *SDE*, 15 July 1939.
25. *Sunderland at War*, a teaching pack edited by E. Longstaffe (1986).
26. *SDE*, 18 September 1939.
27. *Ibid.*, 11 November 1939.
28. Billeting allowances in September 1939 were 10s 6d (52½p) for a single child up to 14, with 8s 6d for each subsequent child. 10s 6d was paid for each child over 14. The government intended to recover up to 6s (30p) on a means test basis.
29. County Borough of Sunderland. *Thirty First Annual Report of the School Medical Service* (1939).
30. The families of agricultural workers often lived on the margins of poverty, now it appeared to some they were being asked to subsidise the children of others.
31. Longstaffe E. (Ed.) *Sunderland at War*, 1986.
32. *SDE*, 14 October 1939.
33. The debate over the re-opening of Bede School became particularly acrimonious. The LEA determined to make a stand over keeping the Collegiate Schools at Northallerton and Richmond. To return them to Sunderland would have meant recognising the complete failure of evacuation. By February 1940 most parents had become openly rebellious. "They decided to notify the committee that they intended bringing home their children . . . at the end of the present term". *SDE*, 19 February 1940.
34. *SDE*, 5 October 1939.
35. *SDE* for 16 October reported one school using "a large room at an old picture house, Boys' Brigade hut, Salvation Army hut, two gardeners' huts, two social centres, quoit club hut, and football club pavilion for classrooms".
36. TWAS T150/107 *Barnes Boys School Log Book 1902-1956.*

37. TWAS SDB/A14/1/88 *Minutes* of the Health Committee (signed), 25 October 1939.
38. *SDE*, 24 March 1943.
39. TWAS SDB/A14/1/88.
40. TWAS SDB/A14/1/90 *Minutes* of the Health Committee (signed), 27 January 1943.
41. *SDE*, 31 March 1943.
42. SDB/A14/1/90, 26 April 1942.
43. County Borough of Sunderland, *Annual Report of the Medical Officer of Health* (1944).
44. *SDE*, 30 March 1943.
45. *SDE*, 16 March 1943.
46. TWAS SDB/A2/1/45 *Minutes* of the Watch Committee (signed), 22 June 1943.
47. TWAS SDB A2/1/44 *Ibid.*, 23 January 1940.
48. However there were 1,539 full-time and 1,223 part-time 'immobile' women. From December 1941 women were gradually conscripted for industry and the services. 'Immobile' women were those with family responsibilities who could not be drafted to areas of labour shortages.
49. TWAS 270/3959 *War work for Sunderland workshops and factories.* Miscellaneous papers.
50. TWAS 270/3956 Sunderland CBC Town Clerk's Department Industrial Development File Number 3. The Ministry of Aircraft Production had built a unit next to Short's Shipyard in Pallion.
51. TWAS 990/40 Mssrs. Bartram and Sons Ltd. *Correspondence with the Admiralty* November 1942 — May 1943.
52. 708/11 *Minutes*, 24 March 1942.
53. *Ibid. Minutes*, 17 November 1941.
54. *Ibid. Minutes*, 27 May 1942.
55. *Ibid.*
56. *SDE*, 8 May 1945.
57. Stevenson J., *British Society 1914-1945* (Allen Lane 1984) p. 460.

April 3rd—10th

SUNDERLAND R.D.

Wings for Victory WEEK

OBJECTIVE £120,000

The cost of three Lancaster Bombers

Sunderland 1945-1987

Sunderland emerged from the Second World War with comprehensive ideas to expand the town's services and infrastructure. A post-war planning sub-committee of the Council was established in 1943[1] to co-ordinate these plans. The needs of housing and industry were paramount. New housing was required to remedy the longstanding overcrowding and the new war damage. In 1947 only seven out of 83 county boroughs in England and Wales suffered higher overall densities of population than Sunderland. Even in 1959 the town's density was still, at 21 persons per acre, in the top quartile for English towns. Industry was likewise required to expand, pursuing a process of diversification into light manufacturing and new technologies.

To meet these pressures the local authority looked towards the open spaces of nearby Ryhope, Tunstall, Silksworth, Herrington, Castletown, Boldon and Whitburn. Not unexpectedly, the expansion policy was opposed by the satellite villages, which considered themselves separate, distinct and threatened communities. They were alarmed at the prospect of being enveloped in the mass of dirty industry and poor housing which characterised Sunderland. Geographical propinquity and functional dependence however enforced their eventual submergence within the expanding mass of Sunderland.

The borough had been extended in 1895, 1928 and 1936, the last two extensions adding nearly half of its 7,000 acres. The 1950 Sunderland Extension Act added a modest 1,637 acres. Under the Local Government (Boundary Commission) Act of 1945, the Corporation made an unsuccessful bid for a wide crescent of land from neighbouring districts, which would have trebled the space for urban expansion. It was not until 1967 that the County Borough and Sunderland Rural District amalgamated. The extended borough included Ryhope, Silksworth, East Herrington and South Hylton, but excluded Boldon and Whitburn. The final extension of Sunderland occurred under the 1974 reorganisation of local government, when Hetton-le-Hole, Houghton-le-Spring and Washington Urban Districts joined Sunderland to form a new borough within Tyne and Wear Metropolitan County.

NEW ESTATES

Sunderland's need for more space was widely acknowledged. In 1952 the Minister of Housing and Local Government approved 5,000 more houses for 15,000 people in the Town Development Plan. The population decrease since 1931 had been reversed; in 1946 the town's population was estimated at 179,000, in 1951 it stood at 181,525[2] and it rose another four per cent by 1961,[3] mainly due to natural birthrates of over 20 per thousand.

The extension resulting from the 1950 Act enabled the growth to be concentrated in a continuous belt of new estates on the western edge of the borough. Between 1951 and 1959 an incredible 10,000 houses were built from Hylton Red House in the north through Pennywell to Farringdon in the south, producing homogeneous tracts of semi-detached council houses. The Council built enthusiastically, sensitive about the town's poor reputation for housing. Anxious to rid the inner wards of their notoriously high densities, confirmed by the 1951 census (Bridge, 39 per acre; Deptford, 44.8; Bishopwearmouth, 32), they transformed the surrounding landscape almost overnight from rural farmland to urban housing.

This process of expansion continued in the 1960s, with new estates at Town End Farm, Downhill, Witherwack, Gilley Law and Mill Hill. Thorney Close ward virtually doubled its population from 7,702 in 1951 to 13,969 in 1971. Over the same period the population of inner areas plummeted; Central ward fell from 13,133 to 8,947.

This short phase of population redistribution effectually ringed the Victorian town on all sides with council housing; only 15 per cent of the building programme was carried out by the private sector. This gave Sunderland one of the most impressive local authority records in the country. In the vast new estates, curved roads and avenues replaced the terraced streets of the old inner town, gardens replaced backyards and grassed spaces replaced derelict bomb-sites.

Farringdon Hall estate in 1950, now covered by the houses of Farringdon, Gilley Law and Doxford Park.

The estates, however, were soon affected by social changes. Even in 1950 the "trees, shrubs and hedges in Thorney Close estate were being destroyed by gangs with axes and saws."[4] The extension of Barnes Park in 1952 and 1955 to provide more open space for recreational use did not curb the vandalism. Nor were the new estates immune from natural population changes and the ageing process. Within a decade, the demographic decline of the inner areas was gradually transferred to the post-war neighbourhoods. Pennywell, a product of the 1950s, fell in population from 10,063 in 1961 to 9,029 in 1971.[5] Decline extended and deepened over the next decade (see fig 1) and every ward except Ryhope and Silksworth averaged declines of between one and two per cent per annum, 1971-81.

The total population living in the inner areas (corresponding more or less to Sunderland in 1900) was much less in the 1950s than the whole population of a century earlier. Here, substantial falls in the numbers of school-age groups helped bring about school reorganisation in the period 1983-87.[6] Younger, better-qualified and more ambitious people tended to move to new estates or distant jobs, further distorting the balance of age, class and type in the older areas. The increased proportion of pensioners had implications for the town's health and social services. In the town as a whole, by 1981 nearly 18 per cent of the population was over 60 years of age, while those over 75 had increased by 24 per cent since 1971.

The immediate post-war policy was to attack the town's notoriously overcrowded slum areas by wholesale demolition. Officially, the borough acknowledged only seven per cent of

The policy of slum clearance (officials preferred the term 'improvements') has been traced in considerable detail by Dennis.[8] The celebrated case of Millfield's housing problems and the authority's response received national attention, a textbook example of the interaction between residents and the planning bureaucracy. Millfield, constructed in the last quarter of the nineteenth century, grew up to serve riverside industry and the shipyards. It was characterised by one-storey, privately-owned cottages, occupied by a close-knit artisan community. Parts of the area were duly scheduled for demolition as the houses did not satisfy approved standards; 80 per cent lacked or shared at least one of the basic facilities. Official interviews with householders painted an appalling picture of neglect and deprivation:

> dingy . . . dirty . . . cobbled . . . no electricity supply . . . dark passages . . . no facilities for washing . . . damp . . . no door on the outside toilet . . . plaster falling off the walls . . . three families share a yard.[9]

But the neighbourhood possessed remarkable community cohesion and, led by Norman Dennis, a sociology lecturer, called for improvement and renovation rather than demolition. A widely publicised campaign against the clearance plans was launched by the residents' association, raising general issues about the powers of authorities and the direction of planning. By 1970 the notion of more adequate consultation, as propounded in 1968 by the national enquiry chaired by a junior minister, Arthur Skeffington, was widely accepted. By then the battle for housing

St. John and St. Patrick's Church School (1972) in the east end, where falling rolls brought about this interesting merger in 1981 of two schools, one Anglican, the other Roman Catholic. The former rectory of St. John's, the Trafalgar Square almshouses, and the South Dock are also visible.

the housing stock as slums, but comparative studies suggested[7] that the figure was nearer 25 per cent, the highest in the country. The 1951 census showed 43 per cent of households either sharing or entirely without piped water; 52 per cent had no fixed bath. Even ten years later the respective figures were 14 per cent and 25 per cent, and in 1971 10 per cent of households still lacked hot water and bath facilities. While building their peripheral estates, the Corporation set out to destroy these slum areas.

rehabilitation and renovation rather than demolition and clearance had been won.

The 1969 and 1974 Housing Acts gave the borough authorities increased powers to improve housing and neighbourhoods. General Improvement Areas (GIAs) were created to focus improvement resources on groups of adjacent streets. Sunderland's first GIA was Hartington Street, Roker, in October 1972. Later, Housing Action Areas were created in Millfield, Hendon and Southwick to remedy deficiencies.

Where demolition took place rather than improvement, as in Hendon, the east end, and Monkwearmouth, new council housing was substituted. The new three- or four-storey maisonettes, as in Barclay Court (1957-60), Lawrence Court and Railway Court (1958-60), were popular at first as fashionable alternatives to the old terraces. Almost as soon as they were completed, however, they were upstaged by the semi-detached, gardened houses of the new peripheral estates, on green-field sites away from the traditional industrial areas. Within a decade the 'courts' began to show signs of wear and tear, sinking under vandalism and vacancy. A quarter of a century after their construction they were demolished or comprehensively remodelled, losing their top floors. In 1986-7 Barclay Court, Monkwearmouth, began to receive this treatment at a cost of £1 million, a remnant of a discredited housing policy.[10]

Sunderland in 1980 had, by national standards, a high proportion (56 per cent) of council-owned housing, with a mere 38 per cent owner-occupied. From 1980 to 1986 about 10 per cent of the council house stock was sold to private buyers; of 8,642 applications to buy, 5,465 had been effected by January 1987. Housing Associations and Co-operatives met the special needs of groups who organised and controlled their own housing.

By 1987, despite problems and deficiencies, Sunderland's houses generally reached a high standard. Less than three per cent still lacked exclusive use of basic amenities such as inside sanitation or suffered from overcrowding, while increasingly houses were centrally heated and insulated.

ECONOMIC TRENDS

Post-war Sunderland epitomised the demise of the northern industrial town. Once a leading shipbuilding centre, and justifiably proud of its engineering achievement, it suffered from the progressive downward spiral of national decline and regional disadvantage.

The town's economic transformation after 1945 was truly dramatic. The immediate post-war era opened with naive confidence that the old stalwarts of heavy industry provided a sound platform for reconstruction and future development. But the massive collapse of the industries upon which Sunderland depended undermined the reconstruction effort and exposed the structural frailties of the local economy.

In 1960 coalmining employed some 18,000 workers in the area, about 20 per cent of the male workforce. By 1971 numbers had fallen to 12,000, and slumped further to 3,500 by 1985, making nonsense of optimistic 1940s predictions.[11] The energy crisis of 1973 and the miners' strike of 1984-85 brought coal to the political forefront; ugly and violent conflict broke out at the colliery gates at Wearmouth, symbolically and physically very close to the heart of the town. By the 1980s it was the town's sole remaining pit, employing 2,000 men, producing 1 million tons annually, and with substantial off-shore reserves.[12] It is scheduled for further capital improvements as part of on-going regional investment.

Shipbuilding pursued a similar downward spiral. In 1964 some 20,000 workers were employed in local yards, nearly ten times as many as there were in 1986. There was a dis-

A striking contrast between later 1950s housing development (Barclay Court), on Dame Dorothy Street, and the nineteenth century terraces of Monkwearmouth/Roker beyond. Roker Park AFC is visible, top right. (Looking north from an aerial position over the river Wear.)

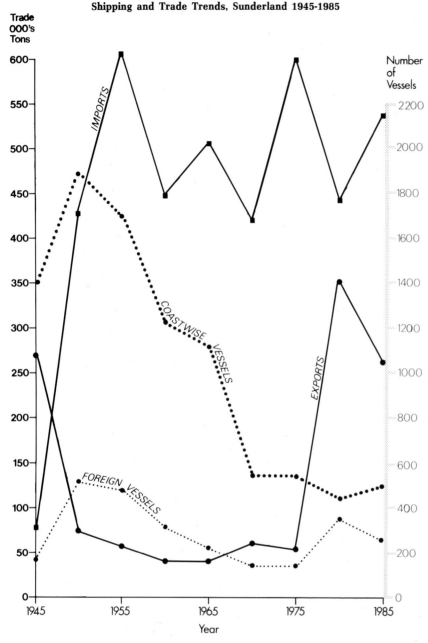

Shipping and Trade Trends, Sunderland 1945-1985

Trade
000's
Tons

Number
of
Vessels

IMPORTS

COASTWISE VESSELS

EXPORTS

FOREIGN VESSELS

Year

tressing catalogue of closures and amalgamations of well-known and long-established firms: Austins, Crowns, Shorts and Laings disappeared between 1954 and 1963; Greenwells, Bartrams, Thompsons and Clarks Engineering had also gone by 1980. Curative and preventive measures were tried to improve competitiveness and shed labour,[13] while rationalisation reduced local firms to two major groupings by the 1970s: Doxfords (Sunderland Shipbuilding and Engineering) and Austin & Pickersgill, on opposite sides of the river. Then nationalisation followed in 1977, on the recommendation of the Geddes Report.[14] Despite government intervention, credit schemes and EEC support, despite the proven ability of local yards to modernise and innovate (notably in the mass-production during the 1970s of SD14 ships at Austin & Pickersgills), Sunderland's falling production paralleled the nation's decline in world shipping. In 1963 Britain occupied second place in world tonnage; in 1983, with half the 1963 deadweight tonnage, it was sixth.

The helplessness of the area in the face of international trends did not prevent an energetic campaign to 'save our shipyards'. Shipbuilding seemed a declining industry, and the question arose of whether the town could survive without it.[15] The close interplay of river and town, yard and community, work and home, noted by Hopkins,[16] was threatened; loyalties, friendships and social networks were loosened, and the busy industrial sites along the river became empty wastes. The River Wear had always served as a barometer of the town's prosperity, at boom times full of life, ships and vitality, at others deserted and depressing. As shipyards and shipping declined, the Port Authority fought a rearguard action, investing £200,000 annually in river improvements, port development and yard construction to keep the port competitive. The figures (excluding coal) revealed limitations: a single commodity, oil, made up 90 per cent of imports, while limestone constituted 80 per cent of exports. The port was a financial liability, though speculation about off-shore oil

Austin and Pickersgill's shipyard, Southwick, in 1985, showing the fabrication sheds and covered berths constructed 1975-77.

raised hopes for a brighter future with new local manufacturing to reward an enterprising promotion and marketing record in the port.

Though uncertainty threatened these major industries, it seemed in the boom conditions of the 1950s that the conditions which had created Victorian wealth might be returning. This optimism continued into the 1960s, with rising living standards, more disposable income and the shorter working week, while the prospect of mass unemployment and industrial collapse was apparently remote. Nevertheless, the Sunderland Junior Chamber of Commerce[17] had indicated by the late 1950s that the high demand generated by the War was ending. The struggle to replace tradi-

1962, grew to a 2,000 workforce by 1970, but shrank by 1984 to a meagre 200. Some companies, like Joblings and Coles Cranes, came under external control (Cornings and Groves respectively) and many lost workers in consequential reorganisation. The vulnerability of branch plants was exposed in nearby Washington. In fact the economic outlook of the 1980s was bleak. Though Sunderland enjoyed Development Area status and was eligible for maximum Urban Aid and EEC grants, the curbs on central, regional and local government spending and greater reliance on market forces implied a difficult future.

Local authorities played a vital part in the struggle for new industry. The co-ordinated

Looking north along the line of the A19 by-pass on the western edge of Sunderland. The Chester Road junction is in the foreground and in the distance the Hylton Bridge over the Wear. On the right the *Sunderland Echo* premises on the Pennywell Industrial Estate are under construction (1974).

tional declining industries focussed on attracting new industry to new sites, away from the river. Significant light industry had been developed already by 1939 at, for example, the Pallion Industrial Estate. Other estates followed, encouraged by the regional incentives of successive governments, at Southwick, Hendon and Pennywell. Television components, radio, and electronic equipment, clothing and mail-order firms appeared, tapping especially the growing female labour market. In 1963, out of a total labour force of about 85,000, 41 per cent were in manufacturing; of these, 5,000 were women. By 1985 nearly half the labour force was female, reflecting the switch from manufacturing to services as well as the role of women in society.

The collapse of manufacturing meant that over 34,000 jobs were lost between 1971 and 1981 alone.[18] Particularly disappointing was the performance of some firms on the post-war industrial estates: Plessey, employing 4,500 in 1970, closed in 1977; Thorn AEI opened in

efforts of Sunderland Borough, Tyne and Wear Council, Washington Development Corporation, and the government scored a major success in 1984 when they succeeded in attracting Nissan to build its new UK factory on Wearside. Whatever the long-term economic prospects for the venture, it provided a much-needed psychological boost, equivalent, the press suggested,[19] to winning the FA cup again. The first phase was a modest one, a £50 million plant employing 500 men; even the second phase announced in mid-1986 did not match optimistic dreams. But it was hoped that Nissan would bring a multiplier effect to local construction, port and engineering firms, and also attract other Japanese companies.

The battle to regenerate jobs continued on a wide front. The local authority and its industrial development service was supplemented by the initiatives of groups and individuals. The Tyne and Wear Enterprise Trust of 1982, supported by the European Social Fund, stimulated and encouraged small

Washington New Town

Washington was designated a new town by the Department of the Environment in July 1964. The idea of a new town in the area was proposed initially by Durham County Council who wanted to raise the quality of the local environment, improve employment opportunities and to counter the area's ailing collieries and dereliction. Located close to and between old industrial areas on Tyneside and Wearside, Washington offered a suitable strategic site for a major new growth pole. The White Paper entitled 'The North East: a programme for regional development and growth', published in November 1963, had included specific proposals for a new town at Washington. After the Minister of Housing and Local Government had issued a draft designation order, and after a local public inquiry, the order was duly confirmed. The Development Corporation was established in September of the same year, and has lasted until 1987.

The New Town designation covered 2,270 hectares (5,610 acres) mainly north of the River Wear, west of Sunderland and south of Gateshead. It incorporated existing historic villages, colliery rows and individual farms, which together housed about 20,000 people in 1964. The Master Plan set out to integrate these scattered communities into an enlarged planned urban environment with an eventual population of 80,000, applying all the accumulated knowledge and wisdom of the British new town movement.

The new town is planned on an axial network of primary and secondary roads serving 18 distinct residential areas and 'villages' and ten industrial estates. The hub of the system is the Galleries, marked by the only high rise building in the new town. Here shops, offices and services are centralised, some of which meet sub-regional, as well as new town, needs.

Each residential area was planned to accommodate about 4,500 people and contain basic community facilities such as schools, churches, and pubs or social centres, as well as a range of basic shops. The 'villages' are recognised by distinct features, especially in their house type and design from which detail the physical growth of Washington can be traced. Some of the older villages suffer from the deficiencies and short-comings of 1960s housing. Other 'villages' provide a mix of types of houses and a more attractive social environment for the expanding residential population.

Nearly 30 per cent of Washington's population is below 15 years of age, and less than seven per cent over 65 years of age. It is the youthfulness and lower proportions of elderly which demographically distinguish it from 'old' Sunderland. The predominant family grouping in Washington (about 55 per cent) is that of parents with unmarried children, which tends to distort the demand for

This view captures very well the atmosphere of the Galleries, a two-deck shopping and business centre.

The designation of Washington New Town led to considerable improvement in the physical landscape. This photograph depicts the removal of coal heaps from the site of the town's F pit.

Some of the newer housing in Albany.

services and employment for women. A range of factory units, purpose-built, with good access and preferential rents, backed by special promotion campaigns, proved attractive even to big multi-national and national companies as well as small starter businesses.

The economic recession of the 1980s however caused unemployment rates to rise rapidly in the new town as many of the branch factories were closed down or relocated elsewhere by their companies. It was the arrival of Nissan in 1985 which provided a much needed psychological boost to the corporation's industrial and promotional policies. And recent signs suggest that the new town is continuing to generate jobs in its quest for sustainable growth.

With a population of about 55,000 in 1987, Washington assumes an important role in the life of the area, albeit secondary to its larger and older neighbour, Sunderland. The Development Corporation's functions are now being taken over by the Borough of Sunderland. As the new town matures it will be interesting to observe how, if at all, the new planned environment will benefit human health, community relations and personal happiness.

educational, health and social services. Sadly, but not unexpectedly the social problems of modern society such as stress, vandalism and drug abuse have not been excluded from Washington. Single parent families have now grown to five per cent of all family groupings in the new town, and in some localities a high proportion of the population are dependent on state and supplementary benefits.

The performance of Washington in providing jobs has generally been good, especially in the 1960s and 1970s, compared with the older, less favoured areas of Sunderland. To replace old declining industries new firms were attracted from the start, especially in light engineering,

Looking west over the Galleries and the centre of Washington New Town. The different styles of housing in the "villages" can be observed as can the relationship between the primary and secondary road system. The A1 can be identified at the top of the photograph.

business enterprise.[20] The Pallion Residents' Enterprises[21] harnessed the enthusiasm and skills of local people in converting a vandalised factory into an industrial sports and leisure complex to serve the community.

In 1987 one of the country's new Urban Development Corporations was established for Tyne and Wear, as part of the government's new national strategy for tackling the persistent decline of inner cities. Under this initiative, local and private business expertise and resources are being harnessed to help regenerate local economies. Much of the Wear estuary, the port area and part of the east end and Hendon Industrial Zone lie within the Development Corporation's boundaries.

UNEMPLOYMENT

The closure of shipyards, collieries and factories was catastrophic for the neighbourhoods and families heavily dependent upon them. Ryhope lost its pit in 1966, where 69 per cent of the village males were employed and the dismay, depression and reaction of its people were the subject of a detailed study.[22] Some welcomed the closure for health reasons, but others were shocked:

> I cried when I got home. I felt the bottom had fallen out of my world. I didn't expect to get another job. I was apprehensive about going to a new colliery . . . making new friends and settling down.

Similar emotions must have coloured reaction to all the other closures in the town, and the psychological, physical, mental and social costs were far-reaching. Sunderland had long recorded rates of unemployment which were among the highest in the region and the country.[23] In January 1986 the figures were 22.7 per cent for the town, 19.5 per cent for the northern region, and 13.9 per cent nationally. Between 1979 and 1985 overall unemployment in the town rose by about 100 per cent.

Unemployment in the 1980s affected some people and districts more than others. 30 per cent of Sunderland's unemployed were between 18 and 24 years, with male rates higher than female, and most males likely to be

out of work for more than two years. Some districts enjoyed unemployment rates no higher than parts of south-east England, while others, sometimes in adjoining streets, might be as high as 63 per cent.[24]

A series of government measures strove to alleviate youth unemployment: Youth Opportunities Programme (1975), Special Temporary Employment Programme (1975), Youth Training Scheme (1983). A local venture, Springboard, was set up in 1975 by Community Service Volunteers and funded by the Manpower Services Commission to provide temporary work for young people.[25] But the lack of permanent employment for three-quarters of those emerging from YTS work meant that a serious problem remained.

'URBAN CRISIS' AND PUBLIC HEALTH

The economic and social malaise of towns like Sunderland was recognised as being of crisis proportions in the 1970s. In November 1977 the town was included as one of 15 'programme' authorities which could take advantage of extra resources to be made available under the 1978 Inner Urban Areas Act. It was required to define inner areas for this purpose.

Two years earlier Sunderland Borough's Planning Department had undertaken its own analysis of the local 'urban crisis'. Relying on indicators such as unemployment, housing and demography in each ward, it defined an area encompassing much of the town's older core and some of its outer estates, and three zones of greatest need were identified[26]: the east end, north Hendon and Bishopwearmouth; Marley Potts, Southwick and west Monkwearmouth; Ford and Pennywell. The population of this area was declining, falling by 25 per cent between 1971 and 1981 to become less than 20 per cent of the town's numbers; further, the area's population was both ageing (20 per cent over 60 years) and youthful (25 per cent under 15 years). The area was extended in 1983 to take in Special Priority Outer Areas at Thorney Close/Farringdon and Castletown/Hylton Red House/Downhill/Town End Farm, for these suburban estates had suffered disproportionately from economic recession and social trends.[27]

The 'areas of need' approach showed the borough Council's early commitment to a policy of 'positive discrimination', where projects were given priority in, and extra resources were channelled to, defined areas. A further measure, the Tyne and Wear Act (1976) allowed the borough to allocate further grants' and loans to zones designated as Industrial Improvement Areas (IIAs) and Commercial Improvement Areas (CIAs). Rundown areas were to be rejuvenated through the preparation of new industrial sites, landscaping, service provision, loans and grants.[28] As IIAs and CIAs, the derelict stretches of the river bank were transformed and revived during the 1980s.

The urban programme had social as well as economic aspects. Eleven neighbourhood

Population change in Sunderland 1971-1981

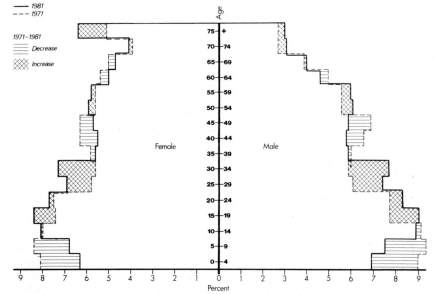

centres were located in areas of need to provide advice about matters of law, tax and housing. Though sometimes perceived as left-wing, they provided decentralised and personalised help for people coping with complex problems.[29] The years after 1945 saw a considerable expansion of welfare and social services, in Sunderland as nationally, to meet the needs of the poor, sick, disabled, elderly and unemployed. Sunderland people suffered from poor health, compared with the national or regional average; thus, infant mortality rates in 1948 were 55 per thousand compared with the 34 of England and Wales. Though Sunderland continued to record significantly higher than average rates for some years, the differences became less alarming as the benefits of immunisation were felt; in 1951, for the first year ever, no child died of diptheria in the town. The overall death rate, however, remained stubbornly 11 per cent higher than it should have been.

National surveys[29] showed health and health-care weaknesses in most north-eastern towns. Sunderland suffered from high death rates of persons under 65, low birth weights and above-average perinatal mortality. These were the result of general environmental factors such as housing and working conditions, pollution and low incomes, and perhaps of local personal preferences in diet, drink and lack of exercise.

In 1948, when the National Assistance Act required local authorities to take responsibility for the aged and infirm, Sunderland had one residential institution, the Highfield Hospital, formerly part of the Union Workhouse. The Council had now to provide alternative accommodation for the elderly, as well as a range of social activity and support services, so new residential units were quickly established at Hendon (1951), Roker (1953), Cedars (1953), Thorney Close (1953), South Hylton (1955), Pennywell (1956) and Hylton Red House (1961). By 1982, 21 local authority homes were established. Subsequent changes in DHSS regulations and the Registered Homes Act encouraged proliferation of private sector accommodation, so by the middle 1980s there were as many private homes as there were belonging to the authority.

In the 12 years after 1975 spending on health and related services for the Sunderland area trebled so far as hospitals were concerned, quadrupled for community health and family practitioner services, and quintupled for the social services.[31] A network of health centres covered the town, initiated in 1956 by the Springwell Centre; and by the 1980s 80 per cent of general practitioners operated from such centres. Simultaneously, social services became more decentralised, comprehensive and specialised. Area social work teams operated so that services could respond readily to growing and changing demand at local level. Meals on wheels, home helps, day community nurseries, warden schemes, workshops for the handicapped, and residential care units were provided to meet special needs. Sunderland can now be proud of the facilities and resources it provides for those in need or 'social distress'.

SOCIETY AND ENVIRONMENT

Sunderland's people in the post-war decades, in common with others throughout the country, went through tremendous social changes: living standards rose, leisure time increased, gender roles changed, new cultural and behavioural patterns emerged. In most respects Sunderland's experience differed little from that elsewhere, though car ownership, for example, remained lower than average, only 48 per cent in the 1980s.

The processes of environmental improvement affected not only the east end slums and the derelict river bank, but the town's commercial centre as well. Between 1966 and 1969 this was redeveloped to provide 250,000 square feet of new shop space, three 19-storey blocks of flats, a bus station and car-parking, at a cost of £3½ million. The scheme scored a modest commercial success, though was not particularly popular with residents. It was soon overtaken, architecturally and commercially, by Newcastle's Eldon Square development. In 1987 work began to roof over and upgrade the shopping area at a cost estimated to be £15 million. At the same time, other new commercial building in Park Lane, Bridge Street, Waterloo Place and elsewhere sought to revive the town centre in face of the challenge from out-of-town supermarkets and the Gateshead Metro Centre.[32] Yet popular opinion continued to bemoan the loss of familiar facades and buildings, and local people were incensed by the demolition of the Victorian Town Hall, seen as having been sacrificed in 1971 on the altar of commercial redevelopment.[33]

Its replacement, the new Town Hall and Civic Centre, was designed to give 'an image to local government'. It stood physically and psychologically aloof from both the commercial centre and the main residential areas. Designed by Sir Basil Spence, Bonnington and Collins, its buildings were massed around a series of hexagonal courts rising up a sloping site and culminating in a theatrical council chamber and mayoral suite. It was intended to

The temporary reconstruction of Sunderland's town centre (east of Crowtree Road) in 1960, prior to the major developments of the 1970s. On Fawcett Street in the distance the dome of the former Subscription Library (1878) and the tower of the Town Hall (1890) are visible.

Fawcett Street in 1962, looking north from Borough Road. The foreground is dominated by the premises of Binns Ltd.

The demolition of the Town Hall, a familiar landmark, in 1971.

centralise all the borough's departments and to produce greater efficiency in local government.[34] It was undoubtedly an architectural and administrative success, but by 1987 both its functions and structure were raising doubts.[35] For Sunderlanders, its brown bricks and tiles, paving and steps, lacked the charisma of the Fawcett Street Town Hall, whose clock tower had stood like a lighthouse marking the heart of the town.

The traditional business quarter at the town centre, straddling the streets eastward from Fawcett Street, was recognised as being of historical and architectural importance. It was designated in 1971, with six other districts[36] as a Conservation Area, to protect its historic buildings from unsympathetic change and encourage environmental enhancement through the collaboration of owners, tenants, developers and planners.

Conservation Areas covered only about 186 acres (75 hectares) of the Borough. More extensive, of course, were the areas rescued from industrial dereliction to be made environmentally attractive and, often, to be used for recreation. The developments here were in direct continuation from the parks and gardens, swimming baths, museum and libraries provided for nineteenth century recreation. In 1976 the 160 acres (65 hectares) of disused Silksworth Colliery were converted to leisure purposes, epitomising the switch from economic productivity to recreational use. At a cost of £1.3 million, two lakes, a ski-slope, an all-weather athletics track and other playing facilities were provided on an unpromising site.[37]

Informal recreational use of the many new open spaces increased markedly, and the planners tried to link them by walkways, corridors and wedges along disused mineral lines, streams and parks. Sunderland carefully protected its open spaces, and some were designated as Sites of Special Scientific Interest, as at Tunstall Hills, Fulwell Quarries, and Hylton Dene; Timber Beach became a Nature Reserve. The Wear and its banks became a recreational corridor stretching up to Washington,[38] though sometimes this development became a battleground for conflicting interests, town and country, housing and farming, industry and leisure interests.

REFERENCES

1. First met 31 October 1943. TWAS, SDB A 59/111.
2. General Registrar, 1951 Census.
3. General Registrar, 1961 Census, Durham, Table III.
4. *SE*, 4 May 1950.
5. General Registrar, 1971 Census.
6. J. Hall, *Falling rolls and re-organisation of secondary schools*, Sunderland Borough, 1983.
7. C. A. Moser and W. Scott, *British Towns: a statistical study of their social and economic differences* (London 1961).
8. N. Dennis, *People and Planning: the sociology of housing in Sunderland* (Faber & Faber, 1970) ibid. *Public participation and planning blight* (Faber & Faber, 1972).
9. *Ibid.* (1970), p. 175.

10. J. Jacques, 'Barclay Court gets £1m revamp', *SE* 6 August 1986.
11. T. Robertson, 'The geology of the Northumberland and Durham Coalfield', in *North East Coast: a survey of industrial facilities*, pp. 1-12, Northern Industrial Group, Newcastle-upon-Tyne.
12. Silk, 'Deep coalmining in North-East England in the 1980s', *Northern Economic Review*, Spring 1983, pp. 28-36.
13. D. Todd, 'Strategies of growth, diversification and rationalisation in the evolution of concentration in British shipbuilding', *Regional Studies* 1983, 18(1) pp. 56-67.
14. R. M. Geddes, *Report of the Shipbuilding Inquiry Committee, 1965-66*, HMSO.
15. *SE*, 11 October 1984.
16. C. H. G. Hopkins, *Pallion 1874-1954: church and people in a shipyard parish* (Wearside Printing Co., 1954).
17. Junior Chamber of Commerce, *The Future of Sunderland*, 1963.
18. I. Stone, J. Stevens and M. Morris, *Economic restructuring and employment changes on Wearside since 1971: employment potential in Sunderland*, report by Sunderland Polytechnic EDU for the EEC/Borough of Sunderland, 1986.
19. *SE* 30 March 1984.
20. I. Stone and J. Stevens, *Small firms and employment potential on Wearside*, Sunderland Borough and Sunderland Polytechnic, 1986. R. Clough, 'Tyne and Wear Enterprise Trust — a new approach to an old problem', *Northern Economic Review*, 1984.
21. C. Robertson, 'Pallion Residents Enterprises Ltd', *Northern Economic Review*, 5, 1982, pp. 11-15.
22. Dept. of Employment and Productivity, *Ryhope: a pit closes; a study in re-deployment*. HMSO, 1970.
23. *The Times*, 'Survey of North-East', 10 February 1969.
24. Tyne & Wear County Council, *Unemployment*, reported in *SE*, 13 April and 6 October 1986.
25. S. Millham, R. Butlock and K. Hosie, *A study of CSV's job creation project in Sunderland* (Dartington Social Research Unit 1977).
26. Borough of Sunderland, *Area of Needs Report*, Programme Planning Unit, 1979.
27. A number of local authorities commissioned CES Ltd to study the urban crisis in outer estates; *Sunday Times*, 12 August 1986.
28. A. T. Rafeek, *Reclamation of Derelict Land*, Planning Dept., Sunderland Borough, 1984; S. J. Cameron et al, *Local Authority aids to industry; an evaluation in Tyne and Wear*, Dept. of Environment, 1982.
29. Anon., *Centres under attack: the case for the centres*. Sunderland Independent Neighbourhood Centres, n.d., c. 1981.
30. D. Black, *Inequalities in Health*, DHSS, 1980.
31. Sunderland Health Authority, District Strategic Plan, 1985.
32. Sunderland Corporation, *The Sunderland Hypermarket Survey*, 1971.
33. D. Donnelly, B. Goodey and M. Menzies, *Perception related survey for local authorities: a pilot study in Sunderland*. Centre for Urban and Regional Studies, Research Memo 20, Birmingham University 1973.
34. L. Wright, 'Sunderland Town Hall and Civic Centre', *Architectural Review* March 1971, p. 162.
35. G. Robertson, 'Civic Centre is cracking up', *SE* 1 July 1986.
36. Under the Civic Amenities Act, 1967, supported by Section 10 of the Town and Country Planning (Amended) Act (1972).
37. In 1965 the provision of playing fields in Sunderland was estimated at only 1.5 acres per thousand people compared with six acres nationally. J. Bridge, 'The chance to share', Education Circular, 1970, TWAS SDB 630/67.
38. *The River Wear Plan*, Sunderland Borough Council, 1978.

Brief Biographies

It virtually goes without saying that the history of a community is very much the story of the contributions made by a mass of diverse individuals. The brief biographies which follow are intended to offer a representative selection indicating the range and variety of Sunderland life stories but without any claim to be comprehensive or definitive. Clearly one limitation has been space. However, in drawing up a final short list of candidates some sort of criteria had to be adopted. The key one is the role of the individual in question in the development of the town whether it be in terms of business, religion, culture, politics, social reform or whatever. This explains amongst other things why local characters like Jack Crawford and Harry Watts are included while an eminent personage like General Sir Henry Havelock is omitted except as the father of Sir Henry Havelock-Allan. Naturally many of the individuals who made vital contributions did not come from Sunderland at all, but this has not been held against them. There is a notable shortage of women in the list but it would have required some very forceful and positive discrimination to include women from a period when they were largely excluded from any significant public life. The twentieth century overall is very largely unrepresented, and this is difficult to explain. Perhaps it has something to do with the problem of perspective, and with the effacement of individuals by the bureaucratisation of much of modern life.

Abbreviations used:

Brockie — Brockie, W. *Sunderland Notables* (Hills, 1894).

Corder — The Corder Manuscripts (see the Guide to Sources).

DBB — *Dictionary of Business Biography.*

DNB — *Dictionary of National Biography.*

Inst. Mech. — *Transactions of the Institution of Mechanical Engineers.*

NECIES — *Transactions of the NE Coast Institution of Engineers and Shipbuilders.*

SE — *Sunderland Echo.*

SDE — *Sunderland Daily Echo.*

SDP — *Sunderland Daily Post.*

SH — *Sunderland Herald.*

SYB — *Sunderland Year Book.*

THE AUSTIN FAMILY (SHIPBUILDERS)

Peter, son of George Austin (farmer) of Houghton and Jane Lawson, was born about 1770. He came to Southwick in 1802 and, with Samuel Moore, worked Brunton's Pottery. Married Jane Moore (1769-1840); their second son *Samuel Peter* (1808-1867) played an important part in developing the shipyard business, which began in the late 1820s. Peter snr. retired in 1846 and died in 1863. By 1834 the shipyard was in the name of Austin & Son, a typical small scale Wear shipyard usually turning out one or two ships in a year. Five ships built in 1838 totalled 1,610 tons but none were built in the following year when a partnership was formed with John & George Mills. This partnership lasted 20 years, while the Austins continued to work on their own account. About 1855-7, Austin built a patent slipway and so extended the repair work which was a characteristic of the family business. Samuel Peter was an original member of the Wear Shipbuilders' Association, served as a member of the Board of Guardians, and was for three years on the Town council. Said to have been "a somewhat rough individual", though, his former school mistress wife Julia Ann (1819-1879) was "a very refined and educated woman". Their son *Samuel Peter II* (1842-1925) joined the firm in 1860. On his father's death in 1867 he continued to manage the yard assisted by his brother *Stanley* (died 1900). Their yard was one of those which persisted in wood construction, building their last wood vessel in 1869. No new ships were built for four years until iron construction began in 1874. The opening of a new graving dock late in 1870 extended the repair facilities. A partnership of a few years duration was formed with George Hunter, who later established his own yard on the Tyne and constructed the *Mauretania.* A Private Limited Company was formed in 1895 and four years later it went public, with W. H. Dugdale as managing director, Samuel Peter II as chairman and his brother Stanley and son *Selwyn Percy* (1871-1922) members of the Board. Samuel Peter II married Marion York daughter of Professor

Spoone; there were three daughters to the marriage. He was very active in the town's politics as a Conservative and was defeated in the 1880 parliamentary election by Storey and Gourley. Served as a magistrate for both Sunderland and Durham, of which county he was Deputy Lieutenant. He did not retire until within a year of his death and left an estate worth £123,683 gross. JFC

Corder MSS; *SH,* 7 June 1867; *Newcastle Daily Journal,* 26 & 30 March 1925.

BACKHOUSE FAMILY (QUAKER BANKERS AND PHILANTHROPISTS)

Prominent north eastern Quaker bankers and businessmen, associated especially with Darlington and Sunderland. *Jonathan Backhouse* (1747-1826) married Ann Pease. Their son *Edward Backhouse I* (1781-1860) married Mary Robson; left Darlington for Sunderland to establish a branch of the family bank there. Lived on Sunniside, and then built Ashburne, the large family house on Ryhope Road, c. 1820. *Edward Backhouse II* (1808-1879) brought up in Sunderland from an early age and became one of the town's foremost citizens. Partner in the family banking and colliery undertakings, but took little active part in them; preferred to concentrate on religious and philanthropic work, especially after a conversion experience at 30. Attended the Nile Street Meeting House. Served as elder, and from 1852 as a Quaker minister (voluntary and unpaid). Preached in Quaker assemblies and a frequent speaker at public meetings. Published *The Religious Society of Friends: Doctrines and Practices in which they agree with their fellow Christians, and others in which they differ* (1870). Conscientious in upholding Quaker principles, including a refusal to pay Church Rates; endured prosecution for this. Built the Pottery Buildings 1866 as a mission and social centre in the east end. Active in its work. Established home for women who 'desired to retrieve their lost character'. Enthusiastic supporter of temperance. A magistrate. Liberal. Co-founder of the *SDE.* Man of wide talents — water colourist, naturalist, traveller, yachtsman, historian. His *Early Church History* (1884) published posthumously, the only volume of an intended series on church history from the Quaker viewpoint. Left a collection of illustrated travel diaries and sketch books. Married Katherine Mounsey in 1856. Lived at Ashburne. Died Hastings 22 May 1879. No children. Buried in the Quaker section of Bishopwearmouth Cemetery, with his wife. *Thomas William Backhouse* (1842-1920) was the son of *Thomas Backhouse* (1810-1857) brother of Edward II. Lived at West Hendon house on Ryhope Road. Coal owner. Keen amateur astronomer with a roof top observatory at his home. Wrote on astronomy. Kept meticulous meteorological records. (See D. Wheeler, *Weather,* Vol. 38. No. 8, August 1983). Poor Law Guardian 1875-1887. School Board member 1880-1903. Inherited Ashburne and bequeathed the house and extensive gardens to the town — the house becoming the College of Art, and the gardens Backhouse Park. GEM

DNB; *SDE* 23 & 28 May 1874. Will *SDE* 19 December 1879 (for Edward B). Maberley Phillips *A History of Banks, Bankers and Banking in Northumberland, Durham and N. Yorks.,* (1894).

BARTRAM, SIR ROBERT APPLEBY (1835-1925) (SHIPBUILDER)

Born at Hylton where his father George (1800-1891) was a master shipwright. After a shipyard apprenticeship, Robert joined his father as a sole partner in 1854 and when his father retired in 1871, Robert in partnership with George Haswell, began building in iron. The yard prospered but almost disappeared in the depression of the mid-1880's. When Haswell retired in 1889, Appleby's sons, George and William, joined in a family partnership. Bartram was also chairman of Samuel Tyzack & Co, steelmakers, and a director of the Sunderland & South Shields Water Co. An active member of the employers' association, he was chairman of the Wear Shipbuilders' Association 1901-1908, and one-time member of the Shipbuilding Conciliation Board. Bartram was first elected to the Hylton School Board in the 1870's, served on Sunderland School Board for 23 years, twice as chairman; he made charitable

donations to education, including 10,000 guineas for four scholarships and to help equip the technical college. Charitable interests included — Sunderland Town & Police Court Mission, the YMCA, the Infirmary and the Blind Institute. A JP from 1892, served on the Board of Guardians, made a freeman in 1921, and later knighted (1922). Bartram was an elder of St. George's Presbyterian Church, which received £4,000 in his will. His first wife, Ann was daughter of shipbuilder William Naisby and his second wife was Agnes Rhind. He left £217,813 gross. JFC

Corder MSS; Shipbuilders' Association archives; Austin & Pickersgill archives; *Shipbuilder,* 1922 & 1925; *DBB.*

THE BINNS FAMILY (RETAILERS)

George Binns I (1781-1836) was a Quaker draper of Lancashire origins who settled in Sunderland soon after 1800 and founded a drapery business in High Street East in 1807. His elder son *Henry* (1810-1890) carried on and developed the drapery business. Henry moved the drapery business westward, first to Villiers Street and then High Street West. (173 High Street West, Bishopwearmouth by 1856.) Henry married twice; by his first wife Elizabeth Bowran he had a large family, including, Henry II (1837-1899) and Joseph John (1839-1922). *Henry II* migrated to S. Africa in 1860 and worked as a sugar planter. He became active in government, and is remembered for his work on Indian immigration and the customs union between the S. African states. Premier of Natal 1897. Knighted 1898. Maintained Quaker allegiance. Died 6 June 1899. Sir Henry's brother *Joseph John* was responsible for the transfer of the family business to Fawcett Street, where he bought two houses for conversion into a shop around 1888. He managed the business himself to 1897. It then became a limited liability company with the name of H. Binns, Son and Co. Ltd., and rapid expansion ensued, under the direction of J. Simpson. The Fawcett Street premises enlarged several times by the annexation of adjoining shops. By 1913 the floor space of the premises was almost two acres, with nearly 400 staff. *George Binns II* (1815-1847) is particularly remembered not as a draper but as a radical and Chartist. Educated at the Quaker School, Ackworth (1826-9) and then trained for the drapery business. Following the death of his father and mother in 1836 he resigned from the Society of Friends the following year and also abandoned his drapery interests to set up with his friend James Williams (qv) as a bookseller, newsagent and stationer at 9 Bridge Street, Bishopwearmouth. Both Binns and Williams were active Chartists and their shop became the centre for Chartist organisation on Wearside. As well as selling books and journals they also published tracts, handbills and poems. Some of this material was by Binns himself; he also was a powerful orator much in demand for reform meetings. After two such meetings on Sunderland Town Moor on 9 and 15 July 1839 he and Williams were arrested on the latter date and charged with attending illegal meetings and using seditious and inflammatory language. Released on bail; finally tried July 1840; when the jury recommended mercy on account of their youthful ages. Both men were imprisoned for six months in Durham Gaol. On release in January 1841 they were led in triumphal procession to Sunderland. Their business partnership was dissolved and Binns set up a drapery shop with a partner, still continuing his active support for Chartism. Nominated as a Chartist candidate for the general election June 1841 but later withdrew; declined to stand at the by-election a few months later. Business difficulties and insolvency in 1842; in Durham Gaol again for debt. Emigrated to New Zealand 1 August 1842, and pursued several occupations in the Colony before dying of consumption at 31 on 5 April 1847. Remembered as "a handsome, high-spirited, talented, true-hearted man — every inch a democrat". Noted for the consistency and integrity with which he held his political principles. Despite his fiery oratory, was genuinely opposed to violence. Both he and James Williams were active temperance reformers. GEM/PJS

George Binns II: SH, 21 January 1848; *Northern Star,* 5 February 1848; Brockie pp. 269-271; Article on George Binns by P. J. Storey in J. O. Baylen and N. J. Gossman (eds.) *Biographical Dictionary of British Radicals, II, 1830-1870* (1984) pp. 62-64. *Binns Family:* Quaker records, Ackworth and TWAS; Corder; Diary of David Binns (1799-1883), nephew of George Binns I, covering the years 1817-1824, together with a fuller account of his life written retrospectively, TWAS 1203/2-3. *SDE* 4 March 1907 has a report of an interview with J. J. Binns and sketch and description of the Fawcett Street premises.

THE BLACK FAMILY (CINEMA OWNERS)

George Black Snr. (d. 1911) toured fairgrounds with waxworks show, and settled in Sunderland. Opened Monkwearmouth Picture Hall 1906 in former St. Stephen's Chapel, Bonner's Field (later owned by Marsh Bros., renamed Bromarsh). Expanded, and turned Tivoli Music Hall, S. Shields and Palace Theatre, Hartlepool into cinemas, also Blyth Theatre Royal. Built Gateshead Palace 1909. By 1914 owned 12 cinemas with *George Jnr.* (1890-1949) as managing director, brothers Alfred and Edward as partners. 1919 sold shares in chain, raising £250,000. 1928 George moved to London, director of General Theatre Corp., 1933 joint managing-director Moss Empires. Alfred and Edward continued in cinemas; opened Regal, Sunderland 1932. Edward became producer with Gainsborough Films, 1937. Made many films with variety artists — Crazy Gang, Arthur Askey, Will Hay — many British cinema successes — *Fanny by Gaslight, Millions Like Us, The Lady Vanishes*. George "king of variety" in London, managing Palladium, Hippodrome, etc. Alfred retained cinema interest till Black's taken over by Rank 1949. George Black banned many stars from radio broadcasting in 1930s. Fears of competition justified, as variety, then cinema, fell to TV's influence. Irony that his sons, George and Alfred Black should be founding directors of Tyne Tees TV. Their mother was May Gibson, a prominent Sunderland amateur and professional performer. Brought up in Sunderland, they were involved in the business from boyhood, cycling between cinemas with reels of film, and in London became partners with their father. During the war they made a major contribution to entertainment for the troops through ENSA and after the war brought American stars to Britain and produced top variety shows nationally, including Blackpool summer shows. Rather than oppose TV the brothers saw its future, and as joint programme directors their variety interests set the predominantly light entertainment tone of TTTV. GP

A. Anderson, *Dream Palaces of Sunderland* (nd? 1983); G. J. Mellor, *Picture Pioneers* (1971).

CANDLISH, JOHN (1816-1874) (MP AND BOTTLE MAKER)

Born at Tarset, near Bellingham, on the North Tyne, the son of a small farmer. The family moved to Sunderland, where his uncle was manager of Pemberton's bottle works, where he worked till the age of 11, when he was apprenticed to a draper named Robert Tate. In 1836 he set up as a draper in his own right, the first of a series of unsuccessful business ventures, as a commercial traveller, a shipbroker, a coal merchant, and in 1844 a shipbuilder in Southwick. His most notable enterprise at this period was the purchase, with George Richmond, of the weekly Tory paper, the *Sunderland Beacon*, but the enterprise failed. After a period as secretary to the Sunderland Gas Company, he set up a bottle-making plant in Trimdon Street, but it was when he moved to Seaham Harbour, and established the Londonderry Bottle Works that he at last became successful. He subsequently acquired the Diamond Hall estate, with its bottleworks, and his enterprise became the largest of its kind in Europe. The profits from bottlemaking were employed in shipbuilding (including the building of iron ships at Middlesbrough), in the purchase in 1864 of Thornley Colliery, and once again in newspapers, this time the *Sunderland News*, a radical weekly which he launched in 1851. Elected to Sunderland Council for the West Ward, he was mayor in 1858 and 1866, and made an alderman in 1862. A borough and county magistrate, chairman of the Board of Guardians, a Wear Commissioner. Elected MP for Sunderland (as a Radical, having early been a Tory) in 1866; re-elected in 1868; retired 1874. A committed Baptist from early manhood. Died in Cannes, where had gone for health, 17 March 1874. Buried Ryhope Road cemetery. Statue to him unveiled 6 October 1875. AH

Brockie pp. 321-33. F. Boase, *Modern English Biography* (London, 1965), IV, pp. 596-7; T. Fordyce, *Local Records* (Newcastle, 1876), pp. 275, 349.

CLANNY, WILLIAM REID (1770-1850) (PHYSICIAN AND INVENTOR)

Clanny was born in Bangor, County Down, of Scottish Presbyterian background. Took a degree in medicine at Edinburgh where he also married Margaret, the daughter of Captain Mitchell of the East India Company. Served for a time as a surgeon in the Royal Navy and was present at the Battle of Copenhagen in 1801. Came to Sunderland and practised as a physician for 45 years although his contribution to the development of the community extended far beyond his professional duties. In 1813 he wrote an article entitled "On the means of procuring a steady light in coal mines without the danger of explosion", revealing the results of his preliminary research. In the same year he became a founder member of the Society for the Prevention of Accidents in Coal Mines. By 1816 when he published "Practical observations on safety lamps for coal mines" he had experimented in person with a safety lamp at the Herrington Mill Pitt. His lamp, and other improvements were, after some initial disputes, recognised for their true worth by his contemporaries including northern coalowners who presented him with a piece of silverware. George Stephenson acknowledged a debt to Clanny's researches and Davy invented his version of a lamp very soon after a visit to Sunderland in August 1815. In 1831, as the chief consultant physician at the Sunderland Infirmary, he was amongst the first to recognise the true nature of cholera. He was a "miasmatist", a believer in disease generated by an "atmosphere highly vitiated by carbonic acid". His book *Hyperanthraxis* (1831) was the first scientific treatise on the subject of cholera. Critics of Clanny at the time of the cholera outbreak regarded him as arrogant and ambitious but this must be assessed against the circumstances in which he was working. Clanny was also very active in cultural pursuits and was a founder and vice-president of the Sunderland Literary and Philosophical Society. He was the author of numerous papers and articles on medical and scientific subjects and a frequent contributor to the *Lancet*. He died on the 10 January 1850. His obituary in the *Sunderland Herald* singled out his lamp as his greatest achievement "... peace will be with the remains of him who has contributed to save thousands of the bare-headed sons of toil and industry from premature and violent death ... for which his memory ought to be dear to all". STM

Brockie, pp. 148-153; *SH*, 11 January 1850.

CLARK, GEORGE (1843-1901) (MARINE ENGINEER)

Born in Sunderland, into an engineering family. His father (1815-83) opened a general engineering business in 1848 and it was there that George began his apprenticeship at 14 years and completed his training at the famous London works of Penn. In the mid-1860's took charge of the works due to his father's ill-health. George Clark established his skill as an engine designer and builder and opened a new works on a nine-acre site at Southwick in 1872, employing 300 men. Became the leading engine builder on the Wear. Active in the Wear Engine Builders' Association which he helped form; following a prolonged strike was active in industrial conciliation. His later years were hampered by poor health. Clark was a director of the Sunderland & South Shields Water Co. He joined the Institution of Mechanical Engineers in 1867, a member of the Institution of Naval Architects, founder member and vice-president of the North East Coal Institution of Engineers and Shipbuilders. A liberal who disagreed with Gladstone on Home Rule; served on Sunderland Town Council and Durham County Council; a freemason. Married Jessie Maud McFarlane, daughter of a school master. He left £105,948 gross. JFC

NECIES, Vol. 17; *Inst. Mech.* 1901; *SDE*, 4 March 1901; *Newcastle Daily Journal*, 5 March 1901; *DBB*; Clarke, *Labour Relations* (1967).

CRAWFORD, "JACK" (1775-1831) ("THE HERO OF CAMPERDOWN")

The son of a keelman of Scottish extraction living in Pottery Bank. He worked on the keels until 1786, then in the merchant navy until 1796 when he left home after a row and was probably picked up by a press gang. He was on the *Venerable* the flagship of Admiral Duncan during Duncan's successful attempt, with a scratch fleet, to prevent the juncture of the Dutch fleet of Admiral van Winter and a French fleet and the landing of an invasion force in Ireland. In the 'pell mell' (and very unorthodox) engagement at Camperdown on the 11 October 1797 the *Venerable*'s flag was shot away with the halliard. It is not clear whether Crawford volunteered, was ordered, or was pushed, or whether he used a marling spike, hammer or pistol butt, but he *did* climb the mast and nail the flag to it. The incident earned him a hero's treatment. His action was re-enacted in tableau in the victory procession in London, he was formally presented to the King and the government later granted him a pension of £30 a year. His home town presented him with a silver medal in March 1798. It is likely that the government propaganda machine lay behind this lionisation. Britain had been an ace from invasion and an "everyman" hero was desperately needed to try and identify the lower orders with a very unpopular war, fought by a nervous and repressive government. Corder thought little of Crawford. He claimed that it was reported by reliable witnesses that Crawford was "drunk, acted without orders, and should have been court martialled". Crawford married the daughter of a Sunderland shipbuilder called Longstaff in 1808. There were three sons and a daughter. Crawford was the second victim of cholera on the 10 November 1831 and was buried in the churchyard of Sunderland Parish Church. A fine headstone was set up on the 6 August 1888. In 1890 what Corder dismissed as a "deplorable monument" was erected. The silver medal had been pawned but eventually found its way, *via* the descendants of Duncan, into the collection of the Borough Museum. STM

Brockie pp. 83-90. "A Tar's Tale of Camperdown" from Clark's *Battles of England* is in the *SYB*, 1906, pp. 35-36, and is a splendidly unhistorical, "boy's own" account. The several different versions are contrasted in the *Monthly Chronicle of North Country Lore and Legend*, (1887) pp. 8-10.

DIXON, THOMAS (1831-1880) (CORKCUTTER)

Born 22 February 1831 on Mark Quay, Low Street, Sunderland, the second son of a cork cutter who later removed to 57 Nile Street. Followed his father's craft and eventually took over the family business at Nile Street, moving in 1868 to 14/15 Sunderland Street, A skilled craftsman noted for his campaign for safer lifebelts. Largely self-educated. Strong interests in literature and art, and eager not only to improve his own mind but to enlarge educational and cultural opportunities for other working men. Secretary to the Sunderland Mechanics Institute in the 1850s, and took part in the agitation for a public free library in Sunderland. As a member of the Education Committee of the Sunderland Industrial Equitable Society (the Cooperative Society) he worked hard to build up the society's library, canvassing its needs by writing to many famous authors asking for free copies of their works. Helped to promote an (evening) Art School in Sunderland in 1857, with the encouragement and advice of the artist William Bell Scott, then based in Newcastle. His artistic interests continued throughout his life. Had lively political and social interests. Keen temperance reformer. A religious searcher — interested in eastern religion and phrenology. From the 1850s began a widespread correspondence on cultural and political matters with men of letters, artists, politicians and reformers, including the artist and social critic John Ruskin. Twenty-five letters from Ruskin to Dixon were published by Ruskin as *Time and Tide by Weare and Tyne — Letters to a working man of Sunderland* (1867). Some extracts of Dixon's letters were included as an appendix. Dixon was also patronised by William Rossetti, Edward Burne Jones, Max Muller *et al*. He befriended the collier-poet Joseph Skipsey. Died 11 July 1880. Buried Holy Trinity, Southwick (no stone survives). A bust and two paintings of Dixon are in Sunderland Museum and Art Gallery. GEM

Brockie, pp. 406-412; J. Patterson, "Thomas Dixon and his correspondents" in *Antiq. Sund.* xii, 1912, pp. 1-12; G. E. Milburn, "Thomas Dixon of Sunderland" in *Sunderland's History*, 2, (1984), pp. 4-45 (with references).

DOXFORD, SIR WILLIAM THEODORE (1841-1916) (SHIPBUILDER)

Born Bishopwearmouth, the first of four sons of a shipwright. After schooling at Bramham College, Doxford joined his father's yard and played an active role in its management until his father's death in 1882, when he took overall charge of a shipyard. This included a marine engine works, and was about to begin building ships of steel. Doxford was very active in the Employers' Association (Chairman 1908-12) where he gave particular attention to labour relations, always anxious to promote conciliation. He was keen to innovate, reflected in both the turret ships, an experimental torpedo boat and a disel engine. A foundation member and second president of the North East Coast Institution of Engineers and Shipbuilders, a vice-president of the Institution of Naval Architects, which he joined in 1878. A Unionist in politics and in 1895 became first Conservative MP to be elected in Sunderland for 40 years, knighted in 1900 Doxford retired from Parliament in 1906. He served on Sunderland Town Council and as a River Wear Commissioner and was a magistrate both of the Sunderland and the County of Durham. His son *Albert Ernest* (1868-1937) followed his father in the active management of the business. William Doxford left £153,946 gross. JFC

Corder MSS: Shipbuilders' Assoc. Archives; Clarke, *Labour Relations* (1967); Clarke, *A Century of Service* (1984). *DBB*; *WWW*; *WWMP*; *SDE*, 2 October 1916; *NECIES* Vol. 33; *Shipbuilder*, 1916.

GOURLEY, EDWARD T. (1826-1902) (SHIPBROKER AND OWNER; MP)

Edward Temperley Gourley, born 8 June 1826, elder son of John Young Gourley, ship captain and owner, and Mary Temperley. Served apprenticeship with John Halcro as a coalfitter before starting on his own account as a ship-chandler and then becoming a shipbroker and owner. Was one of the first to invest largely in steam-shipping. A keen member of the Volunteer movement, he was appointed a lieutenant in the North Durham Militia in 1857, elected Captain of the 1st Company of the 3rd Durham Rifle Volunteer Corps on its formation and on retiring as Lt. Col. in 1881 was appointed Hon. Colonel. He was elected councillor for Bishopwearmouth Ward in 1857, representing the ward until his election as an alderman in 1865. He served as mayor in 1864, 1865 and 1867. A Radical in his political views, he was elected MP for Sunderland in 1868 and held the seat until he retired at the 1900 election, two years before his death. A Home Ruler before Gladstone made Home Rule for Ireland part of Liberal party policy, a believer in Disestablishment and Disendowment of State churches and supporter of local option in the temperance debate, he spoke little in Parliament except to ask questions, particularly on shipping matters. He paid close attention to local interests. Congregationalist. Sunday School teacher and secretary of the local Sunday School Union for several years. Appointed a River Wear Commissioner in 1865, borough (1865) and county (1869) magistrate, and a Deputy Lieutenant for County Durham (1871). Knighted in the 1895 dissolution honours. Died 15 April 1902. Unmarried. PJS

SDE & *SDP* 15 & 21 April 1902. *The Alderman*, 8 April 1876. *The Durham Thirteen*, (1874). *Wearside Review*, I (1886).

THE GRAY FAMILY (CLERGYMEN)

Robert Gray I, (1762-1834), son of a prosperous London silversmith. Educ. Eton and Oxford. Doctor of Divinity, 1802. Bampton lecturer at Oxford 1796. Vicar of Farringdon, Berks. Rector of Crayke, N. Yorks, 1800-1805. Prebendary of Durham, 1805-1834. Rector of Bishopwearmouth, 1805-1827 (the last three appointments due to the patronage of Shute Barrington, Bishop of Durham, 1791-1826). An active Rector of Bishopwearmouth. Initiated the great restoration of St. Michael's church, 1806-1810, transforming the character of the nave and interior from mediaeval to Georgian (with galleries) but retaining the ancient chancel (shortened) and west tower. Took a leading role in establishing a parish elementary school in 1808, replaced in 1812 by a purpose-built school on Low Row (linked with the National Society, 1819) — supported largely by subscriptions. Chaired public meeting 1818, which called for establishment of the infirmary in Bishopwearmouth. Active in promoting the Sunderland Auxiliary of the British and Foreign Bible Society, 1810. Worked with dissenters and Methodists in this, but a stout defender of Church principles. Gray's ecclesiastical stance was moderately Evangelical. Discontinued the collection of the tithe on fish (the "coble teen") which had been assiduously collected by some of his predecessors. Bishop of Bristol, 1827. His episcopal palace burned down in the Reform Bill riots of October, 1831. Married Elizabeth Camplin of Bristol. Fourteen children, six survived to adulthood. Died Clifton, Bristol, 28 September 1834, aged 72. *Robert Gray II*, (1809-1872), twelfth child and seventh son of Dr. Robert Gray I. Born in Bishopwearmouth Rectory. Educated Oxford University. Incumbent of Whitworth, Co. Durham, 1834-1845. Vicar of Stockton, 1845-7. First Bishop of Cape Town, 1847-1872. Married Sophia Myddleton (1836), daughter of Robert Wharton Myddleton of Old Park, Durham. (Some authorities wrongly state that Sophia Myddleton was the wife of Robert Gray I — see Brockie 319, and *Antiq. Sund.* (ii), 1903, p. 67.) *Robert Gray III*, (1787-1838), son of Thomas Gray, a wealthy London jeweller, and nephew of Robert Gray I (Rector of Bishopwearmouth). Educ. privately and at Oriel College, Oxford. Held curacies at Kyloe, Lowick, Stockton and from 1816 to 1819 at Bishopwearmouth under his uncle, sharing actively in Gray's schemes, including the Parish School and the Bible Society of which he was joint secretary for a time. Rector of Sunderland 1819-1838. Sunderland was an evangelical parish and Gray was very much an evangelical Rector, devoting himself assiduously to a community of well over 15,000 people for a reward of about one tenth of that received by his uncle in Bishopwearmouth. He usually employed two curates, paid out of his own stipend. An earnest, puritanical preacher, a strict and tireless pastor, and a keen educationalist establishing a National School, an Infant School and two Sunday Schools in his parish. Into the schools and other parts of his work he poured much of his own private wealth. He was a courageous sick visitor especially at times of epidemic, notably cholera 1831-2, and typhus 1837-8. Contracted typhus (for the second time) early in 1838 and died from the disease on 11 February. The funeral procession and internment in Sunderland Churchyard on 20th February, attracted vast crowds. Ministers of most denominations in the town attended the funeral. The churchwardens and vestrymen acted very quickly after Gray's death to persuade Bishop Maltby to appoint William Webb (one of the Sunderland curates) to the living — Webb was inducted on 10 March 1838. Public meetings were held to discuss a memorial to Gray — it was decided to raise a fund to mount a statue and to endow the parochial schools on Vine Street which became known as the Gray Schools. The statue can still be seen in the main west porch of Holy Trinity Church. Gray married Mary, daughter of Rowland Webster, rope maker of Bishopwearmouth. He left four sons and three daughters. Though there was a rectory near Holy Trinity, Gray also had a residence on Sunniside from where he was buried. GEM

Robert Gray I. Brockie pp. 314-320; H. M. Wood in *Antiq. Sund.* (ii) 1903, 67-68. *Robert Gray II*. Audrey Brooke, *Robert Gray, First Bishop of Cape Town* (Cape Town, 1947). *Robert Gray III*. Brockie pp. 106-115; *A Memorial Sketch of the life of the late Robert Gray, Rector of the parish (of Sunderland) and perpetual curate of St. John's Chapel, Sunderland* (Sunderland, 1838). Various sermons by Gray were published locally, copies of which are in the Sunderland Library.

HAMPSON, REVD JOHN (1760-1819) (CLERGYMAN)

Son of John Hampson senior, a travelling preacher in the Wesleyan connexion. John Hampson junior was educated at Wesley's school at Kingswood and became something of a classical scholar. One of Wesley's travelling preachers from 1776. In April 1785 when stationed in the Sunderland circuit he broke with Methodism over differences with Wesley on matters of connexional government. Subsequent career in the Church of England, probably due to persuasion and encouragement by influential evangelicals in Sunderland parish. Sent to Oxford to get a degree, residing at St. Edmund Hall 1785-7, and then in residence only sporadically up to 1791 when he took his BA, followed by MA in 1792. Probably as early as 1787 he was appointed curate and lecturer at St. John's chapel of ease, a proprietary chapel then in the control of its chief builder, John Thornhill. He was the first evangelical to hold a Church appointment in Sunderland south of the river. Invited Wesley to preach in St. John's, 1 June 1788. In July 1795 he succeeded John Farrer as Rector of Sunderland, a post he occupied until 1819. In this busy parish he held a very influential position both religiously and socially, chairing parish meetings, serving as a county magistrate, and much involved in local government and poor law administration during years of considerable hardship for the working classes. A public meeting in January 1817 thanked Hampson for his continuous attention to the interests of the parish. In 1809 he was able to prevent a duel between two young men of local families over the alleged seduction of the sister of one of them. Published a number of works in Sunderland — various sermons, the *Poetics* of Vida (1793, printed by Thomas Reed) and most importantly the *Memoirs of the Late Revd John Wesley* 1791 (in three volumes printed by James Graham) the first volume of which was in the press when Wesley died. This was the first major biography of Wesley to be published. It contains one of the best early assessment of Wesley, admiring yet also frankly critical on certain matters. GEM

Proceedings of the Wesley Historical Society, ii, 21-22; xx, 131-135. Sunderland Parish Vestry Minutes, DCRO, EP/SU HT 5/3.

HARTLEY, JAMES (1811-1886) (GLASSMAKER)

Born Dumbarton, son of a glass maker who later worked in Bristol and Birmingham. At Smethwick, Hartley senior (who died 1833) entered into partnership with Messrs. Chance to produce crown glass and German sheet glass. His sons, James and John, moved to Sunderland in 1836 and launched their own business, the Wear Glassworks, near the eastern end of Hylton Road. Improved the manufacture of crown glass and in 1847 patented a new process for making rolled plate glass, which was largely responsible for the success of the company. Hartley's plate glass was ideally suited for roofing. The firm was also one of the earliest producers in the world of coloured glass, much used in churches. Hartley occasionally made gifts of entire windows to local churches, eg, the large geometrical window in Park Road Methodist Church, Sunderland, valued in 1887 at £125. By 1860s Hartley was employing 700 men and supplying one third of all the plate glass used in the country. The firm also had a large export trade. Hartley retired from active management in 1868 and was replaced by his son. Town councillor from 1842, Mayor of Sunderland 1851, 1853, 1862. Helped promote the Town Improvement Act, 1851. River Wear Commissioner. Encouraged railway development in Sunderland, and a director of the NE Railway Co. Conservative MP for Sunderland, 1865-1868. Founder member of the Sunderland School Board, 1871 and its first Chairman. The son of pious Wesleyan parents (with a Methodist minister, Robert Dall, as one of his uncles). Hartley was an active Methodist until 1853, serving as Circuit Steward for the Sunderland Wesleyan circuit 1842-1845. In 1853 he became a member of the C of E, and later worshipped at Christ Church. Built Ashbrooke Hall (later renamed Corby Hall) on Ashbrooke Road. Died in London, 24 May 1886. left £147,623. GEM

Brockie pp. 450-459; *DBB* (entry by Catherine Ross); *The Alderman* (Sunderland) iii, No. 68, July 1877, pp. 1-6; Tyne and Wear County Council, *The Glass Industry of Tyne and Wear: Pt. I Glassmaking on Wearside* (1979) pp. 31-3.

HAVELOCK (-ALLAN), SIR HENRY MARSHMAN (1830-1897) (MP)

Born in India, near Calcutta, 6 August 1830, eldest son of (Sir) Henry Havelock (born Ford Hall, Bishopwearmouth, 1795, son of William Havelock, shipbuilder; died Lucknow, Nov. 1857); returned to England to complete his education in 1842 and entered the army in 1846; Lieutenant 1848, Captain 1857; during the Indian Mutiny served as aide-de-camp to his father during the relief of Cawnpore, won VC, twice wounded; created Baronet 1858 — an award intended for his father; served in the Maori War, New Zealand, 1863-64, in Canada 1867-69 and Dublin, 1869; Major 1864, Colonel 1868, Major General 1878. Married 1865 Lady Alice Moreton, 2nd daughter of the 2nd Earl of Ducie; two sons — Henry (b. Dublin 1872) and Allan (b. 1874) — and one daughter (Ethel, b. Montreal 1867, m. 1886 Joseph Albert Pease, MP). Liberal candidate Stroud, Glos. Jan. 1874; MP Sunderland, February 1874 — April 1881; resigned to take command of the 2nd Infantry Brigade at Aldershot; because of ill-health, retired from active list in December 1881 with honorary rank of Lieutenant-General. Liberal/Liberal Unionist MP, SE Durham, 1885-92 (defeated) and 1895-death. A moderate Liberal, who became a Liberal Unionist when the Liberal party split on Home Rule. His time as MP for Sunderland was marred by local suspicions of some of his views, particularly among the Irish electors but also among the more extreme radicals, and by his uneasy relationship with the radical leader, Samuel Storey (q.v.). Havelock was almost certainly not an easy man to get on with. He was killed on 30 December 1897 while visiting troops on the Afghan border during a visit to India. JP (N. Riding & Co. Durham); DL, Co. Durham, 1885; KGB 1887. Alderman, Durham County Council, 1889-death. Baptist. Havelock took the additional surname of Allan in March 1880 following the death of his father's cousin, R. H. Allan, of Blackwell Hall, Darlington, whose heir he was. PJS

DNB; Jamieson, *Durham . . .*; *The Durham Thirteen*; *SDE*, 31 December 1897 & 3 January 1898; Havelock-Alan Papers, N. Yorks. Co. Record Office, Northallerton.

HUDSON, GEORGE (1800-1884) (SHIPOWNER AND PHILANTHROPIST)

In early life a ropemaker. Prospered and became shipowner and shipbuilder. A member of the town council on its inception in 1835, being one of the elected members for Monkwearmouth Ward. Poor Law Guardian. Borough and County magistrate. River Wear Commissioner. Active member of the Church of England. Helped financially in the restoration of St. Peter's, Monkwearmouth, in the 1870s. Liberal benefactor. A retiring, modest man. Bachelor. Lived with spinster sister at 113 Church Street, Monkwearmouth, then at the Grange (a farm) on the Newcastle Road. Died 8 May 1884 aged 83. Buried with his sister at Mere Knolls Cemetery. By his will (dated 1879) he left the residue of his personal estate to establish the George Hudson Charity. The trustees received a sum of nearly £160,000 of which the interest was to be applied to the education, maintenance support and clothing of orphan boys and girls between eight and 14. Two thirds of the recipients at any one time were to be boys, 20 of whom were to be the sons of sailors or pilots belonging to the port of Sunderland, and 20 to be orphans born and living within Monkwearmouth parish. Under the terms of the will an "orphan" was any child whose father was dead or paralysed. Hudson's Charity was not intended to provide any kind of institutional care but to offer help to children who as far as possible were to live at home, and attend local day schools. Medical examinations of children receiving aid were to be held at least quarterly, and medical treatment offered free. By c. 1904, 298 orphans were receiving help, 198 of them boys. The normal assistance to each child was between £12 and £18 p.a. but some received as much as £30 p.a. The Hudson Charity was generally recognised to be of the greatest benefit to the poorer children of Sunderland. GEM

SDE, 10 May 1884; Corder MSS; *Endowed Charities (County Durham and County Boroughs of Sunderland and Gateshead)* 1904 vol. ii 428-430; John Thompson, *Pamphlets on old Monkwearmouth*, pp. 4-5.

HUDSON, GEORGE (1800-1871) (THE 'RAILWAY KING')

Born at Howsham, near York, the son of a farmer. Apprenticed to Bell and Nicholson, drapers, of York. Married Elizabeth Nicholson, and became partner in drapery business, later claiming that with turnover of £35,000 and profits of 25 per cent this was the happiest period of his life. Left £30,000 by relatives, and embarked upon railway speculation. Town councillor, alderman, and in 1837 and 1846 Mayor of York. Founder of the York Banking Company. Founder of the York and North Midland, and Newcastle and Darlington Railway Companies. Promoter and Chairman of the Midland Railway Company. Nicknamed 'the Railway King' by Sydney Smith. £16,000 testimonial raised by his admirers, spent on Albert Gate, Knightsbridge. Also owned Londesborough estate, and Newby Hall, Yorkshire. Elected MP for Sunderland at by-election 1845, the news of his victory being carried to London by train, which travelled for parts of its journey at 75mph. In 1847 with the collapse in railway shares, his fortune and probity were undermined. On investigation, found to have paid dividends out of capital, and to have personally traded in shares, and rails, to his own advantage at the expense of companies he managed. In 1849 forced to resign from the Eastern Counties (who had brought him in as a 'saviour'), Midland, York, Newcastle and Berwick, and York and North Midland Railway boards. Defended his position in Parliament, and undertook to repay his personal obligations. Retained his seat at Sunderland in the general elections of 1847, and 1852, thanks to his successful promotion of the South Docks scheme in the borough. Sought to recoup his fortunes by investing in Spanish railways, but taken ill in Europe. Returned unexpectedly to fight, and win, election for Sunderland in 1857, but defeated 1859. The North Eastern Railway company sought to obtain his Whitby estates and Sunderland Docks in satisfaction of their claims upon him, only settling months before his death. Stood for Parliament for Whitby, 1865, but arrested for debt during campaign, and imprisoned in York Castle for four months. In his late years a revival of sentiment in his favour producd a public banquet in his honour in Sunderland (1869), and a subscription on his behalf which bought him an annuity of £600pa. At death, contemplating development of his West Cliff estate at Whitby, and also considering standing as MP for Sunderland at next election. *The Times*, at his death, noted that 'to the last he had warm friends, and that they were among them men who knew him longest and best'. At his height, courted by all society; 'there was a time when not to know him was to argue oneself unknown'; villified in his fall, but remarkable for his energy and good humour. Never lost his Yorkshire accent, or, according to the *Daily News*, the 'manners appropriate to a provincial shopkeeper of the old school'. Died in London, and buried at Scrayningham, Yorkshire, his funeral cortège from York station being accompanied by civic dignitaries and friends from many parts of the north. AH

R. S. Lambert, *The Railway King 1800-71: A Study of George Hudson and the Business Morals of his time* (London, 1934). A. J. Peacock and D. Joy, *George Hudson of York* (York, 1971). *D.N.B.*, vol. X, pp. 145-7. *The Times*, 16 December 1871. *Durham Chronicle*, 22 December 1871.

KEARNEY, REVD CANON PHILIP (DIED 1856) (ROMAN CATHOLIC PRIEST)

Born Kells, Ireland. Educ. Maynooth College. Appointed priest of Sunderland, October, 1828. Served the congregation worshipping at the chapel on Dunning Street, But also ministered to the Catholics scattered over a wide area (Ryhope, Seaham, Easington, Houghton-le-Spring, Washington, Jarrow, South Shields). Persuaded local Catholics to support the building of a large new church on Bridge Street, opened 15th September, 1835. Kearney helped promote the building of churches elsewhere, eg, St. Michael's, Houghton-le-spring 1837. A keen educationalist. Built school for boys and girls on Pann Lane (behind St. Mary's) and invited the Christian Brothers to staff it from 1836 until 1848. In 1843 Kearney went to Cork to invite a group of nuns belonging to the sisters of Mercy to come to Sunderland to assist in pastoral and educational work. They arrived 15 October 1843, and were accommodated in a large house on Green Street. They taught in the Pann Lane School and promoted other schools in the Convent grounds. Canon of the Cathedral Chapter of the new diocese of Hexham and Newcastle, 1852. Died 16 August 1856 while on a visit to his native Kells. Described as of "a most kind and genial nature, of patriarchal simplicity, a man without guile". GEM

SH, 22 August 1856, p. 5; *St. Mary's (RC Church, Sunderland) Jubilee 1835-1985* (Sunderland, 1985); David Milburn (ed.) *Parish Histories from the Northern Catholic Calendar*, (Durham, 1986) p. 61; *Annals of the Sisters of Mercy* (New York, 1883) vol. (ii), pp. 454-459.

THE LAING FAMILY (SHIPBUILDERS)

Laing, Sir James (1823-1901). Born at Deptford, Laing's father (from a Fifeshire farming family) after training as a doctor joined his brother in a shipyard at South Shields. The family traded in timber and were also ship owners. The young Laing joined his father's firm to serve a normal shipwright's apprenticeship and in 1843 he took charge of the yard, which became one of the largest on the Wear. Laing was always active in the employers' association. A patrician-like figure who was not sympathetic to the trade unions, but recognised their role and was active in the Conciliation Board; he also provided welfare facilities for his workers. Amongst wood shipbuilders, took the lead in using iron for construction. Very active in the commercial affairs of the port; served as a Wear Commissioner from 1859 (Chairman of Commission 1868-1900), first chairman of Hendon Docks; he actively promoted the Chamber of Commerce and became President of the Chamber of Shipping of the United Kingdom. Amongst his directorships were — the Suez Canal Co.; the North Eastern Railway; Sunderland Gas Co., and the Sunderland & South Shields Water Co. In addition there were family holdings in many shipping lines. A member of the Council of the Institution of Naval Architects and served on Bulkhead Committee, and as vice-president on Lloyds Load Line committee. Unsucessfully fought the parliamentary seat for North Durham as a Unionist; a JP in both Durham and Northumberland; a supporter of medical charities, he was a governor of the infirmary; a staunch member of the church of England. He was married twice and left £129,558 gross. *Laing, Phillip* (5 May 1849 — 5, April, 1907). Served as an apprentice in Austin & Mills Shipyard before joining the family yard. His fourth son Hugh (28 May 1871 — 1 January 1930) attended Wellington College and proceeded to an MA at Cambridge. He served an apprenticeship at NE Marine Engineering Co and became a director of the shipyard. He was chairman of the Wear Shipbuilders Association and a member of the Central Board of the national Shipbuilding Employers' Federation. A member of the River Wear Commission and a very active member of the North East Coast Institution of Engineers & Shipbuilders. *Laing, James Jnr.* (1862? — 23 January 1895). Following two and a half years as an apprentice in the Deptford yard, James Jnr. went for 18 months to Denny's Dumbarton shipyard and on his return was engaged in yard management until within six months of his death, having suffered from very poor health in his later years. A member of the Institution of Naval Architects and the North East Coast Institution of Engineers and Shipbuilders. JFC

Corder MSS; Shipbuilders Assoc. Archives; Sunderland Chamber of Commerce; Clarke, *Labour Relations* (1967); *WWW*; *DBB*; *Newcastle Daily Chronicle*, 16 December 1901; *Engineer*, December 1901; *Engineering*, 20 December 1901; *NECIES*, Vol. 12 & Vol. 46.

LONGRIDGE, MICHAEL (1757-1815) (RETAILER AND METHODIST)

Sunderland mercer, and a leading Wesleyan layman. Born in Sunderland, the son of an ironmonger and fitter. His brother, Thomas, became a partner in Hawks and Co, Gateshead, who owned the Bedlington ironworks. Married Elizabeth Bewick in 1782; she died 1789. Lived for some years at Hunters Hall. Joined the Wesleyan Society in Sunderland at age of 17 and remained a loyal and active Methodist to his death. Worshipped at the chapel on Numbers Garth and later a founder member (1793) of the large chapel on Sans Street, in the building of which he invested a considerable sum of money. Served as class leader and local preacher; did much pioneering work in the vast Sunderland circuit. A dedicated educationalist. Largely responsible for launching Sunday Schools in Sunderland in 1786; directed them personally for 16 years. On the re-organisation of the schools in 1802, Longridge became President and occupied this post until his death. His sons also active in the schools (especially George William Longridge). A man of culture and wide reading.

Helped launch the Sunderland Reading Society (the Wesleyan Library) aimed especially at lay preachers; gave many books to it. Active also in the Sunderland Subscription Library and the Religious Tract Society. The author of several tracts and religious books including catechisms and primers for Sunday Schools. Much caught up in the tensions affecting Wesleyanism after the death of Wesley. Played an important role nationally in attempting to resolve these tensions on tolerant lines. Befriended the Wesleyan rebel Alexander Kilham but did not join Kilham's secession (the New Connexion). Died 17 April, 1815. His younger son George William (an ironmonger) lived on in Sunderland; an active conservative Wesleyan. His other son, Michael (b. 1785) made a name at the Bedlington works as a railway engineer of considerable importance; a benevolent and enlightened employer. GEM

Wesleyan Methodist Magazine, 1815, pp. 481-6, 561-8; G. E. Milburn, 'Michael Longridge of Sunderland' in *Bulletin of the Wesley Historical Society, North East Branch*, No. 23 (Feb. 1975) pp. 22-28; E. Martin, *Bedlington Iron and Engine Works 1736-1867* (1974).

McALL, REV. ROBERT WHITAKER (1821-1893) (CONGREGATIONAL MINISTER)

Son of Rev. Dr. R. S. McAll. Trained at the Lancashire Independent (i.e. Congregational) College, Manchester. First Pastorate at the Bethel Chapel, Villiers Streei, Sunderland, from March, 1848. A powerful evangelical preacher, and a man of culture and learning, always seeking to promote knowledge as well as piety. A hymn book edited by McAll for use at the Ebenezer Chapel was published 1852 — a copy is in the Sunderland Local History Library. Well versed in the sciences especially botany and geology. Launched a bible class and a Young men's Mutual Improvement Society which had wide influence. Despite his success, friction developed between him and some of the Bethel deacons, leading to his resignation mid-Feb. 1851. About 240 members left with him and formed a new church, worshipping temporarily at the Bethany Chapel, Hedworth Terrace until the Ebenezer Chapel, Fawcett Street (partly designed by McCall himself) was opened 13 November 1851 at a cost of £2,700. Ebenezer prospered under his ministry; a busy, evangelical, serious congregation. New Congregational causes launched from Ebenezer at Southwick and Seaham. McAll was one of the leading nonconformist ministers in Sunderland around the mid-19th century, always eager to promote interest in religion among those outside the churches, especially intelligent working folk. Helped promote a series of lectures to the working classes of Sunderland in the Lyceum in the winter of 1853-4 and gave the opening lecture on 'Chaos or Cosmos: the Great Artificer, or God in Nature'. Left Sunderland May 1855 to work in Leicester (where he designed another chapel) and later worked in Manchester, Birmingham and Hadleigh. In 1871 on a visit to France he conceived the idea of a protestant mission for the French working class which he launched in January 1872, and directed until his death. The work spread rapidly both in Paris and the provinces. An American McCall Association was founded in 1883, for fund-raising. McAll received a number of honours and awards including: Fellow of the Linnaean Society, 1865; Hon. D. D. (Iowa) 1887, and the Chevalier de la Légion d'Honneur. Died 11 May, 1893. His widow unveiled a memorial window at the Grange Congregational Church (now West Park URC) 30 March, 1898. This church was the successor to Ebenezer. GEM

Anon. *In Memoriam Robert Whitaker McAll* (1898); Eugène Réveillaud *La Vie et L'oeuvre de Robert W. MacAll* (Paris, 1898); WJLP *The Courts of the Lord* (1951).

OGDEN, BERNARD (1769-1850) (QUAKER BUSINESSMAN)

Born in Church Street, Sunderland, grandson of a clockmaker who moved there from Alnwick, and son of Bernard Ogden (1734-1779), brewer and fitter. Ogden was apprenticed after his father's death to a druggist, and in 1789 took over the chemist's shop of his uncle John Maude, at 163 High Street. Helped found Sunderland Branch, Royal Humane Society, 1791, and Dispensary, 1794. As a successful businessman, he soon became prominent in local affairs. Owned copperas works, Deptford. Bridge Commissioner, 1792. Founder-member and secretary, Subscription Library, 1798-1802. Commissioner for Sunderland under 1810 Improvement Act. As a Quaker, helped finance Nile Street Meeting House, 1822. Elected Stallinger, 1811; Freeman 1819. As a senior Freeman, he chaired the unruly Reform Meeting of October 1831. In 1835 he refused requests from municipal reformers to convene a meeting to establish a Sunderland Corporation under the Act of 1835. THC

H. Simpson, "Bernard Ogden", *Antiq. Sund.* xxii (1960), 57-62, and references there.

O'NEILL, JAMES (1838-1913) (TRADE UNIONIST)

Born in Manchester; at 14 he started work in engineering, became an apprentice boilermaker in 1855 and finally was foreman at Brassey's works. Joining the Birkenhead branch of the Boilermakers' Society in 1862 and in addition to other offices was secretary for six years. Elected to the national Executive Council, O'Neill acted as union representative in a number of disputes and won the regard of the Teesside employers in carrying out these duties. Following a period of industrial conflict on the Wear, in 1877, he was elected the full-time delegate for Tyne & Wear (10,256 votes to 2,978). Few trade union leaders won the respect of both immediate employers and the men as he did; receiving testimonials from both the craftsmen, his Executive Council and on his retirement at the end of 1907, from the Wear Shipbuilders' Association. In the depression of the 1880's, after a visit to France he made a most valuable report on European shipbuilding conditions. In 1894, he gave evidence to the Royal Commission on Labour, and a few years later, faced the task of securing the support of the Wearside workers to a wages policy imposed upon them by a national vote. He was very active in securing settlements under the Workmen's compensation Act. His shipbuilding knowledge, negotating skills and keenness to avoid industrial dispute was reflected in offers by the employers to their "technical advisor". A Justice of the Peace; he declined nomination as a Parliamentary candidate. JFC

D. C. Cummings, *A Historical Survey of the Boiler Makers* (1905); Royal, *Commission on Labour*, 1892-4; Reports of the Boilermakers Society, 1877-1913; Wear Shipbuilders Assoc. Archives, 1877-1907; Clarke, *Labour Relations* (1967).

PILE, WILLIAM (1823-1873) (SHIPBUILDER)

Born in Sunderland, son of a shipbuilder (William c. 1795-1858), from a Northumberland farming family, which came to Wearside in the late 18th century. William Pile learned the shipwright's craft under Thomas Lightfoot, for whom he was a foreman for a time before joining his father's shipyard. At 25 opened his own small yard at Fatfield and seven years later, when his brother John began shipbuilding at Hartlepool, William took over the whole of his father's shipyard. Pile was a designer and builder of fine ships, almost regardless of cost, which led to frequent financial problems, had many London customers and his *Roxburgh Castle* was the first of many frigates for Greens of Blackwall. When he wanted to begin iron shipbuilding he owed his timber merchant, William Hay £13,000, apart from other debts. On the formation of a partnership with R. H. Hay, the debts were discharged and five iron ships were built in 1861, but Hay left Pile in 1866. He built the first of his very fine composite vessels in 1863. His workforce is reputed to have grown from 600 to 3,000, at times his workforce may have exceeded even this great size, as he added a graving dock in 1868 and began building marine engines for his iron ships. His output increased to more than 18,000 tons in 1872, but the following year his company went into liquidation. Liabilities were £170,000 and creditors secured a mere one-eighth of this. His output has been estimated to exceed 200 ships. William Pile married Isabella Rickaby (1822-1908) of Coniscliffe, daughter of a miller, by whom he had several children. Pile was described as a "genial pleasant man" and was certainly very much respected in Sunderland. JFC

Corder MSS: *SH*, 6 and 10 June, 1873; D. R. MacGregor, *Merchant Sailing Ships, 1850-1875* (1984).

PRIESTMAN, SIR JOHN (1855-1941) (SHIPBUILDER AND BENEFACTOR)

Born at Bishop Auckland, son of a master baker, who died when John was young. Entering the Bulmer shipyard, Priestman displayed the ability to gain a place in the drawing office and later became chief draughtsman at Pickersgill's. At 25 he designed their first iron ship. In 1882 opened his own shipyard at Southwick. After many fluctuations, in 1894, he secured a patent for a self-trimming trunk vessel. His last ship sold by auction in 1933, the yard having ceased to build ships. His numerous directorships included chairmanship of Enfield Steamship Co., Cliffside SS Co., Brinkburn SS Co., and Bullock's Hall Colliery Co. Ltd., on the board of the Elswick Coal Co., the Sunderland & South Shields Water Co. and Newcastle branch of Phoenix Assurance Co. His vast fortune came from South Africa gold mine investments. He was not a member of any technical society. A Conservative, 23 years on Southwick Urban District Council (21 years chairman), a county councillor and member of school board, Member of River Wear Commission, a Sunderland JP (from 1901) and Freeman (1933); knighted in 1923 and made a baronet in 1934. A keen organist (President Sunderland Organists' Association) donated organs to many churches. An active Anglican (second wife sister of vicar of St. Andrews, Roker). Estimated donated half a million pounds in charitable bequests, including £100,000 for Haig homes, £50,000 for Eye Infirmary and £20,000 for Sunderland Technical College Library. Built St. Andrew's Church, Roker 1906-1907 in memory of his mother, and rebuilt St. Michael's, Bishopwearmouth, 1933-1935, at a cost to himself of £35,000. Founded the Priestman Trust. Left £1,504,774 gross. Bishop Hensley Henson said of him, "his defects were dwarfed by his virtues, the largeness of his nature, and the generosity of his ideals". (Quoted *SE* 14 October 1959.) JFC

Corder MSS; *WWW*; *Shipping World* and *SDE* various issues; *Times*, 6 August 1941; *SDE*, 6 and 8 August 1941; *Engineer*, 1941; *Shipbuilder*, 1941; *DBB*.

THE REED FAMILY (PRINTERS)

The Reeds have run Sunderland's oldest business for two centuries, making notable contributions to the town's civic life. *Thomas Reed* (c. 1700-1799) born at Biddick and his son Peter (1733-1788) were both Master Mariners; Peter and the next three generations were also shipowners. *Thomas II* (1750-1840) established the family firm in High Street East in 1782 and was also a bookseller. *Thomas III* (1795-1883) produced the first of the nautical publications for which the firm became internationally famous in the 1930's. He was a member of the Select Vestry of Sunderland Parish, a Sunderland Improvement Commissioner and Alderman in 1835 and a Poor Law Guardian. *Thomas IV* (1831-1912) expanded the business, particularly maritime publications. A Councillor for 30 years and Chairman of the Parks Committee, he was instrumental in acquiring the land for Barnes Park. One of the first members and from 1881-1897, Colonel of the First Company of Rifle Volunteers, later the 3rd Durham Light Infantry. Brunton was added to the family's name through Thomas IV's second wife. *Harold Brunton-Reed*'s (1880-1964) career saw the introduction of the world famous Reed's *Nautical Almanac* in 1931. *Kenneth Brunton-Reed* (1914-) was responsible for the growth and the diversification of the company in the new areas of the printing, publishing packaging and conference business. He continued the family Territorial involvement as Lieutenant Colonel of 582 LAA/SL Regiment RA (DLI) TA — (the successor to the 3rd and later 7th Durham Light Infantry) — MBE 1945 and TD 1951. *Tony Brunton-Reed* (1940-) is the sixth generation running the firm. NTS

David Bean, *Thomas Reed* (1982); *Alderman* 20 October 1877, pp. 3-4; *SYB*, 1910, pp. 23-24.

REES, REVD ARTHUR AUGUSTUS (1814-1884) (INDEPENDENT MINISTER)

Born Carmarthen 22 February 1815, son of a Welsh land owner. Served briefly as a midshipman.

Converted, and entered St. David's College, Lampeter, to train for the Anglican ministry, graduating in 1839. Invited by William Webb, rector of Sunderland, to become his curate in 1841. Ordained by Bishop Maltby of Durham. Proved a very popular preacher and an assiduous pastor. But his outspoken manner, dogmatic views and impatience with authority led to trouble with both his rector and his bishop. Despite popular demonstrations of support he was obliged to resign the curacy. His farewell sermon preached in St. John's chapel 4 December 1842. Began to hold services in a variety of places and finally raised sufficient money to build the Bethesda Free Church on Tatham Street, 1845. Adult believers baptism soon became the normal practice here. Bethesda had strictly defined doctrines and disciplines to which its members had to adhere, on pain of expulsion. Rees was always a lively and compelling preacher and attracted a considerable congregation. He refused a salary and spurned pew rents; was supported by free-will offerings. Rees was kept in the public eye by his frequent denunciations of contemporary developments. Yet there were many warm tributes to him when he died 16 April 1884. Buried Bishopwearmouth Cemetery. Bethesda was a strongly evangelical church and launched many missions in different parts of the town which were later organised by the Bethesda Evangelisation Society. Rees' widow (née Ann Catherine van de Horst) inherited from him the ownership of Bethesda and sold it to the congregation for £6,000.　　GEM

Brockie, pp. 439-449; SDE 16 April 1886; Stuart K. Hardy, One Man and His Church: The Life of A. A. Rees, unpublished BA dissertation, Sunderland Polytechnic 1984; Rees' farewell sermon in St. John's chapel, Sunderland 4 December 1842, was printed in James Everett, The Midshipman and the Minister (Sunderland, 1867).

SHARP, SIR CUTHBERT (1781-1849) (ANTIQUARIAN)

Sharp was born in Hartlepool, the son of a shipowner and a daughter of Brass Crosby the famous Lord Mayor of London. He was educated at the renowned academy of Dr. Charles Burney at Greenwich. In 1797-1798 Sharp served as an officer in the Essex Fencibles during the bloody events of the French backed Irish rebellion. There followed the interlude of a couple of sessions at Edinburgh University. Trapped in France in 1802 at the end of the Peace of Amiens; held for some time as a paroled prisoner. In 1809 he married Elizabeth, daughter of Thomas Croudace of Lambton and Bainbridge Holme. Indeed he had probably eloped with her because there were two ceremonies, one in Coldstream, then one in Edinburgh. In Hartlepool he became prominent in obtaining an Act of Parliament to improve the harbour; became mayor in 1813 and held the post for three terms. Knighted in 1814. In 1823 became the Collector of HM Customs at Sunderland. It was while he was in Sunderland that he was responsible for the literary and antiquarian work for which he became most well known, his best known works being a History of Hartlepool illustrated with Bewick woodcuts and his Memorials of the Rebellion of 1569. He was on very friendly terms with Sir Walter Scott and shared literary interests with the Duke of Northumberland and the Earl of Durham with whom he published a volume on the legend of the Lambton Worm. Wrote a lot of poetry and made many genealogical collections some of which were used in Surtees' History of Durham. Vice-president of the Sunderland Natural History and Antiquarian Society, Deputy Provincial Grand Master of the Durham Freemasons, Chairman of the Bishopwearmouth Watching and Lighting Board, a vice-president of the Infirmary, a member of the committee of the Subscription Library, a founding member of the Sunderland Beef Steak Club and a leading magistrate. He was also an excellent billiards player! In 1845 he went on to become the Collector at Newcastle. He died on the 17 August 1849.　　STM

Brockie, pp. 141-147; B. Rowland Hills "A Sketch of the life of Sir Cuthbert Sharp with a bibliography of his writings", Antiq. Sund., 1909, pp. 115-123.

SHORT, JOHN YOUNG (1844-1900) (SHIPBUILDER)

Born Sunderland, second of four sons of George Short (1814-63), who was by trade a ship's carpenter, became a shipyard foreman, and in 1850 opened his own yard at Mowbray Quay. John was educated at the Pybus Academy, West Boldon; apprenticed to Tyneside timber merchants Greenwell's. John joined the shipyard in 1865 and worked with brothers George, Thomas and Joseph; in 1869 a move was made to a new yard at Pallion and from 1871 the yard became Short Brothers. By the end of the 1870's it was one of the biggest yards on the river and at Short's death employed about 1,500 workers. Freedom of the Shipwrights' Company was awarded to John Short as well as medals for his ship designs. In addition to managing the family timber business, he became one of the largest shipowners in the port (Chairman of the Sunderland Shipowners' Association in 1898, a River Wear Commissioner from 1885) and was a marine underwriter. A partner in one of the largest collieries at Easington. With his friend William Allen (1837-1903) the Scotia Engine workers introduced the eight-hour day in 1892 and set up an Institute for his workers. A founder member of the Institution of Naval Architects. A Congregationalist, a very effective, enthusiastic speaker, who served on Sunderland Council from 1887, President of Sunderland Liberal Party from 1892; a JP. Brother Joseph (1858-1917) succeeded to the management of the business. J. Y. Short left £384,898.　　JFC

Corder MSS; Archives Short Brothers; J. Westall; Wear Shipbuilders Association; Short Bros, Mowbray Quay to Pallion Yard, 1850-1960 (1950); DBB; Clarke, Labour relations (1967); Shipping World, vols. 3 and 9; SDE, 27 January 1900; Engineer v. 89; Engineering v. 69; New. Chron. January 1900; NECIES vol. 17.

SIMEY, RALPH (1834-1911) (SOLICITOR)

Born Sunderland 1834, son of Thomas Boyes Simey, JP, shipowner; educated at the Grange School; served his articles with Ald. Robert Brown (qv), with whom he then went into partnership for about two years in the late 1850s before going into practice on his own account. In 1861 he married Margaret Iliff, daughter of Dr. Iliff of the Grange School, and they had a family of three sons and six daughters. Also in 1861 he was elected Councillor for Sunderland Ward; he lost his seat at the elections on 1 November 1867 but was elected for Bridge Ward three weeks later, representing it until he retired from the Council in 1879. He was one of the most prominent and able Tories on the Council. He acted as agent for James Hartley in the 1865 parliamentary election and in later elections acted for (Sir) George Elliot in North Durham. In 1880 he was appointed Clerk of the Peace for County Durham and, following the establishment of county councils in 1888, he was also appointed Clerk to Durham County Council, positions he held until his death in 1911. For much of his time as clerk to DCC he worked closely with his former opponent on Sunderland Town Council, Samuel Storey (qv). In 1855 he left Sunderland to live in Durham although he maintained his Sunderland practice, from 1889 in partnership with his wife's nephew, L. S. Iliff. He also acted as Solicitor to the RWC, 1873-1905. He was appointed a Deputy Lieutenant, County Durham, in 1890. He died on 24 June 1911. Ralph Simey was one of the most able, if not the most able, Tory councillors in the 1870s; a clear and forcible public speaker, widely respected both personally and professionally, his political retirement in 1879 robbed local Tories of a strong leader.　　PJS

SDE 26 June 1911; The Alderman, 12 August 1876; Jamieson, Durham . . . (R. Simey and L. S. Iliff).

STEPHENSON, THE REVD GEORGE (1759-1844) (ANGLICAN CURATE)

Son of a fellow of Magdalen College, Oxford, who became vicar of Saltfleetby (Lincs.) and later of Longbenton. George also went to Magdalen, and in 1786 became curate at Bishopwearmouth. He held the post under Egerton, Paley, Gray and Wellesley, until 1829, when he became incumbent of the new town-centre church of St. Thomas. It seems that he never sought preferment. He derived an income from two other parishes, Redmarshall and Kelloe, given him by the Bishop of Durham, but preferred living in Sunderland and playing an active part in that social and political setting. He enjoyed the confidence of his (often absentee) rectors, and Paley entrusted him with the task of editing his sermons. He was a county magistrate for 34 years, treasurer to the Infirmary from 1818, and a leading figure in the Subscription Library from its inception in 1795. He presided over Bishopwearmouth vestry, and laid the foundation stone of the new parish workhouse in 1827. His son, also George Stephenson (1795-1837), solicitor, was very active in local politics and administration. Clerk to the county magistrates, to the Houghton-le-Spring magistrates, to the Board of Guardians, to Bishopwearmouth Improvement Commissioners, to Bishopwearmouth Highways Board; and secretary of, or solicitor to, many other local bodies.　　THC

Antiq. Sund., vol. ix, 12; Brockie p. 53.

STOREY, SAMUEL (1841-1925) & FAMILY (NEWSPAPER PROPRIETOR; MP)

Born at Sherburn, near Durham, 13 January 1841, the sixth son of Robert Storey (1800-1843), farmer, formerly of Monkwearmouth. Educated at St. Andrew's Parish School, Newcastle, where he became a pupil teacher before going to the Durham Diocesan Training College (Bede College), Durham, 1858-59, and then becoming master at Birtley Church of England School, 1860-64. Despite these Church connections, Samuel was brought up by his mother as a Methodist and when he moved to Sunderland he became a member of Dock Street Free Methodist Chapel, Monkwearmouth. Married, 25 April 1864, Mary Ann, daughter of John Addison (1807-70), painter, Cashier and Actuary of Monkwearmouth Savings Bank, and Poor Law Guardian, 1855-70). Late in 1864 he moved to Monkwearmouth and worked as a traveller for Messrs. Glaholm & Robson, rope manufacturers, for about three years, while also setting up as an accountant and in October 1865 starting the Atlas Permanent Building Society with Thomas Steel, a solicitor. The Society survived until 1887. During the 1870s Storey speculated successfully in building land in the expanding residential areas of East Boldon, Monkwearmouth and Bishopwearmouth. From 1870-76 he was Actuary of the Monkwearmouth Savings Bank and 1876-81 a partner in Armstrong, Addison & Co., timber merchants (with his brother-in-law, John George Addison). In 1873 he was one of the founders of the Sunderland Daily Echo, of which he became managing proprietor. 1882-85, in partnership with the Scottish-born, American millionaire iron manufacturer, Andrew Carnegie, and others, he built up a chain of ½d evening newspapers to advocate radical and republican ideas — these papers included the Portsmouth Evening News, Northern Daily Mail, Hartlepool and for a time, the North Eastern Daily and Weekly Gazettes, Middlesbrough. When the Carnegie-Storey Syndicate, as it became known, broke up in July 1885 Storey emerged as the major shareholder in the Portsmouth and Hartlepool papers as well as the Sunderland and Tyneside Echoes. Storey, an ardent Liberal, was Councillor for Monkwearmouth Ward, 1869-77; Alderman, Bridge Ward, 1877-90 (resigned); and Mayor 1876, 1877 and April-November 1880. Leader of the Radical group in the Town Council in the mid-1870s he took a leading role in the establishment of the Sunderland and North Durham Liberal Club (1873) and the Sunderland Liberal Association (1876). Elected MP for Sunderland at a by-election in April 1881 and represented the town until his defeat in 1895. He unsuccessfully contested Newcastle in 1900 but was re-elected for Sunderland as an Independent Tariff Reformer in January 1910, retiring at the December 1910 election on medical advice. After 1895 his interests were concentrated more in the county of Durham than in Sunderland. Presented the Freedom of Sunderland in 1921 and died on 21 January 1925. His first wife, Mary Ann Addison, died in 1877 and he married Sarah, widow of Capt. John Newton of Sunderland, in 1898 but she died in 1908. Six children, all by his first wife; one son and one daughter died in infancy and another daughter in 1895. His second son, Frederick George Storey (1868-1924) was called to the Bar in 1893 and followed his father on to the Town Council (1891-94) and Durham County Council (1898-1907) as well as into newspaper management. His sons, Samuel and Frederick, carried on the twin family interests of politics and newspapers. Samuel (1896-1978) succeeded his grandfather as Chairman of the family newspaper companies (formed into Portsmouth & Sunderland Newspapers Ltd in 1934), represented Monkwearmouth on Sunderland Borough Council, 1927-30, and was elected Conservative MP for Sunderland, 1931-45, moved to Stretford (Manchester) 1950-66, served as Deputy Speaker 1965-66 and was created a baronet in 1960 and a Life Peer (Lord Buckton) in 1966. P & SN is now headed by Lord Buckton's son, Sir Richard Storey. PJS

P. J. Storey, entries on Samuel Storey in J. O. Baylen & N. J. Gossman, eds., *Biographical Dictionary of British Radicals*, vol. 2, 487-490, and D. J. Jeremy, ed., *DBB*, v, pp. 362-366; P. J. Storey, "Samuel Storey of Sunderland (1841-1925): his life and career as a local politician and newspaper proprietor up to 1895", M. Litt. University of Edinburgh, 1978; *SDE*, 22 December 1973 (centenary issue).

SUMMERBELL, THOMAS (1861-1910) (PRINTER; MP)

Born Seaham Harbour, 10 August 1861, son of Thomas Summerbell, a miner, whose family had long lived and worked in the Tunstall/Hylton area as farmers and shipwrights. Thomas left school at 12 and, after briefly trying the grocery trade, served his apprenticeship as a printer, first with George Boggon and then with John Richardson of the *Seaham Weekly News*. He then worked as a journeyman printer at Felling and Jarrow before becoming a reporter on the *Shields and Tynemouth Argus* at South Shields. From c. 1883 worked as a compositor on the *Sunderland Herald & Daily Post* and started his own printing business in Green Street in 1894. Became interested in local politics and trade unionism generally. The Sunderland branch of the Typographical Association appointed him as a delegate to the Sunderland Trades council and in September 1888 he was elected Secretary of the Trades Council, a post which he held until his election to Parliament in 1906. At first a Liberal, he became a member of the Sunderland branch of the Labour Electoral Association, which was formed in October 1889, and in 1892 he joined the Independent Labour Party when a Sunderland branch was formed (February), being elected a vice-president for six months in August 1892. Thereafter he was firmly associated with the cause of independent Labour representation. In November 1892 he stood as a Trades Council candidate in the annual municipal elections in Hendon Ward. He was easily beaten by the long-serving tory councillor, E. R. Dix, but Dix's election as an Alderman a week later led to a by-election in Hendon Ward at which Summerbell defeated a tory candidate. He remained a councillor for Hendon Ward until his death, more than once being re-elected unopposed. By the 1890s his views were strongly Socialistic and he was a keen advocate of municipalisation. As vice-chairman and later chairman of the Corporation's Tramways Committee, was closely involved in, the acquisition of the old tramways system from the company which had begun Sunderland's trams and the system's subsequent expansion and electrification. He was adopted as Labour candidate for Sunderland in 1903 and became the junior member for the borough in 1906. Defeated in the January 1910 election, he collapsed with an apoplexy at a Council meeting on 9 February 1910 and died the following morning. His unremitting capacity for hard work almost certainly contributed to his early death. Apart from his printing business he was a consistent attender at Trades Council and Town Council meetings and in Parliament. Thomas Summerbell was survived by his wife, Mary (nee Allcroft), two sons and a daughter. His elder son, also Thomas (1888-1955), followed in his father's footsteps, carrying on the printing business, serving on the town council, 1930-44 (retired due to poor health), and being elected an Alderman and the town's first socialist mayor in 1935. His younger son, Walter (1896-1963), joined his brother in the family printing business after World War I (during which he was a conscientious objector) and his daughter, Ethel (1898-), obtained a BSc degree from Durham University and became a secondary school teacher — she also acted as mayoress for her bachelor brother, Thomas. PJS

J. M. Bellamy & J. Saville, *Dictionary of Labour Biography*, IV, 165-6 (includes sources); *SYB*; 1907, pp. 16-17, & 1910, pp. 10-12; B. Charlton, "The Origins and the History of Sunderland and District Trades Council (1874-1906)", Ruskin College, Oxford, Labour Diploma thesis, 1985; Sunderland Trades Council, *Annual Reports*, 1902-3, pp. 11-13, 1904-5, pp. 12-13, 1909-10, p. 14, *SDE*, 18 September 1888, pp. 23-24; 15 August 1900, 10 & 14 February 1910, 14 October 1955.

THE THOMPSON FAMILY (SHIPBUILDERS)

Robert Thompson (1797-1860) the son of a ship's captain, for many years worked as a shipwright, foreman or yard manager on the Tyne as well as the Wear, occasionally alone and in partnership, building on his own account. In 1846 he founded the shipyard which became one of the rivers largest shipyards and one of his sons Robert (see below) would establish a yard of almost equal distinction. *Joseph Lowes* (1824-1893) like his brothers learned his trade at his father's side, and became an able designer of ships, and later gave his name to the family yard (J. L. Thompson); his brother John (1825-1891) set up his own short lived yard, Joseph Lowes I intending to introduce iron construction sent his sons *Joseph Lowes II* (1853-1903) and Robert III to learn the techniques in his brother Robert's shipyard. Active Methodists. *Robert Thompson III* (1850-1908) left Gainford school to start his apprenticeship at 15 and became outside manager in his father's yard, became a quarter share partner in 1873; took over the management, with his brother in 1877, on his father's retirement. He extended the company, introduced electrical plant; his other business interests included the Sunderland Forge & Engineering Co Ltd, Skinningrove Iron Co. Ltd. and his shipping interests included the Alpha SS Co. In 1894, the year after his brother retired, the shipyard became a limited liability company. Very interested in all technical matters — a member of Institution of Naval Architects from 1878. Iron & Steel Institute from 1886, a founder member of the North East Coast Institution of Engineers & Shipbuilders, President 1892-4, freeman of the Worshipful Company of Shipwrights, a strong supporter of industrial conciliation, opened a Workmen's Rest Home with library in 1892, active on hospital boards, Durham JP, a Liberal in politics who was a Sunderland town councillor. A member of the United Methodist Free Churches; continued his father's support of Sunderland Football Club, both financially and as a visitor to Roker Park. Married Georgina Andrew of Whitby, four sons and one daughter survived their father, Robert Norman (1878-1951) had a distinguished career in the industry and was knighted. He died on his estate Over Dinsdale Hall and left £159,804. *Robert Thompson II* (1819-1910) decided to leave his father's yard in 1850, but was persuaded to return and soon offered a partnership in 1853. He represented the shipyard at meetings of the employers' association, in which he actively participated on founding his own yard in 1854. He built many very fine composite ships and for a time had one of the largest yards on the river. Served 23 years on the Wear Commission first elected as representative of the importers & exporters of the town. Elected to Southwick Local Government Board in 1863, and was later for nine years chairman of the Southwick UDC. He donated site for council's offices. He twice married, Sarah Barber (1821-66) and later Lilian Clark. He left £159,639. JFC

Corder MSS; Shipbuilders Assoc. papers; Papers of J. L. Thompson; John Thompson, *The Past & the Present of the North Sands Shipyards* (1891); *Memoir of Mr. John Thompson* (1893); J. L. Thompson, *One Hundred Years of Shipbuilding* (1946); *DBB*; *SE*; *NECIES* v. 20 (1903), v. 24 (1908), v. 68 (1951); Clarke (1984).

THE VAUX AND NICHOLSON FAMILIES (BREWERS)

The Vaux Brewery was founded by *Cuthbert Vaux* (1813-1878) while its move to the Castle Street premises in 1875 was overseen by his son *John* (1834-1884). Several other members of the family were involved in brewing, notably *Cuthbert (II)* (1862-1927) who after studying at European breweries pioneered the introduction of bottled ales and stouts. John's daughter Amy married *Frank Nicholson (I)* (1875-1952), a chartered accountant who became the brewery manager and secretary. He was grandson of James Williams of the *Sunderland Times*. After the amalgamation with the North Eastern Breweries Frank (I) became managing director then chairman of the larger company. He became a CBE in 1937 and a knight in 1943. His successors as chairman were his son *Douglas* (1905-1984) and his grandson *Paul* (1938-) while another grandson *Frank (II)* (1954-) became managing director. The three generations of Nicholsons have overseen major expansion in which Vaux has developed from a local concern to the second largest regional brewery in the country. They have all been much involved in commercial and public life. All three chairmen have been High Sheriffs of Durham, while Frank (I) and Douglas were both River Wear Commissioners and chairman of the Brewers Society, Frank (I) also became a Councillor and Mayor and was chairman of the Finance Committee for 24 years while Paul has been chairman of the northern organisation of the CBI and the National Enterprise Board. He became the first chairman of Tyne and Wear Urban Development Corporation in 1987. NTS

Corder MSS, Vols. 9 & 12; *SE*, 29 December 1952; *Times*, 29 December 1984; *Things That Affect Us* No. 90.

WATTS, HARRY (1826-1913) (LIFESAVER AND DIVER)

Born in Silver Street, Sunderland on 15 June. Following brief periods of employment in the Garrison Pottery, then a weaving factory, he went to sea in 1831 as an apprentice to James Leithead. In that year he rescued a fellow apprentice from drowning in Quebec harbour — the first of a series of life-savings. In all he is said to have rescued 39 people (and a dog) although it is difficult to decide whether one should count the young suicidal lady in 1854 who insisted "Oh, let me be in!". From 1861 he was employed as a diver by the RWC which involved him in a number of very perilous situations. He was one of the divers employed in the recovery of the bodies after the Tay Bridge disaster of December 1879. Also did valuable work in flooded mine shafts and in waterwork wells. Married Rebecca Smith in 1846 and they set up house in Silver Street. Ironically she died in 1856 being drowned in the harbour when rushing out to meet the lifeboat carrying in her husband from his grounded vessel. In 1857 he married Sarah Ann Thompson a woman of some property. They had two children. Sarah died in 1884. Also in 1857 Watts was converted to Christianity following a bout of delirium tremens. In 1858 he became a member of the Primitive Methodist Chapel in Flag Lane, though for a while joined the Christian Lay Churches. He became an enthusiastic teetotaller and advocate of temperance. For his lifesaving efforts he received medals from the Royal Humane Society, from his fellow seafarers and from the United Temperance Crusaders. In 1878 his medals were stolen although many of them were later replaced. Watts refused to prosecute the burglar when he was captured. He was introduced to Andrew Carnegie when he visited the town and Carnegie gave him a pension of 25 shillings a week saying of him "The hero who kills men is the hero of barbarism, the hero of civilisation saves the lives of his fellows". Watts died on the 23 April 1913. STM

A. Spencer, *Life of Harry Watts: Sixty Years Sailor and Diver* (1911).

WAYMAN, JOHN WRIGHT (1830-1886) (BUILDING SOCIETY MANAGER)

Born 25 December 1830, son of Watson Wayman, waterman, and his second wife, Margaret Wright; became a clerk in a shipping insurance firm and then in a bank before setting up as a shipbroker and agent. In 1854 he turned to building societies, then in their infancy, beginning the series of Universal Building Societies, a series of terminating societies, with which his name became synonymous — by his death in 1886 he had promoted 37 such building societies under his direct management. He also speculated successfully in building land. He served briefly as Councillor for Sunderland Ward 1861-62 (retired) but in 1867 he was elected at the head of the poll for the new Hendon Ward — an area in which much of his business activity lay and which he helped to create. He represented Hendon, being re-elected unopposed, until his election as an Alderman in 1885. He served as Mayor in 1882 and 1883. His first mayoralty was marred by the Victoria Hall Disaster and he opened a subscription list for the relief of the bereaved parents and for the establishment of a children's convalescent home. Both his mayoralties saw widespread distress in the town due to the ship-building slump and consequent unemployment and he spent much time on the raising and subsequent distribution of relief funds. He served on the Board of Guardians in the early 1870s and the School Board, 1880-82. JP, 1879. Connected with the local branch of the RSPCA. Interested in art and collected paintings. Wesleyan — local lay preacher for 25 years. Married (1) 1854 Elizabeth, daughter of Joseph Curry, master mariner (deceased by 23 March 1837) who died in 1865, aged 30; and (2) 20 November 1866 Annie Maria, daughter of George Turner, Wesleyan minister; having children by both. Wayman was a staunch and locally prominent Conservative. He was popular, an able speaker, though with a tendency to be pompous. He helped to keep the *Sunderland Daily Post* going as a Conservative organ, being associated with it as a shareholder or joint proprietor from its establishment in 1876 until his death on 27 August 1886. His relatively early death after a brief illness following a cerebral haemorrhage precipitated a crisis in his Universal Building Societies. Like the Atlas Permanent Building Society managed by his arch rival, Samuel Storey, which went into liquidation the following year, the Universal was probably a victim of the disastrous 1880s shipbuilding depression; unlike the Atlas, however, the Universal Building Societies fell into the hands of the lawyers and instead of being gradually wound up by an amicably-reached agreement, a number of law suits ensued, complicated by a lack of properly kept books and by apparent financial irregularities on Wayman's part which he was not there to explain, and it was several years before any money could be paid out to depositors: a sad end to a hitherto successful career.   PJS

The Alderman, 23 September 1876, 13 October 1877; *SDP*, 28 & 30 August 1886; *SDE*, 27 August 1886, 2 July 1887, 19 January 1888, 23 June 1891.

THE WEBSTER FAMILY (ROPE MAKERS)

The Websters controlled the world's first rope factory at Deptford, which became one of the country's major rope-making firms, for almost a century and a half. After its opening in 1794 *Rowland Webster (I)* (1759-1809) Mayor of Stockton who married Mary daughter of Rowland Burdon, founded the firm along with Ralph Hills and John Grimshaw. His two sons *Rowland (II)* and *Christopher* went bankrupt in 1821, but the family retained control, Christopher Maling (1812-1894) and *Henry (I)* (1815-1882) ran the firm. Christopher who owned Pallion Hall, left an estate of £257,000. *Henry (II)* (1855-1936) was chairman of the firm until his death.   NTS

Corder MSS, Vol. 13.

WHITE, ANDREW (1792-1856) (MP; BUSINESSMAN)

John White (1764-1833) moved from Stamfordham to Sunderland, where he established himself as a cooper, and subsequently became a prosperous shipowner and proprietor of Bishopwearmouth Ironworks. A Wesleyan and keen Sabbatarian. Active in charitable works (subscribing to the town's dispensary), and in promoting Sunday Schools and the distribution of religious tracts. His second son, *John* (1794-1828) was a director of the Ironworks, active in Sunderland Methodism, and a committee member of the Dispensary and Infirmary. His third son, *Richard* (b. 1804) was a Director of the Ironworks and of Sunderland Joint Stock Bank, as well as having coal interests in Whitwell Colliery; a poor law guardian; and Mayor of Sunderland in 1841. John White's eldest son, *Andrew*, was also a director of the Ironworks and chairman of the Joint Stock Bank. He was a Commissioner of the River Wear and of Sunderland Bridge, Chairman of the Poor Law Guardians, and elected first Mayor of Sunderland following the Municipal Corporations Act (which he had warmly supported) in 1835. A borough and county magistrate; President of the Mechanics Institute and of the Sunderland British and Foreign School; vice-president of the Exchange Newsroom. Re-elected as Mayor in 1836 and 1837, he resigned that office in order to stand for Parliament. Elected MP for Sunderland (Whig/Liberal), defeating David Barclay but declined to stand for re-election 1841 be-

cause of difficulties in his business affairs. From then on took little part in public affairs. Active Wesleyan in younger years. Died at Frederick Lodge, Bishopwearmouth, aged 64. Buried Bishopwearmouth cemetery, his funeral attended by the aldermen, councillors, and most of the leading citizens, and the procession accompanied by the entire Sunderland police force.   JP

Brockie pp. 90-99, 154-60; F. Boase, *Modern English Biography* (London, 1965), III, p. 1309; *Gentleman's Magazine* (July-December 1856), p. 661; W. W. Bean, *Parliamentary Representation of the Six Northern Counties* (Hull, 1890) p. 177; G. E. Milburn, "Wesleyanism in Sunderland", *Antiq. Sund.*, xxvii (1977-79), pp. 19-20; *SH*, October 3 & 10 1856.

WILLIAMSON, SIR HEDWORTH (1797-1861) (LANDOWNER; BUSINESSMAN; MP)

Originally from Nottinghamshire, the Williamson family acquired the manor of Monkwearmouth by marriage and purchase in the late seventeenth century, and in the eighteenth century added the Whitburn estate, developing Whitburn Hall (especially in the nineteenth century) as the principal family residence. Sir Hedworth succeeded his father (also Sir Hedworth) as 7th baronet while a minor, in 1810. Educated at St. John's College, Cambridge, he married in 1826 Anne Elizabeth, daughter of the first Lord Ravensworth. Developed the Monkwearmouth estate, and, with the growth of Monkwearmouth colliery, said in 1841 to have been able to command between 200 and 300 votes. Elected MP for County Durham in 1831, and for the newly-created Northern Division of the County in 1832. Re-elected in 1835, but retired in 1837. A moderate Reformer, later a conservative Whig in politics. Developed (against the wishes of most of the inhabitants of Sunderland) the North Dock, and thereby impoverished himself. A county magistrate, member of the Wear Commission, High Sherriff of County Durham in 1840, Alderman of Monkwearmouth ward, and Mayor of Sunderland 1841-2 and 1847. Resigned the Mayoralty 1847 on succeeding his brother-in-law David Barclay as MP for Sunderland 1847-1852. Died at Whitburn, aged 63, and at his funeral his son, Sir Hedworth, the 8th Baronet, distributed a "dole" to 150 poor citizens of Monkwearmouth Shore and Whitburn.   AH

E. W. Moses, "The Williamsons of East Markham, Nottinghamshire, Monkwearmouth and Whitburn", *Antiq. Sund.*, xxiii (1964). F. Boase, *Modern English Biography* (London, 1965), III, p. 1385. *Gentleman's Magazine* (January-June 1861), pp. 697-8.

WILSON, JOSEPH HAVELOCK (1858-1929) (TRADE UNIONIST)

Founder of the National Amalgamated Sailors' & Firemen's Union, the forerunner of the present National Union of Seamen. Born in High Street, Sunderland, went to sea aged 14. Experienced trade unionism in Australia, joined North of England Sailors' & Seagoing Firemen's Friendly Society 1879. Left the sea 1882, opened "Wilson's Temperance Hotel and Dining Rooms" in High Street, providing union with meeting rooms. North of England Union reluctant to expand beyond Tyne and Wear, Wilson left and founded NASFU August 1887: Samuel Plimsoll became Hon. President. By 1889 had 65,000 members and moved to London, but major defeats by Shipping Federation broke the union in 1894. A new union, the National Sailors' & Firemen's Union, was formed with Wilson as President. Elected MP for Middlesbrough 1892 (first Labour candidate to win a three-cornered fight), sat as Liberal; re-elected 1895, lost 1900, re-elected 1906, retired 1910. Strikes from 1911 brought increasing recognition of NSFU, but war helped more. Already anti-socialist, Wilson became ultra-patriotic and fiercely anti-German; awarded CBE 1918. Elected MP South Shields 1919, defeated 1922 by Will Lawther, made Companion of Honour. NSFU isolated from rest of labour movement, Wilson allied with Shipping Federation, ordering strike breaking against rival unions, expelling many activists. Supported mine-owners 1926, saw General Strike as "communist plot", gave financial support to "Spencer" mining unions in Nottingham. NSFU expelled from TUC 1928. Wilson died in his office 16 April 1929. Left £428.   GP

SDE, 17 April 1929; J. H. Wilson, *My Stormy Voyage Through Life* (1925); J. Bellamy & J. Saville (eds.) *Dictionary of Labour Biography* Vol. iv, pp. 200-208.

WOODCOCK, MRS. ELIZABETH (1752-1842) (PHILANTHROPIST)

Born 25 July 1752, on Queen Street, Sunderland, the daughter of a sailor. Married John Woodcock, son of a prosperous London merchant, and moved to the south with her husband, who died young. With her inherited wealth Elizabeth was able to donate over £20,000 to good causes in her home town. The institutions which benefitted from her gifts and bequests included the Sunderland Shipwrecked Master Mariners Society, the Bishopwearmouth and Sunderland Indigent Sick Society, The Sunderland Lying-In Society (for maternity help), The Orphan Asylum, the Sunderland Dispensary and Infirmary, the Sunderland National (Gray) Schools (an endowment of £1,000), and St. Thomas' Church Bishopwearmouth (£500 to the Building Fund). She also bequeathed £2,000 to trustees to be used on behalf of Church of England Charity schools in Sunderland and Bishopwearmouth, and on behalf of the aged poor. Her most memorable act of charity was the foundation in 1820 of the Maritime Institution, built on land given by her on Crowtree Road, Bishopwearmouth and endowed with a sum of over £4,000. The Institution was a set of ten alms-houses (Maritime Place) open to women who were widows or unmarried daughters of master mariners. Mrs. Woodcock selected the inmates in her lifetime. (The Institution still exists, in new premises in the Ashbrooke area of Sunderland.) In her will she also left £3,000 to the Almshouse Trustees; the dividends of this sum to be used to pay "out-pensions" of £5 twice a year to other poor widows (with the same qualifications mentioned) who continued to live in their own homes. Died 20 March 1842. A memorial was placed in the chancel of St. Michael's, Bishopwearmouth.   GEM

Fordyce (ii) pp. 436, 453-6; *Endowed Charities (County Durham)* 1904, vol. ii, pp. 442-445; M. A. Richardson, *Local Historian's Table Book* (1846) (v) p. 363; Information from Mr. Brian Myers is acknowledged also.

WRIGHT, JOSEPH JOHN (1803?-1878) (SOLICITOR AND CONSERVATIVE ACTIVIST)

At his death, the *Sunderland Herald* described him as worth "a long chapter in the social, policital, and material history of Sunderland". Forty years ago, they said, he was "almost Sunderland itself". Established by father in solicitor's practice in Sunderland 1823. Became moving spirit in project for South Docks, and for enfranchisement of Borough. Altercations over South Docks involved him in duel and citation for contempt by House of Lords. After Reform Act, became principal Tory spokesman in Sunderland, and principal Tory agent for County Durham; said to exert more influence than any other provincial solicitor. Leading solicitor to the Londonderry family; Londonderry praised him in House of Lords. Condemned by erstwhile colleagues as "Judas", but known to friends as "Joe". Twice invited to stand as Tory candidate for Sunderland, at by-elections 1841 and 1845, but declined on grounds of lack private fortune and need to support family. Became principal supporter in town of George Hudson (qv), whom he was instrumental in persuading to come to Sunderland. His son-in-law, William Digby Seymour, was Radical MP for Sunderland 1852-55. Took brother, George Walton-Wright, into partnership 1837, but later described as "too good and amiable a man for a solicitor"; at his death in 1858, aged 51, found he had neglected the firm's book-keeping, run up debts. Wright bankrupted 1859. Lost large sum on Sunderland Docks, £3,000 on railways. Lent £30,000 to son-in-law, further £4,000 to son-in-law W. D. Seymour and his friends. Lost £5,000 on *Sunderland Times*. Moved to Scotland to avoid his creditors, having retired from practice in 1859, and being retained by his sons as a clerk. Spent rest of life in comparative obscurity. Died at Brookfield, aged 75, 28 August 1878.   AH

SH, 6 May 1859; *SE*, 30 August 1872; P. Storey, "Sunderland Newspapers, 1831-1873"; *Antiq. Sund.*, xxvii (1977-79), pp. 105-6; A. Baharie, *Tales and Sketches of Sunderland* (1887), pp. 117-21.

A Guide to Sources

The references associated with each chapter are very detailed and comprehensive and there is no need to repeat them here. However there is a need to give the details of a number of authoritative texts which have been referred to repeatedly, to draw attention to some useful sources which may not have been mentioned because the opportunity to do so did not arise, to clear up some aspects of nomenclature (as with the newspapers of Sunderland) and to elaborate upon the non-published sources which are available in terms of archival materials, maps and museum displays of artefacts. It is not easy to draw a clean line between Sunderland's history and that of the region within which Sunderland has played a significant part, and indeed it would be misleading to try and divorce the two. However it is to be hoped that the sources outlined below present a balanced picture.

BIBLIOGRAPHY

The obvious starting point for the interested researcher is Bowling, H. and Corfe, T. *History in Sunderland: A Guide* (Eyewitness, 1974) although this is now becoming somewhat outdated. Two useful surveys are Craggs, S. *Theses on North East England* (Sunderland Polytechnic, 1983). Potts, G. *A Bibliography of North Eastern History in Periodicals* (forthcoming).

JOURNALS AND PERIODICALS

There are two journals especially which should be consulted for information on a wide range of subjects concerning the history of Sunderland.
Antiquities of Sunderland. The transactions of the Sunderland Antiquarian Society (1900 onwards; index in Vol. XXI (1954). Now published under the title *Sunderland's History*.
Bulletin of the Durham County Local History Society (bi-annual, from 1964 onwards).
In addition there are articles of relevance in:
Archaeologia Aeliana. The transactions of the Society of Antiquaries of Newcastle upon Tyne (1822 onwards; annual).
Bulletin of the North East Group for the study of Labour History.
Durham University Journal.
Northern History, published annually by the School of History of the University of Leeds.
Transactions of the North East Coast Institution of Engineers and Shipbuilders.
Finally some of the volumes of the Surtees Society are concerned with original source material which relates to aspects of the towns development eg. Vol. CXCV G. E. Milburn, *The Diary of John Young 1841-1843* (1983). An index to the Surtees Society publications was compiled by Ms. E. Brown in August 1976.
In view of the considerable number of periodical articles in existence in the list which follows the only articles which appear are those published in the more specialised journals or in journals which are not specifically devoted to the north east region.

BOOKS AND SELECTED ARTICLES

1. GENERAL

Bowling, H. (ed) *Some Chapters on the History of Sunderland* (privately published, 1969).
Brockie, W. *Sunderland Notables* (Hills, 1894).
Burnett, J. *History of the Town and Port of Sunderland* (privately published, 1830).
Clay, M., Milburn, G. E and Miller, S. T. *An Eye Plan of Sunderland and Bishopwearmouth 1785-1790 by John Rain* (Frank Graham, 1984).
Corfe, T. *A History of Sunderland* (Frank Graham, 1973).
Fordyce, W. *History and Antiquities of the County Palatine of Durham* (two volumes, Fullarton, 1857). There is a long account of Sunderland in Vol. 2.
Garbutt, G. *History of Monkwearmouth, Bishopwearmouth and Sunderland* (privately published, 1819).
Mackenzie, E. and Ross, M. *Historical, Topographical and Descriptive View of the County Palatine of Durham* (Mackenzie and Dent 1834, two volumes).
Miller, S. T. *Sunderland Past and Present* (Waterloo Press, 1983).

Mitchell, W. C. *History of Sunderland* (Hills, 1919; reprint by E. J. Morten, 1972).
Page, W. (ed) *Victoria History of the County of Durham* (Constable, St. Catherine's Press, OUP 1905-1928, reprinted in 1968, two volumes).
Potts, T. *Sunderland: A History of the Town, Port, Trade and Commerce* (B. Williams, 1892).
Summers, J. W. *History and Antiquities of Sunderland* (Joseph Tate, 1858).
Surtees, R. *History and Antiquities of the County Palatine of Durham* (Nichols and Bentley, London and Andrews, Durham, 1816-1840, four volumes).
Welford, R. *Men of Mark 'twixt Tyne and Tweed* (Walter Scott, 1895, three volumes).
In addition there are several general studies of specific localities such as Gibson, P. *Southwick on Wear* (Southwick Publications, 1985). County and Borough directories are an invaluable source for the 19th and early 20th centuries. Particularly detailed accounts of Sunderland, with much historical and topographical information, can be found for instance in four County Directories — Whellan's for 1856, 1865 and 1894 and Kelly's for 1910.

2. ECONOMIC DEVELOPMENT

Anon. *Years of Change — Shipyards in the 1880s* (Austin and Pickersgill, 1979).
Baker, J. C. *Sunderland Pottery* (5th Edition, Thomas Reed and Tyne and Wear County Council Museums, 1984).
Baker J. C. and Crowe, K. *A Collectors Guide to Jobling 1930s Decorative Glass* (Tyne and Wear County Council Museums, 1985).
Baker, J. C., Evans, S. et. al. *Pyrex: 60 years of Design* (Tyne and Wear County Council Museums, 1983).
Blair, D. J. 'Spatial Dynamics of Commercial Activity in Central Sunderland' (MA thesis, Durham University, 1977).
Bean, D. *Thomas Reed: The First 200 Years* (Thomas Reed, 1982).
Clarke, J. F. *The Changeover from Wood to Iron Shipbuilding* (Newcastle Polytechnic, 1986).
Corfe, T. *Swan in Sunderland* (Eyewitness and Tyne and Wear County Council, 1979).
Dolan, N. *Scotts Southwick Pottery* (Tyne and Wear County Council Museums, 1988).
Dougan, D. *The History of North East Shipbuilding* (Frank Graham, 1968).
Fox, R. C. *The Demography of Sunderland, 1851,* (Sunderland Polytechnic, Department of Geography and History Occasional Paper No 1, 1980).
James, J. G. *The Cast Iron Bridge at Sunderland* (Newcastle Polytechnic, 1986).
McCutcheon, J. E. *A Wearside Mining Story* (privately published, 1960).
Osler, A. *The Maritime Collections* (Tyne and Wear County Council Museums, 1970).
Ross, C. *The Development of the Glass Industry on the River Wear and Tyne 1700-1900* (Ph.D thesis, Newcastle University, 1987).
Smith, J. W. and Holden, T. S. *Where Ships are Born, 1346-1946* (Thomas Reed and Wear Shipbuilders Association, 1946).
Smith, S. B. 'Wire Rope Making, Sunderland', *Bull. North Eastern Industrial Archaeology Society* No. 7, Nov-Dec 1968.
Smith, S. B. 'Scott's Pottery, Sunderland', *Bull. North Eastern Industrial Archaeology Society* No. 10, Feb 1970.
Baker, J. C. *The Glass Industry of Tyne and Wear Pt. 1 Glassmaking on Wearside* (Tyne and Wear County Council Museums, 1979).
Sturgess, R. W. (ed) *The Great Age of Industry in the North East* (Durham County Local History Society, 1981) Especially J. F. Clarke, 'Shipbuilding on the River Wear 1780-1870' and G. Patterson, 'The Shipping Industry: Life and death at sea'.

3. TRANSPORT AND COMMUNICATIONS

Anon. *Sunderland Transport — The First Hundred Years* (Newcastle upon Tyne, 1979).
Douglas, M. *The Life and Adventures of Martin Douglas Sunderland Keelman* (privately published, 1848).
Lambert, R. S. *The Railway King* (Allen and Unwin, 1934).
Miller, S. T. 'The Progressive Improvement of

Sunderland Harbour and the River Wear, 1717-1859'. (MA thesis, Newcastle University, 1977).
Miller, S. T. 'North versus South; The Docks Dispute at Sunderland in the 1830s', *Industrial Archaeology Review*, Vol. 4, No. 1, Winter 1979-80, pp. 36-50.
Miller, S. T. *The River Wear Commissioners: Extracts from their papers 1717-1846* (Durham County Local History Society, 1980).
Miller, S. T. *Harbour Improvements and Sunderland in the Early Nineteenth Century* (Sunderland Polytechnic, Department of Geography and history, Occasional Paper No. 2, 1981).
Miller, S. T. 'John Murray: "a bold and skilful engineer" ', *Industrial Archaeology Review*, Vol. 6, No. 2, Spring 1982, pp. 102-111.
Murray, J. 'An Account of the progressive improvement of Sunderland Harbour and the River Wear'. *Proc. Inst. of Civil Engineers*, Vol. 6, 1847, pp. 256-277.
Sinclair, N. *The River Wear* (Tyne and Wear County Council Museums, 1984).
Sinclair, N. *Railways of Sunderland* (Tyne and Wear County Council Museums, 1985).
Skempton, A. W. 'The Engineers of Sunderland Harbour 1718-1817' *Industrial Archaeology Review*, Vol. 1, No. 2, Spring 1977, pp. 103-125.
Staddon, S. A. *The Tramways of Sunderland* (Huddersfield, 1964).
Warn, C. R. *Rails Between Wear and Tyne* (Frank Graham, 1982).

4. SOCIETY AND POLITICS

Anon. *Them were the days . . . or were they? Life in Sunderland's East End in the 1930s* (East End History and Community Arts Project, 1985).
Conlin, J. *History of the Sunderland Borough Police Force* (J. A. Jobling, 1969).
McLoughlin, P. *The Johnson Street Bullies* (New Horizon, 1980).
Miller, S. T. *Cholera in Sunderland* (Eyewitness, 1977).
Miller, S. T. 'Cholera in Sunderland 1831-1832', *Jnl. of Regional and Local Studies*, Vol. 3 No. 1, Summer 1983.
Miller, S. T. and Hepplewhite, P. *Public Health in Sunderland in the Nineteenth Century* (1988).
Morris, R. J. *Cholera 1832* (Croom Helm, 1976).
Nossiter, T. J. *Influence, Opinion and Political Idioms in Reformed England: Case Studies from the North East 1832-1874* (Harvester Press, 1975).
Seabrook, J. *Unemployment* (Quartet Books, nd. 1982?) especially chapters 7 and 8.
Storey, P. J. 'Samuel Storey of Sunderland'. (M. Litt. thesis, Edinburgh University, 1975).
Storey, P. J. *Politics and the Press in the later Nineteenth Century* (Sunderland Polytechnic, forthcoming).
Wood, P. 'The Activities of the Sunderland Poor Law Union, 1834-1930' (M. Litt. thesis, Newcastle University, 1975).
Wood, P. 'Finance and the urban Poor Law: Sunderland Union 1834-1914' in Rose, M. E. *The Poor and the City* (1985).
Yearnshire, J. *Back on the Borough Beat* (privately published, 1987).

5. RELIGION

Hart, J. *Bishopwearmouth Parish Church c. 940 to 1982* (Wearside Historic Churches Group, 1982).
Hopkins, C. H. G. *Pallion 1874 to 1954: Church and People in a Shipyard Parish.* (Wearside Printing Co., 1954).
Hopkins, C. H. G. *The Moving Staircase: Sunderland 1939-1972* (Wearside Printing Co., 1972).
Innes, V. *South Hylton Church and Village* (privately published, 1984).
Lavin P. *Alexander Boddy, Pastor and Prophet* (Wearside Historic Churches Group, 1986).
Levy, A. *A History of the Sunderland Jewish Community* (Macdonald, 1956).
Milburn, G. E. *Religion in Sunderland in the mid-nineteenth century* (Sunderland Polytechnic, Department of Geography and History, Occasional Paper No. 3, 1983).
Milburn, G. E. *Church and Chapel in Sunderland 1780-1914* (Sunderland Polytechnic, Department of Geography and History Occasional Paper No. 4, 1988).

Myers, B. A. *The Rectors of the ancient Parish Church of Bishopwearmouth 1195-1975* (Wearside Historic Churches Group, 1975).

6. CULTURE AND LEISURE

Anderson, A. *The Dream Palaces of Sunderland* (Mercia Cinema Society, 1982).

Anon. *Ha'way the Lads: The Road to Wembley* (Ceolfrith Press, 1974).

Appleton, A. *Sunderland and the Cup from 1884 to 1973* (Frank Graham, 1974).

Collingwood, C. S. *Dr Cowan and the Grange School* (1897).

Hall, W. G. 'The Provision of Technical Education in Sunderland to 1908' (M.Ed. thesis, University of Durham, 1964).

Hill, P. and Sinclair, N. *Centenary of the Sunderland Library and Museum* (Sunderland, 1979).

Horsley, J. *Ship to Shore, Maritime Paintings from Seaham to the Tyne* (Tyne and Wear County Council Museums, 1984).

Makkison, J. 'The Development of Further and Higher Education in Sunderland since 1908' (M.Ed. thesis, University of Durham, 1969).

Simmons, W. and Graham, R. *History of Sunderland AFC* (1987).

Sinclair, H. *Cycle Clips: A History of Cycling in the North East*, (Tyne and Wear County Council Museums, 1983).

Took, R. and Van der Merve, P. *Clarkson Stanfield 1793-1867* (Tyne and Wear County Council Museums, 1979).

Watts, Moses, E. (ed) *To Ashbrooke and Beyond: The History of the Sunderland Cricket and Rugby Football Club 1808-1963* (Sunderland, 1963).

7. PLANNING AND DEVELOPMENT POST 1945

Anon. *Washington Legacy, Washington and its Development Corporation 1964-1988* (no publisher, nd).

Blair, D. J. and Hodgson, D. (eds). *Greater Sunderland* (Sunderland Polytechnic, 1974).

Dennis, N. *People and Planning: The Sociology of Housing in Sunderland* (Faber, 1970).

Hole, W. V. Adderson, I. M., Pountney, M. T. *Washington New Town: The early years* (HMSO, 1979).

Holley, S. *Washington: Quicker by Quango. The History of Washington New Town 1964-1983* (Publications for Companies, 1983).

McLelland, G. *Washington: Over and Out. The Story of Washington New Town 1983-1988*, (Publications for Companies, 1988).

Robson, B. T. *Urban Analysis, A Study of City Structure with special reference to Sunderland* (Cambridge University Press, 1969).

8. ARCHITECTURE

Corfe, T. (ed) *The Buildings of Sunderland 1814-1914* (Tyne and Wear County Council Museums, 1983).

Corfe, T., Milburn, G. E., le Roy, M. *Buildings and Beliefs* (Wearside Historic Churches Group, 1984).

Pevsner, N. *County Durham Buildings of England* series (Penguin, 1953; 2nd Edition revised by E. Williamson, 1983).

9. PHOTOGRAPHS AND PRINTS

Anon. *Canny Aad Sunlun* (Sunderland Echo, 1983).

Anon. *Old Sunderland* (Sunderland Museum and Art Gallery, 1951).

Boyle, M. *Wearside at War* (*Sunderland Echo*, 1984).

Meddes, C. *Sunderland revisited: A Selection of Photographs of a By-gone Age* (privately published, 1983).

Pickersgill, A. *Sunderland in Times Past* (Countryside Publications, 1981).

Pickersgill, A. *Sunderland in old picture postcards* (European Library, 1985).

10. URBAN TRAILS

Corfe, T. *Wearmouth Heritage* (Sunderland Civic Society, 1975).

Corfe, T. *The Buildings of Sunderland Town Centre Trail* (Tyne and Wear County Council Museums).

The *Wearside Heritage Trails* series (published by

the Tyne and Wear County Council Museums).
1. Wear Bridge Area.
2. The East End.
3. Monkwearmouth.
4. Tunstall Hills.
5. South Hylton.
6. Around Bishopwearmouth Green.
7. Barnes Park to Hastings Hill.
8. Mowbray Park.
9. Washington.
10. New Silksworth.

SUNDERLAND IN MAPS

Maps are an excellent and essential starting point for historical and environmental research. Maps which could be useful for a study of Sunderland can be found in several scattered locations. This list is confined to maps which are available in the Local Studies Department of the Central Library in Borough Road, Sunderland. The list is further restricted by limitations of space to the 50 most useful or significant maps and is by no means complete or exhaustive. It is chronological with the exceptions of the ordnance Survey maps and a separate section on the plans of the Docks.

The scales given in this list are presented in the way most familiar to map users, they are not always presented in the same way on the map itself.

(1) 1855 Ordnance Survey
Scale: 6″ to 1 mile
            25″ to 1 mile
(2) 1894 Ordnance Survey
Scale: 6″ to 1 mile
            25″ to 1 mile
(3) 1939 Ordnance Survey
Scale: 25″ to 1 mile
(4) 1950 to date Ordnance Survey
Scale: 6″ to 1 mile
            25″ to 1 mile
            50″ to 1 mile

These Ordnance Survey maps form a basic guide to the changing face of Sunderland and especially in the larger 25″ and 50″ to the miles scales show an incredible amount of detail. Later revisions are at scales 1:10,000, 1: 2,500 & 1:1,250

(5) 1728 S. & R. Buck 'The perspective and ichnography of the town of Sunderland'.
Scale: 6″ to 1 mile.
(6) 1737 Burleigh & Thompson 'A plan of the River Wear from Newbridge to Sunderland Bar'.
Scale: 10″ to 1 mile.

One of the most important surveys of the town it includes much information on landownership and the townships bordering the Wear.

(7) 1790 J. Rain 'An Eye Plan of Sunderland and Bishopwearmouth'.
Scale: 50″ to 1 mile (approx).

A most unusual and interesting map, a hand drawn aerial view of late Eighteenth Century Sunderland. It is as charming as it is accurate. It is also available in book form: M. Clay, G. Milburn and S. Miller, *An Eye-Plan of Sunderland and Bishopwearmouth 1785-1790* (Frank Graham, 1984).

(8) 1817 T. Robson 'A plan of Sunderland, Bishopwearmouth and Monkwearmouth'.
Scale: 10″ to 1 mile
Originally published in Garbutt (qv).

(9) 1827 T. Robson 'A correct plan of the harbour and towns of Bishopwearmouth, Sunderland and Monkwearmouth'.
Scale: 6″ to 1 mile (approx).

(10) 1832 Boundary Commission Sunderland.
Scale: 4″ to 1 mile.
Parliamentary boundary only.

(11) 1836 Boundary Commission Sunderland.
Scale: 4″ to 1 mile.
Shows parliamentary, parish and township boundaries.

(12) 1844 T. Robson 'Plan of the Harbour and Towns of Sunderland, Bishopwearmouth and Monkwearmouth'.
Scale: 6″ to 1 mile.

(13) 1851 T. Meik & R. Morgan 'Plan of the town of Sunderland including Bishopwearmouth, Monkwearmouth, Deptford and Southwick'.
Scale: 10″ to 1 mile.

(14) 1866-67 J. G. Campbell & Co. 'Plan of Sunderland'.
Scale: 6″ to 1 mile (approx).
Basic Street Plan.

(15) 1873 T. Younger 'New Plan of the town of Sunderland, Bishopwearmouth, Monkwearmouth and Southwick'.
Scale: 6″ to 1 mile.
Official plan by Borough Surveyor.

(16) 1878 'Borough of Sunderland'.
Scale: 6″ to 1 mile.
This plan is based on the official surveyor's plan but has additional information such as the incidence of various diseases.

(17) 1883 'Infectious diseases in Sunderland in 1883'.
Scale: 6″ to 1 mile.
Based on the official plan and contains similar information to No. 16.

(18) 1883 R. S. Rounthwaite 'Plan of the Borough of Sunderland'.
Scale: 6″ to 1 mile.
Official plan by Borough Surveyor.

(19) 1891 R. S. Rounthwaite 'Plan of the Borough of Sunderland'.
Scale: 6″ to 1 mile.
Official plan.

(20) 1896 'Plan of the Borough of Sunderland'.
Scale: 6″ to 1 mile.
Shows incidence of various infectious diseases, based on official plan.

(21) 1901 J. W. Moncur 'Plan of the Borough of Sunderland'.
Scale: 6″ to 1 mile.
Official plan by Borough Engineer.

(22) 1915 J. W. Moncur 'Plan of the Borough of Sunderland'.
Scale: 6″ to 1 mile.
Official plan by Borough Engineer.

(23) 1920 G. W. Bacon & Co. 'Plan of Sunderland and Southwick'.
Scale: 6″ to 1 mile.
Based on the Ordnance Survey map.

(24) 1930 G. W. Bacon & Co. 'Plan of Sunderland'.
Scale: 6″ to 1 mile.

(25) 1935 R. Ward 'Map of Sunderland and District'.
Scale: 6″ to 1 mile.

(26) 1939 County Borough of Sunderland Town Planning Scheme.
Scale: 6″ to 1 mile.
Based on Ordnance Survey map.

(27) 1953 J. Burrow & Co. 'Street Plan of Sunderland'.
Scale: 4″ to 1 mile.

(28) 1959 G. W. May Ltd 'Sunderland'.
Scale: 6″ to 1 mile.

(29) 1961 'County Borough of Sunderland Industrial Development Plan'.
Scale: 4″ to 1 mile.
Shows land use and sites available for development.

(30) 1964 'County Borough of Sunderland Industrial Development Plan'.
Scale: 4″ to 1 mile.
Shows land use and sites available for development.

(31) 1966 'County Borough of Sunderland Industrial Development Plan'.
Scale: 4″ to 1 mile.
Shows land use and sites available for development.

(32) 1969 'Sunderland Development Plan Town Map'.
Scale: 6″ to 1 mile.

(33) 1970 Geographia Ltd 'Plan of Sunderland'.
Scale: 3″ to 1 mile.

(34) 1971 Borough of Sunderland. Census Enumeration Districts.
Scale: 6″ to 1 mile.

(35) 1973 Borough of Sunderland 'Confidence Areas'.
Scale: 6″ to 1 mile.
A planning map which shows properties in the Borough built before 1961.

Maps of the Docks and Harbour
The docks and harbour area was so important to the development of Sunderland that it deserves a section to itself.

(1) 1700 No cartographer named. 'Sunderland Harbour'.
Scale: 10″ to 1 mile.

(2) 1750 J. Vincent, Engineer to the RWC. 'Sunderland Harbour'.
Scale: 10″ to 1 mile.

(3) 1800 J. Pickernell, Engineer to the RWC. 'Sunderland Harbour'.
Scale: 10″ to 1 mile.

(4) 1850 T. Meik, Engineer to the RWC. 'Sunderland Harbour'.
Scale: 10″ to 1 mile.
(5) 1900 H. Wake, Engineer to the RWC. 'Sunderland Harbour'.
Scale: 10″ to 1 mile.
The above maps are to a constant scale and format and clearly show the port development over its most important period.
(6) 1832 J. Murray. 'Plan of part of the harbour of Sunderland showing a design for a Wet Dock'.
Scale: 25″ to 1 mile.
This is just one example of numerous maps showing plans for projected dock and harbour schemes most of them doomed never to materialise.
(7) 1881 RWC 'General plan of Sunderland Harbour and Docks'.
Scale: 5″ to 1 mile.
(8) 1898 'Reid's New Map of the River Wear from the Sea to Biddick Ford'.
Scale: 4½″ to 1 mile.
This map shows the main industrial sites, ferry crossings, etc, on the banks of the river.
(9) 1909 RWC 'Plan of Sunderland Harbour and docks and the River Wear to Hylton'.
Scale: Main plan 6″ to 1 mile.
Section at 2½″ to 1 mile of River to Biddick.
This map shows sites available for industrial development.
(10) 1929 RWC 'General plan of the Harbour and Docks at Sunderland'.
Scale: 5″ to 1 mile.
(11) 1939 'Andrew Reid's New Map of the River Wear from the Docks to South Hylton'.
Scale: 4½″ to 1 mile.
Shows main industrial sites, etc.
(12) 1949 RWC 'General Plan of Sunderland Harbour and Docks'.
Scale: 4½″ to 1 mile.
(13) 1959 RWC 'General Plan of Sunderland Harbour and Docks'.
Scale: 4½″ to 1 mile.
(14) 1972 Port of Sunderland 'General Plan of Sunderland Harbour and Docks'.
Scale: 4½″ to 1 mile.
(15) 1978 Port of Sunderland 'General Plan of Sunderland Harbour and Docks'.
Scale: 4½″ to 1 mile.

SUNDERLAND NEWSPAPERS

For a complete listing of Sunderland's newspapers with details of all their title changes and dates of copies available in Sunderland Public Library, the British Library, Colindale, and elsewhere, see Manders, F. W. D. (ed) *Bibliography of British Newspapers: Durham and Northumberland* (British Library, 1982) pp. 45-50. Papers are listed here by date of first publication and the titles given are the short ones by which the paper is generally known (some early newspapers especially had long titles intended to indicate their circulation area and/or special interests, eg, the *Sunderland Times and North of England Shipping & Mercantile Gazette*.

On the history of Sunderland's newspapers see:
Milne, M. *Newspapers of Northumberland and Durham* (1971).
Milne, M. 'Survival of the fittest? Sunderland newspapers in the nineteenth century' in Shattock, J. & Wolff, M., eds, *The Victorian Periodical Press: Samplings & Soundings* (1982) pp. 193-223.
Storey, P. J. Sunderland Newspapers 1831-1873, *Antiquities of Sunderland* XXVII, 1977-79 (1980) pp. 101-116.
Storey P. J. articles in SDE 28, 30, 31 December 1981 and 4 January 1982. SDE, 2 December 1923 and 2 December 1973 (50th and 100th anniversary issues).

Sunderland Gazette, weekly; 29 January-7 October 1831; proprietor and publisher Wm. Gracie; politically neutral.
Sunderland Herald, weekly; 28 May 1831-2 April 1881; *Sunderland Daily Herald* 8 April 1880-3 September 1881; sold to and amalgamated with *Sunderland Daily Post* (qv) as *Sunderland Herald & Daily Post*; principal proprietor 1831-38, Thomas Marwood, jun.; proprietors and publishers 1838-40 B. L. White & Thomas Carr, 1841-81 Vint & Carr (Robert Vint, 1841-67, retd.; Thomas Carr 1841-81;

Vint's nephew, J. S. Burton, 1858-72, died, and H. A. Cave, 1866-81); Liberal (Whig).
Sunderland Beacon, weekly; 3 January 1838-26 September 1839, continued as *Northern Times*; publishers including John Candlish and George Richmond, February-August 1839; Conservative.
Northern Times, weekly; 4 October 1839-29 December 1843, continued as *Sunderland Times*; nom. proprietors W. F. and Thomas Marwood, 1839-42; proprietors Garsham Barnes & Charles Beswick, 1843; Conservative.
Sunderland Times, weekly; 5 January 1844-1856, twice weekly 30 December 1856-30 June 1876, *Sunderland Daily Times*, 3 July 1876-3 August 1878, incorporated in *Sunderland Daily Echo*, *Sunderland Weekly Times*, 7 July 1876-31 December 1880, continued as *(Sunderland) Weekly Echo & Times*, 7 January 1881-7 August 1914. Proprietor Garsham Barnes, 1844-August 1851; James Williams, 1857-1868 (died), Mrs Barbara Williams, 1868-1878 (sold to *Echo*). Ed. William Brockie 1860-73. Mild Conservative, 1844-51, strong Conservative 1851-57, Liberal, 1857-78.
Sunderland Mirror, weekly; 14 September 1839-5 November 1840. Conservative.
Sunderland News, weekly; 5 July 1851-19 May 1855; proprietor. John Candlish; Radical.
Sunderland Examiner, weekly; nos. 1-35, 2 January-27 August 1852, nos. 36-65, 16 September 1853-7 April 1854; continued as *Northern Examiner*, 12 May 1854-11 January 1856 (discontinued) transferred to Newcastle, September 1854. Proprietor John Hardinge Veitch, 1852-54 (died 26 April 1854). Liberal.
Sunderland Advertiser, weekly; 12 Nov. 1853-?.
Sunderland Daily News & Shipping List, morning; ?27 September-2 October 1854 — ? autumn 1865; 4 extant copies, nos. 735, 794, 1152 & 2658, 30/1/1857, 9/4/1857, 3/6/1858, 1/5/1863; proprietor, publisher and printer, John Barnes.
Sunderland Telegram, weekly; 28 August-18 December 1858; proprietors William and Henry Pickering; Conservative.
Sunderland (Penny) Weekly News, 6 January 1865-27 March 1868; proprietor Joseph Cowen *Newcastle Chronicle*; Radical.
Sunderland Daily Shipping News, 6 November 1865-31 December 1913; proprietors of *Sunderland Herald*.
Sunderland Sentinel, weekly; 26 August 1867-?early November 1878, extant copies 1867-10 July 1869; proprietor and publisher William Williams; Conservative.
Sunderland Evening Chronicle, 6 July 1870-3 May 1871; Conservative.
Sunderland Daily Echo, 22 December 1873 to date; 19th century; Radical.
Sunderland Daily Post, 21 July 1876-3 September 1881, continued as *Sunderland Herald & Daily Post*, 5 September 1881-15 November 1902, continued as *Sunderland Daily Post & Herald*, 17 November 1902-21 July 1906 (discontinued); Conservative 1876-87, Unionist 1887-1906.
Sunderland Daily Mail, 14 November 1898-30 June 1899, continued as *Sunderland Morning Mail*, 1 July 1899-13 August 1901, incorporated in *North Mail*, Newcastle; Unionist.
Sunderland Weekly News. 10 December 1898-6 May 1899; weekly attached to *Sunderland Mail*.
Sunderland Weekly News, 4 September-9 October 1931.

PHOTOGRAPHS

By far the biggest collection is that held at Sunderland Museum (qv). The Local Studies Department of the Central Library also has a useful collection. The Sunderland Antiquarian Society has a number of glass 'lantern' slides some of which are of considerable interest (eg, 'Brunnel's Bridge' of 1832). Apart from these deposits attention is drawn here to three others.

The William Waples collection:
In the Masonic Lodge on Ryhope Road there is the famous Waples Collection of some 40,000 photographs, prints, negatives and glass slides. Many of them are of things like freemasons' regalia and of buildings, scenes and people of little relevance to the study of the history of Sunderland. However

1,000 of them are of Sunderland in the period between the 1890s and 1935; many of them of excellent quality (when the sky was not good enough Waples sometimes 'spliced' in a patch of clear sky with a few clouds) and many of them of great interest. Waples was the advertising manager for Binns. He came to Sunderland in 1908 and died in 1968 aged 84.

The Auty-Hastings collection:
This lesser known collection is held by the Local History Section of the Newcastle Central Library. Between 1850-1890 Matthew Auty was running a photographic business in Tynemouth. From the 1880s he was taking local views and selling them in postcard form. In 1895 the business was taken over by Godfrey Hastings who continued the postcard line. The Library holds a total of some 15,000 photographs. In fact only 100 or more are of Sunderland and many of them are of the Roker-Seaburn region. Their quality is superb. Apart from those there are many more which cover life in the villages and towns of County Durham and which are catalogued in a systematic way.

The Billy Bell collection:
Unlike the others this is not in the possession of an institution but is a collection which has been built up by a private individual well known for his illustrated talks on 'Old Sunderland'. It has received some publicity recently and a video film has been made which reveals a sample of the material. Some of the items are actually available in other collections as well but very many of them are quite unique. They are also catalogued in a very systematic way.

Other private collections
Stuart Miller and Geoffrey Milburn have both built up two considerable collections of prints and slides related to the history of Sunderland. The former contains much material related to the river Wear, and the latter to churches and chapels. Many of the photographs are historical and show features no longer extant.

MAJOR LOCAL COLLECTIONS OF BOOKS AND ARCHIVAL MATERIALS

Dean and Chapter Muniments
The Dean and Chapter Muniments contain material relating to parts of Sunderland north of the Wear.
The most important medieval material is:
(i) deeds, 12th century and later, relating to Southwick and Monkwearmouth;
(ii) accounts, 14th-century and later, of the Durham Priory cell at Monkwearmouth, relating to Hylton, Southwick, Monkwearmouth and Fulwell;
(iii) halmote rolls, end of 13th century and later, relating to Southwick, Monkwearmouth and Fulwell.
After the dissolution of Durham Priory in 1539 the cathedral was refounded under a dean and chapter and re-endowed with the priory's estates. Leases and other estate records for these Dean and Chapter lands, including a few estate plans of the late 18th and early 19th centuries, survive from 1541 to c. 1860.

Durham County Record Office
Since 1974 the Durham County Record Office (Shire Hall, Durham City) has had, with one exception, no administrative responsibility for the records of the Sunderland area. The exception relates to its role as Diocesan Record Office for the Diocese of Durham and in that capacity the Durham Record Office is responsible for Church of England parish records in Sunderland. The archives of the ancient parishes of Bishopwearmouth and Monkwearmouth form the core of these holdings (dating from 1567 and 1735 respectively, earlier documents for Monkwearmouth being lost in an 18th century fire). The records of the parish of Sunderland, Holy Trinity, date from its creation in 1719. As the population of the Sunderland area grew in the 19th century so new parishes were formed from the three existing parishes. In most cases the registers of baptisms, marriages and burials are held in the Record Office but in addition there are records relating to the formation of the parish and the building of the church, records of church administration and finance, and records of church societies.

A number of official records held in the Durham Record Office which related to the Sunderland area were transferred to the newly established Tyne & Wear Archives in the years following 1974, but some Sunderland documents are still held at Durham, including the archives of the Sunderland Gas Co. Also to be found at Durham are records of county-wide organisations and institutions which were active in the borough of Sunderland or its immediate vicinity, eg, records of the Durham County Council and its predecessors, the Court of Quarter Sessions; records of the pre-vesting colliery companies deposited by British Coal; the Durham Miners' Association records.

The Durham Record Office also holds copies of the 1841, 1851, 1861, 1871 and 1881 census returns for Sunderland and has an extensive collection of Ordnance Survey six inch and 25 inch plans for the urban area, dating from the 1850s.

Durham Diocesan Records

The Durham Diocesan Records are the archives of the central spiritual administration of the bishops of Durham. Most of the surviving records of this administration have now been deposited in the Department of Palaeography and Diplomatic of the University of Durham, and are housed at 5 The College, Durham. They run from the 15th century to the 20th century and cover a wide geographical area; today the diocese of Durham is roughly coterminous with the historic county of Durham, including the Sunderland area, but from the mediaeval period until the creation of Newcastle diocese in 1882 it also took in most of Northumberland. As well as the obvious material relating to the careers of Church of England clergy, church fabrics, churchyards, parsonage houses, parochial endowments, ecclesiastical jurisdictions and boundaries, and diocesan boards, committees and societies, the diocesan records also include a range of other documents: among these are parish register transcripts (covering approximately 1760-1840 for most parishes), marriage licence applications, some registrations of nonconformist meeting-houses, tithe plans and apportionments drawn up following the 1836 tithe commutation legislation, and, of particular significance, the records of ecclesiastical visitations (or inspections) and of church courts. Visitation records can be extremely informative, especially from the late 18th century onwards; for instance, the returns sent in by clergy at the 1792 episcopal visitation include population figures and notes on schools, hospitals and charities and on the progress of nonconformity and Roman Catholicism in most parishes in the diocese. And ecclesiastical courts, today concerned chiefly with questions of alterations to church fabrics and furnishings, and the occasional clergy discipline case, until relatively recently also dealt with all manner of other cases: these included non-attendance at church, the correction of manners and morals, matrimonial disputes, numerous allegations of defamation, quarrels over the right to hold pews, and attempts to enforce payments of church rates and tithes. In addition, estates of deceased persons were dealt with by ecclesiastical courts up to 1858; church court records contain many references to probate matters and disputed wills, and the Durham Probate Records, also deposited in the Department of Palaeography, include original wills proved and records of probate administrations granted in the diocese of Durham between 1540 and 1858.

Complementary to the Durham Diocesan Records, and also held in the Department of Palaeography, are the Durham bishopric estate and financial records, again dating from the 15th century to the 20th century. The bishopric estates, administered since the 19th century by the Church Commissioners (until 1948 known as the Ecclesiastical Commissioners) were extensive, particularly in the historic county of Durham. In the Sunderland area they included large blocks of copyhold and leasehold property south of the river Wear, and certain details concerning these properties and their tenants can generally be traced through the estate records.

Family History Centre

On the corner of Lindon Road and Queen Alexandra Road stands the Church of Jesus Christ of Latter Day Saints, attached to which is the newly re-named

Family History Centre, an access point for one of the most amazing collections of archival data. Genealogical research plays a significant part in the Mormon faith. As a result the central archive in Salt Lake City holds the most extensive collection of genealogical data in the world. The Centre at Sunderland holds, or can obtain, a wide variety of records covering the whole of Britain and beyond. Amongst other things, the Centre has a microfilm copy of the St. Catherine's House index of civil registration references covering births, deaths and marriages up to the 1920s, the International Genealogical Index (updated in 1988) and a wealth of parish register and census data including much relating to the Sunderland area. Anyone interested in genealogical research is welcome to make use of the facilities although this must be by appointment in view of the pressure of demand and physical limitations of space and microfilm reader time.

Methodist Collections

The Tyne and Wear Archives Service provides the main repository for local Methodist records. However other collections of Methodist materials should be noted. The John Rylands University Library of Manchester (Deansgate Building) houses the national Methodist Church Archives and should always be consulted by local historians since there may well be material relevant to their enquiries in the holdings. In addition to primary sources the Methodist Church Archives contain an abundance of important secondary material including connexional minutes, magazines, and newspapers. The Wesley Historical Society has a north eastern branch which publishes a bi-annual Bulletin and endeavours to preserve photographs, books, pamphlets, ephemera and connexional magazines. These may be consulted by arrangement.

Sunderland Antiquarian Society

Founded in 1900 the Society continues to encourage interest in the history of Sunderland through meetings, research and publications. Its membership stands at 120. The archives, which have been donated and collected over the years consist of an impressive collection of books, photographs, slides, paintings and maps which are available for the use of members and, by arrangement of visitors. The archival material includes interesting items on archaeology, local history, theatre posters of the music halls, and political posters. The large collection of maps and plans dates from 1611. A copy of Rain's Eye Plan is also on deposit and copies of this may be purchased. The library holds many volumes from the 17th century onwards and a vast newspaper collection. The Society's publication, Antiquities of Sunderland, is now produced under the title Sunderland's History.

Sunderland Central Library, Local Studies Department

The Department holds a bookstock of over 8,000 volumes either about the locality, published in the locality or written by someone in the locality. Some of these date from the 18th century. Only part of the collection is actually displayed on the open shelves. A wide range of local and regional periodicals is also available. There is a considerable collection of local newspapers dating from 1831, most of which are available to readers only on microfilm. An index covers the whole newspaper series. The county and town directories, dating from 1827, constitute an invaluable source of information. Also available to researchers are electoral rolls from 1832. Census returns on microfilm (1841-1881), a collection of 10,000 illustrations, photographs and slides and around 3,000 maps (see separate list). The Corder Manuscripts in 38 volumes are a unique compendium of material (mainly biographical and topographical) relating to Sunderland. A collection of ephemera has been started and the recently acquired Lilburne Collection has added valuable material to this relating to matters such as the first Wearmouth bridge, the cholera outbreak of 1831-1832 and the Sunderland Volunteers.

Tyne and Wear Archives Service

The Tyne and Wear Archive Service cares for extensive collections of documents reflecting the history of the communities which make up industrial

Wearside and Tyneside and dating from the 12th to the 20th centuries, though most are from the last 300 years.

Local government records are extensive. Early authorities such as those for Monkwearmouth Parish did little more than care for the poor and maintain the highways. From 1835 council and committee minutes cover many key aspects of Sunderland's development such as public health, town planning and industrial growth and decline. Evidence from other statutory bodies such as Poor Law Unions, Burial Boards and School Boards is abundant. Outstanding are the records of the River Wear Commissioners. They chart the progress of Sunderland as a major port from the early 18th century. The work of the commissioners is intimately linked to coal exports and shipbuilding, the twin pillars of modern growth on Wearside.

Tyne and Wear Archives Service is authorised by the Lord Chancellor to hold public records. These include Customs and Excise Registers, court and health service collections. Amongst the latter is detailed material from Sunderland's hospitals including the General Hospital and the Royal Infirmary. Recently Washington Development Corporation deposited the records of the 'new town'.

The activities of Wearside business and commercial firms are well represented, notably shipbuilding and related industries. For example the records of Sunderland Shipbuilders Ltd which was formed by a merger of Doxford, Laing and Thompson in 1966. The collection dates back to the late 18th century and contains details of the workforce and technical innovations such as turret ships. The records of smaller enterprises giving a broader picture of maritime activities include the notebooks of John and Andrew White, 19th century shipowners and the Neptune Steamship Protecting and Indemnity Association.

Other categories on deposit are private family papers (eg, the Ogdens, influential Quakers); the records of non-conformist churches, often including baptismal registers; community organisations (eg, Sunderland Rotary Club); professional associations and trade unions (eg, Transport and General Workers Union) and political groups (eg, Sunderland Labour Party). Some archives have regional or sub-regional significance and often have a direct bearing on Sunderland. This category includes English (Industrial) Estates, the Northumberland and Durham Miners Permanent Relief Fund and the records of Tyne and Wear County Council.

TYNE AND WEAR MUSEUMS SERVICE

(i) Source materials
Sunderland museum and Art Gallery
In addition to material on display at Museums in Sunderland (see below) there is a large reserve collection which is available for research and study by prior arrangement. It falls into four main groups:

1. Photographs
Sunderland Museum holds approximately 12,000 photographs, among them some of the earliest views of the town, such as a view of the iron bridge taken in 1854 by Edward Backhouse. They include a large number taken during the mid 19th and early 20th centuries; and a series of views of the town, particularly of the East End and of public houses, taken by Dr. J. Dixon Johnson in the 1940s and 1950s. Other photographs show areas such as Monkwearmouth and Deptford before they were demolished by the Borough Council in the 1960s. The majority of these photographs are filed by street name. There are separate sections for churches and for the river; the latter includes photographs mainly taken for the River Wear Commissioners from 1863 which are often the only known views of buildings which once stood on the river banks. Further significant collections show Wearside ships and shipbuilding, other Wearside industries, aspects of community life such as football, and notable Sunderland people particularly those involved in civic life at the end of the 19th century. Photographs of Sunderland railways, trams and buses are held at Monkwearmouth Station Museum.

2. Topographical Paintings and Prints
In its fine art collections the Museum holds a range

of paintings and prints from the 18th century, many of which pre-date photographs. Subjects which are particularly well represented are the river, the Iron Bridge and churches. They include many views by the prolific A. J. Moore (1852-1915), an amateur artist who copied some of his paintings from photographs as well as by leading North East professional artists such as C. H. Bell (1823-1896) and J. W. Carmichael (1799-1868).

3. *Ephemera*
There are around 9,000 items in the ephemera collections including a wide range of posters, notices, letterheads and invoices. Subjects which are particularly well covered are 19th century politics, commerce, collieries, the World Wars and shipbuilding and ship-owners. Indexes exist for most of the collection covering subject, individuals or firms and location in the town. There is also a collection at Monkwearmouth Station Museum covering land transport (particularly Sunderland Corporation Transport).

4. *Maps*
In addition to the maps located in the Local Studies department, of which the 50 most useful are listed in this section, the Museum has specialist collections of maps such as those showing property and estates dating from the beginning of the 18th century to the end of the 19th. Some areas of Sunderland, such as Southwick, are well covered. The central commercial area of Sunderland from the river to Borough Road and from the Docks to Silksworth Row is covered by the insurance maps produced by G. E. Goad between 1894 and 1959. These give details of the structure of buildings whether stone or brick, wood or glass, and name the functions and users of each property. A slightly wider area is covered by 10' to the mile Ordnance Survey series of 1856. Ordnance Survey maps also include 6" to the mile coverage for County Durham. Durham is well represented by a collection of County maps starting with that of Christopher Saxton in 1576; though the scale is necessarily small some show interesting features such as important houses and their owners, collieries and wagonways.

Because of limitations of space and staff, this material can only be consulted by prior appointment.

(ii) *Displays*
Sunderland Museum and Art Gallery
Many of the Museum's displays relate to the history and natural history of Wearside. *The Sunderland Story* traces the history of the town from the time of the Neolithic settlement at Hasting Hill about 3000BC. Later archaeological material includes Bronze-age cist burials, also from Hasting Hill, stray Roman finds and the important Saxon material such as stained glass, found during the excavations at the St. Peter's Monastery site during 1959-1974. Further displays cover the Medieval period and Sunderland's role in the Civil War. The growth of Sunderland since the 1790s is covered in an audio-visual presentation, while there are individual displays on many of the topics covered in this book such as the Iron Bridge, the Corporation, MP's, Churches and the First and Second World Wars. One area is devoted to Victorian and Edwardian commerce and includes a re-construction of Reynold's pawnbrokers shop. The entertainment displays feature 'Wallace', the lion from a menagerie, which has been one of the most popular exhibits since the Museum opened on the present site in 1879. The displays covering the River Wear Commissioners include a suit worn by one of their divers, Ralph Scott, while an adjacent section on the Sunderland lighthouses includes optics from the 1856 South Pier and 1903 Roker lighthouses.

While *The Sunderland Story* concentrates on the community life of the town, middle-class domestic life is shown in the 1790s, 1860s and 1930s period rooms on the second floor of the Museum.

Three of Sunderland's best-known industries are featured in separate displays. Shipbuilding is shown through models of sail and steam vessels built on Wearside and a working model of a Doxford marine engine of 1951. The exhibits in the *Glassmaking on Wearside* gallery range from bottles and engraved glasses of the 18th and 19th centuries to recent Pyrex. The spectacular part of the glass collection is the table service made for the Marquis of

Londonderry in 1824. Sunderland's pottery industry is shown by a comprehensive display of ceramics made on Wearside, most notably the 19th century pink lustre-ware; transfers on these reflect the historical and social developments of the period.

The permanent collection of paintings, prints and drawings includes works by British artists ranging from Sir Edwin Landseer to Allen Jones. It includes several works with local connections such as spectacular paintings by the Sunderland-born artist Clarkson Stanfield as well as views of Wearside by artists as diverse as T. M. Hemy and L. S. Lowry. Similarly the silver gallery shows a wide range of silver from the 16th to 18th centuries, but also includes items with specific local connections such as Sunderland church plate. Sunderland's new cultural ties are reflected in the Japanese Art display.

The extensive natural sciences collections cover the Tyne and Wear and County Durham areas. *The North East Before Man* gallery concentrates on local Permian geology and includes a 240,000,000 years old fossil of one of the oldest vertebrate animals in the world capable of gliding flight; this was found at Eppleton Quarry in 1978. The *Local Wildlife* display shows animals and plants in the sea, river, moorland and urban environments. It includes live exhibits, such as the salt and fresh-water aquaria.

The Museums Education Service provides activities, events for visitors and quiz sheets for children. It also offers facilities for schools and colleges including loans, handling sessions, in-service training and help with projects and course work.

Grindon Close Museum
The Museum occupies the upper floor of an Edwardian house which previously belonged to two of Sunderland's major shipbuilding families — the Doxfords and then from 1916-1954, the Shorts. Appropriately the displays are of Edwardian rooms such as the children's nursery and the kitchen, and shop interiors, including a post office, chemist and dentist's surgery.

Monkwearmouth Station Museum
One of the great attractions of Thomas Moore's masterpiece of 1848 is that the building has changed little since the 19th century. The imposing classical exterior has been restored to its 1848 condition. Other restored features include the ticket office, the footbridge, the waiting shelter and the siding area which houses restored rolling stock. The railway atmosphere of the building is preserved by the trains which pass through the station on the Newcastle-Sunderland railway line.

The Museum displays include a section on George Hudson, who was responsible for the station being built in such an impressive style; the centre-piece of this is Sir Francis Grant's well-known portrait of Hudson. Other displays cover the British Steam Locomotive 1835-1954, which features a fine selection of models; Wearside Railways; and Cycling in the North-East of England.

Washington 'F' Pit Museum
The Museum consists of the winding engine house for headgear of the 'F' pit, which was one of a string of collieries in the Washington area. The engine house was built in 1903, but the engine itself was second-hand and had been constructed by Grange & Co of Durham in 1888. It has been adapted to be driven by electrical motor for demonstration purposes.

Ryhope Pumping Engines Museum
This is not run by the Tyne and Wear Museums Service but can be conveniently appended here. It stands just off Stockton Road near Ryhope General Hospital. It was renovated by and is cared for by a group of volunteers. The Pumping Station has been described as 'the finest single industrial monument in the North East'. The two great 100hp beam engines and their pump were supplied by R. & W. Hawthorn of Newcastle and commissioned in 1869. The building itself is an impressive Gothic edifice set in attractive grounds. There is also a small museum illustrating aspects of water pumping, supply and use and an entertaining display of articles of sanitary ware called the 'Clean and Decent'.

CONTACTS
The guide to sources was compiled and edited by Geoffrey Milburn, Stuart Miller and Neil Sinclair. The section on Sunderland Newspapers was contributed by Patricia Storey. There follows a list of the names of the other individual contributors together with the addresses and telephone numbers of the institutions which they represent.
Margaret McCollum, Assistant Keeper, Department of Palaeography and Diplomatic, 5 The College, University of Durham. (Tel: Durham 3743610.)
David Butler, Archivist, Durham County Record Office, County Hall. (Tel: Durham 3864411.)
Fenwick Davidson, Chief Librarian, Family History Centre, Alexandra Road, Sunderland. (Tel: Wearside 5285787.)
John Almond, Chairman, Ryhope Engines Trust, 5 Birchfield Road, Sunderland. (Tel: Wearside 5142259.)
Vera Stevens, Secretary, Sunderland Antiquarian Society, 16 Grizedale Court, Seaburn, Sunderland. (Tel: Wearside 5487541.)
Philip Hall, Local Studies Librarian, Sunderland Central Library, Borough Road, Sunderland. (Tel: Wearside 5141235.)
Peter Hepplewhite, Education Officer, Tyne and Wear Archives Service, Blandford House, Blandford Square, Newcastle-upon-Tyne. (Tel: Tyneside 2326789.)
Neil Sinclair, Curator, Sunderland Museum and Art Gallery, Borough Road, Sunderland. (Tel: Wearside 5141235.)
Geoffrey Milburn, Editor, Wesley Historical Society (NE), 8 Ashbrooke Mount, Sunderland. (Tel: Wearside 5284682.)
Alison Peacock, Methodist Church Archives, John Rylands University Library of Manchester, Oxford Road, Manchester M13. (Tel: Manchester 8345343.)
Pat Mussett, Senior Assistant Keeper, Department of Palaeography and Diplomatic, The Prior's Kitchen, The College, Durham. (Tel: Wearside 3743615.)

Appendix 1
THE POPULATION OF SUNDERLAND

A. BEFORE 1801 (ESTIMATES)

1481 1,300; *1681* 3,090; *1781* 20,940; (estimates based on parish registers from W. Hutchinson, *History and Antiquities of County Durham* [1794]).
c.1642 3,762 (estimate from Poor Rate books by D. A. Kirby, *Transactions of the Institute of British Geographers*, 1972, pp. 86-7.

B. 1801-1901 (CENSUS RETURNS)

The Parishes of Bishopwearmouth, Monkwearmouth and Sunderland are those existing in 1801. Townships or civil parishes were areas which could have a separate poor rate or overseer of the poor.

	Acreage	1801	1811	1821	1831	1841	1851	1861	1871	1881	1891	1901
i. *Bishopwearmouth Parish*	9,225	7,806	8,810	11,542	16,590	27,092	35,035	50,541	67,253	88,102	103,048	118,851
			(1.2)	(3.1)	(4.3)	(6.3)	(2.9)	(4.4)	(3.3)	(3.1)	(1.6)	(1.5)
Bishopwearmouth Township	2,669	6,126	7,060	9,477	14,462	24,206	31,824	45,673	59,032	74,441	87,648	99,437
Bishopwearmouth Panns Township	6	564	476	483	363	298	316	272	264	195	68	5
Burdon Township	1,135	69	107	149	162	114	123	95	116	104	125	195
Ford Township	1,029	602	712	791	911	1,720	1,922	2,036	2,477	2,631	2,737	2,954
Ryhope Chapelry	1,585	254	255	368	365	423	475	2,082	4,576	6,024	7,541	10,414
Silksworth Township	1,993	138	150	210	252	267	305	289	396	401	426	446
Tunstall Township	808	53	50	64	75	64	70	94	392	4,306	4,503	5,400
ii. *Monkwearmouth Parish*	5,180	6,293	6,504	7,644	9,428	12,493	16,911	23,440	29,041	36,358	41,866	49,171
			(0.3)	(1.7)	(2.3)	(3.2)	(3.5)	(3.8)	(2.3)	(2.5)	(1.5)	(1.7)
Fulwell Township	737	85	145	118	158	134	169	208	318	527	1,038	2,989
Hylton Township	2,593	312	363	320	420	550	546	487	638	1,533	1,313	1,715
Monkwearmouth Township	550	1,103	1,091	1,278	1,498	2,155	3,366	3,343	5,507	8,355	9,125	9,929
Monkwearmouth Shore Township	287	4,239	4,264	4,924	6,051	7,742	10,109	15,139	16,641	17,765	20,077	21,810
Southwick Township	1,013	554	641	1,004	1,301	1,912	2,721	4,263	5,937	8,178	10,313	12,728
			(1.5)	(5.6)	(2.9)	(4.6)	(4.2)	(5.6)	(3.9)	(3.7)	(2.6)	(2.3)
iii. *Sunderland Parish*	220	12,412	12,289	14,725	17,060	17,022	19,058	17,107	16,861	15,333	14,558	14,238
			(−0.9)	(1.9)	(1.5)	(—)	(1.1)	(−1.0)	(−0.1)	(−0.9)	(−0.5)	(−0.2)
The three parishes (1)		26,511	27,603	33,911	43,078	56,607	71,004	91,088	113,155	139,793	159,472	182,260
			(0.4)	(2.2)	(2.7)	(3.1)	(2.5)	(2.8)	(2.4)	(2.3)	(1.4)	(1.4)
Sunderland Parliamentary Borough (2)		24,998	25,821	31,891	49,735	53,335	66,618	82,474	104,179	124,720	141,328	158,735
Sunderland Municipal Borough (3)		24,444	25,180	30,887	39,434	51,423	63,897	78,211	98,242	116,542	131,015	146,077
			(0.3)	(2.3)	(2.8)	(3.0)	(2.4)	(2.2)	(2.6)	(1.9)	(1.2)	(1.1)

Figures in brackets show annual average percentage rate of growth from previous decade.
For comparison the percentage figures for England and Wales are given.

			1811	1821	1831	1841	1851	1861	1871	1881	1891	1901
England & Wales			(1.4)	(1.8)	(1.6)	(1.4)	(1.3)	(1.2)	(1.3)	(1.4)	(1.2)	(1.2)

(1) Sunderland Poor Law Union of 1836, comprised the whole of the three original parishes of Bishopwearmouth, Monkwearmouth and Sunderland, except for the township of Burdon, which was in Easington Union.
(2) Sunderland Parliamentary Borough was created by the Great Reform Act of 1832 and comprised the townships of Sunderland, Bishopwearmouth, Bishopwearmouth Panns, Monkwearmouth, Monkwearmouth Shore and Southwick. It returned two members to Parliament.
(3) Sunderland Municipal Borough was created in 1836 from the townships of Sunderland, Monkwearmouth, Monkwearmouth Shore and as much of Bishopwearmouth as lay within a radius of one mile of the centre of Wearmouth Bridge. The boundary was extended in 1867 and 1895.

C. 1911-1981 (CENSUS RETURNS [1])

	1911	1921	1931(2)	1941	1951	1961	1971(3)	1981(4)
Sunderland Borough	151,159	159,055	185,824	N.A.	181,524	189,686	212,995	294,894

(1) The many changes in boundaries makes calculation of sub-area population figures impossible.
(2) Boundary extension to include Southwick UD.
(3) boundary extension to include Sunderland RDC.
(4) Boundary extension to form Sunderland Metropolitan District within Tyne and Wear County.
Sources: Census Volumes 1801-1981. VCH Durham Vol II, (1907), pp. 261-274. Compilation and calculations by George Patterson.

Appendix 2
PARLIAMENTARY ELECTION RESULTS, SUNDERLAND, 1832-1983

Sunderland was a 2-member constituency from 1832 until its division into two single-member constituencies (North and South) under the 1948 Representation of the People Act. Results are given in detail for the 2-member period showing, first, the number of 'plumpers', i.e. electors voting for one candidate only, and, secondly, the 'splits', i.e. electors using both their votes and so expressing either their personal preference or the party or electoral alliance decided on, if any, by their principal candidate. From 1874 voting was generally based on straight party lines whereas previously electoral alliances between candidates could, and did, change from election to election. Before the 1872 Ballot Act made voting secret polling lists showing which electors voted for which candidate(s)are available for all Sunderland elections except 1833, 1835 and 1868, either published in local newspapers soon after the poll (marked * in the list below), or as printed Poll Books (marked † below). The date given is that on which the poll was held — general election polls were not held on the same day throughout the country until 1918 — until then they were spread out over some three weeks with the boroughs generally polling early and the counties later. Results for the earlier elections are drawn from a variety of sources which do not necessarily agree: the press, which often printed unofficial figures supplied by the candidates' agents, the official declaration, polling lists. Where conflict has occurred, the most likely result has been selected here. Party allegiances are indicated after the name of each candidate:

C = Conservative
L = Liberal
LU = Liberal Unionist
U = Unionist
UFT = Unionist Free Trader

Lab = Labour
NL = National Liberal
Com = Communist
Co L = Coalition Liberal
Ind TR = Independent Tariff Reformer

†14 December 1832 General Election. Registered Electors: 1,378; voted: 1,132.

	Sir William Chaytor (L)	Capt. Hon. Geo. Barrington (L)	David Barclay (L)	Ald. William Thompson (C)
Plumpers	42	38	124	32
Chaytor/Barrington	315	315	—	—
Chaytor/Barclay	77	—	77	—
Chaytor/Thompson	264	—	—	264
Barrington/Thompson	—	31	—	31
Barrington/Barclay	—	139	139	—
Thompson/Barclay	—	—	65	65
Result:	698	523	405	392

4 April 1833 by-election, Capt. Barrington having accepted the Chiltern Hundreds:

Ald. William Thompson (C)	574
David Barclay (L)	557

8 Jan. 1835 General Election. Reg. Electors: 1,359; voted: 1,108.

Ald. William Thompson (C)	844 (96 plumpers)
David Barclay (L)	708 (119 plumpers)
Sir William Chaytor (L)	392 (57 plumpers)

No published voting list has been found for this election; W. W. Bean, *Parl. Rep. of the six Northern Counties*, gives the number of plumpers but not the splits.

†26 July 1837 General Election. Reg. Electors: 1,532; voted: 1,176.

	Ald. William Thompson (C)	Andrew White (L)	David Barclay (L)
Plumpers	329	37	77
Thompson/White	217	217	—
Thompson/Barclay	140	—	140
White/Barclay	—	374	374
Result:	686	628	591

30 June 1841 General Election. Reg. Electors: 1,691
Ald. Wm. Thompson (C) and David Barclay (L) were returned after George Binns (Chartist) was nominated but declined to go to the poll. Ald. Thompson subsequently resigned to stand for his native county of Westmorland.

†16 Sept. 1841 by-election.

Viscount Howick (L)	706
M. Wolverley Attwood (C)	462

Lord Howick became 3rd Earl Grey.

*14 Aug. 1845 by-election.

George Hudson (C)	627
Col. Thomas Perronet Thompson (L)	498

*3 Aug. 1847 General Election, Reg. Electors: 1,692; voted: 1,322.

	George Hudson (C)	David Barclay (L)	Wm. Arthur Wilkinson (L)
Plumpers	160	61	330
Hudson/Barclay	532	532	—
Hudson/Wilkinson	186	—	186
Barclay/Wilkinson	—	53	53
Result:	878	646	569

*21 Dec. 1847 by-election, Barclay having accepted the Chiltern Hundreds:

Sir Hedworth Williamson (L)	707
Wm. Arthur Wilkinson (L)	578

*8 July 1852 General Election. Reg. Electors: 1,973; voted: 1,540.

	George Hudson (C)	Wm. Digby Seymour (L)	Henry Fenwick (L)
Plumpers	175	322	249
Hudson/Seymour	389	389	—
Hudson/Fenwick	302	—	302
Seymour/Fenwick	—	103	103
Result:	866	814	654

Seymour stood for re-election on being appointed Recorder of Newcastle-upon-Tyne.

*2 Jan. 1855 by-election. Reg. Electors: 2,176.

Henry Fenwick (L)	956
Wm. Digby Seymour (L)	646

*28 March 1857 General Election. Reg. Electors: 2,493; voted: 1,991.

	Henry Fenwick (L)	George Hudson (C)	Ralph Walters (L)
Plumpers	218	176	524
Fenwick/Hudson	735	735	—
Fenwick/Walters	169	—	169
Hudson/Walters	—	169	169
Result:	1,122	1,080	862

*30 April 1859 General Election. Reg. Electors: 2,729; voted: 2,079.

	Henry Fenwick (L)	Wm. Schaw Lindsay (L)	George Hudson (C)
Plumpers	65	30	460
Fenwick/Lindsay	1,196	1,196	—
Fenwick/Hudson	263	—	263
Lindsay/Hudson	—	65	65
Results:	1,524	1,291	788

*12 July 1865 General Election. Reg. Electors: 3,468; voted: 2,617.

	Henry Fenwick (L)	James Hartley (C)	John Candlish (L)
Plumpers	89	382	261
Fenwick/Hartley	823	823	—
Fenwick/Candlish	914	—	914
Hartley/Candlish	—	130	130
Result:	1,826	1,335	1,305
(Declaration):	(1,826)	(1,355)	(1,307)

Fenwick stood for re-election on appointment as a Lord of the Admiralty.

*28 Feb. 1866 by-election. Reg. electors: 3,468.

John Candlish (L)	1,430
Henry Fenwick (L)	1,296

17 Nov. 1868 General Election. Reg. electors: 11,364; voted: 8,186.

	John Candlish (L)	Edward T. Gourley (L)	Thomas C. Thompson (L/C)
Plumpers	148	614	931
Candlish/Gourley	3,844	3,844	—
Candlish/Thompson	2,221	—	2,221
Gourley/Thompson	—	428	428
Result:	6,237	4,901	3,596

7 July 1874 General Election. Reg. Electors: 14,008; voted: 9,853.

	Edward T. Gourley (L)	Sir Henry M. Havelock (L)	Lawrence R. Bailey (C)
Plumpers	162	109	3,472
Gourley/Havelock	5,711	5,711	—
Gourley/Bailey	299	—	299
Havelock/Bailey	—	100	100
Result:	6,172	5,920	3,871

31 March 1880 General Election. Reg. Electors: 15,021; voted: 11,396.

	Edward T. Gourley (L)	Sir Henry M. Havelock-Allan (L)	Edward Broke (C)
Plumpers	146	42	3,596
Gourley/H-Allan	6,890	6,890	—
Gourley/Brooke	603	—	603
H-Allan/Brooke	—	63	63
Result:	7,639	6,995	4,262

11 April 1881 by-election, Sir Henry Havelock-Allan having accepted the Chiltern Hundreds on being appointed to an active military command:
Samuel Storey (L) returned unopposed.

25 Nov. 1885 General Election. Reg. Electors: 17,978; voted: 14,468.

	Samuel Storey (L)	Edward T. Gourley (L)	Samuel P. Austin (C)
Plumpers	177	166	5,732
Storey/Gourley	7,370	7,370	—
Storey/Austin	748	—	748
Gourley/Austin	—	223	223
Result:	8,295	7,759	6,703

4 July 1886 General Election. Reg. Electors: 17,978; voted: 12,901.

	Samuel Storey (L)	Edward T. Gourley (L)	William Stobart (LU)
Plumpers	238	75	5,575
Storey/Gourley	6,522	6,522	—
Storey/Stobart	210	—	210
Gourley/Stobart	—	242	242
Results:	6,970	6,839	6,027

2 July 1892 General Election. Reg. Electors: 22,282; voted: 18,030.

	Samuel Storey (L)	Edward T. Gourley (L)	Hon. F.W. Lambton (LU)	John S.G. Pemberton (C)
Plumpers	67	44	174	34
Storey/Gourley	9,324	9,324	—	—
Storey/Lambton	241	—	241	—
Storey/Pemberton	79	—	—	79
Lambton/Pemberton	—	—	7,841	7,841
Gourley/Pemberton	—	48	—	48
Gourley/Lambton	—	138	138	—
Result:	9,711	9,554	8,394	8,002

15 July 1895 General Election. Reg. Electors: 22,962; voted: 17,973.

	Wm. Theodore Doxford (C)	Edward T. Gourley (L)	Samuel Storey (L)
Plumpers	9,393	67	110
Doxford/Gourley	265	265	—
Doxford/Storey	175	—	175
Gourley/Storey	—	7,900	7,900
Result:	9,833	8,232	8,185

4 Oct. 1900 General Election. Reg. Electors: 24,423; turnout 78.3%.

	Wm. Theodore Doxford (C)	John S.G. Pemberton (C)	William Hunter (L)	Alexander Wilkie (Lab)
Plumpers	358	178	255	62
Doxford/Pemberton	8,954	8,954	—	—
Doxford/Hunter	245	—	245	—
Doxford/Wilkie	60	—	—	60
Hunter/Wilkie	—	—	8,578	8,578
Hunter/Pemberton	—	292	292	—
Wilkie/Pemberton	—	142	—	142
Result:	9,617	9,566	9,370	8,842

5 Dec. 1910 General Election. Reg. Electors: 27,610; voted: 22,443 (81.2%).

	Hamar Greenwood (L)	Frank W. Goldstone (Lab)	William Joynson-Hicks (U)	Samuel Samuel (U)
Plumpers	717	188	113	104
Greenwood/Goldstone	11,022	11,022	—	—
Greenwood/J-Hicks	192	—	192	—
Greenwood/Samuel	66	—	—	66
Goldstone/Samuel	—	24	—	24
J-Hicks/Samuel	—	—	9,938	9,938
J-Hicks/Goldstone	—	57	57	—
Result:	11,997	11,291	10,300	10,132

17 Jan. 1906 General Election. Reg. Electors: 27,650; turnout 85.5%.

	James Stuart (L)	Thomas Summerbell (Lab)	David H. Haggie (U)	John S.G. Pemberton (UFT)
Plumpers	1,294	833	2,450	524
Stuart/Summerbell	11,323	11,323	—	—
Stuart/Haggie	193	—	193	—
Stuart/Pemberton	810	—	—	810
Summerbell/Pemberton	—	974	—	974
Summerbell/Haggie	—	300	300	—
Pemberton/Haggie	—	—	4,936	4,936
Result:	13,620	13,430	7,879	7,244

14 Dec. 1918 General Election. Reg. Electors: 73,131; turnout 56.4%.

	Sir Hamar Greenwood (Co L)	Ralph M. Hudson (C)	Frank W. Goldstone (Lab)
Plumpers	6,997	8,754	3,726
Greenwood/Hudson	15,858	15,858	—
Greenwood/Goldstone	4,791	—	4,791
Hudson/Goldstone	—	1,086	1,086
Result:	27,646	25,698	9,603

Sir Hamar Greenwood stood for re-election on being appointed Chief Secretary to the Lord Lieutenant of Ireland.

17 Jan, 1910 General Election. Reg. Electors: 27,610; voted: 24,110 (87.2%).

	Samuel Storey (Ind T.R.)	James Knott (C)	James Stuart (L)	Thomas Summerbell (Lab)
Plumpers	93	128	490	252
Storey/Knott	11,976	11,976	—	—
Storey/Stuart	201	—	201	—
Storey/Summerbell	64	—	—	64
Knott/Summerbell	—	35	—	35
Stuart/Summerbell	—	—	10,707	10,707
Stuart/Knott	—	131	131	—
Result:	12,334	12,270	11,529	11,058

24 April 1920 by-election. Reg. Electors: 76,216; turnout 55.4%.

Sir Hamar Greenwood (Co L)	22,813
Dr V. H. Rutherford (Lab)	14,379
Ernest M. Howe (L)	5,065

15 Nov. 1922 General Election. Reg. Electors: 74,970; turnout 81.6%.

	Walter Raine (C)	Luke Thompson (C)	Sir Hamar Greenwood (NL)	David B. Lawley (Lab)	Dr. V. H. Rutherford (Lab)	L. Andrew Common (L)
Plumpers	561	289	7,104	227	138	2,132
Raine/Thompson	23,192	23,192	—	—	—	—
Raine/Greenwood	2,408	—	2,408	—	—	—
Raine/Lawley	332	—	—	332	—	—
Raine/Rutherford	381	—	—	—	381	—
Raine/Common	1,127	—	—	—	—	1,127
Thompson/Greenwood	—	349	349	—	—	—
Thompson/Lawley	—	150	—	150	—	—
Thompson/Rutherford	—	416	—	—	416	—
Thompson/Common	—	195	—	—	—	195
Greenwood/Lawley	—	—	625	625	—	—
Greenwood/Rutherford	—	—	271	—	271	—
Greenwood/Common	—	—	8,301	—	—	8,301
Lawley/Common	—	—	—	673	—	673
Lawley/Rutherford	—	—	—	11,676	11,676	—
Common/Rutherford	—	—	—	—	608	608
Result:	28,001	24,591	19,058	13,683	13,490	13,036

6 Dec. 1923 General Election. Reg. Electors: 76,916; turnout 77.9%.

	Walter Raine (C)	Luke Thompson (C)	L. Andrew Common (L)	Sir Hamar Greenwood (L)	David B. Lawley (Lab)	Thomas W. Gillinder (Lab)
Plumpers	145	177	545	435	296	49
Raine/Thompson	22,865	22,865	—	—	—	—
Raine/Common	143	—	143	—	—	—
Raine/Greenwood	167	—	—	167	—	—
Raine/Lawley	116	—	—	—	116	—
Raine/Gillinder	61	—	—	—	—	61
Thompson/Common	—	146	146	—	—	—
Thompson/Greenwood	—	129	—	129	—	—
Thompson/Lawley	—	50	—	—	50	—
Thompson Gillinder	—	12	—	—	—	12
Common/Greenwood	—	—	20,750	20,750	—	—
Common/Gillinder	—	—	359	—	—	359
Common/Lawley	—	—	495	—	495	—
Greenwood/Lawley	—	—	—	300	300	—
Grenwood/Gillinder	—	—	—	253	—	253
Lawley/Gillinder	—	—	—	—	12,450	12,450
Result:	23,497	23,379	22,438	22,034	13,707	13,184

29 Oct. 1924 General Election. Reg. Electors: 78,361; turnout 72%.

	Luke Thompson (C)	Walter Raine (C)	Jeremiah MacVeagh (Lab)	L. Andrew Common (L)	Ian C. Hannah (L)
Plumpers	237	214	17,475	1,691	102
Thompson/Raine	27,731	27,731	—	—	—
Thompson/MacVeagh	72	—	72	—	—
Thompson/Common	543	—	—	543	—
Thompson/Hannah	29	—	—	—	29
Raine/MacVeagh	—	61	61	—	—
Raine/Common	—	582	—	582	—
Raine/Hannah	—	20	—	—	20
MacVeagh/Hannah	—	—	236	—	236
MacVeagh/Common	—	—	3,979	3,979	—
Hannah/Common	—	—	—	13,344	13,344
Result:	28,612	28,608	21,823	20,139	13,731

30 May 1929 General Election. Reg. Electors: 101,875; turnout 81.1%.

	Dr Marion Phillips (Lab)	Alfred Smith (Lab)	Sir Walter Raine (C)	Luke Thompson (C)	Dr. Eliz. T. Morgan (L)	Sir John W. Pratt (L)
Plumpers	411	370	296	167	240	358
Phillips/Smith	29,602	29,602	—	—	—	—
Phillips/Raine	133	—	133	—	—	—
Phillips/Thompson	59	—	—	59	—	—
Phillips/Morgan	970	—	—	—	970	—
Phillips/Pratt	619	—	—	—	—	619
Smith/Raine	—	146	146	—	—	—
Smith/Thompson	—	168	—	168	—	—
Smith/Morgan	—	427	—	—	427	—
Smith/Pratt	—	372	—	—	—	372
Raine/Thompson	—	—	28,371	28,371	—	—
Raine/Morgan	—	—	79	—	79	—
Raine/Pratt	—	—	155	—	—	155
Thompson/Morgan	—	—	—	59	59	—
Thompson/Pratt	—	—	—	113	—	113
Morgan/Pratt	—	—	—	—	19,525	19,525
Result:	31,794	31,085	29,180	28,937	21,300	21,142

Death of A. Smith.

26 March 1931 by-election. Reg. Electors: 103,363; turnout 73.1%.

L. Thompson (C)	30,497
J.T. Brownlie (Lab)	30,075
Dr. Elizabeth T. Morgan (L)	15,020

27 Oct. 1931 General Election. Reg. Electors: 103,559; turnout 81.1%.

	Luke Thompson (C)	Samuel Storey (C)	Dr. Marion Phillips (Lab)	Denis N. Pritt (Lab)
Plumpers	979	297	711	521
Thompson/Storey	52,050	52,050	—	—
Thompson/Phillips	175	—	175	—
Thompson/Pritt	182	—	—	182
Storey/Phillips	—	43	43	—
Storey/Pritt	—	199	—	199
Phillips/Pritt	—	—	28,778	28,778
Result:	53,386	52,589	29,707	29,680

14 Nov. 1935 General Election. Reg. Electors: 103,928; turnout 79.0%.

	Stephen N. Furness (NL)	Samuel Storey (C)	Gordon E.G. Catlin (Lab)	Mrs. Eliz. Leah Manning (Lab)
Plumpers	415	591	497	316
Furness/Storey	47,339	47,339	—	—
Furness/Catlin	829	—	829	—
Furness/Manning	418	—	—	418
Storey/Catlin	—	331	331	—
Storey/Manning	—	499	—	499
Catlin/Manning	—	—	30,826	30,826
Result:	49,001	48,760	32,483	32,059

5 July 1945 General Election. Reg. Electors: 90,729; turnout 77.2%.

	Fred K. T. Willey (Lab)	Richard Ewart (Lab)	Stephen N. Furness (NL)	Samuel Storey (C)	Thomas A. Richardson (Com)
Plumpers	550	300	503	324	517
Willey/Ewart	34,912	34,912	—	—	—
Willey/Furness	437	—	437	—	—
Willey/Storey	321	—	—	321	—
Willey/Richardson	2,549	—	—	—	2,549
Ewart/Furness	—	420	420	—	—
Ewart/Storey	—	88	—	88	—
Ewart/Richardson	—	991	—	—	991
Furness/Storey	—	—	27,704	27,704	—
Furness/Richardson	—	—	302	—	302
Storey/Richardson	—	—	—	142	142
Result:	38,769	36,711	29,366	28,579	4,501

SUNDERLAND NORTH

23 Feb. 1950. Electors: 54,416; turnout 84.3%.

F.T. Willey (Lab)	24,810
S. Hudson (C)	17,469
J.L. Hurst (L)	3,614

25 Oct. 1951. Electors: 52,652; turnout 83.7%.

F.T. Willey (Lab)	23,792
R. Kendall (C)	20,302

26 May 1955. Electors: 60,255; turnout 75.7%.

F.T. Willey (Lab)	24,237
A.M.H.Y.M. Herbert (C)	21,401

8 Oct. 1959. Electors: 57,763; turnout 80.5%.

F.T. Willey (Lab)	24,341
P.E. Heselton (C)	22,133

15 Oct. 1964. Electors: 56,856; turnout 76.3%.

F.T. Willey (Lab)	24,024
P.E. Heselton (C)	18,195
R.C. Middlewood (Ind C)	1,157

31 March 1966. Electors: 56,197; turnout 74.5%.

Rt. Hon. F.T. Willey (Lab)	25,438
P.L. Rost (C)	16,423

18 June 1970. Electors: 60,921; turnout 69.8%.

Rt. Hon. F.T. Willey (Lab)	25,779
J.M. Reay-Smith (C)	16,728

28 Feb. 1974. Electors: 75,028; turnout 73.9%.

F.T. Willey (Lab)	28,933
J.D.S. Brown (C)	17,533
J.A. Lennox (L)	9,015

10 Oct. 1974. Electors: 75,560; turnout 67.0%.

F.T. Willey (Lab)	29,618
J.D.S. Brown (C)	13,947
J.A. Lennox (L)	7,077

3 May 1979. Electors: 72,994; turnout 69.5%.

F.T. Willey (Lab)	29,213
L.J. Keith (C)	16,311
J.A. Lennox (L)	5,238

9 June 1983. Electors: 78,520.

R. Clay (Lab)	24,179
C. Lewis (C)	16,983
D. McCourt (L)	11,090

SUNDERLAND SOUTH

23 Feb. 1950. Reg. Electors: 65,833; turnout 83.3%.

R. Ewart (Lab)	27,192
H. Wilkinson (C)	22,012
C.J. Kitchell (L)	5,604

25 Oct. 1951. Reg. Electors: 65,928; turnout 82.2%.

R. Ewart (Lab)	27,257
P.G. Williams (C)	26,951

13 May 1952. by-election following the death of Ewart.
Reg. Electors: 65,453; 72.7%.

P.G. Williams (C)	23,114
A.G.S. Whipp (Lab)	21,939
R.F. Leslie (L)	2,524

26 May 1955. Reg. Electors: 61,615; turnout 77.4%.

P.G. Williams (C)	24,727
E. Armstrong (Lab)	22,953

8 Oct. 1959. Reg. Electors: 68,014; turnout 80.4%.

P.G. Williams (C)	27,825
E. Armstrong (Lab)	26,835

15 Oct. 1964. Reg. Electors: 66,239; turnout 75.8%.

G.A.T. Bagier (Lab)	25,900
P.G. Williams (C)	24,334

31 March 1966. Reg. Electors: 63,554; turnout 75.5%.

G.A.T. Bagier (Lab)	27,567
P.E. Heselton (C)	20,398

18 June 1970. Reg. Electors: 67,751; turnout 70.2%.

G.A.T. Bagier (Lab)	26,840
D.A. Orde (C)	20,722

28 Feb. 1974. Reg. Electors: 75,968; turnout 75.2%.

G.A.T. Bagier (Lab)	28,296
M.T. Wright (C)	19,700
W.J. Nicholson (L)	9,098

10 Oct. 1974. Reg. Electors: 78,464; turnout 68.1%.

G.A.T. Bagier (Lab)	28,623
Sir J.C.B. Riddell (C)	15,593
W.J. Nicholson (L)	7,828

3 May 1979. Reg. Electors: 79,130; turnout 70.0%.

G.A.T. Bagier (Lab)	29,403
J.R. Harris (C)	21,002
P.M. Barker (L)	4,984

9 June 1983. Reg. Electors: 75,124.

G.A.T. Bagier (Lab)	22,869
A. Mitchell (C)	17,321
J. Anderson (SDP)	9,865

APPENDICES

Appendix 1: *The Population of Sunderland* was compiled by George Patterson.
Appendix 2: *Parliamentary Election Results, Sunderland, 1832-1983* was compiled by Patricia Storey.

Lists of black and white illustrations

The abbreviation SM/TWMS in the attributions attached to certain illustrations stands for Sunderland Museum (Tyne and Wear Museums Service). Full details of the coloured illustrations are given on the pages on which they appear.